Engineering Economics for Aviation and Aerospace

I0882175

It is essential for all engineers and practitioners to have a fundamental understanding of cost structure, estimating cash flows, and evaluating alternative projects and designs on an economic basis. *Engineering Economics for Aviation and Aerospace* provides the tools and techniques necessary for engineers to economically evaluate their projects and choices.

Offering a comprehensive understanding of the theory and practical applications of engineering economics, this book explains and demonstrates the principles and techniques of engineering economics and financial analysis as applied to the aviation and aerospace industries. The authors use time value of money, interest, and Microsoft Excel functions to evaluate the cash flows associated with a single project or multiple projects. They use different engineering economics tools to evaluate individual projects or select the best of multiple alternatives.

Fully updated to reflect the latest information on, and practical insights into, the field of engineering economics, this second edition of *Engineering Economics for Aviation and Aerospace* continues to provide students of aviation and industrial economics, as well as practitioners, with the necessary mathematical knowledge to evaluate alternatives on an economic basis.

Bijan Vasigh is President and Founder of Aviation Consulting Group and Professor of Economics and Finance in the College of Business at Embry-Riddle Aeronautical University, Daytona Beach, Florida, USA.

Javad Gorjidooz is Professor of Finance and Chair of the Business Administration Program in the School of Business at Embry-Riddle Aeronautical University, Prescott, Arizona, USA.

Engineering Economics for Aviation and Aerospace

Second Edition

Bijan Vasigh and Javad Gorjidooz

Routledge
Taylor & Francis Group
LONDON AND NEW YORK

Second edition published 2025

by Routledge
4 Park Square, Milton Park, Abingdon, Oxon, OX14 4RN

and by Routledge
605 Third Avenue, New York, NY 10158

Routledge is an imprint of the Taylor & Francis Group, an informa business

First edition published by Routledge 2017

British Library Cataloguing-in-Publication Data
A catalogue record for this book is available from the British Library

Library of Congress Cataloging-in-Publication Data
Names: Vasigh, Bijan author | Gorjidooz, Javad, 1951– author
Title: Engineering economics for aviation and aerospace / Bijan Vasigh and Javad Gorjidooz.
Description: Second edition. | Abingdon, Oxon ; New York, NY : Routledge, 2025. | Includes bibliographical references and index.
Subjects: LCSH: Aerospace engineering—Cost control | Engineering economy
Classification: LCC TL872 .V37 2025 | DDC 338.4/76291—dc23/eng/20250327
LC record available at https://lccn.loc.gov/2024056585

ISBN: 978-1-032-74542-8 (hbk)
ISBN: 978-1-032-74540-4 (pbk)
ISBN: 978-1-003-46975-9 (ebk)

DOI: 10.4324/9781003469759

Typeset in Times New Roman
by Apex CoVantage, LLC

Contents

Figures

Tables

About the Authors

Bijan Vasigh, PhD, is the president and founder of Aviation Consulting Group and a professor of economics and finance in the College of Business at Embry-Riddle Aeronautical University, Daytona Beach Florida. He has focused his consulting and teaching on the theory, modeling, and application of transport finance instruments, and he provides expert opinions in court cases. He is the author of North America's leading aviation textbooks, including *An Introduction to Air Transport Economics: From Theory to Application, Foundation of Airline Finance: Methodology and Practices*, and *Aircraft Valuation in Volatile Market Conditions*.

Dr. Vasigh's work has led to formal collaborations with multiple domestic government agencies and foreign governments, such as the International Civil Aviation Organization, the Association of Unmanned Vehicle Systems International, the International Air Transport Association (IATA) Learning Center, and NASA on a grant on "Determination of Statewide Economic Benefits of the Small Aircraft Transportation System (SATS)."

He has been interviewed and quoted by national and international news media, including *The Washington Post*, *The Wall Street Journal*, NBC News, CBS News, *USA Today*, *Forbes*, *Bloomberg Business*, National Public Radio Marketplace, *Voice of Russia*, *El Pais* (Spain), *Rzeczpospolita* (Poland), *Trinidad Express*, *Cuba News*, and *The Guardian* (United Kingdom), among others.

Dr Javad Gorjidooz is a professor of finance and Chair of the Business Administration Program in the School of Business at Embry-Riddle Aeronautical University, Prescott, Arizona, USA. He has an MBA and a PhD from Indiana University at Bloomington, Indiana, with majors in accounting, economics, and finance. He also has a diploma in airline finance and accounting management from IATA Training.

Dr. Gorjidooz has over 30 years of experience in teaching a variety of courses in finance, economics, and aviation finance. He has written and coauthored many articles concerning the aviation industry that have been published in numerous peer-reviewed academic journals such as the *Journal of Air Transportation*, the *International Business and Economics Research Journal*, *Journal of Business and Economic Research*, and *Journal of American Academy Business Review*.

Dr. Gorjidooz has been a member of many ACBSP accreditation site visit teams, evaluating business programs across the United States. He was the recipient of 2009, 2010, and 2011 CIBER scholarships to attend faculty development programs in Vietnam, China, and India in the area of global business and research. He also gave a speech on his economic impact analysis of an international airport at the Busan Global Forum in Busan, Korea, and young adults at the FBLA State and National Leadership Conferences on topics such as empowering young adults to better prepare for investing and retirement. Dr Gorjidooz has received many awards and recognitions for scholarly activities, intellectual contributions, and professional services.

Foreword

To an aerospace engineer educated in the post-Sputnik era of science-heavy curricula, the economics of engineering were an afterthought at best. Fortunately, that is no longer the case. Today, aviation and aerospace education recognize the complex interconnectivity of engineering and economics.

This book by Dr. Bijan Vasigh and Dr. Javad Gorjidooz deserves much credit. First published in 2017, *Engineering Economics for Aviation and Aerospace* has served as an ideal learning tool for a generation of engineers hoping to understand the economic impacts of tradeoffs. Now in its second edition, the book remains the most comprehensive resource available for undergraduate and graduate students, as well as a reference for many industry professionals.

While offering a solid foundation in principles and financial analysis of engineering economics, the book sets itself apart by its application to the aviation industry, an industry with unique risks and costs.

Its chapters clearly lay out the concepts of nominal and effective interest rates, time value of money, present worth analysis, life cycle costs, annual worth analysis, rate of return, breakeven analysis, and payback period analysis, among others. Simultaneously, the authors explore a broad spectrum of aviation-relevant engineering questions, including design, manufacturing, and machinery decisions. Engineers learn to assess the viability of individual projects and to choose the best option among multiple alternatives.

One of the text's primary focuses is on the industry's most complex and expensive question: the decision to build and sell a new aircraft. This is for good reason. Wrong judgments have led to massive losses and caused companies to quit the industry entirely. As those who are likely to invest in this book are aware, air transport also requires the infusion of large amounts of capital from government, particularly for airport infrastructure and maintenance. One critical chapter is devoted to the evaluation of such public-sector projects via cost/benefit analysis.

The expertise contained in this book can benefit both engineers and industry executives alike. In the wake of the coronavirus pandemic upending commercial aviation, its sections on risk and uncertainty in the aviation industry are particularly compelling. The book covers everything from the deregulation of the airlines in 1978 to the aviation industry's current cost structure. Its final chapters on cost estimation and decision theory will benefit anyone in our industry seeking to make better economic decisions. Both chapters begin with discussions of past failures: Lockheed's L-1011 Tristar and the supersonic Concorde jet. The L-1011 lost $2.5 billion before it was canceled because Lockheed failed to properly estimate production costs and the breakeven number of aircraft sold, and the Concorde, which made its last commercial flight in October 2003, could never overcome its costs, particularly its high fuel consumption amid rising oil prices.

Such mistakes are not presented by Dr. Vasigh and Dr. Gorjidooz to stifle the spirit of innovation in aviation, a spirit displayed more than a century ago by the Wright Brothers and still seen today among students at Embry-Riddle Aeronautical University. Both authors are revered faculty members whose knowledge and passion for the industry come through in this book's pages just as it does in their classrooms.

Indeed, this updated volume – full of real-world examples and practical applications – makes the challenging process of learning engineering economics highly tangible and relevant. Students and practitioners who use this book will be prepared to engineer the new aircraft of tomorrow and make sound economic decisions for the future of the global aviation industry.

P. Barry Butler, PhD
President
Embry-Riddle Aeronautical University

Preface

The new edition of *Engineering Economics for Aviation and Aerospace* is designed to offer a comprehensive exploration of the theoretical underpinnings and real-world applications of economic principles within the context of engineering, with a specific focus on the aviation and aerospace industries. Building upon the success of the first edition, this updated version aims to provide readers with the latest information and practical insights into the field of engineering economics, tailored to the unique challenges and opportunities encountered in aviation and aerospace.

Our primary goal is to bridge the gap between theory and practice by offering a balanced approach that combines academic rigor with practical relevance. Each chapter is meticulously crafted to elucidate fundamental concepts while illustrating their practical implications through real-world examples and case studies drawn from the aviation and aerospace sectors. By delving into topics such as cost analysis, project evaluation, risk assessment, and decision-making techniques, the authors give readers a deeper understanding of how economic principles are applied to solve complex engineering problems in these dynamic industries.

One of the key features of this edition is its providing a diverse array of engineering economics tools and techniques, allowing readers to assess the viability of individual projects or select the optimal solution among multiple alternatives. Whether analyzing the lifecycle costs of aircraft systems, evaluating the economic feasibility of airport expansions, or optimizing supply chain management strategies for aerospace manufacturers, the tools and methodologies presented in this book will equip readers with the skills needed to make informed decisions in a rapidly evolving industry landscape.

Designed to be accessible to both undergraduate and graduate students, as well as serving as a valuable reference for professionals working in the aviation and aerospace sectors, this edition of *Engineering Economics for Aviation and Aerospace* is intended to serve as a comprehensive resource for anyone seeking to understand and apply economic principles in the context of engineering challenges and opportunities. We hope that this book will inspire readers to explore the intersection of engineering and economics and empower them to contribute meaningfully to the advancement of the aviation and aerospace industries.

Whether you're a seasoned engineer looking to sharpen your skills or a student just beginning your journey in the world of engineering, we hope that this book will serve as a valuable resource, a guiding light illuminating the path to success in the dynamic and challenging field of engineering economics. Engineers often find themselves making choices with significant financial implications, such as selecting materials, designs, or project plans. Studying engineering economics enhances engineers' ability to integrate financial considerations into their decision-making processes, fostering success in their projects and contributing to the overall efficiency of engineering endeavors.

Engineering projects can fail for a variety of reasons, often stemming from issues related to breakeven estimation, demand projection, communication, and resource management. Successful engineering projects require meticulous planning, proactive risk management, clear market analysis, and adaptable production planning to navigate the complexities inherent in large-scale endeavors.

Airbus' venture into the superjumbo market with the A380 was bold and ambitious. The aircraft was designed to revolutionize air travel, offering unprecedented capacity and luxury to passengers while providing airlines with a cost-effective solution for high-density routes. However, the reality didn't quite match the vision, and one of the critical missteps was in the calculation of the breakeven point for the A380 program.

In 1988, Airbus began development of an ultra-high-capacity airliner to break the dominance that Boeing had enjoyed in this market segment since the early 1970s with its 747. However, the A380, known for its iconic double-deck design and capacity to carry many passengers, faced challenges as airlines increasingly favored more fuel-efficient, long-range twin-engine aircraft. As a result of these factors, Airbus struggled to reach its projected sales targets for the A380, leading to significant financial losses. The company had to make the difficult decision to withdraw the A380 from production prematurely, halting further investment in a program that had failed to meet expectations. Airbus officially announced the decision to cease production of the A380 on February 14, 2019.

This book provides the tools and techniques necessary for engineers to economically evaluate their decisions and designs. For example, the supersonic Concorde aircraft was the most sophisticated aircraft, flying at twice the speed of sound and known by many people as an aviation icon and an engineering phenomenon. But the very high costs of research and development, in addition to expensive operating costs, made the commercial operation of Concorde uneconomical. After producing 20 aircraft, in 1979, the program was terminated because of the lack of demand by airlines due to these high operating costs.

Most of the engineering economics and financial mathematic books available in the market either take a pure theoretical approach or offer limited applied application without justification. In this book, we have seamlessly integrated both theoretical approaches and well-justified applications. This book is intended to provide students and practitioners with the necessary mathematical knowledge and techniques to evaluate, analyze, and solve engineering economics problems especially in the field of aviation and aerospace.

For students and practitioners, this book explains the concepts and applications carefully and clearly, assisting readers to understand the materials and help them to apply the tools and techniques to engineering economics situations.

Acknowledgements

Writing a textbook is a challenging and complex endeavor that requires extensive research, meticulous attention to detail, and a significant amount of time and effort. It is a process that can often be daunting, but we have been incredibly fortunate to receive support and encouragement from many individuals who have played an essential role in helping us bring this book to completion.

We are especially grateful to Dr. Barry P. Butler, President of Embry-Riddle Aeronautical University, for his unwavering support. Dr. Butler took the time to read the book and provided invaluable feedback that has significantly enhanced the quality of this edition. His expertise and thoughtful suggestions were crucial in refining the content and ensuring its accuracy and relevance.

We received a great deal of assistance and encouragement from several individuals and would like to take this opportunity to gratefully recognize their contributions and assistance. Many Embry-Riddle Aeronautical University graduate students assisted in the preparation of this manuscript. We owe a special debt to graduate assistants Vaclav Kuncak, Adam Zaraszczak, Sharath Chandra Balan, and Mariya Zarubina. The authors would like to recognize Bompally Vivek Rao, Ali Mazhar, Zachary Shega, Christian Spann and many students in the Engineering Economics course at Embry-Riddle Aeronautical University, Prescott Campus who had the opportunity to read, critique, and provide feedback. We would like to thank our reviewers and other professionals who offered helpful suggestions and criticisms.

We are also deeply grateful to the following individuals for their invaluable contributions to the first edition of this book. Their expertise, guidance, and support have been instrumental in laying the foundation for this second edition. First and foremost, we extend our heartfelt thanks to Brian Pearce, Chief Economist at IATA, for his insightful feedback and unwavering encouragement. We also wish to acknowledge Zane Rowe, Chief Financial Officer and Executive Vice President of VMware, whose meticulous research and dedication significantly enriched the content of the first edition. Our gratitude also goes to Barry Humphreys, formerly Director of External Affairs and Route Development at Virgin Atlantic Airways, and Jean-Marc Bourreau, Chief Operating Officer at IOS Partners, for their critical reviews and thoughtful suggestions, which greatly enhanced the quality of the initial manuscript. Special thanks to Robin Sobotta and Billy McGrane at Embry-Riddle Aeronautical University for their exceptional support and assistance.

We are also thankful for the support of Andy Humphries and Kelly Cracknell, Production Editor at Routledge. Their expertise and dedication ensured clarity and coherence throughout the text. Additionally, we greatly appreciate Jaya Dalal, our copyeditor, whose encouragement and meticulous attention to detail helped us deliver a top-quality product.

Finally, we extend our sincere appreciation to our readers for their constructive feedback on the first edition. Your comments and suggestions have been instrumental in shaping this revised and expanded second edition. To all who contributed to the first edition, we extend our heartfelt gratitude and look forward to your continued support and collaboration.

Thank you,

Bijan Vasigh
Javad Gorjidooz

Abbreviations

AOC	Annual operating cost
ASM	Available seat miles
CAPM	Capital asset pricing model
CASM	Cost per available seat mile
CD	Certificate of deposit
CR	Current ratio
DOT	Department of Transportation
EBIT	Earnings before interest and taxes
FV	Future value
IATA	International Air Transport Association
IRR	Internal rate of return
LCC	Life cycle costing
LIBOR	London Interbank Offered Rate
NASDAQ	National Association of Securities Dealers Automated Quotations
NPV	Net present value
P/E	Price-to-earnings ratio
PI	Profitability index
PV	Present value
RASM	Revenue per Available Seat Mile
ROA	Return on assets
ROE	Return on equity
ROI	Return on investment
RPM	Revenue passenger mile
SEC	Security Exchange Commission
SML	Security market line
TC	Total cost
VC	Variable cost
WACC	Weighted average cost of capital

1 Introduction to the Air Transport Industry

Engineers often face decisions regarding resource project viability, allocation, and market analysis. Understanding economic principles allows engineers to make informed decisions by considering factors such as risk assessment, cost-effectiveness, and resource allocation. For example, engineers use tools like breakeven analysis to evaluate the economic viability of projects and determine the optimal course of action.

Aircraft and parts manufacturers and airlines are actively seeking ways to minimize their carbon footprint and reduce the environmental impact of air travel. Efforts include exploring alternative fuels such as biofuels to make aviation more sustainable. The industry is also actively working on various strategies to reduce its emissions including investing in more fuel-efficient aircraft, improving operational efficiency. Jet engines in service today are well over 70% more fuel efficient per seat mile than the aircraft in the 1960s.

Air transportation provides an economical and reliable mode of moving passengers and cargo with no comparable substitute, especially for the long-haul market. As the demand for air travel continues to grow, the air transport sector recognizes the imperative to balance its expansion with environmental stewardship, striving for a future where aviation is both efficient and environmentally conscious. The growing middle class in emerging economies has played a pivotal role in driving the demand for air transportation. Additionally, the proliferation of international tourism has significantly contributed to the surge in air travel demand.

Aircraft manufacturers leverage innovative technologies such as fly-by-wire programs to improve the economic efficiency and ecofriendliness of commercial aviation. A key task in any manufacturing facility is to continuously seeking ways to improve efficiency and reduce costs. Engineering economics applies economic principles to engineering projects; for instance, a jet engine manufacturer could evaluate the costs and benefits of investing in fuel-efficient and environmentally friendly engines. Air transport continues to create tremendous value for its customers and others in the value chain such as airports, aircraft manufacturers, jet engine producers, and travel facilitators, and in this chapter, we give overviews of these.

Introduction to Economics

Despite being a vital component of the global economy, airlines often contend with thin profit margins due to factors such as susceptibility to external shocks (fuel price volatility, economic downturns, political tensions, and pandemics). The cyclicality of the industry, where demand can be highly sensitive to economic conditions, further amplifies the challenge of maintaining consistent profitability. Economic variables affect air travel demand in a variety of ways, requiring a comprehensive analysis of factors influencing consumer behavior and industry dynamics because understanding their impacts is crucial for airlines, policymakers, and researchers.

DOI: 10.4324/9781003469759-1

> Microeconomics is the study of individual economic units such as households, businesses, and individual markets and how these economic agents make decisions regarding the allocation of resources, consumption, production, and pricing of goods and services.

Economics is the study of how societies allocate limited productive resources to satisfy their unlimited needs. At its core, it revolves around the fundamental principle that our wants surpass the resources available and how to effectively satisfy as many of them. This basic principle sets the stage for addressing pivotal economic questions: What goods and services should be produced and distributed, and how and for whom? Economics has two subcategories, microeconomics and macroeconomics based on scale.

Microeconomics

Microeconomics focuses on the decisions made by individuals and businesses, examining specific industries and the behavior of individual decision-making units. This subcategory of economics addresses the essential questions of what to produce, how to produce, and for whom to produce. For instance, in a significant move for the aviation industry, Airbus decided to terminate the production of its A380 aircraft. This decision reflects changing market dynamics, particularly the declining demand for large, four-engine planes in favor of smaller, more fuel-efficient models.

Microeconomics shapes many facets of the air transport industry. One notable application is in pricing strategies, where microeconomic principles help airlines set optimal ticket prices by considering factors such as demand, competition, and cost structures. Market structure analysis, a core microeconomic concept, assists in understanding whether the industry operates under conditions of perfect competition, monopolistic competition, oligopoly, or monopoly. Additionally, microeconomics guides airlines in conducting cost–benefit analyses for decisions related to routes, aircraft acquisitions, and operational efficiency. The impact of government regulations and deregulation on the industry is assessed through microeconomic lenses, providing insights into market entry, competition levels, and pricing strategies. Understanding consumer behavior, labor market dynamics, and the efficient allocation of resources within airlines are further applications of microeconomic principles. From investment decisions to environmental considerations and government interventions, microeconomics serves as a valuable tool for analyzing and optimizing various aspects of the air transport sector.

Supply, representing the quantity producers are willing to offer at various prices, is influenced by factors like production costs, technology, regulations, the number of producers, and government policies. The relationship between the price of a product and the quantity that producers are willing to supply is represented by the supply curve, illustrating how the quantity supplied changes in response to changes in price. The supply of air transportation is intricately shaped by a multitude of factors inherent

> In economic terms, supply refers to the quantity of a good or service that producers are willing and able to offer for sale in the market at various prices during a specific period. The law of supply describes the relationship between the price of a good or service and the quantity that producers are willing and able to supply in a given period all other things being equal.

to the aviation industry. The availability of aircraft within an airline's fleet, influenced by decisions on acquisition, maintenance, and retirement, is a fundamental determinant. Other factors include product price and operational costs such as fuel prices, labor expenses, and airport fees.

Regulatory constraints also directly impact the feasibility of providing air transportation services, including safety standards and air traffic control regulations, as do airport infrastructure such as capacity and efficiency. Technological advancements can enhance operational efficiency and impact the supply of air transportation, and number of firms in the market affects overall supply; more producers often mean a higher total supply, while fewer producers may limit the overall supply. Finally, the supply of air transportation is always affected by unforeseen global events such as shortages. The intricate interplay of these factors requires airlines to adapt and make strategic decisions to ensure a reliable and efficient supply of air transportation services.

The law of supply is a fundamental economic principle that applies to various industries, including air transport; it describes the relationship between the price of a good or service and the quantity that producers are willing and able to supply in a given period when all other things are equal. The law of supply is characterized by a direct relationship: As the price of a good or service increases, its supply increases as well. In the context of air transportation, this means that that as airfares increase, the supply of air transportation will also increase, and conversely, as prices decrease, the quantity supplied will decrease. This relationship is typically depicted graphically as an upward-sloping supply curve on a supply and demand diagram.

Demand and the Law of Demand

> Demand, in economics, refers to the quantity of a good or service that consumers are willing and able to purchase at various prices during a specific period. The law of demand is a fundamental economic principle that describes the inverse relationship between the price of a good or service and the quantity demanded by consumers, assuming other factors remain constant.

Conversely, demand, reflecting the quantity consumers are willing to purchase, is impacted by preferences, income levels, and related goods' prices. Economic growth also plays a pivotal role, as thriving economies typically lead to heightened business and leisure travel demands. Technological advancements, such as online booking platforms and mobile applications, contribute to the accessibility of air travel and also influence consumer preferences. Travel trends in both tourism and business directly impact air travel demand, and government policies and regulations ranging from visa requirements to safety standards influence the ease and attractiveness of air travel as well. Environmental concerns have also become increasingly relevant, with a growing emphasis on sustainable practices affecting consumer choices and shaping the demand for environmentally friendly travel options. Unforeseen events including global crises and geopolitical tensions can have immediate and lasting impacts on air travel demand.

Other factors that influence demand for air transportation include income and airfare prices. Higher incomes typically correlate with increased willingness and ability to engage in air travel for both business and leisure, and airfares substantially affect demand inversely proportionate to ticket prices. The demand for air transportation is also significantly influenced by the availability and price of alternative modes of transportation (e.g., trains, buses, cars). If alternative modes are readily available, efficient, and competitively priced, travelers may opt for these options instead of air transportation. Finally, marketing and promotional activities by airlines, government policies and regulations, seasonal variations, and perceptions of security and safety also play crucial roles in shaping air transportation demand.

Understanding demand is essential for businesses, policymakers, and stakeholders as it helps analyze and predict market trends, consumer behavior, and the impacts of external factors such as pandemics on the buying decisions of individuals and households. The COVID-19 pandemic substantially reduced air travel demand both internationally and domestically. According to the International Air Transport Association, global airline traffic declined by 66% in 2020, and by 58% in 2021 compared with 2019, producing economic losses of $244 billion in 2020 and $146 billion in 2021 across the value chain. Total traffic in 2023 rose 36.9% compared to 2022. Globally, full-year 2023 traffic was at 94.1% of 2019 levels.

In contrast with the law of supply, the law of demand is describes an inverse relationship between the price of a good or service and the quantity demanded by consumers when all things are equal: As the price of a good or service rises, the quantity demanded by consumers decreases, and conversely, as the price falls, the quantity demanded increases, and the equilibrium point occurs where supply and demand intersect. Changes in any supply or demand determinants lead to shifts in these curves, affecting the market's stability. Price, a result of this interaction, acts as a signal to guide producers and consumers. A nuanced understanding of these microeconomic principles is vital for comprehending market dynamics and aiding decision-making for businesses, policymakers, and consumers.

Macroeconomics

In contrast, macroeconomics takes a holistic approach, studying the overall economic behavior of a society. It delves into macroeconomic objectives such as price stability, employment, economic growth, and efficiency. By exploring these macroeconomic factors, economists gain insights into the broader economic landscape, including inflation, unemployment, and overall economic progress.

Macroeconomics studies the behavior and performance of an economy as a whole; it focuses on aggregate indicators such as unemployment rates, inflation, and overall economic growth. Macroeconomists analyze how different factors such as government fiscal policies and monetary policies affect the economy on a large scale.

The Airline Industry Before Deregulation

In 1938, the US Civil Aeronautics Act transferred federal responsibilities for nonmilitary aviation from the Bureau of Air Commerce to a new independent agency, the Civil Aeronautics Authority (Bunke, 1954). The 1938 Act created the Civil Aeronautics Board (CAB) and the Civil Aeronautics Administration as well as issuing air carrier route certificates and regulating airfares. The Civil Aeronautics Board (CAB) was responsible for issuing and overseeing aircraft and pilot certification and suspension.

The newly established CAB also became responsible for investigating aircraft accidents. Before deregulation, there were 16 trunk airlines in the United States; trunk was the generic name for the common carriers that provided scheduled national and international air service. Government assistance through protection, subsidy, promotion, and regulation was considered necessary for the new industry's development. For example, at that time, railroads were still the dominant form of both passenger and freight transportation, so railroad companies were specifically prohibited from having any financial interests in airlines. The fear was that very rich and powerful railroad firms would crush the competition from the embryonic airline industry.

Forty years later, by 1978, six of the original 16 trunk airlines had left the market and no new trunk airline had been allowed to come into existence. The 10 that had survived accounted for 90% of the US air carrier market. During the era of regulation, the airline industry was stable, mainly attributed to CAB's control over the airline industry (Kahn, 1988). The fixed prices and routes meant that airlines were ensured of a certain profit, but the only form of competition that existed was nonprice based: Airlines had to compete based on quality of service and other non-price-related factors. CAB's extreme regulation also made it nearly impossible for any new airline to enter the industry because operations costs would be insurmountable for newcomers. In 1978, the supersonic commercial jet era was two years old (Concorde flights between Europe and the United States had begun in 1976), and the CAB machinery of airline regulation had slowed significantly.[1]

The Airline Industry After Deregulation

The Airline Deregulation Act of 1978 aimed to promote competition, reduce government involvement, and provide consumers with lower fares and choices. Following deregulation, airlines gained more freedom to set their own routes and prices, leading to increased competition and significant changes in the industry's structure.[2]

This law modified the historic Federal Aviation Act of 1958 in the area of economic regulation of airlines by the federal government.[3] The deregulation legislation was the result of several years of industry, academic, and congressional debate over the role that the CAB had played in the economic regulation of the airline industry. The CAB's primary role was to protect the industry through government intervention and regulation, limiting competition among airlines via methods including pricing and route controls and caps on new airlines. By the mid-1970s, the aforesaid restrictions seemed inappropriate to most industry observers, consumer advocates, and politicians. The resulting Airline Deregulation Act of 1978 was signed into law by President Jimmy Carter with an effective date of October 24, 1978. It included a number of provisions including eventually eliminating the CAB. The act removed controls on domestic airline air fares and routes, imposed a 180-day limit on CAB's response to almost any issue (including requests for the economic certification of new airlines), and mandated an "essential air service" program to provide federally subsidized air service to rural areas. There were also new labor protection provisions to provide job protection for employees displaced by deregulation, and the act changed the final approval process for airline mergers.[4]

Airline deregulation opened the airline industry to intense competition because there were no longer any controls over airlines' prices or routes; indeed, this era birthed the entry of low-cost carriers into the market. Along with the entry of new low-cost carriers came hub-and-spoke airline networks and revenue management; managing costs and focusing on revenue became the primary focus of all the airlines, which proved extremely costly for the legacy carriers since they could not cope with all their legacy costs. A previously stable industry suddenly looked extremely unstable due to the sudden volume of changes.

The dominant players in the US airline industry, Delta, American, Southwest, and United, collectively wield significant influence, consistently maintaining a market share well above 75%. This contrasts with the European market, which exhibits a more fragmented landscape.

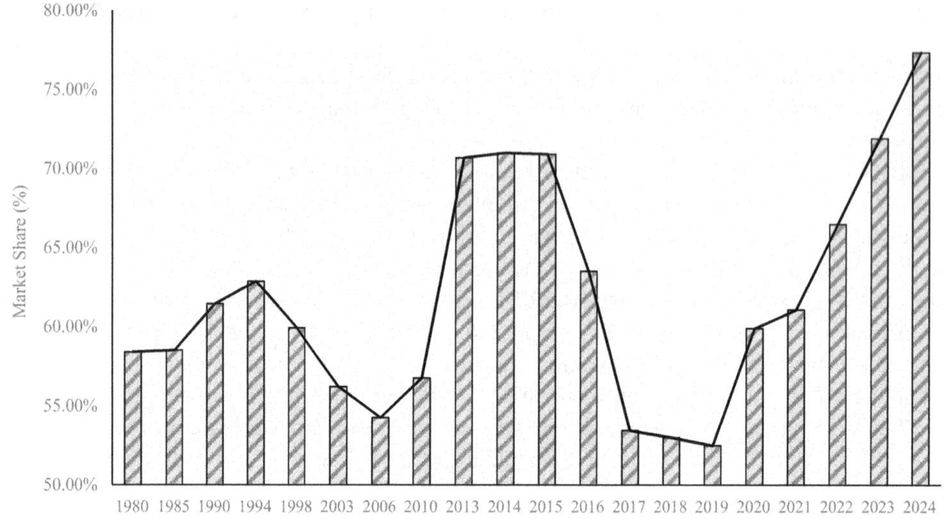

Figure 1.1 Market shares for four US domestic carriers: 1980–2024.[5]

Figure 1.1 illustrates the dynamic shifts in market share among the top four US carriers. The concentrated market control by these airlines is a consequence of numerous mergers and bankruptcies. This trend is anticipated to persist in the coming years, solidifying their stronghold on the industry. Passengers could once choose from a variety of large and medium-sized carriers, today the choices are much more limited, and with fewer competitors, airfares increase as customer service declines.

The return on capital in the airline industry is historically extremely poor; for years, airlines were generating returns far below their cost of capital, although in 2012, the industry began experiencing a positive shift. Over subsequent years, return on invested capital (ROIC) saw a consistent upward trend, attributed to factors such as increased load, declining fuel prices, industry consolidation, and increasing ancillary revenues. ROIC reached its pinnacle around 2016 and 2017, approximately 10%. However, the landscape underwent a dramatic transformation with the onset of the COVID-19 pandemic, leading airlines into substantial losses.

Deregulation in the US was quickly followed by the same in European and Asian countries within a few years; a crucial step in Europe was also privatizing airlines and airports. Air transport privatization and deregulation was pioneered by Great Britain under the Thatcher government with its privatization of British Airlines and the British Airports Authority in 1987. Privatization was intended to provide impetus for airlines and airports to be operated more efficiently and competitively. For instance, following airline industry deregulation, the number of aircraft being leased rather than bought increased; as of 2022, as much as 50% of the aircraft around the world was leased, and that number was expected to continue to rise. Leasing is particularly popular with new and low-cost airlines.

Airline Profitability

Total airline industry 2024 revenues are expected to grow 7.6% year over year to a record $964 billion; expense growth is expected to be slightly lower at 6.9% for a total of $914 billion.

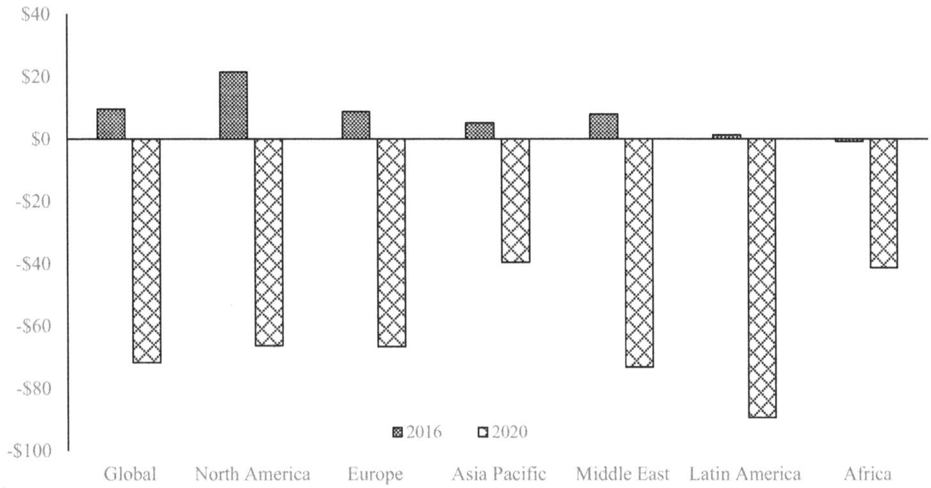

Figure 1.2 Airlines' profits per passenger, 2016 and 2020.[6]

The sector is witnessing a resurgence in travel demand, with an estimated 4.35 billion people taking advantage of air travel in 2023, nearly approaching the prepandemic levels of 4.54 billion in 2019. However, the cargo segment is expected to experience a dip, as volumes are projected to be 57.8 million tons, down from the 61.5 million tons transported in 2019, attributed to a slowdown in international trade.

Despite this, the industry is set to stabilize and prosper, with total revenues forecasted to grow by 9.7% year over year, surpassing the $800 billion threshold for the first time since 2019 ($838 billion). Moreover, expense growth is expected to remain relatively contained, with an 8.1% annual increase. This positive trajectory signals a robust recovery for the airline industry in 2023 (Figure 1.2). We include 2015, 2016, and 2023 to highlight the impacts of COVID-19.

However, recovery has been excellent since the economic meltdown, and the industry is only expected to grow further in the coming years; the global airline industry has transformed itself with major gains in efficiency. The recovery from COVID-19 has been fast and rapid, as clearly reflected in the high passenger load factor of 75% in 2023.[7] The result is a positive operating profit that is higher than last year.[8] The operating profit reached $22,400 million for airlines, for reasons including bankruptcies and consolidations, lower fuel prices and labor costs, and high demand for air travel. Figure 1.3 presents the combined operating profits of all the airlines in the world since 1990; it is notable that the operating profits largely follow a cyclical pattern. In the last two decades, the three most significant events that impacted the profitability were the 9/11 attacks, the economic meltdown of 2008, and the COVID-19 crisis.

Although the current state of the airline industry is looking bright, airline economists are unanimously worried about the sustainability of the current levels of profit for a number of reasons for concern. Importantly, for instance, fuel and labor prices are expected to rise, and a large number of forecasted retirements is expected to increase demand for pilots and flight attendants. Indeed, attrition is expected to increase labor costs; attrition refers to losing employees through normal means such as retirement and resignation while not filling the vacant positions, and the increasing pressure on current employees could lead to seeking pay increases.

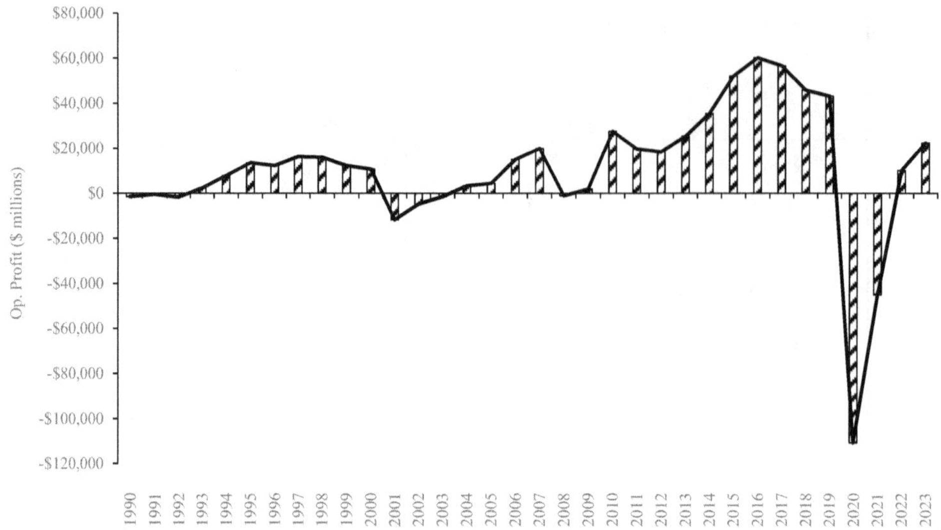

Figure 1.3 Global airline profitability: 1990–2023.[9]

The Air Transport Industry

The air transport industry is an essential component of the world economy, providing infrastructure and services that enable global trade, tourism, and economic development. The industry's impact extends far beyond its direct economic contributions, influencing various sectors and fostering international connectivity. The transport industry has evolved over the last 40 years. Technological changes and productivity growth spurred the number of passengers to an all-time high of $4.723 billion in 2019. In 2021, due to the coronavirus pandemic, the estimated number of scheduled passengers amounted to just over 2.2 billion people.

The commercial aviation value chain represents a network of interlinked entities with the airline industry being the central node, as can be observed in Figure 1.4.[10] Suppliers are upstream, and distributors are downstream, and we discuss both later in this chapter. The introduction of very-large-body aircraft like Boeing B-747 and Airbus A-380 has significantly increased passenger capacity. On the manufacturing side, the industry consists of a few aircraft and jet engine manufacturers.

Aircraft Manufacturers

Entering the commercial aircraft industry requires high investments to develop and manufacture aircraft, avionics, and engines (Vasigh and Azadian, 2022). Since the dawn of aviation, many aircraft manufacturing companies have gone out of business or merged with peers. In Europe, Junkers was a major German aircraft manufacturer that produced some of the best-known aircraft over the course of its 50-plus years: commercial aircraft (F-13), helicopters, and military jets. The company produced a total of 322 F13s, mainly between 1920 and 1925, and most went into service in Germany and Russia (Kay and Couper, 2004). Junkers even built the first all-metal airplane using a tubular structure protected with corrugated sheet iron. However, in 1969, the company was acquired by Messerschmitt-Bölkow-Blohm, a German aerospace company, and the Junkers name disappeared.

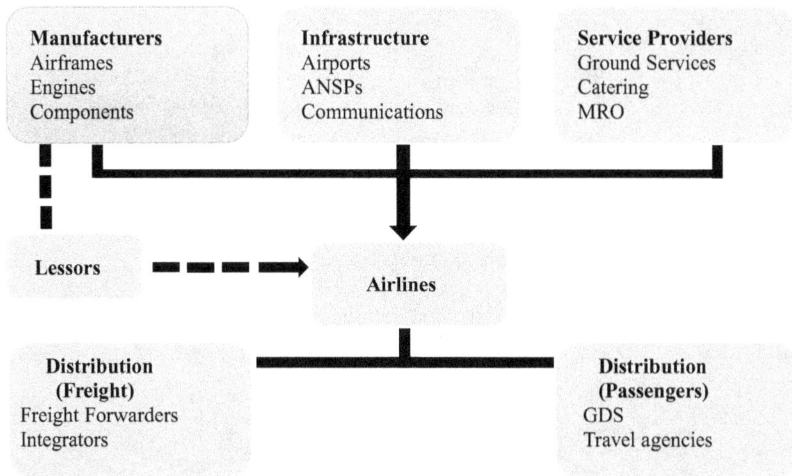

Figure 1.4 Commercial aviation value chain. MRO—maintenance, repair, and overhaul.

Source: Tretheway and Markhvida (2013).

Aircraft manufacturing has been dominated by two main entities: Boeing and Airbus, although after World War II, four prominent players emerged in the business of building commercial jets: Boeing, McDonnell, Douglas, and Lockheed. Douglas manufactured commercial aircraft that could also be used as military aircraft (DC-6), and McDonnell Aircraft and the Douglas Aircraft Company merged in 1967.[11] In 1982, McDonnell Douglas decided that all new aircraft models would have the designation MD, and the company produced several well-known commercial and military aircraft such as the MD-80, MD-90, and DC-10 airliner and F-15 Eagle air-superiority fighter jets. In 1996, McDonnell Douglas announced plans to build a 400-seat jumbo jet to challenge the monopoly status of Boeing's 747 in that category. The MD-11, built from 1990 until 2001 was the last commercial aircraft of McDonnell Douglas during the 1990s before it was acquired by Boeing (Gray, 1996), marking the end of McDonnell Douglas commercial aircraft production.[12]

Lockheed produced a wide assortment of commercial aircraft including the Electra, Super Constellation, and L-10111 TriStar; however, the company lost $2.5 billion on the L-1011 program between 1968 and 1984 on a total of 250 aircraft.[13] The collapse of the L-1011 led Lockheed to exit commercial aircraft manufacturing and focus exclusively on military aircraft (Sandler and Hartley, 2007). The Boeing Company was founded by William Boeing in 1916, and Boeing's real start in commercial aviation came through the mail. The US Postal Service awarded Boeing a contract to fly the mail between San Francisco and Chicago in 1927, and Boeing developed the Model 40A to fly this route (Vasigh et al., 2012). Boeing's growth has been immense since then and the only major competition Boeing currently faces is from Airbus. The various mergers and acquisitions in the aircraft manufacturing industry are shown in Figure 1.5, including the formation of Boeing and Lockheed Martin. Boeing's merger with McDonnell Douglas was a significant event in the aerospace industry: This merger, announced in December 1996 and completed in August 1997, created the world's largest aerospace company and a leading manufacturer of commercial jetliners, defense, space, and security systems.

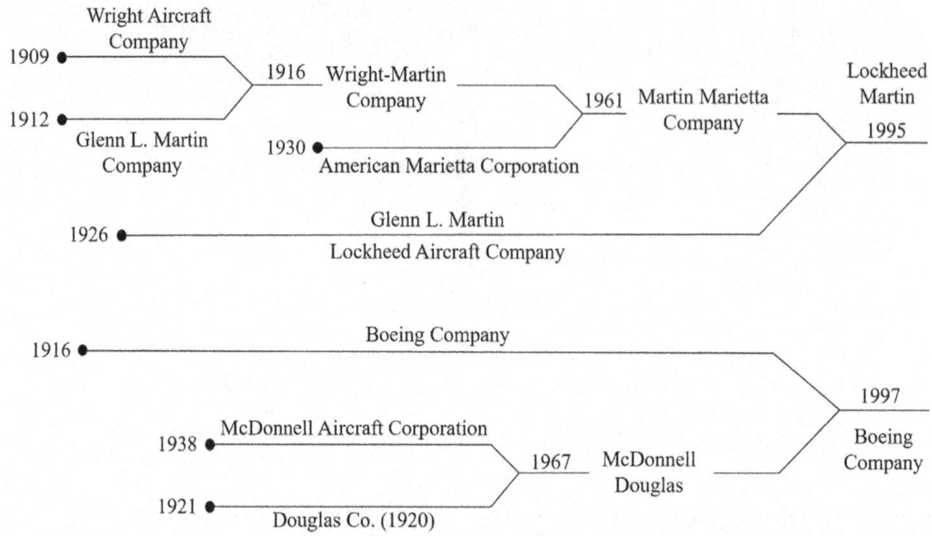

Figure 1.5 US commercial aircraft manufacturer mergers.[14]

Boeing started to design passenger aircraft throughout the late 1920s and early 1930s, progressively building aircraft that could hold more passengers and cargo. In 1952, Boeing began to build a prototype of the 707, which became Boeing's first commercial jetliner with both military and government applications. A total of 916 Boeing 707s were delivered to customers from 1958 to 1982 (Eden, 2008). Before the introduction of the 707, US airlines had preferred Douglas and Lockheed aircraft, but that all changed after the 707 became the first US-manufactured jetliner, and Boeing became the premier aircraft manufacturer for airlines around the world. In addition to the 707, Boeing designed and produced the 727, 737, 747, 757, 767, 777, and 787. Boeing's newest widebody aircraft, the 777X, is the world's largest twin-engine plane in production.[15] The jet is expected to enter service in 2025, although the timeline is years behind schedule.

Airbus was formed in 1970 as a consortium of smaller aircraft manufacturers in mainly Germany and France but was operating more as an alliance until the owners decided to create the European Aeronautic Defense and Space Company (EADS) in 2000. EADS was just recently rebranded to the more commonly known subdivision Airbus.[16] With the delivery of the A-380, Airbus is currently the manufacturer of the largest commercially used airliners. However, this specific aircraft has been below sales target, and the company's political structure, with ownership and production spread across multiple countries, often sparks debates during economic downturns and potential facility shutdowns.

The first Airbus aircraft was the A300, a twin engine, with its first flight in 1972. Today, Airbus is producing its bestseller A320 family (A318, A319, A320, A321) that is also available with a new engine option (the A320neo). In the wide-body segment, Airbus is still offering the A330, its new A350 with composite material, and its flagship, the A380, which in a full-economy seating, would fit more than 850 people. However, as we noted, sales were slower than expected, with only Emirates ordering a significant number.[17] A380 production stopped in 2021, with the last aircraft delivered to Emirates in 2021. For Emirates, the A380 represents a characteristic aircraft that will be difficult to replace, and in fact the company has been buying used A380s and adding them to their fleet.

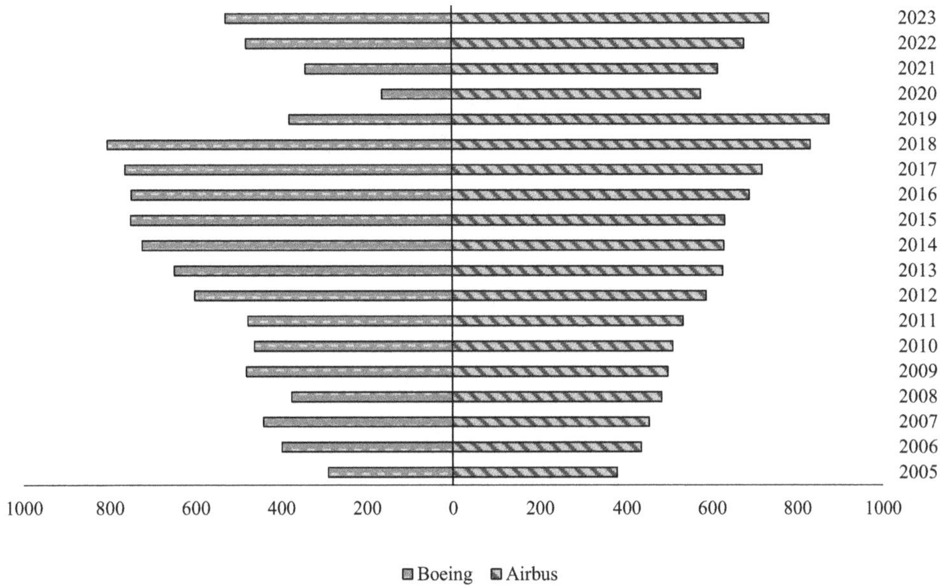

Figure 1.6 Airbus vs Boeing: number of deliveries: 2005–2023.[18]

Despite its acknowledged status as an engineering marvel, the A380 is considered to be an unsuccessful project. Airbus faced several production obstacles along the way, and the shifting airline demand caused less orders than expected. Moreover, Airbus initially incorrectly estimated the breakeven cost of A380, and final breakeven turned out to be nearly double the initial estimate. For these reasons, Airbus took a heavy financial loss from the aircraft.

Today, the market is shifting from nearly even split in favor of Airbus: In 2018, Airbus surpassed Boeing in number of ordered and manufactured aircraft, primarily because of Boeing's manufacturing and safety issues. Recently, Boeing has struggled to deliver promised aircraft on time and in expected quality; the 737 MAX has in particular shown many safety hiccups, production delays, and questionable operation.

Figure 1.6 shows the growth of both Airbus and Boeing over nearly two decades based on the number of overall deliveries. Another important aspect, as mentioned above, is the even growth enjoyed by both companies, making the aircraft manufacturing industry an almost perfect duopoly. Due to the impressive performance of the A300B4 model, the A300 and A310 became the first family of twin-engine aircraft to become extended-range twin operations-certified.[19]

Recently, smaller companies such as Bombardier and Embraer have started to encroach on some of Boeing's and Airbus's market share (Figure 1.7). Embraer is the world's third-largest commercial aircraft manufacturer, and both its and Bombardier's entry into the 140-seat range of aircraft proved to be crucial in the narrow-body market. However, as we later discuss, Bombardier left the market and fully shifted its focus to business jets. Figure 1.8 shows the current manufactures of different types of aircraft used in commercial aviation. It can be observed that the smaller the capacity of the aircraft the more manufacture is present in the market.

Beyond Bombardier and Embraer, other smaller companies developing narrow bodies and regional jets include Mitsubishi, COMAC, and Sukhai.

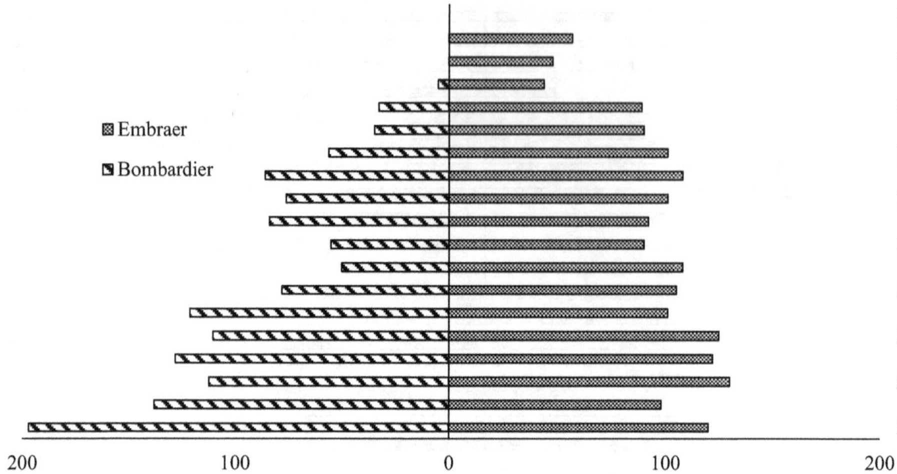

Figure 1.7 Bombardier vs Embraer: number of commercial aviation deliveries: 2005–2023.[20]

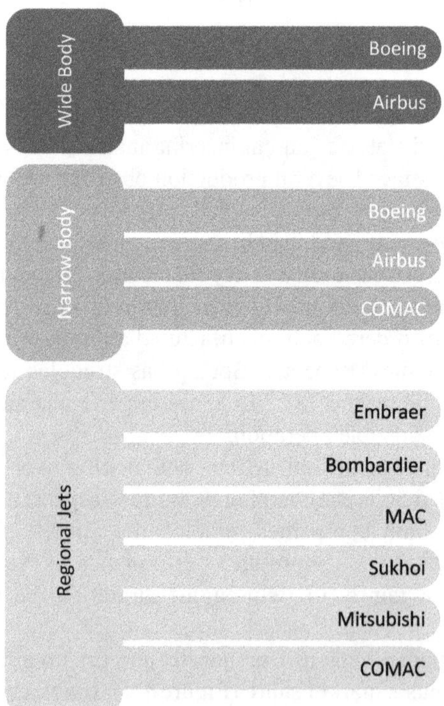

Figure 1.8 Overview of aircraft manufacturers.

Bombardier

Bombardier was founded in 1942 to market snowmobiles and became one of the world's biggest manufacturers of aircraft and trains; the company became famous for its CRJ and C-series aircraft. In 2017, facing manufacturing issues, low sales, and a dispute with Boeing regarding sales to US airlines, Bombardier decided to sell the majority stake of its C-Series commercial

To overcome financial difficulties, Bombardier has undertaken strategic measures including divesting from several branches. These divestitures aim to streamline operations, reduce costs, and refocus resources on core business areas. Bombardier completed four major sales in the aerospace sector: the CSeries to Airbus, the Q400 to Longview Aircraft, the CRJ to Mitsubishi Heavy Industries), and its Belfast aerostructure operations to Spirit AeroSystems.

program to Airbus. This move was prompted by the challenges encountered in competing with Embraer's E-Jet and the high costs associated with the C-Series jet. In 2020, Bombardier ceased production of the CRJ, and Mitsubishi Aircraft stepped in to acquire the program. Mitsubishi's intention is to offer maintenance and spare parts for the currently operational fleet of CRJ aircraft worldwide. Following these strategy shifts, Bombardier announced a shift in focus to its series of business jets (Global 7500, Global Express, Challenger 650, and Challenger 3500) and discontinued the production of commercial aircraft.

Embraer

ERJ 145 and E-jet family are examples of Embraer's manufacturing efforts. The E-Jet family has played a pivotal role in revolutionizing regional air travel, presenting lucrative business opportunities for numerous airline operators. Over the past 21 years since its inaugural flight, this series of narrow-body airliners with short to medium range has maintained consistent, impressive production of over 1,600 units. Introduced as the successor to Embraer's ERJ family, the E-Jet marked a significant leap in size for the Brazilian manufacturer. On February 19, 2002, the E-Jet prototype took its maiden flight, and two decades later, it stands as a testament to continuous commercial success. Notably, Embraer retired the proud ERJ 145 family a few years ago.

Mitsubishi's Regional Jet is another regional jet manufacturer. Launched in 2008, this project encountered significant challenges, leading to repeated setbacks and a failure to meet its 2013 rollout target. The situation worsened in October 2020 when the project was put on hold due to additional glitches and a sharp decline in demand for new aircraft amid the COVID-19 pandemic. Reflecting on the setbacks, Mitsubishi acknowledges today that a lack of initial understanding of the highly complex certification process for commercial aircraft and insufficient resources for long-term development were critical lessons learned from the MRJ/SpaceJet project. In the short term, Mitsubishi Heavy Industries Regional Jets (MHIRJ) in Canada is continuing its CRJ program acquired from Bombardier.

Sukhoi Civil Aircraft

Russian aircraft company Sukhoi Civil Aircraft produces the regional Sukhoi Superjet 100 (SSJ100). The aircraft commenced commercial operations in mid-2011, and as of April 2024, about 164 SSJ100s had been delivered. The flying fleet of SSJ100s worldwide had accumulated over 300,000 flight hours by that date. Notably, the SSJ100 distinguished itself as the first airliner designed with an integrated approach, optimizing performance by coordinating the design of both engine and airframe. In 2012, the SSJ100 received the European Aviation Safety Agency (EASA) Type Certificate, and it holds certifications from various authorities, including the Russian IAC AR, as well as the civil aviation authorities of Indonesia, Laos, and Mexico. An additional milestone was reached in January 2016 when the SSJ100 achieved Cat IIIA certification from EASA. Since the inception of the program, a total of 147 SSJ100s have been delivered. Looking ahead, the SSJ-New development suggests a maturation of the aircraft type. Russia has a strong commitment to enhance its fleet with domestically built aircraft due to the effort to reach global independence and improve its current geopolitical situation.

After Russia's invasion of Ukraine, Western countries imposed heavy sanctions against the Russian aviation industry. These sanctions were part of broader measures aimed at penalizing Russia for its aggression and deterring further military actions. The sanctions targeted various aspects of the Russian aviation sector, including aircraft manufacturing, exports, and related technologies. The Sukhoi Superjet 100 has been attempting to make its comeback with more Russian parts since trade sanctions have limited access to foreign components. Airlines that operate the aircraft have been having a tough time keeping the SJ100 airborne because of a shortage of parts, mainly for the aircraft's SaM146 turbofan engine.[21]

Commercial Aircraft Corporation of China

Commercial Aircraft Corporation of China (Comac) produces the Comac C919, a narrow-body airliner developed by China's state-owned aerospace company. The C919 is China's first domestically produced narrow-body passenger plane.

The C919 program was initiated in 2008, and production started in December 2011, with the first prototype rolling off the assembly line in November 2015. The aircraft's first flight occurred over Shanghai in May 2017, and the first commercial flight took place in 2023. However, challenges including technical issues and supply chain disruptions led to significant delays in the project. Comac encountered additional setbacks in securing local certification from China's aviation regulator, the Civil Aviation Administration of China, by the end of 2021. Nevertheless, all these issues seem to be sorted out, and the company has managed to secure an impressive number of over 1,200 orders including non-Chinese orders from Hainan Airlines and the non-Chinese entity GE Capital Aviation Services, now known as AerCap, which has placed an order for 10 C919 s.

Comac also produces a regional jet, ARJ21. This aircraft, developed independently by China for which Comac holds complete intellectual property rights, achieved a significant milestone with its official delivery to its first overseas customer, TransNusa, on December 18, 2022. The ARJ21 has proven its success and utility since its introduction in 2008, marking a noteworthy accomplishment in China's aviation industry. Recently Comac announced that it has more than 1,000 orders for the C919, but most of those are from Chinese airlines and aircraft lessors. At the Singapore Airshow, Comac took orders from Tibet Airlines, a Chinese entity, for 40 C919 single-aisle planes.[22]

Moreover, Comac's C929 wide-body jet project has progressed into the detailed design stage. However, the absence of any mention regarding the involvement of the Russian firm suggests that the joint venture with Russia may have encountered difficulties or fallen apart. The C929, a collaborative effort between China and Russia, was envisioned as a significant project to produce a wide-body jet, but recent statements from Comac seem to suggest a shift in the partnership dynamics.

Jet Engine Manufacturers

The 21st century has witnessed the emergence of innovative technologies that promise to reshape the jet engine industry. Electric and hybrid propulsion systems, along with artificial intelligence and advances in materials science, are paving the way for more sustainable and autonomous air travel. Concepts like distributed propulsion and blended-wing body designs hint at a future where aircraft are not only more efficient but also fundamentally different in their configurations.

The world jet engine market is dominated by four gargantuan manufacturers that produce engines for commercial airlines around the world, although apart from commercial and military aircraft, jet engine technology is used in industrial and marine applications. Developing new engines requires huge initial investments in labor, capital, equipment, and technology; engines are a very significant cost of aircraft ownership and operation. Advances in aircraft engines have contributed to higher fuel efficiency of commercial fleets. Since 1980, the average fuel burn per aircraft seat mile has been reduced significantly. However, the complexity and the technological advancements have led to the formation of a large, consolidated, oligopolistic industry with the following firms: General Electric (GE), Rolls-Royce, Pratt &Whitney (P&W),[23] CFM International (CFMI), and International Aero Engines (IAE), a consortium with Pratt & Whitney as the main company.

CFMI is a partnership between General Electric and Snecma, the French state-owned engine manufacturer. IAE was formed in 1983 between P&W, Rolls-Royce, Daimler-Benz, Fiat, and Japan Aero Engines; Rolls-Royce sold all its shares to P&W in 2012. CFMI has generally been the provider of engines for narrow-body aircraft; P&W has a smaller presence in the commercial aircraft market but is a big player in the military contracting field. These consortia have created the interesting situation that manufacturers are both partners and competitors concurrently.

Aircraft Leasing

Aircraft leasing has gained popularity in the aviation industry due to its flexibility and efficiency. By choosing to lease instead of purchase outright, airlines can avoid the substantial upfront costs associated with acquiring aircraft. This financial model allows them to spread the expenses over time through manageable lease payments. Moreover, leasing enables airlines to adjust their fleet sizes according to fluctuating market demands without committing to long-term ownership. This ability is particularly valuable during periods of economic uncertainty or rapid changes in passenger traffic. Additionally, leasing provides access to newer aircraft models equipped with advanced technology and fuel efficiency, enhancing airlines' competitiveness. With lessors assuming some risks like depreciation and maintenance costs, airlines can focus on core operations while enjoying the benefits of a modern fleet. As air travel continues to globalize and demand rises, leasing offers a scalable solution for airlines to expand their fleets swiftly and effectively, catering to evolving market needs.

Over half of the commercial aircraft coming into market are leased, and smaller airlines lease an even higher percentage of their fleet. A lease is a contract by which the lessor grants the airline the right to use the aircraft in exchange for a series of lease payments. Major leasing companies generally provide maintenance, financial, and technical services. AerCap and Air Lease Corporation are the two global leaders in aircraft leasing, with a combined fleet of approximately 2,316 aircraft. Table 1.1 and Figure 1.9 show the fleet values and market shares of the top 10 leasing companies.

In 1973, Steven Házy co-founded the aircraft leasing business that became International Lease Finance Corporation (ILFC) and led the company from its start in 1973 until his departure in 2010.[24] In 2014, AerCap completed its acquisition of ILFC from American International Group (AIG). The transaction provided AIG $3 billion in cash and 97.6 million AerCap shares.[25] The combined company is the largest aircraft leasing firm in the world by fleet value, with a fleet of over 1,809 aircraft (Table 1.1). In 2010, S. Hazy, after terminating his relationship with ILFC, founded Air Lease Corporation (ALC). ALC is the second-largest commercial aircraft and engine lessor in the world by fleet value, with a fleet of 507 aircraft.

Airports

The US Federal Aviation Administration (FAA) categorizes airports as commercial service, primary, cargo service, reliever, and general aviation. Generally, commercial airports are publicly

Table 1.1 The Total Fleet Value of the Top 10 Leasing Companies

Rank 2023	*Leasing Company*	*Total Fleet Value ($m)*	*Total Fleet*
1	Aercap	47,939	1,809
2	Air Lease Corporation	21,709	507
3	Avolon	19,810	587
4	SMBC Aviation Capital	17,647	506
5	BOC Aviation	16,451	426
6	BBAM	15,052	456
7	ICBC Financial leasing	10,051	428
8	Aviation Capital Group	9,676	347
9	CDB Aviation	9,554	269
10	Bocom Leasing	9,550	270

Source: *Airfinance*.

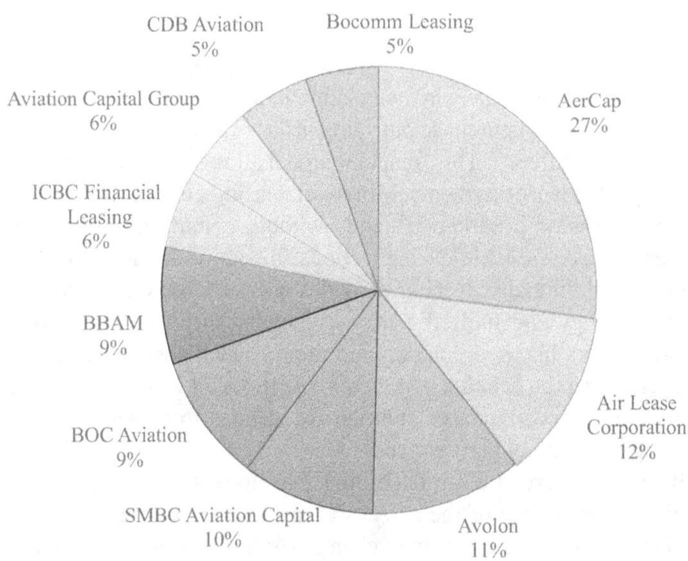

Figure 1.9 Market share of top 10 aircraft leasing companies globally.[26]

owned airports that receive scheduled passenger service and have at least 2,500 passenger enplanements annually.[27] Cargo airports serve only cargo, not passenger, air transportation with a total annual landed weight of more than 100 million pounds.[32] Reliever airports are airports the FAA has designated for relieving congestion at commercial airports and increase general air travel access to regional communities.

As of January 2024, Airports Council International (ACI) serves 757 members, operating 2,109 airports in 191 countries. ACI is organized, structured, and governed in a federal manner and includes ACI World and five regions: Africa, Asia-Pacific and Middle East, Europe, Latin America and the Caribbean, and North America. According to the ACI World Airport Traffic Report, there are roughly 2,000 commercial airports in the world, and around 41,000 civilian and military commercial airports around the world in total.[28] This is an indication of the volume of passengers and the importance of proper connectivity around the world.

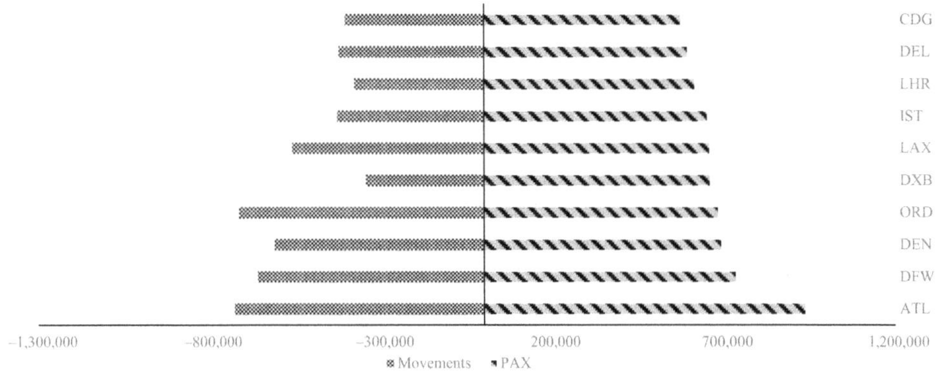

Figure 1.10 Top 10 world airports by passenger traffic (in 100s) and total aircraft movements.[29]

The trend toward airport privatization began in the United Kingdom with the Transport Act of 1981. The Act established the framework for privatizing British Airports by creating a holding company. Thatcher administration privatized seven commercial airports and transferred the ownership to private company via the British Airport Authority. The airports privatized are London Heathrow, Gatwick, Stanstead, Southampton, Edinburgh Airport, Aberdeen Airport, and Glasgow Airport.

Privatization of airports ensures that the airports function in an efficient manner since there is now adequate motivation for proper management of the airport. Although privatized airports have a few disadvantages, the process of privatization has helped airports earn a bigger role in the air transport industry value chain. Worldwide airport passenger numbers increased to over 6.6 billion in 2022. Figure 1.10 presents the world's busiest airports of 2022.

Atlanta remains the world's busiest airport with nearly 100 million passengers annually, but with the rapidly growing economies, airports around Asia are making market share gains. Airports Beijing Airport and airports in India, Dubai, and Turkey have experienced significant growth in passengers and aircraft movement.[30]

Air Navigation Service Providers

Air navigation service providers (ANSPs) historically operated as government agencies financed by taxes and charges; this structure reflected the role of ANSPs as a form of policing of the skies. In the late 1980s, under pressure from a radically expanding air transport industry, the commercialization of ANSPs began in New Zealand and Australia in 1987 and 1988, respectively. Commercialization has intensified in particular in Europe, where most states now operate air traffic control as a business. However, individual member states are still in the process of aligning the various previously national navigation centers into the European navigation system. Both Africa and Asia have witnessed significant increases in commercial air navigation provision. In the Americas, however, apart from Canada, the traditional governmental model has continued to prevail.

Ground Handling and Catering

Ground handling is the services provided to aircraft, passengers, and cargo at an airport; it is an essential service that encompasses all the activities around the aircraft, terminal, and cargo warehouse, focusing on the load being carried. Catering, providing the in-flight and club meals, is another important service requirement in the airline industry, and the quality of this service can be a significant factor in retaining customer loyalty and satisfaction.

Global Distribution and Computer Reservation Systems

Global distribution systems (GDSs) are global computerized reservation networks used as a single point of access for reserving airline seats, hotel rooms, and rental cars by reservation and travel agents. Most travel companies use a GDS to book flights, hotels, and cars. A number of GDSs currently distribute airline schedules, seat availability by booking class, and other relevant booking class information worldwide. Individual airlines can use the GDS to see their own published information but more importantly to monitor their competitors. The companies dominating the GDS market are Amadeus,[31] Galileo (owned by Travelport), Sabre, Travelport,[32] and Worldspan. Amadeus, Sabre, and Galileo are among the top global distribution systems available today. Airline reservation systems (ARS) are the user side system for any airline or GDS.[33] GDSs have four integrated functional components (see Figure 1.11).

Similar to the ARS, the passenger's name record is maintained in the GDS system, and computerized reservation systems (CRSs) contain information about air carrier schedules, availability, fares, and fares rules, and users can make reservations or issue tickets. Some airlines prefer direct sales to travelers, but the overhead of maintaining the networks that would allow this compels them to work with GDSs.

United Airlines was the first airline to install their in-house CRS, called Apollo, in travel agencies in 1976. American Airlines quickly followed suit, and by the end of the year, 130 reservation offices had installed the Sabre GDS. European airlines began developing their own GDSs, Amadeus and Galileo,[34] that were very similar to the systems developed in the United

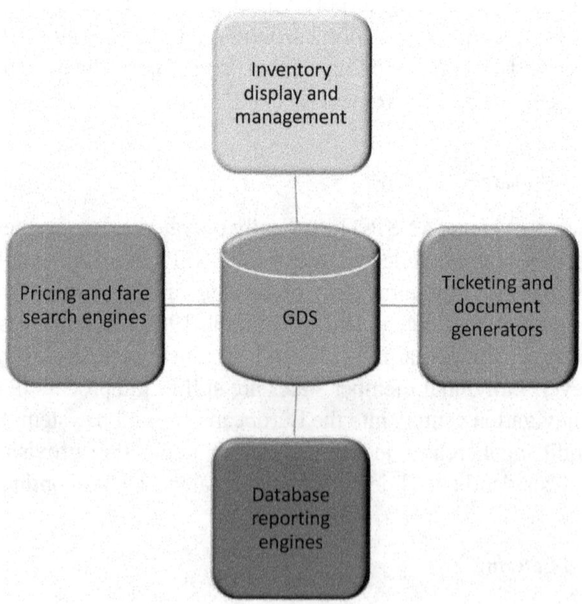

Figure 1.11 A global distribution system.

States. The GDS called Abacus was developed by a consortium of Southeast Asian Airlines, and TravelSky is the GDS used in China.

As we described earlier, concentrations in the sector have left only four global players, which gives them tremendous power. Low-cost carriers avoid GDS fees by only offering tickets through their own distribution channels. However, Ryanair, the exemplary European low-cost carrier, has recently started to offer bookings through a GDS. Lufthansa started an initiative to reduce dependency on reservation system providers by adding a GDS fee to all GDS bookings, making their own distribution network 8–16 Euros cheaper per ticket.

Expedia-Owned Brands

- ebookers
- Expedia
- Expedia.com
- CarRentals.com
- Expedia Affiliate Network
- Expedia Local Expert
- HomeAway
- Hotels.com
- Hotwire Group
- Orbitz
- Travelocity
- Vrbo
- Trivago
- Venere.com
- Wotif.com

While a GDS more globally manages all relevant booking information, reservation details, and prices, CRSs manage the reservation process for travelers, particularly booking tickets. Today, online travel agents are integral components of the air travel sector, utilizing both GDSs and CRSs on behalf of both airlines and travelers for a fee.

Online Travel Agents

Travel agents render services for passenger travel such as advice and planning; arranging tours, accommodations, and passenger and baggage transportation; issuing tickets. With the advent of the World Wide Web, particularly Web 2.0, the demand for these services from individual providers decreased, and travel agent activity moved online.

Worldwide online travel sales accounted for US$475 billion in 2022, and global travel and tourism is estimated to reach to $1 trillion by 2030.[35] Expedia, launched in 1996 by Microsoft and sold in 2001, has become one of the most successful electronic-commerce sites.[36] Expedia acquired Travelocity from Sabre Corporation for $280 million.[37] In November 2014, Expedia completed its acquisition of Australia-based Wotif Group, and in September 2015 acquired Orbitz Worldwide for $1.6 billion. Expedia, through brands such as Trivago, Hotels.com, and Hotwire, as well as its eponymous operation, earned $12 billion in gross bookings in 2022. Expedia uses Amadeus, Sabre, and other GDSs for flights and Worldspan and Pegasus for hotels along with its own and consolidators' reservations.

Freight Forwarders and Integrators

Freight forwarders organize shipments of goods from the manufacturer or producer to the final point of distribution. A forwarder does not move the goods but acts as an expert in the logistics network, contracting with carriers to move cargo ranging from raw agricultural products to manufactured goods. Another freight distributor in the aviation value chain is an integrator, a company providing door-to-door delivery of freight and an entire range of services associated with that such as planning, tracking, shipping, clearance, complex supply chain management, and other general and customized services. Some of the most well-known US integrators are DHL, UPS and FedEx.

Airline Profitability

In the commercial aviation sector, just about every member in the aforementioned value chain enjoys a decent level of profits. One of the enduring ironies of the industry is that the companies that actually move passengers from one place to another, the most crucial link in the chain, struggle to break even. This comparative failure of airlines can be attributed to multiple major factors. For one, the bargaining power of suppliers is high, with powerful labor unions especially at hub operations, concentrated oligopolies in aircraft and engine manufacturing, local monopolies at airports, and increasing concentration in the supply of services.

For example, aircraft manufacturing is currently a duopoly run by Boeing and Airbus. The consolidation of the aerospace industry in North America reached a climax on December 15, 1996, when then Boeing CEO Phil Condit and McDonnell Douglas CEO Harry Stonecipher, announced that the two aerospace giants would merge in a $13.3 billion stock-for-stock transaction. Airbus, on the other hand, was formed out of a consortium of four major manufacturers in Europe, making it a near monopoly in the European market, although many small manufacturers exist there as well. GDSs also now have high bargaining power of the GDS because each of the three major ones – Travelport, Amadeus and Sabre – is insulated from competition by their market power.

Buyers also have high bargaining power in that they have many options with low switching costs, which restricts airlines' potential revenues. The competition is high, partly because of the economics (high sunk costs per aircraft, low marginal cost per passenger, perishable product, and limited economies of scale), but also because of government constraints restricting consolidation through exit or cross-border merger. The threat of substitute services is also rising, with improving technology for web conferencing reducing the need to travel for business and competition from high-speed rail in short-haul markets, particularly in Europe, where the rail infrastructure is more accessible and taking the train is common more prevalent. Finally, airports play a vital role in restricting the possible profits of airlines since most major airports in the world are quasi-monopolistic. That is, despite the existence of surrounding airports, some airports dominate the market in their regions, such as London Heathrow.

To remain in contention in such a competitive industry and to sustain their recent growth, airlines need to evolve further and try to incorporate decisive changes in their operations. Airlines could invest in analyzing customer preferences, which would in turn enable them to build more solid customer bases, leading to increased market share and profits. Airlines could also move toward more digitization to reduce operating costs; for example, systems that can enable real-time resource planning and allocation drive greater utilization. Tech-enabled engines can notify maintenance and operations centers of performance issues while an aircraft is still in the air and request that a replacement part be waiting when it lands. Such measures can reduce downtime and greatly improve performance, driving down costs while also bolstering passenger satisfaction through more frequent on-time arrivals and departures. Airline managers need to be ruthless in cutting costs in areas that are not relevant to safety, reputation, branding, or customer value.

Finally, airlines should continue to seek partnerships that will be more targeted and synergistic than the traditional alliances that now dominate. Those alliances allow route sharing on a broad basis, but they aren't tailored narrowly enough to allow airlines to strategically fill in specific gaps. For example, Qantas, which was already part of the oneworld Alliance, recently forged such a targeted partnership with Emirates;: Qantas did not have the traffic to fly profitably to multiple cities in Europe, although there was significant demand among its loyal customer bases; Emirates had sufficient demand to access a large number of destinations in Europe, but it did not have a loyal base of local customers in Australia. The new partnership gave Qantas access to many more destinations in Europe and let Emirates access an extremely loyal base of customers.

Airline Mergers and Bankruptcies

The airline industry is very competitive and susceptible to external shocks, and as a result is fearfully turbulent. Since 1978, more than 250 new airlines have been started in the United States, and nearly all of them failed.

The air transport industry has advanced dramatically since its first flight in 1903, primarily improving after deregulation in 1978, which drastically altered the landscape and competitive nature for airlines. Delta Air Lines pioneered the hub-and-spoke model, which was subsequently replicated by the other major US carriers. While the legacy carriers initially benefited from deregulation, the hub-and-spoke model and new competition also exposed them to many drawbacks, namely their inability to adapt quickly to an ever-changing environment. Low-cost carriers took advantage of the inflexibility inherent in the model and adopted a point-to-point system that allowed for greater versatility in a volatile market. The period between 2000 and 2010 was particularly rough for the industry, which faced steep declines in travel, spikes in fuel prices, and labor disputes, all culminating in a record 20 airlines filing for either Chapter 7 or Chapter 11 bankruptcy.[38]

Filing for Chapter 11 protections buys a company time to devise a new business plan to pay off its creditors. A bankruptcy judge can impose a new contract – and new wage cuts – on a union, approve the transfer of pension obligations to the federal government, and agree to eliminate some debts altogether. There are also a few disadvantages associated with bankruptcy protection, among the biggest being the high costs. The debtor must pay for its own legal advisers as well as for those of its creditors; the total cost of an airline bankruptcy can be hundreds of millions of dollars. If the company can't find enough cash to pay back loans and cover legal fees, it is liquidated.

Bankruptcies are a way for capital to reorganize in a more efficient way; they help to move the industry to a more efficient structure where consumers get good services at reasonable prices and airlines can actually make money, although airlines are never going to consistently make money year after year because it is an industry that is inherently volatile. The most common consequence of a bankruptcy in the airline industry is a merger or consolidation of multiple carriers to rescue the firm facing bankruptcy. A clear indication of that trend is depicted in Figure 1.12, which gives an account of all the major airline mergers in the past 15 years.

Airline mergers have both pros and cons. For passengers, mergers mean fewer carriers, which can lead to increasing prices as customers have fewer options. For airlines, the merged entities are more competitive, although it is challenging to efficiently merge large companies and manage the employees and assets in a cost-effective and efficient manner. The merger of American Airlines and US Airways could be the last major merger in the United States since the

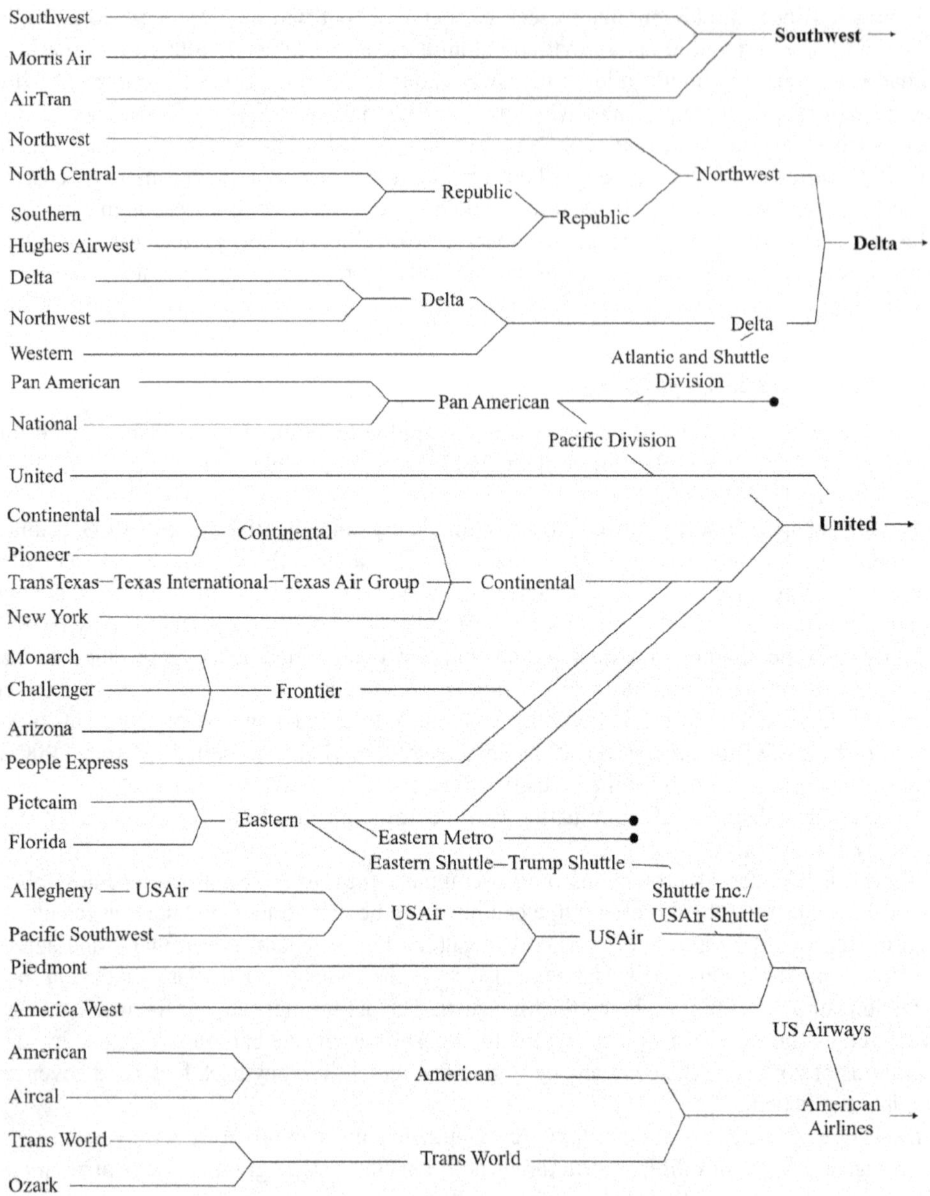

Figure 1.12 The consolidation of the US airline industry.

Source: Adopted from *Introduction to Airline Economics* (Vasigh et al., 2014).

Department of Justice (DOJ) would definitely consider any further mergers among the major carriers to be large scale collusion and prevent it from happening. Monopolies are banned in the United States. However, the US airline industry is concentrated among four major players, whereas in Europe, the market is divided more equally. The four major US airlines controlled 67.3% of their market in 2022, while Europe's top 10 airlines administered roughly only 40% of total flights.[39]

Summary

Engineering economics is a branch of economics that focuses on the analysis, evaluation, and comparison of the costs and benefits of engineering projects and decisions. It involves applying economic principles and techniques to solve engineering problems and make informed decisions. By applying concepts such as present and future value, net present value, internal rate of return, and annuities, engineering economics helps professionals determine the most cost-effective and beneficial approaches to project evaluation, investment decisions, cost management, and resource allocation. In this chapter, we have given an overview of the components of the air transport industry and the aviation value chain and their various economic implications for the industry, airlines, and customers themselves.

Discussion Questions and Problems

1.1 What were the primary strategic motivations behind Boeing's decision to merge with McDonnell Douglas, and how did this consolidation impact the competitive landscape of the aircraft manufacturing industry?
1.2 What are the main purposes of airline computer reservation systems (CRSs)?
1.3 Would you expect aircraft and jet engine manufacturers to have the same degree of control over price? Why?
1.4 What is the difference between airline CRS and GDS?
1.5 Discuss the pros and cons of airline consolidations.
1.6 Explain the main functions of global distribution systems.
1.7 What is required for the airline industry to continue its profitability?
1.8 Explain what the major network airlines should do to minimize the competitive threat posed by the low-cost airlines?
1.9 Why does the airline industry continue to dominate the world transportation system?
1.10 What has been the impact of the introduction of wide-body aircraft on economic development in the world?
1.11 From an engineering point of view, how can airlines reduce aircraft operating costs and increase revenue?
1.12 What is the economic rationale behind airline mergers?
1.13 Describe engineering economics and define its role in decision-making.
1.14 Has airline deregulation been good for the airline industry as a whole?
1.15 What impact has deregulation had on commercial airline profitability?

Notes

1 Presentation to the Aeronautical Law Committee of the Business Law Section of the International BAR Association at its Annual Meeting in Vancouver, B.C. on 15 September 1998. Published: 2008–03–26.
2 Deregulation refers to the Airline Deregulation Act of 1978 (92 Stat. 1705).
3 NewMyer, D. A. (1990). The Impact of Deregulation on Airports: An International Perspective. *Journal of Aviation/Aerospace Education & Research.*
4 Wolfe, H. P. & NewMyer, D. A. (1985). *Aviation Industry Regulation.* Carbondale, IL: Southern Illinois University Press.
5 Sources: Airlines in the U.S. Ranked by Domestic Market Share 2011–2021 | Statista (2023, June 22). *Statista.* www.statista.com/statistics/445683/united-states-domestic-market-share-of-leading-airlines/; Market Share of the Top American Airlines, 1977–2022 | The Geography of Transport Systems (2022, June 25). *The Geography of Transport Systems | the Spatial Organization of Transportation and Mobility.* https://transportgeography.org/contents/chapter5/air-transport/airline-market-share-united-states/.

6 Source: Statista (2023, December 1). *Worldwide Net Profit per Passenger by Region 2020*. www.statista.com/statistics/602658/net-profit-per-passenger-by-airline-region/.
7 Bureau of Transportation Statistics, December 2023.
8 Statista, 2023.
9 Sources: www.statista.com/statistics/227242/operating-income-of-commercial-airlines-worldwide/. www.statista.com/statistics/227242/operating-income-of-commercial-airlines-worldwide/. Operating Profit of Airlines Worldwide 2023 | Statista (2023, November 2). *Statista*. www.statista.com/statistics/227242/operating-income-of-commercial-airlines-worldwide/.
10 Tretheway, M. W. & Markhvida, K. (2013). The Aviation Value Chain: Economic Returns and Policy Issues. *Journal of Air Transportation Management*.
11 *Los Angeles Times*, Los Angeles, CA, October 9, 2004.
12 Boeing Announces Phase-Out of MD-11 Jetliner Program, Seattle, June 3, 1998.
13 *The New York Times*, December 8, 1981.
14 Compiled by the authors from data published by Boeing and Lockheed-Martin. Adopted from Vasigh, et al. (2012). *Aircraft Finance: Strategies for Managing Costs in a Turbulent Industry*.
15 Unlike the Airbus A350, a completely new design, Boeing's next-generation 777X builds off the successful track record of its classic 777 planes, particularly the historically popular 777–300ER.
16 Airbus History. *Flight International*, October 29, 1997.
17 A380 Superjumbo Lands in Sydney. *BBC News*, October 25, 2007.
18 Sources: www.aerosociety.com/news/airbus-boeing-2016-orders-and-deliveries/ https://about.ch-aviation.com/blog/2023/02/10/airbus-vs-boeing-deliveries-2022/#:~:text=In%20total%2C%20Airbus%20delivered%20676,a%20whopping%2072%25%20in%202020. https://dsm.forecastinternational.com/2018/01/26/airbus-boeing-report-december-and-full-year-2017-commercial-aircraft-orders-and-deliveries/.
19 U.S. Department of Transportation Federal Aviation Administration, Advisory Circular, AC:120–42B, June 13, 2008.
20 Sources: http://ir.bombardier.com/modules/misc/documents/77/77/92/55/14/Bombardier-Financial-Report-2015-en.pdf. https://aviationweek.com/air-transport/aircraft-propulsion/embraer-delivers-108-commercial-aircraft-2016–69. https://aviationweek.com/air-transport/embraer-commercial-aircraft-deliveries-slip-slightly-2017. www.prnewswire.com/news-releases/embraer-delivers-181-total-jets-in-2018-300792990.html. www.prnewswire.com/news-releases/embraer-sa-embraer-delivers-198-total-jets-in-2019-301007476.html. https://airinsight.com/embraer-airliner-deliveries-only-four-more-than-in-2020/. www.prnewswire.com/news-releases/embraer-delivers-80-jets-in-4q22-and-159-in-2022-301749807.html.
21 *Simple Flying*, December 30, 2023.
22 *VOA*, February 20, 2024.
23 Pratt & Whitney is a subsidiary of Raytheon Technologies (RTX). The company is best known for its JT8 and JT9 engines.
24 Company Annual Reports, 2010.
25 Johnsson, J. & Tracer, Z. (2014). AerCap Finishes $7.6 Billion ILFC Deal as AIG Narrows Aim. *Bloomberg*.
26 Source: *Air Finance Journal*.
27 DOT, FAA, Airport Categories, 2024.
28 Aeronewstv (2015). *How Many Commercial Airports are there in the World?*
29 Sources: www.afar.com/magazine/the-busiest-airports-in-the-world; https://aci.aero/2023/04/05/international-travel-returns-top-10-busiest-airports-in-the-world-revealed/ www.stratosjets.com/blog/busiest-us-airports/.
30 ACI World Reports and press release.
31 Owned by the Amadeus Group with headquarters in Madrid, Spain.
32 Travelport provides travel agencies and other travel-related businesses with access to a wide range of travel content, including airline reservations, hotel bookings, car rentals, and other travel services.
33 Travel Technology Company, December 20, 2014.
34 Now owned by Travelport.
35 Statista.
36 *The Economist*, June 21, 2014.
37 *Forbes*, January 25, 2015.
38 Tolkin, J. (2010). *Airline Bankruptcy: The Determining Factors Leading to an Airline's Decline*. CMC Senior Theses. Paper 88.
39 Bureau of Transportation Statistics, December 2015.

References

Bunke, H. (1954). Commercial Aviation and the Civil Aeronautic Act of 1938. *Southern Economic Journal*, 20(4).

Eden, P. E. (2008). *Civil Aircraft Today: The Worlds Most Successful Commercial Aircraft*. London, UK: Amber Books.

Gray, B. (1996). Boeing, McDonnell Douglas Merger Talks Break Down. *Financial Times*.

Kahn, A. (1988). Surprises of Airline Deregulation. *American Economic Review, Papers and Proceedings*, 78(2).

Kay, L. & Couper, P. (2004). *Junkers Aircraft and Engines, 1913–1945*. London: Putnam Aeronautical Books.

Sandler, T. & Hartley, K. (2007). *Handbook of Defense Economics, Defense in a Globalized World* (Vol. 2). North Holland.

Vasigh, B. & Azadian, F. (2022). *Aircraft Valuation in Volatile Market Conditions*. Springer International Publishing.

2 Foundations of Engineering Economics and Finance

Today, most companies that hire engineers are expecting them not only to participate in the decision-making process by evaluating the projects' technical aspects but also to provide an economic assessment of projects of different sizes. Engineers are expected to perform cost analyses, compare alternatives, and make decisions by considering both the technical and the financial virtues of projects. Engineering economics equips engineers with skills and techniques that will allow them to analyze, evaluate, and compare alternatives on an economic basis. In practice, engineering economics involves decision-making based on cash flows associated with a given project, life of the project, and interest rates. In this chapter, we discuss the fundamental concepts of engineering economics and introduce the basics of evaluating the financial merit of projects. We will make a distinction between simple and compound interest, calculate the future value of a single present amount, the present value of a future single sum, and the future and present values of streams of nonequal amounts. The concept of time value of the money will also be discussed.

Definition of Engineering Economics

Engineering economics is a study of the processes involved in selecting projects to pursue based on their economic viability, which derives from factors such as cash flows, interest rates, and project life of each project, and the interest rates. These comparisons can be accomplished using tools and techniques that simplify the evaluation of alternatives. Therefore, engineering economics can be defined as a science that equips engineers with a collection of skills, tools, and techniques to allow them to analyze, evaluate, and compare alternatives on an economic basis.

In real life, many factors affect whether to pursue a project including the safety, health, and welfare of the public; environmental impacts; ethical and political issues; and public acceptance. For instance, let us consider the Heathrow airport expansion project. Heathrow airport is one of the busiest airports in Europe and in the world. This airport is owned by the private Heathrow Airport Holdings. During 2014, Heathrow had over 470,000 flights[1] (roughly 1,290 flights a day) and served 73.4 million passengers, mostly international (93%). However, this busy airport that is desired by many airlines and passengers has only two runways, so expansion has been discussed. The expansion project, which includes building a third runway and another terminal, is expected to increase airport capacity and in turn notably increase revenue. However, the decision on this project is not based merely on the expected financial gain. Factors such as

DOI: 10.4324/9781003469759-2

carbon emission, noise pollution, and the creation of new direct and indirect jobs are just some of those that are considered in addition to economic factors for the decision on the merits of the expansion project.

Interest and Time Value of Money

Starting a new project or expanding an existing business requires capital. Often, companies must acquire the needed capital from investors to carry out new projects, but investors expect to see returns on their investments with interest. Consider renting a car. You pay the rental car company to borrow the car for a contracted period and return it at the end of the period but have the privilege of using it during that period. Similarly, when companies need to borrow money from investors, they are expected to return the capital (the rental car) and pay for the privilege of having control of the invested capital for the given period.

In 2012, Delta Air Lines acquired the Trainer refinery facility, which was on the brink of closing. The main motivation of this rather unconventional decision was to protect the airline against the refining margins.[2] During that time, fuel was one of the highest-cost items for the airline, and while jet fuel prices are largely dictated by the price of oil, the refining margins are times be significant. According to Delta, acquiring the refinery cost them $150 million.[3] Thus, Delta needed to acquire $150 million capital from investors, who expected returns with interest; for Delta, that interest payment is the cost of receiving the capital to buy the refinery.

Interest is either simple or compound. Simple interest is charged simply to the principal borrowed; compound interest is charged on the principal and on the amount of interest the borrower owes to the lender at each period, as if it is another loan. We discuss the details of these two concepts further in this chapter, but in short, understanding the difference involves understanding the concept of the time value of money: The basis of time value of money is that a dollar in hand today is worth more than a dollar to be received at some time in the future. It should be noted that this difference is not simply due to inflation but because if you have the money today, you could invest it and earn interest. Thus, when a borrower defers the payment of interest to the lender in a long-term loan, it is as if the borrower borrowed additional money from the lender, and the lender is entitled to gain interest on this additional amount.

In understanding the time value of money and interest, we need to note that the time value of money is not the same for everyone. Consider the rental car example. For a tourist, having a car for a day provides convenient. For a part-time Uber driver, having a car for a day means some additional revenue. For a professional taxi driver, however, a car is the main tool of business, and having a car for a day could mean the only revenue.[4] The same analogy applies for companies. The time value of money for each company highly depends on its ability to generate revenue based on the available capital. On the other side of the spectrum, lenders expect a different amount of interest for foregoing their capital for the loan period, and that expected interest depends on factors such as economic conditions, market size, risk, demand for loan, and loan period. That is why, for instance, different banks announce different interest rates for real estate loans.

Simple Interest

Simple interest is paid only on the principal borrowed at the end of the loan period. Under simple interest, borrowers provide no additional payment during the loan, and lenders only receive the principal and the interest at the end of the loan period.

Example 2.1

If you deposit \$1,000 in a savings account at the beginning of the year and receive \$1,060 at the end of the year, you have earned \$60 in interest in one year. The interest rate you earned on this savings account is 6% per year. The interest rate is calculated by dividing the dollar amount of interest over the principal and multiplying it by 100 to obtain a percentage:

$$\text{Interest Rate }(\%) = \frac{\$60}{\$1000} \times 100$$

$$\textit{Interest Rate} = 6\%$$

$$i = \frac{I}{P} \times 100$$

where i = interest rate expressed in percentage, I = dollar amount of interest accrued in one year, and P = principal (present value). Simple interest is calculated for one year as follows: Interest = principal × annual interest rate, or

$$I = P \times i$$

Example 2.2

If you deposit \$1,000 in a savings account that is paying a simple interest rate of 6% per year, you will earn \$60 in interest at the end of the first year as follows:

$$I = \$1{,}000 \times 6\% = \$60$$

For a multiyear period, total simple interest accrued is calculated as

$$\boldsymbol{I = P \times i \times n}$$

where n = the number of periods, usually in years (Figure 2.1).

Example 2.3

You deposit \$1,000 in a savings account paying a simple interest rate of 6% for four years. How much interest do you owe four years later?

Solution:

Using the multiyear equation for total simple interest, you can calculate the interest earned after four years as follows:

$I = \$1{,}000 \times 6\% \times 4$
$I = \$240$

Figure 2.1 How to calculate total interest.

At the end of the four years, you have accumulated $1,240, the sum of the principal and the accumulated four years of interest:

Amount at the end of year 4 = Principal + Accrued interest in four years
Amount at the end of year 4 = $1,000 + $240 = $1,240
$F = P + P \times i \times n$
$F = P\,[1 + (i \times n)]$

where F = the future value or the total accumulated amount at the end of the nth period.

In Example 2.3, because interest is paid on the principal only, the interest accrued in preceding interest periods is ignored in calculating the interest for each period, and interest is only calculated based on the original principal.

Example 2.4

DirectJet borrowed $10,000,000 with simple interest rate of 5% and with total principal and interest due in five years. Calculate the annual interest and total interest paid on this loan:

Annual interest = $10,000,000 × 0.05 = $500,000
Total interest at the end of year five = $500,000 × 5 = $2,500,000
Total interest and principal due at the end of year five = $12,500,000

The principal and interest are paid at the end of year five. The amount due at the end of each year increases by the constant amount of annual interest of $500,000. The interest accrued at the end of each year does not earn interest in the following years because the interest is simple. Figure 2.1 presents the details of annual interest, amount owed at the end of each year, and total amount due at the end of year five.

Simple interest is one of the fundamental concepts in engineering economics. However, in practice, simple interest loans are not common and are usually offered for short terms. One example of simple interest loans is the fixed rate short-term loans known as payday loans, also called cash advances. Payday loans are small loans (e.g., $50 to $1000) that are given for a short period of time (e.g., 14 days), and the borrowers are expected to return the principal with the interest (e.g., $15 for $100 loan). Despite the name, these loans are not technically related to actual paydays.

Compound Interest

In practice, interest is normally compounded, meaning it is paid on the principal and the accrued interest at any given period. In other words, the interest at the end of each period is added to the principal, both principal and interest earn interest in the next period, and that process continues through the end of the period. Note that in this scenario, there is no payback until the end of the loan period.

The interest for the first period is calculated as

$$\mathbf{I} = \mathbf{P} + (\mathbf{P} \times \mathbf{i})$$
$$\mathbf{I} = \mathbf{P} \times (1 + \mathbf{i})$$

The interest for the second period is calculated as

$$\mathbf{I} = (\mathbf{P} + (\mathbf{P} \times \mathbf{i})) \times \mathbf{i}$$

The interest for each period is calculated as follows:

Interest per period = (Principal + Accrued interest) × (Interest rate)

Example 2.5

Legacy Regional Airport (LRA) is a vibrant airport that serves both general aviation and commercial airlines. LRA borrowed $200 million from Bank One at 5% compound interest for four years to build a parking garage. Calculate the interest per year and total interest LRA pays to Bank One:

Interest at the end of year one = $\$200 \times 0.05 = \$10$
Total amount due at the end of year one or beginning of year two = $\$200 + \$10 = \$210$

Interest at the end of year two = $\$210 \times 0.05 = \$10.5$
Total amount due at the end of year two = $\$210 + 10.5 = \$220.5$

Interest at the end of year three = $\$220.5 \times 0.05 = \$11.025$
Total amount due at the end of year three = $\$220.5 + 11.025 = \$231.525$

Interest at the end of year four = $\$231.525 \times 0.05 = \$11.576$
Total amount due at the end of year four = $\$231.525 + \$11.576 = \$243.10$

Total interest paid at the end of year four on this loan is the difference between the total amounts due at the end of year four minus the loan principal: $243.10 – $200 = $43.10 million total interest paid at the end of year four.

To highlight the difference between simple and compound interest, let's rework Example 2.4 assuming interest is compounded annually. The detailed calculation of annual interest accrued

Table 2.1 Calculating Compound Interest

End of Year	*Loan Principal*	*Interest Rate*	*Interest Due*	*Amount Owed*	*Amount Paid*
0	$10,000,000	5%	0	0	0
1	$10,000,000	5%	$500,000	$10,500,000	0
2	$10,500,000	5%	$525,000	$11,025,000	0
3	$11,025,000	5%	$551,250	$11,576,250	0
4	$11,576,250	5%	$578,813	$12,155,063	0
5	$12,155,063	5%	$607,753	$12,762,816	$12,762,816
Total Interest			$2,762,816		

Table 2.2 Difference between Accrued Simple and Compound Interest

Year	*Simple Interest*	*Compound Interest*	*The Increased Interest*
1	$500,000	$500,000	$0
2	$500,000	$525,000	$25,000
3	$500,000	$551,250	$51,250
4	$500,000	$578,813	$78,813
5	$500,000	$607,753	$107,753
Total Increased Accrued Interest due to Compounding Interest			$262.816

on this loan is tabulated in Table 2.1. This table shows the effect of changing interest from simple to compounding on annual interest accrued, total interest accrued, and total amount paid on this loan. The interest accrued at the end of each year earned interest in the following years because the interest was compounding.

Table 2.2 shows the accrued simple and compound interests on this loan, reflecting the higher total accrued interest because of compounding. As the table shows, the difference between simple and compound interest increases exponentially as time passes. Accordingly, compound interest is beneficial for investors (lenders) for longer-term loans.

Interest Rates

Many entities that need money will borrow money if they believe their return on capital will be higher than the cost of borrowing. But for airlines, airports, and manufacturers, borrowing is a powerful way to raise money to finance growth and expansion. The US airline debt pile hit $340 billion in 2021 as COVID-19 choked travel, and that amount has to be repaid with interest and fees.[5] At the end of fiscal year 2023, the total US national debt was expected to be $34 trillion.[6]

Whether we borrow money for a new project, expansion of existing facilities, or liquidity for unforeseen expenses, we rely mainly on financial institutions. A financial institution is a firm that facilitates financial transactions such as investments, loans, and deposits between lenders and borrowers. Figure 2.2 gives a graphical depiction of the role of financial institutions.

Globally, interest rates are controlled and managed by some form of government agency. In the United States, the Federal Reserve (the Fed) drives interest rates; founded in 1781, the Fed is the central bank of the United States. To stimulate economic growth, many central banks have kept their policy interest rates very low. The central banks in Denmark, Sweden,

Figure 2.2 The role of financial institutions.

Switzerland, and Japan, have decided on negative rates on commercial banks' excess funds held on deposit at their central banks.[7] This pushes banks to use that money instead of depositing it; the negative interest rate aims to increase investments and trigger the economy by incentivizing banks to lend. In the United States, the Fed can increase the supply of money by changing short-term interest rates, lowering the discount rate that banks pay on short-term loans from the Fed.

Short-Term Interest Rates

Short-term interest rates include discount, interbank lending, prime, Treasury bill (T-bill), and certificate of deposit (CD) rates.

Discount Rate

Commercial banks and other depository institutions from time to time borrow money from the Fed to cover temporary deposit drains, and the discount rate is the rate the Fed charges commercial banks and other depository institutions. Discount window is a term for credit facilities through which financial institutions borrow Fed funds. Federal Reserve banks offer three discount window programs to depository institutions: primary credit, secondary credit, and seasonal credit, each with its own interest rate.[8] The Fed sometimes changes the discount rate to to encourage or discourage borrowing by financial institutions. During 2022–23, the Fed increased interest rates significantly to reduce the high inflation rate of 9.1% over the year ending June 2022, the largest increase in 40 years (Table 2.3).[9]

Federal Fund Rate

Commercial banks and other depository institutions are required to maintain a certain amount of deposit at the Fed to meet their financial obligation; when an institution expects to have more end-of-day cash than it needs, the bank can lend the excess to another bank that expects a shortfall, and the federal funds rate is the rate on such loans: The lower the federal fund rate, the less expensive it is to borrow money. Federal fund transactions neither increase nor decrease money supply and bank reserve; rather, they just redistribute reserves. Figure 2.3 presents historical federal fund rates.[10]

The Prime Rate

The prime interest rate is what commercial banks charge their most-favored customers, such as large corporations. The prime rate is a benchmark for business and consumer loans, and it is often used as a benchmark for credit card and small-business loans. For example, a bank may charge a local business the prime rate plus two or three percentage points on a loan. The Federal

Table 2.3 Federal Reserve Interest Rate Changes: March 2022–July 2023

Meeting date	*Rate change*	*Target range*
March 15–16, 2022	+25 basis points	0.25%–0.5%
May 3–4, 2022	+50 basis points	0.75%–1%
June 14–15, 2022	+75 basis points	1.50%–1.75%
July 26–27, 2022	+75 basis points	2.25%–2.5%
Sept. 20–21, 2022	+75 basis points	3%–3.25%
Nov. 1–2, 2022	+75 basis points	3.75%–4%
Dec. 13–14, 2022	+50 basis points	4.25%–4.5%
Jan. 31-Feb. 1, 2023	+25 basis points	4.5%–4.75%
March 21–22, 2023	+25 basis points	4.75%–5%
May 2–3, 2023	+25 basis points	5%–5.25%
July 25–26, 2023	+25 basis points	5.25%–5.5%

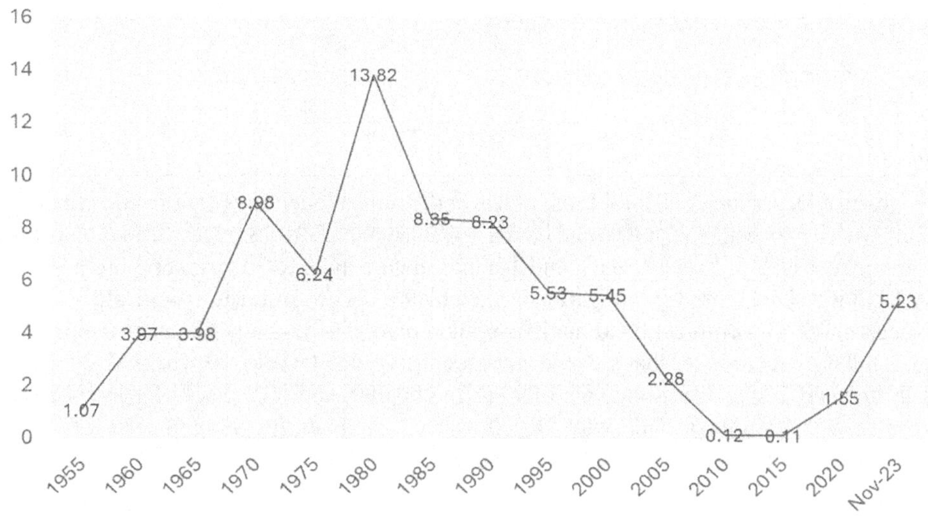

Figure 2.3 Federal fund rates: 1955–2023.[11]

Reserve has no direct control on the prime rate, but the change in prime rate tends to be closely correlated to changes in the target federal funds rate.

London Interbank Offered Rate

Every day, the Intercontinental Exchange publishes a common interest rate known as the London Interbank Offered Rate, LIBOR. LIBOR is the estimated average interest that leading banks in London are expected to be charged if they borrow from other banks. The rate is published daily by Thomson Reuters for loans of different periods (e.g., one day, one week, three months, or one year loan time) and for different currencies (e.g., US dollar, British pound, Euro, Japanese yen). Many lenders and borrowers set interest rates against LIBOR (Figure 2.4).[12] Additionally, to protect borrowers against usury, many governments impose limits on maximum interest rates. In the United States, the states are responsible for setting the maximum interest rates.

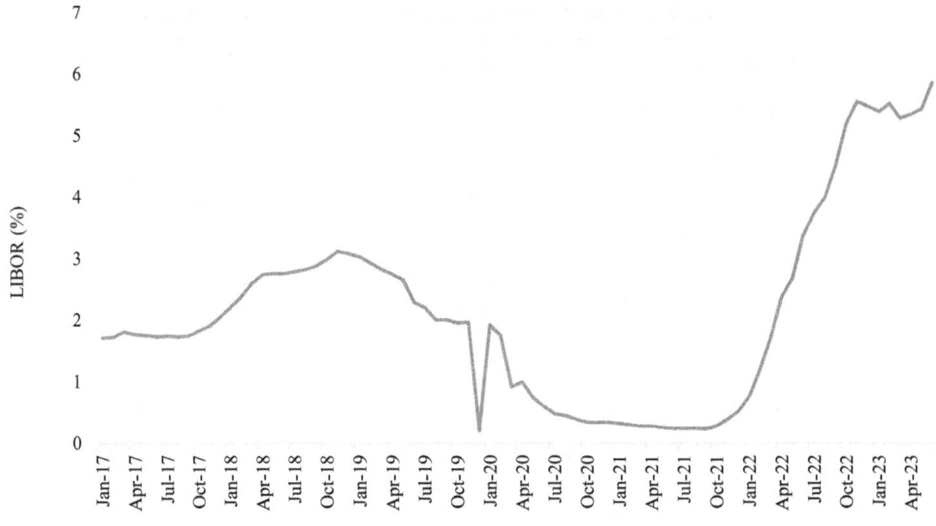

Figure 2.4 LIBOR for 12-month loans in USD.

T-bills

The Treasury Department sells all bills, notes, and bonds at auction with a fixed interest rate. The difference between bills, notes, and bonds is maturity date: T-bills mature in less than a year; T-notes mature in 2, 3, 5, or 10 years; and T-bonds mature in 20 to 30 years or more.

A T-bill is a short-term debt obligation backed by the US government, specifically the Treasury Department. Government bond markets remain pivotal in virtually all of the major economies. T-bill have face values that are paid at the maturity date: 4 weeks, 13 weeks, or 26 weeks.[13] T-Bills are sold in denominations of $1,000 to $5,000,000, and all are sold for less than their face value. For example, a T-bill with $1,000 worth at the maturity could be sold for $950. In this example, the discount rate is 5.26%, because $50 is 5% of $950.

$$\textit{Interest rate earned} = \frac{\$50}{\$950}$$

$$\textit{Interest rate earned} = 5.26\%$$

As another example, a business firm could buy a 26-week T-bill with face value of $1000 for $950.68 at the time of purchase, effectively earning an annualized yield of 10.24% on the investment.

Treasury notes are an additional type of debt for the U.S. government. Maturity is between one and ten years but unlike the T-bills, it does not only pay out the face value at the end but also pays out coupon payments every six months. The coupon rate (e.g. 5% of the face value) is determined before the note is sold. Treasury notes are well accepted investments as there is a large secondary market that adds to their liquidity.

CDs

Checking and saving accounts are called demand deposits. A demand deposit is an account where the customer can deposit money and withdraw money at any time by going to the bank and completing a withdrawal; by law, the banks have to give the money by financial institutions that pays interest if the money remains in the account for a specified period. CDs are similar to standard savings accounts with the exception that the owner cannot withdraw the funds before maturity. CDs state that the customer has a specified amount of deposit, usually for a given period, at fixed interest and are among the safest of investments.

Example 2.6

Assume that the US government issues $10 million in bonds, which are essentially IOUs,[14] and agrees to redeem the bonds in 182 days. A financial institution buys this T-bill at a price of $9,900,000. What is interest on a yearly basis for this type of debt?

$$Interest\ Rate\ Charged = \frac{Face\ Value - Purchase\ Price}{Face\ Value} \times \frac{365}{Time\ until\ maturity\,(in\ days)} \times 100\%$$

$$Interest\ Rate\ Charged = \frac{10{,}000{,}000 - 9{,}900{,}000}{10{,}000{,}000} \times \frac{365}{182} \times 100\%$$

$$Interest\ Rate\ Charged = 2\%$$

Typically, governments are charged much lower interest than businesses because their risk of default is zero: If the US government runs out of money, it can always print more and deflate the debt. This is different for the European Union due to their different monetary system with the European Central Bank. That is why countries like Greece are now paying higher interest: There is high debt, and the risk of default is high.

Example 2.7

A private customer has excess cash in his saving account and would like to increase his return on that money. The bank is willing to offer him a higher interest rate if they can plan to have that money for a specific period. The customer opens a CD that allows the bank to invest that money for the agreed time, and the customer receives a slightly higher return on his investment.

Long-Term Interest Rates

Long-term interest is a central variable in economic growth and stability. Long-term interest rates refer to interest on financial securities, mainly bonds, that mature no sooner than 10 years. These rates are important because long-term debt matters to actors all along the aviation value chain as they consider potential projects or extending existing lending periods. Bonds are a long-term debt instrument in which an investor lends money to a borrower for a defined period at a set rate. There are three important things to know about any bond: par value or face value, coupon rate, and maturity date.

Face (par) value refers to the stated value of the financial instrument at the time it is issued, and all bonds are redeemed at face value when they reach maturity. Corporate bonds normally have a par value of $1,000, but this amount can vary greatly for government bonds. Par value is typically different from the market price. The coupon rate is the interest rate that a bond pays to the bondholders; when a bond is issued, it promises to pay a fixed coupon payment until it matures. For example, a $1,000 face value bond with a coupon interest rate of 7.5% pays a $75 coupon payments annually. The maturity date of a bond is the date when the borrower returns the face value of the bond to the investor. There are four basic kinds of bonds, all defined by who is selling the debt: U.S. government bonds, called Treasury bonds, bonds from other government agencies, corporate bonds, and state and local governments bonds.

T-notes

T-notes mature within 10 years, but unlike T-bills, they do not only pay out the face value at maturity; they also pay out coupon payments every six months; the coupon rate (e.g., 5% of face value) is determined before the note is sold. T-notes are well-accepted investments as there is a large secondary market that adds to their liquidity.

T-bonds

T-bonds are the government's longest-term bonds; they pay out face value at maturity in addition to the six-month coupon payments, but they mature in 20–30 years. If the Fed wants to increase the money supply in circulation, it buys government bonds with cash; conversely, if the Fed wants to decrease the money supply, it sells bonds from its account. The escalating debt crisis in several European countries such as the debt crisis in Greece sent investors to the haven of US government bonds.[15]

Municipal Bonds

The federal government is not the only public entity that issues debt securities: the states, counties, and other governmental agencies can also issue debt instruments including bonds to finance their projects. Municipal bonds (munis) offer slightly lower interest rates than the federal government bonds, but they have a few advantages compared to federal and corporate bonds. First, the interest on munis is exempt from federal taxes. Second, depending on the type of project, munis may be secured by the state or local government agencies. The Security Industry and Financial Markets Association reported that the US municipal bonds outstanding as of the fourth quarter of 2023 was about $4.1 trillion.[16]

Table 2.4 Overview of Different Government Loans

Loan type	*Characteristics*
T-bills	• Mature after 28 days, 91 days, 182 days, or 364 days • Only pay at maturity; no coupon payments • Issued by the federal government
T-notes	• Mature in 2–10 years • Pay face value at maturity and coupon payments every six months • Issued by the federal government
T-bonds	• Mature in 20–30 years • Pay face value at maturity and coupon payments every six months • Issued by the federal government
Municipal bonds	• Maturity varies • Pay face value at maturity and, depending on time to maturity, coupon payments every six months • Issued by state, county, or city authority • Special bond structures (e.g., revenue bonds) for specific projects are possible.

Revenue Bonds

Airports commonly turn to the capital markets to finance long-term construction projects such as terminals and parking facilities by issuing revenue bonds. The revenues from passenger facility charges, landing fees, parking charges, and other fees collected by the airport are used to secure the bonds.

Corporate Bonds

Firms issue corporate bonds to raise money for capital investments; bondholders in return receive regular interest payments stipulated when the bond is issued. One of the most well-known risks in the bond market is default, when the bond issuer cannot pay the contractual interest or principal. Some bonds are backed (secured) by physical assets and therefore can be liquidated in case of default; secured corporate bonds are backed by collateral that the issuer can sell to repay if the bond defaults before or at maturity, for instance a specific aircraft or plant and equipment. Secured bonds and securitization provide a dependable source of aircraft funding for many industries.

Credit rating agencies assign credit grades to debtors' ability to pay back debt or risk of default. The three largest credit agencies are Moody's Investors Service, Standard & Poor's and Fitch,[17] and these ratings determine the terms of lending including interest rates on bonds. Figure 2.5 shows different corporate bonds from the aviation sector. The graphs reveal that the later the maturity, the higher the yield and thus the cost of borrowing. Notably, Boeing and Rolls-Royce, with much lower volatility than the airlines, pay much less for their debt than airlines because airlines have a higher likelihood of default.

Now that we have clarified the simple and the compound interest and introduced the different types of short- and long-term debt, we focus on the next two potential investor concerns: future value of present investment and present value of future gain, concepts that are two sides of the same coin in relating to investors' estimates of their investment outcomes for a given period at a given rate.

Future Value of a Single Present Amount

In this section, we are interested in finding out the outcome of investment in a project with a given compound interest rate for a certain time. We assume that the only payback will happen at the end of the investment period. To facilitate calculation, we are using the following notations:

$F =$ Future value, future sum of money at the end of period n, or future worth
$P =$ Present value, single sum of money at the present time, or present worth
$i =$ Interest rate per period, compound rate, or discount rate
$n =$ Number of periods (usually years)
$(F/P, I, n) =$ Future value of present amount interest factor at interest rate i for period n
$(P/F, i, n) =$ Present value of future amount interest factor at i for period n

Assume we invest the present P at interest i for one year. The future value at the end of year one is equal to principal (P) plus one year interest (P_i), and it is calculated as follows:

$$F_1 = P + P \times i$$
$$F_1 = P \times (1 + i)$$

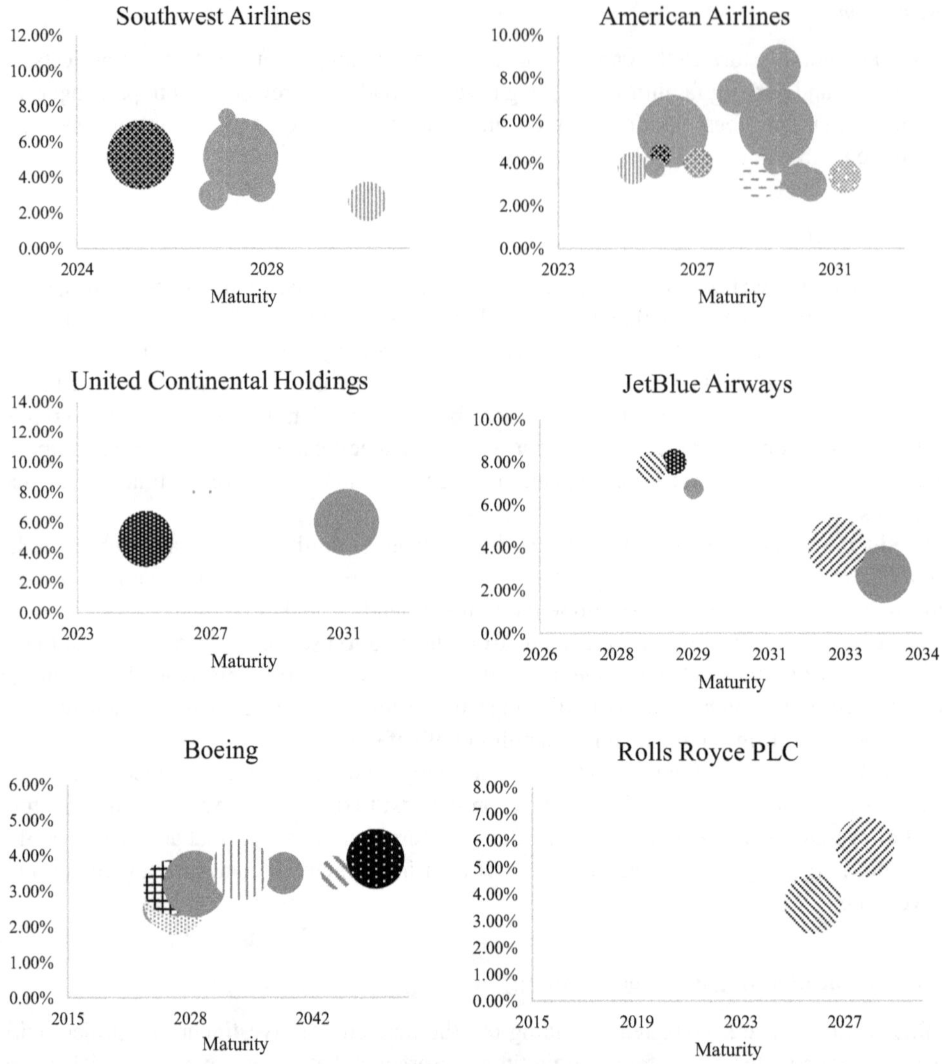

Figure 2.5 Bond rates and maturity dates for different airlines and manufacturing companies.

The future value at the end of two years is calculated as follows:

$$F_2 = [P \times (1+i)] \times (1+i)$$
$$F_2 = P \times (1+i)^2$$

The future value at the end of three years is calculated as follows:

$$F_3 = [P \times (1+i)^2] \times (1+i)$$
$$F_3 = P \times (1+i)^3$$

The future value at the end of four years is calculated as follows:

$$F_4 = \left[P \times (1+i)^3\right] \times (1+i)$$
$$F_4 = P \times (1+i)^4$$

This relationship can be generalized to calculate the future value of a single present sum if it is compounded annually at rate of *i* % for *n* years:

$$\boldsymbol{F_n = P \times (1+i)^n}$$

Example 2.8

A fixed-based operation (FBO) currently has \$50 million set aside to purchase equipment in five years. If the \$50 million is invested at 6%, how much will be accumulated in five years to purchase the equipment?

The cash flow diagram is shown in Figure 2.6. We will use this type of diagram throughout the book to visualize the movement of money in different periods; in each figure, the horizontal line represents time axes, and labels are the ends of each period; that is, 1 represents the end of period one. The arrows represent the cash flows for the party we are solving the problem for. Arrows above the timeline represent positive cash flows (income or gain) and arrows below the timeline indicate negative cash flows (cost and expenses).

For this problem, we draw the diagram from the perspective of the FBO. The FBO is setting aside \$50 million at the beginning of the period, reflected with an arrow below the timeline in Figure 2.6. There is no cash flow over the five years of the investment, but at the end of year five, FBO collects the principal and compounded interest, reflected as an arrow above the timeline in Figure 2.6.

We are interested in finding the gain after five years of the investment, that is F_5:

$$F_n = P \times (1+i)^n$$
$$F_5 = \$50(1+0.06)^5$$
$$F_5 = \$50(1.3382)$$
$$F_5 = \$66.91 \text{ million}$$

At F_5, FBO will have accumulated \$66.91 million to purchase the equipment.

In equation $\boldsymbol{F_n = P \times (1+i)^n}$, $(1+i)^n$ is simply a future value of present amount interest factor and can be expressed as $(F/P, i, n)$. For all the examples and discussions in this and the

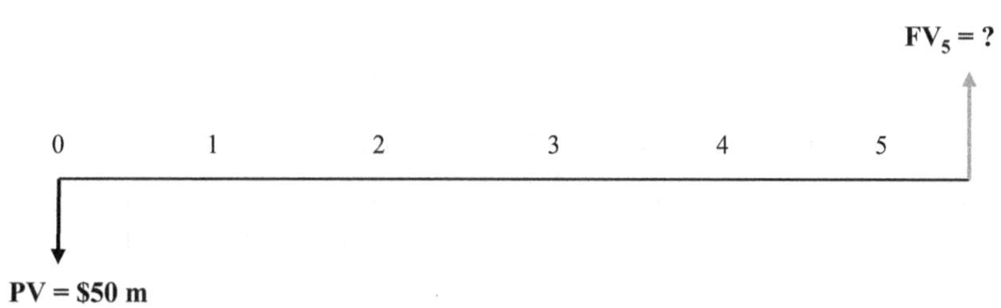

Figure 2.6 Cash flow diagram for a given P and finding F at the end of year five.

subsequent chapters of this book, we precalculated these interest factors, and they are tabulated in Appendix A in Tables A1 to A34. Therefore, this equation can also be expressed as follows:

$$\boldsymbol{F} = \boldsymbol{P} \times (\mathbf{F/P}, \boldsymbol{i}, \boldsymbol{n})$$

Using Example 2.6, the future value at F_5 is calculated as

$$F_n = P(1+i)^n$$
$$F_5 = \$50(1+0.06)^5$$

or

$$F_5 = \$50(\mathrm{F/P},\ 6\%, 5).$$

Table 2.5, a subset of Table A11, gives an interest factor (F/P, 6%, 5) of 1.3382, which we enter into the previous relationship to calculate future value at F_5:

$$FV_5 = \$50\mathrm{m}(1.3382)$$
$$FV_5 = \$66.91\ \mathrm{million}$$

Present Value of a Single Future Sum

One of the critical measures for project evaluation and selection is the present worth of the future gain from performing a project (investment). Present worth is often calculated by reverse calculating the future expected gain in a process called discounting; discounting is the reverse of compounding, which we introduced earlier in this chapter. To calculate the present value of a single future sum, we simply solve the following equation for P, the present value:

$$F = P \times (1+i)^n$$
$$\boldsymbol{P} = \boldsymbol{F} \times \frac{1}{(1+\boldsymbol{i})^n}$$

Table 2.5 Compound Interest Factors: 6%

n	*Single Payment*		*Uniform Payment Series*				*Arithmetic Gradient*	
	F/P	*P/F*	*F/A*	*A/F*	*P/A*	*A/P*	*P/G*	*A/G*
1	1.0600	0.9434	1.0000	1.0000	0.9434	1.0600	0	0
2	1.1236	0.8900	2.0600	0.4854	1.8334	0.5454	0.8900	0.4854
3	1.1910	0.8396	3.1836	0.3141	2.6730	0.3741	2.5692	0.9612
4	1.2625	0.7921	4.3746	0.2286	3.4651	0.2886	4.9455	01.4272
5	**1.3382**	0.7473	5.6371	0.1774	4.2124	0.2374	7.9345	1.8836
6	1.4185	0.7050	6.9753	0.1434	4.9173	0.2034	11.4594	2.3304
7	1.5036	0.6651	8.3938	0.1191	5.5824	0.1791	15.4497	2.7676
8	1.5938	0.6274	9.8975	0.1010	6.2098	0.1610	19.8416	3.1952
9	1.6895	0.5919	11.4913	0.0870	6.8017	0.1470	24.5768	3.6133
10	1.7908	0.5584	13.1808	0.0759	7.3601	0.1359	29.6023	4.0220

Example 2.9

DirectJet's engineering department is planning to purchase power backup equipment in five years at a cost of $500,000. How much should DirectJet set aside today earning 10% interest to accumulate $500,000 in five years? The easiest way to answer problems in economic analysis is to draw a cash flow timeline or diagram. Figure 2.7 is a cash flow diagram showing just one outflow or disbursement of $500,000 at F_5:

$$P = F \times \frac{1}{(1+i)^n}$$
$$P = F \times \frac{1}{(1+0.10)^5}$$
$$P = \$500{,}000 \times 0.6209$$
$$P = \$310{,}450$$

In the equation calculated for Figure 2.7, the term $\frac{1}{(1+i)^n}$ is simply a present value of future amount interest factor and can be expressed as (P/F, i, n). Using the Appendix A tables, equation $\mathrm{P} = \mathrm{F} \times \frac{1}{(1+i)^n}$ can also be articulated as

$$\mathbf{P} = \mathbf{F} \times (\mathbf{P/F, i, n}).$$

Using Example 2.9, the present value, the amount that DirectJet should set aside today, is calculated as follows:

$$\mathrm{P} = \mathrm{F} \times \frac{1}{(1+i)^n}$$
$$\mathrm{P} = \mathrm{F(P/F, i, n)}$$
$$\mathrm{P} = \$500{,}000\ (\mathrm{P/F}, 10\%, 5)$$

Table 2.6, a subset of Table A16, shows that the interest factor (P/F, 10%, 5) is 0.6209, which we enter into the previous relationship to calculate present value:

$$\mathrm{P} = \$500{,}000\ (0.6209)$$
$$\mathrm{P} = \$310{,}450$$

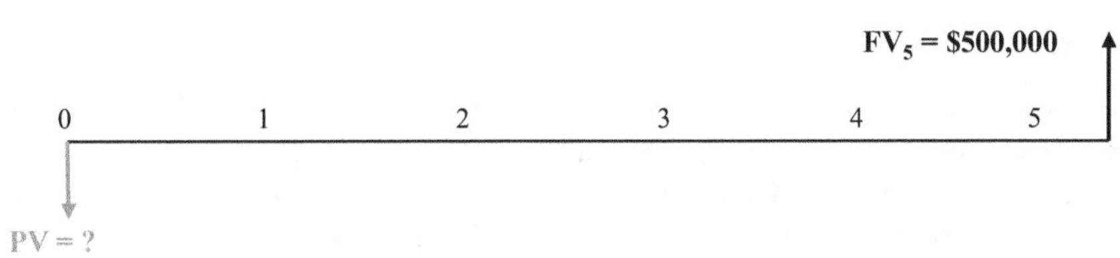

Figure 2.7 Cash flow diagram for a given F at F_5 and finding P.

Table 2.6 Compound Interest Factors: 10%

n	*Single Payment*		*Uniform Payment Series*				*Arithmetic Gradient*	
	FV/PV	*PV/FV*	*FV/A*	*A/FV*	*PV/A*	*A/PV*	*PV/G*	*A/G*
1	1.1000	0.9091	1.0000	1.0000	0.9091	1.10000	0	0
2	1.2100	0.8264	2.1000	0.47619	1.7355	0.57619	0.8264	0.4762
3	1.3310	0.7513	3.3100	0.30211	2.4869	0.40211	2.3291	0.9366
4	1.4641	0.6830	4.6410	0.21547	3.1699	0.31547	4.3781	1.3812
5	1.6105	0.6209	6.1051	0.16380	3.7908	0.26380	6.8618	1.8101

Example 2.10

Johnson Regional Airport (JRA) is planning to construct a new terminal and has received proposals for a total cost of $800 million payable at the beginning of the project or a total cost of $1200 million payable at the end of the project in four years. If construction time is the same under both proposals and JRA earns 10% interest on its investment, which proposal is cost efficient?

This problem can be answered in two ways:

1. Compare the future value of $800 million at the end of four years with the $1,200 million.

$$F = \$800 \times (F/P, 10\%, 4)$$
$$F = \$800 \times (1.4641)$$
$$F = \$1{,}171$$

Since the future value of $800 million in four years is less than $1,200, paying $800 million today is the most cost efficient.

2. Compare the present value of $1,200 million with the $800 million today.

$$P = \$1200 \times (P/F, 10\%, 4)$$
$$P = \$1200 \times (0.6830)$$
$$P = \$820$$

Since the present value of $1,200 million is more than $800 million, paying $800 million today is the most cost efficient.

So far, we have discussed compounding and discounting cash flow to calculate future and present value, respectively. However, it is often necessary in practice to account for multiple payments. Fortunately, the process is a straightforward of combining multiple single cash flows, which we will next discuss.

Example 2.11

Assume you plan to put some money into a savings account that pays 6% interest over the next four years. You will put into the account $100 at F_1, $200 at F_2, $300 at F_3, and $400 at F_4. How much money will you have in that account at F_4? To find out, using $\mathbf{F_n} = \mathbf{P} \times (1+\mathbf{i})^{\mathbf{n}}$, first calculate the future value of each cash flow at F_4 and simply add them together. Detailed calculations are presented in Figure 2.8.

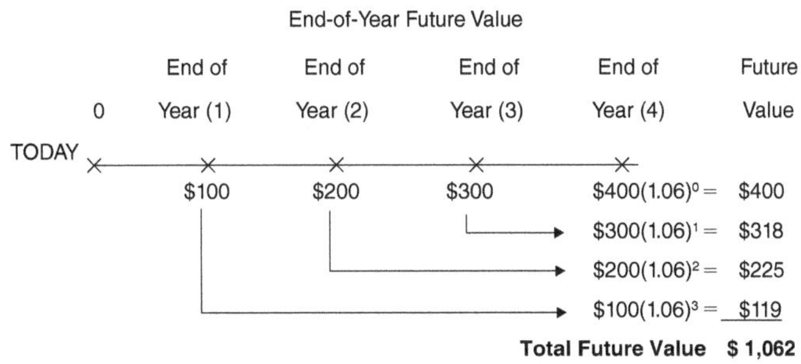

Figure 2.8 Future value of a stream of unequal cash flows.

Future Value of Unequal Cash Flows

To calculate the future value of a steam of nonequal cash flows at the end of *n* periods, we simply calculate the future value of each cash flow at the end of the nth period and then add them.

Example 2.12

Suppose you were offered a stream of payments: $400 in one year, $300 in two years, $200 in three years, nothing in year four, and $100 in five years. Assuming you earn 6% on your investment, what is the present value of this stream of payments? Equation $\mathbf{P} = \mathbf{F} \times \frac{1}{(1+\boldsymbol{i})^{n}}$ can be articulated as follows:

$$P = F \times \frac{1}{(1+i)^{n}}$$
$$P = F \times (1+i)^{-n}$$
$$\mathbf{P} = \mathbf{F} \times (1+\boldsymbol{i})^{-\boldsymbol{n}}$$

Using this equation, first calculate the present value of each payment and simply add them together at the end. Detailed calculations are presented in Figure 2.9.

The Rule of 72

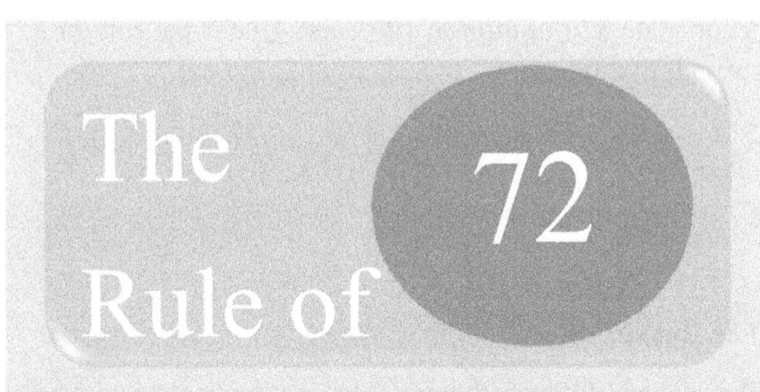

The Rule of 72 is a quick and simple method used in finance and investment to estimate the number of years it will take for an investment to double in value given a fixed annual rate of return: It states that you can determine approximately how many years it will take to double a given sum of money at a

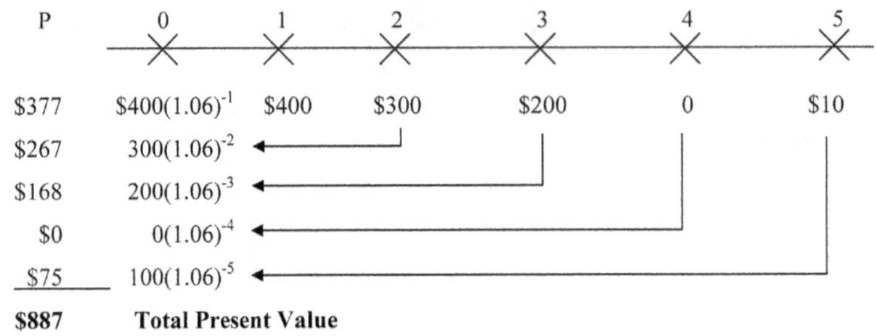

Figure 2.9 Present value of a stream of unequal cash flows.

given compound interest rate. It also states that you can determine approximately the interest rate that doubles a given sum of money within a given number of years simply by dividing the number 72 by the compounded interest rate or the number of years.

$$\text{Approximate number of years (n)} = \frac{72}{\textbf{Interest rate }(\%)}$$

$$\text{Approximate interest rate (i)} = \frac{72}{\textbf{Interest rate }(\%)}$$

Example 2.13

Municipal Agency currently has $5 million in an investment account and needs $10 million to complete a terminal renovation. If the agency earns 8% compound interest on its investment, how long will it take for Municipal to accumulate $10 million to complete the project? Under the rule of 72, it will take nine years:

$$n = \frac{72}{8} = 9 \text{ years}$$

Example 2.14

A regional airport is planning to complete an in-line system of conveyer belts and explosive detection machines for baggage screening process in 10 years that will cost $20 million. If the airport currently has $10 million in an investment account, at what interest rate can the airport accumulate $20 million in 10 years? Under the rule of 72, at 7.2%, the airport can double its current investment:

$$i = \frac{72}{10}$$

$$i = 7.2\%$$

The Rule of 100

The rule of 100 states that you can determine approximately how many years it will take to double a given sum of money at a given simple interest rate. It also states that you can determine the simple interest rate that doubles a given sum of money within a given number of years: Simply divide the number 100 over the simple interest rate or over the number of years:

$$\text{Approximate number of years (n)} = \frac{100}{\textbf{Interest rate }(\%)}$$

$$\text{Approximate interest rate (i)} = \frac{100}{\textbf{Number of Years}}$$

Example 2.15

Rework Example 2.13 assuming the municipal agency earns 8% simple interest instead of compound interest on its investment. Under the rule of 100, it will take 12.5 years to accumulate \$20 million:

$$n = \frac{100}{8}$$
$$n = 12.5 \text{ years}$$

Example 2.16

Rework Example 2.14 and determine the simple interest rate for the regional airport to accumulate \$20 million in 10 years. Under the rule of 100, the airport will double its current investment at 10% simple interest:

$$i = \frac{100}{10}$$
$$i = 10\%$$

Summary

In this chapter, we introduced engineering economics and provided an overview of its application in evaluating investments in aviation-sector projects including loans. Engineers need to comprehend the time value of money due to its direct influence on the economic viability of engineering projects, and this understanding is pivotal for several reasons. Engineers frequently assess investment opportunities, and knowledge of the time value of money aids in comparing options by determining net present value or internal rate of return.

There are two types of interest: simple, which is charged based on the principal borrowed, and compound, charged based on the principal and accrued interest; in practice, interest is normally compounded. Since the interest rate is the price or cost of borrowing money, interest rates vary just like prices of other products for many reasons such as economic conditions, inflation rates, time to maturity, and default risk. There are short-term and long-term interest rates. Short-term rates include discount rates, the federal fund rate (overnight interbank lending rate), the prime rate, the London interbank offered rate, Treasury bill rates, and certificate of deposit rates. Long-term rates include rates on Treasury bonds and notes, municipal bonds, corporate bonds, and mortgages.

For this chapter, we established and derived the equations to calculate the future value of a single amount, present value of a single future sum, and future and present values of streams of unequal amounts. It is fundamental that you as readers clearly understand the concept of time value of money, the financial equations, and the use of interest factors because the rest of this book is based on these concepts: Understanding the time value of money empowers engineers to make informed decisions that ensure the success and sustainability of engineering endeavors.

Discussion Questions and Problems

2.1 Jet Airways borrowed $1,000,000 for one year to improve its liquidity and paid back $1,060,000 as principal plus interest at the end of the year. What is the dollar amount of interest and interest rate on this loan?

2.2 You are investing $10,000 in a CD with simple interest of 5%. How much interest will you accumulate on this CD at the end of four years?

2.3 EZjET Flying operating out of Melbourne, Australia, is considering borrowing $5,000,000 with a simple interest rate of 6% with total principal and interest due in four years. How much interest will accrue at the end of each year and what is the total amount of interest due in four years?

2.4 DirectJet Engineering is planning to purchase equipment in eight years that will cost $14,000,000. It invested a lump sum of money in a CD that pays 5% simple interest per year for eight years. How much did DirectJet invest in this CD if it is worth $14,000,000 at F_8?

2.5 MyJet borrowed $100 million at 7% compound interest for four years to expand its operations. Calculate the interest per year and total interest paid by the company in four years.

2.6 DirectJet has invested million in a money market account that pays 8% interest per year. It is planning to use the amount accumulated at F_6 to for new equipment. How much will be accumulated in this money market account in six years?

2.7 Funjet is planning to expand its operation to Asia Pacific by ordering five Boeing 787 Dreamliners with delivery in five years; the B787's lower fuel consumption and superior long-haul capability are expected to improve the company's profitability as well. It has $1 billion dollars in an investment account today that it expects to have grown to $1.34 billion in five years. If Funjet has $1.34 billion in five years, what annual compounded interest rate did the company earn?

2.8 DirectJet needs $7,320,500 to replace equipment, and they have deposited $5,000,000 in an investment account that pays 10% per year compounded annually. How many years will it take for DirectJet to accumulate at least $7,320,500 in this account?

2.9 You are investing $10,000 in an account that pays 7% interest compounded annually. What is the future value of this investment at the end of five years?

2.10 Jet Services Avionics (JSA) is planning to purchase a new warehouse at the airport in Phoenix five years from now at an estimated cost of $2,000,000. How much should JSA set aside today earning 8% interest to accumulate $2,000,000 in five years?

2.11 DirectJet is planning to purchase new power backup equipment and has been given the options of paying $500,000 today or $700,000 at the end of four years. At a discount rate of 10%, which option is cost efficient?

2.12 You have made an agreement to receive consulting fees of $50,000, $65,000, $80,000, and $100,000 at the end of each year for the next four years. If you deposit these fees into an investment account that pays 10% interest per year over the next four years, how much money will you have in that account at F_4?

2.13 You are leasing a warehouse with annual lease payments of $100,000, $120,000, $135,000, $155,000, and $180,000 at the beginning of each year for the next five years. If you earn 8% of your investment, how much in lump sum do you have to deposit today to be able to make all lease payments for the next five years?

2.14 Johnson Regional Airport currently has $500 million in an investment account that pays 12% per year compounded. JRA needs $1000 million to build a new terminal; assuming 12% on future investments, approximately how many years will it take for JRA to accumulate $1000 million to complete the project?

2.15 In Problem 2.14, assuming JRA earns 12% simple interest instead of compound interest on its investment and assuming all other relevant information, approximately how many years will it take for Johnson Regional to accumulate $1000 million to complete the project?

2.16 DirectJet is planning to purchase two Airbus A350-1000 s at €320 million each in eight years. DirectJet currently has €320 million in an investment account. At approximately what compound interest rate can they accumulate €640 million in eight years to acquire the two aircraft?

2.17 In Problem 2.16, assume all relevant data, at approximately what simple interest rate can DirectJet accumulate €640 million in eight years to acquire the two aircraft?

Notes

1 Facts and Figures, Heathrow Media Centre.
2 How Cheap Oil Has Delta Air Lines Jet Fooled. *Forbes*, January 21, 2015.
3 Delta Buys Refinery to Get Control of Fuel Costs. *The New York Times*, April 30, 2012.
4 Uber and Lyft Have Devastated L.A.'s Taxi Industry, City Records Show. *Los Angeles Times*, April 18, 2016.
5 www.bloomberg.com/news/articles/2021-09-13/airlines-debt-burden-hits-340-billion-as-covid-chokes-travel.
6 www.usdebtclock.org.
7 www.bankofengland.co.uk/knowledgebank/what-are-negative-interest-rates, September 2021.
8 www.frbdiscountwindow.org, December 15, 2023.
9 Source: Fed's Board of Governors.
10 Board of Governors of Federal Reserve System, 2023.
11 Source: *macrotrends.net*. www.macrotrends.net/2015/fed-funds-rate-historical-chart.
12 www.statista.com/statistics/247841/12-month-london-interbank-offered-rate/.
13 The maturity structure of government paper including bonds spans a wide range.
14 An IOU is a signed document acknowledging debts such as bonds.
15 *The Wall Street Journal*, June 29, 2015.
16 www.sifma.org/resources/research/us-municipal-bonds-statistics/.
17 www.forbes.com/advisor/investing/bond-ratings/, May 15, 2023.

3 Annuities and Gradient Series

The concept of annuity holds significant importance for engineering projects due to its implications for project finance, budgeting, and investment analysis. Engineering projects typically require substantial upfront investments followed by a stream of future cash flows. Understanding annuities helps engineers and project managers evaluate the project's financial feasibility by assessing the present value of these cash flows and comparing them to initial investment costs. This analysis guides decision-making regarding project initiation, expansion, or termination. Many large engineering projects such as an airport or an aerospace manufacturing plant require fundraising. and many institutions borrow money from banks or issue bonds to partially finance their projects. These lending instruments allow the owners or managers to make periodic payments of constant amounts to pay off the loan. These payment streams of equal amounts are called annuities or uniform series.

In the previous chapter, we discussed the concept of time value of money and how investors expect to collect interest on their capital that they lend to borrowers. We focused on investment scenarios in which borrowers only make one payment at the end of the loan period. In practice, however, investors expect to receive partial payment during the loan period. For instance, on a 30-year mortgage loan, you are expected to make a payment every month. Clearly, considering the time value of money, regular paybacks to investors change everything, and we need a new approach to evaluate these types of loans.

An annuity is a constant cash flow that takes place at regular intervals; common intervals are annual, semiannual, quarterly, and monthly. In this chapter, we discuss simple annuities, where uniform series of payments are made, and gradient series, in which the amount of payments change throughout the course of a loan. In this chapter, we develop engineering economics formulas and apply the commonly used interest factors to calculate the equivalences of cash flow streams, which are essential for economic decision-making. Cash flows occur in many forms, but the focus of this chapter is on annuities, a uniform series, and gradient series in which payments increase or decrease by constant amounts or constant percentages. In this chapter, we are referring to ordinary annuities where equal payments are made at the end of each period; if payments are made at the beginning of each period, that is called annuity due.

Annuities or Uniform Series

An annuity is defined as a uniform set of payments (A) that occur consecutively over a given period. Usually, the time intervals for the payments are annually, semiannually, quarterly, and monthly. There are many examples of annuity in practice. Common forms include mortgages, pension funds, aircraft or property leases, car loans, insurance premiums, and retirement planning. Let us consider the case of aircraft leasing. Considering the large investment needed to

DOI: 10.4324/9781003469759-3

purchase an aircraft and the volatility of the airline business, many airlines prefer to lease their fleets instead of owning them under one of lease types, operating or capital.

Under an operating lease, rather than the airline, the financial company (e.g., banks, leasing companies, or even another airline) that owns the plane accepts the ownership risk, and the leasing airline pays to use the asset as an expense. These leases are usually shorter than the nominal life of an aircraft and can carry operating restrictions, such as only within certain regions. Operating leases are very common in the airline industry and may be accompanied by other services (e.g., wet lease, where the lessor is generally another airline and provides an aircraft, complete crew, ground staff, maintenance, and insurance to the lessee, or dry lease, where the lessor is generally a financing company and provides only the aircraft without crew, maintenance, and insurance). During the lease period, the leasing airline makes monthly payments to the asset owner and returns the asset at the end of the lease.

Under capital leases, the leasing airlines intend to own the leased aircraft at the end of the contract. Capital leases are usually longer, and payments are usually higher than those with operating lease, but the leasing airline can take ownership of the aircraft at a lower price than fair market value of the asset at the time. That is, capital leases allow an airline to gradually pay for an aircraft at the same time it generates revenue operating it. One of the major advantages of this type of lease for the leasing airline is that it can claim depreciation on the aircraft for tax benefit. We discuss depreciation in detail in Chapter 11.

As can be anticipated, when choosing a lease type, airlines and leasing companies need to evaluate the worth of a contract. For instance, an airline may be interested in assessing the annuity payments required by a lease; this can be done by transforming the annuity payments to a present value equivalent. On the other side, a leasing company might be interested in how much in total they would collect by the end of the lease, that is, the future value of an annuity. In this section, we discuss the engineering economics tools needed to answer these questions. There are four formulas related to annuities: future value of an annuity (*F/A*), annuity of a future single sum (*A/F*), present value of an annuity (*P/A*), and annuity of a present amount (*A/P*).

Future Value of an Annuity

F/A is simply the sum of the future value of all payments at the end of the n period; it has broad application across financial domains, providing valuable insights into long-term savings, investments, loan repayments, and insurance planning. Individuals use *F/A* to determine how much they need to save regularly to achieve a specific retirement goal, and lenders use it to calculate the total interest paid on loans with fixed periodic payments. Overall, *F/A* is a versatile tool used in various financial contexts to estimate the future worth of regular cash flows and make informed decisions about savings, investments, borrowing, and insurance planning. We can express that in the following equation:

$$F = A(1+i)^{n-1} + A(1+i)^{n-2} + \ldots + A(1+i)^{3} + A(1+i)^{2} + A(1+i)^{1} + A$$

which can be simplified as

$$\mathrm{F} = \mathrm{A} \times \left[\frac{(1+i)^{n} - 1}{i} \right]$$

In aviation, it is customary to plan for major expected future expenditures. For instance, aircraft must go through mandatory inspections based on their flight hours and cycle times, A, B, C, and

D checks; A and B checks are lighter, whereas C and D checks are thorough, time consuming, and expensive. D check, which is performed about every six years, is particularly expensive as it consumes labor and takes the plane out of operation for months. Under current airline practices, an aircraft might undergo D check multiple times, but because of the notable cost, some forego the plane if the remaining economic life of the asset and its current market value do not justify the cost of the inspection. D check expenditures for larger fleets require airlines to plan and collect capital to pay for these inspections.

Example 3.1

Monark Airline has a mandatory D check in six years and in preparation is planning to deposit \$5 million in an investment account at the end of each year for six years. If Monark earns 5% return on its investment, how much will it accumulate in this investment account to complete the D check in six years? Figure 3.1 shows the cash flow diagram.

$$F_A = \$5 \times \left[\frac{(1+0.05)^5 - 1}{0.05}\right]$$

$$F_A = \$5 \times \left[\frac{1.2763 - 1}{0.05}\right]$$

$$F_A = \$5 \times \left[\frac{0.2763}{0.05}\right]$$

$$F_A = \$5 \times [5.526]$$

$$F_A = \$27.63 \text{ million}$$

In the equation denoting *F/A*, the term $\left[\frac{(1+i)^n - 1}{i}\right]$ is a future value of an annuity interest factor and can be expressed as (*F/A*, i, n) as follows:

$$F_A = A(F/A, i, n)$$

Using Example 3.1, we can use this equation to calculate the future value of Monark's annual investments. From Table 3.1, a subset of Table A11, we enter interest factor (F/A, 5%, 5) 5.5256 into (*F/A*, i, n) to calculate *F/A* for Monark's potential investments:

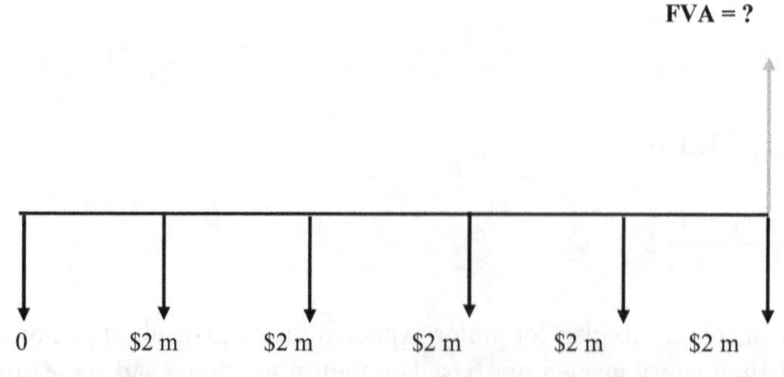

Figure 3.1 Annuity cash flow diagram for \$5 million at the end of each year for six years.

Table 3.1 Compound Interest Factors: 5%

n	*Single Payment*		*Uniform Payment Series*				*Arithmetic Gradient*	
	F/P	*P/F*	*F/A*	*A/F*	*P/A*	*A/P*	*P/G*	*A/G*
1	1.0500	0.9524	1.0000	1.0000	0.9524	1.0500	0	0
2	1.1025	0.9070	2.0500	0.4878	1.8594	0.5378	0.9070	0.4878
3	1.1576	0.8638	3.1525	0.3172	2.7232	0.3672	2.6347	0.9675
4	1.2155	0.8227	4.3101	0.2320	3.5460	0.2820	5.1028	1.4391
5	1.2763	0.7835	5.5256	0.1810	4.3295	0.2310	8.2369	1.9025
6	1.3401	0.7462	6.8019	0.1470	5.0757	0.1970	11.9680	2.3579
7	1.4071	0.7107	8.1420	0.1228	5.7864	0.1728	16.2321	2.8052
8	1.4775	0.6768	9.5491	0.1047	6.4632	0.1547	20.9700	3.2445
9	1.5513	0.6446	11.0266	0.0907	7.1078	0.1407	26.1268	3.6758
10	1.6289	0.6139	12.5779	0.0795	7.7217	0.1295	31.6520	4.0991

$$F_A = \$2 \times [5.5256]$$
$$F_A = \$27.63 \text{ million}$$

A sinking fund is a financial tool that is commonly used in engineering and other industries to set aside money over time to repay a debt or fund future expenditures. It involves making regular contributions to a designated fund that accumulates over time to cover a specific financial obligation or investment. For example, if an airline issues bonds to collect needed capital, it uses the sinking fund to ensure repayment. This fund provides a guarantee that the face value of the bonds will be repaid at a predetermined maturity date.

To calculate the annuity of a future sum, we solve the future value of annuity equation for A as follows:

$$\mathrm{F} = \mathrm{A} \times \left[\frac{(1+i)^n - 1}{i}\right]$$

$$A = F \times \left[\frac{i}{(1+i)^n - 1}\right]$$

Example 3.2

An employee of the AvParts, a newly hired engineer, has determined that she will need \$2,400,000 when she retires in 40 years to live comfortably. Assuming she earns 10% on her investment, how much will she need to invest at the end of each year in equal amounts for 40 years to accumulate \$2,400,000? To find the answer, we enter the information in the annuity equation:

$$A = F \times \left[\frac{i}{(1+i)^n - 1}\right]$$

$$A = \$2,400,000 \times \left[\frac{0.10}{(1+0.10)^{40} - 1}\right]$$

$$A = \$2,400,000 \times \left[\frac{0.10}{45.2593 - 1}\right]$$

$$A = \$2,400,000 \times 0.0023$$

$$A = \$5,520$$

In the equation that calculates annuity, the term $\left[\frac{i}{(1+i)^n - 1}\right]$ is an annuity of a future amount interest factor and can be expressed as (A/F, I, n). Therefore, the annuity equation can also be articulated as follows:

$$A = F(\text{A/F}, i, n)$$

Using Example 3.2, we use the previous equation to calculate the amount that she needs to invest at the end of each year in equal amounts for 40 years to accumulate $2,400,000:

$$A = F(\text{A/F}, i, n)$$

$$A = \$2,400,000(\text{A/F}, 10\%, 40)$$

From Table 3.2, a subset of Table A16, we enter interest factor (A/F, 10%, 40) 0.0023 into the previous relationship to calculate the annuity of a future amount:

$$A = \$2,400,000 \times (0.0023)$$

$$A = \$5,520$$

The employee should invest $5,520 per year to achieve her goal of accumulating $2,400,000 for her retirement.

Present Value of an Annuity

The present value of an annuity is simply the sum of the present value of all payments at t = 0 (the present, i.e., time 0). We can express that concept in the following equation:

Table 3.2 Compound Interest Factors: 10%

n	*Single Payment*		*Uniform Payment Series*				*Arithmetic Gradient*	
	F/P	*P/F*	*F/A*	*A/F*	*P/A*	*A/P*	*P/G*	*A/G*
31	19.1943	0.0521	181.944	0.0055	9.4790	0.10550	78.6395	8.2962
32	21.1138	0.0474	201.138	0.0050	9.5264	0.10497	80.1078	8.4091
33	23.2252	0.0431	222.252	0.0045	9.5694	0.10450	81.4856	8.5152
34	25.5477	0.0391	245.477	0.00401	9.6086	0.10407	82.7773	8.6149
35	28.1024	0.0356	271.025	0.0037	9.6442	0.10369	83.9872	8.7086
40	45.2593	0.0221	442.593	0.0023	9.7791	0.10226	88.9525	9.0960
45	72.8905	0.0137	718.905	0.0014	9.8628	0.10139	92.4544	9.3740
50	117.391	0.0085	1163.91	0.0009	9.9148	0.10086	94.8889	9.5704

$$P = A\times\frac{1}{(1+i)^{1}} + A\times\frac{1}{(1+i)^{2}} + \ldots + A\times\frac{1}{(1+i)^{n-1}} + A\times\frac{1}{(1+i)^{n}}$$

We obtain A of the previous equation as follows:

$$P = A\times\left[\frac{1}{(1+i)^{1}} + \frac{1}{(1+i)^{2}} + \frac{1}{(1+i)^{3}} + \ldots + \frac{1}{(1+i)^{n-1}} + \frac{1}{(1+i)^{n}}\right]$$

The last equation can be further simplified as

$$P = A\times\left[\frac{1}{i} + \frac{1}{i\times(1+i)^{n}}\right]$$

and that equation can be articulated into

$$P = A\times\left[\frac{[(1+i)^{n} - 1]}{i\times(1+i)^{n}}\right]$$

The final equation obtained can be used to calculate the present value of an annuity for uniform series. The present value of annuity formula has numerous practical applications across various financial scenarios. Business owners use present value of annuity to estimate the present value of future cash flows. Individuals use it to calculate the present value of their future retirement income streams, such as pension or annuity payments.

Present worth of future annuity is a critical measure in evaluating investment projects that promise future revenue. Air cargo transportation often requires a location at the airport for receiving, processing, transhipping, and loading air cargo. Leasing cargo facilities is a major source of revenue for airports, and these facilities, or extra services such as refrigerated warehouses for perishable products, can act as a major attractor of airlines to a given airport. Indeed, airlines provide airports revenues in the form of landing fees, parking fees, ramp access fees, and so forth.

Airport authorities have few options for planning, development, construction, and marketing the cargo facilities. Airports can take charge of the development and do it in house. Clearly, this option gives airports more control and flexibility and eventually better revenue. Additionally, airport-owned facilities tend to have lower rent, which makes them more attractive for airlines and more marketable. This is because airports often have access to cheaper capital through government funding or tax-exempt bonds. On the other hand, using outside developers frees airports of the investment risk of building, maintaining, and marketing the facilities. In this approach, airports enter long-term agreements with third parties to develop the facilities and provide the airports with monthly revenue from leasing/using the facility. Indeed, a critical measure in helping airport authorities in planning cargo facilities is the estimated present worth of the expected annuity to be collected from tenants.

Example 3.3

DirectJet is signing a lease agreement for a property to service aircraft. The lease payments are \$2.5 million per year for 10 years. If DirectJet can earn 6% on its investment, what is the present value of these payments? See Figure 3.2.

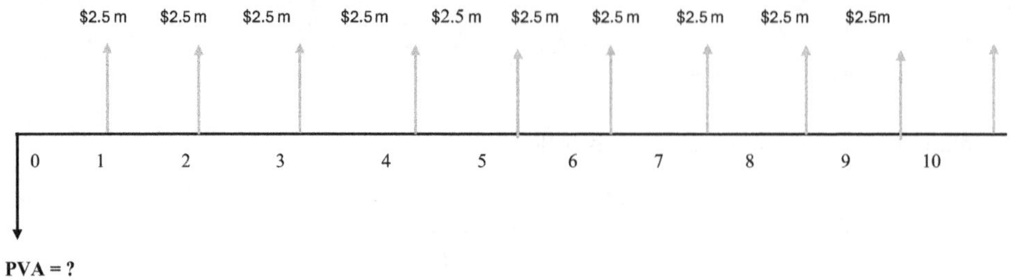

Figure 3.2 Annuity cash flow diagram: Example 3.3.

Entering the information in equation $P = A \times \left[\frac{[(1+i)^n - 1]}{i \times (1+i)^n}\right]$ into the following, we can calculate the present value of the lease payments:

$$P = \$2{,}500{,}000 \times \left[\frac{[(1+0.06)^{10} - 1]}{0.06 \times (1+0.06)^{10}}\right]$$
$$P = \$2{,}500{,}000 \times [7.3601]$$
$$P = \$18{,}400{,}250$$

Table 3.3 shows the present value of each payment and the sum of present value of all payments. The difference from the answer in Example 3.3 is due to rounding.

The term $\left[\frac{[(1+i)^n - 1]}{i \times (1+i)^n}\right]$ is the present value of an annuity interest factor and can be expressed as (P/A, i, n). Therefore, the equation can also be articulated to the following:

$$P = A(\text{P/A}, i, n)$$

Using Example 3.3, we can calculate the present value of DirectJet's annual lease payments using the previous equation as follows:

$$P = A(\text{P/A}, i, n)$$
$$P = \$2{,}500{,}000(\text{P/A}, 6\%, 10)$$

From Table 3.4, a subset of Table A12, enter present value interest factor (P/A, 6%, 10) 7.3601 in the previous equation and calculate the present value of all lease payments:

$$P = \$2{,}500{,}000 \times (7.3601)$$
$$P = \$18{,}400{,}250$$

Annuity of a Present Value

An annuity of present value refers to a series of equal cash flows received or paid at regular intervals over a specified period, with the present value of these cash flows calculated at the

Table 3.3 Calculating Present Value of an Annuity

Period (n)	*Lease payment (A)*	*Interest rate (i)*	*Present value (PV)*
0	0	6%	0
1	$2,500,000	6%	$2,358,491
2	$2,500,000	6%	$2,224,499
3	$2,500,000	6%	$2,099,048
4	$2,500,000	6%	$1,980,234
5	$2,500,000	6%	$1,868,145
6	$2,500,000	6%	$1,762,401
7	$2,500,000	6%	$1,662,643
8	$2,500,000	6%	$1,568,531
9	$2,500,000	6%	$1,479,746
10	$2,500,000	6%	$1,395,987
Total	**$25,000,000**		**$18,399,725**

Table 3.4 Compound Interest Factors: 6%

n	*Single Payment*		*Uniform Payment Series*				*Arithmetic Gradient*	
	F/A	*P/F*	*F/A*	*A/F*	*P/A*	*A/P*	*P/G*	*A/G*
1	1.0600	0.9434	1.0000	1.0000	0.9434	1.0600	0	0
2	1.1236	0.8900	2.0600	0.4854	1.8334	0.5454	0.8900	0.4854
3	1.1910	0.8396	3.1836	0.3141	2.6730	0.3741	2.5692	0.9612
4	1.2625	0.7921	4.3746	0.2286	3.4651	0.2886	4.9455	01.4272
5	1.3382	0.7473	5.6371	0.1774	4.2124	0.2374	7.9345	1.8836
6	1.4185	0.7050	6.9753	0.1434	4.9173	0.2034	11.4594	2.3304
7	1.5036	0.6651	8.3938	0.1191	5.5824	0.1791	15.4497	2.7676
8	1.5938	0.6274	9.8975	0.1010	6.2098	0.1610	19.8416	3.1952
9	1.6895	0.5919	11.4913	0.0870	6.8017	0.1470	24.5768	3.6133
10	1.7908	0.5584	13.1808	0.0759	7.3601	0.1359	29.6023	4.0220
11	1.8983	0.5268	14.9716	0.0668	7.8869	0.1268	34.8702	4.4213
12	2.0122	0.4970	16.8699	0.0593	8.3838	0.1193	40.3369	4.8113
13	2.1329	0.4688	18.8821	0.0530	8.8527	0.1130	45.9629	5.1920
14	2.2609	0.4423	21.0151	0.0476	9.2950	0.1076	51.7128	5.5635
15	2.3966	0.4173	23.2760	0.0430	9.7122	0.1030	57.5546	5.9260

beginning of the annuity term. In engineering projects, understanding annuity of present value is crucial for financial analysis, budgeting, and investment evaluation. Engineers may evaluate investment opportunities for project enhancements, technology upgrades, or efficiency improvements. An annuity of present value helps in assessing the financial viability of such investments by calculating their net present value (NPV) or internal rate of return (IRR). Projects with a positive NPV or IRR greater than the discount rate are considered financially attractive and viable.

To calculate the annuity of a present value, we solve the present value of annuity equation for A as follows:

$$P = A \times \left[\frac{[(1+i)^{n} - 1]}{i \times (1+i)^{n}} \right]$$

$$A = P \times \left[\frac{i \times (1+i)^{n}}{(1+i)^{n} - 1} \right]$$

This equation describes a loan payment and is used often for financial planning purposes. Individuals use it to calculate mortgage and car payments, aviation companies use it to determine the uniform payments on their loans received from financial institutions, and airlines can use it to calculate their aircraft lease payments.

Example 3.4

EZjET Airlines is expanding its operation and needs three Boeing 737 MAX priced currently at \$114 million. EZjET approaches International Financial Corporation (IFC) to finance the purchase. IFC agrees to grant a loan to EZjET to finance the entire purchase price at 8% compound interest for 20 years. What will be EZjET's annual loan payment? To calculate the annual loan payments, we use the annuity of a present value equation:

$$A = \$114,000,000 \times \left[\frac{0.08 \times (1+0.08)^{20}}{(1+0.08)^{20} - 1} \right]$$

$$A = \$114,000,000 \times \left[\frac{0.3729}{3.6610} \right]$$

$$A = \$114,000,000 \times (0.1019)$$

$$A = \$11,616,600$$

To use standard compound interest factor notation, the present value of an annuity can be expressed with the following equation:

$$A = P(A/P,\ i,\ n)$$

where interest factor (A/P, i, n) can be found in the tables in Appendix A.

To calculate EZjET's annual payment on the \$114 million loan (Table 3.5), using standard compound factor notation, enter the data given in Example 3.4 into the following equation:

$$A = \$114,000,000(A/P,\ 8\%,\ 20)$$

$$A = \$114,000,000 \times (0.1019)$$

$$A = \$11,616,600$$

Amortization and Amortization Schedule

In the previous section, we discussed loan payments as annuity payments of a present loan; as we mentioned in Chapter 4, the payment consists of principal and the compound interest for the privilege of having the capital during the course of the loan. We described how to calculate the annuity payment for a given loan based on the interest rate and length of the loan. In practice, however, investors and lenders often prefer to separate the payment into the interest and principal so that part of each payment contributes to interest and the remainder of each payment goes toward retiring the principal.

Amortization is the distribution of a single cash flow into smaller cash flows, and the amortization schedule outlines how each payment is divided between interest and principal over

Table 3.5 Amortization Schedule for EZjET (in USD 1000)

Period	*Payment Date*	*Beginning Balance*	*Schedule Payments*	*Total Payments*	*Principal*	*Interest*	*Ending Balance*
1	7/1/2023	114,000.00	11,616.60	11,616,60	2,496.60	9,120.00	111,503.40
2	7/1/2024	111,503.40	11,616.60	11,616.60	2,696.33	8,920.27	108,807.07
3	7/1/2025	108,807.07	11,616.60	11,616.60	2,912.03	8,704.57	105,895.04
4	7/1/2026	105,895.04	11,616.60	11,616.60	3,145.00	8,471.60	102,750.04
5	7/1/2027	102,750.04	11,616.60	11,616.60	3,396.60	8,220.00	99,353.44
6	7/1/2028	99,353.44	11,616.60	11,616.60	3,668.32	7,948.28	95,685.12
7	7/1/2029	95,685.12	11,616.60	11,616.60	3,961.79	7,654.81	91,723.33
8	7/1/2030	91,723.33	11,616.60	11,616.60	4,278.73	7,337.87	87,444.60
9	7/1/2031	87,444.60	11,616.60	11,616.60	4,621.03	6,995.57	82,823.56
10	7/1/2032	82,823.56	11,616.60	11,616.60	4,990.71	6,625.89	77,832.85
11	7/1/2033	77,832.85	11,616.60	11,616.60	5,389.97	6,226.63	72,442.88
12	7/1/2034	72,442.88	11,616.60	11,616.60	5,821.17	5,795.43	66,621.71
13	7/1/2035	66,621.71	11,616.60	11,616.60	6,286.86	5,329.74	60,334.84
14	7/1/2036	60,334.84	11,616.60	11,616.60	6,789.81	4,826.79	53,545.03
15	7/1/2037	53,545.03	11,616.60	11,616.60	7,333.00	4,283.60	46,212.03
16	7/1/2038	46,212.03	11,616.60	11,616.60	7,919.64	3,696.96	38,292.39
17	7/1/2039	38,292.39	11,616.60	11,616.60	8,553.21	3,063.39	29,739.19
18	7/1/2040	29,739.19	11,616.60	11,616.60	9,237.47	2,379.13	20,501.72
19	7/1/2041	20,501.72	11,616.60	11,616.60	9,976.46	1,640.14	10,525.26
20	7/1/2042	10,525.26	11,616.60	10,525.26	9,683.24	842.02	0.00
Total					**114,000.0**		

the life of the loan. This schedule consists of a number of payments, the balance at the beginning of each period, total payments per period, dollar amount of principal and interest paid each period, and the balance at the end of the period.

> *Amortizing means spreading out the cost of an asset over the duration of its lifespan. Note, amortization is not used for tangible assets. It is used for intangible assets such as trademarks, patents on inventions, licenses, and goodwill.*

The amortized schedule is often set in a way that larger portion of payment in the beginning of the loan payback goes to cover the interest (as high as 80% to 90%). As the loan approaches maturity, the share of principal payback increases because the interest portion is mostly paid back already. Disregarding the share of interest and principal, the payment instalments are often the same. There are several methods for calculating the share of interest vs principal for payment. Consider Example 3.5.

Example 3.5

Principal Borrowed:	$100,000.00	**Annual Payments:**	12
Regular Payment amount:	$599.55	**Total Payments:**	360 (30 years)
Interest-only payment:	$500.00	**Annual interest rate:**	6.00%
Total Repaid:	$215,838.00	**Periodic interest rate:**	0.5000%
Total Interest Paid:	$115,838.00	**Debt Service Constant:**	7.1946%
		Total interest paid as a percentage of Principal:	115.838%

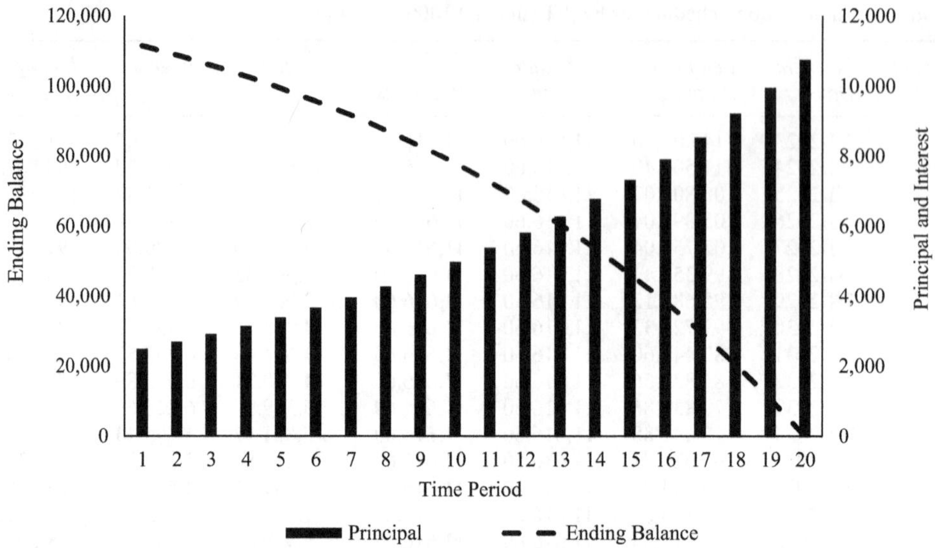

Figure 3.3 Amortization schedule.

Using these numbers and annuity of present value, we can calculate the annuity payment as \$599.55. Now, Figure 5.3 shows how this payment is contributing to paying back interest and principal throughout the length of the loan.

Annuity Due

Annuity due is like ordinary annuity except that payments are made at the beginning rather than the end of the period. Because payments are made at the beginning of each interval, both future and present values of annuity due will earn one extra period of interest. Therefore, to calculate the future value of an annuity due, we multiply future value of ordinary annuity by (1 + i):

$$F_{ordinary} = A \times \left[\frac{(1+i)^n - 1}{i} \right]$$

$$F_{due} = A \times \left[\frac{(1+i)^n - 1}{i} \right] \times (1+i)$$

$$F_{ordinary} = A(F/A,\, i,\, n)$$
$$F_{due} = A(F/A,\, i,\, n) \times (1+i)$$

Similarly, to calculate the present value of an annuity due, we multiply the present value of ordinary annuity by (1 + i):

$$P_{ordinary} = A \times \left[\frac{[(1+i)^n - 1]}{i \times (1+i)^n} \right]$$

$$P_{due} = A \times \left[\frac{[(1+i)^n - 1]}{i \times (1+i)^n} \right] \times (1+i)$$

$$P_{ordinary} = A(P/A,\ i,\ n)$$
$$P_{due} = A(P/A,\ i,\ n) \times (1+i)$$

In Example 3.5, if DirectJet makes the lease payment of $2.5 million per year at the beginning of each year for 10 years, the present value of the annuity due payments can be calculated as follows:

$$P_{due} = A\left(\frac{P}{A},\ i,\ n\right) \times (1+i)$$

$$P_{due} = \$2{,}500{,}000(P/A,\ 6\%,\ 10) \times (1+6\%)$$
$$P_{due} = \$2{,}500{,}000 \times (7.3601) \times (1.06)$$
$$P_{due} = \$19{,}504{,}265$$

Capitalized Cost

Capitalized cost (CC) in engineering economics refers to the present worth of a project with an infinite life. In other words, CC is a lump sum needed today (t = 0) to support an infinite life project simply on the earned interest only. CC usually applies to public projects such as airports, bridges, dams, and long-term private projects such as hospitals and private airports. Since most present value interest factors are the same after 50 to 100 years depending on interest rates, perpetual annuity can be used to determine the present worth of infinite life projects as CC. When acquiring capital assets like equipment or machinery, CC includes not only the purchase price but also additional expenses incurred to prepare the asset for use. By capitalizing expenditures, engineering projects can align costs with the revenue generated or benefits derived from the asset over time. Depreciation, a key component of CC, reflects the systematic allocation of the asset's cost over its useful life.

Since it is difficult to calculate CC for a project with a stream of infinite cash flows when they vary from year to year or they occur irregularly, it is necessary first to convert those cash flows to a uniform series or annuity and then use perpetual annuity to calculate the CC of that project. CC can also be defined as the present worth of an annuity that will last forever. To drive the CC equation, we use the present value of annuity formula, assuming n approaches infinity.

$$\mathrm{P} = \mathrm{A} \times \left[\frac{[(1+i)^n - 1]}{i \times (1+i)^n} \right]$$

Dividing both the numerator and the denominator of that equation by $(1+i)^n$ gives the following:

$$P = A\left[\frac{1 - \dfrac{1}{(1+i)^n}}{i} \right]$$

In this equation, if n $\rightarrow \infty$, the numerator decreases to 1, and the equation is simplified as follows:

$$P = CC = A \times \frac{1}{i}$$

$$CC = \frac{A}{i}$$

In other words, CC is equal to annuity payment divided by interest rate.

Example 3.6

An insurance agent approaches you and makes an offer of paying you $1,000 per year forever. If you earn 10% in your savings account, what is the value of this offer to you? In other words, what is the maximum price you are willing to pay for this offer?

To find the maximum price for this offer, we calculate the CC of this annuity at an interest rate of 8%:

$$CC = \frac{\$1,000}{0.10}$$
$$CC = \$10,000$$

The answer is $10,000 because if you deposited $12,500 in a savings account, every year you would receive $1,000 $(\$10,000 \times 0.10 = \$1,000)$ in interest. So long as the money is deposited in your account and interest rate remains at 10%, you will receive $1,000 per year forever.

Arithmetic Gradient Series

In engineering economics, not all cash flows are uniform series or annuity series; they can be graduating annuities. Graduating annuity is a stream of payments or cash flows that occur at the end of each period for a given period, similar to annuities but payments are not constant, although they change uniformly. Understanding and analyzing gradient series is essential for engineering projects as they provide valuable insights into project economics, cash flow dynamics, and financial performance over time. By incorporating gradient series analysis into project evaluation and decision-making processes, engineers can make informed choices that optimize project outcomes and maximize return on investment. An arithmetic gradient series is a graduated annuity series, in which cash flows uniformly increase or decrease by a constant amount.

> *The gradient series is a financial concept used in engineering economics and project evaluation. It is a series of cash flows that change by a constant amount from one period to the next. In other words, each cash flow in the series increases or decreases by the same amount over time.*
>
> *In engineering projects, gradient series often arise in scenarios where costs or revenues change incrementally over the project's lifespan. For example, the annual maintenance costs of an aircraft may increase by a certain percentage each year due to inflation or escalating service fees.*

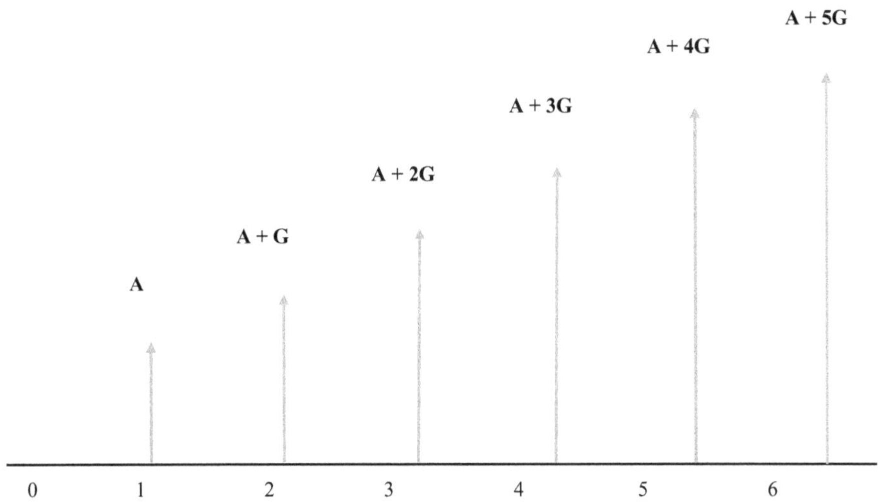

Figure 3.4 Arithmetic gradient series.

Figure 3.4 presents an arithmetic gradient cash flow series in which A is the base amount that occurs at the end of year one and G is the gradient amount; the increase in cash flows starts at the end of year two and continues through the end of the cash flow period.

Present Value of an Arithmetic Gradient Series

The present value of an arithmetic gradient series represents the current worth of a series of cash flows that increase or decrease by a constant amount over time. This financial concept is essential in engineering economics for evaluating the economic feasibility of projects with changing cash flows. To drive an equation for calculating the present value of an arithmetic gradient, we divide the cash flow series in Figure 3.4 into two series. First series is an annuity of A amount per year for six years. Second series is the gradient amount G, a series of G amount in year two that increases by the same amount every year as shown in Figure 3.5.

To calculate the present value of the first cash flow series, we use the equation

A A A A A A
↑ ↑

$$P_1 = A \times \left[\frac{[(1+i)^n - 1]}{i \times (1+i)^n} \right]$$

To calculate the present value of the second cash flow series, we use

$$P_2 = \frac{G}{i} \times \left[\frac{(1+i)^n - 1}{i \times (1+i)^n} - \frac{n}{(1+i)^n} \right]$$

This equation derived from the cash flows in Figure 3.5. The present value of all gradient amounts is calculated to present time value, add them all together, and simplify it to derive the equation.

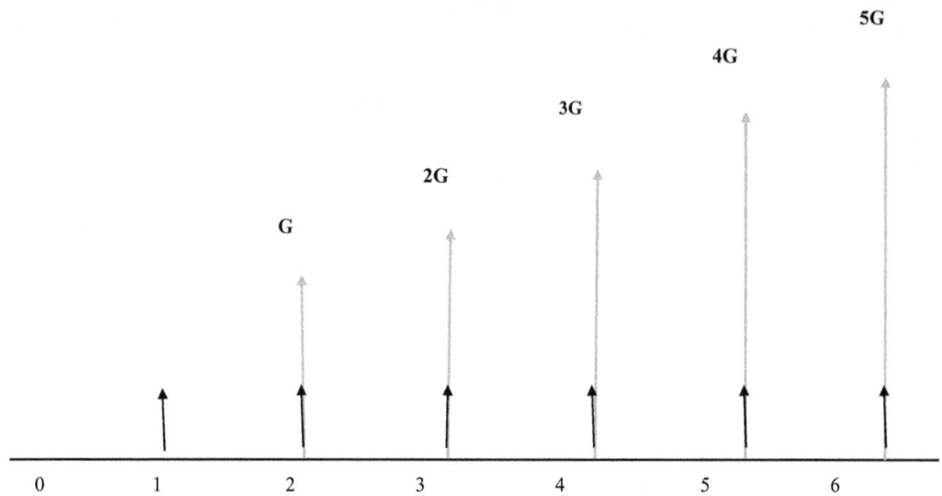

Figure 3.5 Cash flow diagram of an arithmetic gradient series.

To calculate the present value of the whole arithmetic gradient series, we add the previous two equations into one general equation as follows:

$$P_G = A \times \left[\frac{[(1+i)^n - 1]}{i \times (1+i)^n} \right] + \frac{G}{i} \times \left[\frac{(1+i)^n - 1}{i \times (1+i)^n} - \frac{n}{(1+i)^n} \right]$$

To use standard compound interest factor notation, this equation can also be articulated to the following:

$$P_G = A(P/A,\ i,\ n) + G(P/G,\ i,\ n)$$

where interest factors (P/A, i, n) and (P/G, i, n) are precalculated and presented in Appendix A.

Example 3.7

An aerospace engineer is signing up a consulting agreement with an airport in Solomon Islands. The length of the contract is seven years and consulting fees are \$200,000 at the end of year one, increasing by \$20,000 per year starting at the end of the second year through the end of the contract. Assuming the engineer earns 8% return on his investment, what is the present value of his consulting contract?

Figure 3.6 presents the cash flow diagram for this contract. The \$200,000 is the base amount $(A = \$200{,}000)$ and the \$20,000 increase per year is the gradient amount $(G = \$20{,}000)$.

To calculate the present value of the arithmetic gradient series in Example 3.7, we apply the data given in the example into the equation as follows:

$$P_G = \$200{,}000(P/A,\ 8\%,\ 7) + \$20{,}000(P/G,\ 8\%,\ 7)$$

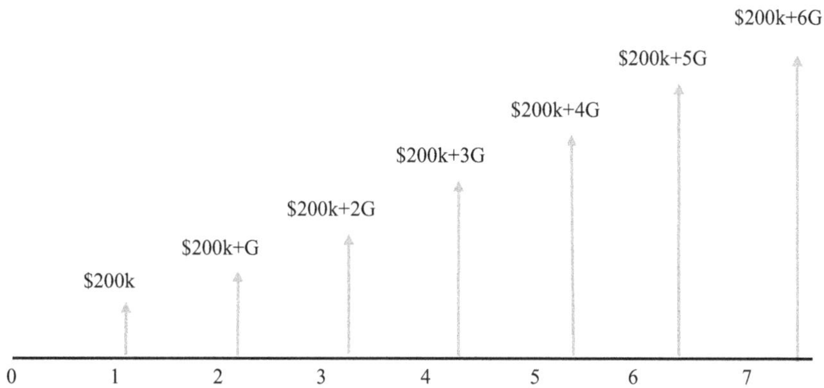

Figure 3.6 Cash flow diagram of an arithmetic gradient series: Example 3.7.

Table 3.6 Compound Interest Factors: 8%

n	*Single Payment*		*Uniform Payment Series*				*Arithmetic Gradient*	
	F/P	*P/F*	*F/A*	*A/F*	*P/A*	*A/P*	*P/G*	*A/G*
1	1.0800	0.9259	1.0000	1.0000	0.9259	1.0800	0	0
2	1.1664	0.8573	2.0800	0.4808	1.7833	0.5608	0.9573	0.4808
3	1.2597	0.7938	3.2464	0.3080	2.5771	0.3880	2.4450	0.9487
4	1.3605	0.7350	4.5061	0.2219	3.3121	0.3019	4.6501	1.4040
5	1.4693	0.6806	5.8666	0.1705	3.9927	0.2505	7.3724	1.8465
6	1.5869	0.6302	7.3359	0.1363	4.6229	0.2163	10.5233	2.2763
7	1.7138	0.5835	8.9228	0.1121	5.2064	0.1921	14.0242	2.6937
8	1.8509	0.5403	10.6366	0.0940	5.7466	0.1740	17.8061	3.0985
9	1.9990	0.5002	12.4876	0.0801	6.2469	0.1601	21.8081	3.4910
10	2.1589	0.4632	14.4866	0.0690	6.7101	0.1490	25.9768	3.8713

From Table 3.6, a subset of Table A14, enter annuity interest factor (P/A, 8%, 7) 5.2064 and gradient interest factor (P/G, 8%, 7) 14.0242 into the previous equation and calculate the present value of this arithmetic gradient series:

$$P_G = \$200{,}000(5.2064) + \$20{,}000(14.0242)$$
$$P_G = \$1{,}041{,}280 + \$280{,}484$$
$$P_G = \$1{,}321{,}764$$

Annuity of an Arithmetic Gradient Series

The annuity of an arithmetic gradient series represents the equivalent uniform cash flow stream that has the same present value as the gradient series. This concept is important in engineering economics for evaluating projects with changing cash flows over time. To convert an arithmetic gradient series into an annuity or uniform series, we divide the cash flow series in Figure 3.7 into two series, first the cash flow series of the base amount A_1, which is a constant amount per year

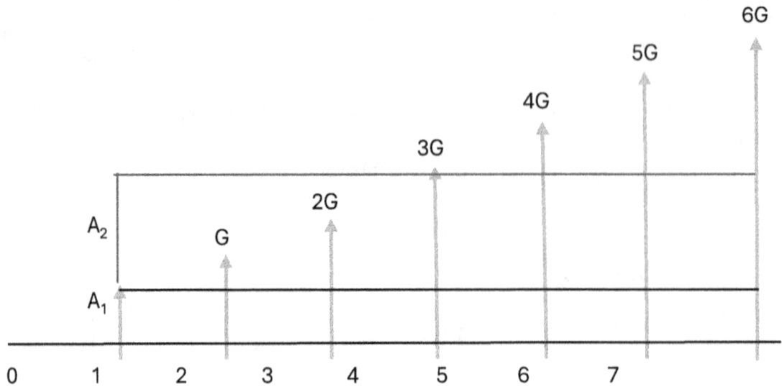

Figure 3.7 Cash flow diagrams of arithmetic gradient series.

for seven years. Second, we convert the cash flow series of the gradient amount G to a uniform series of A_2 per year using the following equation:

$$A_2 = G \times \left[\frac{1}{i} - \frac{n}{(1+i)^n - 1} \right]$$

The total annuity or uniform series of an arithmetic gradient series (A_G) is simply the sum of the annuity series A_1 and annuity series A_2:

$$A_G = A_1 + A_2$$

Entering the first equation into this one provides us with a formula to convert an arithmetic gradient series to an annuity series as shown:.

$$A_G = A_1 + G \times \left[\frac{1}{i} - \frac{n}{(1+i)^n - 1} \right]$$

In Example 3.7, to convert the engineer's consulting fees over the seven years into a uniform series, we enter the information in Example 3.7 into the converted equation to calculate the uniform amount:

$$A_G = \$200,000 + \$20,000 \times \left[\frac{1}{0.08} - \frac{7}{(1+0.08)^7 - 1} \right]$$

$$A_G = \$200,000 + \$20,000 \times [12.50 - 9.8063]$$

$$A_G = \$200,000 + \$20,000 \times [2.6937]$$

$$A_G = \$200,000 + \$53,874$$

$$A_G = \$253,874$$

To use standard compound interest factor notation, the equation can also be articulated as follows:

$$A_G = A_1 + G(A/G, i, n)$$

where interest factor (A/G, i, n) is precalculated and presented in Appendix A.

To calculate the annuity of the arithmetic gradient series in Example 3.7, using standard compound factor notation, we apply the data given in the example into the equation as follows:

$$A_G = \$200,000 + \$20,000(A/G,\ 8\%,\ 7)$$

From Table 3.7 for 8%, a subset of Table A14, the gradient interest factor (A/G, 8%, 7) is 2.6937. We now enter the interest factor in the previous relationship to calculate the annuity of this arithmetic gradient series:

$$A_G = \$200,000 + \$20,000(2.6937)$$
$$A_G = \$200,000 + \$53,874$$
$$A_G = \$253,874$$

Understanding and accurately calculating the annuity of an arithmetic gradient series is crucial for engineers to assess the economic feasibility and profitability of projects, optimize financial performance, and make informed investment decisions.

Future Value of an Arithmetic Gradient Series

The future value of an arithmetic gradient series represents the total worth of a series of cash flows that increase or decrease by a constant amount over time at a specified future point. In engineering economics, understanding and calculating the future value of such gradient series is crucial for evaluating the economic feasibility and profitability of projects with changing cash flows. To drive an equation for calculating the future value of an arithmetic gradient, we divide the cash flow series in Figure 3.4 into two series: first, the series for the base amount annuity A per year for six years, and second, the series for gradient amount G in year two that increases by the same amount per year as shown in Figure 3.5.

To calculate the future value of the first cash flow series (the annuity series), we use the following equation:

$$F_1 = A \times \left[\frac{(1+i)^n - 1}{i}\right]$$

Table 3.7 Compound Interest Factors: 8%

n	*Single Payment*		*Uniform Payment Series*				*Arithmetic Gradient*	
	F/P	*P/F*	*F/A*	*A/F*	*P/A*	*A/P*	*P/G*	*A/G*
1	1.0800	0.9259	1.0000	1.0000	0.9259	1.0800	0	0
2	1.1664	0.8573	2.0800	0.4808	1.7833	0.5608	0.9573	0.4808
3	1.2597	0.7938	3.2464	0.3080	2.5771	0.3880	2.4450	0.9487
4	1.3605	0.7350	4.5061	0.2219	3.3121	0.3019	4.6501	1.4040
5	1.4693	0.6806	5.8666	0.1705	3.9927	0.2505	7.3724	1.8465
6	1.5869	0.6302	7.3359	0.1363	4.6229	0.2163	10.5233	2.2763
7	1.7138	0.5835	8.9228	0.1121	5.2064	0.1921	14.0242	2.6937
8	1.8509	0.5403	10.6366	0.0940	5.7466	0.1740	17.8061	3.0985
9	1.9990	0.5002	12.4876	0.0801	6.2469	0.1601	21.8081	3.4910
10	2.1589	0.4632	14.4866	0.0690	6.7101	0.1490	25.9768	3.8713

To calculate the future value of the second cash flow series, we use the next equation:

$$F_2 = \frac{G}{i} \times \left[\frac{(1+i)^n - 1}{i} - n \right]$$

This equation derived from the cash flows in Figure 3.5. The future value of all gradient amounts is calculated at the end of the period; add them all together and simplify it to derive the equation.

To calculate the future value of the whole arithmetic gradient series, we add the above two equations into one general equation as follows:

$$F_G = A \times \left[\frac{(1+i)^n - 1}{i} \right] + \frac{G}{i} \times \left[\frac{(1+i)^n - 1}{i} - n \right]$$

To use standard compound interest factor notation, this equation can also be articulated as follows:

$$F_G = A(F/A,\, i,\, n) + \frac{G}{i}\left[(F/A,\, i,\, n) - n\right]$$

where interest factor (F/A, i, n) is precalculated and presented in Appendix A.

Example 3.8

A dispatcher who works for Frankfurt International Airport would like to retire in 20 years. He is planning to invest \$10,000 at the end of year one and increase that amount by a constant amount of \$1,000 per year for 20 years. Assuming he is earning 12% on his long-term investment, how much can he accumulate in his retirement account by the end of 20 years?

We simply enter information in the future value of arithmetic gradient series equation:

$$F_G = \$10{,}000(F/A,\, 12\%,\, 20) + \frac{\$1{,}000}{0.12}\left[(F/A,\, 12\%,\, 20) - 20\right]$$

From Table A18 for 12%, we enter annuity interest factor (F/A, i, n) 72.0524 in the previous equation:

$$F_G = \$10{,}000(72.0524) + \frac{\$1{,}000}{0.12}[72.0524 - 20]$$

$$F_G = \$720{,}524 + \$433{,}770$$

$$F_G = \$1{,}154{,}294$$

To calculate a future arithmetic gradient, you can also calculate the present of the series and then calculate the future of that present single amount at the end of the period. Using Example 3.8, first we calculate the present arithmetic gradient and then calculate its future value.

First, use the present gradient series equation to calculate the present gradient series.

$$P_G = \$10{,}000(P/A,\, 12\%,\, 20) + \$1{,}000(P/G,\, 12\%,\, 20)$$

Table A18, we enter annuity interest factor (P/A, 12%, 20) 7.4694 and gradient interest factor (P/G, 12%, 20) 44.9676 into the previous relationship and calculate the present value of this arithmetic gradient series:

$$P_G = \$10{,}000(7.4694) + \$1{,}000(44.9676)$$
$$P_G = \$74{,}694 + \$44{,}968$$
$$P_G = \$119{,}662$$

Next, we use the equation to calculate the future value of the dispatcher contributions to the retirement account at the end of 20 years.

$$F_{20} = 119{,}662 \times (1 + .12)^{20}$$
$$F_{20} = 119{,}662 \times (9.6463)$$
$$F_{20} = \$1{,}154{,}296$$

Geometric Gradient Series

The geometric gradient series is a financial concept used in engineering economics to model cash flows that change by a constant percentage or growth rate over time (g). In contrast to arithmetic gradient series where cash flows change by a constant amount, in geometric gradient series, each cash flow increases or decreases by a constant percentage from one period to the next. Figure 3.8 presents a geometric gradient cash flow series in which A_1 is the base amount that occurs at the end of year one and g is the gradient rate, the constant percentage increase in cash flows starting at the end of year two and continues through the end of the cash flow period.

Present Value of a Geometric Gradient Series

To calculate the present value of a geometric gradient, we used the following equation:

$$P_g = A_1 \times \left[\frac{1 - \left[\frac{1+g}{(1+i)}\right]^n}{i - g} \right]$$

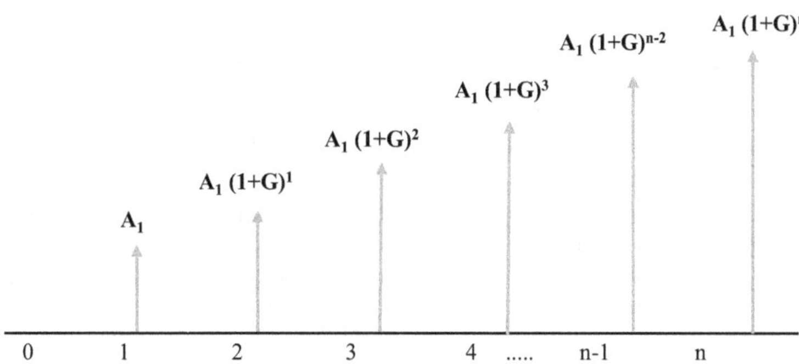

Figure 3.8 Geometric gradient series.

This equation is valid as long as $i \neq g$.

This equation is used often to determine the levels of activity where the change in the next period's cash flow is a percentage of the previous period's cash flow.

Example 3.9

Cirrus Aircraft is leasing a property for an aircraft hangar for 10 years. The first lease payment is \$20,000 and it is due at the end of the first year. Starting the second year, the lease payments will increase by a constant 5% per year through the end of 10 years of the lease contract. If Cirrus can earn 10% return on its investment, how much should Cirrus deposit as a lump sum today in that investment account to be able to pay the lease payments every year for the next 10 years?

In this example, $A_1 = \$20{,}000$, $g = 5\%$, $i = 10\%$, $n = 10$ years, $P_g = ?$

To calculate present value of this geometric gradient series, we use the following equation:

$$P_g = A_1 \times \left[\frac{1 - \left[\frac{1+g}{(1+i)} \right]^n}{i-g} \right]$$

$$P_g = A_1 \times \left[\frac{1 - \left[\frac{1+0.05}{(1+0.10)} \right]^{10}}{0.10-0.05} \right] \quad P_g = \$20{,}000 \times \left[\frac{1-0.6280}{0.05} \right]$$

$$P_g = \$20{,}000 \times (7.44)$$
$$P_g = \$148{,}800$$

If interest rate is equal to the growth rate, we cannot use the above equation, the present value of the geometric gradient can be calculated using the equation shown below:

$$P_g = \frac{n \times A_1}{1+i}$$

Annuity of a Geometric Gradient Series

The annuity of a geometric gradient series represents the equivalent uniform cash flow stream that has the same present value as the gradient series. In engineering economics, this concept is essential for evaluating projects with changing cash flows over time. To convert a geometric gradient to an annuity or a uniform series, it is best to calculate the present value of the geometric gradient and then calculate the annuity of that present single amount for a 10-year period.

Assume that Example 3.9 asked you to calculate the annuity of the lease payments over the 10-year period. First, we would have calculated the present value of the geometric gradient series as shown in Example 3.9. Next, we calculate the annuity of the present value as follows:

$$P_g = \$148{,}800$$
$$A = P(A/P, i, n)$$
$$A = \$148{,}800(A/P, 10\%, 10)$$

From Table A16 for 10%, enter annuity interest factor (A/P, 10%, 10) 0.16275 into the previous relationship and calculate the annuity of the present amount:

$$A = \$148{,}800 \times (0.16275)$$
$$A = \$24{,}217$$

In other words, instead of depositing a single sum of $148,800, Cirrus can make its lease payments by depositing a uniform series of $24,217 at the end of each year for 10 years. In engineering projects, the annuity of a geometric gradient series helps in financial analysis, budgeting, and decision-making. It provides a simplified way to represent the cash flows of projects with changing revenues or costs over time, facilitating comparison and evaluation of alternatives.

Future Value of a Geometric Gradient Series

To calculate the future value of a geometric gradient, like witharithmetic gradients, it is best to calculate the present value of the series and then calculate future value of that present single amount at the end of the period.

Example 3.10

Unite Technologies offers retirement benefits to its employees and matches up to 5% of the employees' contributions. An engineer who was just hired by Unite started with a salary of $100,000 in the first year with an increase of 4% per year for 30 years. The employee who wants to take advantage of matching by employer will contribute 5% of his salary every year. If the employee can earn 10% return on his retirement investment, how much will he accumulate in his retirement account at the end of 30 years? For geometric gradient series, first we calculate the present value of the series and then calculate the future value of that present amount.

Total contributions by employee and employer in the first year = $100,000 (0.05 + 0.05) = $10,000. This amount will increase by the same percentage increase of employee's salary or by 4%.

First use the following equation to calculate present value of the geometric gradient:

$$P_g = \$10{,}000 \times \left[\frac{1 - \left[\frac{1+0.04}{(1+0.10)} \right]^{30}}{0.10 - 0.04} \right]$$

$$P_g = \$10{,}000 \times \left[\frac{1 - 0.1859}{0.06} \right]$$

$$P_g = \$10{,}000 \times (13.5683)$$

$$P_g = \$135{,}683$$

Second, calculate the future value of the present amount at the end of 30 years:

$$F_{30} = \$135{,}683 \times (1 + .10)^{30}$$
$$F_{30} = \$135{,}683 \times (17.4494)$$
$$F_{30} = \$2{,}367{,}587$$

Shifted Cash Flow Series

Not all cash flow series start at the end of the first year. In that case, we have to calculate the present value of the cash flow stream at the beginning of the year when the payment starts and then shift it as a single amount to t = 0.

Example 3.11

You are considering an investment opportunity that provides no revenues in the first four years, but starting at the end of year five, revenue is expected to be \$20,000 per year for five years. If you earn 8% on your investment, what is the maximum price that you are willing to pay for this investment opportunity? The maximum price that you are willing to pay for this investment is the present value of these cash flows discounted at 8% to time 0. Figure 3.9 presents the cash flow diagram.

To calculate the present value of cash flows at time 0, we first calculate the present value of the cash flow at the beginning of year five or end of year four (P_4) and then shift P_4 to time 0 to calculate P_0.

$$P_4 = \$20,000(P/A, 8\%, 6)$$

Enter annuity interest factor (P/A, 8%, 6) 4.6229 from Table A14 for 8% into the previous equation to calculate the present value:

$$P_4 = \$20,000 \times (4.6229)$$
$$P_4 = \$92,458$$

Next, we calculate the present value of P_4 at t = 0 as follows:

$$P_0 = P_4(P/F, 8\%, 4)$$

Enter the present interest factor 0.7350 (P/F, 8%, 4) from Table A14 into the previous equation to calculate the present value:

$$P_0 = \$92,458 \times (0.7350)$$
$$P_0 = \$67,957$$

By the same reasoning, not all cash flow series continue to the end of a given period. If we need to calculate the future value of cash flows at the end of the period, first we calculate the future value of cash flows at the end of the year when cash flow stops and then shift that future value to the end of the period.

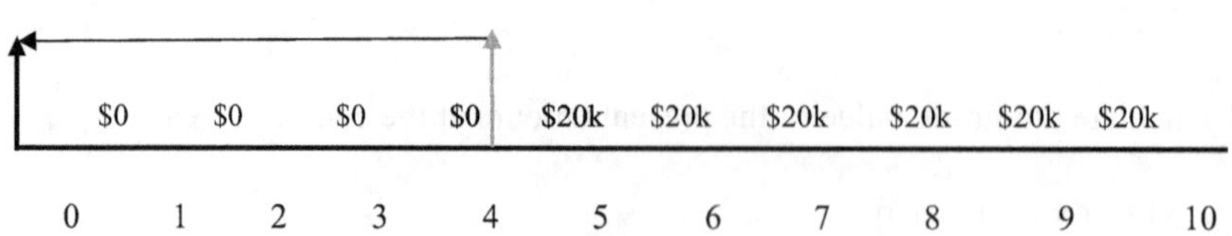

Figure 3.9 Shifted cash flow series.

Example 3.12

Booz Allen Jackson is planning to replace equipment in 10 years. The company is investing \$20,000 at the end of each year for the first five years with no additional investment. If Booz Allen can earn 9% from its investment, how much can it accumulate at the end of 10 years? Figure 3.10 presents the cash flow diagram.

To calculate the future value of cash flows at the end of 10 years, we first calculate the future value of the cash flow at the end of year five (F_5) where the last deposit occurs and then shift the F_5 to the end of year 10 to calculate F_{10}.

$$F_5 = \$20{,}000\left(F/A,\ 9\%,\ 5\right)$$

From Table A15 for 9%, enter annuity interest factor (F/A, 9%, 5) 5.9847 into the previous relationship and calculate the future value at the end of five years (F_5):

$$F_5 = \$20{,}000\left(5.9847\right)$$
$$F_5 = \$119{,}694$$

Next, we calculate the future value of F_5 at F_{10} as follows:

$$F_{10} = F_5\left(F/P,\ 9\%,\ 5\right)$$

From Table A15, enter interest factor (F/P, 9%, 5) 1.5386 into the previous relationship and calculate the future value at F_{10}:

$$F_{10} = \$119{,}694 \times \left(1.5386\right)$$
$$F_{10} = \$184{,}161$$

Calculating Equivalences in Excel

This section presents how to run the financial equations referenced in this chapter using Microsoft Excel functions. To calculate future value of an annuity in Excel, first we open the future value function. This formula is listed under the financial formulas option. Once this step is accomplished, the user can answer the formula questions and then Excel will solve this function.

Example 3.13

Calculate the future value of \$5 million at the end of each year for six years at 5% interest. As shown in Figure 3.11, enter 5% or 0.05 in the Rate line for interest rate, 6 in the Nper line for

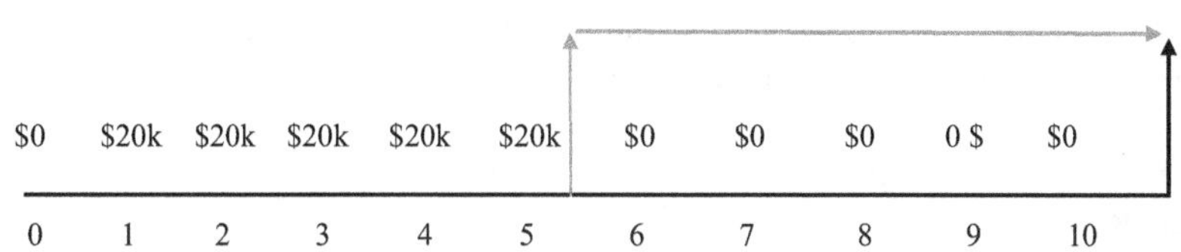

Figure 3.10 Shifted cash flow series.

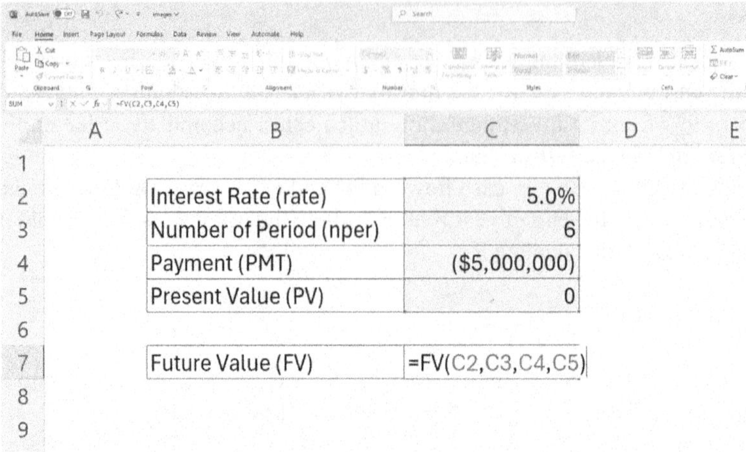

Figure 3.11 Excel future value function.

period, –5,000,000 in the PMT line as an annuity amount, and 0 for PV. Excel will calculate the solution for future value of an annuity which in this case is $34,009,564. Note that PMT (annuity amount) is entered as a negative number to get a positive solution for future value of the annuity.

Alternatively, one can simply enter the following function in cell B6 and press the enter key to get the result in that cell.

= FV(i%,n,–A,0)

The present value of an annuity function in Excel is as follows:

= PV(i%,n,–A,0)

In Example 3.3, entering = PV(6%,10,–2500000,0) in a cell and pressing return gives $18,400,217 as the present value of an annuity of $2.5 million for 10 years at 6% (Figure 3.12). Again, we use a negative value for the annuity payment to get positive present value.

The Excel functions to calculate the annuity of a future amount and the annuity of a present amount are as follows; PMT is the payment or annuity amount:

Annuity of a future amount = PMT(i%,n,0,–F)
Annuity of a present amount = PMT(i%,n,0,–p)

Figures 3.13 and 3.14 show Excel calculation of an annuity of a future value and an annuity of a present value respectively.

The Excel functions to calculate period and interest rate in an annuity series where NPER is the period and RATE is the interest rate (Figure 3.15):

Period = NPER(i%,A,P,F)
Interest Rate = RATE(n,A,P,F)

In both equations, either P or F is 0.

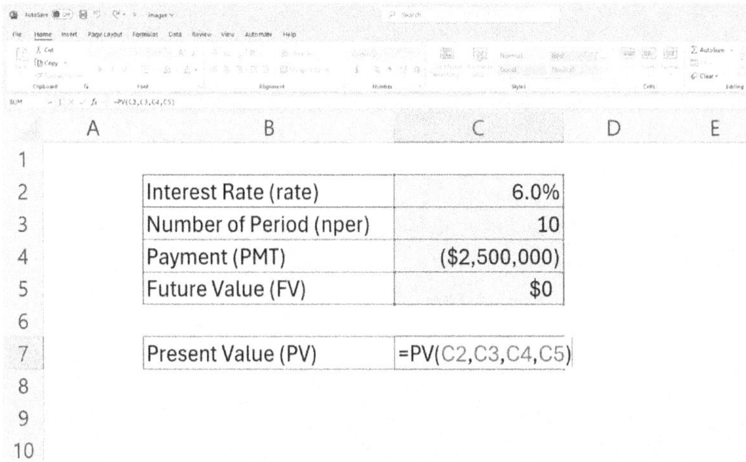

Figure 3.12 Calculating present value of an annuity in Excel.

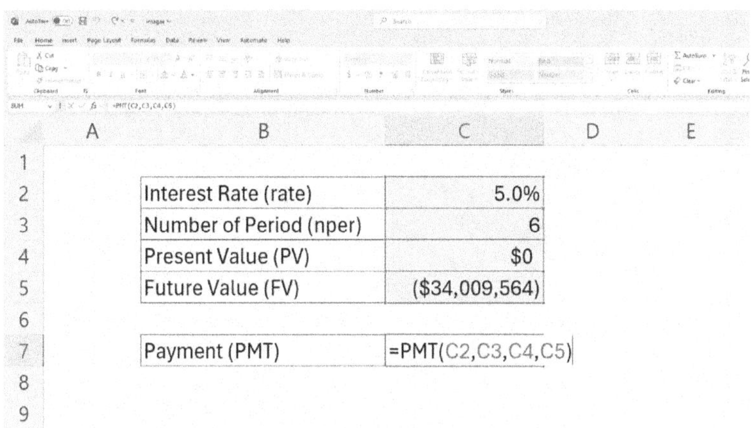

Figure 3.13 Calculating annuity of a future amount in Excel.

To use Excel to calculate the present value of an arithmetic gradient or geometric gradient, we use the following equation where NPV is present value or present worth:

= NPV (i%, Cell [1]:Cell [n])

Example 3.14

If you have an arithmetic gradient series with the base amount of $100,000 in year one and gradient amount of $10,000 per year starting the second year through year five, assume 10% and calculate the present value of this series using Excel. Figure 3.18 shows the cash flows in cells B2 through B6, the Excel function in cell B8, and the result in cell B8.

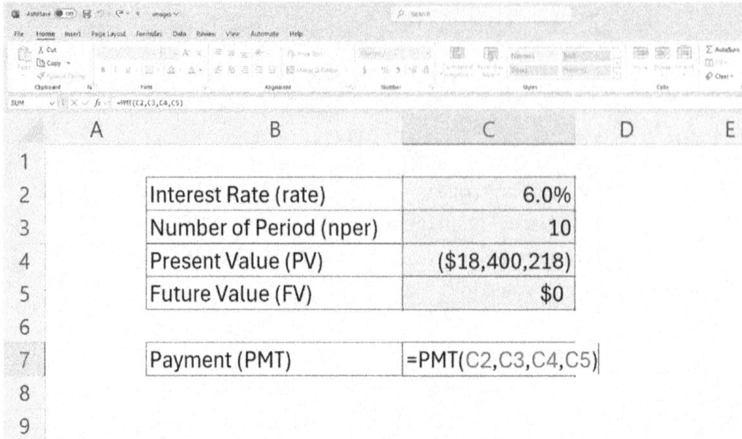

Figure 3.14 Calculating annuity of a present amount in Excel.

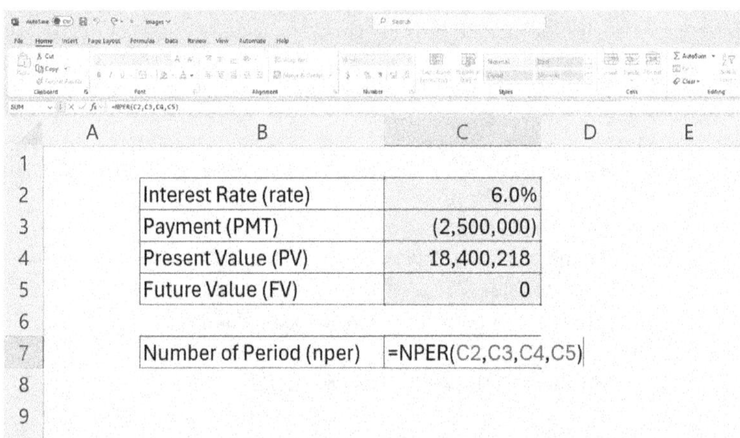

Figure 3.15 Calculating period of an annuity series in Excel.

Summary

The concept of annuity holds significant importance for engineering projects due to its implications for project finance, budgeting, and investment analysis. Engineering projects typically require substantial upfront investments followed by a stream of future cash flows. Understanding annuities helps engineers and project managers evaluate the project's financial feasibility by assessing the present value of these cash flows and comparing them to initial investment costs. This analysis guides decision-making regarding project initiation, expansion, or termination.

In this chapter, we defined annuity as a uniform set of payments that occur consecutively over a given period. The most common payment intervals are yearly, semiannually, quarterly, and monthly. In addition, the most common form of annuities is seen in mortgages, pension funds, aircraft leases, property leases, car loans, insurance premiums, and retirement planning. There are two types of annuities which differ based on the timing of annuity payments, ordinary

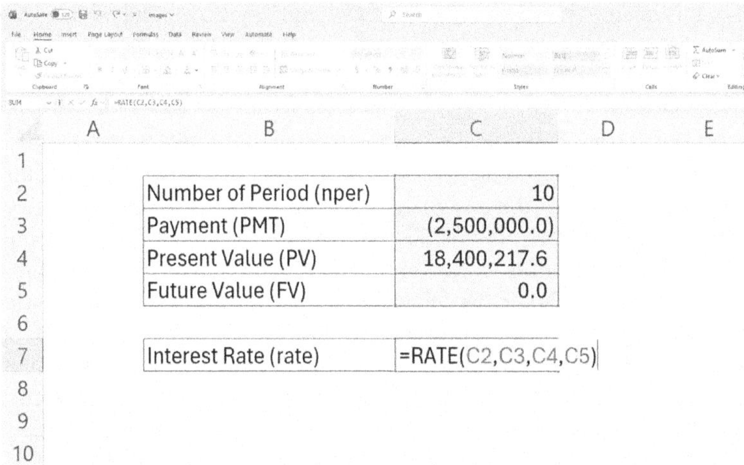

Figure 3.16 Calculating interest rate of an annuity series in Excel.

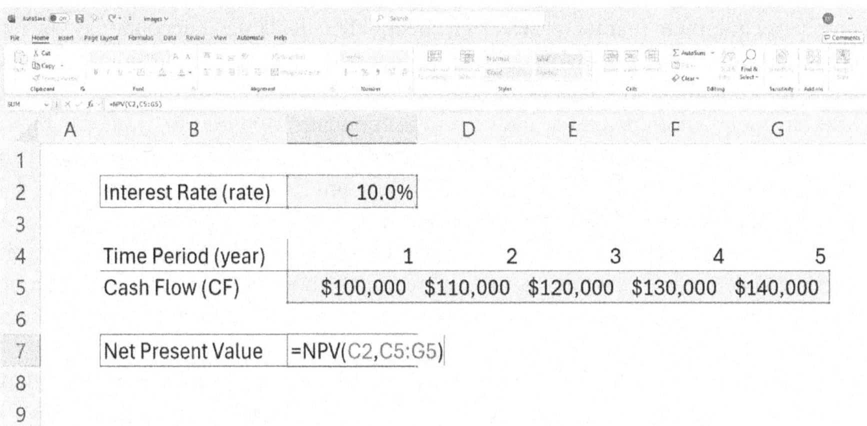

Figure 3.17 Excel calculation of the present value of an arithmetic gradian series.

annuity and annuity due. An ordinary annuity is when payments are made at the end of each period, while in annuity due, payments are made at the beginning of the period. Ordinary annuity is commonly used in engineering economics practices and therefore in this book, the word annuity is referred to ordinary annuity with end-of-the-period convention.

This chapter derived and presented the economic equations to calculate the future value of an annuity and to calculate an annuity of a future sum known as sinking fund which is used often for financial planning purposes. Individuals and aviation companies have short- and long-term financial goals to achieve and they use this formula to determine the uniform series needed to be invested in an interest-bearing account to accumulate a future sum to finance their future goals. It also presented economic equations to calculate the present value of an annuity series and to calculate an annuity of a present amount known as amortization which is often used in mortgages, personal and commercial loans. Individuals and businesses often buy capital equipment on credit. They can use this formula to calculate their annual or monthly payments and to determine whether the payments fit within their budget.

In addition, this chapter presented the economic equations to calculate the present value of an arithmetic gradient series, to convert an arithmetic gradient series to a uniform series, to calculate future value of an arithmetic gradient series, and to calculate the present value of a geometric gradient series.

Furthermore, we present how to calculate the present and future value of shifted cash flow series are presented. Shifted series are streams of cash flows that do not start at the end of year one or do not end at the end of the designated year. To calculate the present value of a shifted series, the present value of cash flow series is calculated at the beginning of the year where payments start, and that amount is shifted to time 0 by multiplying it with the present value of future amount (P/F) interest factor. To calculate the future value of a shifted series, the future value of the cash flow series is calculated at the end of the year where payments stop, and that amount is shifted to the end of the designated year by multiplying it with the future value of a present amount (F/P) interest factor. In conclusion, the application of all the derived formulae using Excel functions is presented.

Discussion Questions and Problems

3.1 A leasing company is considering investing $500,000 at the end of each year for 5 years to purchase equipment that increases its efficiency. The investment account pays 6% interest compounded annually. How much will the company accumulate in this account to purchase the equipment in 5 years?

3.2 You have a newborn daughter and plan to accumulate $400,000 for your daughter's college education in 18 years. Assuming you earn 8% of your investment, how much will you need to invest at the end of each year in equal amount for 18 years to accumulate 400,000?

3.3 An airport in Japan is planning to purchase a parcel of land for building additional executive hangars in 5 years. The price of land currently is $5,000,000. The average inflation rate is 5% per year in the next 5 years. How much should the airport invest in a uniform amount per year for 5 years in an account that pays 10% interest annually to be able to purchase the land in 5 years?

3.4 Your son just graduated from high school, and he has been accepted for undergraduate program at an Ivy League university. The cost of attending the university is $40,000 per year for tuition and room and board due at the end of each year for four years. How much do you have to deposit in a lump sum today in a bank account that pays 7% interest per year to be able to pay for your son's college education for the next four years?

3.5 United Engine Leasing (UEL) is planning to lease an executive hangar for $100,000 per year for 10 years. The company may build a 3200 square feet hangar at the cost of $960,000 with $5,000 maintenance cost per year. Assume UEL can borrow at 6% and be able to sell the hangar at the end of 10 years for $500,000. Using present value analysis, should UEL lease or build the hangar?

3.6 Travelers flying in and out of an international airport should soon get free wireless speeds that would be ten times faster than the current service in the terminals (5 megabits per second). The airport has recently awarded a $7.5 million contract to Bingo Wireless Inc. to upgrade, manage, and operate the Wi-Fi network at the airport for 10 years. What would be the annual cost of offering free Wi-Fi to airport travelers? Assume a minimum acceptable rate of return (MARR) of 8% for the airport.

3.7 In Problem 3.4 assuming all relevant information, if the cost of attending the university is $40,000 per year due at the beginning instead of ending of each year for four years, how much do you have to deposit in a lump sum to be able to pay for your son's college education for the next four years?

3.8 A newly graduated electrical engineer is signing up for a five-year consulting agreement with the Dubai International Airport to improve the efficiency of the airport energy consumption. The length of the contract is seven years, and consulting fees are $100,000 at the end of year one increasing by $20,000 per year starting at the end of the second year through the end of the contract. Assuming the engineer earns 10% return on his investment, what is the present value of his consulting contract?

3.9 A new airline in México has started a new nonstop flight from Mexico City to Boston in the United States. The airline requires an average sales revenue of at least $10,000,000 per year for four years to break even. If sales are $5,000,000 in year one, how much should the sales increase by a constant amount per year in order for the airline to reach its breakeven target in four years? Airline uses a MARR of 8%.

3.10 Huntington has budgeted $2,000,000 per year for an expansion over the next eight years. Huntington spent $1,000,000 at the end of the first year on this expansion. What should be the constant amount of annual increase in spending so that Huntington uses its total budgeted amount by the end of eight years? Huntington uses a MARR of 9%.

3.11 A newly hired engineer would like to retire in 25 years. She is planning to invest $12,000 at the end of year one and increase that amount by a constant amount of $1,200 per year for 25 years. Assuming that the engineer is earning 10% on her long-term investment, how much can she accumulate in her retirement account at the end of 25 years?

3.12 Spirit Mechanic is estimating a total payroll expense of $1,000,000 at the end of the first year. Starting the second year, the payroll expenses will increase by a constant 6% per year through the end of the 10-year study period. How much should Spirit deposit as a lump sum today in an investment account that pays 8% interest to be able to pay the payroll expenses every year for the next 10 years?

3.13 In Problem 5.12, assume all relevant information, what is the annuity (uniform series) of payroll expenses per year over the next 10 years?

3.14 Star Technology offers retirement benefits to its employees and matches up to 5% of the employee's contribution. An engineer who was just hired by Star Technology started with a salary of $150,000 in the first year with increase of 4% per year for the next 30 years. The employee who wants to take advantage of matching by employer, will contribute 5% of his salary every year. If the employee can earn 10% return on his retirement investment, how much will he accumulate in his retirement account at the end of 30 years?

3.15 Rockwell Machine is considering building a manufacturing plant that takes three years to complete. The plant is expected to generate a revenue of $500,000 per year at the end of each year of operation for 10 years (years 4 through 13). If Rockwell earns 8% on its investment, what is the maximum price that Rockwell is willing to pay for this investment opportunity?

3.16 An aviation company is planning to replace equipment in 10 years with an expected cost of $1,500,000. The company is planning to invest an equal amount of money at the end of each year only for the first 5 years with no further investment through year 10. If the company can earn 12% on its investment, how large must the size of uniform deposit be in the first five years to accumulate $1,500,000 at the end of the 10 years?

3.17 Precision Machine is signing a 10-year lease contract with a lease payment schedule of $40,000 at the end of each year for the first 5 years, $60,000 at the end of year 6 and increases by $20,000 at the end of each year through year 10. If Precision could earn 8%

on its investment, how much does Precision need to deposit today to make all scheduled lease payments in the next 10 years?

3.18 Legacy Airport, which anticipates significant increase in the number of passengers, is planning to construct a 5-story parking garage in 10 years. The current cost of parking construction is about $20,000,000. The average annual rate of inflation in the next 10 years is 4%. How much does Legacy have to deposit in equal amounts at the end of each year to be able to build the parking garage in 10 years? Assume an interest rate of 7%.

3.19 An airport manager is planning to pay $40,000 per year for 10 years for weather monitoring and reporting services. The cost of buying weather monitoring equipment is $200,000 with $3,000 maintenance cost per year. Assuming the life of the equipment is 10 years and airport can borrow at 8%, should the airport manager buy the equipment?

3.20 DirectJet has started a new route from Dubai Airport in the United Arab Emirate (UAE) to Islamabad Airport in Pakistan. DirectJet requires an accumulated sales revenue of at least $30,000,000 at the end of year 5 to break even. DirectJet is earning 10% on its investment. If sales are $4,000,000 in year one, how much should the sales increase by a constant amount per year in order for DirectJet to reach its breakeven target in 5 years?

3.21 Golden Aerospace Company has budgeted $500,000 per year for an expansion over the next 10 years. Golden earns 8% return on its investment and spent $200,000 at the end of the first year on this expansion. What should be the constant annual increase in spending so that Golden uses its total budgeted amount by the end of 10 years?

3.22 Precision Machine maintenance payment schedule division B for the next 10 years is given in the following table. If Precision could earn 6% on its investment, how much does it need to deposit today to make all scheduled payments for the next 10 years?

Precision's Payments Schedule

End of the Year	*Payments*
1	$50,000
2	$50,000
3	$50,000
4	$50,000
5	$50,000
6	$100,000
7	$120,000
8	$140,000
9	$160,000
10	$180,000

4 Nominal and Effective Interest Rates

In the past two chapters, the interest rates were compounded annually. The majority of investment projects evaluated by professional engineers, and almost all financial institutions, use interest rates that are compounded more frequently than once a year. Common interest compounding time frames are daily, monthly, semiannually, annually, and continuously compounding. More frequent compounding means that the investors receive a higher return, whereas less frequent compounding results in receiving a lower return. For instance, most credit card companies compound interest daily; that results in effective annual rates that exceed the annual stated interest rates.

The focus of this chapter is to enable practitioners and professional engineers to make a distinction between nominal and effective interest rates as applied to engineering projects and financial activities of aviation and aerospace companies. Nominal and effective interest rates are common in business practices, financial management, and engineering economics. This chapter presents the process of converting nominal interest rates to effective interest rates.

Nominal versus Effective Interest Rates

As we described, for most projects evaluated by professional engineers in aviation, aerospace, and financial institutions, interest can be compounded semiannually, quarterly, monthly, daily, and potentially continuously. The effective interest rate, or annual equivalent rate, is the actual rate of interest earned or paid. If interest is given per year (stated interest rate or nominal rate) but compounded more frequently than once a year, then effective interest rate per year is greater than the nominal interest rate per year. Every nominal interest rate must be converted into an effective rate before it can be used for financial decision-making purposes. Each type of interest rate must be analyzed in order to solve various cases where interests are expressed in different manners (Figure 4.1).

For the airline industry, the single largest capital expenditure is the cost of aircraft. Therefore, many airline companies use either commercial bank loans or leasing companies to finance their capital needs. In 2023, Boeing Commercial Market Outlook (CMO) forecast demand for more than 42,000 new airplanes over the next 20 years. With the strong increase in demand for new and fuel-efficient commercial aircraft for foreseeable future, the aircraft finance markets play an important role in offering a broad and balanced range of financing options at competitive prices to support the airline industry.

Airlines pay explicit interest on commercial loans and implicit interest on leasing arrangements. Although the interest rates on commercial loans and lease agreements are coded in annual percentage rates, the loan and lease payments are often made more frequently than annually. Therefore, the effective interest rates are higher than the stated interest rates on the loan and lease agreements. Next we describe calculating effective interest rates.

DOI: 10.4324/9781003469759-4

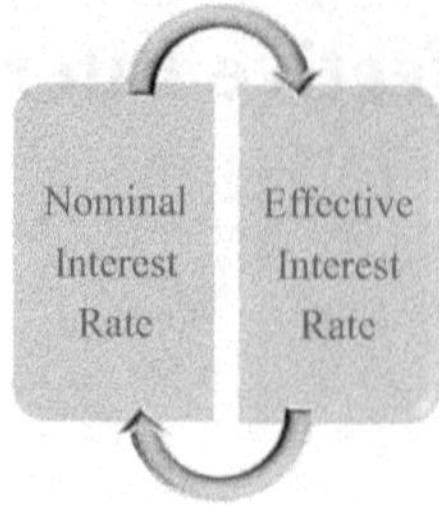

Figure 4.1 Nominal and effective interest rates.

Calculating Effective Interest Rate

The effective interest rate, also known as the effective annual rate or annual equivalent rate, is the actual interest rate that an investor earns or a borrower pays after accounting for compounding over a given period. Unlike the nominal interest rate, which is the stated rate without considering compounding, the effective interest rate reflects the impact of compounding within a specific time frame, providing a more accurate measure of financial cost or yield. The effective interest rate can be calculated using the relationship between nominal rate and effective rate as follows:

$$i_{EAR} = \left(1 + \frac{r}{m}\right)^{m} - 1$$

where i = effective rate per some stated period, r = nominal rate for the same period, and m = frequency of compounding per the same period.

Example 4.1

For a nominal rate of 12% per year, calculate the annual effective rate if interest is compounded a) semiannually, b) quarterly, c) monthly, and d) daily. We apply the previous equation to calculate the effective rates:

a. $$i_{year} = \left(1 + \frac{0.12}{2}\right)^{2} - 1$$

$$i_{year} = 0.1236 \text{ or } 12.36\%$$

b. $$i_{year} = \left(1 + \frac{0.12}{4}\right)^{4} - 1$$

$$i_{year} = 0.1255 \text{ or } 12.55\%$$

c. $$i_{year} = \left(1 + \frac{0.12}{12}\right)^{12} - 1$$

$$i_{year} = 0.1268 \text{ or } 12.68\%$$

d. $$i_{year} = \left(1 + \frac{0.12}{365}\right)^{365} - 1$$

$$i_{year} = 0.1275 \text{ or } 12.75\%$$

As you notice, the higher the compounding frequency, the higher the effective rate.

We can also calculate effective semiannual rate and effective quarterly rate when interest is compounded monthly and the interest rate is 1% per month. To calculate effective rate semiannually and quarterly, we need to calculate the semiannual and quarterly nominal rates. A nominal interest rate can be calculated for any period that is greater than compounding period as follows:

$$r_{\text{semiannually}} = 1\% \times 6 \text{ month} = 6\%$$
$$r_{\text{quarterly}} = 1\% \times 3 \text{ month} = 3\%$$

Now, we can calculate the effective rate semiannually and quarterly where interest is compounding monthly. In other words, frequency of compounding is six times semiannually (there are 6 months in a semiannual period) and frequency of compounding is three times quarterly (there are 3 months in a quarter):

$$r_{\text{semiannually}} = 1\% \times 6 = 6\%$$
$$i_{\text{semiannually}} = \left(1 \times \frac{0.06}{6}\right)^{6} - 1$$
$$i_{\text{semiannually}} = 6.15\%$$
$$r_{\text{quarterly}} = 1\% \times 3 = 3\%$$
$$i_{\text{quarterly}} = \left(1 \times \frac{0.03}{3}\right)^{3} - 1$$
$$i_{\text{quarterly}} = 3.03\%$$

If we have nominal interest rate per year, we can also calculate nominal rate per quarter and per semiannual as follows:

Assuming nominal interest rate is 12% per year, then

$$r_{\text{semiannually}} = 12\% / 2 = 6\%$$
$$r_{\text{quarterly}} = 12\% / 4 = 3\%$$

Table 4.1 presents the effective interest rates per year for different periods and different interest rates.

Table 4.1 Effective Annual Interest Rates for Selected Nominal Rates

Nominal Rate	*Annual Compounding*	*Semiannual Compounding*	*Quarterly Compounding*	*Monthly Compounding*	*Daily Compounding*
4%	4%	4.04%	4.06%	4.07%	4.08%
5%	5%	5.06%	5.09%	5.12%	5.13%
6%	6%	6.09%	6.14%	6.17%	6.18%
7%	7%	7.12%	7.19%	7.23%	7.25%
8%	8%	8.16%	8.24%	8.30%	8.33%
9%	9%	9.20%	9.31%	9.38%	9.42%
10%	10%	10.25%	10.38%	10.47%	10.52%
12%	12%	12.36%	12.55%	12.68%	12.75%
15%	15%	15.56%	15.87%	16.08%	16.18%
18%	18%	18.81%	19.25%	19.56%	19.72%
20%	20%	21.00%	21.55%	21.94%	22.13%
24%	24%	25.44%	26.25%	26.82%	27.11%
25%	25%	26.56%	27.44%	28.07%	28.39%
30%	30%	32.25%	33.55%	34.49%	34.97%

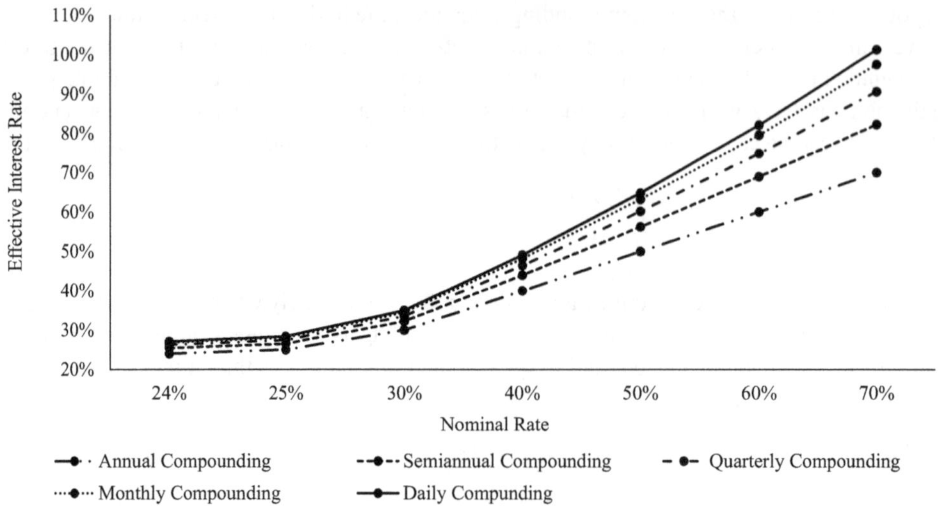

Figure 4.2 Effective interest rates for various nominal rates.

Figure 4.2 provides a visual illustration of the increasing amounts of effective rates as the frequency of compounding keeps increasing and the nominal rates are changed. Since at lower nominal rates, the effective rates are close to the nominal rates, nominal rates from 25% to 70% are used to illustrate the changes in effective interest rates.

Continuous Compounding

If compounding is increasingly frequent, the compounding period becomes increasingly shorter; then, m, the number of compounding periods, increases. Continuous compounding is a concept in finance where interest is calculated and added to the principal balance an infinite number of times in each period. This means that interest is effectively being compounded constantly, leading to the maximum possible amount of compound interest that can be earned or paid.

If interest is compounded continuously, then m approaches infinity ($m \longrightarrow \infty$):

$$i_{effective} = \left(1+\frac{r}{m}\right)^{\overset{\infty}{\nearrow}\, m\times n} - 1$$

An important theory in calculus is

$$\lim_{m\to\infty}\left(1+\frac{1}{m}\right)^{m} = \lim_{x\to 0}\left(1+x\right)^{\frac{1}{x}} = e = 2.7182$$

As m approaches infinity, x becomes 0, and this equation reduces to the following:

$$i_{effective} = e^{r} - 1$$

Therefore, if an investor puts \$1,000,000 in an account paying 10% interest, under continuous compounding the effective rate is

$$i_{effective} = e^{0.10} - 1$$
$$i_{effective} = 1.1049 - 1$$
$$i_{effective} = 10.49\%$$

Example 4.2

Shelden Financial charges stated 12% interest per year on its loans. The interest is, however, compounded continuously. What is the annual effective rate charged by this financial company?

$$i_{effective} = e^{12} - 1$$
$$i_{effective} = 1.1275 - 1$$
$$i_{effective} = 0.1275$$
$$i_{effective} = 12.75\%$$

Converting Effective Rate to Nominal Rate

Sometimes effective rate may be given, and we are asked to calculate the nominal rate. We use both of the equations mentioned above to calculate the nominal rate. Table 4.2 presents the nominal interest rates per year when interest is compounded for different periods and different effective interest rates.

Figure 4.3 graphically displays the nominal rates calculated for various effective rates, using different frequencies of compounding. Note that this graph reflects the opposite relationships to those the depiction of effective rate calculated from nominal rates in Figure 4.2. The nominal rates keep decreasing as the compounding periods increase.

Table 4.2 Nominal Annual Interest Rates for Selected Effective Annual Rates

Effective Interest Rate	*Annual Compounding*	*Semiannual Compounding*	*Quarterly Compounding*	*Monthly Compounding*	*Daily Compounding*
4%	4%	3.96%	3.94%	3.93%	3.92%
5%	5%	4.94%	4.91%	4.89%	4.88%
6%	6%	5.91%	5.87%	5.84%	5.83%
7%	7%	6.88%	6.82%	6.78%	6.77%
8%	8%	7.85%	7.77%	7.72%	7.70%
9%	9%	8.81%	8.71%	8.65%	8.62%
10%	10%	9.76%	9.65%	9.57%	9.53%
12%	12%	11.66%	11.49%	11.39%	11.33%
15%	15%	14.48%	14.22%	14.06%	13.98%
18%	18%	17.26%	16.90%	16.67%	16.56%
20%	20%	19.09%	18.65%	18.37%	18.24%
24%	24%	22.71%	22.10%	21.71%	21.52%
25%	25%	23.61%	22.95%	22.52%	22.32%
30%	30%	28.04%	27.12%	26.53%	26.25%

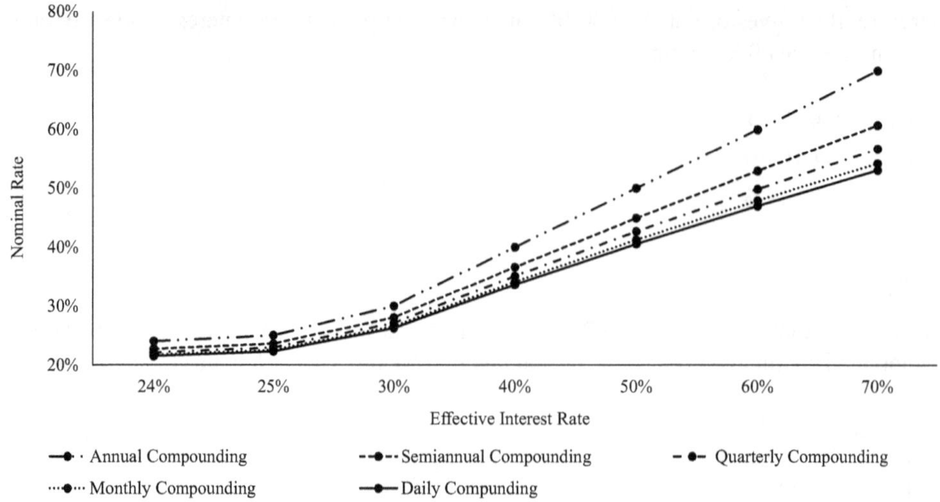

Figure 4.3 Nominal rates for various effective interest rates.

Example 4.3

Wilshire Financial charges an effective rate of 17% per year. If interest is compounded quarterly, what is the nominal rate per year?

Enter the given information in the following equation and solve for nominal rate of r:

$$i_{effective} = \left(1+\frac{r}{m}\right)^{m} - 1$$

$$0.17 = \left(1+\frac{r}{4}\right)^{4} - 1$$

$$1.17 = \left(1+\frac{r}{4}\right)^{4}$$

Obtain the power of ¼ as follows:

$$(1.17)^{1/4} = \left(1+\frac{r}{4}\right)$$

$$1.04 = 1+\frac{r}{4}$$

$$0.04 = \frac{r}{4}$$

$$r = .16$$

$$r = 16\%$$

Comparing Compounding Periods and Payment Periods

In this section, it is important to differentiate between payment periods and compounding periods and to be able to reconcile them; Figure 4.4 displays frequencies of compounding.

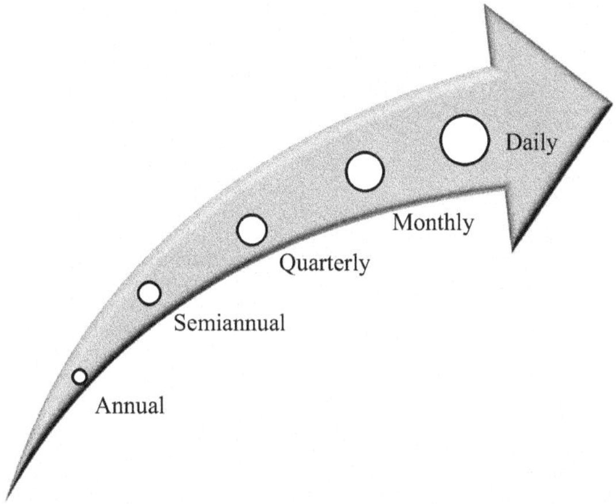

Figure 4.4 Frequent compounding.

In many projects analyzed by engineers, the payment periods (PPs) or frequency of making payments may not be the same as compounding periods (CPs) or frequency of compounding interest.

For example, consider a situation where you are depositing \$1,000 per month in a savings account that pays 6% interest per year compounded quarterly. In this case the PP is monthly, and CP is quarterly, and therefore PP < CP. Alternatively, consider a situation where you are depositing \$1000 every quarter in a savings account that pays 6% interest per year compounded monthly. In this case the PP is quarterly, and CP is monthly, and therefore PP > CP. Therefore, it is essential to recognize the PP and CP for single amounts, uniform series, and gradient series before calculating the equivalences. Ultimately, PP has to equal CP (PP = CP) before we attempt to calculate equivalences. In the following sections, we are differentiating between PP and CP for single amounts, for uniform series, and for gradient series, and then we decide how to reconcile those to calculate equivalences.

Single-Amount Factors

We have two alternative methods to calculate present and future value of a single amount when interest is compounded more frequently that once a year.

Matching the Compounding Period to Payment Period

Under this method, we first calculate the effective interest rate to match PP and enter that in the formula for either present value or future value of a single amount to calculate the equivalences.

Example 4.4

Westwood Company has borrowed \$100 million at 6% per year compounded semiannually. The principal and interest are due in 10 years. Calculate the equivalence future value of this loan in 10 years.

First, we calculate the effective rate per year:

$$Effective\ rate = \left(1+\frac{0.06}{2}\right)^2 - 1$$

$$Effective\ rate = 6.09\%$$

Now we enter the loan amount and the effective interest rate in $F = P\times(1+i)^n$ to calculate the future amount:

$$F_{10} = \$100\times(1+.0609)^{10}$$
$$F_{10} = \$100\times(1.8061)$$
$$F_{10} = \$180.61\text{ million}$$

Matching the Payment Period to Compounding Period

Under this method, we convert the period from annual to semiannual and from 10 years to 20. The interest rate per year is 6% but because it is compounded semiannually, it is 3% per semiannual period. Now period is semiannual and interest is compounding semiannually. That is, PP = CP, and therefore we are ready to calculate the future value.

For annual compounding, the F can be calculated as follows:

$$F = P\times(1+i)^n$$

For m frequency of compounding per year, the F is calculated using the next equation, where the interest rate is divided by the frequency of compounding and period is multiplied by the frequency of compounding.

$$F = P\times\left(1+\frac{i}{m}\right)^{n\times m}$$

To use standard compound interest factor notation, that equation can be articulated to this next equation as follows:

$$F = P\left(F/P,\frac{i}{m},n\times m\right)$$

In Example 4.4, using standard compound interest factor notation, the equivalent future value can be calculated as follows:

$$F = 100\left(F/P,\frac{6\%}{2},10\times 2\right)$$

That relationship can be simplified to

$$F = 100(F/P, 3\%, 20)$$

From Table A9 for 3%, enter single amount interest factor (F/P, 3%, 20) 1.80611 into the previous equation to calculate the future value of the single amount:

$$F = 100(1.80611)$$
$$F = 180.611$$

In Example 4.4, we can also use standard future value of a single amount formula by dividing interest rate by frequency of compounding per year two and multiplying the period in years by frequency of compounding per year two as follows:

$$F = P \times \left(1 + \frac{i}{2}\right)^{2n}$$

We now enter the information from Example 4.4 into the last equation to calculate future value equivalence; keep in mind that the period is semiannual:

$$F = \$100 \times \left(1 + \frac{0.06}{2}\right)^{2\times10}$$
$$F = \$100 \times (1 + 0.03)^{20}$$
$$F = \$100 \times (1.8061)$$
$$F = \$180.61 \text{ millions}$$

Annuities and Gradients

There are three alternatives for calculating equivalences for annuities and gradient series: when PP = CP, when PP > CP, and when PP < PP.

When Payment Period Equals Compounding Period

In annuities or gradient series when PP = CP, we simply adjust our equations to reflect PP. Let's look at Example 4.5.

Example 4.5

Western is purchasing aircraft structural components, fairings, and wing flaps for its aircraft from a Middle Eastern manufacturer. Western is planning to purchase \$2,000,000 worth of aircraft components at the end of the first quarter and increase that amount by \$250,000 per quarter for five years. How much should Western set aside today earning 12% per year compounded quarterly to be able to pay for purchases in the next five years?

In this example, we are asked to calculate the present value of this arithmetic gradient series; as you can see, PP = CP, which is quarterly. Because PP and CP are quarterly, there is no need to calculate the annual effective rate. Instead, we use the following equation, divide annual interest rate by 4, and multiply period by 4 to convert them to quarterly:

$$P_G = A\left(P/A, \frac{i}{4}, 4n\right) + G\left(P/G, \frac{i}{4}, 4n\right)$$
$$P_G = \$2{,}000{,}000\left(P/A, \frac{12\%}{4}, 4\times5\right) + \$250{,}000\left(P/G, \frac{12\%}{4}, 4\times5\right)$$
$$P_G = \$2{,}000{,}000\,(P/A, 3\%, 20) + \$250{,}000(P/G, 3\%, 20)$$

From Table A9 for 3%, enter annuity interest factor (P/A, 3%, 20) and gradient interest factor (P/G, 3%, 20) in the previous equation to calculate the present value of the arithmetic gradient:

$$P_G = \$2,000,000 \times (14.8775) + \$250,000 \times (126.7987)$$
$$P_G = \$29,755,000 + \$31,699,675$$
$$P_G = \$61,454,675$$

When Payment Period Exceeds Compounding Period

This is the only situation where effective rate must be calculated because CP < PP. Calculating effective rate to match PP allows for calculating the present or future value of an annuity series or gradient series.

Example 4.6

Dontae Inc. is planning to deposit $500,000 per year for five years to purchase new equipment. The interest rate is 8% per year compounded quarterly. How much can Dontae accumulate at the end of 5 years? In this example, payments are made annually, and interest is compounded quarterly and therefore PP > CP.

To achieve PP = CP, we have to calculate the annual effective rate:

$$i_{year} = \left(1 + \frac{0.08}{4}\right)^4 - 1$$
$$i_{year} = 8.24\%$$

Now, we can enter information from Example 6.6 into this equation:

$$F = A \times \left[\frac{(1+i)^n - 1)}{i}\right]$$

$$F = \$500,000 \times \left[\frac{(1+0.0824)^5 - 1)}{0.0824}\right]$$

$$F = \$500,000 \times \frac{0.4857}{0.0824}$$
$$F = \$500,000 \times 5.8944$$
$$F = \$2,947,200$$

Example 4.7

Aircraft Competence Training (ACT) is a program developed by Mesa Aircraft manufacturer focusing on learning by doing. Monarch Airlines is sending a group of employees for ACT training during the next year to improve their dispatch reliability and in-house capability, as well as ensure the safety of their operations. The cost of training is $100,000 per quarter for the next four quarters. Monarch is planning to recover the training cost through maintenance cost savings in the next four years following the training period. How much can Monarch save on maintenance cost per year in order to recover the training cost in four years? Interest rate is 12% per year compounded monthly.

There are two steps to obtaining the answer.

1. Calculate the future value of training cost at the end of year one as shown in Figure 4.5.

Because PP = CP = quarterly, we use the following to calculate the future value at the end of the first year:

$$F = A\left(F/A, \frac{i\%}{4}, n\times 4\right)$$
$$F = \$100,000\left(F/A, \frac{12\%}{4}, 1\times 4\right)$$
$$F = \$100,000(F/A, 3\%, 4)$$

From Table A9 for 3%, enter the annuity interest factor into the previous equation:

$$\text{F} = \$100,000\ (4.1836)$$
$$\text{F} = \$418,360$$

2. The future value in step 1 becomes the present value of the maintenance cost savings for the next four years, so we need to calculate the annuity of that present amount. In step 2, PP is annual, and CP is quarterly and therefore PP > CP. We need to calculate effective rate per year to match the annual PP:

$$\text{i}_{\text{year}} = \left(1 + \frac{0.12}{4}\right)^4 - 1$$
$$\text{i}_{\text{year}} = 12.55\%$$

Now, we enter the this information into the next equation to solve for annuity amount:

$$\text{A} = \text{P}\times\left[\frac{i\times(1+i)^{\text{n}}}{(1+i)^{\text{n}} - 1}\right]$$
$$\text{A} = \$418,360\times\left[\frac{0.1255\times(1+0.1255)^4}{(1+0.1255)^4 - 1}\right]$$
$$\text{A} = \$418,360\times\frac{0.2014}{0.6047}$$
$$\text{A} = \$418,360\times 0.3331$$
$$\text{A} = \$139,355.72$$

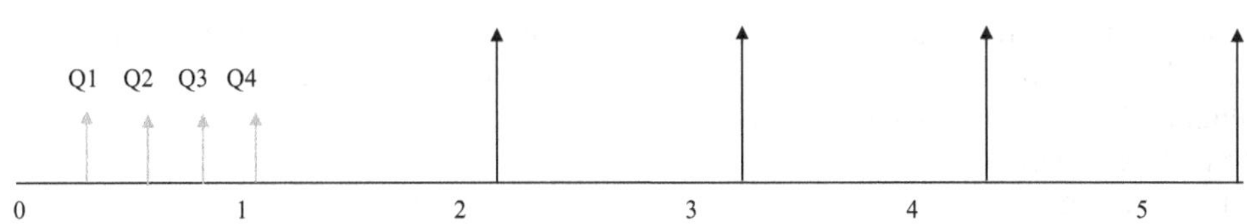

Figure 4.5 Annuity series cash flows: Example 4.7.

When Payment Period Is Shorter than Compounding Period

To calculate equivalences, we move payments to match CP. For example, if compounding period is quarterly and payments are made monthly, PP < CP. When PP < CP, then interperiod payments do not earn interest.

There will be no interest earned until the third payment is made. Now the sum of all three payments earns interest because interest is compounded quarterly. By the same reasoning, the fourth and fifth payments will not earn interest, but the sixth will, and now the sum of all payments and accrued interest in the first quarter will earn interest. In this example, we add the monthly payments together for three months to make the quarterly payment match the compounding period.

Example 4.8

Great Lake Aircraft Production is planning to deposit \$100,000 per month in an account for five years to accumulate enough money to build a new aircraft hangar. If the account pays 8% interest per year compounded quarterly, how much would Great Lake accumulate at the end of five years?

In this example, PP < CP, and we need to calculate quarterly payments to match the compounding period:

$$\text{Quarterly Payment} = \$100{,}000 \times 3 = \$300{,}000$$

Now, we can rewrite the problem as Great Lake is depositing \$300,000 per quarter for five years. At interest rate of 8% per year compounded quarterly, what is the future value of all payments at the end of five years? Now PP = CP = quarterly, and we can use the following equation to calculate the accumulated amount:

$$F = A\left(F/A, \frac{i\%}{4}, n \times 4\right)$$

$$F = \$300{,}000\left(F/A, \frac{8\%}{4}, 5 \times 4\right)$$

$$F = \$300{,}000(F/A, 2\%, 20)$$

From Table A8 for 2%, enter the annuity interest factor into the previous equation to calculate the total accumulated amount:

$$\text{F} = \$300{,}000 \times 24.2974$$
$$\text{F} = \$7{,}289{,}220$$

We can reverse Example 4.8 as follows:

Great Lake Aircraft Production is planning to accumulate \$7,289,220 at the end of five years to build a new aircraft hangar. How much does Great Lake have to deposit at the end of each month for five years to accumulate \$7,289,220? Assume Great Lake earns 8% interest per year compounded quarterly.

In this example, PP < CP, and we need to calculate quarterly payments to match the compounding period:

Monthly payments = A
Quarterly payments = A × 3 = 3A

Now, we can rewrite the problem as Great Lake is planning to accumulate \$7,289,220 at the end of five years to build a new aircraft hangar. How much does Great Lake have to deposit at the end of each quarter for five years to accumulate \$7,289,220?

$$\begin{aligned}
\$7,289,220 &= 3A\left(F/A,\frac{8\%}{4},5\times 4\right)\\
\$7,289,220 &= 3A(F/A,2\%,20)\\
\$7,289,220 &= 3A(24.2974)\\
\text{3A (Quarterly Payments)} &= 300,000\\
\text{A (Monthly Payments)} &= \frac{300,000}{3} = \$100,000
\end{aligned}$$

Calculating Effective Rate and Equivalences in Excel

Excel's functions allow for efficiently calculating effective interest rates and then analyzing the data to aid in decision-making and financial planning. This section presents a short review of how to run financial equations using Microsoft Excel functions. In Excel, two functions are used to convert between nominal and effective interest rates:

= EFFECT(nominal rate, compounding frequency per year)
= NOMINAL(effective rate, compounding frequency per year)

To find effective rate, insert a function and execute the following steps:

First, select a cell. Then, click the Insert Function button. To calculate effective rate in Excel, first click the Formulas tab on the top row, then open the financial functions and click EFFECT. Enter nominal rate per year and frequency of compounding per year in the window that appears on the screen, and the answer appears on the next line. Alternatively, type =EFFECT(r, m) in a cell and hit Enter for a result.

Example 4.9

For a nominal rate of 12% per year, calculate the annual effective rate if interest is compounded semiannually, quarterly, monthly, and daily in Excel. Figure 4.6 shows examples of calculating the effective annual interest rate for four different compounding periods in Excel. Because effective semiannual rate is called for here, locate and click on EFFECT, enter the nominal rate per quarter of 12% in cell B2 and enter m = 2 since semiannual occurs two times per year, then click OK:

= EFFECT(12%, 2)   Answer: 0.1236   12.36%

Next, effective semiannual rate is requested, so enter the nominal rate per year (12%) to obtain effective rate per quarter, entering m = 4 for quarterly (Figure 4.7):

= EFFECT(12%, 4)   Answer: 0.1255   12.55%

	A	B
1	Nominal Rate (r)	12%
2	Compounding Periods (m)	2
3		
4	Semiannual	
5	Effective Rate	=EFFECT(B1,B2)

	A	B
1	Nominal Rate (r)	12%
2	Compounding Periods (m)	2
3		
4	Semiannual	
5	Effective Rate	12.36%

Figure 4.6 Calculating semiannual effective rate in Excel.

	A	B
1	Nominal Rate (r)	12%
2	Compounding Periods (m)	4
3		
4	Quarterly	
5	Effective Rate	=EFFECT(B1,B2)

	A	B
1	Nominal Rate (r)	12%
2	Compounding Periods (m)	4
3		
4	Quarterly	
5	Effective Rate	12.55%

Figure 4.7 Calculating quarterly effective rate in Excel.

	A	B
1	Nominal Rate (r)	12%
2	Compounding Periods (m)	12
3		
4	Monthly	
5	Effective Rate	=EFFECT(B1,B2)

	A	B
1	Nominal Rate (r)	12%
2	Compounding Periods (m)	12
3		
4	Monthly	
5	Effective Rate	12.68%

Figure 4.8 Calculating monthly effective rate in Excel.

To calculate monthly effective rate, use m = 12 in the following formula (Figure 4.8):

$$= \text{EFFECT}(12\%, 12) \qquad \text{Answer}: 0.1268 \qquad 12.68\%$$

For daily compounding, m must be 365 (Figure 4.9):

$$= \text{EFFECT}(12\%, 365) \qquad \text{Answer}: 0.1275 \qquad 12.75\%$$

Conversely, you can also use Excel functions to calculate the nominal rate if an effective rate and the frequency of compounding are given, specifically, =NOMINAL(i, m).

Example 4.10

For an effective rate of 12% where interest is compounded semiannual, quarterly, monthly, and daily, calculate the nominal rates. For semiannual, we enter the effective rate (r) as 12% and m = 2 (Figure 4.10):

$$= \text{NOMINAL}(12\%, 2) \qquad \text{Answer}: 0.1166 \qquad 11.66\%$$

	A	B
1	Nominal Rate (r)	12%
2	Compounding Periods (m)	365
3		
4	Daily	
5	Effective Rate	=EFFECT(B1,B2)

	A	B
1	Nominal Rate (r)	12%
2	Compounding Periods (m)	365
3		
4	Daily	
5	Effective Rate	12.75%

Figure 4.9 Calculating daily effective rate in Excel.

	A	B	C
1	Effective Rate (i)	12%	
2	Compounding Periods (m)	2	
3			
4	Semi-Annual		
5	Nominal Rate	=NOMINAL(B1,B2)	

	A	B
1	Effective Rate (i)	12%
2	Compounding Periods (m)	2
3		
4	Semi-Annual	
5	Nominal Rate	11.66%

Figure 4.10 Calculating semiannual nominal rate in Excel.

	A	B	C
1	Effective Rate (i)	12%	
2	Compounding Periods (m)	4	
3			
4	Quarterly		
5	Nominal Rate	=NOMINAL(B1,B2)	

	A	B
1	Effective Rate (i)	12%
2	Compounding Periods (m)	4
3		
4	Quarterly	
5	Nominal Rate	11.49%

Figure 4.11 Calculating quarterly nominal rate in Excel.

For quarterly, m must be 4 as follows (Figure 4.11):

$$= \text{NOMINAL}(12\%,4) \qquad \text{Answer}: 0.1149 \qquad 11.49\%$$

For monthly compounding, m = 12 in the formula (Figure 4.12):

$$= \text{NOMINAL}(12\%,12) \qquad \text{Answer}: 0.1139 \qquad 11.39\%$$

For daily compounding, enter m = 365 (Figure 4.13):

$$= \text{NOMINAL}(12\%,365) \qquad \text{Answer}: 0.1133 \qquad 11.33\%$$

Summary

Professional engineers and almost all financial institutions use interest rates that are compounded more frequently than once a year in their evaluations of project viability. With higher frequency of compounding interest comes greater rates of return, that is an incentive for lenders to compound interest very frequently.

	A	B	C
1	Effective Rate (i)	12%	
2	Compounding Periods (m)	12	
3			
4	Monthly		
5	Nominal Rate		=NOMINAL(B1,B2)

	A	B
1	Effective Rate (i)	12%
2	Compounding Periods (m)	12
3		
4	Monthly	
5	Nominal Rate	11.39%

Figure 4.12 Calculating monthly nominal rate in Excel.

	A	B	C
1	Effective Rate (i)	12%	
2	Compounding Periods (m)	365	
3			
4	Daily		
5	Nominal Rate		=NOMINAL(B1,B2)

	A	B
1	Effective Rate (i)	12%
2	Compounding Periods (m)	365
3		
4	Daily	
5	Nominal Rate	11.33%

Figure 4.13 Calculating daily nominal rate in Excel.

For instance, credit card companies generally compound interest daily on your balance. The nominal interest rate is usually given per year and to calculate nominal rates per quarter or monthly, we simply divide the annual rate by four for quarterly rate and by twelve for monthly. To calculate the effective rate per quarter or per month, we have to calculate the effective rates for quarterly and monthly compounding. The resulting effective rates are greater than their nominal rates for the same period. Therefore, every nominal interest rate must be converted into an effective rate before it can be used for financial decision-making.

If the frequency of compounding period approaches infinity ($m \to \infty$), continuous compounding will occur, and the effective interest rate can be calculated based on that.

It is also important to differentiate between payment periods and compounding periods. In many projects analyzed by engineers, PP can differ from CP. If PP = CP, then there is no need to calculate the effective rate; we adjust interest rate and period to conform with PP. If PP is different from CP, then we need to reconcile them. In case of PP > CP, then we have to calculate the effective rate to correspond to PP. If PP < CP, then interperiod payments will not earn interest, and we need to sum up payments to conform to the compounding period. In the last section of this chapter, we discussed using Excel to calculate effective and nominal rates.

Discussion Questions and Problems

4.1 For a nominal rate of 8% per year compounded monthly, calculate quarterly, semiannual, and annual effective rates.

4.2 Reward Credit Card Company charges stated 18% annual interest on credit card balances. The interest is compounded daily. Assuming 360 days per year, calculate monthly, quarterly, and annual effective rates.

4.3 West Coast Financial Company charges stated 10% per year on its loans. The interest is compounded continuously. What is the effective annual rate the company charges?

4.4 Sapphire Financial Company charges a stated 18% interest rate on credit card balances. The interest is compounded continuously. Calculate the following:

a. Nominal rate per month
b. Effective rate per month

c Nominal rate per quarter
d Effective rate per quarter
e Nominal rate per semiannual
f Effective rate per semiannual
g Effective rate per year

4.5 Mesa Bank charges an effective rate of 19.56% per year. If interest is compounded monthly, what is the nominal rate per year?

4.6 General Financial Company charges an effective rate of 12.75% per year. What is the nominal rate per year if interest is compounded continuously?

4.7 Major Aviation has borrowed $120 million at 8% per year compounded semiannually. The principal and interest are due in 10 years. How much does Major Aviation have to pay in 10 years to pay off the loan?

4.8 Global Aviation Group is planning to accumulate $5,000,000 in six years for future expansion. How much does Global Aviation have to set aside today earning 8% per year compounded quarterly to accumulate $5,000,000 in six years?

4.9 Sky Aviation is purchasing aircraft structural components, fairings, and wing flaps for its signature aircraft from Group Aerospace Manufacturing. Sky is planning to purchase $1,000,000 at the end of the first quarter and increase that amount by $200,000 per quarter for five years. How much should Sky set aside today, earning 8% per year compounded quarterly, to be able to pay for purchases in the next five years?

4.10 Gold Coast Aviation Competence Training (GCACT) is a learning-by-doing concept approved by the airworthiness authorities. Atlantic Airlines, aiming to improve is dispatch reliability and in-house capability, as well as ensure the safety of their operations, is sending a group of employees for GCACT training during the next year. The cost of training is $50,000 per month for one year. Atlantic is planning to recover the training cost through maintenance cost savings in the next five years following the training period. How much must Atlantic save on maintenance cost per year to recover the training cost in five years? Interest rate is 12% per year compounded monthly.

4.11 Kazak Airline is planning to deposit $200,000 per month in an account for four years to accumulate enough money to build a new aircraft hangar. If the account pays 8% interest per year compounded quarterly, how much would Kazak accumulate at the end of four years?

4.12 Pacific Airlines is planning to accumulate $500,000 to fund a scheduled engine overhaul in three years. How much should Pacific deposit every month in an account that pays 10% interest per year compounded semiannually to accumulate the cost of engine overhaul in three years?

4.13 Reward Credit Card Company charges 24% annual interest on credit card balances. The interest is compounded daily. What is the effective annual interest rate charged on this credit card balance? Assume 360 days in a year.

4.14 Reward Financial Company charges 18% interest on credit card balances. The interest is compounded continuously. Find the following:

a. Nominal rate per month
b. Effective rate per month
c. Nominal rate per quarter
d. Effective rate per quarter
e. Nominal rate per semiannual
f. Effective rate per semiannual
g. Effective rate per year

4.15 General Financial charges an effective rate of 19.72% per year. What is the nominal rate per year if interest is compounded continuously?

4.16 Eastern Aviation Group (EAG) is planning to accumulate \$1,000,000 in five years for future expansion. How much does EAG have to set aside today earning 8% per year compounded quarterly to accumulate \$1,000,000 in five years?

4.17 Monark Airline is planning to accumulate \$2 million for a required inspection D check in three years. How much should Monark set aside at the end of each quarter for three years to accumulate \$2 million to pay for the required inspection? Assume an interest rate of 8% per year compounded quarterly.

4.18 Royal Aerospace Manufacturing is considering purchasing a property in five years to expand its operations and planning to deposit \$500,000 in an investment account at the end of each year for five years. If Royal earns 12% per year compounded quarterly, how much will Royal accumulate in this account to purchase the property in five years?

References

Airbus (2023). *Global Market Forecast 2023–2042.*
Boeing (2023a). *Commercial Aircraft Finance Market Outlook.*
Boeing (2023b). *Commercial Market Outlook.*

5 Present Worth Analysis

Present worth (PW) analysis is a very popular technique used by professional engineers to evaluate projects. To evaluate a single project, PW analysis comprises calculating the equivalence of all project cash flows, both inflows and outflows, using a given minimum acceptable rate of return (MARR) to the present time ($t = 0$). Based on the equivalence, one may accept or reject the project. PW analysis requires equivalent service lives for competing, mutually exclusive alternatives.

The focus of this chapter is to enable readers and practitioners to use PW to evaluate single projects, compare mutually exclusive alternatives, and independent projects. This chapter also presents the concept of a capitalized cost that is equivalent to PW for projects with infinite lives. In the sections that follow, we address the PW calculation of single projects, the criteria for accepting or rejecting projects, and the comparison and selection among mutually exclusive alternatives and independents projects.

Measuring Project Cash Flows

Engineering economics involves analyzing the costs and benefits of engineering projects to make informed decisions. Whether it's deciding on the design of a new product, selecting a manufacturing process, or evaluating the feasibility of infrastructure projects, engineers need to consider the financial implications of their decisions. In engineering economics, PW plays a fundamental role in assessing the financial viability of engineering projects and investments. PW theory, also known as present value analysis, is a financial technique used to evaluate the profitability of investments by comparing the present value of expected cash inflows and outflows over the project's life.

Cash flow measurement is essential for evaluating the financial health and performance of a business or investment. It encompasses the movement of money in and out of a business or investment over a specific period, offering insights into liquidity, solvency, and operational efficiency. The primary tool for assessing cash flow is the cash flow statement, which categorizes cash flows into operating, investing, and financing activities. Economic cash flows generate both inflows (revenue) and outflows (expense) streams. In engineering economics, we are interested in measuring the incremental after-tax cash flows resulting from an investment proposal. In general, there are three major sources of cash flows associated with a new project: first cost (initial outlay), net annual cash flows (cash inflows less cash outflows per year), and terminal cash flow (or salvage value) (Figure 5.1).

By utilizing comprehensive cash flow measurement techniques and management strategies, businesses can make informed decisions, mitigate risks, and enhance financial performance in both the short and long terms.

DOI: 10.4324/9781003469759-5

Figure 5.1 Net cash flow.

First Cost

Initial investment in engineering economics is called first cost and denoted by P. First cost includes all cash flows that are necessary to get the project in running order. These cash flows include the following: cost of the new equipment; design and testing; new buildings for manufacturing; shipping, handling, and installation; training on proposed equipment; required nonexpense cash outlays such as working capital requirement; and research and development.

Lockheed Martin's F-35 fighter jet, the world's most expensive weapons program, was estimated to cost $412 billion in 2022 according to the US Defense Department. With maintenance and operating fleet, the cost estimate is about $1.3 trillion.[1]

Net Annual Cash Flow

Net annual cash flows (NACFs) are the sum of incremental after-tax cash inflows and outflows per year over the project's life and are a measure of a company's financial health. NACF is the cash receipts minus cash payments over a given period (usually a year) but must include the amounts charged off for depreciation, depletion, and amortization.

Annual cash flows might include the following:

- Cash receipts from the sale of goods and the services (inflows)
- Cash receipts relating to future contracts (inflows)
- Cash receipts from royalties, patents, and other revenue (inflows)
- Cash payments to suppliers for goods and services (outflows)
- Cash payments to employees (outflows)
- Payments or refunds or tax payments (outflows)

Note: We should not include sunk costs and financial cost of the project.

$$NACF = \left[(R - AOC - D) \times (1 - T) \right] + D$$

where NACF = net annual cash flow, R = annual revenue, AOC = annual operating cost, D = annual depreciation, and T = marginal tax rate.

In that equation, we add back depreciation to NACF at the end because depreciation is an expense that does not require an outlay of cash.

Terminal Cash Flow

Terminal cash flow (salvage value) includes any incremental cash flows resulting at the termination of the project. The salvage value is an important part of any project valuation. A manager needs to understand how terminal cash flows are estimated and what factors impact these values. Retiring an aircraft or selling pieces of assets generate terminal cash flows. For almost all projects, it is very difficult to estimate the terminal cash flow, but it is critical to forecast it as accurately as possible. These cash flows include net of tax on a project's salvage value, recovery of any nonexpense cash outlay such as working capital associated with the project, and any terminal cash flow needed such as disposal of obsolete equipment.

Example 5.1

Majestic Aircraft Company (MAC) is a manufacturer of single-engine, high-performance turboprop aircraft. The company specializes in manufacturing advanced composite structures for military and commercial aviation customers, space systems, and other agencies. MAC is considering purchasing a new machine for \$75,000. The shipping and handling cost is \$1,000, installation cost is \$2,500, training for one employee is \$5,000, and the machine requires increasing the working capital of \$6,000. Expected annual revenue from this machine is \$25,000 and expected annual operating cost is \$4,000. The machine will be depreciated based on a straight-line method over a five-year life toward zero salvage value. Assuming a tax rate of 40% and \$7,000 value of the machine at the end of five years, calculate the following:

a) First cost
b) NACF
c) Terminal cash flow

a. $P = \$75,000 + \$1,000 + \$2,500 + \$5,000 + \$6,000$
   $P = \$89,500$
b. To calculate NACF, first we need to calculate depreciation per year using straight-line method. The annual depreciation is calculated by dividing the sum of purchase price of the machine plus shipping, handling, and installation costs over the useful life of the machine:

$$D = \frac{(\$75,000 + \$1,000 + \$2,500)}{5}$$

$$D = \$15,700$$

$$NACF = [(\$25,000 - \$4,000 - \$15,700) \times (1 - 0.40)] + \$15,700$$
$$NACF = [(\$5,300) \times (1 - .40)] + \$15,700$$
$$NACF = \$18,880$$

c. $TCF = [\$7,000 \times (1 - 0.40)] + \$6,000$
   $TCF = \$10,200$

In this section, we learned how to calculate the net of tax annual cash flows associated with a given project, and taxes, similar to inflation, must be considered to determine the real payoff of a project. In most engineering problems, however, taxes will affect alternatives similarly and that allows us to compare alternatives accurately without considering tax effects.

Evaluating a Single Project

As we described, PW analysis is intended to guide professionals in deciding on whether a project or investment is economically justified, that is, whether the project or investment is profitable.

In the airline industry, most capital expenditure decisions are about acquisition of aircraft that facilitate the airline's growth, profitability, sustainability, and efficient business operation. PW analysis is probably the most popular and the most accurate technique available to engineers for project evaluation.

There are numerous examples of projects in the aviation industry requiring PW analysis, for example, when an aircraft manufacturer decides to build a new aircraft; to determine that, the aircraft manufacturer needs to consider all cash flows, both inflows and outflows associated with the investment. PW is simply equal to present value of net cash flows minus the first cost. An appropriate MARR for each project is needed to calculate PW. Note that in engineering economics, P now represents the first cost, and present value is called PW; all costs have a negative sign; and net cash flows are calculated per period:

$$\text{PW} = -\text{P} + \text{sum of present values of all net annual cash flows}$$

Or

$$\text{PW} = -\text{P} + \sum_{t=1}^{n} \left(\frac{\text{NACF}_t}{(1+i)^t} \right)$$

$$NACF = Annual\ cash\ inflow - Annual\ cash\ outflow$$
$$PW = -P + NACF_1\,(P/F, i\%, 1) + NACF_2\,(P/F, i\%, 2) \ldots + NACF_n\,(P/F, i\%, n)$$

If net annual cash flows have a format of an annuity series, then PW is calculated as follows:

$$PW = -P + A(P/F, i\%, n)$$

The criteria to select or to reject a project are summarized in Table 5.1.

Example 5.2

MAC is considering purchasing composite wing fixtures for the assembly of its signature aircraft. The cost of the assembly system is \$4 million with a life expectancy of 20 years and annual operating cost of \$250,000. MAC anticipates a stream of \$1,000,000 in revenue per year for 20 years. Using PW analysis and assuming a MARR of 10%, is this investment economically justified?

The initial investment or first cost is \$4 million. The net cash flow per year is calculated as follows:

$$\text{Net cash flow per year} = \$1{,}000{,}000 - \$250{,}000$$
$$\text{Net cash flow per year} = \$750{,}000$$
$$PW = -P + A(P/A, i\%, n)$$
$$PW = -\$4{,}000{,}000 + \$750{,}000 \times (P/A, 10\%, 20)$$

Table 5.1 Present Worth Analysis Accept-and-Reject Criteria

Present Worth	*Selection Criteria*
$PW > 0$	Accept the project because it produces a return that is greater than MARR.
$PW = 0$	Accept the project because it produces a return that is equal to MARR.
$PW < 0$	Reject the project because it produces a return that is less than MARR.

From Table A16 for 10%, enter the interest factor in the previous equation and calculate PW:

$$PW = -\$4,000,000 + \$750,000 \times (8.5136)$$
$$PW = -\$4,000,000 + 6,385,200$$
$$PW = \$2,385,200$$

Because PW is positive, this project is economically justified.

Example 5.3

Consider Boeing's decision to manufacture the new B787 Dreamliner. The cash flows involve initial costs for design and development, production and operation, and testing and support, all of which are cash outflows. Cash inflows include receiving revenue over a few years from customers' purchase deposits, full aircraft payments, and spare parts. Both cash inflows and outflows are based on market demand, which depends on many factors including economic cycles, production level, and all the other host of events that impact air transportation domestically and internationally. The Boeing 787 Dreamliner is the most advanced airplane with a body made of 50% composites and 20% aluminum.[2] The lower weight of composites than of aluminum is the main contributor to the fuel efficiency of the aircraft, which that is known to be 20% more efficient than similarly sized aircraft as well as emitting 20% less pollutants and having a 30% lower maintenance cost.

To evaluate this major investment, Boeing needed to estimate the cash outflows including the initial investment and the cost of production per unit. It also needed to forecast the cash inflows including deliveries per year and price per unit. The Boeing development and production costs added up to about $32 billion dollars in 2011 when the first airplane was delivered, of which half was development cost and the other half was production cost (Gates and Dominic 2011). The retail prices for the 787 class of airplanes vary from $220 million to $280 million with average of approximately $250 million (The Boeing Company).[3]

To determine the production cost of 787 class airplanes, although it is difficult to assign a total cost to each airplane due to the early stage of production without having reached breakeven yet, the report indicated that the 787 class costs between $160 million and $190 million to produce, costing an average of approximately $175 million per airplane for the 235 units delivered by January 2015 (The Boeing Company). Boeing anticipated that the total number of orders for this aircraft would be approximately 3,500 units for 20 years between 2010 and 2030. The average cost of production will be expected to decrease starting 2015 to about $120 million per airplane due to economies of scales.

Table 5.2 summarizes the cash flows for the development of B787 Dreamliner. We assumed the following:

- Cash flows occurred at the end of each year.
- The $16 billion development cost occurred at the end of 2005.
- The $16 billion production cost occurred evenly at the ends of 2006 through 2010.
- The production cost and the revenue per aircraft remained the same from 2011 through 2014 at $175 million and $250 million, respectively.
- No deposit was made when the orders were placed, and revenue was received when the delivery was made.
- The production cost and the revenue per aircraft remained the same from 2015 through 2030 at $120 million and $250 million, respectively.

Table 5.2 Forecast of Costs and Revenues for Development of B787 Dreamliner

Year	*Cost*	*Revenue*
2005 Development cost. Assume development cost occurred at the end of 2005	\$16 billion	
2006–2010 Production cost	Total cost: \$16 billion Average cost per year: \$3.2 billion	
2011 Delivery: 32 units	Estimated cost per unit: \$175 million	Estimated revenue per unit: \$250 million
2012 Delivery: 93 units	Estimated cost per unit: \$175 million	Estimated revenue per unit: \$250 million
2013 Delivery: 69 units	Estimated cost per unit: \$175 million	Estimated revenue per unit: \$250 million
2014 Delivery: 41 units	Estimated cost per unit: \$175 million	Estimated revenue per unit: \$250 million
2015–2030 Delivery of average 210 units per year, based on the Boeing forecast of 3,500 delivery for 20 years between 2011 to 2030	Average cost per unit: \$120 million	Estimated revenue per unit: \$250 million

Table 5.3 Net Cash Flows per Year for the B787 Dreamliner (in USD billions)

Year	*Cash outflows*	*Cash inflows*	*Net Cash flows*
2005	–\$16	0	–\$16
2006–2010 per year	–\$3.20	0	–\$3.20
2011	–\$5.60	\$8	\$2.40
2012	–\$16.26	\$23.25	\$6.99
2013	–\$12.08	\$17.25	\$5.17
2014	–\$7.18	\$10.25	\$3.07
2015–2030 per year	–\$25.20	\$52.50	\$27.30

Because of the risky nature of this project, we assume a MARR of 15% to evaluate the project. Cash inflows, outflows, and net cash flows are summarized in Table 5.3.

We are using formulas from Chapters 4 and 5: present value of future amount, present value of annuities, and present value of shifted series to calculate the PW of this investment as follows:

$$\begin{aligned} PW = &-\$16 - \$3.2(P/A,15\%,5) + \$2.4(P/F,15\%,6) + \$6.99(P/F,15\%,7) \\ &+ \$5.17(P/F,15\%,8) + \$3.07(P/F,15\%,9) \\ &+ \$27.3(P/A,15\%,16) \times (P/F,15\%,9) \end{aligned}$$

From Table A21 for 15%, enter the interest factors in the previous equation and calculate PW:

$$\begin{aligned} PW = &-\$16 - \$3.2(3.3522) + \$2.4(0.4323) + \$6.99(0.3759) + \$5.17(0.3269) \\ &+ \$3.07(0.2843) + \$27.3(5.9542) \times (0.2843) \\ PW = &-\$16 - \$10.73 + \$1.04 + \$2.63 + \$1.69 + \$0.87 + \$46.21 \\ PW = &\ \$25.71\ \textit{billion} \end{aligned}$$

The investment in the 787 Dreamliner over a 25-year period, is profitable and therefore it is economically justified: the PW of \$25.71 billion means that in 2005's dollar value, the investment will net Boeing \$25.71 billion.

Bond Valuation

> *A bond is a debt instrument issued by a company or governmental agencies to raise large sums of money to fund their projects. A bond is known as a fixed-income security because it pays its holder a fixed sum on a regular schedule for a fixed term.*

A bond is a debt instrument issued by major corporations and federal and local government agencies to raise large sums of money to fund their projects. Bonds are usually sold at discount prices. When you purchase a bond, you will receive a bond certificate that contains the following information:

- Face value, par value, or maturity value (V), which is usually \$1,000 for corporate bonds and thousands for government bonds. This amount is received at bond maturity date.
- Coupon rate (c) is the rate used to determine the amount of interest payment you receive periodically.
- Interest rate or required yield (i) is the required return that would motivate an investor to buy the bond.
- Maturity date is the year in which the investors receive the face value of the bond. The number of periods to maturity is normally denoted as n. For a bond making annual payments, the number of periods to maturity is n years. If the bond makes semiannual payments, the number of periods to maturity is n × 2. Another notation for this is f, which denotes frequency of interest payments: f = 1 implies annual payments and f = 2 implies semiannual payments.

The dollar amount of interest payment (I) received per period is determined by the following equation:

$$I = \frac{V \times c}{f}$$

PW of a bond or bond price that makes payments annually is calculated as follows:

$$PW_{Bond} = I\left(P/A, i, n\right) + V\left(P/F, i, n\right)$$

If a bond makes semiannual payments, the equation becomes

$$PW_{Bond} = I\left(P/A, \frac{i}{2}, n \times 2\right) + V\left(P/F, \frac{i}{2}, n \times 2\right)$$

The simplified mathematical equation to determine the value of a bond, or bond price, is the following:

$$Bond\ price = I \times \frac{1}{i}\left[1 - \left[\frac{1}{(1+i)^n}\right]\right] + \frac{V}{(1+i)^n}$$

Example 5.4

A bond with a face value of \$1,000 and coupon rate of 6%, makes annual payments and has a time to maturity of 20 years. Analyze the change in bond price over the duration to maturity for two scenarios, one with the required yield of 8% and another with the required yield of 4%.

Scenario 1: Required yield of 8%

When n = 20 years, the bond value is as follows:

$$Bond\ price = \$60 \times \frac{1}{0.08}\left[1 - \left[\frac{1}{(1+0.08)^{20}}\right]\right] + \frac{\$1000}{(1+0.08)^{20}}$$

$$Bond\ price = \$803.64$$

When n = 10 years, the bond value is as follows:

$$Bond\ price = \$60 \times \frac{1}{0.08}\left[1 - \left[\frac{1}{(1+0.08)^{10}}\right]\right] + \frac{\$1000}{(1+0.08)^{10}}$$

$$Bond\ price = \$865.80$$

When n = 0 years, that is, at maturity, the bond value is

$$Bond\ price = \$60 \times \frac{1}{0.08}\left[1 - \left[\frac{1}{(1+0.08)^{0}}\right]\right] + \frac{\$1000}{(1+0.08)^{0}}$$

$$Bond\ price = \$1{,}000$$

Scenario 2: Required yield of 4%

When n = 20 years, the bond value is calculated as follows:

$$Bond\ price = \$60 \times \frac{1}{0.04}\left[1 - \left[\frac{1}{(1+0.04)^{20}}\right]\right] + \frac{\$1000}{(1+0.04)^{20}}$$

$$Bond\ price = \$1{,}271.81$$

When n = 10 years, the bond value is as follows:

$$Bond\ price = \$60 \times \frac{1}{0.04}\left[1 - \left[\frac{1}{(1+0.04)^{10}}\right]\right] + \frac{\$1000}{(1+0.04)^{10}}$$

$$Bond\ price = \$1{,}162.22$$

When n = 0 years, at maturity, the bond value is

$$Bond\ price = \$60 \times \frac{1}{0.04}\left[1 - \left[\frac{1}{(1+0.04)^{0}}\right]\right] + \frac{\$1000}{(1+0.04)^{0}}$$

$$Bond\ price = \$1{,}000$$

The change in value over the 20 years is presented in Table 5.4. Figure 5.2 graphically displays the bond valuation changes over the 20 years.

Table 5.4 Bond Valuation

Scenario 1: Required yield of 8%		*Scenario 2: Required yield of 4%*	
Time to maturity	*Price of Bond*	*Time to maturity*	*Price of Bond*
20	$803.64	20	$1,271.81
19	$807.93	19	$1,262.68
18	$812.56	18	$1,253.19
17	$817.57	17	$1,243.31
16	$822.97	16	$1,233.05
15	$828.81	15	$1,222.37
14	$835.12	14	$1,211.26
13	$841.92	13	$1,199.71
12	$849.28	12	$1,187.70
11	$857.22	11	$1,175.21
10	$865.80	10	$1,162.22
9	$875.06	9	$1,148.71
8	$885.07	8	$1,134.65
7	$895.87	7	$1,120.04
6	$907.54	6	$1,104.84
5	$920.15	5	$1,089.04
4	$933.76	4	$1,072.60
3	$948.46	3	$1,055.50
2	$964.33	2	$1,037.72
1	$981.48	1	$1,019.23
0	$1,000.00	0	$1,000.00

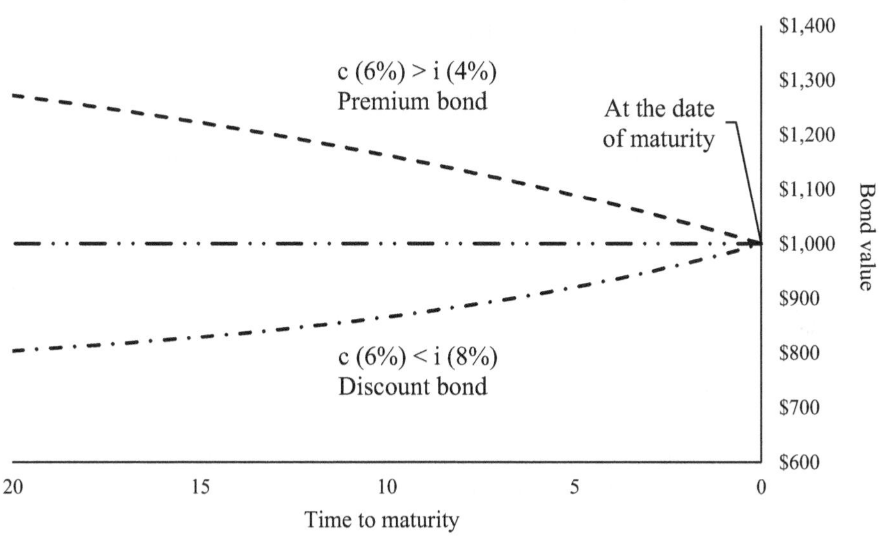

Figure 5.2 Bond valuation.

Example 5.5

Legacy Air issued a 10-year bond with face value of $10,000 and a coupon rate of 7%. An investor purchased this bond at a 10% discount. Will the investor make 8% return per year compounded semiannually?

To answer this problem, we calculate PW of bond at 8%:

If PW = 0, investor makes exactly 8%
If PW > 0, Investor makes more than 8%
If PW < 0, Investor makes less than 8%

$$\text{Semiannual interest (I)} = (10,000) \times .07/2 = 350$$
$$\text{First cost (P)} = 10,000\ (1 - .10) = 9,000$$

To calculate PW, since PP = CP = semiannual, we convert everything to semiannual.

$$PW = -P + I(P/A, i\%/2, n \times 2) + V(P/F, i\%/2, n \times 2)$$
$$PW = -9,000 + 350(P/A, 8\%/2, 10 \times 2) + 10,000(P/F, 8\% / 2, 10 \times 2)$$
$$PW = -9,000 + 350(P/A, 4\%, 20) + 10,000 \times (P/F, 4\%, 20)$$
$$PW = -9,000 + 350(13.59033) + 10,000 \times (0.45639)$$
$$PW = -9000 + 4,756.62 + 4563.90 = 320.22$$

Since PW > 0, the investor will make more than 8%.

Calculating Present Bond Value in Excel

The value of a bond can be calculated in Excel functions. The present value function normally returns a negative value because the purchase of anything is a cash outflow. Hence, a negative sign is used before the Excel function to ensure that the value returned is positive.

To calculate the present value of a bond, use the following formula:

= −PV (rate, nper, pmt, fv)

where rate is the required yield for the bond, nper is the time to maturity on the bond (represented as number of periods), pmt is the coupon payment made in each period, and fv is the future value or face value of the bond.

The present value for a bond with a face value of $1,000 and time to maturity of 20 years with annual coupon rate of 6% and required yield of 8% is calculated as

= −PV (8%, 20, 60, 1000)

and gives $803.64 ; Figure 5.3 gives the step-by-step process. The coupon payment can also be entered as a product of the annual coupon rate and the face value:

$$6\% \times \$1000 = \$60$$

Changing the required yield to 4% uses the following formula:

= −PV(4%, 20, 60, 1,000)

and gives $1,271.81 (Figure 5.4).

	A	B	C	D
1	Face value	$1,000		
2	Coupon rate	6%		
3	Time to maturity		20 years	
4				
5	Scenario 1			
6	Interest rate or YTM	8%		
7				
8	Time to maturity	Price of Bond		
9	20	=-PV(B6,A9,(B2*B1),B1)		
10	19	PV(rate, nper, pmt, [fv], [type])		
11	18	$812.56		
12	17	$817.57		

	A	B	C
1	Face value	$1,000	
2	Coupon rate	6%	
3	Time to maturity		20 years
4			
5	Scenario 1		
6	Interest rate or YTM	8%	
7			
8	Time to maturity	Price of Bond	
9	20	$803.64	
10	19	$807.93	
11	18	$812.56	
12	17	$817.57	

Figure 5.3 Calculating bond value in Excel.

	A	B	C	D
1	Face value	$1,000		
2	Coupon rate	6%		
3	Time to maturity		20 years	
4				
5	Scenario 2			
6	Interest rate or YTM	4%		
7				
8	Time to maturity	Price of Bond		
9	20	=-PV(B6,A9,(B2*B1),B1)		
10	19	PV(rate, nper, pmt, [fv], [type])		
11	18	$1,253.19		
12	17	$1,243.31		

	A	B	C
1	Face value	$1,000	
2	Coupon rate	6%	
3	Time to maturity		20 years
4			
5	Scenario 2		
6	Interest rate or YTM	4%	
7			
8	Time to maturity	Price of Bond	
9	20	$1,271.81	
10	19	$1,262.68	
11	18	$1,253.19	
12	17	$1,243.31	

Figure 5.4 Calculating bond value in Excel.

PW analysis is applied to calculating whether an investment in a bond is sound as well as to calculating bond value to determine if you will make at least a required rate of return on your purchase.

Example 5.6

DirectJet Airline is a major carrier in the US and has an extensive network of operations. DirectJet has decided to issue bonds with face value of $1,000, coupon rate of 8%, with 10 years to maturity. The interest is paid semiannually, and the bond is currently priced at $920. If you require a minimum rate of return of 10% compounded semiannually, is this a good investment for you?

To answer this question, we calculate the present worth of this bond at 10% MARR (i.e., i = 10%). If PW is positive or 0, it means you earn at least your minimum rate of return, and it is a good investment. If PW is negative, it means you are not making the MARR on this investment and therefore it is not a viable investment.

First, the semiannual interest payment can be calculated using the following equation:

$$I = \frac{V \times c}{f}$$
$$I = \frac{\$1{,}000 \times 0.08}{2}$$
$$I = \$40$$

In this example, the interest is paid semiannually and the discount rate is 10% compounded semiannually, and therefore like payment, the required rate of return and the number of periods are converted to semiannual. Calculate actual bond PW using the following equation:

$$PW_{Bond} = I\left(P/A, \frac{i}{2}, n \times 2\right) + V\left(P/F, \frac{i}{2}, n \times 2\right)$$

However, to determine if buying this bond is a sound investment, we add the previous PW to the to the negative cash outflow for the purchase:

$$PW_{Bond} = -\$920 + \$40\left(P/A, \frac{10\%}{2}, 10 \times 2\right) + \$1{,}000\left(P/F, \frac{10\%}{2}, 10 \times 2\right)$$
$$PW_{Bond} = -\$920 + \$40(P/A, 5\%, 20) + \$1{,}000(P/F, 5\%, 20)$$

From Table A11 for 5%, enter the interest factors into the previous relationship to calculate PW:

$$PW_{Bond} = -\$920 + \$40(12.4622) + \$1{,}000(0.3769)$$
$$PW_{Bond} = -\$920 + \$498.49 + \$376.90$$
$$PW_{Bond} = -\$920 + \$875.39$$
$$PW_{Bond} = -\$44.61$$

Because PW < 0, purchasing this bond is not economically justified.

The airline industry often issues billions of dollars of bonds to fund aircraft purchases or expansion through mergers and acquisition. Airlines also use Enhanced Equipment Trust Certificates (EETCs), which are basically corporate secured debt instruments that rely on the creditworthiness of the airline and are secured using the aircraft as collateral. EETCs are often used by foreign airline companies to obtain fairly inexpensive capital from US investors who may not otherwise be seeking investment opportunities in foreign companies.

EETCs are also used by aircraft leasing companies to purchase large fleets of aircraft and lease them to several airlines. Doric Nimrod Air France Alpha Limited[4] issued two tranches of EETCs in 2012 in the total amount of $587.5 million to fund the acquisition of four Airbus A380 aircraft and in turn lease them to Emirates Airlines.

Types of Project Alternatives

When multiple projects are under consideration, one has to determine whether the projects are mutually exclusive or independent from each other because they are analyzed differently.

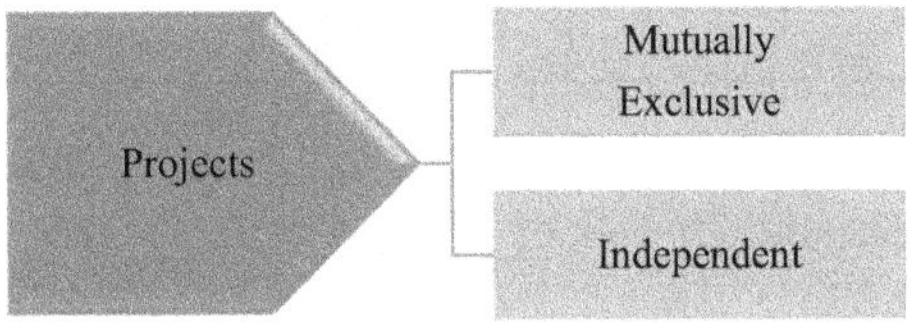

Figure 5.5 Mutually exclusive and independent projects.

Mutually Exclusive Projects

When projects are mutually exclusive, selecting one automatically rejects the others even if they might be profitable projects. So choosing between these projects means choosing the one that contributes the most to the value of the firm. An example of a mutually exclusive project is when an airline needs a new aircraft and must choose only one between the B767, B777, B787, A330, and A350. Considerations might include price, efficiency, maintenance cost, consistency with the rest of its fleet, noise, and pollution. There are two types of mutually exclusive alternatives: cost based and revenue based. When multiple projects provide the same service and produce the same revenue in the same time, they are called cost-based alternatives, and the project is selected that gives the highest PW; in cost-based alternatives, usually the revenue is not provided. When multiple mutually exclusive projects produce different amounts of revenue in the same period, they are revenue based, and again, the project is selected that gives the highest PW.

Independent Projects

Projects are independent if selecting one has no impact on the others. Independent projects evaluation does not require common lives. Examples of independent projects for an airport include building a new terminal, runway, weather monitoring station, concession area, or parking garage. If all these projects are economically justified and there is no budget limitation, the airport might undertake all of them because they all contribute to the airport's value.

Doing Nothing

This is a scenario where none of the projects is being selected. If none of the projects is economically justified, the decision-makers will likely do nothing, leaving the firm's value unchanged.

Mutually Exclusive Equal-Life Alternatives

The focus of engineering economics primarily is on mutually exclusive cost-based alternatives. However, all engineering economics techniques can be used to evaluate mutually exclusive and independent projects that are cost or revenue based.

Many companies are contemplating incorporating alternative energy into their processes. For instance, many airlines are considering retiring inefficient aircraft that are still operable for many years with new and more efficient aircraft that requires significant cash flows at the time of replacement. PW analysis can also be used to guide these decisions.

Example 5.7

MAC engineers are introducing a new process for their new engine design, and they need to choose between a robotics and a nonrobotics testing system that will ensure that their new

Table 5.5 Cash Flows for Testing Both Systems: Example 5.7

	Robotics	*Nonrobotics*
Testing system and support equipment (first cost)	−$1,500,000	−$2,250,000
Annual operating cost	−$700,000	−$500,000
Rebuild cost in year 3	−$200,000	$0
Salvage value	$50,000	$100,000
Estimated life, years	8	8

signature program does indeed work for every engine produced. Table 5.5 presents the cash flows associated with both alternatives. Assume a MARR of 10%, which of the two mutually exclusive testing systems should be selected?

To select the best alternative, calculate the PW of both systems:

$$\text{PW} = -\text{P} + \sum_{t=1}^{n}\left(\frac{NACF_t}{(1+i)^t}\right)$$

$$PW_R = -\$1,500,000 - \$700,000 \times (P/A,10\%,8) - \$200,000 \times (P/F,10\%,3)$$
$$+\$50,000 \times (P/F,10\%,8)$$

From Table A16 for 10%, enter the interest factors into the previous relationship and calculate PW:

$$PW_R = -\$1,500,000 - [\$700,000 \times (5.3349)] - [\$200,000 \times (0.7513)] + [\$50,000 \times (0.4665)]$$
$$PW_R = -\$1,500,000 - \$3,734,430 - \$150,260 + \$23,325$$
$$PW_R = -\$5,361,365$$

Perform the calculation for the nonrobotics system:

$$PW_{NR} = -\$2,250,000 - \$500,000(P/A,10\%,8) + \$100,000(P/F,10\%,8)$$

From Table A16 for 10%, enter the interest factors into the last equation and calculate PW:

$$PW_{NR} = -\$2,250,000 - [\$500,000 \times (5.3349)] + [\$100,000 \times (0.4665)]$$
$$PW_{NR} = -\$2,250,000 - \$2,667,450 + \$46,650$$
$$PW_{NR} = -\$4,870,800$$

Because the nonrobotics system has the higher PW, it will be the selected alternative.

Airports are also looking for most cost-effective alternative energy light sources. In the following example, decision-makers are analyzing solar cells versus power lines.

Example 5.8

Legacy Regional Airport (LRA) is conveniently located in the center of the City of Ho Chi Minh, Vietnam. The airport offers commercial service to Paris and regularly scheduled charter flights to different destinations. Since the new management assumed responsibility for the airport, passenger traffic has increased more than 15%. To accommodate the new traffic by opening night flights, LRA has the following two options to light the taxiways and runways: solar cells or a new power line.

Solar cells will have a first cost of \$24,000 including installation. Annual operating costs for inspection and cleaning are expected to be \$2,500. The solar cells will have a useful life of 10 years with an expected salvage value of 20% of the first cost. A new power line will have a first cost of \$18,000. The annual operation cost is expected to be \$3,000 in year one and to increase by a constant amount of \$500 per year starting the second year through the end of 10 years of life. The power line will stay in place and therefore has zero salvage value. If LRA uses a 12% MARR for these projects, which option should be selected?

From Table A18 for 12%, enter the interest factors into the following equations to obtain PW:

$$
\begin{aligned}
PW_{SC} &= -\$24,000 - \$2,500(P/A,12\%,10) + (0.20)\times(\$24,000)\times(P/F,12\%,10) \\
PW_{SC} &= -\$24,000 - \$2,500(5.6502) + (0.20)\times(\$24,000)\times(0.3220) \\
PW_{SC} &= -\$24,000 - \$14,126 + \$1,546 \\
PW_{SC} &= -\$36,580
\end{aligned}
$$

$$
\begin{aligned}
PW_{PL} &= -\$18,000 - \$3,000\,(P/A,12\%,10) - \$500(P/G,12\%,10) \\
PW_{PL} &= -\$18,000 - \$3,000\,(5.6502) - \$500(20.2541) \\
PW_{PL} &= -\$18,000 - \$16,951 - \$10,127 \\
PW_{PL} &= -\$45,078
\end{aligned}
$$

The solar cell system has the higher PW and therefore should be selected.

Mutually Exclusive Different-Life Alternatives

In PW analysis, projects must be evaluated over the same period. For example, if one project has a five-year life and a second has a 10-year life, evaluating them over five years ignores the cash flows from the remaining five years of the longer-life project. However, evaluating them over 10 years ignores the returns on the cash flows of the shorter-life project for the last five years. Here we describe three approaches to comparing projects with different lives: study period, least common multiple, or capitalized cost (CC).

Study Period

The study period is used when a company needs, for example, equipment for only a fixed period and not beyond that. The assumptions of this approach are as follows:

- Once the time is established, only cash flows within that period are evaluated and cash flows outside of the study time frame are disregarded.
- If project life is longer than the study period, use market value of the project at the end of the study period as the salvage value of the project.
- If project life is shorter than the study period, the cash flows for the period through the end of the study period must be estimated, and if there is a salvage value, that also needs to be adjusted to reflect the market value at the end of the study period.

In the examples and problems in this book, the study period would not be greater than the life of any projects because we do not have information to estimate the cash flows behind the project's life. In addition, when the life of a project is greater than the study period, the project's salvage value moves to the end of the study period because we do not have information to determine the market value of the equipment at the end of the study period.

Example 5.9

DirectJet is considering improving customer service. DirectJet is looking into offering one of two free services onboard its aircraft: live television (LT), with a first cost $50 million and annual operating cost of $10 million for 10 years and no salvage value, or high-speed internet (HSI), with first cost of $30 million and annual operating cost of $8 million for five years. DirectJet's MARR is 10%. Using a study period of five years, which alternative is cost effective (Table 5.6)?

Using a five-year study period, and Table A16 for 10%, calculate PW for both alternatives as follows:

$$PW_{LT} = -\$50{,}000{,}000 - \$10{,}000{,}000(P/A, 10\%, 5)$$
$$PW_{LT} = -\$50{,}000{,}000 - \$10{,}000{,}000(3.7908)$$
$$PW_{LT} = -\$50{,}000{,}000 - \$37{,}908{,}000$$
$$PW_{LT} = -\$87{,}908{,}000$$

$$PW_{HSI} = -\$30{,}000{,}000 - \$8{,}000{,}000(P/A, 10\%, 5)$$
$$PW_{HSI} = -\$30{,}000{,}000 - \$8{,}000{,}000(3.7908)$$
$$PW_{HSI} = -\$30{,}000{,}000 - \$30{,}326{,}400$$
$$PW_{HSI} = -\$60{,}326{,}400$$

Based on a study period of five years, HSI has the highest PW and therefore is the more cost effective.

Least Common Multiple

The second alternative to compare projects with different lives is the least common multiple (LCM). Under this alternative, the analysis period is the LCM of the projects' lives. For example,

Table 5.6 Cash Flows for Both Alternatives: Example 5.9

Year	*LT*	*HSI*
0	–$50,000,000	–$30,000,000
1	–$10,000,000	–$8,000,000
2	–$10,000,000	–$8,000,000
3	–$10,000,000	–$8,000,000
4	–$10,000,000	–$8,000,000
5	–$10,000,000	–$8,000,000
6	–$10,000,000	
7	–$10,000,000	
8	–$10,000,000	
9	–$10,000,000	
10	–$10,000,000	

if one project has four years of life and the alternative project has six years, the analysis period is the LCM of 4 and 6, which is 12 years. In other words, we add 6 to itself and add 4 three times to reach a 12-year analysis period.

LCM makes three assumptions; the third is not always realistic as cash flows for second and third cycles may change due to inflation or deflation: The service is needed for the LCM analysis period; projects replace themselves to reach LCM year; and cash flows will not change during the replacement periods. In Example 5.9, the LCM period for LT and HSI is 10 years. Therefore, we compare one life cycle of LT with two cycles of HSI as shown in Table 5.7.

Using LCM of 10 years, and Table A16 for 10% interest, calculate PW of both projects as follows:

$$PW_{LT} = -\$50,000,000 - \$10,000,000(P/A,10\%,10)$$
$$PW_{LT} = -\$50,000,000 - \$10,000,000(6.1446)$$
$$PW_{LT} = -\$50,000,000 - \$61,446,000$$
$$PW_{LT} = -\$111,446,000$$

$$PW_{HSI} = -\$30,000,000 - \$30,000,000(P/F,10\%,5) - \$8,000,000(P/A,10\%,10)$$
$$PW_{HSI} = -\$30,000,000 - [\$30,000,000 \times (0.6209)] - [\$8,000,000 \times (6.1446)]$$
$$PW_{HSI} = -\$30,000,000 - \$18,627,000 - \$49,156,800$$
$$PW_{HSI} = -\$97,783,800$$

Based on a period of 10 years and using LCM, HSI has the higher PW and is therefore the more cost-effective alternative. Assuming that passengers value the two services equally, DirectJet should offer high-speed internet.

Capitalized Cost

CC is the third alternative for comparing projects. This approach assumes infinite lives for alternative projects. In other words, this approach assumes that projects replace themselves indefinitely and therefore LCM = ∞. CC is particularly useful when the life of at least one of the projects is a prime number and therefore LCM is the product of their lives and possibly a very

Table 5.7 Cash Flows for Both Alternatives under the Least Common Multiple Approach

Year	*LT*	*HSI*	
		First Cycle	*Second Cycle*
0	–$50,000,000	–$30,000,000	
1	–$10,000,000	–$8,000,000	
2	–$10,000,000	–$8,000,000	
3	–$10,000,000	–$8,000,000	
4	–$10,000,000	–$8,000,000	
5	–$10,000,000	–$8,000,000	–$30,000,000
6	–$10,000,000		–$8,000,000
7	–$10,000,000		–$8,000,000
8	–$10,000,000		–$8,000,000
9	–$10,000,000		–$8,000,000
10	–$10,000,000		–$8,000,000

Capitalized cost is the present worth of a project that will last forever. Facilities such as airport terminals, runways, shipyards, subway systems, and railroads fall into this category, since they have useful lives of 30 years or more.

large number. For example, if the life of project A is 9 years and life of project B is 13 years, then, the LCM is 9 × 13, or 117 years and it would be very time consuming to use LCM. Therefore, it is best to use CC.

Under this approach, first we calculate the PW of the projects over their original lives. Second, we calculate the annuity of their PW over their original lives, and third, we assume that projects replace themselves infinitely; therefore, using CC, we calculate the PW of each alternative over an infinite period. Finally, we apply PW selection criteria to choose the best project. The assumptions of CC are similar to LCM: The service is needed infinitely, projects replace themselves indefinitely, and cash flows do not change during the infinite replacement periods. Using Example 5.9 and CC, compare DirectJet's two mutually exclusive alternatives of live television or high-speed internet.

First, calculate PW of each alternative over their original lives:

$$PW_{LT} = -\$50,000,000 - \$10,000,000(P/A,10\%,10)$$
$$PW_{LT} = -\$50,000,000 - \$10,000,000(6.1446)$$
$$PW_{LT} = -\$50,000,000 - \$61,446,000$$
$$PW_{LT} = -\$111,446,000$$

$$PW_{HSI} = -\$30,000,000 - \$8,000,000(P/A,10\%,5)$$
$$PW_{HSI} = -\$30,000,000 - \$8,000,000(3.7908)$$
$$PW_{HSI} = -\$30,000,000 - \$30,326,400$$
$$PW_{HSI} = -\$60,326,400$$

Second, calculate the annuity of their PW over their original lives. The interest factors are taken from Table A16 for 10%.

$$A_{LT} = -\$111,446,000(A/P,10\%,10)$$
$$A_{LT} = -\$111,446,000(0.16275)$$
$$A_{LT} = -\$18,137,837$$
$$A_{HSI} = -\$60,326,400(A/P,10\%,5)$$
$$A_{HSI} = -\$60,326,400 \times (0.26380)$$
$$A_{HSI} = -\$15,914,104$$

Third, as projects are replacing themselves infinitely, the annuities A_{LT} and A_{HSI} continue to infinity, and we calculate PW over an infinite period:

$$PW_{LT\,\&\,\infty} = -\frac{\$18,137,837}{0.10}$$
$$PW_{LT\,\&\,\infty} = -\$181,378,370$$
$$PW_{HSI\,\&\,\infty} = -\frac{\$15,914,104}{0.10}$$
$$PW_{HSI\,\&\,\infty} = -\$159,141,040$$

Based on CC, assuming infinite replacement of projects by themselves, HSI service has the higher PW and DirectJet should still offer high-speed internet.

CC is also useful when we compare two mutually exclusive projects where one project has infinite life (long-term alternative) and the other one has a finite life (short-term alternative).

Example 5.10

Royal Aviation Group (RAG) is evaluating two mutually exclusive alternatives: Alternative A with a first cost of \$80 million and annual operating cost of \$1 million for an infinite life (long-term project) or Alternative B with a first cost of \$25 million and annual operating cost of \$5 million with a life of 10 years (short-term project). RAG uses a MARR of 10%. Which project should be selected based on CC?

First, calculate PW of Alternative A for an infinite life:

$$\text{PW A},_{\infty} = \text{CCA} = -\$80,000,000 - \$1,000,000/0.08$$
$$\text{PW A},_{\infty} = \text{CCA} = -\$80,000,000 - \$12,500,000$$
$$\text{PW A},_{\infty} = \text{CCA} = -\$92,500,000$$

Second, calculate PW of Alternative B, assuming that it replaces itself infinite time in two steps:

1. Calculate the annuity of all cash lows for Alternative B over the original life:

$$\text{AB} = -\$25,000,000\,(\text{A/P},\ 8\%,\ 10) - \$5,000,000$$
$$\text{AB} = -\$25,000,000\,(0.17401) - \$5,000,000$$
$$\text{AB} = -\$4,350,250 - \$5,000,000$$
$$\text{AB} = -\$9,350,250$$

2. Assuming Alternative B replaces itself indefinitely, calculate CC for Alternative B:

$$\text{PW B},_{\infty} = \text{CCB} = \text{AB/i} = -\$9,350,250/0.08$$
$$\text{PW B},_{\infty} = \text{CCB} = -\$116,878,125,$$

RAG should select Alternative A, the long-term project, because it has the higher CC.

Evaluating Independent Projects

As we defined earlier, independent projects are projects that have no impact on each other when one is accepted or rejected; an airline with a portfolio of independent projects that are all economically justified and it has no budget constraints, then it should undertake the entire portfolio of projects.

However, sometimes only limited funds are available for investment and, at least in the short run, no additional capital is available from external sources; this situation is referred to as capital rationing. Capital might need to be rationed if the decision unit is not an entire firm but a division with a specific capital allocation for investment determined by the parent company. Capital constraints also characterize the work of government agencies that must allocate fixed appropriations among competing alternations.

As with all other project types we have discussed, using PW analysis and following these procedures will help the airline determine the project or projects that contribute the most to firm value: Calculate the PW of all projects at company's MARR; eliminate all projects that have negative PW; bundle all projects into sets with total investment equal to or less than the given budget; calculate total PW of all sets and select the set with the highest total PW.

Example 5.11

DirectJet is considering the following four independent projects:

- Installing 10 electronic kiosks at its Chicago hub. The kiosks expedite passenger check-in and allow travelers to view seat assignments, make seat changes, review itineraries, and print boarding passes. The total cost of kiosks, annual operating cost, and annual revenue are provided in Table 5.8.
- Offering Wi-Fi onboard its airplanes with cash flows presented in Table 5.8.
- Providing live television service onboard its airplanes with cash flows summarized in Table 5.8.
- Leasing an additional Embraer 170 to add to its fleet with cash flows shown in Table 5.8.

DirectJet has a limited budget of $17 million with a MARR of 8%. Use PW analysis to determine which alternatives, if any, DirectJet should undertake to maximize its profits.

First, calculate PW for each alternative using Table A14 for 8%:

$$PW_{EK} = -\$500{,}000 + \left[(\$200{,}000 - \$50{,}000)\times(P/A,8\%,10)\right] + \$10{,}000(P/F,8\%,10)$$
$$PW_{EK} = -\$500{,}000 + \left[(\$150{,}000)\times(6.7101)\right] + \$10{,}000(0.4632)$$
$$PW_{EK} = -\$500{,}000 + \$1{,}006{,}515 + \$4{,}632$$
$$PW_{EK} = \$511{,}147 > 0 \quad \textit{economically justified}$$

$$PW_{WF} = -\$1{,}000{,}000 + (\$50{,}000 - \$10{,}000)\times(P/A,8\%,25)$$
$$PW_{WF} = -\$1{,}000{,}000 + (\$40{,}000)\times(10.6784)$$
$$PW_{WF} = -\$573{,}008 < 0 \quad \textit{eliminate WF, because it is not economically justified}$$

$$PW_{LT} = -\$2{,}500{,}000 + (\$500{,}000 - \$20{,}000)\times(P/A,8\%,10) + \$50{,}000(P/F,8\%,10)$$
$$PW_{LT} = -\$2{,}500{,}000 + (\$480{,}000)\times(6.7101) + \$50{,}000(0.4632)$$
$$PW_{LT} = -\$2{,}500{,}000 + \$3{,}220{,}848 + \$23{,}160$$
$$PW_{LT} = \$774{,}008 > 0 \quad \textit{economically justified}$$

Table 5.8 DirectJet Airlines Independent Project Cash Flows

	Electronic Kiosks (EK)	*Wi-Fi (WF)*	*Live Television (LT)*	*Embraer 170 (EM)*
Investment (lease deposit)	–$500,000	–$1,000,000	–$2,500,000	–$15,000,000
Annual operating cost	–$50,000	–$10,000	–$20,000	–$1,000,000
Annual revenue	$200,000	$50,000	$500,000	$4,000,000
Salvage value (deposit return)	$10,000	0	$50,000	$2,000,000
Life in years	10	25	10	20

Table 5.9 DirectJet Airlines Possible Bundles, Total Investments, and PWs

Project or Bundle	*Total Investments Must be ≤ $17,000,000*	*Total Present Worth*
EK	−$500,000	$511,147
LT	−$2,500,000	$744,008
EM	−$15,000,000	$14,883,300
EK & LT	−$3,000,000	$1,255,155
EK & EM	−$15,500,000	$15,394,447

$$\begin{aligned} PW_{EM} &= -\$15,000,000 + (\$4,000,000 - \$1,000,000) \times (P/A, 8\%, 20) \\ &\quad + \$2,000,000(P/F, 8\%, 20) \\ PW_{EM} &= -\$15,000,000 + (\$3,000,000) \times (9.8181) + \$2,000,000(0.2145) \\ PW_{EM} &= -\$15,000,000 + \$29,454,300 + \$429,000 \\ PW_{EM} &= \$14,883,300 > 0 \quad \textit{economically justified} \end{aligned}$$

The table shows that the Wi-Fi project is not profitable and therefore is eliminated. Table 5.9 shows the possible project bundles of the remaining projects that fit within the budget.

This table shows that investing in the electronic kiosks and the Embraer 170 have the highest PW and therefore, those two will be selected.

Calculating Present Worth in Excel

Here, we describe how to calculate PW in Excel. The PW equation in Excel is called net present value and denoted as NPV:

$$= \textbf{NPV}\left(\textbf{rate, Cell}\left[\textbf{1}\right]:\textbf{Cell}\left[\textbf{n}\right]\right) + \textbf{Cell}\left[\textbf{0}\right]$$

where rate is the MARR and (Cell [1]: Cell [n]) is the range of cash flows from period 1 through period n. Cell [1] is the NACF in Year 1, Cell [n] is the NACF in year n (the last year), and Cell [0] is the first cost or initial investment that occurs at the present time (year 0); the latter is negative.

Example 5.12

An investment of $100,000 results in the NACFs in Table 5.10 for eight years. Calculate the PW of this investment using Excel financial equation and a MARR of 10%.

The cash flow in year 0 is the first cost, and NACFs are in years one through eight. Excel NPV can be used to calculate the PW as visually depicted in Figure 5.6.

Life Cycle Costing

At the beginning of any project, it is imperative to understand and forecast the associated costs. Life cycle costs are costs associated with various phases of a product life cycle, and life cycle costing (LCC) refers to evaluating the entire life cycle from inception to disposal of equipment or asset. LCC allows for calculating the most cost-effective options among competing alternatives. Many times, redundant equipment is needed to avoid expected costly failures and reduce risk, and both general aviation and commercial aircraft have many redundant parts to minimize

Table 5.10 Cash Flows

Year	*NACF*
0	−100,000
1	$25,000
2	$20,000
3	$15,000
4	$14,000
5	$18,000
6	$20,000
7	$20,000
8	$20,000

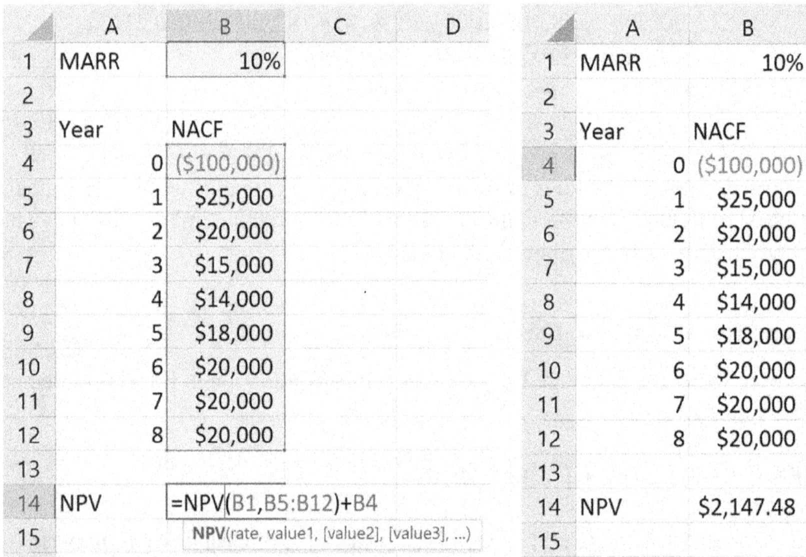

Figure 5.6 Calculating present worth in Excel.

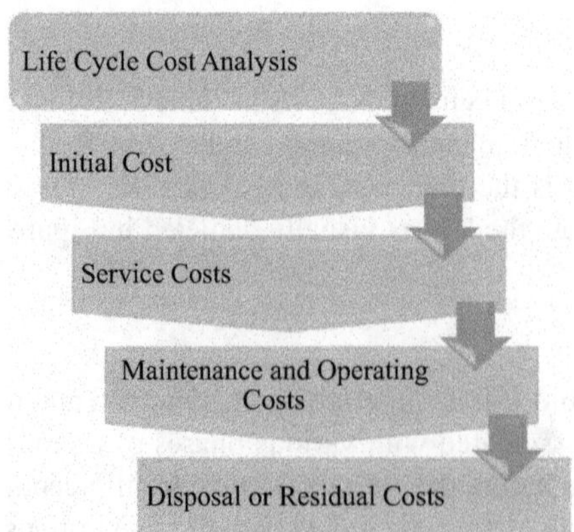

Figure 5.7 Life cycle costing.

the LCC of the aircraft. For example, Cirrus SR22 aircraft have two alternators, two batteries, two GPSs, and an extra flight instrument. In the case of prevention, cost management is aimed at avoiding adverse outcomes.

LCC entails analyzing a number of project criteria such as the project evaluation period and initial and future project cash flows following accepted economic and risk analysis techniques and then analyzing the results to make a decision. For an aviation project, LCC will entail examining all the factors that affect an investment over its lifetime from design to retirement stage, like aircraft range; noise (cabin and community); development, marketing, production, maintenance, operating, and phaseout cost; weight and payload capacity (aircraft); schedule reliability; and warranty commitment cost

For example, to make the Boeing 787 Dreamliner more efficient, engineers designed the plane to use more composite materials in its airframe than any previous Boeing commercial aircraft. The B787 comprises 50% composites, versus 20% in the B777, which reduced the weight of the B787 by 20% compared with the conventional aluminum design and increased its efficiency by about 20%. In Example 5.13, MAC is choosing between three new training aircraft based on PW analysis and LCC.

Example 5.13

MAC is considering choosing between developing three separate models (A, B and C) of aircraft scheduled for training purposes. The expected costs of the three models are presented in Table 5.11. Calculate which will be the most cost-effective for MAC using a MARR of 10%. The costs in year 0 are the initial costs of the projects, and from then on, the costs provided are the estimated total costs, including service, maintenance, and operating costs for the following four years.

Calculate NPV in Excel, as discussed in the previous section. Since these are all cost-based alternatives, the project with the highest NPV, Model A, is the most cost effective and therefore the MAC must choose.

Summary

Engineering economics involves analyzing the costs and benefits of engineering projects to make informed decisions. Whether it's deciding on the design of a new product, selecting a manufacturing process, or evaluating the feasibility of infrastructure projects, engineers need to consider the financial implications of their decisions. In engineering economics, present worth theory plays a fundamental role in assessing the financial viability of engineering projects and investments. Present worth theory, also known as present value analysis, is a financial technique used to evaluate the profitability of investments by comparing the present value of expected cash inflows and outflows over the project's life.

Table 5.11 Life Cycle Costing

Years	*A*	*B*	*C*
0	–$200,000	–$250,000	–$300,000
1	–$90,000	–$50,000	–$15,000
2	–$40,000	–$20,000	–$15,000
3	–$20,000	–$20,000	–$15,000
4	–$10,000	–$20,000	–$15,000
NPV	**–$336,732.46**	**–$340,670.04**	**–$347,547.98**

This chapter presented how to calculate PW to determine if a project is economically justified including comparing alternative projects. PW analysis entails calculating the equivalence of all cash flows, both inflows and outflows, associated with a project, discounted at MARR to the present time ($t = 0$). If PW is equal to or greater than 0, the project is economically justified and accepting it increases the value of the firm. If PW is negative, it should be rejected.

When multiple projects are under consideration, they can be mutually exclusive – that is, selecting one necessarily rejects the others – or independent, meaning that selecting one has no impact on the others. There are two types of mutually exclusive alternatives: cost based and revenue based alternatives. The former are projects that provide the same service and produce the same amount of revenue in the same period, and PW analysis determines the most cost-effective project. In cost-based alternatives, usually the revenue is not provided. PW analysis requires equivalent service lives for comparing mutually exclusive alternatives. Least common multiples are used to calculate a common life for both alternatives. If one or both projects have infinite life, then $LCM = \infty$, and capitalized cost is used to evaluate those projects. In contrast, evaluating independent projects does not require common lives and therefore LCM is not needed.

At the beginning of any project, it is imperative to understand and forecast the costs associated with the project. The last section of the chapter discusses life cycle costing, evaluating the entire life cycle from inception to disposal of equipment or asset. LCC allows for determining the most cost-effective option among competing alternatives to manufacture products from design stage to phaseout to product disposal. PW analysis allows for calculating the equivalences of all costs to present-day value for all project stages of all competing products to select the optimal alternative.

Discussion Questions and Problems

5.1 Majestic Aircraft Company (MAC) is considering purchasing new equipment for \$200,000, with shipping and handling of \$4,000 and installation cost of \$6,000. MAC is sending an employee for training to operate the equipment for \$12,000, and working capital of \$15,000 is needed to get the equipment up and running. The expected annual revenue from this machine is \$50,000, and expected annual operating cost is \$10,000. The equipment will be depreciated on the straight-line method over a seven-year life toward zero salvage value. MAC is expecting to sell the equipment at \$8,000 at the end of the seven years. Assuming tax rate of 40% calculate the following:

a. First cost (P)
b. Net annual cash flow (NACF)
c. Terminal cash flow (TCF)

5.2 Samsung Aviation is considering purchasing equipment to manufacture a part of the wing fixture for an aircraft. The cost of the system is \$5 million with a life expectancy of 10 years and annual operating cost of \$200,000. Samsung is using a MARR of 12% and expecting annual revenue of \$1.5 million for 10 years and a terminal cash flow of \$25,000. Using present worth analysis, is this investment economically justified?

5.3 How much would an investor pay to purchase a bond today that is redeemable in four years for its par value or face value of \$1,000 and pays an annual coupon of 5% on the par value? Assume the required rate of return for a bond in this risk class is 4%.

5.4 DirectJet has a bond issue with a face value of \$1,000 and coupon rate of 7%, with 10 years to maturity. The interest is paid semiannually, and the bond is currently selling at a 10% discount. Assuming your MARR is 8% compounded semiannually, is this a good investment?

5.5 EZjET Airline has a new bond issue with a face value of $1,000 and a coupon rate of 8%, with 10 years to maturity, and interest is paid semiannually. What is the maximum price you are willing to pay for this bond if your required rate of return is 6% compounded semiannually?

5.6 An airline has a new bond issue with a face value of $1,000 and acoupon rate of 6%, with 10 years to maturity, and interest is paid semiannually. What is the maximum price you are willing to pay for this bond if your required rate of return is 8% compounded semiannually?

Hint: To earn exactly 8% return on this bond, its PW should be 0 at MARR of 8%. Therefore, set the PW = 0 and solve for price, which is the same as the first cost (P).

5.7 Legacy Regional Airport (LRA) has the following two options to light the taxiways and runways:

- Solar cells, with a first cost of $250,000 including the installation cost. Annual operating cost for inspection and cleaning is expected to be $15,000. The solar cells will have a useful life of 10 years with an expected salvage value of 15% of the first cost.
- A new power line, with a first cost of $150,000. The annual operation costs are expected to be $10,000 in year one and increase by a constant amount of $2,000 per year from the second to the 10th year. The power line will stay in place and therefore has zero salvage value.

If LRA uses a MARR of 10% for these projects, which option should be selected to light the runways and taxiways at LRA?

5.8 MyJet Airlines is planning to expend its operation to India. It needs a hangar in Bangalore for its new nonstop route from Frankfurt to Bangalore and has the following two leasing options: Location A, with a first cost of $20,000,000, an annual lease payment of $4,000,000 for four years, and a deposit return of $1,000,000, or Location B, with a first cost of $25,000,000, an annual lease payment of $3,000,000 for six years, and a deposit return of $2,000,000.

MyJet has a MARR of 8%. Using present worth analysis, which location is cost efficient?

5.9 DirectJet is considering improving customer service by offering one of the following two free services onboard its aircraft: free live television with a first cost of $70 million and annual operating cost of $5 million for 10 years with no salvage value or free high-speed internet with first cost of $25 million and annual operating cost of $15 million for five years. DirectJet's MARR is 9%. Using a study period of five years, which alternative is cost efficient?

The following table presents the cash flows for both alternatives.

Year	*Live Television*	*High-Speed Internet*
0	−$70,000,000	−$25,000,000
1	−$5,000,000	−$15,000,000
2	−$5,000,000	−$15,000,000
3	−$5,000,000	−$15,000,000
4	−$5,000,000	−$15,000,000
5	−$5,000,000	−$15,000,000
6	−$5,000,000	
7	−$5,000,000	
8	−$5,000,000	
9	−$5,000,000	
10	−$5,000,000	

5.10 Using the information in Problem 5.9, use LCM to compare live television high-speed internet for DirectJet.

5.11 Using the information in Problem 5.9, use CC to compare live television with high-speed internet for DirectJet.

5.12 A bond has a face value of $1,000 and was issued five years ago at a coupon rate of 10%. The bond has a maturity period of five years. If the current market interest rate is 14%, what should be the price of the bond today?

5.13 Two machines with the following cost estimates are under consideration to manufacture computer drives to play HD movie discs. Assuming a MARR of 8%, which alternative should be selected using PW analysis?

	Machine A	*Machine B*
Equipment (first cost)	−$200,000	−$300,000
Annual operating cost per year	−$60,000	−$40,000
Salvage value	$20,000	$40,000
Estimated life, years	4	6

5.14 MyJet is considering the following three mutually exclusive projects with different lives.

- Project A with first cost of $100 million and operating cost of $1.2 million per quarter. This project is considered permanent (i.e, has an infinite life).
- Project B with first cost of $25 million and operating cost of $3 million per quarter with 10-year life.
- Project C with first cost of $10 million and operating cost of $0.8 million per quarter with four-year life.

Using PW analysis and assuming a MARR of 12% per year compounded quarterly, which project should be selected by MyJet?

5.15 DirectJet is considering five independent projects with the cash flows shown in the following table. DirectJet has a limited budget of $10 million with a MARR of 6%. Using PW analysis, determine which alternatives, if any, should DirectJet undertake to maximize its profits.

	Project A	*Project B*	*Project C*	*Project D*	*Project E*
Net investment	−$2,000,000	−$3,000,000	−$5,000,000	−$10,000,000	−$15,000,000
Annual operating cost	−$50,000	−$100,000	−$200,000	−$500,000	−$1,000,000
Annual revenue	$600,000	$600,000	$650,000	$1,500,000	$2,250,000
Salvage value	$100,000	200,000	$300,000	$500,000	$800,000
Life, years	5	10	15	20	25

5.16 Determine CC for $2,000,000 at time 0, $500,000 in years one through five, and $1,000,000 per year from year six on. Use an interest rate of 6% per year.

5.17 DirectJet is planning to invest in a new electronic ticket system. The investment is expected to produce profit from its rental of $300,000 in the first year it is in service. The profit is expected to decrease by $50,000 each year thereafter. At the end of six years assume the salvage value is 0. Calculate the present worth at 12%.

5.18 Calculate CC for an infinite series of annual payments of $100,000 using an interest rate of 5% compounded annually.

Notes

1 www.bloomberg.com/news/articles/2022-09-28/lockheed-f-35-s-cost-grows-modestly-by-its-standards-to-412-billion.
2 Boeing Celebrates the Premiere of the 787 Dreamliner (Press release). *Boeing*, July 8, 2007.
3 Final Assembly Begins on Another Boeing 787 Dreamliner (Press release). *Boeing*, February 15, 2008.
4 EETC: The next generation of debt financing for airlines around the globe? By Mehtap Cevher Conti. Marketrealist.com, October 25, 2013.

References

The Boeing Company (2015a). *787 Dreamliner Program Fact Sheet*. Retrieved on March 15, 2016. www.aversan.com/10-fun-facts-about-the-787-boeing-dreamliner.

The Boeing Company (2015b). *Boeing 787–10 Dreamliner Fact Sheet*. Retrieved on March 15, 2016. www.aversan.com/10-fun-facts-about-the-787-boeing-dreamliner.

The Boeing Company (2015c). *Boeing 787: Orders and Deliveries*. Retrieved on March 15, 2016. www.aversan.com/10-fun-facts-about-the-787-boeing-dreamliner.

The Boeing Company (2015d). *Boeing Commercial Airplanes Prices*. Retrieved on March 15, 2016. www.aversan.com/10-fun-facts-about-the-787-boeing-dreamliner.

The Boeing Company (2015e). *Current Year Deliveries*. Retrieved on March 15, 2016. www.aversan.com/10-fun-facts-about-the-787-boeing-dreamliner.

Nathanson, S. (2014). United Airlines Launches a $949 Million Equipment Trust Certificate. *Marketrealist.com*. Retrieved on March 15, 2016. www.seattletimes.com/business/boeing-celebrates-787-delivery-as-programs-costs-top-32-billion.

Skift (2019). *The Most Amazing Airline Failures of the Past 15 Years*.

Strategic Analysis of Ozjet Airlines Company Tourism Essays UK (2013). Retrieved on March 15, 2016. www.grin.com/en/e-book/76304/the-australian-airline-industry-and-the-case-of-ozjet.

6 Annual Worth Analysis

Annual worth (AW) analysis is a simple technique used by professional engineers to evaluate single, multiple, and competing alternative projects. To evaluate a single project, AW analysis consists of calculating the sum of annual equivalent amount (annuity amount) of all cash flows, both inflows and outflows, associated with a project. AW analysis is generally preferred over present worth (PW) analysis because it is simpler calculate and it does not require equal service lives for comparing mutually exclusive alternatives. The focus of this chapter is to enable readers to use AW to analyze projects, but we also present the capital recovery of investments, for instance with equipment, the annual revenue needed to recover the cost of the equipment (first cost), any nonrecurring costs, and the equipment salvage value at a given interest rate over the life of the project.

Motivation for Using AW

In the previous chapter, we discussed using PW analysis to evaluate projects, and this approach is very effective for single projects, mutually exclusive projects with the same lifespan, and independent projects.

However, as mentioned in Chapter 5, with two projects that have unequal lives, PW analysis becomes complicated. For such a scenario, we must assume that the projects in question are repeatable. Consequently, we need to find the least common multiple (LCM) of their lives and repeat the projects to be able to evaluate their overall present worth throughout the length of LCM.

For instance, consider a company that needs to acquire a new aircraft for its operations. Usually based on range, performance, commonality with the remaining fleet, and some other factors, operators can narrow down their options to a given make and model. Let's assume the company decided to get a Boeing $737-700$C to carry its personnel and equipment between operation sites. The $737-700$C is a short- to medium-range, narrow-body jet airliner; the 700C variation is a convertible version that can switch between carrying passengers and cargo. The seats can be removed to convert the main cabin to cargo capacity, and the aircraft has a large door on the left side for cargo loading. This option is particularly important for companies with logistics as well as personnel transportation needs. For instance, the US Navy and US Air Force have used the variations of Boeing $737-700$ for transportation of generals and for cargo delivery.

The next critical question is whether they should purchase or lease the plane. The current price for a new $737-700$C is approximately \$80 million with a life expectancy of 25 years. On the other hand, the monthly leasing rate for a 2001 $737-700$C is estimated at around \$250,000 per month for a 10-year lease. To use PW analysis here, since the lives of these options are not equal, we need to consider a 50-year time horizon, the LCM, that covers buying the aircraft

DOI: 10.4324/9781003469759-6

two consecutive times or leasing it five times. This approach not only requires more extensive calculations but also makes it harder to interpret. This complexity can be avoided by using AW. AW provides a yearly worth of doing a project, does not require LCM for projects with different life spans, and is easier to interpret for companies that do annual budgeting.

Evaluating Single Projects

Whereas PW analysis is probably the most popular technique for evaluating single and independent projects and mutually exclusive projects with equal lives, AW is commonly used to evaluate mutually exclusive alternatives with different lives because AW does not require an LCM. Evaluating AW for a single project involves a comprehensive evaluation of its financial performance, value generation, and overall contribution to the organization within a year. In analyzing AW, we rely on the equations that we discussed in Chapter 3.

Essentially in this approach, we first convert all cash flows including first cost, nonrecurring cost, and salvage value to an equivalent annuity worth for the life span of the project. Then we add them all together with annual cash flows such as annual operating cost (AOC) and annual revenue as long as they are a constant amount per year. If AOC or annual revenue are not constant per year, then we must convert those to equivalent annuity worth to calculate AW. Table 6.1 presents the criteria for accepting or rejecting a project using AW. We follow the table with examples of calculating AW for a single project with different cash flow formats.

Example 6.1

Johnson Regional Airport (JRA) is a small airport offering domestic commercial services all over the United States. Due to significant increases in the number of flights and high passenger traffic, JRA is considering building a new rental car complex. The initial investment is estimated to be \$2,000,000 with a salvage value of \$200,000 at the end of the 10-year life of the project. In addition, there is a single nonrecurring cost of \$400,000 incurred in year five for repairs. Calculate AW for this investment assuming JRA uses a MARR of 10%. The cash flow diagram of this project is presented in Figure 6.1.

To calculate AW for JRA's investment in a rental car building, we first convert all cash flows associated with the project to an equivalent annuity worth and then add them together. The compound interest factors are taken from Table A16 for 10% interest:

$$\begin{aligned}\text{Annuity of the first cost} &= -\$2,000,000(A/P,10\%,10)\\ &= -\$2,000,000(0.16275) \qquad = -\$325,500\\ \text{Annuity of the salvage value} &= \$200,000(A/F,10\%,10)\\ &= \$200,000(0.06275) \qquad = \$12,550\end{aligned}$$

Table 6.1 Accept-and-Reject Criteria for AW Analysis

Annual Worth	*Selection Criteria*
AW > 0	Accept the project because the AW of revenue exceeds the AW of costs and therefore, it is economically justified.
AW = 0	Accept the project because the AW of revenue is equal to the AW of costs and therefore, it is economically justified.
AW < 0	Reject the project because the AW of revenue is less than the AW of costs and therefore, it is not economically justified.

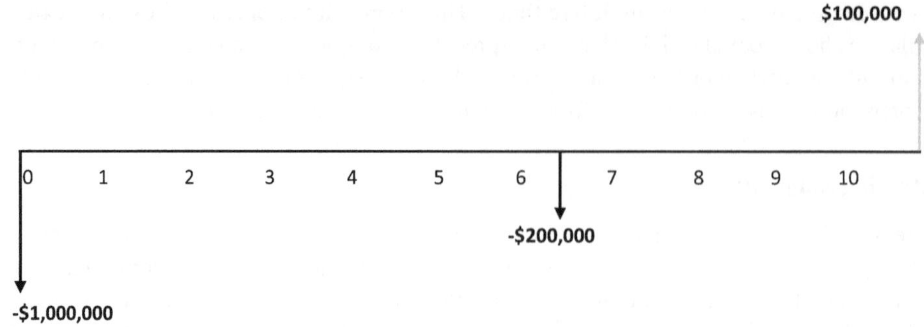

Figure 6.1 Cash flow diagram: Example 6.1.

$$\begin{aligned}\text{Annuity of the repair cost} &= -\$400{,}000(P/F,10\%,5)(A/P,10\%,10)\\ &= -\$400{,}000(0.62092)(0.16275) = -\$40{,}422\\ AW &= -325{,}500+12{,}550-40{,}422\\ AW &= -\$353{,}372\end{aligned}$$

According to AW, building the rental car complex will cost JRA $353,372 per year for 10 years, and therefore, JRA should collect revenue of that amount per year to break even on this investment. In other words, this investment is economically justified if JRA collects at least a revenue of $353,372 per year.

Example 6.2

Majestic Aircraft Company (MAC) is a manufacturer of single-engine, high-performance turboprop aircraft. MAC is considering purchasing composite wing fixtures for the assembly of its signature aircraft. The cost of the assembly system is $3 million with life expectancy of 10 years and AOC of $200,000 with zero salvage value. MAC anticipates a stream of $1,000,000 in revenue per year for 10 years from this project. Using AW analysis and assuming MAC uses a MARR of 10%, is this investment economically justified? The cash flow diagram of this project is presented in Figure 6.2.

First, we calculate net annual cash flows (NACF) for years 1 through 10:

$$NACF = \$1{,}000{,}000 - \$200{,}000 = \$800{,}000$$

Since NACFs are constant per year, to calculate AW of the project, we simply calculate the annuity of the first cost and add it to the NACF:

$$\begin{aligned}AW &= -\$3{,}000{,}000(A/P,10\%,10)+\$800{,}000\\ AW &= -\$3{,}000{,}000\times(0.16275)+\$800{,}000\\ AW &= -\$488{,}250+\$800{,}000\\ AW &= \$311{,}750\end{aligned}$$

In this example, because AW is greater than 0, the project is economically justified.

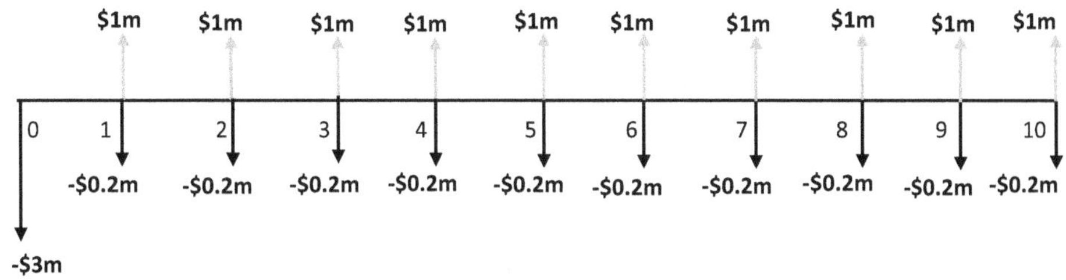

Figure 6.2 Cash flow diagram: Example 6.2.

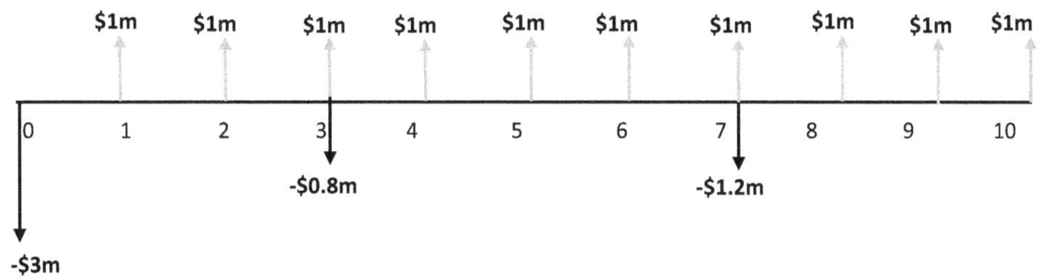

Figure 6.3 Cash flow diagram: Example 6.3.

Example 6.3

In Example 6, assume there is no AOC but there are rebuild costs of $800,000 in year three and $1,200,000 in year seven. Assuming everything else remains the same, recalculate the AW of the project. The cash flow diagram is presented in Figure 6.3.

Because revenues are constant per year, to calculate AW of the project, we calculate the equivalent annuity values of the first cost and rebuild costs and simply add them all to the annual revenue:

$$AW = \text{Equivalent annuity values of all costs} + \text{Annual revenue}$$

To calculate the equivalent annual values of all costs, we shift all costs to present time by calculating the present worth of all costs (PW_{Cost}) and then calculate the equivalent annuity of that amount over a 10-year period:

$$\begin{aligned}
PW_{Cost} &= -\$3,000,000 - \$800,000(P/F,10\%,3) - \$1,200,000(P/F,10\%,7) \\
PW_{Cost} &= -\$3,000,000 - \$800,000 \times (0.7513) - \$1,200,000 \times (0.5132) \\
PW_{Cost} &= -\$3,000,000 - \$601,040 - \$615,840 \\
PW_{Cost} &= -\$4,216,880
\end{aligned}$$

$$\begin{aligned}
\text{Equivalent Annuity Values of all cost} &= -\$4,216,880(A/P,10\%,10) \\
\text{Equivalent Annuity Values of all cost} &= -\$4,216,880 \times (0.16275) \\
\text{Equivalent Annuity Values of all cost} &= -\$686,297
\end{aligned}$$

To calculate AW for the project, we simply add the AW of all costs to the annual revenue:

$$AW = -\$686,297 + \$1,000,000$$
$$AW = +\$313,703$$

Because AW of the project is greater than 0, this project is economically justified. As you notice, depending on the format of the cash flows, there are many ways to calculate the AW of a project. In fact, when it comes to time value of money, there is more than one way to find the solution to any problem.

Example 6.4

In Example 6.4, assume no AOC but rebuild costs of $\$800,000$ in year three and $\$1,200,000$ in year seven. In addition, there is no uniform annual revenue but revenue of $\$4,000,000$ and $\$5,000,000$ occurs in years four and eight, respectively. Assume everything else remains the same and recalculate AW. The cash flow diagram is presented in Figure 6.4.

To calculate the AW of the project, we first shift all cash flows to the present time by calculating the PW of all cash flows:

$$PW = -\$3,000,000 - \$800,000(P/F,10\%,3) - \$1,200,000(P/F,10\%,7) \\ + \$4,000,000(P/F,10\%,4) + \$5,000,000(P/F,10\%,8)$$
$$PW = -\$3,000,000 - \$800,000 \times (0.7513) - \$1,200,000 \times (0.5132) \\ + \$4,000,000 \times (0.6830) + \$5,000,000 \times (0.4665)$$
$$PW = -\$3,000,000 - \$601,040 - \$615,840 + \$2,732,000 + \$2,332,500$$
$$PW = +\$847,620$$

Now calculate AW of the present amount over the life of the project:

$$AW = \$847,620(A/P,\ 10\%,\ 10)$$
$$AW = \$847,620 \times (0.16275)$$
$$AW = \$137,950$$

Because $AW > 0$, this project is economically justified.

Example 6.5

Monarch Airport is considering building a new terminal. This project is permanent, with a first cost of \$500 million and additional investment of \$50 million every 10 years. No salvage value

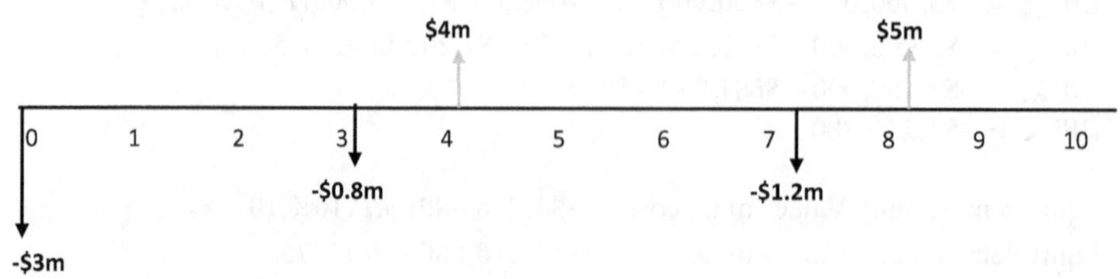

Figure 6.4 Cash flow diagram: Example 6.4.

is expected. The revenue from the new terminal is expected to be \$100 million per year. AOC is \$15 million per year. Monarch uses a MARR of 10%. Use AW analysis to determine whether this project is economically justified:

$$\text{AW of Revenue} = \$100\text{ m}$$
$$\text{AW of AOC} = \$15\text{ m}$$
$$\text{AW of P} = \$500\text{ m}(0.10) + \$50\text{ m}(\text{A/F},10\%,10) = \$50\text{ m} + \$50\text{ m}(0.06275)$$
$$\text{AW of P} = -\$50\text{ m} - \$3.14\text{ m} = -\$53.14\text{ m}$$
$$\text{AW of the Project} = -\$53.14\text{ m} - \$15\text{ m} + \$100\text{ m} = \$31.86\text{ m}$$

Because AW is positive, this project is economically justified.

Project AW can also be calculated by adding capital recovery (*CR*) of the first cost and all other nonrecurring costs to annuity of the net annual cash flows (*A of NACF*) as follows:

$$CR + A\ of\ NACF = AW$$

Capital Recovery

Capital recovery (CR) of investment in equipment is the uniform annual revenue needed to recover the cost of the equipment (first cost), any nonrecurring costs, and the salvage value at a given interest rate over the life of the project. In other words, CR is the annuity of the first cost, any nonrecurring costs and the salvage value over the economic life of the equipment.

This concept is particularly of interest in aircraft financing. Purchasing a new aircraft imposes various acquisition and maintenance costs on airlines. Airlines make a down payment for ordering a new aircraft and often arrange some payment plan with a financial company to pay for the aircraft. Through the life cycle of the aircraft, aside from recurring maintenance and operating costs, there are multiple C and D checks that impose notable cost. Eventually, airlines are expected to sell their airplanes to recover a salvage value based on the market price of the aircraft at the time of retirement. In view of these expenditures, airlines are interested in estimating the annual cost to recover the capital invested in acquiring the new aircraft.

> *Capital recovery is a fundamental concept in engineering economics, crucial for evaluating the financial feasibility of projects or investments. Capital recovery involves calculating the annual payments necessary to recover the initial investment incorporating both principal and interest. The process considers the time value of money, reflecting the opportunity cost of capital and ensuring a fair comparison of alternatives.*

Figure 6.5 Calculating annual worth.

This concept is closely related to breakeven analysis, which we will discuss in detail in Chapter 9. The following formula is used to calculate CR:

$$\begin{aligned} \text{Where: } CR &= \text{Capital recovery} \\ P &= \text{First cost (initial investment)} \\ C_{NR} &= \text{Non-recurring cost occurs in year } n_t \\ S &= \text{Salvage value} \\ i &= \text{MARR} \\ n &= \text{Time period} \end{aligned}$$

Example 6.6

Consider Example 6.2 for MAC, where the NACF is an annuity series. Calculate the CR, the annuity of NACF, and the AW of this project.

First, we calculate the CR using a simplified version of the equation, where there is no non-recurring cost and no salvage value:

$$\begin{aligned} CR &= -P(A/P,i,n) \\ CR &= -\$3{,}000{,}000(A/P,10\%,10) \\ CR &= -\$3{,}000{,}000\times(0.16275) \\ CR &= -\$488{,}250 \end{aligned}$$

Second, because NACF is constant per year, the A of NACF is the same as NACF per year:

$$A \text{ } of \text{ } NACF = NACF = \$1{,}000{,}000 - \$200{,}000 = \$800{,}000$$

Third, calculate AW:

$$\begin{aligned} AW &= \text{CR} + A \text{ } of \text{ } NACF \\ AW &= -\$488{,}250 + \$800{,}000 \\ AW &= \$311{,}750 \end{aligned}$$

Because AW > 0, the project is economically justified.

Example 6.7

Legacy Regional Airport (LRA) is planning to build a parking garage because of significant increases in the number of flights and high passenger traffic. The initial investment is estimated to be \$100 million now with \$10 million in 10 years. AOC is \$15 million, with annual revenue of \$35 million and a salvage value of \$20 million at the end of 20 years. Calculate the CR, annuity of net annual cash flows, and AW of this project at a MARR of 8%:

$$\begin{aligned} CR &= [-\$100\text{ m} - \$10\text{ m}(P/F,8\%,10)]\ [(A/P,8\%,20)] + \$20(A/F,8\%,20) \\ CR &= [-\$100\text{ m} - \$10\text{ m}(0.21455)] \times [0.10185] + \$20\text{ m}(0.02185) \\ CR &= [-\$100\text{ m} - \$2.15\text{ m}] \times [0.10185] + \$0.44\text{ m} \\ CR &= -\$10.40 + \$0.44 \\ CR &= -\$9.96\text{ m} \end{aligned}$$

The NACF can be either the AOC or the annual revenue, or a combination of both. The distribution of NACF can be an annuity series or a gradient series or have no format. If the NACF is an annuity series, then the A of NACF will be the same as the NACF per year. Otherwise, we have to calculate the annuity of the NACF:

A of NACF $= \$35\text{ m} - \$15\text{ m} = \$20\text{ m}$
The AW of the project is simply the sum of CR and the A of NACF.
$\text{AW} = -\$9.96\text{ m} + \$20\text{ M} = \$10.04\text{ m}$

Since AW > 0, the parking garage project is economically justified.

Example 6.8

Majestic Manufacturing Company (MMC) purchased a diagnostic system for $500,000. The life of the system is 10 years with a salvage value of $50,000. AOC is $50,000 in year one, increasing by $10,000 per year starting in year two through the end of year 10. The annual revenue from this system is estimated to be $180,000 per year. Calculate the CR, A of NACF, and AW for this diagnostic system assuming MMC uses a MARR of 7%.

First, calculate CR as follows:

$$\text{CR} = -\$500{,}000(\text{A/P},7\%,10) + \$50{,}000(\text{A/F},7,10)$$
$$\text{CR} = -\$500{,}000(0.14238) + \$50{,}000(0.07238)$$
$$\text{CR} = -\$71{,}190 + \$3{,}619$$
$$\text{CR} = -\$67{,}571$$

Second, since AOC has a format of arithmetic gradient series, convert it to an annuity series by calculating A of AOC:

$$\text{A of AOC} = -\$50{,}000 - \$10{,}000(\text{A/G},7\%,10)$$
$$\text{A of AOC} = -\$50{,}000 - \$10{,}000(3.94607)$$
$$\text{A of AOC} = -\$50{,}000 - \$39{,}461$$
$$\text{A of AOC} = -\$89{,}461$$

Third, calculate the A of NACF:

$$\text{A of NACF} = -\$89{,}461 + \$180{,}000 = \$90{,}539$$

Fourth, calculate the AW of the diagnostic system:

$$\text{AW} = -\$67{,}571 + \$90{,}539$$
$$\text{AW} = \$22{,}968$$

Since project AW is greater than 0, the project is economically viable.

Evaluating Mutually Exclusive Projects

In Chapter 5, we discussed mutually exclusive projects, projects that selecting one from the group will necessarily reject all the other options.

For instance, in the 1990s, Boeing had to choose to aircraft to compete with Airbus's 3XX (later A380) and considered two options: the 747X or the Sonic Cruiser. The 747X was an extension of the 747 – 400 series with more capacity and better fuel efficiency. The alternative was a Sonic Cruiser with distinctive delta wing canard that promised 15%–20% faster speed than the conventional airliner. Considering the required capital and market demand, it only made sense to pursue one of these options. The market interest in 747X was moderate to low, so Boeing eventually chose the Sonic Cruiser, which later became the 787 Dreamliner.

Congestion is a significant problem at many major airports around the world. Congestion imposes costs on both the passengers and the airline industry, and the traditional solution is to expand the current infrastructure in the most afflicted areas such as runways, gates, terminals, and parking areas. And expanding current facilities can entail multiyear capital investments. Current landing fees solely depend on aircraft weight; another way to reduce congestion is through peak-load landing charges that are higher when demand is higher during the peak time. Peak-load pricing aims to shift demand to off-peak hours to accommodate runway slots.

To evaluate mutually exclusive alternatives, we simply calculate the AW of each alternative and select the one alternative with the highest AW. In the following sections, we evaluate mutually exclusive projects with equal and nonequal lives.

AW Analysis of Equal-Life Alternatives

AW analysis of equal-life alternatives is one of the most used analysis techniques for engineering economists. Projects with equal lives have the same duration or lifespan, making their analysis simple because there's no need to adjust for different timeframes; equal project lives streamlines the evaluation process. Annual equivalent worth measures investment value by determining equal payments on annual basis. AW of equal-life alternatives measures cash flows as equal payments for different projects. As shown in Example 6.9, we simply calculate the AW of each project and select the one with the highest AW. However, it's essential to remember that while equal project lives simplify comparisons, all other factors are not necessarily identical; differences must still be carefully evaluated alongside the equal project lives to make informed decisions.

Example 6.9

The Kirby Chambliss Red Bull Air Race Team wishes to evaluate the two alternative machines presented in Table 6.2 for engine testing. Use AW with MARR of 12% per year to select the best alternative.

Table 6.2 Mutually Exclusive Alternatives: Example 6.9

	Machine A	*Machine B*
First cost	–\$250,000	–\$350,000
AOC	–\$80,000	–\$50,000
Life, years	5	5
Salvage value	\$20,000	\$25,000

To select the best alternative, calculate AW for machine A and machine B:

$$
\begin{aligned}
AW &= CR + A \text{ of } AOC \\
AW_A &= [-\$250{,}000(A/P,12\%,5) + \$20{,}000(A/F,12\%,5)] - \$80{,}000 \\
AW_A &= [-\$250{,}000 \times (0.27741) + \$20{,}000 \times (0.15741)] - \$80{,}000 \\
AW_A &= [-\$69{,}353 + \$3{,}148] - \$80{,}000 \\
AW_A &= -\$66{,}205 - \$80{,}000 \\
AW_A &= -\$146{,}205
\end{aligned}
$$

$$
\begin{aligned}
AW_B &= [-\$350{,}000(A/P,12\%,5) + \$25{,}000(A/F,12\%,5)] - \$50{,}000 \\
AW_B &= [-\$350{,}000 \times (0.27741) + \$25{,}000 \times (0.15741)] - \$50{,}000 \\
AW_B &= [-\$97{,}094 + \$3{,}935] - \$50{,}000 \\
AW_B &= -\$93{,}159 - \$50{,}000 \\
AW_B &= -\$143{,}159
\end{aligned}
$$

Because $AW_B > AW_A$, machine B is is the economically viable option.

AW Analysis of Non-Equal-Life Alternatives

As mentioned earlier, the advantage of AW over PW analysis is that the equal-life service requirement is met without using the LCMs of alternatives with different lives because the AW calculated over one life cycle is exactly the same for any multiple life cycles. When analyzing AW for non-equal-life alternatives in engineering economics, it's crucial to standardize cash flows for meaningful comparisons. This involves extending or truncating cash flows to a common time frame and then annualizing them to equivalent annual values. By spreading out cash flows over the common time frame and discounting them appropriately, the present worth of each alternative can be determined. Example 6.10 demonstrates the repeatability of the AW over multiple life cycles.

Example 6.10

JRA is purchasing a Cessna 150 for $115,000 to conduct primary flight instruction. The cash flows associated with this project are presented in Table 6.3. Evaluate this project using AW analysis over one and two life cycles. JRA uses a MARR of 10%.

a. Calculate AW over one life cycle. Figure 6.6 shows the cash flows for one life cycle.

$$AW = -\$115{,}000(A/P,10\%,5) + \$20{,}000(A/F,10\%,5) - \$40{,}000 + \$85{,}000$$

Table 6.3 Cash Flows for Cessna 150: Example 6.10

First Cost	$115,000
AOC	$40,000
Annual revenue	$85,000
Salvage value	$20,000
Life, years	5

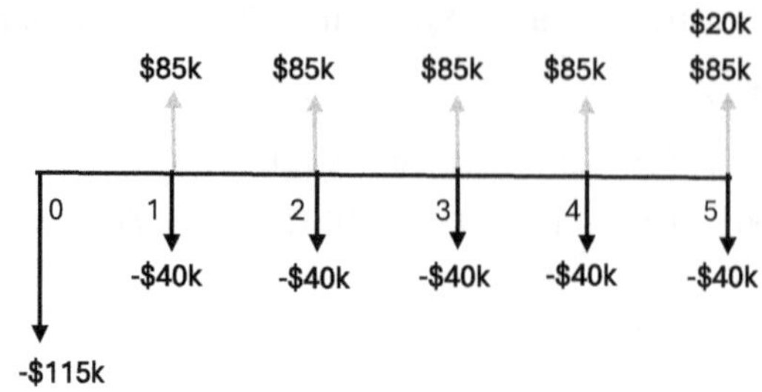

Figure 6.6 Cash flows for one life cycle: Example 6.10.

Enter the interest factors from Table A16 into the previous relationship:

$$\text{AW} = -\$115{,}000 \times (0.2638) + \$20{,}000 \times (0.1638) + \$45{,}000$$
$$\text{AW} = -\$30{,}337 + \$3{,}276 + \$45{,}000$$
$$\text{AW} = \$17{,}939$$

Because AW is greater than 0, the project is economically justified.

b. Calculate AW over two life cycles. Figure 6.7 shows cash flows for two life cycles.

$$\text{AW} = [-\$115{,}000 - \$115{,}000(\text{P/F},10\%,5)] \times [(\text{A/P},10\%,10)] + [\$20{,}000(\text{F/P},10\%,5) + \$20{,}000] \times [(\text{A/F},10\%,10)] - \$40{,}000 + \$85{,}000$$

Enter the interest factors from Table A16 into the previous equation:

$$\text{AW} = [-\$115{,}000 - \$115{,}000 \times (0.6209)] \times [0.16275] + [\$20{,}000 \times (1.6105) + \$20{,}000] \times [0.06275] + \$45{,}000$$
$$\text{AW} = -\$30{,}337 + \$3{,}276 + \$45{,}000$$
$$\text{AW} = \$17{,}939$$

As you notice, AW is the same for both one and two life cycles. The AW is also the same over multiple life cycles.

Evaluating Independent Projects

Investment decisions are made based on the results, prioritizing projects with positive NPV, IRR exceeding the cost of capital, and favorable financial metrics. This method ensures that stakeholders make well-informed decisions that maximize the value of their investments and align with strategic objectives. Independent projects are projects that have no impacts on any others if any one if them is chosen. For example, an airline's replacing an old aircraft is independent from replacing the computer reservation system.

When evaluating independent projects, several important subjects need to be considered to ensure a thorough and accurate analysis. One important aspect is accurately estimating all cash inflows and outflows associated with each project, including initial costs, operating costs, maintenance costs, and any expected revenues. The timing of these cash flows must be considered as it can significantly impact the present value and overall AW of the project. Furthermore, it is important to evaluate the risks associated with each project, including market risks,

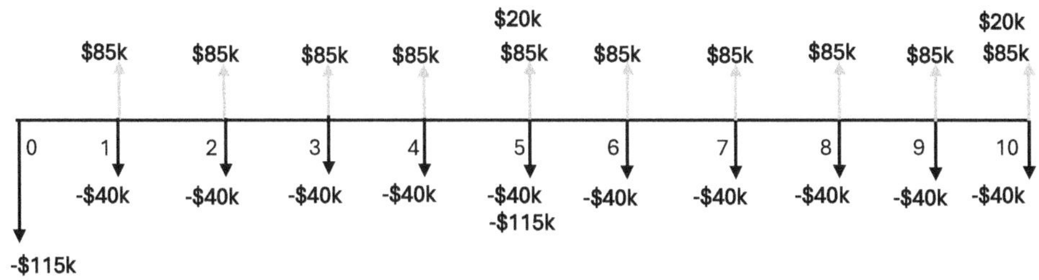

Figure 6.7 Cash flows for two life cycles: Example 6.10.

financial risks, and operational risks. Evaluating independent projects based on AW entails calculating AW for each project and accepting all with an AW at least 0 as long as there is no budget constraint. If there is a budget limitation, then we use the PW approach as explained in Chapter 5.

Example 6.11

Majestic Oil Company is producing jet fuel from crude oil in its refinery in Texas. It is considering producing synthetic rubber, rubber cement, car battery cases, and linoleum from byproducts of the crude oil. The cash flows for those byproducts are presented in Table 6.4. Using AW and assuming a MARR of 7%, which if any of the following alternatives should Majestic select?

AW of synthetic rubber:

$$AW_{SR} = -\$100{,}000(A/P,7\%,8) + \$10{,}000(A/F,7\%,8) - \$30{,}000 + \$65{,}000$$
$$AW_{SR} = -\$100{,}000 \times (0.16747) + \$10{,}000 \times (0.09747) - \$30{,}000 + \$65{,}000$$
$$AW_{SR} = -\$16{,}747 + \$975 - \$30{,}000 + \$65{,}000$$
$$AW_{SR} = \$19{,}228 > 0$$

AW of rubber cement:

$$AW_{RC} = -\$150{,}000(A/P,7\%,8) + \$12{,}000(A/F,7\%,8) - \$40{,}000 + \$85{,}000$$
$$AW_{RC} = -\$150{,}000 \times (0.16747) + \$12{,}000 \times (0.09747) - \$40{,}000 + \$85{,}000$$
$$AW_{RC} = -\$25{,}121 + \$1{,}170 - \$40{,}000 + \$85{,}000$$
$$AW_{RC} = \$21{,}049 > 0$$

AW of car battery cases:

$$AW_{CB} = -\$200{,}000(A/P,7\%,8) + \$15{,}000(A/F,7\%,8) - \$75{,}000 + \$100{,}000$$
$$AW_{CB} = -\$200{,}000 \times (0.16747) + \$15{,}000 \times (0.09747) - \$75{,}000 + \$100{,}000$$
$$AW_{CB} = -\$33{,}494 + \$1{,}462 - \$75{,}000 + \$100{,}000$$
$$AW_{CB} = -\$7{,}032 < 0$$

AW of linoleum:

$$AW_{L} = -\$85{,}000(A/P,7\%,8) + \$8{,}000(A/F,7\%,8) - \$50{,}000 + \$65{,}000$$
$$AW_{L} = -\$85{,}000 \times (0.16747) + \$8{,}000 \times (0.09747) - \$50{,}000 + \$65{,}000$$
$$AW_{L} = -\$14{,}235 + \$780 - \$50{,}000 + \$65{,}000$$
$$AW_{L} = \$1545 > 0$$

Table 6.4 Majestic Byproduct Independent Projects: Example 6.11

	Synthetic Rubber	*Rubber Cement*	*Car Battery Cases*	*Linoleum*
First cost	$100,000	$150,000	$200,000	$85,000
AOC	$30,000	$40,000	$75,000	$50,000
Annual revenue	$65,000	$80,000	$100,000	$65,000
Salvage value	$10,000	$12,000	$15,000	$8,000
Life, years	8	8	8	8

Majestic should accept synthetic rubber, rubber cement, and linoleum projects since they have positive AWs.

AW of Permanent Projects

As explained in Chapter 3, sometimes the life of projects is long enough that we can consider them as permanent projects. Let us consider Next Generation Air Transportation System (NextGen). NextGen proposes transforming America's air traffic control system from a radar-based system with radio communication to a satellite-based system with GPS technology. The GPS technology will be used to shorten routes, save time and fuel, reduce traffic delays, increase capacity, and permit controllers to monitor and manage aircraft with greater safety margins. Radio communications will be increasingly replaced by data exchange and an automation system that reduces the amount of information the air crew must process at one time. As a result of these changes, planes will be able to fly closer together, take more direct routes, and avoid delays caused by airport stacking as planes wait for an open runway.[1] NextGen requires massive federal investment for R&D, feasibility study, development, implementation, and maintenance.

Analyzing AW for projects with indefinite lifespans requires a different approach from that for projects with finite lifespans. Permanent projects are typically evaluated using CC, which considers the project's cash flows as if they continue indefinitely. CC is calculated as

$$CC = \frac{AW}{i}$$

To calculate AW for an infinite life project, we use CC and start with

$$\mathrm{CC} = \frac{\mathrm{AW}}{\mathrm{i}}$$

$$\mathrm{AW} = \mathrm{CC} \times (\mathrm{i})$$

For an infinite life project, the first cost becomes the CC, and AW of the first cost is calculated as

$$\mathrm{AW} = \mathrm{PV} \times (\mathrm{i})$$

For recurring cash flows, we calculate their AWs over the life cycle of their occurrences. All nonrecurring cash flows are shifted to present time value, and then AW is calculated using the previous equation.

Example 6.12

By understanding these concepts and applying the appropriate formulas, engineers and decision-makers can effectively evaluate AW for permanent projects. For example, suppose Johnson International Airport (JIA) is considering building a new five-story parking garage with a first cost of $100 million. This project is considered to be permanent with an estimated annual operating cost of $500,000 per year and a resurfacing cost of $2,000,000 every five years. The annual revenue from this parking garage is estimated to be $8,000,000 per year for the first five years, $12,000,000 per year for the next five years, and $15,000,000 per year thereafter. JIA uses a MARR of 10%. Use AW analysis to determine if this project is economically justified:

$$\begin{aligned}
AW_P &= -\$100{,}000{,}000 \times (0.10) = -\$10{,}000{,}000 \\
AW_{AOC} &= -\$500{,}000 \\
AW_{Resurfacing} &= -\$2{,}000{,}000(A/F,10\%,5) \\
AW_{Resurfacing} &= -\$2{,}000{,}000 \times (0.1638) \\
AW_{Resurfacing} &= -\$327{,}600 \\
AW_{Revenue} &= \$8{,}000{,}000 + \$4{,}000{,}000(P/F,10\%,5) + \$3{,}000{,}000(P/F,10\%,10) \\
AW_{Revenue} &= \$8{,}000{,}000 + \$4{,}000{,}000 \times (0.6209) + \$3{,}000{,}000 \times (0.3855) \\
AW_{Revenue} &= \$8{,}000{,}000 + \$2{,}483{,}600 + \$1{,}156{,}500 \\
AW_{Revenue} &= \$11{,}640{,}100
\end{aligned}$$

To calculate total AW of the project, we add the AW_P, AW_{AOC}, $AW_{Resurfacing}$, and $AW_{Revenue}$ together as follows:

$$\begin{aligned}
AW_{Total} &= -\$10{,}000{,}000 - \$500{,}000 - \$327{,}600 + \$11{,}640{,}100 \\
AW_{Total} &= \$812{,}500 > 0
\end{aligned}$$

Because AW for the parking garage project is positive, it is economically justified.

Calculating AW in Excel

This section presents how to use Excel functions to calculate AW; Excel is an efficient way to handle complex financial calculations, especially when evaluating permanent projects with indefinite lifespans. Excel's AW formula is as follows:

$$= \mathbf{PMT(i\%,\ n,\ PV,\ FV)}$$

To calculate the AW of a project, we enter the following formula into a cell:

$$= \mathbf{PMT(i\%,\ n,\ PV,\ FV) + NACF}$$

where i is the MARR, n is the period, P is the first cost, F is the salvage value, and NACF is annual cash inflows less annual cash outflows.

Example 6.13

An investment in equipment costing $100,000 results in NACF of $50,000 per year for five years and a salvage value of $20,000 at the end of five years when the equipment will be disposed of. Assuming a MARR of 10%, calculate the AW of this investment in Excel.

Figure 6.8 shows the Excel solution for the project in Example 6.13. The cash flow in cell B3 is the first cost, the cash flow in cell B4 is the salvage value, and the cash flow in cell B7 is the NACF. The function to calculate the AW is presented in cell C9, and the solution appears when you hit Enter. As you notice, the NACF represents a uniform series, first cost has a positive sign, and salvage value is negative. To obtain the correct answer, you need to pay close attention to the cash flow signage.

Example 6.14

EZjET Airlines purchased a tow truck for $300,000. The operating cost will be $5,000 per year. The airline expects to sell the tow truck for $50,000 five years from now. What is the equivalent AW of the truck assuming the interest rate is 10%?

$$AW = -\$300{,}000 \times (A/P,10\%,5) + \$50{,}000 \times (A/F,10\%,5) - \$5{,}000$$
$$AW = -\$300{,}000 \times (0.2638) + \$50{,}000 \times (0.1638) - \$5{,}000 = -\$75{,}950$$

To calculate AW for this example using Excel, enter the cost of equipment (the first cost) in cell B3, the salvage value in cell B4 with a negative sign, and the operating cost per year in cell B7 as the NACF. The function to calculate the AW is presented in cell C9, and the solution appears when you hit Enter. The results are presented in Figure 6.9.

	A	B	C	D
1				
2				
3	P	100,000		
4	S	–20,000		
5	n	5		
6	MARR	10%		
7	NACF	50,000		
8				
9	AW	$26,896	= PMT(10%,5,B[3],B[4]) + B[7])	
10				
11				

Figure 6.8 Calculating annual worth in Excel: Example 6.13.

	A	B	C	D
1				
2				
3	P	300,000		
4	S	–50,000		
5	n	5		
6	MARR	10%		
7	NACF	5,000		
8				
9	AW	$75,950	= PMT(10%,5,B[3],B[4]) + B[7]	
10				
11				

Figure 6.9 Calculating annual worth in Excel: Example 6.14.

The examples presented in this chapter offer a comprehensive analysis of AW across diverse scenarios and conditions. By methodically examining financial performance, value generation, and nonfinancial contributions, these frameworks provide a nuanced understanding of a project's yearly impact. Moreover, the insights generated from these evaluations are invaluable for informing strategic decision-making and future planning.

Summary

Annual worth analysis is a simple technique used by professional engineers to evaluate single, multiple, competing alternatives, and independent projects. To evaluate a single project, AW analysis consists of calculating the annual equivalent amount (annuity amount) of all cash flows, both inflows and outflows, associated with a project and simply adding them together. If AW of a project is equal to or greater than 0, the project is economically justified and accepting it increases the value of the firm.

AW analysis is generally preferred over present worth because it is simple to calculate and does not require equal service lives to compare mutually exclusive alternatives. AW of a project can also be calculated by adding the capital recovery to the annuity of net annual cash flows (A of NACF). CR of an investment in equipment is the uniform annual revenue needed to recover the cost of the equipment and any nonrecurring cash flows over the life of the project. CR can be calculated by simply adding the equivalent annuity of the first cost, any nonrecurring costs, and the salvage value over the economic life of the equipment. The NACF can be of annual operating cost, annual revenue, or the difference between the annual revenue and annual operating cost. The distribution of NACF can be an annuity series or a gradient series or have no particular format. If the format of NACF is an annuity series, then the A of NACF will be the same as the NACF per year. Otherwise, we have to calculate the annuity of the NACF to calculate AW. To evaluate mutually exclusive alternatives using AW analysis, we simply calculate the AW of each alternative over its original life and select the one alternative with the highest AW. The last section of this chapter discussed calculating AW in Excel.

Discussion Questions and Problems

6.1 Royal Aviation Corporation (RAC) is undertaking a project that requires purchasing equipment with the first cost of \$5,000,000, one time rebuild cost of \$400,000 at the end of year five, and a salvage value of \$250,000 at the termination of the project in 10 years. RAC uses a MARR of 9%. Calculate the annual worth of cash flows associated with this project.

6.2 RAC is considering purchasing a piece of equipment to manufacture a part of the wing fixture for an aircraft. The cost of the system is \$5 million with life expectancy of 10 years and with no salvage value. The annual operating cost of the system is \$400,000 and RAC anticipates a stream of \$1,500,000 in revenue at the end of each year for 10 years. Using AW analysis and assuming a MARR of 10%, is this investment economically justified?

6.3 Majestic Heavy Industries (MHI) purchased a diagnostic system for \$500,000. The life of the system is eight years with a salvage value of \$100,000. The annual operating cost is \$50,000 in year one increasing by \$20,000 per year starting in year two through the end of year 8. Calculate the CR, A of NACF, and AW for this diagnostic system assuming MHI uses a MARR of 9%.

6.4 Monarch Aviation is manufacturing an aircraft equipped with an airframe parachute system, a whole-plane parachute recovery system capable of lowering the entire aircraft to the ground in an emergency. Assume the cost of the parachute system installation is

$4 million with life expectancy of 10 years, salvage value of $200,000, and no annual operating cost but rebuild costs of $500,000 at the end of year four and $600,000 at the end of year eight. If the added revenue stream of $1,200,000 at the end of each year for 10 years is anticipated, given a MARR of 8%, is this investment economically justified?

6.5 Royal Aviation Services (RAS) is a premier aviation service provider of ground handling, passenger services, cargo aircraft handling, loading and offloading, etc. RAS is considering purchasing equipment for $400,000 with a salvage value of $50,000 at the end of its eight-year life. The annual operating cost is $20,000. There is no annual revenue, but revenues of $300,000 and $400,000 are expected in years three and six, respectively. RAS uses a MARR of 10%. Is the purchase of this equipment economically justified?

6.6 Inflight Internet Services Company is a provider of in-flight broadband internet service and other connectivity services for commercial and business aircraft. It is considering a new system of satellite Wi-Fi technology. The cost of the system is $4 million, with a rebuild cost of $500,000 in year five and a salvage value of $200,000 at the end of the 10-year life of the system. Assuming a MARR of 12%, what is the capital recovery of this system?

6.7 Majestic Aircraft Company (MAC) manufactures a single-seat, single-jet engine, multirole light fighter jet. It is supersonic and highly maneuverable and is the smallest and lightest in its class of contemporary combat aircraft. MAC undertook a project with a first cost of $50 million to construct aluminum–lithium alloys, carbon-fiber composites, and titanium alloy steels for airframe and fuselage to make the aircraft lighter and stronger. The annual operating cost was $3 million; the salvage at the end of 25 years of operation was $4 million. Assuming a MARR of 10%, calculate the CR and AW of the costs.

6.8 Johnson Aerospace Company (JAC) purchased a diagnostic system for $2,000,000. The life of the system is eight years with a salvage value equal to 10% of the first cost. The annual operating cost is $100,000 in year one increasing by $50,000 per year starting in year two through the end of year eight. Calculate the CR, A of NACF, and AW for this diagnostic system assuming JAC uses a MARR of 9%.

6.9 JAC wishes to evaluate the following two alternative machines for engine testing of its signature aircraft. Use AW analysis with MARR of 11% per year to select the most cost-effective alternative.

	Machine A	*Machine B*
First cost	−$500,000	−$800,000
AOC	−$120,000	−$40,000
Life, years	10	10
Salvage value	$50,000	$100,000

6.10 Amazing Flight Academy (AFA) is purchasing 10 Cessna 150 s for $1,100,000 to conduct primary flight training. The cash flows associated with this project are presented as follows. Evaluate this project using AW analysis over a 10-year period. AFA uses a MARR of 10%.

First cost	$1,100,000
AOC	$100,000 in the first year increasing by $50,000 per year
Annual revenue	$300,000 in year one increasing by $75,000 per year
Salvage value	$80,000
Life, years	10

6.11 Royal Mobile Company is producing jet fuel from crude oil in its refinery in Texas. It is considering three mutually exclusive alternatives to improve the efficiency of its refinery. The cash flows for the three alternatives are shown in the following table. Using AW and assuming a MARR of 7%, determine which alternative Royal Mobile should select.

	Alternative 1	*Alternative 2*	*Alternative 3*
First cost	$300,000	$500,000	$800,000
Annual operating cost	$85,000	$65,000	$45,000
Salvage value	$50,000	$70,000	$100,000
Life, Years	4	6	8

6.12 Dutch Mobile Company is producing jet fuel from crude oil in its refinery in Mexico. It is considering three mutually exclusive alternatives to improve the efficiency of its refinery. The cash flows for the three alternatives are shown in the next table. Using AW and assuming a MARR of 8%, determine which alternative Dutch Mobile should select.

	Alternative 1	*Alternative 2*	*Alternative 3*
Fist cost	$300,000	$500,000	$800,000
AOC	$50,000 in year One increasing by $20,000 per year	$65,000	$30,000 in year one growing at 5% per year
Salvage value	$50,000	$70,000	$100,000
Life, years	4	6	10

6.13 Synthetic Product Manufacturing (SPM) is considering four capital investment proposals with no budget limitation. The projects are independent from each other and have the following cash flows. SPM is using a MARR of 6%. Based on AW analysis, which of the following projects should be undertaken, if any?

	Project A	*Project B*	*Project C*	*Project D*
First cost	$100,000	$150,000	$200,000	$250,000
AOC	$30,000	$40,000	$75,000	$80,000
Annual revenue	$65,000	$80,000	$100,000	$120,000
Salvage value	$10,000	$12,000	$15,000	$20,000
Life, years	10	10	10	10

Note

1 Federal Aviation Authority, NextGen Fact Sheet, 2007.

7 Rate of Return Analysis

Rate of return analysis (ROR) is yet another popular technique used by professional engineers to evaluate projects. This technique is also used often by investors to evaluate the ROR of their investments in a single asset or security, portfolio of securities, or mutual funds. As long as the rate of return on an investment is equal to or greater than the minimum acceptable rate of return (MARR), the investment is economically justified. ROR analysis, like present worth (PW) analysis, requires equivalent service lives for comparing mutually exclusive alternatives. In addition, mutually exclusive projects are evaluated two at a time on the basis of the incremental cash flows evaluation to select the optimal project.

The focus of this chapter is to enable readers to use ROR analysis to evaluate projects to select economically justified independent projects. In the sections that follow, we address calculating ROR for single projects, the criteria for accepting or rejecting projects, and comparing and selecting projects. In addition, it presents the possibility of multiple RORs and describes the use of modified ROR analysis.

The rate of return (ROR) is the foundation of financial analysis, serving as a critical measure of an investment's profitability and the effectiveness of its allocation. ROR provides a comprehensive view of how well resources are being utilized to generate earnings. By transforming raw data into actionable insights, the ROR guides investors and decision-makers in their pursuit of growth, sustainability, and financial health. Understanding and leveraging this metric is essential for making informed investment choices and achieving long-term success.

Rate of Return Calculation

Newnan[1] defines ROR as the interest rate at which PW and annual worth are 0, while Blank[2] defines it "as the rate paid on the unpaid balance of borrowed money, or the rate earned on the uncovered balance of an investment, so that the final payment or receipt brings the balance to exactly zero with interest considered".

In this book, the ROR, which is also called internal rate of return (IRR), is defined as the interest rate (i*) that sets PW for all cash flows, both inflows and outflows, to 0. We use this definition as presented in the following equation to calculate ROR:

$$PW = \sum_{t=1}^{n} \left[\frac{CFt}{(1+i^*)^t} \right] = 0$$

DOI: 10.4324/9781003469759-7

Where: CF_t = cash flow in period t
i^* = rate of return
n = number of periods

The advantages of ROR analysis over PW and AW analyses are that ROR measures project attractiveness in terms that are commonly and easily understood by both engineers and business leaders and that you need to accurately estimate MARR to calculate PW and AW, but it is not needed for calculating ROR.

Example 7.1

DirectJet has borrowed \$1,228.92 million from a local bank to expand its fleet of B787s. DirectJet will pay back this loan with payments of \$200 million per year for 10 years. What is the ROR of this loan to the local bank?

Figure 7.1 shows the cash flow diagram. To find ROR, we set the PW of all cash flows to zero.

$$\begin{aligned} PW &= 0 \\ PW &= \$1,228.92 + \$200(P/A,\ i^*,\ 10) = 0 \\ \$200(P/A,\ i^*,\ 10) &= \$1,228.92 \end{aligned}$$

To simplify that equation, we divide both sides by \$200 million to find the interest factor:

$$\frac{\$200(P/A,\ i^*,10)}{\$200} = \frac{\$1,228.92}{\%200}$$

$$(P/A,\ i^*,\ 10) = 6.1446$$

Knowing that the interest factor is 6.1446, we go to Appendix A in the textbook for interest factor values, and in each table, we look for the value in column under A/P for a 10-year period. We find the interest factor of 6.1446 in Table A16 for 10% interest, and we conclude that rate of return is 10%:

$$ROR = i^* = 10\%$$

If we could not find the exact interest factor value in the tables, then we would interpolate between the two closed values.

ROR ranges from −100% to infinity. The extreme downside return is when ROR = −100%. This means that the investment is totally lost. The upside return is open and theoretically unlimited. The criteria to select or to reject a project are summarized in Table 7.1.

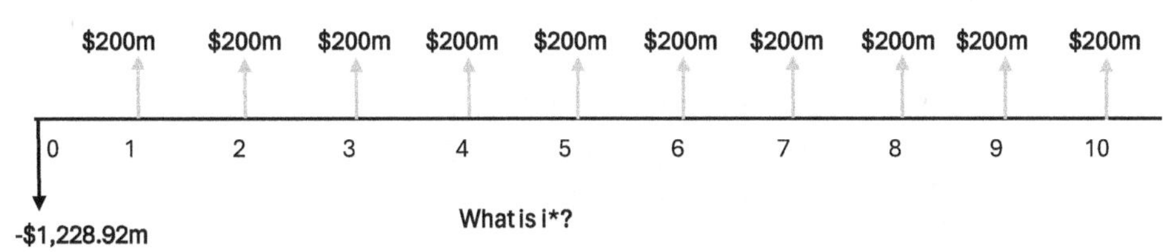

Figure 7.1 Cash flow diagram: Example 7.1.

Table 7.1 Accept-and-Reject Criteria for Rate of Return

ROR	*Selection Criteria*
ROR > MARR	Accept the project because it is economically justified.
ROR = MARR	Indifference about the project, but it is still economically justified.
ROR< MARR	Reject the project because it is not economically justified.

Trial and Error

In Example 7.1, there was only one interest factor $(\text{P/A, i*}, 10)$, and that allowed us to calculate the interest factor and reference it to the interest factors in Appendix A to find the corresponding interest rate. In Example 7.2, there are two interest factors, $[(\text{P/A, i*}, 10) \& (\text{P/F, i*}, 10)]$; therefore, we must use trial and error to find the correct rate of return.

Example 7.2

In Example 7.1, assume that DirectJet pays \$500 million at the end of 10 years in addition to annual payments of \$200 million. What is the rate of return on this loan to the local bank? If the local bank uses a 10% MARR, is this investment economically justified?

Similar to Example 7.1, we set the PW of all cash flows to 0 to find the ROR:

$$\text{PW} = 0$$
$$\text{PW} = \$1,228.92 + \$200(\text{P/A, i*, } 10) + \$500(\text{P/F, i*, } 10) = 0$$

Trial and error simply involves applying different interest rates to calculate the PW of the cash flows where the one interest rate that sets the PW of all cash flows to 0 is the ROR. If there is no interest rate that sets the PW to 0, then we select the two interest rates that provide the PWs closest to 0 and 0 interpolate.

Normally we start with an initial i* of 10% that we enter into the PW function. If PW is positive, then we increase i*; if PW is negative, then we decrease i*. For a typical investment, as we increase i*, PW is expected to decrease, and as we decrease i*, PW is expected to increase. In Example 7.2, because PW at 10% interest is positive, \$192.75 million, we increase i* to 12% for the second trial.

This trial also results in a positive PW of \$62.12 million. For the third trial of 13%, we get another positive PW, but it is getting closer to 0. With the fourth trial at 14%, PW was negative. Therefore, we know that i* lies between 13% and 14%, and this provides enough information to make a decision because the MARR is 10% but we are asked to calculate the ROR on this loan. Now we begin the trial-and-error process.

In the first trial, we enter i* of 10% into the PW equation:

$$\text{Try i*} = 10\%$$
$$\text{PW} = -\$1,228.92 + \$200(\text{P/A, } 10\%, 10) + \$500(\text{P/F, } 10\%, 10)$$
$$\text{PW} = -\$1,228.92 + \$200\ (6.1446) + \$500\ (0.3855)$$
$$\text{PW} = -\$1,228.92 + \$1,228.92 + \$192.75$$
$$\text{PW} = +\$192.75$$

Because PW is positive, we increase i* to 12% for the second trial:

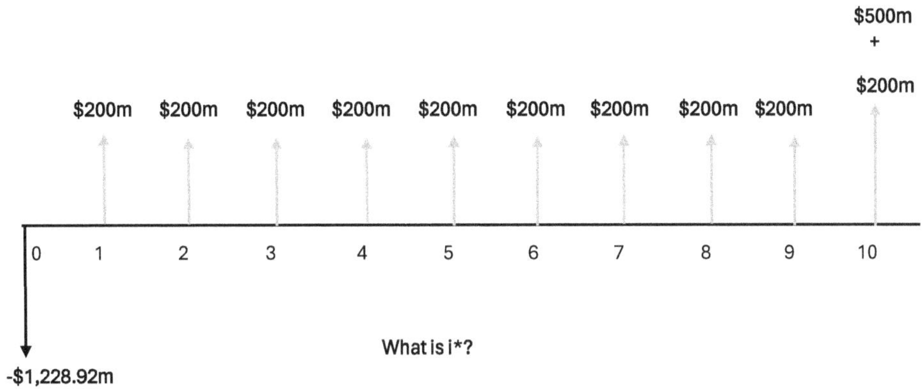

Figure 7.2 Cash flow diagram: Example 7.2.

$$
\begin{aligned}
&\text{Try } i^* = 12\% \\
&\quad PW = -\$1,228.92 + \$200(P/A,\ 12\%,\ 10) + \$500(P/F,\ 12\%,\ 10) \\
&\quad PW = -\$1,228.92 + \$200\ (6.1446) + \$500\ (0.3855) \\
&\quad PW = -\$1,228.92 + \$1,228.92 + \$192.75 \\
&\quad PW = +\$192.75
\end{aligned}
$$

Because PW is still positive, we increase i* to 13% for the third trial:

$$
\begin{aligned}
&\text{Try } i^* = 13\% \\
&\quad PW = -\$1,228.92 + \$200(P/A,\ 13\%,\ 10) + \$500(P/F,\ 13\%,\ 10) \\
&\quad PW = -\$1,228.92 + \$200\ (5.4262) + \$500\ (0.2946) \\
&\quad PW = -\$1,228.92 + \$1,085.92 + \$147.30 \\
&\quad PW = +\$3.62
\end{aligned}
$$

Because PW is still positive, we increase i* to 14% for the fourth trial:

$$
\begin{aligned}
&\text{Try } i^* = 14\% \\
&\quad PW = -\$1,228.92 + \$200(P/A,\ 14\%,\ 10) + \$500\ (P/F,\ 14\%,\ 10) \\
&\quad PW = -\$1,228.92 + \$200\ (5.2161) + \$500\,(0.2697) \\
&\quad PW = -\$1,228.92 + \$1,043.22 + \$134.85 \\
&\quad PW = -\$50.85
\end{aligned}
$$

Because PW changes sign from positive at 13% to negative at 14%, i* lies between 13% and 14%. Now, we will interpolate to calculate i*. Usually, the relationship between interest rates and their corresponding PW is not a linear function, as shown in Figure 7.3.

However, for interest rates that are only one or possibly two percentage points apart, we can assume that the relationship is linear, and we can interpolate to determine the approximate i* as presented in Figure 7.4.

To interpolate between 13% and 14%, we set up information as shown in Table 7.2.

Now we form two equal fractions. For the fraction on the left side, the numerator is the difference between 13% and 13% + X%, which is X%, and the denominator is the difference between 13% and 14%, which is 1%. Similarly, on the right side, the numerator is the difference between

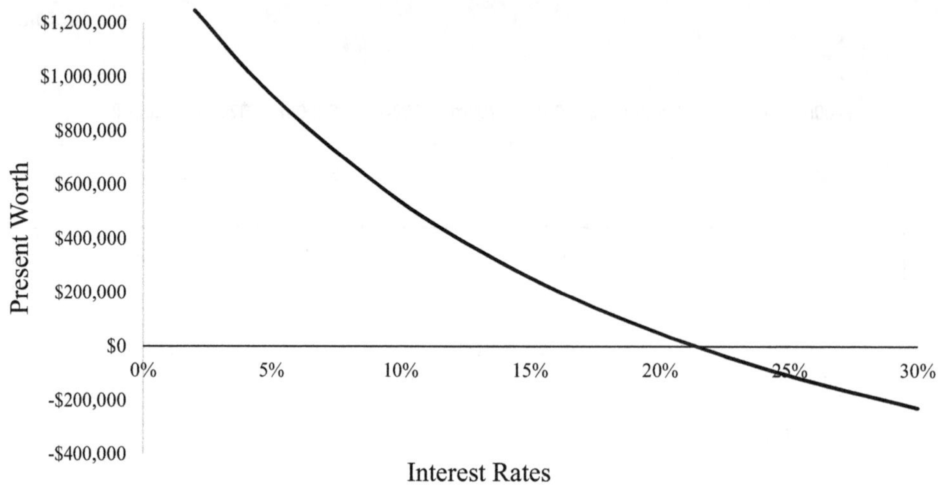

Figure 7.3 Present worth as a function of the interest rate.

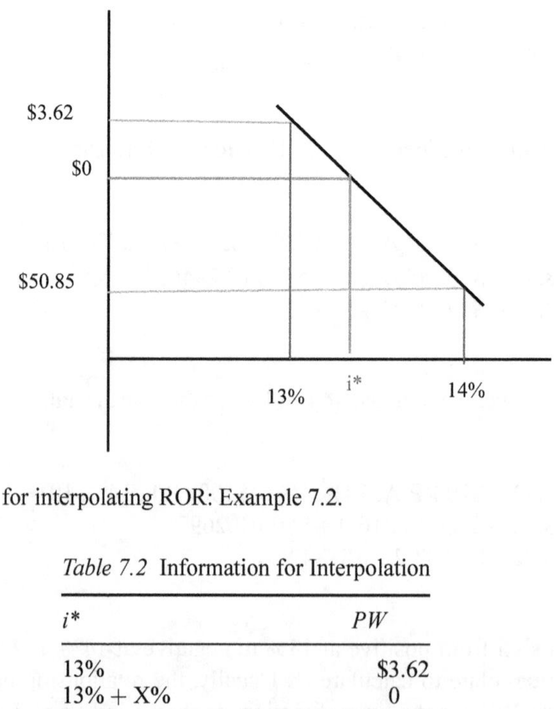

Figure 7.4 Endpoints for interpolating ROR: Example 7.2.

Table 7.2 Information for Interpolation

i^*	PW
13%	$3.62
13% + X%	0
14%	−$50.85

the $3.62 million and 0, which is $3.62 million; the denominator is the difference between $3.62 million and −$50.85 million, which is $54.47 million.

$$\frac{X\%}{1\%} = \frac{3.62}{54.47}$$

Now we cross multiply and solve for X%.

$$X\% = \frac{\$3.62}{\$54.47}$$
$$X\% = 0.07\%$$

Therefore, ROR $= i^* = 13\% + 0.07\% = 13.07\%$. Since ROR exceeds the MARR of 10%, this investment by the local bank is economically justified.

Because the relationship between different ranges or boundaries is not linear, to obtain the accurate ROR, we have to interpolate between the two closest ranges. In this example interpolating between 10% and 14% would not have given the accurate answer. The rule of thumb is to interpolate between one to two percentages boundaries.

Rate of Return on Bonds

Many airlines including financially well-established airlines issue bonds to finance new aircraft. At the 2015 Dubai Airshow, Emirates Airline's chairman announced a bond issue of \$1 billion to finance 30 new aircraft with an additional cash infusion to help. The airline has around 270 additional aircraft on order: 46 Boeing 777–300ERs, 115 Boeing 777–9Xs, 35 Boeing 777–8Xs, and 74 Airbus A380s.[3]

Individuals and companies tend to invest in bonds because bonds are considered much safer than stocks. With bonds, you receive the annual interest and the face value of bond at maturity. Therefore, there is uncertainty associated with this investment. Since most bonds are sold at discount, below their par value, one would wonder about the ROR on bonds. Example 7.3 shows how to calculate the ROR on bonds, which can be compared with the required ROR or MARR to determine whether the investment in bond is economically justified.

Example 7.3

DirectJet has a new bond issue with face value of \$1,000 and coupon rate of 6%, with 10 years to maturity. If you pay \$850 for this bond, what would be your ROR if interest is paid annually?

Use the following equations to calculate the annual interest payment, set PW to 0, and use trial and error to solve for the interest rate:

$$I = \frac{(\$1,000) \times (0.06)}{1} = \$60$$
$$PW = -\$850 + \$60(P/A, i^*, 10) + \$1,000(P/F, i^*, 10) = 0$$

In bond valuation, ROR can be calculating using either trial and error or approximate rate, which is very close to ROR. Once we calculate the approximate rate with the next equation, we can interpolate between the two whole percentage boundaries of the approximate rate:

$$\text{Approximate Rate} = \frac{I + \frac{V - P}{n}}{\frac{(V + P)}{2}}$$

where I = dollar amount of periodic interest, V = bond face value, P = bond market price or value, and N = number of years to maturity.

The approximate rate for Example 7.3 is calculated as follows:

$$\text{Approximate Rate} = \frac{\$60 + \frac{(\$1000 - \$850)}{10}}{\frac{(\$1000 + \$850)}{2}}$$

$$\text{Approximate Rate} = \frac{\$60 + 15}{925} = \frac{\$75}{925} = 8.11\%$$

The approximate rate of 8.11% indicates that the actual rate of return is between 8% and 9%. Therefore, we calculate bond PW at 8% and 9% and interpolate between the two to get bond ROR:

$$\begin{aligned}
&\text{Try } i^* = 8\% \\
&\quad PW = -\$850 + \$60(P/A, 8\%, 10) + \$1{,}000(P/F, 8\%, 10) \\
&\quad \text{PW} = -\$850 + \$60(6.71008) + \$1{,}000(0.46319) \\
&\quad \text{PW} = -\$850 + \$402.60 + \$463.19 \\
&\quad \text{PW} = \$15.79
\end{aligned}$$

$$\begin{aligned}
&\text{Try } i^* = 9\% \\
&\quad PW = -\$850 + \$60\,(P/A, 9\%, 10) + \$1{,}000\,(P/F, 9\%, 10) \\
&\quad \text{PW} = -\$850 + \$60\,(6.41766) + \$1{,}000\,(0.42241) \\
&\quad \text{PW} = -\$850 + \$385.06 + \$422.41 \\
&\quad \text{PW} = \$42.53
\end{aligned}$$

Interpolate between 8% and 9%:

i*	PW
8%	\$15.79
8% + X%	0
9%	−\$42.53

$$X\% = \frac{\$15.79}{2\,\$58.32}$$

$$X\% = 0.27\%$$

$$\text{ROR} = i^* = 8\% + 0.27\% = 8.27\%$$

Using approximate rate of 8.10% and interpolating between 8% and 9%, we calculated the actual ROR of 8.27%.

Evaluating Mutually Exclusive Projects

As we defined earlier, mutually exclusive projects are projects that cannot be executed simultaneously; selecting one necessarily rejects all the others even if they are profitable. Using ROR analysis to select the best project among the competing alternatives, we need to evaluate two projects at a time, calculate the incremental cash flows between the two alternatives, determine the equal service life and, depending on whether the projects are revenue based or cost based, select one of them, or do nothing.

Incremental Cash Flows

Professional engineers often use ROR to select among mutually exclusive alternatives, but a complication often arises if two projects both have positive PWs and RORs that are greater than the MARR. But if one has a higher PW but the other has a higher IRR, which criterion should we use?

Example 7.4

Consider the two mutually exclusive alternatives shown in Table 7.3. Alternative A is larger than alternative B: Assuming a MARR of 10%, which alternative should be selected?

Notice that both projects have positive PWs and RORs that are greater than MARR, but PW favors project B, whereas ROR favors project A.

Example 7.5

Now consider the two mutually exclusive projects C and D shown in Table 7.4. Alternative C has decreasing cash inflow, whereas alternative D has increasing cash inflow. Assuming a MARR of 10%, which alternative should be selected?

Table 7.3 Mutually Exclusive Projects of Different Sizes

	Project A	*Project B*
First cost	−$1,000,000	−$10,000,000
AOC	−$50,000	−$500,000
Annual revenue	$300,000	$2,500,000
Life	10	10
PW	$536,142	$2,289,134
ROR	21.41%	15.10%

Table 7.4 Mutually Exclusive Projects with Different Cash Flows

Year	*Project C*	*Project D*
0	−$9,000,000	−$10,000,000
1	$5,000,000	$1,000,000
2	$4,000,000	$2,000,000
3	3,000,000	$3,000,000
4	2,000,000	$4,000,000
5	1,000,000	$5,000,000
6	500,000	$6,000,000
PW	$3,374,369	$4,039,432
ROR	27.50%	19.71%

As was the case in Example 7.4, in Example 7.5, both projects have positive PWs and RORs that are greater than MARR, but PW favors project D, whereas ROR favors project C.

Because basing the choice on an individual project's ROR might not result in selecting the best project, as shown in Examples 7.4 and 7.5, calculate the incremental cash flows between the larger and the smaller first cost alternatives, call it Δ project, and evaluate the Δ project. If ROR of Δ project (Δi*) is greater than MARR, then Δ project is a good project, and we select the project with the larger first cost. Otherwise, we select the project with the smaller first cost. The criteria for selecting Δ project using ROR analysis are presented in Table 7.5.

Table 7.6 shows the incremental cash flows for both alternatives A and B and the Δ project in Example 7.4.

$$\Delta\text{Project} = \text{Project B} - \text{Project A}$$

In other words,

$$\text{Project B} = \text{Project A} + \Delta\text{Project}$$

The Δ project has positive PW and ROR (Δi*) greater than MARR; therefore, it is economically justified. Because Δ project is profitable, we select project B. By selecting project B, we are theoretically selecting project A and an additional profitable project (Δ Project). On the other hand, if we select project A, we are actually giving up a profitable project that would have otherwise increased the value of the firm. Table 7.7 shows the cash flows for projects C and D and incremental cash flows for Δ project in Example 7.5. In this example, because Δ project has positive PW and ROR (Δi*) that is greater than MARR, we select project D with the larger first cost.

Examples 7.4 and 7.5 illustrate why we should use incremental cash flows to evaluate mutually exclusive alternatives rather than comparing alternatives simply based on their individual rate of returns.

Table 7.5 Accept-and-Reject Criteria for Δ Project

*Δi**	*Selection Criteria*
Δi* > MARR	Accept the Δ project because it is economically justified. Select the alternative with the larger first cost.
Δi* = MARR	Indifferent about the Δ project. Indifferent about the alternatives. Select either first cost alternative.
Δi* < MARR	Reject the Δ project because it is not economically justified. Select the alternative with the smaller first cost

Table 7.6 Cash Flows for Projects A & B and Δ Project

	Project A	*Project B*	*Δ Project*
First cost	−$1,000,000	−$10,000,000	−$9,000,000
AOC	−$50,000	−$500,000	−$450,000
Annual revenue	$300,000	$2,500,000	$2,200,000
Life	10	10	10
PW	$536,142	$2,289,134	$1,752,992
ROR	21.41%	15.10%	Δi* = 14.36%

Table 7.7 Cash Flows for Projects C & D and Δ Project

Year	*Project C*	*Project D*	*Δ Project*
0	−\$9,000,000	−\$10,000,000	−\$1,000,000
1	\$5,000,000	\$1,000,000	−\$4,000,000
2	\$4,000,000	\$2,000,000	−\$2,000,000
3	3,000,000	\$3,000,000	0
4	2,000,000	\$4,000,000	\$2,000,000
5	1,000,000	\$5,000,000	\$4,000,000
6	500,000	\$6,000,000	\$5,500,000
PW	\$3,374,369	\$4,039,432	\$1,665,063
ROR	27.50%	19.71%	Δi* = 12.70%

Cost-Based Alternatives

Cost-based competing alternatives are projects that provide the same service and produce the same amount of revenue in the same period. The focus of ROR analysis is to determine the most cost-effective project. In cost-based alternatives, usually the revenue is not provided since both projects generate the same amount of revenue, and because one project is needed, Do-nothing is not an option. The selection criteria are based on the evaluation of the Δ project.

Example 7.6

Mega Cargo airline is considering express delivery to Hanoi in Vietnam and therefore is looking for leasing storage facilities in Hanoi. It is evaluating the lease options for the two locations in Table 7.8. Using ROR analysis and assuming a MARR of 12%, which location should be selected by Mega?

Table 7.9 shows the incremental cash flows for the Δ project.

$$
\begin{aligned}
&\text{PW}\Delta = -\$1{,}500{,}000 + \$350{,}000\ (\text{P/A}, \Delta i^*, 8) + \$500{,}000\ (\text{P/F}, \Delta i^*, 8) = 0\\
&\text{Try}\Delta i^* = 12\%\\
&\text{PW}\Delta = -\$1{,}500{,}000 + \$350{,}000\ (\text{P/A}, 12\%, 8) + \$500{,}000\ (\text{P/F}, 12\%, 8) = 0\\
&\text{PW}\Delta = -\$1{,}500{,}000 + \$350{,}000 \times (4.9676) + \$500{,}000 \times (0.4039)\\
&\text{PW}\Delta = -\$1{,}500{,}000 + \$1{,}738{,}660 + \$201{,}950\\
&\text{PW}\Delta = \$440{,}610
\end{aligned}
$$

Since at Δi* = MARR, the PW of Δ project is positive; this indicates that Δi* > MARR, and Δ project is economically justified. Therefore, the project with larger first cost, location Y, should be selected.

If there are more than two alternatives, we first place them in order of their first cost from the lowest to the highest. Then we compare the first two alternatives. The survivor of the first two alternatives is compared with the third alternative. This process continues until one project has survived and that is the selected alternative.

Revenue-Based Alternatives

When mutually exclusive projects that are being evaluated produce different amounts of revenue in the same period, they are revenue based. ROR analysis determines the most profitable alternative. With revenue-based alternatives, doing nothing becomes an option because it could

Table 7.8 Mega Storage Facility Options in Hanoi, Vietnam

	Location X	*Location Y*
First cost	−$2,000,000	−$4,000,000
AOC	−$500,000	−$150,000
Deposit return	$500,000	$1,000,000
Life, year	8	8

Table 7.9 Incremental Cash Flows for Δ Project

	Location X	*Location Y*	*Δ Project*
First cost	−$2,000,000	−$3,500,000	−$1,500,000
AOC	−$500,000	−$150,000	$350,000
Deposit return	$500,000	$1,000,000	$500,000
Life, year	8	8	8

be that no project is economically justified. The selection criteria, like cost-based alternatives, are based on the evaluation of the Δ project.

Example 7.7

DirectJet is considering purchasing a number of aircraft to expand its operations to either Central America or Latin America. The estimated initial investment, AOC, annual revenue, and potential salvage value for both alternatives are presented in Table 7.10. Which alternative should DirectJet select given a MARR of 8% and using ROR analysis and a study period of 10 years?

Because these projects are revenue based, doing nothing is an option; the smaller first cost project is compared with doing nothing, and the survivor of those two is compared with the second project. Table 7.11 shows incremental cash flows between doing nothing and Central America expansion.

$$PW_{\Delta} = -\$300 + (\$100 - \$50)\,(P/A, \Delta i^{*}, 10) + \$30\,(P/F, \Delta i^{*}, 10) = 0$$

Using trial and error, we start with the MARR:

$$\begin{aligned}
\text{Try}\Delta i^{*} &= 8\% \\
PW_{\Delta} &= -\$300 + (\$100 - \$50)\,(P/A, 8\%, 10) + \$30\,(P/F, 8\%, 10) \\
PW_{\Delta} &= -\$300 + \$50 \times (6.7101) + \$30 \times (0.4632) \\
PW_{\Delta} &= -\$300 + \$335.51 + \$13.90 \\
PW_{\Delta} &= \$49.401
\end{aligned}$$

Since PW of the Δ project is positive, Δi* > MARR, and Δ project is economically justified. Therefore, we eliminate Do-Nothing, and Central America expansion (CAE) survives. Now we compare CAE with Latin America expansion (LAE) (Table 7.12).

shows incremental cash flows between Central America Expansion and Latin America Expansion.

$$PW_{\Delta} = -\$400 + (\$50 + \$20)\,(P/A, \Delta i^{*}, 10) + \$20\,(P/F, \Delta i^{*}, 10) = 0$$

Table 7.10 Airline Expansion Plan

	Central America Expansion	*Latin America Expansion*
First cost	−\$300 million	−\$700 million
AOC	−\$50 million	−\$30 million
Annual revenue	\$100 million	\$150 million
Salvage value	\$30 million	\$50 million
Life, years	10	10

Table 7.11 Airline Incremental Cash Flows for $\Delta_{CAE\text{-}DN}$ Project

	Do-Nothing	*Central America Expansion*	$\Delta_{CAE\text{-}DN}$ *Project*
First cost	\$0.0	−\$300 million	−\$300 million
AOC	\$0.0	−\$50 million	−\$50 million
Annual revenue	\$0.0	\$100 million	\$100 million
Salvage value	\$0.0	\$30 million	\$30 million
Life, years	10	10	10

Table 7.12 Airline Incremental Cash Flows for $\Delta_{LAE\text{-}CAE}$ Project

	CAE	*LAE*	$\Delta_{LAE\text{-}CAE}$ *Project*
First cost	−\$300 million	−\$700 million	−\$400 million
AOC	−\$50 million	−\$30 million	\$20 million
Annual revenue	\$100 million	\$150 million	\$50 million
Salvage value	\$30 million	\$50 million	\$20 million
Life, years	10	10	10

Using trial and error, we start with the MARR:

$$
\begin{aligned}
&\text{Try}\Delta i^* = 8\% \\
&PW_{\Delta} = -\$400 + \$70\ (,8\%,\ 10) + \$20\ (,8\%,\ 10) \\
&PW_{\Delta} = -\$400 + \$70 \times (6.7101) + \$20 \times (0.4632) \\
&PW_{\Delta} = -\$400 + \$469.71 + \$9.26 \\
&PW_{\Delta} = \$78.97
\end{aligned}
$$

Because PW of the Δ project is positive, $\Delta i^* >$ MARR and Δ project is economically justified. Therefore, we eliminate CAE, and DirectJet should choose the Latin America expansion project.

Equal-Life Service Requirement

ROR analysis of mutually exclusive projects requires not only evaluating incremental cash flows but, similar to PW analysis, comparing equal life service. Example 7.8 shows how to compare nonequal lives of mutually exclusive alternatives.

Example 7.8

Royal Aviation Manufacturing is considering selecting one of two cost-based projects to improve efficiency in its operations. Royal uses a MARR of 8%. Using ROR analysis, determine which project should be selected.

Table 7.14 shows the cash flows for both projects over a least common multiple life of six years. We compare two life cycles of Project A with one life cycle of Project B. This table also shows the incremental cash flows between the two alternatives (Δ project).

$$PW_{\Delta} = -\$500{,}000 + \$20{,}000\ (P/A, \Delta i^*, 6) + \$330{,}000\ (P/F, \Delta i^*, 3) + \$20{,}000\ (P/F, \Delta i^*, 6) = 0.$$

Using trial and error, we start with the MARR:

$$\text{Try}\ \Delta i^* = 8\%$$
$$PW_{\Delta} = -\$500{,}000 + \$20{,}000(P/A, 8\%, 6) + \$330{,}000(P/F, 8\%, 3) + \$20{,}000(P/F, 8\%, 6)$$
$$PW_{\Delta} = -\$500{,}000 + \$20{,}000(4.62288) + \$330{,}000(0.79383) + \$20{,}000(0.63017)$$
$$PW_{\Delta} = -\$500{,}000 + \$92{,}457.60 + \$261{,}963.90 + \$12{,}603.40$$
$$PW_{\Delta} = -\$500{,}000 + \$367{,}024.90$$
$$PW_{\Delta} = -\$132{,}975.10$$

Since PW of the Δ project is negative, $\Delta i^* <$ MARR, and Δ project is not economically justified. Therefore, we eliminate Project B and select Project A.

Example 7.9

Legacy Regional Airport (LRA) serving traffic within a relatively lightly populated area in southern France. The airport is considering two mutually exclusive projects, purchasing a weather monitoring system with five-year life or a jet fuel service station with approximately 10-year life. The cash flows for both alternatives are presented in Table 7.15. LRA uses a MARR of 10%. Which alternative should LRA select based on the ROR analysis?

Table 7.13 Royal Aviation Projects

	Project A	*Project B*
First cost	−\$300,000	−\$900,000
AOC	−\$80,000	−\$60,000
Salvage value	\$70,000	\$90,000
Life, years	3	6

Table 7.14 Royal Aviation Incremental Cash Flows for $\Delta_{B\text{-}A}$ Project

Year	*Project A*		*Project B*	Δ_{B-A} *Project*
	First Cycle	*Second Cycle*		
0	−\$400,000		−\$900,000	−500,000
1	−\$80,000		−\$60,000	\$20,000
2	−\$80,000		−\$60,000	\$20,000
3	−\$80,000 + \$70,000	−\$400,000	−\$60,000	\$350,000
4		−\$80,000	−\$60,000	\$20,000
5		−\$80,000	−\$60,000	\$20,000
6		−\$80,000 + \$70,000	−\$60,000 + \$90,000	\$40,000

Table 7.15 Legacy Regional Airport Projects

	Weather Monitoring System	*Jet Fuel Service Station*
First cost	−\$200,000	−\$800,000
Net annual cash flow	\$80,000	\$170,000
Salvage value	\$20,000	\$50,000
Life, years	5	10

Table 7.16 Legacy Regional Airport Incremental Cash Flows for $\Delta_{\text{WMS-DN}}$ Project

	Do-Nothing	*Weather Monitoring System*	$\Delta_{LAE\text{-}CAE}$ *Project*
First cost	\$0.0	−\$200,000	−\$200,000
Net annual cash flow	\$0.0	\$80,000	\$80,000
Salvage value	\$0.0	\$20,000	\$20,000
Life, years	5	5	5

Because these projects are revenue-based alternatives, doing nothing becomes an option. Table 7.16 shows incremental cash flows between Do-Nothing and the weather monitoring system.

$$PW_{\Delta} = -\$200,000 + \$80,000\ (P/A, \Delta i^*, 5) + \$20,000\ (P/F, \Delta i^*, 5) = 0$$

Using trial and error, we start with the MARR:

$$\begin{aligned}
&\text{Try } \Delta i^* = 10\% \\
&\quad PW_{\Delta} = -\$200,000 + \$80,000\ (P/A, 10\%, 5) + \$20,000\ (P/F, 10\%, 5) \\
&\quad PW_{\Delta} = -\$200,000 + \$80,000 \times (3.7908) + \$20,000 \times (0.6209) \\
&\quad PW_{\Delta} = -\$200,000 + \$303,264 + \$12,418 \\
&\quad PW_{\Delta} = \$115,682
\end{aligned}$$

Since PW for Δ project is positive, Δi* > MARR, and Δ project is economically justified. Therefore, we eliminate doing nothing and compare the weather monitoring system (WMS) with the jet fuel station (JFS).

Table 7.17 shows the cash flows for both projects over a life of 10 years. We compare two life cycles of WMS with one life cycle of JFS. This table also shows the incremental cash flows between the two alternatives (Δ project).

To evaluate the ROR for Δ project (Δi*), we set the PW of all cash flows for Δ project to 0 as follows:

$$\begin{aligned}
&\quad PW_{\Delta} = -\$600,000 + \$90,000\ (P/A, \Delta i^*, 10) + \$180,000\ (P/F, \Delta i^*, 5) \\
&\qquad\quad + \$30,000\ (P/V, \Delta i^*, 10) \\
&\text{Try} \Delta i^* = \text{MARR} = 10\% \\
&\quad PW_{\Delta} = -\$600,000 + \$90,000\ (P/A, 10\%, 10) + \$180,000\ (P/F, 10\%, 5) \\
&\qquad\quad + \$30,000\ (P/F, 10\%, 10) \\
&\quad PW_{\Delta} = -\$600,000 + \$90,000\ (6.1446) + \$180,000\ (0.6209) + \$30,000\ (0.3855) \\
&\quad PW_{\Delta} = -\$600,000 + \$553,014 + \$111,762 + \$11,565 \\
&\quad PW_{\Delta} = \$76,341
\end{aligned}$$

Table 7.17 Legacy Regional Incremental Cash Flows for $\Delta_{JFS\text{-}WMS}$ Project

Year	*Weather Monitoring System (WMS)*		*Jet fuel service Station (JFS)*	$\Delta_{JFS\text{-}WMS}$ *Project*
	First Cycle	*Second Cycle*		
0	−$200,000		−$800,000	−600,000
1	$80,000		$170,000	$90,000
2	$80,000		$170,000	$90,000
3	$80,000		$170,000	$90,000
4	$80,000		$170,000	$90,000
5	$80,000 + $20,000	−$200,000	$170,000	$270,000
6		$80,000	$170,000	$90,000
7		$80,000	$170,000	$90,000
8		$80,000	$170,000	$90,000
9		$80,000	$170,000	$90,000
10		$80,000 + $20,000	$170,000 + $50,000	$120,000

Because PW_Δ at MARR of 10% is positive, ROR of the Δ project (Δi*) is greater than MARR, and therefore, Δ project is economically justified. Hence, JFS should be selected.

Evaluating Independent Projects

Projects are independent when one of a group can be selected without affecting any of the others. Evaluating independent projects does not require common lives. The ROR approach to evaluating independent projects is to calculate the ROR of each project, eliminate those projects with ROR less than MARR, and accept the rest of them because they contribute to firm value as long as there is no budget limitation. If there is a budget constraint, then we use PW as explained in Chapter 5. Project quality is not crucial. The only condition for selecting a project is whether the benefit/cost ratio is greater or equal to 1.0.

Example 7.10

Legacy Regional Airport is considering four independent projects with the cash flows presented in Table 7.18. LRA uses a MARR of 9% and has no budget constraint. Using ROR analysis, which of the projects in Table 7.18 should the airport select to maximize the value of the airport?

The ROR for each project is calculated by setting the PW of all cash flows to 0 and solve for i*:

New parking garage:

$$PW = 0$$
$$-\$200 - 10\,(P/A, 9\%, 10) + \$50\,(P/A, 9\%, 10) = 0$$
$$\$200 = (\$50 - \$10)\,(P/A, 9\%, 10)$$
$$\$200 = \$40\,(P/A, 9\%, 10)$$
$$(P/A, 9\%, 10) = 5$$

In Appendix A, compound interest factors, we look in columns under P/A for 10 years with different interest rates until we find an interest rate at which the interest factor is 5. If we cannot find the exact interest factor in the tables, then we interpolate between the two closed interest factors as follows:

Table 7.18 Legacy Regional Airport Independent Projects

	New Parking Garage	*New Runway*	*Expanding C Pier*	*Expanding F Pier*
First cost	−$200 million	−$300 million	−$500 million	−$800 million
Estimated annual operating cost	−$10 million	−$20 million	−$25 million	−$30 million
Estimated annual revenue	$50 million	$45 million	$85 million	$100 million
Life, years	10	20	25	25

i*	(P/A, *i**, 10)
15%	5.0188
15% + X%	5.0
16%	4.8332

$$\frac{X}{1} = \frac{0.0188}{0.1856}$$

$$X\% = \frac{0.0188}{0.1856} = 0.10\%$$

Therefore, ROR = i* = 15.10% > MARR, and the new parking garage is economically justified.

New runway:

$$PW = -\$300 - 20\ (P/A, 9\%, 20) + \$45\ (P/A, 9\%, 20) = 0$$
$$\$300 = (\$45 - \$20)\ (P/A, 9\%, 20)$$
$$\$300 = \$25\ (P/A, 9\%, 20)$$
$$(P/A, 9\%, 10) = 12$$

i*	(P / A, *i**, 20)
5%	12.4622
5% + X%	12.0
6%	11.4699

$$\frac{X}{1} = \frac{0.4622}{0.9923}$$

$$X = \frac{0.4622}{0.9923}$$

$$X = 0.47\%$$

Therefore, ROR = i* = 5.47% < MARR, and the new runway is not economically justified.

Expanding C Pier:

$$PW = -\$500 - 25\ (P/A, 9\%, 25) + \$85\ (P/A, 9\%, 25) = 0$$
$$\$500 = (\$85 - \$25)\ (P/A, 9\%, 25)$$
$$\$500 = \$60\ (P/A, 9\%, 25)$$
$$(P/A, 9\%, 25) = 8.3333$$

i*	(P/A, i*, 25)
11%	8.4217
11% + X%	8.3333
12%	7.8431

$$\frac{X}{1} = \frac{0.0884}{0.5786}$$

$$X = \frac{0.0884}{0.5786}$$

$$X = 0.15\%$$

Therefore, ROR = i* = 11.15% > MARR, and expanding C Pier is economically justified.

Expanding F Pier:

$$PW = -\$800 - 30\ (P/A, 9\%, 25) + \$100\ (P/A, 9\%, 25) = 0$$
$$\$800 = (\$100 - \$30)\ (P/A, 9\%, 25)$$
$$\$800 = \$70\ (P/A, 9\%, 25)$$
$$(P/A, 9\%, 25) = 11.4286$$

i*	(P/A, i*, 10)
7%	11.6536
7% + X%	11.4286
8%	10.6748

$$\frac{X}{1} = \frac{0.2250}{0.9788}$$

$$X = \frac{0.2250}{0.9788} = 0.23\%$$

Therefore, ROR = i* = 7.23% < MARR, and expanding F Pier is not economically justified. Therefore, of the four projects LRA is considering, only the new parking garage and C Pier expansion are economically justified.

Complications with ROR

Most investments start with an initial investment followed by a stream of positive cash flows over the life of the project. For projects with this pattern of cash flows, where the initial investment or first cost is negative and the rest of the cash flows are positive, there is only one unique ROR for that project. If the ROR is greater that the firm's MARR, then both PW and AW are positive, and all three techniques mutually indicate that the project is economically justified. Next we discuss complications with ROR analysis.

Multiple Rates of Return

For unconventional projects where there is more than one infusion of capital (initial investment) over the original life of the project or there are multiple sign changes in the cash flow stream, there is possibility of more than one ROR. In that case, no RORs are valid, and we should use PW and AW, where only one PW and one AW exist for each project. Alternatively, we could use modified ROR analysis as explained later in this chapter.

Example 7.11

Consider a project with unconventional cash flow stream presented in Table 7.19. Calculate ROR.

Table 7.20 presents different interest rates and their corresponding PWs. Note that PW becomes 0 at 2.387% and 16.75%. By definition, those are the two RORs for this project.

The two RORs for Example 7.10 are also depicted in Figure 7.5.

ROR Reinvestment Rate Assumption

PW analysis implicitly assumes that the generated cash flows from a project can be reinvested at MARR, while ROR analysis implies that a firm can reinvest the generated cash flows from a project at the ROR. Although there may be many projects available to yield MARR, the firm may not find another project that provides the same ROR. Therefore, assuming reinvestment rate with PW analysis seems more reasonable than doing so with ROR.

Modified Rate of Return Analysis

Modified rate of return (MROR) was developed to allow decision-makers the intuitive appeal of the ROR but be able to eliminate the problem of multiple RORs with the ability to directly specify the appropriate reinvestment rate. The idea behind MROR is to shift all negative cash flows after first cost to time 0 at MARR and add it to the first cost. In addition, shift all positive cash flows to the end of the project at the rate of MARR, add it to the salvage value, and call it terminal cash flow. The MROR is an interest rate (mi*) that sets PW for all cash flows, first costs, and terminal cash flows to 0. The criteria to select or to reject a project are summarized in Table 7.21.

Table 7.19 Cash Flow Stream of an Unconventional Project

Year	*Cash Flows*
0	251,000
1	−550,000
2	300,000

Table 7.20 Interest Rates and Corresponding PWs

Interest Rate	*Present Worth*
0.00%	$1,000
2.38%	$0
5%	−$701
10%	−$1,066
15%	−$418
16.75%	$0
20%	$1,000

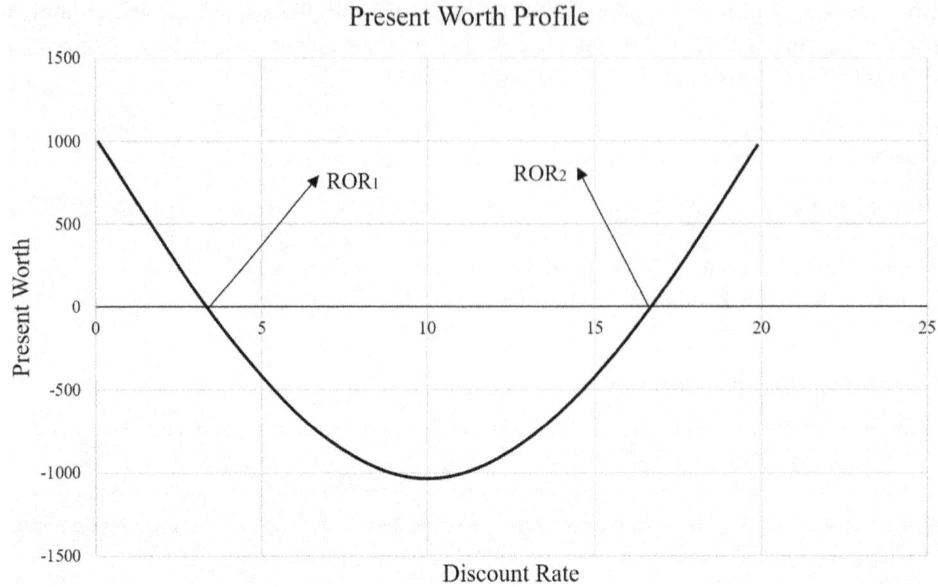

Figure 7.5 Multiple rates of return.

Table 7.21 Accept-and-Reject Criteria for Modified Rate of Return

MROR (mi)*	*Selection Criteria*
MROR (mi*) > MARR	Accept the project because it is economically justified
MROR (mi*) = MARR	Indifference about the project, but it is still economically justified.
MROR (mi*) < MARR	Reject the project because it is not economically justified.

Example 7.12

In Example 7.11, calculate the MROR assuming MARR is 10%:

$$\text{First cost} = -\$550{,}000\ (\text{P/F}, 10\%, 1)$$
$$\text{First cost} = -\$550{,}000 \times (0.9091)$$
$$\text{First cost} = -\$500{,}005$$
$$\text{Terminal cash flow} = \$251{,}000\ (\text{F/P}, 10\%, 2) + \$300{,}000$$
$$\text{Terminal cash flow} = \$251{,}000 \times (1.2100) + \$300{,}000$$
$$\text{Terminal cash flow} = \$303{,}710 + \$300{,}000$$
$$\text{Terminal cash flow} = \$603{,}710$$
$$PW = 0$$
$$-500{,}005 + \$603{,}710\ (F/P, mi^*, 2) = 0$$
$$\$500{,}005 = \$603{,}710\ (F/P, mi^*, 2)$$
$$(F/P, mi^*, 2) = 0.8282$$

We now go to Appendix A for compound interest factors, and in each table, we look for 0.8282 in the columns under F/P for two years. If we could not find the exact interest factor value in the tables, then we would interpolate between the two closed values.

i*	(F/P, mi*, 2)
9%	0.8417
9% + X%	0.8282
10%	0.8264

$$\frac{X}{1} = \frac{0.0135}{0.0153}$$

$$X = \frac{0.0135}{0.0153} = 0.88\%$$

Therefore, MROR = mi* = 9.88% < MARR, and this project is not economically justified.

Calculating ROR in Excel

This section presents how to calculate ROR using Excel functions. The ROR equation in Excel is called Internal Rate of Return and denoted as IRR. To calculate IRR, we enter the following function in a cell:

= IRR(Cell [0]:Cell [n])

where (Cell [0]:Cell [n]) is the range of cash flows from period [0] to period [n]. Cell [0] is the first cost or initial investment (Year 0), and Cell [n] is the NACF in year n (the last year).

Example 7.13

The cash flows for an investment for five years are presented in Table 7.22. Calculate ROR of this investment using Excel.

Figure 7.6 shows the Excel solution for the project in Example 7.13. The cash flow in year 0 is the first cost, and NACFs are in years one through five. The function is in cell B9, and the solution appears when you hit Enter. As you will note, the NACFs do not represent a uniform series: Enter them in a cell, enter IRR, and hit Enter. Excel makes it very easy to use trial and error.

Table 7.22 Cash Flows for Five Years for Calculating ROR

Year	*NACF*
0	–$200,000
1	$40,000
2	$60,000
3	$80,000
4	$60,000
5	$40,000

	A	B
1		
2	**Year**	**NACF**
3	0	($200,000)
4	1	$40,000
5	2	$60,000
6	3	$80,000
7	4	$60,000
8	5	$40,000
9	ROR	=IRR(B3:B8)

	A	B
1		
2	**Year**	**NACF**
3	0	($200,000)
4	1	$40,000
5	2	$60,000
6	3	$80,000
7	4	$60,000
8	5	$40,000
9	ROR	12.26%

Figure 7.6 Calculating ROR in Excel.

Summary

Rate of return analysis is used often by professional engineers and individual investors to evaluate the return on their investments and select the best alternative among the competing alternatives. ROR is defined as the interest rate (i*) that sets present worth of all cash flows, both inflows and outflows, to 0. Although PW and AW are easier to calculate, the ROR is the most frequently used and is easily understood by professional engineers, leaders, and individual investors: If ROR > MARR, accept the project; if not, reject the project. If ROR = MARR, we are indifferent about the project.

When ROR analysis is used to select the best project among mutually exclusive alternatives, the project with the best ROR might not be the best project, as we showed in this chapter. Therefore, the incremental cash flows between the larger and the smaller alternatives based on their first cost (known as Δ project) need to be calculated, and the Δ project or the extra project is to be evaluated. If Δ project is economically justified, the project with the larger first cost is selected; otherwise, we select the project with smaller first cost. If ROR ≥ MARR, then Δ project is economically justified, and the project with higher first cost is to be selected. If ROR < MARR, then Δ project is not economically justified, and the project with lower first cost is to be selected.

Comparing mutually exclusive alternatives is not only based on evaluating incremental cash flows or Δ project but also requires equivalent service lives. In comparing cost-based competing alternatives, doing nothing is not an option, whereas it is for revenue-based alternatives. If there are more than two alternatives, we first place them in order of their first cost from the lowest to the highest. Then, we compare the first two and compare the survivor with the third. This process continues until one project has survived and that is the selected alternative.

Using ROR to evaluate independent projects involves calculating ROR for each project, eliminating projects if ROR < MARR, and accept the rest of them because they contribute to firm value as long as there is no budget limitation. If there is a budget constraint, then we use PW as explained in Chapter 5. ROR can be complicated if there are multiple and also because of the underlying reinvestment rate assumption. We presented modified rate of return (MROR) to eliminate ROR complications. The selection criteria are the same for both ROR and MROR.

The ROR equation in Excel is called Internal Rate of Return and denoted as IRR. To calculate ROR, simply enter the project's cash flows into IRR.

Discussion Questions and Problems

7.1 Define rate of return.

7.2 What are the ROR criteria for accepting or rejecting a project?

7.3 What are the differences between ROR and PW analysis in evaluating mutually exclusive alternatives?

7.4 What are the complications of ROR analysis and how can they be resolved?

7.5 Heritage Airways is planning to expand its fleet by purchasing five B737s at $465 million. A local bank is lending Heritage $465 million with the agreement that Heritage will pay the bank $80 million per year for the next 10 years. What is the ROR for the bank on this investment (loan)?

7.6 In Problem 7.5, assume that Heritage pays $100 million at the end of 10 years in addition to the annual payments of $80 million. What would be the ROR on this loan to the bank? If the bank's MARR is 14%, is this investment economically justified?

7.7 Avian Air Cargo is considering an investment of $10 million to purchase facilities with life expectancy of 10 years and annual operating cost of $400,000 in year one that increases $50,000 per year from the second year through the life of the project. Avion anticipates a stream of $2,500,000 in revenue per year from this project for 10 years. Calculate the ROR for this project and explain whether is is economically justified. Assume MARR is 12%.

7.8 Royal Aviation Consulting Group is issuing a new bond with a face value of $1,000 and a coupon rate of 10% paid annually, with 10 years to maturity. As an investor, if you purchase this bond at price of $920 and hold it to maturity, what will be your ROR on this investment?

7.9 Legacy Airport has a new bond issue with face value of $1,000 and coupon rate of 8%, with 10 years to maturity. As an investor, if you pay $850 to purchase this bond, what will be your ROR on this bond assuming interest is paid semiannually?

7.10 DirectJet has a bond issue with face value of $1,000 and coupon rate of 8%, with 10 years to maturity. The interest is paid annually. You are considering purchasing this bond at $1050. Assuming MARR of 6% compounded semiannually, what is your ROR on this bond and is this investment economically justified?

7.11 DirectJet is considering leasing one of the following hangars for 10 years. Using ROR and assuming MARR of 12%, which hangar should the airline lease?

	Hangar A	*Hangar B*
First cost	−$2,000,000	−$3,000,000
Annual operating cost	−$500,000	−$200,000
Deposit return	$400,000	$800,000
Life, years	10	10

7.12 Heritage Airways is considering a new route to Ho Chi Minh City, Vietnam, or Sydney, Australia. The first cost, AOC, expected annual revenue, and potential salvage value for both alternatives are presented in the following table. Assume a MARR of 10% and a study period of 10 years. Which alternative route should Heritage Airways select?

	Ho Chi Minh City Route Vietnam	*Sydney Route Australia*
Initial investment (First cost)	−$300 million	−$500 million
Annual operating cost	−$50 million	−$80 million
Annual revenue	$100 million	$180 million
Salvage value	$30 million	$50 million
Life, years	10	10

7.13 Legacy Airport is considering two mutually exclusive projects: purchasing a weather monitoring system with five-year life or a jet fuel service station with approximately 10-year life. The cash flows for both alternatives are presented in the following table. Legacy uses a MARR of 8%. Which alternative should it select based on ROR analysis?

	Weather Monitoring System	*Jet Fuel Service Station*
First cost	−$300,000	−$600,000
AOC	−$40,000	−$20,000
Annual revenue	$120,000	$180,000
Salvage value	$20,000	$50,000
Life, years	5	10

7.14 Royal Racing Motor Corporation is considering the following two mutually exclusive project for improving the efficiency of their fighter jects. Select the best alternative using ROR analysis with a MARR of 10%.

	Project A	*Project B*
First cost	−$350,000	−$470,000
Annual operating cost	−$50,000	−$30,000
Salvage value	$35,000	$47,000
Life, years	2	4

7.15 Mid-East Airfreight is considering two mutually exclusive projects for operational improvement. The cash flows for both alternatives are presented in the next table. Using a MARR of 10%, which alternative should Mid-East select based on ROR analysis?

	Project C	*Project D*
First cost	−$1,000,000	−$6,000,000
Net annual cash flow	$500,000	$1,500,000
Salvage value	$100,000	$400,000
Life, years	3	9

7.16 Majestic Aviation Corporation is evaluating the following two mutually exclusive alternatives to improve the strength of the cockpit door for their signature aircraft. Majestic uses a MARR of 10%. Select the best alternative using ROR analysis.

	Project A	*Project B*
First cost	−$400,000	−$900,000
Annual operating cost	−$80,000	−$50,000
Salvage value	$40,000	$90,000
Life, years	4	6

7.17 Legacy Regional Airport is considering three independent projects with cash flows presented in the following table. The airport uses a MARR of 12% and has no budget constraint. Using ROR analysis, which of the independent projects, if any, should be selected to maximize the value of the airport?

	New Parking Garage	*Expanding Existing Terminal*	*Building New Terminal*
First cost	−$120 million	−$540 million	−$780 million
Estimated annual operating cost	−$5 million	−$25 million	−$30 million
Estimated annual revenue	$25 million	$85 million	$150 million
Life, years	20	25	25

7.18 Legacy International Airport is considering an investment of $5 million in constructing facilities to provide jet fuel to the airlines with life expectancy of 10 years and AOC of $300,000 in year one, increasing by $50,000 per year from the second year through the life of the project. Legacy anticipates a stream of $2.5 million revenue in year one with an annual increase of 8% per year through the end of 10 years. Calculate MROR for this project and explain whether it is economically justified. Legacy is using a MARR of 10%.

Notes

1 Lewis, N., et al. (2021). *Engineering Economic Analysis* (14th Edition). Oxford University Press.
2 Blank, L. & Tarquin, A. (2021). *Basics of Engineering Economy* (3rd Edition). McGraw-Hill.
3 Saadi, D. (2016, March). *The National Business*.

References

Blank, L. & Tarquin, A. (2021). *Basics of Engineering Economy* (3rd Edition). McGraw-Hill.
Lewis, N., et al. (2021). *Engineering Economic Analysis* (14th Edition). Oxford University Press.

8 Public-Sector Projects and Cost–Benefit Analysis

The transition from government ownership to the free-market system has gone especially well for air transport industry. From the start, the government's objective was to create strong partnership between the public and private sectors. Throughout the world, governments were turning over to the private sector everything from airports and airlines to public utilities.[1]
From time to time, outdated air navigation systems,[2] crumbling bridges, and shabby airport terminals remind us of the need for increased investment in maintaining transport infrastructure. In the United States, most airports request funding from the Federal Aviation Administration (FAA) for airport improvement or expansion projects such as adding or expanding terminals. One method the FAA uses in considering these requests is cost–benefit analysis (CBA). Private-sector projects tend to use the analysis techniques we discussed in the previous chapters; for public-sector projects, CBA is a common method of evaluating the costs to the public of proposed projects: When the ratio of public benefits to public costs is equal to or greater than 1, the project is economically justified. CBA, similar the rate of return analysis, is based on evaluating the incremental cash flows when mutually exclusive projects are being evaluated. Present or annual worth values are utilized to calculate benefit/cost (B/C) ratios. If present worth values are applied, then the equivalent service lives for mutually exclusive alternatives are required.

The focus of this chapter is to enable readers and practitioners to use CBA to evaluate single public projects, compare mutually exclusive public alternatives, and select among independent public projects. In the chapter, we address calculating B/C ratios for single public project using present or annual worth as well as modified B/C ratios.

Public-Sector vs Private-Sector Projects

In previous chapters, we have evaluated projects in the private sector, and the criterion we used was the economic justification of the projects. In other words, if projects had positive present worth (PW), we accepted them. Public projects are owned by the public sector: federal, state, county, city, and other government agencies. Public-sector investments are usually intended to benefit the public in some way.

Most public-sector investments are in infrastructure (e.g., airports, highways, roads, bridges, dams, hospitals, police and fire departments, courts and prisons, public housing, and clean energy projects). The US Federal Aviation Administration (FAA) has clear and thorough guidelines for project-level cost–benefit analysis, CBA,[3] that it uses to calculate benefit/cost (B/C) ratios for airport projects competing for funding under the Airport Improvement Program (AIP). For any projects requesting AIP funds, total discounted benefits must exceed total discounted costs.

Other public-sector investments are designed to support public leisure activities such as parks and recreation, lakes, museums, sport arenas, convention centers, and libraries. The government

DOI: 10.4324/9781003469759-8

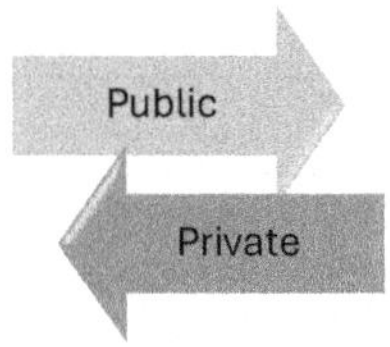

Figure 8.1 Public vs private.

also invests in projects to defend the country such as military bases, weaponry, artillery, and software. Although these projects are very important, we cannot evaluate them based on maximizing worth. Generally, the public sector or government exists to serve the public and the investment decisions they make should reflect that goal. As long as the public benefits exceed the costs to the public, or B/C ratio ≥ 1, the public project is economically justified.

The government also uses CBA to consider regulatory proposals that would be costly to implement but that would have potentially large benefits to society, such as the HHS Covid-19 campaign during April 2021 to March 2022.[4]

Public projects have a number of common characteristics, such as size. Most public projects such as airports, highways, and public transportation require significant initial investment, possibly distributed over several years. In recent years, we have seen accelerated partnerships between public entities and private companies, as funding for large public projects becomes more challenging. Another common feature is lifespan: Public projects such as airports, bridges, dams, and highways are considered permanent.

Additionally, public-sector investments are usually developed to benefit the public in some way; while the goal of the private sector is to maximize the company's worth, the goal of public projects is to provide services to the public at minimized cost and no profit. Some public-sector investments have negative impacts on some groups even as they benefit others, and the negative consequences of public projects are called disbenefits and are usually estimated in monetary units.

Let's look at the benefits and disbenefits of constructing an international airport as a public project. The primary benefits will be the airport's vast economic impact. Commercial airports are often economic engines that drive local, regional, and national economies. Airports are significant generators of economic activities including creating jobs, payroll, and total output for the economy. Table 8.1 presents total impacts of the 485 commercial airports, broken down into on-airport activities, capital improvement projects (CIP), and visitor categories. Total impacts show the combined effects of the direct and multiplier impact. These economic impacts are a considerable contribution to the national economy. In total, we found that US commercial airports generate an annual payroll of $358 billion, produce a $1.135 trillion annual output, and support 9.6 million jobs.

An international airport will open a country to the global air transportation network. Airports accommodate the travel needs of business and leisure visitors in the country and beyond; with airports, communities have access not just to other parts of their own countries but every airport in the world. Airports drive business growth: New airports increase the value added by manufacturers, retail and wholesale trades, and service business volume. Airports are also industry magnets; they are commonly found in the center of commercial and industrial development. Some industrial facilities are located at or near airports because they have a direct need for access to air transport. New industries not only provide more employment and improve community economies but also increase tax revenues for local governments.

Table 8.1 Economic Benefits of Commercial Airports in the United States

Impact Measure	*On-Airport*	*CIP*	*Visitor*	*U.S. Total*
Employment	3,490,640	176,160	5,929,540	9,596,340
Payroll	$177,019 m	$5,114 m	$175,727 m	$357,860 m
Economic Output	$617,630 m	$31,600 m	$485,949 m	$1,135,179 m

Source: NCI-NA 2014.

New airports also help retain existing industry. Air transportation has become increasingly important to local industry representatives by helping them retain and improve their competitive positions in local, national, and international markets. Commercial airports are now driving the new urban form. Airports are no longer just aviation infrastructures; they are becoming multimodal, multifunctional enterprises that generate significant commercial development within and well beyond their boundaries. Major airports are expanding to include shopping malls, entertainment amenities, theme restaurants, electronic shops, internet cafés, and other businesses to form so-called airport cities. Airports are also integral to cargo logistics and supply chains. Global supply chains are becoming firms' new competitive edge. Speed, reliability, and agility are becoming as important as price in many high-value sectors.

However, there are major disbenefits to an international airport, most obviously the noise. Noise from aircraft and from traffic going to and from airports is easily perceived and annoying and will be frequent with an international airport. Airports also generate air pollution through combustion of jet fuel, inefficiency of engine on approach, fuel dumping by aircraft releases, vehicles traveling to and from airport, and various emissions from construction. These activities contribute to emission of carbon monoxide, nitrogen oxide, nitrogen dioxide, and ozone, which in turn contribute to greenhouse gases and in turn climate change. Airports will also have impacts on local biodiversity (plants and animals); habitat loss occurs when previously green areas are built on. Airports can also have negative community impacts, especially if they are not well thought out. House values around airports can fall due to noise, air pollution, and other negative impacts. The number of children attending schools in the area could fall, as could the number of people participating in community activities. In contrast to airport benefits, which can be fairly easily converted into monetary value, it is not always easy to monetize disbenefits.

However, sometimes disbenefit is clearly estimable. For example, a city official issues $50 million, 10-year bond with coupon rate of 5% paid annually to build a new high school to accommodate the growing numbers of middle school graduates and the high-school-age children of families who are moving to this city. The city increases property taxes per year in equal amounts for the next 10 years to pay off the interest and the $50 million bond face value to bondholders. In this example, the benefits are clear for students and their families as well as all who would benefit from the school, but there is a disbenefit to property owners who do not have students in high school, or perhaps any children.

While the benefits are not as clearly estimable, the disbenefits can be clearly calculated. If the city can earn 5% on its investment, the annual disbenefit comes to $6,475,000, and it is the AW of the $50 million today at 5% interest rate as follows:

AW = PW (A/P, 5%, 10)
AW = $50,000,000 (0.1295)
AW = $6,475,000

CBA of Single Projects

As we discussed earlier, public-sector projects are often evaluated based on the B/C ratio, and there are two types of ratio, conventional and modified; in this section, we look at the conventional ratio. PW, AW, and FW are utilized to calculate B/C ratios; benefits, disbenefits, and all costs must be converted to a common equivalent worth (PW, AW, and FW) at MARR using the following equation:

$$Conventional\ B/C\ Ratio = \frac{Benefits - Disbenefits}{First\ cost + AOC \quad Salvage\ value\left(Savings\right)}$$

$$Conventional\ B/C\ Ratio = \frac{B - D}{P + AOC - S}$$

where B = benefits, D = disbenefits, P = first cost or initial investment, AOC = annual operating cost, and S = salvage value or savings.

Using PW requires equivalent service lives for mutually exclusive alternatives. CBA, similar to rate of return analysis, is based on incremental cash flows for mutually exclusive projects. *In this chapter and only this chapter, costs will have positive signs*. The criteria to select or to reject a project are summarized in Table 8.2.

Example 8.1

Legacy Regional Airport (LRA) is owned and operated by the Legacy Airport Authority (LAA). LRA is conveniently located in the southwestern United States and offers commercial services all over the United States and a few foreign destinations. Due to significant increases in the number of flights and high passenger traffic, the LAA is considering a proposal to build a new rental car complex. The initial investment is estimated to be \$200 million with an annual operating cost of \$5 million. This is a 20-year project with annual benefit (revenue from car rental companies) of \$35 million, disbenefit to the public of \$2 million per year, and a salvage value of \$20 million. Using conventional B/C ratio with MARR of 8%, is this project economically justified?

To calculate the B/C ratio, we need to convert all costs, benefits, and disbenefits to a common equivalent worth. Because most of the information is provided in annual worth, we convert the rest to AW:

AW of benefits = \$35 million
AW of disbenefits = \$2 million
AW of AOC = \$5 million

Table 8.2 Accept-and-Reject Criteria for B/C Ratio

	Selection Criteria
B/C > 1	Accept the project because it is economically justified.
B/C = 1	Indifference about the project, but it is still economically justified.
B/C < 1	Reject the project because it is not economically justified.

$$\text{AW of initial investment (P)} = \$200\ (A/P, 8\%, 20) = \$200\ (0.10185) = \$20.37 \text{ million}$$
$$\text{AW of salvage} = \$20\ (A/F, 8\%, 20) = \$20\ (0.02185) = \$0.44 \text{ million}$$

$$B/C = \frac{\$35 - \$2}{\$20.37 + \$5 - \$0.44}$$
$$B/C = \frac{\$33}{\$24.93}$$
$$B/C = 1.32 > 1$$

Because the B/C ratio is greater than 1, the car rental complex project is economically justified.

Example 8.2

A city water department is planning to spend \$5,000,000 to build a treatment plant to remove certain heavy metals from well water. The plant's operating cost is \$1,000,000 per year. Public health benefits are expected to be \$2,000,000 per year. The life of the project is 20 years with no salvage value. At 5% per year, evaluate this project using conventional B/C ratio with PW:

$$\text{PW of benefits} = \$2{,}000{,}000\ (P/A, 5\%, 20)$$
$$\text{PW of benefits} = \$2{,}000{,}000\ (12.46221)$$
$$\text{PW of benefits} = \$24{,}924{,}420$$
$$\text{PW of first cost} = \$5{,}000{,}000$$
$$\text{PW of AOC} = \$1{,}000{,}000\ (P/A, 5\%, 20)$$
$$\text{PW of AOC} = \$1{,}000{,}000\ (12.46221)$$
$$\text{PW of AOC} = \$12{,}462{,}210$$

$$B/C = \frac{\$24{,}924{,}420 - 0}{\$5{,}000{,}000 + \$12{,}462{,}210}$$
$$B/C = \frac{\$24{,}924{,}420}{\$17{,}462{,}210}$$
$$B/C = 1.43 > 1$$

Because the B/C ratio of the project is greater than 1, the project is economically justified.

Example 8.3

Monarch Airport is considering the construction of a new terminal. This project is permanent, with first cost of \$500 million and additional investment of \$50 million every 10 years. No salvage value is expected. The revenue from the new terminal (benefits) is expected to be \$100 million per year, and the disbenefits are estimated at \$4 million per year. AOC = \$15 million per year. Monarch uses a MARR of 10%. Using a conventional B/C ratio with AW, determine whether this project is economically justified:

$$\text{AW of Benefits} = \$100\text{m}$$
$$\text{AW of Disbenefits} = \$4\text{m}$$
$$\text{AW of AOC} = \$15\text{m}$$
$$\text{AW of P} = \$500\text{m}\,(0.10) + \$50\text{m}\,(A/F, 10\%, 10) = \$50\text{m} + \$50\text{m}\,(0.06275)$$
$$\text{AW of P} = \$50\text{m} + 3.14\text{m} = 53.14\text{m}$$

$$BC = \frac{\$100\,m - \$4\,m}{\$53.14\,m + \$15\,m} = \frac{\$96\,m}{\$68.14\,m} = 1.41 > 1$$

Because the B/C ratio of the new terminal is greater than 1, it is economically justified.

Example 8.4

In Example 8.3, calculate conventional B/C ratio using PW:

$$\text{PW of Benefits} = \$100\,m/0.10 = \$1{,}000\,m$$
$$\text{PW of Disbenefits} = \$4\,m/0.10 = \$40\,m$$
$$\text{PW of AOC} = \$15\,m/0.10 = 150\,m$$
$$\text{PW of P} = \$500\,m + \$50\,m\,(A/F, 10\%, 10)/0.10 = \$500\,m + \$50\,m\,(0.06275)/0.10$$
$$\text{PW of P} = \$500\,m + \$31.38\,m = \$531.38$$
$$BC = \frac{\$1{,}000\,m - \$40\,m}{\$531.38\,m + \$150\,m} = \frac{\$960\,m}{\$681.38\,m} = 1.41 > 1$$

Because the B/C ratio of the new terminal is greater than 1, it is economically justified.

Evaluating Cost-Based Mutually Exclusive Alternatives

To select among the mutually exclusive alternatives using conventional B/C ratio, we first arrange alternatives in order of their total cost expressed in equivalent worth; then we compare two alternatives at a time. Comparing mutually exclusive alternatives introduces the problem of different sizes: Projects with a larger initial investment might have a higher PW but a lower B/C ratio than projects with a smaller initial investment. Similar to ROR analysis in Chapter 7, to overcome this problem, we evaluate mutually exclusive alternatives based on the incremental cash flows or create a Δ project and then evaluating it.

Cost-based competing alternatives have no direct benefits; the implied benefits come from cost savings to the public when we compare the alternatives. Therefore, calculate the B/C ratio of the Δ project (ΔB/C), and there are more than two alternatives, compare the survivor of the first two with the next one and continue this process continues until one project survives. Using PW to calculate the B/C ratio requires equal service lives for comparison, although most public projects are considered permanent and therefore generally have equal lives. Finally, for cost-based mutually exclusive alternatives, doing nothing is not an option since there is no direct benefit associated with the alternatives. The Δ project selection criteria are presented in Table 8.3.

Example 8.5

Legacy Regional Airport (LRA) is considering solar and power line alternatives to light the airport. The costs associated with each alternative are shown in Table 8.4. Use conventional

Table 8.3 Accept-and-Reject Criteria for Δ Project

ΔB/C Ratio	*Selection Criteria*
$\Delta B/C > 1$	Since Δ project is economically justified, select the alternative with the larger total cost.
$\Delta B/C = 1$	Indifferent about the Δ project. Indifferent about the alternatives. Select either alternatives.
$\Delta B/C < 1$	Since Δ project is not economically justified, select the alternative with the smaller total cost.

Table 8.4 Cash Flows for Two Alternatives

	Power Line	*Solar Cell*
First cost	$10 million	$20 million
AOC to public	$5 million	$2 million
Salvage value	$0	$5 million
Estimated life, years	10	10

B/C analysis with AW to determine which alternative should be selected. LRA uses a MARR of 10%.

Because these alternatives are cost based projectdoing do nothing is not an option; the benefits come from the AOC saving. Table 8.5 presents the incremental cash flows for the Δ Project.

$$\text{AW of P} = \$10\,(\text{A/P}, 10\%, 10) = \$10\,(0.16275) = \$1.6275$$

$$\text{AW of Benefits} = \$3$$

$$\text{Modified B/C} = \$5\,(\text{A/F}, 10\%, 10)$$

$$\text{Modified B/C} = \$5\,(0.06275) = \$0.3136$$

$$\Delta\text{B/C} = \frac{\Delta\text{B} - \Delta\text{D}}{\Delta\text{TC} - \Delta\text{S}}$$

$$\Delta\text{B/C} = \frac{\$3 - \$0}{\$1.6275 - \$0.3136}$$

$$\Delta\text{B/C} = \frac{\$3}{\$1.314}$$

$$\Delta\text{B/C} = 2.28 > 1$$

Because the ΔB/C ratio is greater than 1, the Δ project is economically justified. Select solar power, which has the largest total cost.

Evaluating Benefit-Based Mutually Exclusive Alternatives

Benefit-based projects have direct benefits to the public. To evaluate benefit-based mutually exclusive alternatives using B/C ratio, we follow the same procedure for cost-based alternatives except that doing nothing is now an option. First, compare that option with the project with the lowest total cost is compared; then compare the survivor with the next alternative in line and continue doing so until there is a final surviving best alternative.

Example 8.6

LRA is considering three mutually exclusive alternatives shown in Table 8.6 (in millions) to accommodate its increasing traffic. Using conventional B/C ratio with MARR of 8%, which project should LRA select?

Because projects have different lives, it is best to use AW, and therefore we first convert all cash flows to AW (Table 8.7):

AW of first cost for NEPG = $200 (A/P, 8%, 15) = $200 (0.11683) = $23.37
AW of first cost for CAE = $500 (A/P, 8%, 25) = $500 (0.09368) = $46.84

Table 8.5 Cash Flows for Both Alternatives and Incremental Cash Flows for Δ Project.

	Power Line	*Solar Cell*	$\Delta_{SC\text{-}PL}$
First cost	$10 million	$20 million	$10 million
AOC	$5 million	$2 million	$3 million (Benefits)
Salvage value	$0	$5 million	$5 million
Estimated life, years	10	10	10

Table 8.6 Legacy Regional Airport Mutually Exclusive Projects

	New Economy Parking Garage (NEPG)	*Concourse A Expansion (CAE)*	*Concourse B Expansion (CBE)*
First cost	$200	$500	$300
Estimated AOC	$10	$20	$15
Estimated annual revenue	$50	$100	$85
Disbenefit incurred at t = 0	$20	$10	$10
Salvage value	$20	$50	$30
Life, years	15	25	20

Table 8.7 Legacy Regional Airport Mutually Exclusive Projects in AW (in USD millions)

	New Economy Parking Garage	*Concourse A Expansion*	*Concourse B Expansion*
AW of first cost	$23.37	$46.84	$30.56
AW of AOC	$10	$20	$15
AW of benefits	$50	$100	$85
AW of disbenefits	$2.34	$0.94	$1.02
AW of salvage value	$0.74	$0.68	$0.66
Life, years	10	10	10

$$\begin{aligned}
\text{AW of first cost for CBE} &= \$300\ (A/P, 8\%, 20) = \$300\ (0.10185) = \$30.56 \\
\text{AW of D for NEPG} &= \$20\ (A/P, 8\%, 15) = \$20\ (0.11683) = \$2.34 \\
\text{AW of D for CAE} &= \$10\ (A/P, 8\%, 25) = \$10\ (0.09368) = \$0.94 \\
\text{AW of D for CBE} &= \$10\ (A/P, 8\%, 20) = \$10\ (0.10185) = \$1.02 \\
\text{AW of S for NEPG} &= \$20\ (A/F, 8\%, 15) = \$20\ (0.03683) = \$0.74 \\
\text{AW of S for CAE} &= \$50\ (A/F, 8\%, 25) = \$50\ (0.01368) = \$0.68 \\
\text{AW of S for CBE} &= \$30\ (A/F, 8\%, 20) = \$30\ (0.02185) = \$0.66
\end{aligned}$$

Because all cash flows are converted to AW and AW is used to calculate conventional B/C ratios, project life is irrelevant, and we eliminate it.

Because these projects are benefit based, doing nothing is an option. First, we calculate total costs of all projects and rearrange them in order of increasing total costs in AW, and we add doing nothing as the first alternative. As before, we compare the first two alternatives and continue pairing each survivor with the next alternative until there is a final survivor. We now rearrange projects in Table 8.8 and add doing nothing as the first alternative.

Δ Project = NEPG – DN

Table 8.8 Legacy Regional Airport Projects in Order of Their Total Cost (in USD millions)

	Do Nothing	*NEPG*	*CBE*	*CAE*
AW of total cost	$0	$33.37	$45.56	$66.84
AW of benefits	$0	$50	$85	$100
AW of disbenefits	$0	$2.34	$1.02	$.94
AW of salvage value	$0	$0.74	$0.66	$0.68
Life, years	10	10	10	10

Table 8.9 Comparison of Doing Nothing with New Economy Parking Garage (in USD millions)

	Do Nothing	*NEPG*	*Δ Project NEPG – DN*
AW of total cost	$0	$33.37	$33.37
AW of benefits	$0	$50	$50
AW of disbenefits	$0	$2.34	$2.34
AW of salvage value	$0	$0.74	$0.74
Life, years	10	10	10

Table 8.9 presents the cash flows for two projects and the incremental cash flows for the Δ Project.

$$\Delta \text{B/C} = \frac{\$50 - \$2.34}{\$33.37 - \$0.74}$$

$$\Delta \text{B/C} = \frac{\$47.66}{\$32.63}$$

$$\Delta \text{B/C} = 1.46 > 1$$

Because ΔB/C >1, the Δ project is economically justified. Therefore, we eliminate doing nothing and compare the New Economy Parking Garage with the Concourse B Expansion.

$$\Delta \text{ Project} = \text{CBE} - \text{NEPG}$$

Table 8.10 presents the cash flows for NEPG and CBE and incremental cash flows for the Δ Project.

$$\Delta \text{B/C} = \frac{\$35 - (-\$1.32)}{\$12.19 - (-\$0.08)}$$

$$\Delta \text{B/C} = \frac{\$36.32}{\$12.27}$$

$$\Delta \text{B/C} = 2.96 > 1$$

Because ΔB/C > 1, the Δ project is economically justified. NEPG is eliminated, and we compare CBE with CAE: Δ Project = CAE – CBE. Table 8.11 presents the cash flows for both and for the Δ Project.

$$\Delta \text{B/C} = \frac{\$15 - (-\$0.08)}{\$21.28 - \$0.02}$$

Table 8.10 New Economy Parking Garage vs Concourse B Expansion (in USD millions)

	NEPG	*CBE*	*Δ Project CBE – NEPG*
AW of total cost	$33.37	$45.56	$12.19
AW of benefits	$50	$85	$35
AW of disbenefits	$2.34	$1.02	−$1.32
AW of salvage value	$0.74	$0.66	−$0.08
Life, years	10	10	10

Table 8.11 Concourse B Expansion vs Concourse A Expansion (in USD millions)

	CBE	*CAE*	*Δ Project CAE – CBE*
AW of total cost	$45.56	$66.84	$21.28
AW of benefits	$85	$100	$15
AW of disbenefits	$1.02	$.94	-$0.08
AW of salvage value	$0.66	$0.68	$0.02
Life, years	10	10	10

$$\Delta B/C = \frac{\$15.08}{\$21.26}$$

$$\Delta B/C = 0.71 < 1$$

Because $\Delta B/C = < 1$, the Δ project is not economically justified. Therefore, CAE is eliminated, LRA should select the Concourse B expansion.

Evaluating Independent Projects

The B/C approach to evaluating independent projects is to calculate the B/C ratio of each project, eliminate projects with a B/C ratio less than 1, and accept the rest because they contribute to the growth of the public institution as long as there is no budget limitation. If there is a budget constraint, then we use PW as explained in Chapter 5. Examples of independent projects for an airport include building of a new terminal, runway, food court, parking garage, rental car complex, or concession area; concourse or hangar expansion; new weather monitoring equipment, airport flight information screens, etc.

Example 8.7

LAA is entertaining the four independent proposals presented in Table 8.12 for LRA. LAA uses a MARR of 10% and has no budget constraint. Using B/C ratio and PW, which projects in Table 8.12 are economically justified?

First, calculate the conventional B/C ratios of all alternatives using PW at 10% MARR.

B/C ratio for new parking garage:

$$PW\ (P) = \$100$$

$$PW\ (AOC) = \$5\ (P/A,\ 10\%,\ 20) = \$5\ (8.5136) = \$42.57$$

$$PW\ (B) = \$30\ (P/A,\ 10\%,\ 20) = \$30\ (8.5136) = \$255.41$$

$$PW\ (D) = \$5$$

$$PW\ (S) = \$10\ (P/F,\ 10\%,\ 20) = \$10\ (0.1486) = \$1.49$$

Table 8.12 Legacy Regional Airport Independent Projects (in USD millions)

	New Parking Garage	*Flight Information Screen*	*Gate Expansion*	*Hangar Expansion*
First cost (P)	\$100	\$2	\$40	\$8
AOC	\$5	\$0.2	\$2	\$0.4
Annual benefits (B)	\$30	\$0.8	\$4	\$3
Disbenefits (D)	\$5	\$0	\$1	\$1
Salvage value	\$10	\$0.2	\$2	\$0.5
Life, years	20	6	25	10

$$\text{BC} = \frac{\$255.41 - \$5}{\$100 + \$42.57 - \$1.49}$$

$$\text{BC} = \frac{\$250.41}{\$141.08}$$

$$\Delta\text{B/C} = 1.77 < 1$$

B/C ratio for flight information screen:

$$\text{PW (P)} = \$2$$

$$\text{PW (AOC)} = \$0.2\ (\text{P/A, 10\%, 6}) = \$0.2\ (4.3553) = \$0.87$$

$$\text{PW (B)} = \$0.8\ (\text{P/A, 10\%, 6}) = \$0.8\ (4.3553) = \$3.48$$

$$\text{PW (D)} = \$0$$

$$\text{PW (S)} = \$0.2\ (\text{P/F, 10\%, 6}) = \$0.2\ (0.5645) = \$0.11$$

$$\text{BC} = \frac{\$3.48 - \$0}{\$2 + \$0.87 - \$0.11}$$

$$\text{B/C} = \frac{\$3.48}{\$2.76}$$

$$\text{B/C} = 1.26 < 1$$

B/C ratio for gate expansion:

$$\text{PW (P)} = \$40$$

$$\text{PW (AOC)} = \$2\ (\text{P/A, 10\%, 25})$$

$$\text{PW (AOC)} = \$2\ (9.0770) = \$18.15$$

$$\text{PW (B)} = \$4\ (\text{P/A, 10\%, 25}) = \$4\ (9.0770) = \$36.31$$

$$\text{PW (D)} = \$1$$

$$\text{PW (S)} = \$2\ (\text{P/F, 10\%, 25}) = \$2\ (0.0923) = \$0.18$$

$$\text{BC} = \frac{\$36.31 - \$1}{\$40 + \$18.15 - \$0.18}$$

$$\text{BC} = \frac{\$35.31}{\$57.97}$$

$$\text{B/C} = 0.61 < 1$$

B/C ratio for hangar expansion:

$$\text{PW (P)} = \$8$$

$$\text{PW (AOC)} = \$0.4\ (\text{P/A, 10\%, 10}) = \$0.4\ (6.1446) = \$2.46$$

$$PW(B) = \$3\ (P/A, 10\%, 10) = \$3\ (6.1446) = \$18.43$$
$$PW(D) = \$1$$
$$PW(S) = \$0.5\ (P/F, 10\%, 10) = \$0.5\ (0.3855) = \$0.19$$
$$BC = \frac{\$18.43 - \$1}{\$8 + \$2.46 - \$0.19}$$
$$BC = \frac{\$17.43}{\$10.27}$$
$$B/C = 1.70 < 1$$

Of the four proposals under review by Legacy Airport Authority, the new parking garage, flight information screen, and hangar expansion for Legacy Regional Airport have B/C ratios that are greater than 1 and are therefore economically justified.

Modified CBA

Modified CBA is another technique for evaluating public projects. The modified B/C ratio is the profitability index of a public project, and it indirectly measures the return of a public project to the public. For a modified B/C ratio, the denominator consists of only the initial investment and the salvage value associated with first cost, and all other cash flows are placed in the numerator. In other words, modified B/C ratio compares the net benefits to initial investment as shown:

$$\text{Modified B/C} = \frac{\text{Net Benefits}}{\text{Initial Investment}}$$

where Net Benefits = benefits – disbenefits – operating cost + savings and initial investment = first cost + nonrecurring cost – salvage value. Entering net benefit details into that equation results in its expanded formula:

$$\text{Modified B/C} = \frac{B - D - AOC + \text{Savings}}{P - \text{Salvage Value}}$$

This equation is also used to determine the rate of return on public investments. It is often used to rank and fund projectsthe highest: Public institutions usually fund the project with highest ratio first and then continue with the next highest until the entire budget is utilized.

Although modified B/C ratio yields a different value than conventional B/C ratio, it does not change the decision to accept or reject a project: Both the conventional and modified ratios consistently provide the same answer because the accept-or-reject criteria are the same for both.

Example 8.8

U.S. Airports Authority (USAA) owns and operates three airports in the southeastern United States. The airports are conveniently located in a triangle format. Gator International Airport (GIA) is the largest airport with enplanement of 60 million per year and offers commercial services to major cities within the central and eastern parts of the United States and major cities abroad. Gator Regional Airport (GRA) is located approximately 100 miles southwest of GIA with enplanement of 30 million offering domestic commercial services to the US southwest, west, and northwest. Gator Reliever Airport is located approximately 30 miles from GIA offers commercial services to all cities in the southeast, east, and northeast of the United States.

USAA has received a proposal to build a new food court at GIA. The information about this proposal is summarized in Table 8.13. USAA uses a MARR of 12%. Use both conventional and modified B/C ratios with PW to determine if the food court project is economically justified.

Conventional B/C ratio:

PW of First cost = \$6,000,000 + \$1,500,000 (P/F, 12%, 5)
PW of First cost = \$6,000,000 + \$1,500,000 (0.5674)
PW of First cost = \$6,851,100
PW of AOC = \$500,000 (P/A, 12%, 10) + \$100,000 (P/G, 12%, 10)
PW of AOC = \$500,000 (5.6502) + \$100,000 (20.2541)
PW of AOC = \$2,852,100 + \$2,025,410
PW of AOC = \$4,877,510
PW of Benefits = \$3,000,000 (P/A, 12%, 10)
PW of Benefits = \$3,000,000 (5.6502)
PW of Benefits = \$16,950,600
PW of Disbenefits = \$1,000,000
PW Salvage value = \$1,200,000 (P/F, 12%, 10)
PW Salvage value = \$1,200,000 (0.3220)
PW Salvage value = \$386,400

$$\text{Conventional BC} = \frac{\$16,950,000 - \$1,000,000}{\$6,851,100 + \$4,877,510 - \$386,400}$$

$$\text{Conventional BC} = \frac{\$15,950,000}{\$11,342,210}$$

$$\text{Conventional BC} = 1.41 > 1$$

Modified B/C Ratio:

$$\text{Modified BC} = \frac{\$16,950,000 - \$1,000,000 - \$4,877,510}{\$6,851,100 - \$386,400}$$

$$\text{Modified BC} = \frac{\$11,072,490}{\$6,464,700}$$

$$\text{Modified BC} = 1.71 > 1/$$

Both conventional and modified B/C ratio are greater than 1, meaning the food court project is economically justified.

Table 8.13 Food Court Project for Gator International Airport

First cost	\$6,000,000 now and \$1,500,000 upgrade cost five years from now
AOC	\$500,000 in the first year with increase of \$100,000 per year starting the second year
Annual benefits (revenue)	\$3,000,000
Disbenefits at time 0	\$1,000,000
Salvage value	\$1,200,000
Life, years	10

Calculating B/C Ratio in Excel

This section presents how to calculate conventional or modified B/C ratios using PW in Excel. Unlike for our previous tasks, Excel does not have a B/C ratio function. We can, however, calculate conventional B/C ratio using the following formula:

$$B/C = \frac{\left[(PW\ of\ B)-(PW\ of\ D)\right]}{\left[\text{PW of P} + \text{PW of AOC} - \text{PW of S}\right)}$$

The following equation in Excel will produce modified B/C ratio:

$$B/C = \frac{\text{PW of B} - \text{PW of D} - \text{PW of AOC} + \text{PW of Savings}}{\text{PW of P} - \text{PW of S}}$$

Example 8.9

USAA has received a proposal for hangar expansion at GRA. The cash flows associated with the Hangar Expansion are as follows:

First cost is \$2,000,000. AOCs are \$100,000 per year for the first three years, \$150,000 per year for years four to seven, and \$100,000 per year for years 8–10. Benefits less disbenefits are \$500,000 per year for the first three years, \$800,000 per year for years four to seven, and \$500,000 per year for years 8–10. Salvage value is \$400,000, life is 10 years, and MARR is 10%. Using Excel, calculate both conventional and modified B/C ratios and determine whether the project is economically justified. Figure 8.2 shows the Excel solutions for both conventional and modified B/C ratios. Both conventional B/C ratio and modified B/C ratio are greater than 1, and therefore the hangar expansion is economically justified.

Summary

Public projects are owned by the public sector and comprise federal, state, county, city, and other government agencies. Public-sector investments should usually benefit the public; projects

	A	B	C
1	A	B	C
2			
3	First cost	$2,000,000	
4	Salvage value	$400,000	
5	Life/ years	10	
6	MARR	10%	
7			
8	Year	AOC	Benefits - Disbenefits
9	1	100,000	500,000
10	2	100,000	500,000
11	3	100,000	500,000
12	4	150,000	800,000
13	5	150,000	800,000
14	6	150,000	800,000
15	7	150,000	800,000
16	8	100,000	500,000
17	9	100,000	500,000
18	10	100,000	500,000
19			
20	Conv. B/C Ratio	1.31	=NPV(10%,C9:C18)/(B3+NPV(10%,B9:B18)-
21			PV(10%,10,,B4))
22	Mod. B/C Ratio	1.42	1.42

	A	B	C
1	A	B	C
2			
3	First cost	$2,000,000	
4	Salvage value	$400,000	
5	Life/ years	10	
6	MARR	10%	
7			
8	Year	AOC	Benefits - Disbenefits
9	1	100,000	500,000
10	2	100,000	500,000
11	3	100,000	500,000
12	4	150,000	800,000
13	5	150,000	800,000
14	6	150,000	800,000
15	7	150,000	800,000
16	8	100,000	500,000
17	9	100,000	500,000
18	10	100,000	500,000
19			
20	Conv. B/C Ratio	1.31	1.31
21			
22	Mod. B/C Ratio	1.42	=(NPV(10%,C9:C18)-NPV(10%,B9:B18))/(B3-
23			PV(10%,10,,B4))

Figure 8.2 Calculating benefits vs cost in Excel.

should provide services to the public at no profit. Public-sector projects are often evaluated based on cost–benefit analysis: If the benefit/cost ratio exceeds 1, the project is economically justified.

Cost-based mutually exclusive alternatives do not have direct benefits. The implied benefits come from cost savings to the public when we compare the alternatives. Doing nothing is not an option for cost-based mutually exclusive alternatives because there is no direct benefit associated with the alternatives. If there are more than two alternatives, then the survivor of the first two alternatives is compared with the next alternative in line until one project survives.

To evaluate benefit-based mutually exclusive alternatives using B/C ratio, we follow the same procedure for cost-based alternatives except that do nothing is now an option. First, the project with the lowest total cost is compared with doing nothing. The survivor of these two alternatives is compared with the next alternative until there is a final survivor. If $\Delta B/C$ ratio ≥ 1, select the project with the higher total cost; if $\Delta B/C$ ratio < 1, select the project with lower cost.

Modified B/C ratio is calculated similar to profitability index, where the denominator is only the initial investment and all other cash flows are placed in the numerator. In other words, modified B/C ratio compares the net benefits to initial investment. Although the modified B/C ratio is different from the conventional ratio, it does not change the decision to accept or reject a project.

Discussion Questions and Problems

8.1 What are the characteristics of private-sector and public-sector projects?

8.2 What are the benefits of an airport to its community?

8.3 What are the disbenefits of an airport to its community?

8.4 Explain the process of evaluating cost-based mutually exclusive alternatives.

8.5 Explain the process of evaluating benefit-based mutually exclusive alternatives.

8.6 Majestic Water Department is planning to spend $2,000,000 to build a treatment plant to remove certain heavy metals from well water. The plant's operating cost is $100,000 per year. Public health benefits are expected to be $200,000 per year. The life of the project is 20 years with no salvage value. At 10% per year, evaluate this project using conventional B/C ratio with AW.

8.7 Legacy Airport Authority (LAA) is considering building a new terminal. This project is permanent, with first cost of $800 million and additional investment of $50 million every 10 years. No salvage value is expected. The revenue from the new terminal (benefits) is expected to be $150 million per year, and disbenefits are estimated to be $10 million per year. AOC are $25 million per year. LAA uses a MARR of 10%. Using a conventional B/C ratio with AW, determine whether this project is economically justified.

8.8 Monarch International Airport is considering building a new parking garage with a first cost of $400 million and additional investment of $20 million every 10 years. This is a permanent project with no salvage value. The revenue from the new terminal (benefits) is expected to be $250 million per year, and disbenefits are estimated to be $5 million per year. AOC are $25 million per year. Legacy uses a MARR of 12%. Using a modified B/C ratio with AW, determine whether this project is economically justified.

8.9 LAA is considering constructing a reliever airport in Faridville County, which is about 30 miles away from Legacy International Airport (LIA), to reduce current congestion at LIA. The initial investment is estimated to be $1.200 million with AOCof $50 million in year one increasing by $10 million per year. This is a 20-year project with annual benefit (airport revenues) of $200 million in year one increasing by $20 million per year and disbenefit to the public of $5 million per year. LAA is planning to sell the airport to Faridville County at a price of $500 million at the end of 20 years, which is considered the salvage value of the project. Using conventional B/C ratio with PW and a MARR of 8%, is this reliever airport project economically justified?

8.10 U.S. Airport Authority (USAA) is considering building a construction of a new terminal at Gator Regional Airport. This project is permanent with first cost of $800 million and additional investment of $100 million every 10 years. No salvage value is expected. The revenue from the new terminal (benefits) is expected to be $150 million per year, and disbenefits are estimated to be $4 million per year. AOC is $25 million per year. USAA uses a MARR of 12%. Using a conventional B/C ratio with AW, determine whether this project is economically justified.

8.11 LAA has received a proposal for building a new luggage conveyer belt. The information about this proposal is summarized in the following table. LAA uses a MARR of 10%. Using both conventional and modified B/C ratios with PW, determine if the conveyer belt project is economically justified.

First cost	$4 million now and $2 million five years from now
AOC	$200,000 in the first year with increase of $50,000 per year starting the second year
Annual benefits (revenue)	$2.5 million
Disbenefits at time 0	$500,000
Salvage value	$200,000
Life, years	10

8.12 Busan Global is considering two alternative bridges to connect the city to an island. The costs associated with both bridges are shown in the next table. The bridges are considered permanent, and MARR is 8%. Assume that both bridges have equivalent use but that Bridge B is shorter than Bridge A, with lower user travel cost but higher construction cost. Which alternative should Busan Global select based on conventional B/C analysis?

(in millions)	*Bridge A*	*Bridge B*
First cost	$50	$80
AOC	$4	$5
Repair cost every 10 years	$2	$2.5
Users travel costs per year	$20	$10
Estimated life, years	∞	∞

8.13 USAA is considering adding a new runway at the Gator Reliever Airport to land the largest jets. USAA has three options for the runway surface: asphalt, concrete, and a mixture of both; the benefit from all three alternatives is the same. Therefore, these projects are cost based, and their cash flows are provided in the following table. Using conventional B/C ratio with MARR of 9%, which alternative should be selected?

(in millions)	*Asphalt*	*Concrete*	*Mixture*
First cost	$250	$350	$400
AW of resurface cost	$30	$20	$10
Disbenefit at construction time	$5	$10	$12
Life, years	20	20	20

8.14 LIA is considering three mutually exclusive alternatives shown in the next table below for airport improvement. Using conventional B/C ratio with MARR of 8%, which project should LIA select?

(in millions)	*Concourse A Expansion*	*Concourse B Expansion*	*New Runway*
First cost	$300	$400	$500
Estimated AOC	$15	$20	$25
Benefits, estimated annual revenue	$85	$100	$120
Disbenefit, incurs at time 0	$15	$20	$18
Life, years	∞	∞	∞

8.15 USAA is entertaining three independent proposals presented in the table for GRA. USAA uses a MARR of 12% and has no budget constraint. Using B/C ratio and PW, which of the following projects are economically justified as maximizing services to the public?

(in USD millions)	*New Parking Garage*	*Flight Information Screen*	*Gate Expansion*
First cost	$120	$3	$50
AOC	$5	$0.5	$3
Annual benefits	$25	$1.0	$6
Disbenefits at time	$5	$0	$2
Salvage value	$15	$0.4	$5
Life, years	20	5	25

Notes

1 Goodman, J. & Loveman, G. (1991, December). Does Privatization Serve the Public Interest? *Harvard Business Review*.

2 The current air traffic management system is based on radar, voice communications, and ground navigational aids and will ultimately be unable to deal with predicted air traffic growth.

3 2020 FAA Airport Benefit cost analysis guidance.

4 *American Journal of Preventive Medicine* (2024, May 6). www.ajpmonline.org/article/S0749-3797(24)00110-7/fulltext.

References

Federal Aviation Administration (2020). *FAA Airport Benefit Cost Analysis Guidance*. Retrieved on May 15, 2024. www.faa.gov/sites/faa.gov/files/regulations_policies/policy_guidance/benefit_cost/FAA_Airport_Benefits_Guidance.pdf.

Goodman, J. & Loveman, G. (1991, December). Does Privatization Serve the Public Interest? *Harvard Business Review*.

Turner, S., et al. (2024). Benefit-Cost Analysis of the HHS Covid-19 Campaign: April 2021–March 2022. Retrieved on May 15, 2024. www.ajpmonline.org/article/S0749-3797(24)00110-7/fulltext.

9 Breakeven and Payback Period

Aviation industry actors such as airports, airlines, aircraft manufacturers, and fixed-based operators continuously face decisions regarding whether to buy or lease equipment for operations. Breakeven can be analyzed to assist managers in deciding.

Breakeven is the point at which a project's total costs equal its total revenue, resulting in zero profit. Breakeven analysis contributes to effective cash flow management by helping businesses anticipate periods of positive cash flow and plan for potential cash shortages before reaching that point. Therefore, the annual usage rate (annual production or consumption units) must be equal to or greater than breakeven to make the project economically acceptable. Breakeven analysis can also be applied to two mutually exclusive alternatives such as buying versus making. In comparing the alternatives, the intention is to determine the indifference point between the two alternatives; in other words, at breakeven, both alternatives become equally attractive, whereas if one parameter exceeds the other, one alternative is more attractive.

Some companies have a required period as a policy for recovering their investments. Payback period (PP) is a simple technique to quickly determine the period needed to recover the first cost. Conventional PP assumes that interest rate (i) is 0, whereas discounted PP utilizes the minimum acceptable rate of return (MARR).

The focus of this chapter is to empower readers to use breakeven analysis to evaluate single projects and select among mutually exclusive alternatives. We also aim to enable readers to quickly utilize conventional and discounted payback periods to determine the economic viability of projects. In the following sections, we briefly address calculating breakeven as well as both conventional and discounted PPs.

Industry Insight

WOW Air was an Icelandic low-cost airline known for its budget transatlantic flights. WOW expanded rapidly but faced financial challenges due to intense competition, high fuel costs, and overexpansion. The airline attempted to restructure and find investors to alleviate its financial woes but ultimately ceased operations in March 2019, leaving passengers stranded and causing disruption in the aviation industry.

Breakeven analysis plays a crucial role in decision-making and assessing the feasibility of projects. When considering the acquisition or retirement of aircraft, breakeven analysis becomes crucial; airlines need to assess the breakeven point for new or existing aircraft types to make informed decisions about fleet composition considering

DOI: 10.4324/9781003469759-9

factors such as fuel efficiency and operational costs. Aviation investments typically involve long-term commitments and are heavily influenced by shifting economic conditions throughout the investment horizon. Despite these challenges, it is imperative to execute the analysis correctly. History has shown that inaccurate breakeven analysis can lead to catastrophic consequences, even for major companies like Airbus.

Lockheed's L-1011 Tri Star Airbus, a wide-bodied commercial jet capable of carrying between 260 and 400 passengers, faced a crucial moment during 1971 Congressional hearings. Seeking federal guarantee for an additional $250 million in bank credit due to financial distress, Lockheed aimed to secure the necessary funds to complete the program. The debate during these hearings largely revolved around the estimated breakeven sales, with Lockheed's chief executive asserting that this point would be reached at sales between 195 and 205 aircraft. Despite Lockheed having secured only 103 firm orders and 75 optional ones at the time of the hearings, a significant discrepancy emerged. According to a naive estimate of the breakeven sales level, it was determined to be around 287 aircraft, considerably higher than Lockheed's initial forecast.

Originally, Lockheed had aspired to capture 35% to 40% of the total free-world market for wide-bodied airbuses in the medium-range category, but this too proved overly optimistic and unattainable. Lockheed, facing challenges with below-target sales, ultimately withdrew from the commercial aircraft business. The production of a total of 250 TriStar jets marked the end of Lockheed's ventures into commercial passenger airliners due to failing to reach breakeven.

The production of the L1011 was initiated in 1968. The first flight of the L1011 took place in November 1970, and it entered service in April 1972. However, Lockheed, facing continuous financial challenges and L1011 sales disappointments announced in 1981 that it would not break even, opting to manufacture only 250 units instead of the initially planned 500. As a result, production ceased in 1984. On January 5, 1970, the stock reached a high of $3.382. However, negative news related to the production issues of the L1011 and investors' lack of confidence led to a sharp decline, with the stock dropping to $1.237 by June 29, 1970. The macroeconomic situation worsened, and additional problems with the L1011 caused Lockheed's shares to further decrease to $0.522 on December 24, 1973. Despite these challenges, there was a turnaround in Lockheed's stock performance after December 23, 1974. The stock rebounded from its low, fluctuating around $0.582, and maintained an upward trend for several years reaching double digits per share. This resurgence was attributed to lucrative military contracts and successful projects undertaken by Lockheed during this period.

The Airbus A380, known as one of the most iconic aircraft in history, also stands out as one of the costliest for both its purchasers and the manufacturer. Despite its engineering superiority, the A380 became a significant failure for Boeing due to an initial miscalculation of breakeven. Originally, Boeing projected a breakeven point of 270 units for the A380 program, but this estimate proved to be far from reality. The actual figure required for breakeven escalated to a staggering 420 units.

Over the years, the precise breakeven point underwent several readjustments. Boeing's chief financial officer had previously expressed optimism, stating that Airbus anticipated selling more than 750 planes throughout the project's lifespan. However, this ambitious target remained unmet, with just over 250 A380 aircraft delivered before Airbus decided to halt production. The upfront development costs for the A380 ranged from $17 billion to $25 billion, and Airbus barely broke even on production costs as the $445 million price tag for each aircraft fell short of covering the production expenses. Facing these financial constraints, Airbus made the strategic decision to cease A380 production in 2021, marking the end of an era for this ambitious but economically challenging aircraft.

Breakeven Analysis

In this capital-intensive industry, where substantial upfront investments are required for research, development, and production, breakeven analysis plays a pivotal role in estimating costs and setting prices. Breakeven analysis aids in evaluating the financial risks associated with new aircraft programs, enabling management to allocate resources effectively and manage risks proactively. The Boeing 787 Dreamliner experienced numerous delays during its development, resulting in increased development costs and pushing back the breakeven point for the program.

The concept of breakeven, originating from finance, is used in different fields from economics to business to physics. In essence, breakeven analysis is a simple approach of estimating the minimum quantity of sales (or production) needed to cancel out their cost; in other words, at breakeven, total cost equals revenue, yielding zero profit. After breakeven, revenue contributes directly to profit. This understanding is fundamental for assessing profitability.

Similarly, breakeven can be viewed as the point of indifference between two available options. For instance, one of the noteworthy changes in the Boeing 787 Dreamliner is the replacement of traditional aluminum body with new composite material that can provide the required strength but with much less weight, which significantly improved the fuel efficiency. Boeing says that the 787 is about 20% more fuel efficient than the 767, which it was intended to replace. Consequently, the higher cost of using composite material than aluminum can be justified by the resulting fuel savings. Now, let us consider this tradeoff between saving on fuel cost and saving on using cheaper material. Since 2014, we observed a decreasing trend on jet fuel prices. Indeed, as fuel price decreases, there should be a point where the fuel cost saving equals the extra cost of adopting composites, and that point is breakeven: Traditional aluminum and the new composites become economically indifferent.

Other examples of breakeven include considering the time value of money (opportunity cost of money) where $i > 0\%$ or without it where $i = 0\%$. The latter is simple and is used often. In this chapter, we describe breakeven analysis for project evaluation. We also discuss payback period (PP).

Elements of Breakeven Analysis

Given the enormous expenses involved in compliance with stringent regulatory standards, research and development, and production, understanding the breakeven point is essential for strategic planning and financial stability. Breakeven is defined in relation to total cost and total revenue. For Boeing and Airbus, accurately forecasting this point helps in setting realistic sales targets, optimizing production processes, and managing resources efficiently. However, risk lies in manufacturing problems, the volatile nature of the aerospace market, fluctuating fuel prices, economic downturns, and random shocks.[1]

Misjudging breakeven can lead to significant financial losses, inventory issues, and reduced market competitiveness. Thus, continuous and precise breakeven analysis is indispensable for these aerospace giants to navigate financial risks and maintain their market leadership. While cost is particularly discussed in Chapter 12, in this chapter, we briefly review the cost concepts necessary for understanding and performing breakeven analysis. The key to understanding is recognizing the difference between fixed and variable costs.

In practice, acquiring some resources or assets requires a commitment for a certain time when the commitment cannot be nullified or altered. For instance, renting a business space often requires a contract of a fixed period during which a tenant is obligated to pay the property owner for the privilege whether the tenant uses the property. Costs that remain unchanged by an operator's actions are defined as fixed.

In contrast, in operating a small manufacturing business, the consumption of raw material will depend on its rate of production, and consequently, the cost of raw material varies based on the production variations. Costs that do depend on the operator's actions or other variations (e.g., in output) are variable. Table 9.1 presents few examples of fixed and variable costs.

Fixed costs by definition are linear, but as discussed in Chapter 12, variable costs can be linear or nonlinear. We mostly assume linear cost relationships in this chapter, but the analysis can be extended to accommodate for nonlinear variable costs. Figure 9.1 presents the relationships between variable and fixed costs against quantity of output.

Nonlinear variable costs are more realistic due to economies of scales. In practice, as production volume increases, the variable cost per unit usually decreases, creating the nonlinear cost curve shown in Figure 9.2. Because nonlinear variable costs are more realistic, nonlinear revenue function are as well. As variable cost decreases per unit, assuming a constant price, the revenue per unit will increase, resulting in the nonlinear revenue curve shown in Figure 9.3. This means that there might be two possible solutions to breakeven since both total cost and total revenue curves are nonlinear.

Table 9.1 Fixed vs Variable Costs

Fixed Costs	*Variable Costs*
• Building & equipment	• Raw materials
• Building rental costs	• Direct labor
• Equipment leases	• Sales commission
• Depreciation	• Inventory
• Insurance	• Packaging supplies
• Management salaries	• Shipping costs
• Utilities	• Marketing & advertising

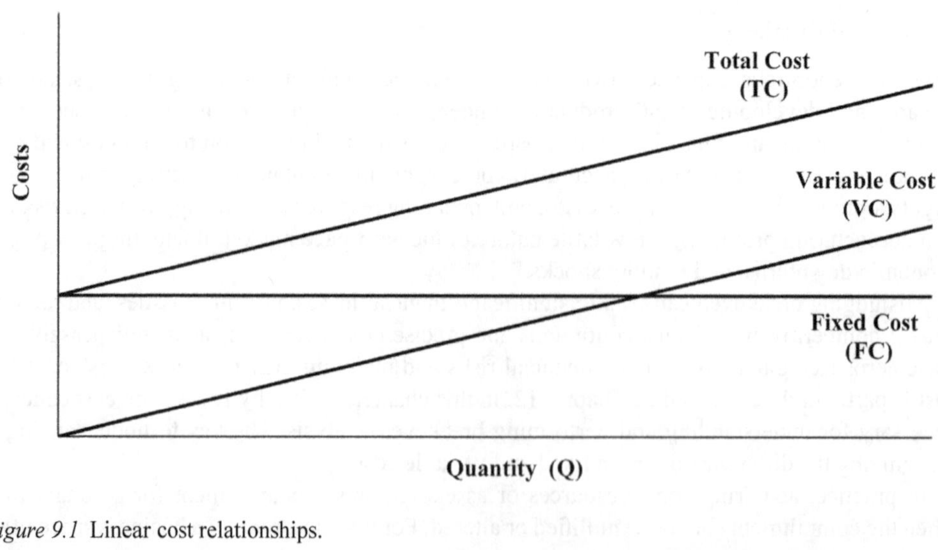

Figure 9.1 Linear cost relationships.

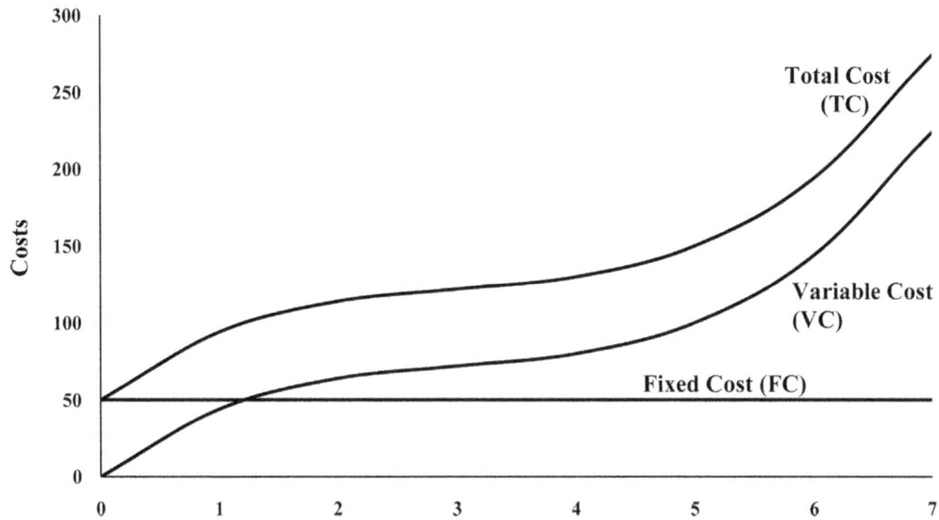

Figure 9.2 Nonlinear cost curves.

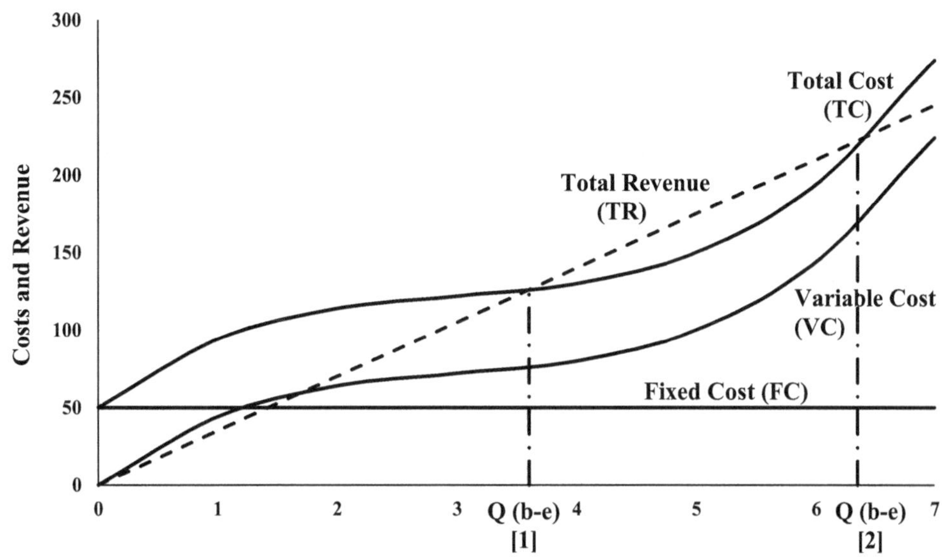

Figure 9.3 Nonlinear cost curves and total revenue.

Next, we begin describing the basic analysis to calculate breakeven for a single project without considering the time value of money.

Single Project When Interest Is 0

In this section, we start by performing breakeven analysis without considering the time value of money (i.e., $i = 0$). Breakeven quantity (Q_{BE}) corresponds to the intersection of total revenue and total costs curves. At that point, total revenue is equal to total cost, with profit equal to zero. Figure 9.4 shows the linear relationships among costs and revenue.

$$Total\ Revenue\ (TR) = Quantity\ of\ output\ (Q) \times Price\ per\ unit\ (P)$$
$$\text{TR} = \text{Q} \times \text{P}$$

In this section and only for this section, where $i = 0$, P represents the price per unit and not the first cost:

$$Total\ Costs = Fixed\ Costs + Variable\ Costs$$
$$Variable\ costs = Quantity\ of\ output\ (Q) \times Variable\ cost\ per\ unit\ (V)$$
$$\mathbf{TC = FC + V \times Q}$$
$$\text{At } \mathbf{Q_{BE}}, \ \mathbf{TR = TC}$$

We now enter the previous equations and solve for Q, breakeven:

$$\mathbf{TR = TC}$$
$$\text{Q} \times \text{P} = \text{FC} + \text{Q} \times \text{V}$$
$$\text{FC} = \text{Q} \times \text{P} - \text{Q} \times \text{V}$$
$$\text{FC} = \text{Q} \times (\text{P} - \text{V})$$
$$\mathbf{Q_{BE} = \frac{FC}{P - V}}$$

As can be seen, breakeven analysis is algebraically and graphically easy to understand. As shown in Figure 9.5, at breakeven, the profit is zero. At any level of output less than breakeven,

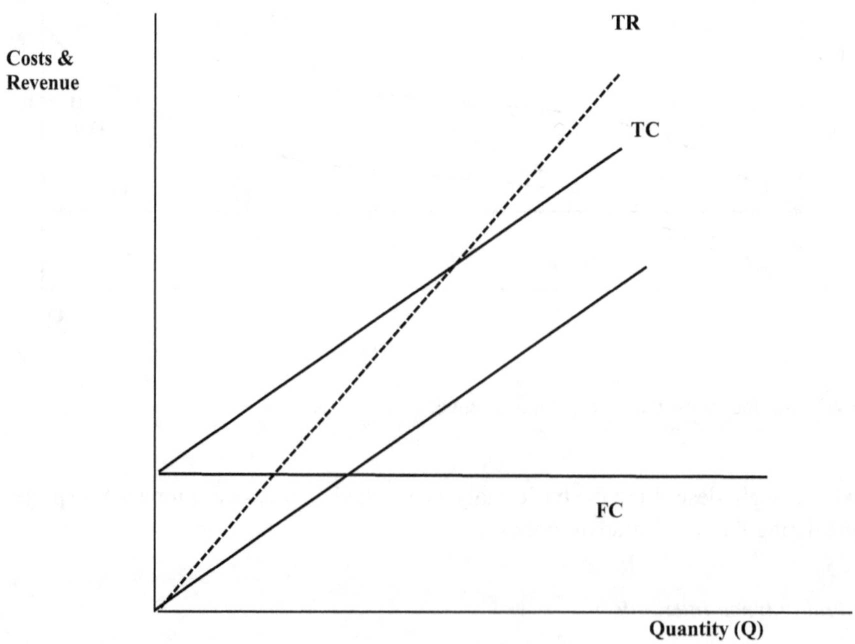

Figure 9.4 Linear costs and revenue functions.

$$\text{Profit} = \text{TR - TC}$$

$$\text{Profit} = \text{Q}\times\text{P - FC} - \text{Q}\times\text{V}$$

$$\mathbf{Profit = Q \times (P - V) - FC}$$

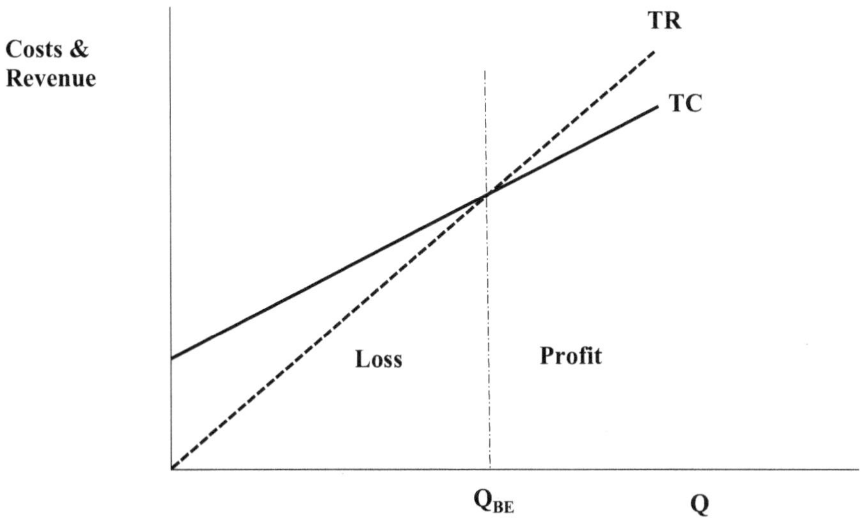

Figure 9.5 Breakeven point (Q_{BE}).

the firm incurs a loss, and at any quantity greater than breakeven, the firm makes a profit. The profit is the difference between total revenue and total costs.

Example 9.1

AirJet International, an aerospace company, has invested \$200 million to build sharklet wingtips for commercial airplanes. The variable cost per unit is \$200,000, and price per unit is about \$280,000. What is the breakeven point, and what is the profit if the company sells 3,000 units per year?

Breakeven is calculated as follows:

$$Q_{BE} = \frac{\$200,000,000}{\$280,000 - \$200,000}$$

$$\text{Q}_{\text{BE}} = 2,500 \text{ units}$$

and the profit is

$$\text{Profit} = 3,000 \times (\$280,000 - \$200,000) - \$200,000,000$$

$$\text{Profit} = \$40,000,000$$

Analyzing different scenarios involves examining how changing different factors affect breakeven and overall financial performance. For instance, higher production costs can lead to higher breakeven points. Due to ballooning production costs, Boeing has spent $32 billion on the B787 ; estimates for the number of aircraft sales needed to break even vary between 1,300 and 2,000. As of October 2024, the company has booked a total of 1,916 orders and made 1,130 deliveries while recording zero fatalities and no hull losses.

Two Alternatives with Interest = 0

Breakeven analysis can also be applied to two mutually exclusive alternatives, for instance, buying versus making. In comparing the alternatives, the intention is to determine the indifference point between the two alternatives. In other words, at breakeven point, both alternatives become equally attractive, whereas if one parameter exceeds the other, one alternative becomes more attractive. We set the total costs of one alternative equal to the total costs of the other alternative and solve for breakeven. Usually, one alternative has larger fixed costs and smaller variable cost per unit than the other, but the second has smaller fixed costs but larger variable cost per unit.

Example 9.2

Jet Aviation, an aircraft manufacturer, has two alternatives to manufacture security approved cockpit doors to meet the FAA new standards for commercial airplanes: fixed cost of $1,000,000 with variable cost per unit of $8,000 or fixed cost of $600,000 with variable cost per unit of $12,000. The door is designed to resist incursion by anyone trying to enter the cockpit using physical force. The FAA requirements include the door, its means of attachment to the surrounding structure, and the attachment structure on the bulkhead itself. What is the breakeven quantity of a cockpit door that makes the manufacturer indifferent between these two alternatives?

To find breakeven, we set the total cost of alternative 1 equal to the total cost of alternative 2 and solve for the unknown quantity:

$$TC_1 = TC_2$$
$$\text{TC}_1 = \$1{,}000{,}000 + \$8{,}000\text{Q}$$
$$\text{TC}_1 = TC_2 = \$600{,}000 + \$12{,}000\text{Q}$$

$$\$1{,}000{,}000 + \$8{,}000\text{Q} = \$600{,}000 + \$12{,}000\text{Q}$$
$$\$1{,}000{,}000 - \$600{,}000 = \$12{,}000\text{Q} - 8{,}000\text{Q}$$
$$\$400{,}000 = \$4{,}000\text{Q}$$
$$\text{Q} = 100$$

Figure 9.6 gives a graphical representation of the alternatives and their relative costs.

As shown in Figure 9.7, the breakeven quantity reference point is the intersection of the two linear total cost relationships that correspond to a breakeven quantity of 100 units. For an output level of less than 100 units, alternative 2 is preferred with smaller fixed cost and larger variable cost per unit, while for output greater than 100 units, Alternative 1 is selected with relatively fixed cost and smaller variable cost per unit. This argument makes sense because at breakeven point of 100 units, both alternatives have the same total costs. If the manufacturer wants to make more than 100 units, it makes sense to select the alternative with lower variable cost per unit, which is alternative 1.

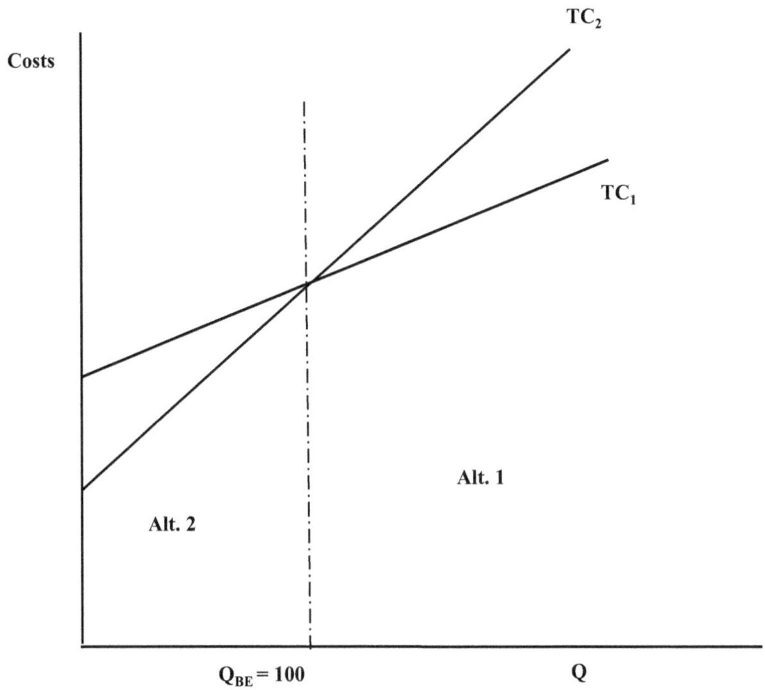

Figure 9.6 Breakeven quantity between two alternatives.

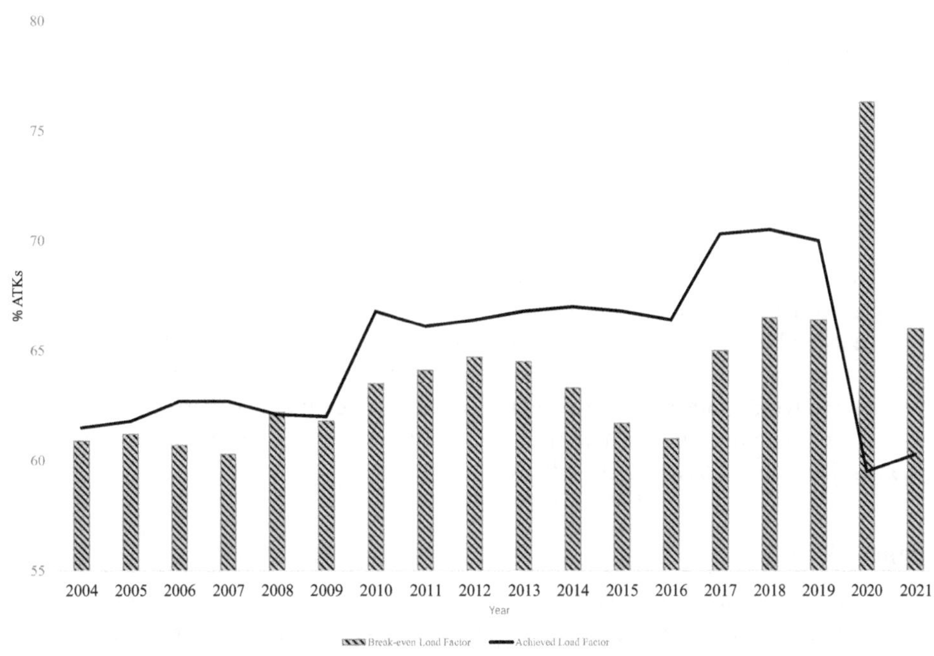

Figure 9.7 Average achieved and breakeven load factor.

Source: IATA Industry Statistics Fact Sheet.

Single Project with Interest Greater than 0

In the previous sections, we ignored the time value of money in calculating breakeven; in this section, the time value of money is significant. To calculate breakeven in this setting, we utilize present worth (PW) and annual worth (AW) as discussed in previous chapters. With these approaches, we evaluate the overall cash flow during the length of a project, considering positive and negative transactions while accounting for the time value of money.

To calculate breakeven for a single project where interest rate is greater than 0, we set the PW or AW of the project to 0 and solve for breakeven of the parameter of interest (e.g., interest rate), the parameter that makes the two projects equally attractive, for instance quantity per year, interest rate, or first cost. For example, the rate of return (ROR) of a single project (i^*) is the breakeven interest rate of that project, as we discussed in Chapter 7. AW is preferred when variable cost is annual.

Example 9.3

Using Example 9.1, calculate the breakeven quantity per year assuming a 20-year project, a MARR of 10%, and all other relevant data from the example.

Because we are asked to calculate quantity per year, we set AW to 0:

$$
\begin{aligned}
\text{AW} &= 0 \\
-\$200{,}000{,}000(\text{A/P}, 10\%, 20) + (\$280{,}000 - \$200{,}000) \times \text{Q} &= 0 \\
\$200{,}000{,}000 \times (0.11746) &= \$80{,}000\ \text{Q} \\
\$23{,}492{,}000 &= \$80{,}000\ \text{Q} \\
\text{Q}_{\text{BE}} &= 294 \text{ units per year}
\end{aligned}
$$

The breakeven quantity can be now compared with the expected total output per year. If the expected total output is much greater, then there is no need for concern, and the company can comfortably undertake the project. On the other hand, if the expected total output is much less than breakeven, then the company should not undertake the project.

Mutually Exclusive Alternatives with Interest Greater than 0

Breakeven analysis can also be utilized to compare mutually exclusive alternatives. With interest rate greater than 0, we can set the total cost (TC) of one alternative equal to TC of the second alternative using PW or AW to find the parameter that is common to both alternatives. ROR for the extra project (Δ project), (Δi^*), as calculated in Chapter 7, is the breakeven interest rate for two alternatives; at breakeven, we are indifferent between the two alternatives as they provide the same economic value. AW is preferred to PW when the variable costs are annual basis or when projects do not have the same lives.

Example 9.4

EuroJet designs and manufactures turbine engines for transport category aircraft. Advanced testing systems will ensure that their new signature program called Cool-Start does indeed work for every engine produced. Let us assume that EuroJet has two cost-based testing systems, Turboprop and Turbofan. Table 9.2 presents the costs associated with both alternatives. Assuming a MARR of 8%, at what breakeven engine quantity per year will EuroJet be indifferent in undertaking either of the alternatives?

Table 9.2 Cash Flows for Turboprop and Turbofan

	Turboprop	*Turbofan*
Robot and support equipment (first cost)	–$1,500,000	–$2,250,000
AOC	–$700,000	–$550,000
Rebuild cost in year three	–$200,000	$0
Rebuild cost in year five	$0	–$300,000
Salvage value	$50,000	$100,000
Estimated life, years	10	10
Labor wages per hour	$40	$30
People	6	8
Number of engine tested per hour	3	6

AW of TC of Turboprop (TP) = AW of TC of Turbofan (TF):

$$\text{Turboprop variable cost per unit } \left(V_{TP}\right) = \frac{\$40 \times 6}{3} = \$80$$

$$\begin{aligned}
AW_{TP} &= -\$1,500,000\ (A/P), 8\%, 10) - \$200,000\ (P/F, 8\%, 3) \times (A/P, 8\%, 10) \\
&\quad + \$50,000\ (A/F, 8\%, 10) - \$700,000 - \$80\ Q \\
AW_{TP} &= -\$1,500,000 \times (0.1490) - \$200,000 \times (0.7938) \times (0.1490) \\
&\quad + \$50,000 \times (0.0690) - \$700,000 - \$80\ Q \\
AW_{TP} &= -\$223,500 - \$23,655 + \$3,450 - \$700,000 - \$80\ Q \\
AW_{TP} &= -\$943,705 - \$80\ Q
\end{aligned}$$

$$\text{TF variable cost per unit } \frac{\$30 \times 8}{6} = \$40$$

$$\begin{aligned}
AW_{TF} &= -\$2,250,000\ (A/P, 8\%, 10) - \$300,000\ (P/F, 8\%, 5) \times (A/P, 8\%, 10) \\
&\quad + \$100,000\ (A/F, 8\%, 10) - \$550,000 - \$40\ Q \\
AW_{TF} &= -\$2,250,000 \times (0.1490) - \$300,000 \times (0.6806) \times (0.1490) \\
&\quad + \$100,000 \times (0.0690) - \$550,000 - \$40\ Q \\
AW_{TF} &= -\$335,250 - \$30,423 + \$6,900 - \$550,000 - \$40\ Q \\
AW_{TF} &= -\$908,773 - \$40\ Q - \$943,705 - \$80\ Q = -\$908,773 - \$40\ Q \\
\$40\ Q &= \$34,932 \\
Q &= 873
\end{aligned}$$

Therefore, for output of fewer than 873 engines, the Turboprop system is preferred with smaller fixed cost, while for more than 873 engines, the Turbofan with smaller variable cost per unit is optimal.

Airline Breakeven Load Factor

One of the most common yet simple measurements of an airline's operation is load factor: simply, the percentage of an airline's seats that is filled by revenue passengers. For example, when we say that United Airlines (UA) has a load factor of 80% on its route from Chicago, Illinois, to Phoenix, Arizona, we mean that on average 80% of UA airplanes seats were occupied by paying customers. Load factor, however, does not include any consideration of airline revenue or operating costs. In other words, it does not give any indication of whether UA's Chicago–Phoenix route is economically justified. Therefore, load factor alone is not useful because it can easily distort an airline's financial image. For the load factor to be meaningful, it needs to be compared with the breakeven load factor, which is the percentage of the airplane seats that must be filled with paid customers for the airline to break even at its current cost structure. The difference between the two load factors indicates the profitability of the airline. To calculate load factor and breakeven load factor, we need to know the following:

- Available Seat Mile (ASM) = Number of seats in an airplane times number of miles flown.
- Revenue per Passenger Mile (RPM) = Number of occupied seats by paid passengers times number of miles flown.
- Total Cost (TC) = Total fixed and variable costs of flights per year.
- Total Revenue (TR) = Total revenues collected from passengers per year.
- Cost per Available Seat Mile (CASM) $= \dfrac{\text{Total Costs}}{\text{ASM}}$
- Revenue per Revenue Passenger Mile (RRPM) $= \dfrac{\text{Total Revenue}}{\text{RPM}}$

$$\text{Load Factor (LF)} = \frac{\text{RPM}}{\text{ASM}}$$

$$\text{LF}_{\text{B-E}} = \frac{\text{CASM}}{\text{RRPM}}$$

Example 9.5

DirectJet Airlines has frequent flights from Seoul, Korea, to Tokyo, Japan. Assuming the following information, calculate LF and breakeven load factor and determine if the airline's route is economically justified:

$$\begin{aligned} \text{ASM} &= 57{,}800 \text{ million} \\ \text{RPM} &= 41{,}616 \text{ million} \\ \text{Total revenue} &= \$6{,}936 \text{ million} \\ \text{Total cost} &= \$6{,}358 \text{ million} \end{aligned}$$

Calculate LF as follows:

$$\text{Load Factor}\left(\text{LF}\right) = \frac{41{,}616}{57{,}800}$$

$$\text{LF} = 0.72 \text{ or } 72\%$$

To calculate breakeven LF, calculate CASM and RRPM and enter them in the next equation:

$$\text{CASM} = \frac{\text{Total Costs}\left(\text{TC}\right)}{\text{Available Seat Miles}\left(\text{ASM}\right)}$$

$$\text{CASM} = \frac{\$6{,}358 \text{ million}}{57{,}800 \text{ million}} = \$0.110$$

$$\text{R/RPM} = \frac{\text{Total Revenue (TR)}}{\text{Revenue per Passenger Miles (RPM)}}$$

$$\text{R/RPM} = \frac{\$6{,}936 \text{ million}}{\$41{,}616 \text{ million}} = \$0.167$$

$$\text{Break-even Load Factor} = \frac{\$0.110}{\$0.167} = 0.66 \text{ or } 66\%$$

Because the airline's LF is greater than breakeven LF, the Seoul–Tokyo route is economically justified.

To present a more comprehensive outlook of airline LFs and breakeven thresholds, we use available ton kilometers (ATK). ATK combines passenger and cargo capacity of airlines because they often provide both services. Figure 9.7 presents the load factor and the breakeven trend according to IATA.

As the figure shows, during the financial crisis of 2008–9 and COVID-19, achieved LF fell below breakeven LF emphasizing the economic hardship.

Payback Period Analysis

Bombardier Aerospace, a transportation company, faced challenges related to its commercial aircraft division in the early 21st century. The development of the Bombardier CSeries (now known as the Airbus A220) faced delays and cost overruns, putting pressure on Bombardier's finances. Despite efforts to secure orders and investments, Bombardier struggled to achieve profitability in its commercial aircraft segment. Eventually, Bombardier sold a majority stake in the CSeries program to Airbus in 2018, and the remaining stake was acquired by Airbus in 2020.

Another analysis that is commonly used in assessing projects is payback period. The objective of this analysis is to estimate the period needed to recover the initial investment (i.e., the first cost) considering the cash flow during the life of a project. Clearly, shorter PPs are more desirable. This method is often used by companies that have a small amount of working capital or companies in an industry that experiences rapid changes in technology. Another application of PP analysis is as an initial indicator that a project may be feasible and worthy of a full economic evaluation. We discuss two payback period analyses: conventional and discounted. In the former, we ignore the time value of money, while for the latter the interest rate is assumed to be nonzero.

Conventional PP is very simple to calculate and easy to understand; however, it has two major shortcomings: It ignores cash flows beyond the recovery period and therefore does not always select the best economically justified alternative, and assuming $i = 0$ ignores time value of money, which is the whole basis of the economic evaluation of alternatives. To eliminate the second shortcoming, we can incorporate the time value of money into payback analysis. This adjustment will result in discounted PP analysis, where $i > 0$.

Conventional Payback Period Analysis

Conventional payback period (N_P) analysis quickly determines the period needed to recover first cost. N_P assumes that $i = 0$, while discounted PP utilizes MARR. The focus of this section

Table 9.3 Nonuniform NACFs: Example 9.7

Year	*NACF*
1	\$1,750,000
2	\$1,500,000
3	\$1,250,000
4	\$1,000,000
5	\$1,000,000
6	\$1,000,000
7	\$1,000,000
8	\$1,000,000
9	\$1,000,000
10	\$1,000,000

is N_p. We calculate the conventional PP for projects with a uniform and nonuniform net annual cash flows (NACFs).

PP with Uniform NACFs

If a project has uniform NACFs, then we use the following equation to calculate (N_p):

$$N_P = \frac{\text{First Cost}}{\text{Net Annual Cash Flow}}$$

$$N_P = \frac{\text{PV}}{\text{Net Annual Cash Flow}}$$

Example 9.6

Jet Aviation is considering purchasing a machine costing \$5,000,000 to produce wing parts from composite carbon fiber. A uniform NACF of \$1,250,000 is expected for 10 years over the physical life of the asset with zero salvage value. What is the conventional PP for this machine?

Utilizing the last equation, PP is calculated as follows:

$$N_P = \frac{\$5,000,000}{\$1,250,000}$$

$$N_P = 4 \text{ years}$$

PP with Nonuniform NACFs

If a project has nonuniform NACFs, then we calculate the cumulative NACFs and use the following equation to calculate N_p:

$$N_P = (\frac{P - \textit{The cumulative cash flow in } (n-1) \textit{ year}}{\textit{Net Annual Cash Flow in year } n}$$

where n is the number of years that the cumulative cash flow exceeds the first cost for the first time and P is the first cost.

Table 9.4 Cumulative NACFs: Example 9.7

Year	*NACF*	*Cumulative NACF*
1	\$1,750,000	\$1,750,000
2	\$1,500,000	\$3,250,000
3	\$1,250,000	\$4,500,000
4	\$1,000,000	\$5,500,000
5	\$1,000,000	\$6,500,000
6	\$1,000,000	\$7,500,000
7	\$1,000,000	\$8,500,000
8	\$1,000,000	\$9,500,000
9	\$1,000,000	\$10,500,000
10	\$1,000,000	\$11,500,000

Example 9.7

In Example 9.6, assume the aircraft company has the nonuniform NACFs presented in Table 9.3. All other relevant information remains the same.

We first calculate the cumulative NACFs shown in Table 9.4.

The cumulative NACFs in Table 9.4 indicate that by year four, cumulative NACF exceeds the first cost for the first time; therefore, n = 4. With the first cost of \$5 million, PP is calculated as follows:

$$\mathrm{N_P} = (4-1) + \frac{\$5,000,000 - \$4,500,000}{\$1,000,000}$$

$$N_P = (3) + 0.5$$

$$N_P = 3.5 \text{ years}$$

The discounted payback period is a financial metric used to evaluate the time it takes for an investment to recoup its initial cost considering the time value of money. Unlike the traditional PP, which considers only the total cash flows without discounting, the discounted PP discounts future cash flows to their present value using a predetermined discount rate.

$$PW = -P + \sum_{t=1}^{NDP} \frac{NACFt}{(1+i)^t} = 0$$

Discounted PP Analysis

By calculating discounted payback period (N_{DP}), we eliminate the second shortcoming of $\mathrm{N_P}$ by assuming $i > 0$ or considering the time value of money in PP analysis. To find the $\mathrm{N_{DP}}$ of a project, we set PW of all cash flows to 0 and solve to the period as shown:

$$PW = -P + \sum_{t=1}^{NDP} \frac{NACFt}{(1+i)^t} = 0$$

If NACFs are an annuity or a uniform series, then this equation can be simplified:

$$\mathrm{PW = -P + NACF\,(P/A,\, i,\,} N_{DP}) = 0$$

Example 9.8

Using all relevant information in Example 9.6 for Jet Aviation and assuming a MARR of 10%, calculate N_{DP} is calculated as follows:

$$\begin{aligned} PW &= -\$5{,}000{,}000 + \$1{,}250{,}000\,(P/A, 10\%, N_{PD}) = 0 \\ \$5{,}000{,}000 &= \$1{,}250{,}000\,(P/A, 10\%, N_{DP}) \\ (P/A, 10\%, N_{DP}) &= 4 \end{aligned}$$

We now go to Appendix A for compound interest factors for 10% interest and look for the interest factor under column P/A. If we find the exact interest factor in that column, then the corresponding period under column n is N_{DP}. If we could not find the exact interest factor under column P/A, then we would interpolate between the two closed values. In this example, the interest factor of 4 is between five and six years, and therefore we interpolate between five and six years as follows:

$$\begin{aligned} \frac{n}{5} &= \frac{(P/A, i^*, N_{DP})}{3.7908} \\ \frac{5+X\%}{6} &= \frac{4}{4.33} \\ \frac{X\%}{1\%} &= \frac{0.2092}{0.5645} \\ X &= \frac{0.2092}{0.5645} \\ X &= 0.37\% \end{aligned}$$

Therefore, $N_{DP} = 5.37$ years. This number can be compared with the required payback period in a company policy to determine whether to consider evaluating the project or reject it.

Calculating Breakeven and Payback Periods in Excel

This section presents how to calculate breakeven in Excel when $i = 0$ or $i > 0$. Excel does not have a financial function to calculate breakeven; it is possible, however, to do so with the following formula:

$$Q_{BE} = \frac{FC}{P - V}$$

We can also calculate breakeven in Excel with this equation:

$$\begin{aligned} &\text{Profit} = Q \times (P - V) - FC \\ &Q_{BE} \times (P - V) - FC = 0 \end{aligned}$$

To calculate breakeven for a single project where $i > 0$, we set the PW or AW of the project to 0 and solve for breakeven of the parameter. AW is preferred when variable cost is expressed as annual:

$$\begin{aligned} AW &= 0 \\ AW &= -P\,(A/P, i, n) - AOC + (p - v) \times Q_{BE} = 0 \\ P\,(A/P, i, n) + AOC &= (p - v) \times Q_{BE} \end{aligned}$$

$$Q_{BE} = \frac{P(A/P,i,n) + AOC}{(p - v)}$$

where P = first cost, p = price per unit, and v = variable cost per unit.

Example 9.9

Jet Aviation is considering purchasing equipment costing \$700,000 with expected eight-year life to produce wing strut fairings and sell them at \$600 each. The variable cost per unit is \$250, and AOC is \$50,000 per year. Use Excel to determine the quantity of wing strut fairings Jet Aviation should produce per year to break even. Assume Jet Aviation uses a MARR of 9%.

Figure 9.8 shows a calculation of breakeven quantity. We enter the equation for breakeven quantity where interest $i = 0$ in cell [B8] and the equation for breakeven quantity where $i > 0$ in [B12]. The solutions are provided in cell [B9] and cell [B13] for breakeven quantities where $i = 0$ and $i > 0$, respectively.

We also describe how to calculate conventional and discounted PPs in Excel. The following is the formula for the conventional period, entered into a cell, and the next formula is used to calculate the discounted period:

$$N_P = \frac{PV}{NACF}$$

$$N_P = NPER(i\%, A, P, F)$$

Example 9.10

EuroJet is considering purchasing equipment costing \$4,000,000 to produce wing parts for airplanes from composite carbon fiber. A uniform net annual cash flow of \$800,000 is expected for 10 years over the economic life of the equipment with salvage value of \$400,000. Assuming EuroJet uses a MARR of 8%, calculate both conventional and discounted payback periods.

Figure 9.9 shows a PP calculation in Excel. We enter the equation for N_P in cell [B7] as shown; salvage value is ignored because it occurs beyond the recovery period. We also enter the equation for N_{DP} in [B11] as shown. The solutions are provided in cell [B8] and cell [B12] for N_P and N_{DP}, respectively.

	A	B	C
1			
2	First Cost	\$570,000	
3	AOC	\$50,000	
4	Life/years	6	
5	MARR	9%	
6	Variable cost per unit	\$250	
7	Price per unit	\$600	
8			
9	**Break-even quantity**	=((B2/B4)+B3)/(B7-B6)	
10	**MARR = 0**		
11			
12	**Break-even quantity**	**505.90**	
13	**MARR = 9%**		

	A	B	C	D
1				
2	First Cost	\$570,000		
3	AOC	\$50,000		
4	Life/years	6		
5	MARR	9%		
6	Variable cost per unit	\$250		
7	Price per unit	\$600		
8				
9	**Break-even quantity**	**414.29**		
10	**MARR = 0**			
11				
12	**Break-even quantity**	=(PMT(B5,B4,-B2,0)+B3)/(B7-B6)		
13	**MARR = 9%**			

Figure 9.8 Breakeven quantity with zero and nonzero interest.

	A	B
1		
2	First Cost	$4,000,000
3	AOC	$800,000
4	Life/years	10
5	MARR	8%
6	Salvage Value	$400,000
7		
8	**Conventional Payback**	=B2/B3
9	**MARR = 0**	
10		
11	**Discounted Payback**	**6.11**
12	**MARR = 8%**	

	A	B	C
1			
2	First Cost	$4,000,000	
3	AOC	$800,000	
4	Life/years	10	
5	MARR	8%	
6	Salvage Value	$400,000	
7			
8	**Conventional Payback**	**5**	
9	**MARR = 0**		
10			
11	**Discounted Payback**	**=NPER(B5,B3,-B2,B6)**	
12	**MARR = 8%**		

Figure 9.9 Calculating conventional and discounted payback periods with zero and nonzero interest in Excel.

Summary

Estimating payback periods and determining breakeven quantities are crucial for aircraft manufacturers in assessing the financial viability and profitability of their products. Companies interested in recovering their investment quickly to finance other profitable projects often use payback period analysis. Aircraft manufacturing involves substantial upfront investments in research, development, design, testing, and production. Estimating breakeven helps manufacturers understand how long it will take to recover these initial investments through sales of the aircraft.

Indeed, Airbus 380 and Lockheed's L-1011 TriStar are notable examples of projects that faced significant challenges due to incorrect estimations, including of breakeven. This chapter presents two new techniques for professional engineer decision-makers: breakeven analysis, and payback period analysis. Understanding the breakeven point allows companies to evaluate their vulnerability to changes in market conditions, costs, or technological advances. It serves as a tool for risk management, enabling businesses to identify potential financial challenges and develop strategies to mitigate risks proactively. The breakeven point of a given product, procedure, etc. is the point at which the cost equals the revenue generated, meaning profit is zero. For a single project, the annual usage rate (annual production or consumption units) must be equal to or greater than breakeven to make the project economically acceptable.

Breakeven can be analyzed considering time value of money where $i > 0\%$ or without it where $i = 0\%$. The latter method is simple and used often. With $i = 0$, breakeven is equal to project's fixed cost over the difference between price and variable cost per unit. To calculate the breakeven point of a single project where $i > 0$, we set the PW or AW of the project to 0 and solve for the breakeven of the parameter. AW is preferred when variable cost is annual. Breakeven also be applied to two mutually exclusive alternatives. To calculate the breakeven point between two alternatives, the point of indifference between the two, we set the total costs of one equal to the total costs of the other and solve for breakeven.

Conventional payback period (N_p) is a simple technique that quickly determines the period needed to recover the initial investment, but it has two major shortcomings: It ignores the cash flows beyond the recovery period, and it ignores the time value of money. Discounted payback period (N_{DP}) incorporates the time value of money. To find the N_{DP} of a project, we set PW of all cash flows to zero and solve the period.

Discussion Questions and Problems

9.1 At Av-Parts Aviation Support System, the main product is sharklet wingtips for commercial airplanes. The fixed cost for manufacturing the wingtips is $1,500 million. The average variable cost is $500,000, and Av-Parts Aviation sells the wingtips at an average price of $900,000. Calculate

a) the breakeven point and
b) the profit if the company sells 4,000 units per year.

9.2 EuroJet, the manufacturer of the AE-900 aircraft, spent about $15 billion at the beginning of the project for design, development, production, and testing, all fixed costs. The variable cost per unit is $270 million. The average price is $320 million.

a) What is the breakeven quantity?
b) What price should EuroJet charge for each AE-900 to break even at 200 units?
c) At a price of $320 million per unit, how much does the variable cost per unit have to be reduced to break even at 200 units?

9.3 DirectJet Airlines has frequent flights from Singapore to Hong Kong. Based on the following information, calculate the load factor and the breakeven load factor, and determine whether this Singapore–Hong Kong route is economically justified.

$$\begin{aligned} \text{ASM} &= 2{,}284 \text{ million} \\ \text{RPM} &= 1{,}957 \text{ million} \\ \text{Total revenue} &= \$388 \text{ million} \\ \text{Total cost} &= \$365 \text{ million} \end{aligned}$$

9.4 EZjET Airlines is reviewing the flight route to North America from China. This route has a load factor of 82%. EZjET has a target breakeven load factor of 75%. It has 45,000 million available seat miles and total revenue of $5,400 million. Based on target breakeven point, what is EZjET's cost per available seat mile?

9.5 A commercial aircraft manufacturer has two alternatives to manufacture security approved cockpit doors to meet the FAA new standards for commercial airplanes. The first has a fixed cost of $2,000,000 with variable cost of $10,000 per unit. The second has a fixed cost of $1,200,000 with variable cost of $20,000 per unit. What quantity of cockpit doors will make the manufacturer indifferent to the two alternatives?

9.6 Jet Aviation's main product is sharklet wingtips for commercial airplanes. The fixed manufacturing cost is $150 million, the average variable cost, is $50,000, and Jet Aviation sells the wingtips for an average of $90,000. Calculate the breakeven quantity per year assuming a 10-year project with no salvage value and a MARR of 10%.

9.7 Majestic Air Company LLC manufactures inflatable aircraft evacuation slides, and it is considering a more advanced machine to manufacture the slides with a first cost of $12 million and annual operating cost of $500,000. The economic life of the machine is 10 years with a required rebuild cost of $1,000,000 in four years and salvage value of $2,000,000. The machine requires six people to operate at $50 per hour including fringe benefits. In an eight-hour shift per day, they produce eight units. Assuming a MARR of 8% and a sale price of $15,000 per unit, what is the breakeven quantity per year?

9.8 EuroJet designs and manufactures turbine engines for transport aircraft. Advanced testing systems will ensure that their new signature program entitled Cool-Start works for every engine produced. EuroJet is choosing between one of the two cost-based testing systems described in the next table. Assuming a MARR of 10%, at what quantity per year will EuroJet be indifferent to the alternative systems?

	System A	*System B*
Robot and support equipment (first cost)	–$1,200,000	–$2,500,000
AOC	–$600,000	–$500,000
Rebuild cost in year five	–$200,000	$0
Salvage value	$120,000	$200,000
Estimated life, years	10	10
Labor wages per hour	$50	$30
People	6	10
Number of engine tested per hour	4	6

9.9 AvProp Aircraft Company produces prop-driven airplanes and is considering buying propeller systems of three-blade composite carbon fiber from Hartzell Inc. at $24,000 per unit. It is also considering making its propeller systems in house with equipment costing $12 million, AOC of $300,000, variable cost of $12,000 per unit, and estimated salvage value of 8% of the end of 10 years. At what breakeven quantity will AvProp be indifferent between making and buying propellers systems? Assume AvProp uses a MARR of 10%.

9.10 Jet Aviation is considering purchasing a machine costing $8,100,000 to produce wing parts from composite carbon fiber for airplanes. A uniform NACF of $1,500,000 is expected for 10 years over the physical life of the asset with zero salvage value. What is the conventional payback period for this machine?

9.11 In problem 9.10, assume Jet Aviation has nonuniform net annual cash flows as presented in the following table. All other relevant information remains the same. What is the conventional payback period for this machine?

Year	*NACF*
1	$2,000,000
2	$1,750,000
3	$1,500,000
4	$1,250,000
5	$1,000,000
6	$750,000
7	$500,000
8	$500,000
9	$500,000
10	$500,000

9.12 Using all relevant information in problem 9.10 for Jet Aviation and assuming a MARR of 10%, calculate the discounted payback period.

9.13 Jet Aviation is considering purchasing a machine costing $15 million with expected 10-year life to produce aircraft parts and sell them at $4500 each. Jet Aviation is expecting to sell 1,000 units per year with AOC of $500,000 in year one that will increase by $50,000 per year in year two through the end of 10 years. Jet Aviation uses a MARR of 12% and is expecting no salvage or residual value. What is the discounted payback period for this equipment?

9.14 Boeing, the manufacturer of the B787 Dreamliner, spent about $16 billion at the beginning of the project for design, development, production, and testing, considered fixed costs. The variable cost per unit is \$170 million. What price should Boeing charge per B787 to break even at 200 units?

9.15 DirectJet is reviewing the flight route from Pittsburgh to San Francisco. This route has a load factor of 80%. DirectJet has a target breakeven load factor of 70%. DirectJet has 56,000 million available seat miles and total revenue of \$5,376 million. Based on target breakeven point, what is DirectJet's cost per available seat mile?

9.16 FAA requires slides on all commercial aircraft doors where the floor is 6 feet or more above the ground. Air Cruisers Company LLC manufactures evacuation slides and is considering a more advanced machine to manufacture slides with a first cost of \$10 million and AOC of \$800,000. The economic life of the machine is 10 years with a required rebuild cost of \$2,000,000 in five years and salvage value of \$1,500,000. The machine requires five people to operate at \$60 per hour including fringe benefits. In an eight-hour shift per day, they produce 10 units. Assuming a MARR of 12% and a sale price of \$12,000 per unit, what is the breakeven quantity per year?

9.17 BizJet Aircraft Company is the leading designer and manufacturer of light and midsize business jets. Jet Aviation is selling parts for its aircraft through BizJet's parts department. It is considering purchasing a machine costing \$2,500,000 with expected 10-year life to produce right and left landing gear bulkheads and sell them at \$1500 each. BizJet is expecting to sell 500 units per year with AOC of \$50,000 in year one that will increase by \$20,000 per year starting the second year through the end of 10 years. BizJet uses a MARR of 9% and is expecting no salvage or residual value. What is the discounted payback period for this equipment?

Note

1 The Boeing 737 MAX represents a significant manufacturing crisis that profoundly impacted Boeing as an aircraft manufacturer. The issue stemmed from a flaw in the aircraft's Maneuvering Characteristics Augmentation System, which was designed to prevent stalls but was found to have contributed to two fatal crashes. These tragedies resulted in the grounding of the entire 737 MAX fleet worldwide and triggered extensive investigations, regulatory scrutiny, and legal challenges.

10 Engineering Cost Estimation

This chapter presents a detailed description of the cost structure of the aviation industry. The aviation industry is known for its high fixed costs and sensitivity to various economic factors. Cost-effectiveness is critical for an airline's ability to survive and compete.

Understanding cost structures is crucial for financial planning and risk mitigation. It helps in forecasting future expenses, conducting sensitivity analyses to assess the impact of external factors, and developing risk management strategies to reduce economic uncertainties. In-depth understanding of cost structures and accurate estimation are among the most important functions of engineer economists. The accuracy of the cost estimation plays a pivotal role in the financial sustainability of any company.

As a well-known case in point, Lockheed entered the commercial aircraft market in the early 1960s by producing their L-1011 TriStar. The new aircraft featured a twin-aisle interior with a maximum of 400 passengers and a three-engine layout. Lockheed faced strong competition first from the McDonnell Douglas DC-10, and later from the Boeing 747 (Phillip, 1998). After producing about 250 aircraft, Lockheed withdrew from the commercial aircraft business in 1984 due to inadequate demand and cost overruns.[1] The program did not earn back its development costs because Lockheed had failed to properly estimate the production costs and the breakeven number of aircraft sold.[2]

Professional engineering practices require cost rather than revenue estimation, and our focus with this chapter is to enable students and practitioners to understand the fundamental cost concepts including total costs, fixed costs, variable costs, direct costs, indirect costs, opportunity costs, and incremental costs and, especially, cost estimation.

Types of Costs

Cost is defined as the direct and indirect resources (materials, human capital, expertise, technology, and equipment) used to produce a certain output. For example, the cost of producing an aircraft includes the resources used to create the complex manufacturing plant, research and development, labor, material, and intellectual properties. Understanding costs is crucial for decision-making in various contexts, whether it be pricing strategies, budgeting, investment decisions, or assessing the economic viability of a project. After a steep rise in the price of oil in 2008, many airlines looked for different practices to reduce fuel cost and consumption. Airlines frequently apply various strategies to reduce costs and improve operational efficiency in an industry known for its tight profit margins and sensitivity to economic conditions. For instance airlines might replace older, less fuel-efficient planes with newer models like the more fuel-efficient Boeing 787 or Airbus A350.

DOI: 10.4324/9781003469759-10

> *In economics, cost refers to the quantitative measure of resources, whether financial, material, or labor, required to produce goods or services. In engineering, this encompasses expenses related to designing, manufacturing, constructing, and maintaining infrastructure, machinery, or systems. It includes factors such as raw materials, labor wages, equipment usage, energy consumption, and overhead expenses.*

Cost management should be closely aligned with the corporate culture, tailored productivity and efficiency targets, and carefully selected cost cutting measures. Southwest Airlines (LUV), by only flying Boeing 737s has been able to drastically lower the cost of training, maintenance, and inventory. Fleet homogeneity has enabled LUV to achieve significant cost reductions in labor and inventory spare holding costs. Modern technology such as automated check-in, electronic boarding passes, and self-service kiosks can streamline operations and reduce the need for manual intervention. Some airlines and airports have introduced biometric boarding passes, allowing passengers to use their fingerprints or facial recognition to board instead of traditional paper or electronic boarding passes.

A fundamental understanding of controlling costs is essential to ensure shareholders earn an optimum rate of return on the investment. In business, cost is usually a monetary valuation of effort, intellectual property, materials, forgone opportunities, resources, risks incurred, and time and utilities consumed. All expenses are costs, but not all costs are expenses (such as those incurred in acquisition of an income-generating asset). Expenses are a subset of costs that are specifically related to the ongoing operations of the business and are recognized on the income statement. Costs, on the other hand, include a wider range of expenditures incurred in the process of generating revenue, including the cost of goods sold and nonoperating costs.

Engineers often work within budget constraints and need to efficiently allocate resources such as time, labor, materials, and capital. Understanding the costs associated with various alternatives helps in making informed decisions and is crucial for financial analysis, budgeting, and decision-making. Costs in economics are categorized as fixed or variable. In the following section, we describe a wide range of understood costs in industry, including how to identify cost as fixed, variable, or total.

Fixed Costs

Figure 10.1 shows the structure of different costs. Fixed costs are independent of output; they remain constant throughout the relevant range of production and may be considered sunk for the relevant range (Figure 10.2). Typical fixed costs differ widely among industries. Retail shops such as restaurants are an example of a low fixed cost industry, but the aviation industry, auto manufacturers, and drilling operations usually have very high fixed costs.

A major portion of the cost of producing a new aircraft is the fixed costs for research and development of a prototype along with the new physical plants and infrastructure. Airbus spent eight years and around $14.7 billion developing the A350-XWB.[3] The A350 is the first Airbus with both wing structure and fuselage made largely of carbon fiber-reinforced polymer.

An aircraft's fixed costs are the same no matter how much the airplane flies. Fixed costs can create economies of scale, which are reductions in per-unit costs through increasing production volume. If a firm has high fixed costs, profits fall when sales fall, which adds some risk to the firm's stocks. Conversely, the same high-fixed-costs company will experience an abundance of profits when sales start to rise because any revenue increases are applied across a constant cost level.

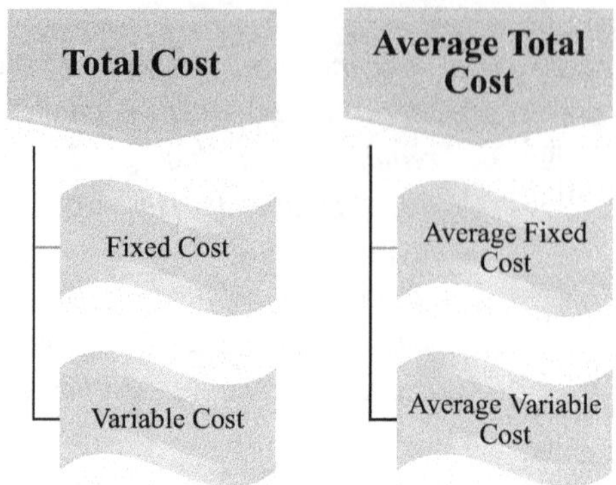

Figure 10.1 Cost structures.

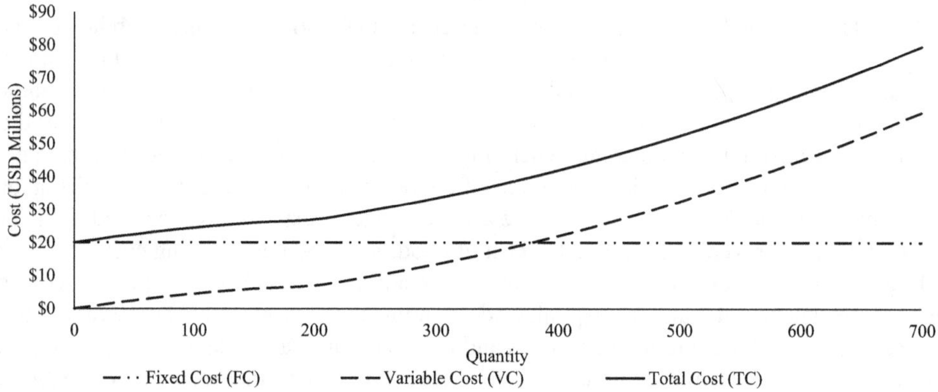

Figure 10.2 Short-run cost curves.

As previously mentioned in our earlier discussion, the airline industry is highly capital intensive, requiring massive financial assets to operate effectively. The high costs both fixed and variable have historically resulted in lower profitability and higher chance of financial insolvency. Fixed costs include aircraft ownership, airport slot and terminals, crew member salaries (annual contracts), insurance, jet engines, maintenance,[4] ownership of hanger and other physical assets, plant and equipment, and regulatory fees and charges.

Variable Costs

A variable cost is an expense that varies in relation to changes in the volume of production and activity. It can be a constant amount per unit produced or used such that total variable cost will change proportional to the volume of activity (Figure 10.2). Airlines incur a wide range of variable costs that are based on number of passengers, number of departures, volume of cargo carried, and many other factors. The variable cost per unit also fluctuates with changes in production levels. Other variable costs include aircraft fuel, some labor costs, supplies, and replacement parts.

In the airline industry, maintenance costs can be fixed or variable depending on the type of maintenance. Engine overhauls are based on the number of hours the engine has been in operation. The more the aircraft is flown, the more wear and tear the engine experiences, necessitating more frequent overhauls. Common variable airline costs include catering, labor and crew expenses, fuel, landing fees and air navigation charges, maintenance,[5] and oil.

Understanding the distinction between fixed and variable costs is essential for airlines to manage their operations efficiently. Fixed costs are expenses that remain constant regardless of the number of flights or passengers. For airlines, these include significant commitments such as aircraft lease payments and hangar rental fees, which persist irrespective of whether a plane flies one route or several.

Variable costs are expenses that change in direct proportion to the level of production. Fuel stands out as a primary variable cost for airlines, with its magnitude closely tied to the number of miles flown.

Total Costs

Total cost refers to the sum of all expenses incurred in producing a particular product or services; it encompasses both fixed and variable costs. Total cost analysis is a critical tool in many industries. It provides valuable insights into the financial aspects of production, enabling informed decision-making, efficient resource allocation, and sustainable growth:

$$TC = Total\ Cost$$
$$TFC = Total\ Fixed\ Cost$$
$$TVC = Total\ Variable\ Cost$$
$$TC = TFC + TVC$$

Because fixed and variable costs are positive at all levels of output, the total cost will always be positive irrespective of output level. When estimating cost, they can be approximated by either a linear cost function or an exponential function within the relevant range. The general linear cost function is given by

$$TC(Q) = FC + \beta \times Q$$

where TC (Q) is the total cost, FC is the fixed cost, Q is the number of items of output, and β is the average variable cost per unit, also called is the marginal cost. In a linear cost function, slope β represents the cost per unit, which is the marginal cost of producing one more unit of output. The intercept represents the fixed costs, which are incurred regardless of the level of output.

Variable costs fluctuate in direct proportion to level of production or other operational factors. With a linear total cost function, the total variable cost naturally becomes a linear function (constant variable cost), as illustrated in the following equation for better understanding all the elements of cost involved in any process of estimation:

For example,

$$TC(Q) = 20{,}000 + 400 \times Q$$

In this equation, FC is 20,000 and b is 400, and FC remains constant even if the production level is zero. $400 \times Q$ represents the variable cost, which increases proportionally with the quantity of output produced. For each unit of output produced (q), there is an additional variable cost of $400.

So, if an airline operates 20 flights ($Q = 20$) on this route, the total cost would be

$$TC(20) = 20{,}000 + 400 \times 20$$
$$TC(20) = 20{,}000 + 400 \times 20$$
$$TC(20) = 28{,}000$$

The linear cost function is a basic model used for conceptual understanding, but real-world cost functions in aviation may involve nonlinear relationships.

Example 10.1

A manufacturing company, JetParts, is seeking to develop a certain new aircraft. Assume the fixed cost for the project to be $20 million. Table 10.1 and Figures 10.2 and 10.3 give other elements of the cost to produce this aircraft the figures to demonstrate variations in cost plotted against the quantity of a product produced.

Example 10.2

Assume the total cost of flying a passenger aircraft is a linear function, comprising a fixed cost to operate a flight and variable costs based on the number of passengers onboard. Jet Aviation has

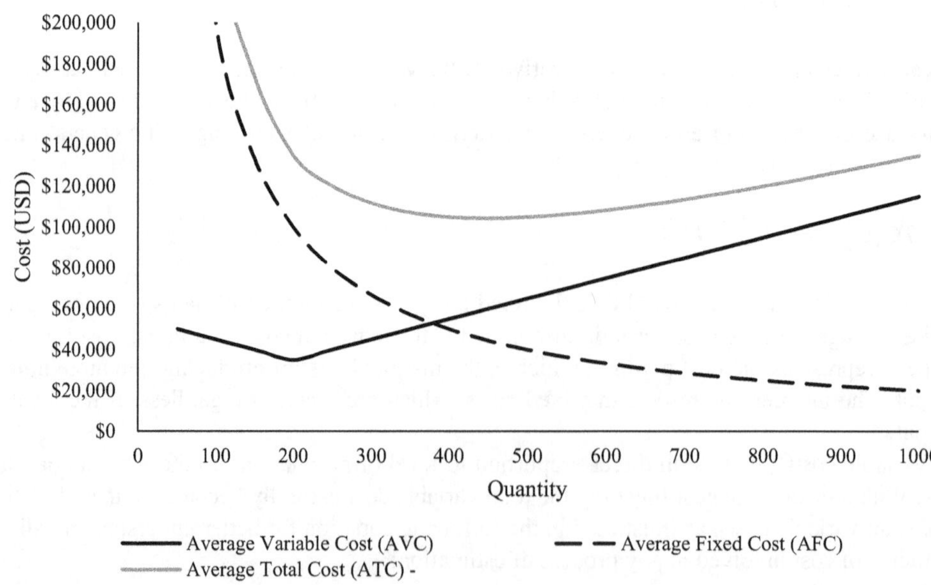

Figure 10.3 Average fixed, variable, marginal, and total cost curves.

Table 10.1 Short-Run Cost Schedule: Example 10.1

Quantity	*Fixed Cost*	*Variable Cost*	*Total Cost*	*Average Variable Cost*	*Average Fixed Cost*	*Average Total Cost*
0	\$20,000,000	\$0	\$20,000,000	–	–	–
50	\$20,000,000	\$2,500,000	\$22,500,000	\$50,000	\$400,000	\$450,000
100	\$20,000,000	\$4,500,000	\$24,500,000	\$45,000	\$200,000	\$245,000
150	\$20,000,000	\$6,000,000	\$26,000,000	\$40,000	\$133,333	\$173,333
200	\$20,000,000	\$7,000,000	\$27,000,000	\$35,000	\$100,000	\$135,000
250	\$20,000,000	\$10,000,000	\$30,000,000	\$40,000	\$80,000	\$120,000
300	\$20,000,000	\$13,500,000	\$33,500,000	\$45,000	\$66,667	\$111,667
350	\$20,000,000	\$17,500,000	\$37,500,000	\$50,000	\$57,143	\$107,143
400	\$20,000,000	\$22,000,000	\$42,000,000	\$55,000	\$50,000	\$105,000
450	\$20,000,000	\$27,000,000	\$47,000,000	\$60,000	\$44,444	\$104,444
500	\$20,000,000	\$32,500,000	\$52,500,000	\$65,000	\$40,000	\$105,000
550	\$20,000,000	\$38,500,000	\$58,500,000	\$70,000	\$36,364	\$106,364
600	\$20,000,000	\$45,000,000	\$65,000,000	\$75,000	\$33,333	\$108,333
650	\$20,000,000	\$52,000,000	\$72,000,000	\$80,000	\$30,769	\$110,769
700	\$20,000,000	\$59,500,000	\$79,500,000	\$85,000	\$28,571	\$113,571

fixed costs of \$10,000 per block hour and equipment and variable costs per passenger of \$30/hour. What is the total cost at varying levels of output?

$$TC = \$10{,}000 + \$30 \times Q$$

If the airline carriers 100 passengers, the total cost per block-hour is

$$TC = \$10{,}000 + \$30 \times 100$$
$$TC = \$13{,}000 \text{ per hour}$$

Cubic Cost Function

Quadratic or cubic cost specifications are frequently used to estimate manufacturing costs. A cubic specification for a total cost function is appropriate when the scatter diagram shows that the total cost initially increases at a decreasing rate followed by increasing at an increasing rate throughout the range of output. Cubic cost functions are often used in economics and business particularly when there are economies or diseconomies of scale. The general formula for a cubic cost function is as follows

$$TC(Q) = FC + \beta Q + \gamma Q^2 + \delta Q^3$$

β, γ and δ are the parameters of the function.
For example,

$$TC(Q) = 200 + 80 \times Q - 6 \times Q^2 + 0.25 \times Q^3$$
$$At\ Q = 0,$$
$$FC = TC = \$200$$
$$TVC = 80 \times Q - 6 \times Q^2 + 0.25 \times Q^3$$

Marginal cost is the cost incurred by producing one more unit of a good or service. It represents the change in total cost when production output increases by one unit. In aircraft manufacturing, marginal cost refers to the additional cost incurred by producing one more aircraft. This includes the costs associated with manufacturing additional parts, assembly labor, materials, and any other variable costs directly related to increasing production output.

$$MC = \frac{\Delta TC}{\Delta Q}$$

Marginal Costs

Marginal cost is defined as the change in the total cost resulting from producing one additional unit of output, in the airline industry, typically one additional passenger or one additional flight. Marginal cost is crucial for airlines as it helps them make decisions regarding flight frequencies, capacity management, pricing, and aircraft selection. When plotted on a graph, marginal cost curves can take a U shape, decreasing to a certain point before beginning to rise but continuing to decrease as long as the economy of scale is achieved. As soon as production enters diseconomies of scale, the marginal costs begin to rise again. In the airline industry, the marginal costs of providing an additional seat are likely insignificant, such as providing food and drink and luggage handling for one more person or additional fuel consumption.

Marginal costs are used in production decisions. If the price charged for a product is greater than the marginal cost, then the revenue will be greater than the added cost, and hence it is viable to continue production, whereas if the price charged is less than the marginal cost, the company is losing money and should cease or rethink production.

Mathematically, marginal cost is the change in total cost resulting from a change in the quantity of output produced by a company in the short run. Marginal cost indicates how much total cost changes for a given change in the quantity of output and is found by dividing the change in total cost by the change in quantity of output:

$$MC = \frac{\Delta Total\ Cost}{\Delta Quantity\ of\ Output}$$

$$MC = \frac{\Delta TC}{\Delta Q} = \frac{dTC}{dTC}$$

To calculate marginal cost, we need to take the change in total cost divided by the change in total output or taking the first derivative of the total cost function.

Example 10.3

Assume the total cost function is given by the following equation. Determine the marginal cost and identify the level of output that minimizes it:

$$TC(Q) = 200 + 80 \times Q - 6 \times Q^2 + 0.25 \times Q^3$$

Marginal cost is the derivative of the total cost function, as follows:

$$MC(Q) = 80 - 12 \times Q + 0.75 \times Q^2$$

Given the marginal cost, to determine the level of production that minimizes it, we just need to set the derivative of the marginal cost {MC (Q)} to 0:

$$\frac{d\,MC(Q)}{d\,Q} = -12 + 1.5 \times Q$$

$$\frac{d\,MC(Q)}{d\,Q} = 0$$

$$-12 + 1.5 \times Q = 0$$

$$Q = 8$$

Hence a quantity of eight units will minimize the marginal cost.

Average Costs

Average cost is primarily known as per unit total cost, or total cost divided by the quantity of output produced. Average cost is also the sum of average fixed cost and average variable cost (Figure 10.3). Average cost provides insights into how efficiently resources are being used in production.

Average total cost (ATC) is a measure used in engineering economics to represent the average cost of producing each unit of output. To find the average total cost, we just divide the total cost by the total number of units produced:

$$ATC = \frac{TC}{Q}$$

While average cost is a general term, there are three specific average costs: average total, average variable, and average fixed; we discuss the latter two in the next sections. Average total cost (ATC) refer to the per unit cost that includes all fixed costs and all variable costs and is a key factor in short-run production decisions evaluated against the price, which is per unit revenue. Comparing price with average cost gives a direct indication of whether a firm is making a profit or incurring a loss. Many managers want to know the cost per unit associated with producing a good because ATC can be used to determine the price of the product:

$$Average\ Total\ Cost = \frac{Total\ Cost}{Quantity\ of\ Output}$$

$$ATC = \frac{TC}{Q}$$

From Example 12.3, the average total cost is

$$ATC = \frac{200 + 80 \times Q - 6 \times Q^2 + 0.25 \times Q^3}{Q}$$

Example 10.4

Jet Services International (JSI) is one of the leading manufacturers of turbofan engines. JSI would like to analyze the variations in ATC and marginal cost for manufacturing a new engine. The estimated initial cost of the project is $1,000,000,000 Table 10.2 gives the other projected costs.

Figure 10.4 shows, among other trends, that when the marginal cost is less than the ATC, ATC declines, and when the marginal cost is higher than ATC, ATC increases. Additionally,

Table 10.2 Jet Services International Project Costs: Example 10.4 (in USD millions)

Quantity (Q)	*Total Cost*	*Average Total Cost*	*Marginal Cost*
0	$1,000		
10	$6,000	$600	$500
20	$9,000	$450	$300
30	$11,500	$383	$250
40	$15,000	$375	$350
50	$19,500	$390	$450
60	$25,000	$417	$550
70	$31,800	$454	$680
80	$40,200	$503	$840
90	$50,500	$561	$1,030
100	$63,000	$630	$1,250
110	$78,000	$709	$1,500
120	$95,800	$798	$1,780

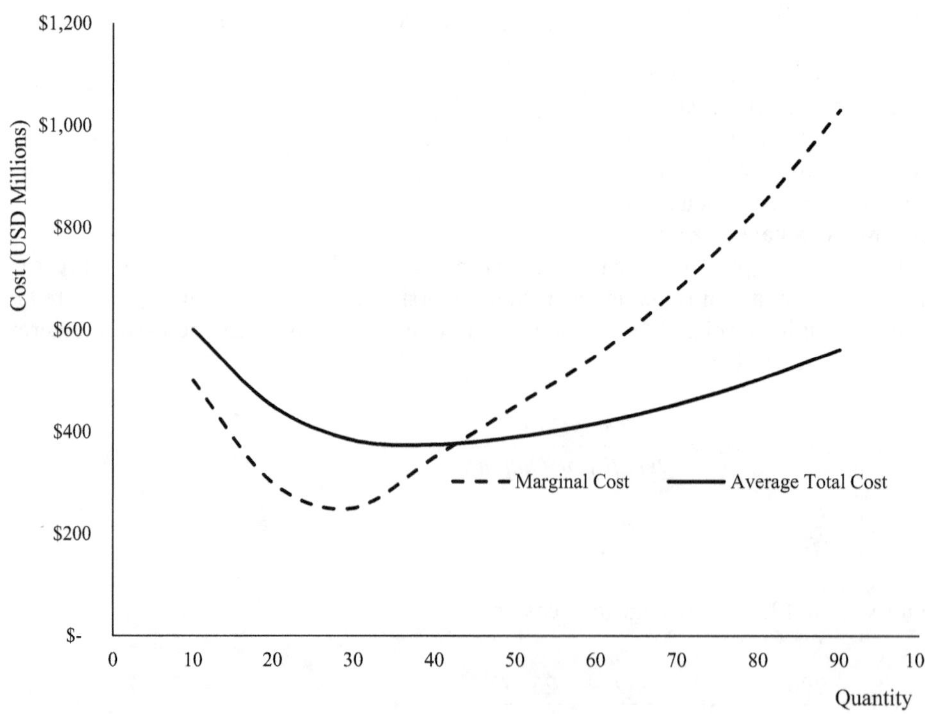

Figure 10.4 Marginal cost and average total cost.

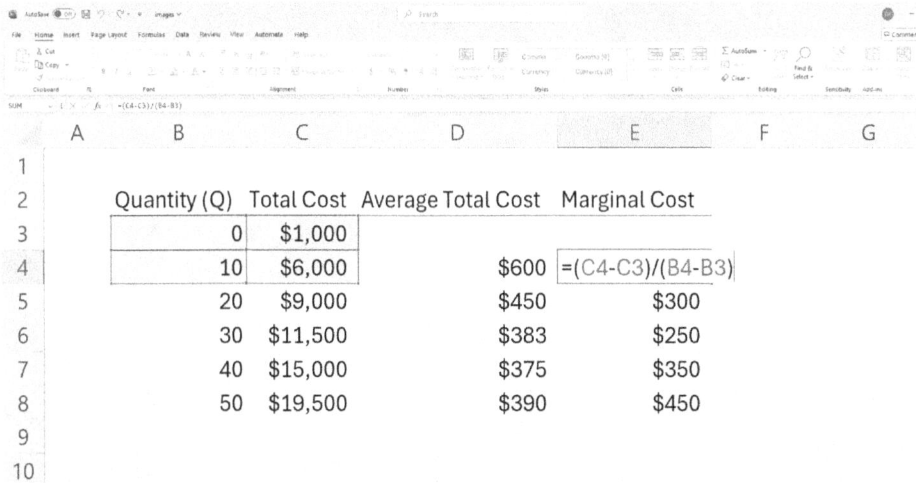

Quantity (Q)	Total Cost	Average Total Cost	Marginal Cost
0	$1,000		
10	$6,000	$600	=(C4-C3)/(B4-B3)
20	$9,000	$450	$300
30	$11,500	$383	$250
40	$15,000	$375	$350
50	$19,500	$390	$450

Figure 10.5 Calculating marginal cost in Excel.

when the marginal cost = ATC, there is a minimum or maximum ATC. This concept could also be applied to a university setting. Imagine that you are currently have a 3.5 in a class. If your next grade on an assignment is higher than your average, your average will increase and vice versa. Marginal cost is calculated in Excel using the total cost as shown in Figure 10.5.

In the airline industry, the cost per unit (e.g., flight, seat mile) decreases with increased aircraft utilization. For example, DirectJet leases jet bridges for $120,000 per year and operates the aircraft 3,000 times per year, and the airline cost per aircraft operation for a jet bridge is $40. If DirectJet leases the same jet bridge but operates 4,000 flights annually, its cost per aircraft operation decreases to $30.

Average Fixed Cost

Short-run production analysis makes use of three average cost measures: average total, fixed, and variable costs calculated as $ATC = AFC + AVC$. For airlines, average fixed and variable costs can be compared using the cost per available seat miles (CASM). Operating expenses represent the average variable cost, while the difference between total expenses and operating expenses gives the average fixed cost. Figure 10.6 graphically displays how to calculate average fixed cost (AFC) per unit. Figure 10.7 gives CASMs for the major US carriers for the third quarter of 2015.

The costs for plants and equipment to produce goods and services are fixed costs: Whether only one unit is made or 100, the costs do not change. AFC, or fixed cost per unit, is calculated as total fixed cost divided by the quantity of output produced. Since the fixed cost does not vary with output, AFC declines as the level of activity increases (Figure 10.8).

Example 10.5

From Example 10.3, determine the average fixed cost given

$$TC\left(Q\right) = 200 + 80 \times Q - 6 \times Q^2 + 0.25 \times Q^3$$

Figure 10.6 Fixed cost per unit.

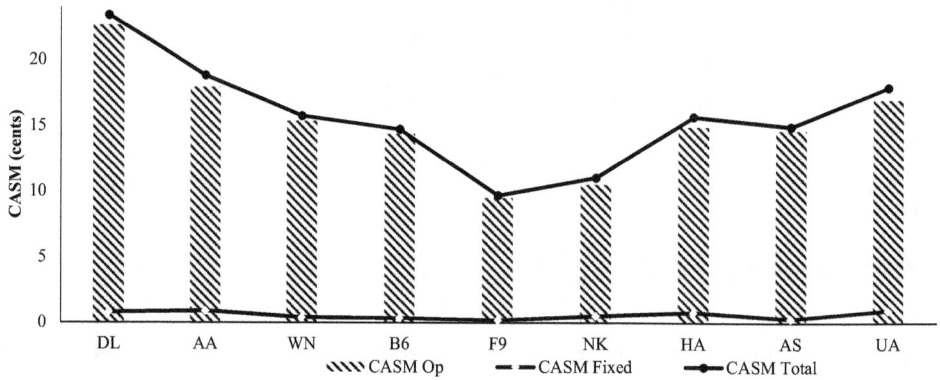

Figure 10.7 CASM comparison 2024.

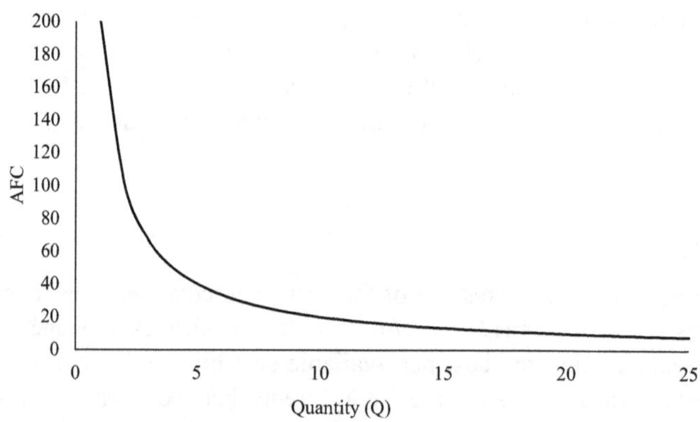

Figure 10.8 Average fixed cost curve.

The fixed cost from that equation is 200, and hence AFC is

$$AFC = \frac{200}{Q}$$

Average Variable Cost

Average variable cost (AVC) is used in economics and engineering to measure the cost per unit of variable inputs needed to produce a given level of output. A good example of a variable cost is fuel: If one mile of flight requires 10 gallons of fuel, then every mile requires 10 gallons, but every flight might not require 10 gallons of fuel. Variable costs can vary linear to production

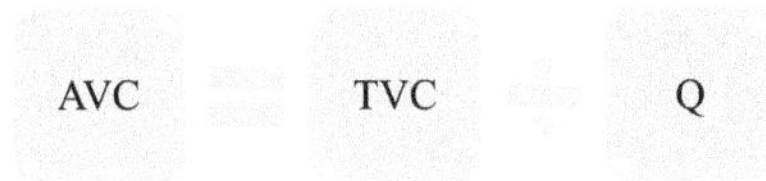

Figure 10.9 Variable cost per unit.

level, as in the more the aircraft flies, the higher the total variable cost (fuel burn). Total variable costs (TVC) vary in direct proportion to volume, for instance being if the aircraft does not fly and just stays at the gate. AVC is calculated as TVC divided by the quantity of output produced and is typically referred to as per unit total variable cost (Figure 10.9). Understanding AVC alongside other cost measures such as AFC and marginal cost can provide valuable insights into the efficiency of production processes.

Example 10.6

Consider Example 10.3. Determine the level of production that minimizes AVC given

$$TC(Q) = 200 + 100 \times Q - 8 \times Q^2 + 0.25 \times Q^3$$

First, find the AVC by dividing TVC by unit produced (Q). TVC is the same as the total cost minus the fixed cost of 200:

$$AVC(Q) = 100 - 8 \times Q + 0.25 \times Q^2$$

To determine the level that minimizes the average cost, the first derivative of AVC (Q) must be found and equated to 0:

$$\frac{d\,AVC(Q)}{d\,Q} = -8 + 0.5 \times Q$$
$$\frac{d\,AVC(Q)}{d\,Q} = 0$$
$$-8 + 0.5 \times Q = 0$$
$$Q = 16$$

Hence a quantity of 12 units will minimize AVC, as shown in Figure 10.10, which depicts the relationship between quantity and AVC for this equation.

Analyzing price and average cost give a firm three short-term alternatives as follows. First, it can produce at a profit; that is, if the price is equal to or greater than the average total cost, the firm generates a profit and can decide to continue operations. The firm can also produce at a loss. Some firms decide to continue production even if they will take a loss in the short run; a firm's managers might choose this alternative when the price is greater than the average variable cost but less than the average total cost. The loss from production is less than the fixed cost loss that would be incurred by shutting down production, which is a firm's final option. A firm chooses to shut down operations in the short run and incur the loss of fixed cost if the price is less than average variable cost, that is, if the loss from production is greater than the fixed cost loss incurred by shutting down production.

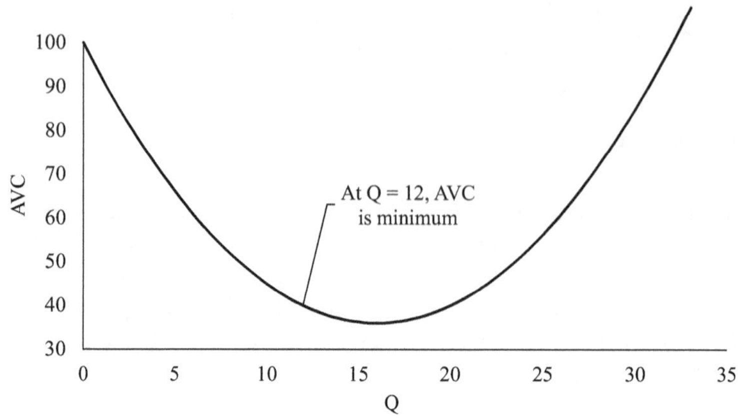

Figure 10.10 Minimum AVC with change in quantity: Example 10.6.

Economies of scale refer to the cost advantages of increasing the scale of operations. These advantages arise from spreading fixed costs over higher output, leading to lower average costs per unit of production or service.

Diseconomies of scale refer to when the average cost of production increases as the scale of operations grows beyond a certain point.

Economies and Diseconomies of Scale

Economies of scale are a fundamental concept in engineering economics and are often a key driver of industry consolidation and the growth of large corporations. Economies of scale refer to the notion that average cost falls as the firm expands. Airlines frequently claim that mergers can lead to economies of scale and provide cost efficiencies. Merging can allow airlines to optimize their fleet by retiring older, less fuel-efficient aircraft and streamlining the types of planes in operation; merging allows airlines to optimize their workforce by eliminating duplicative roles and improving labor productivity.

Economies of scale are evident in the airline industry in the sense that each additional passenger on the plane reduces per unit costs for the flight. Large airlines can negotiate bulk purchases of aviation fuel, obtaining discounts due to their significant purchasing power. This results in a lower average cost per gallon of fuel than smaller airlines pay. Airlines using a hub-and-spoke network can achieve economies of scale by consolidating passenger traffic through major hubs. This allows for more efficient use of aircraft, reduced turnaround times, and streamlined operations, contributing to lower unit costs.

Unfortunately, economies of scale, as a phenomenon, do not go on indefinitely. There is a point when long-run average costs will begin to rise as scale increases. This is known as diseconomy of scale. This occurs when a company's average unit cost increases due to increased output, which also increases AVC, such as when the number of aircraft landing at an airport exceeds runway capacity. In a metropolitan area, unprecedented surges in the number of vehicles during peak hours resulted in diseconomies of scale for the transportation system, causing gridlock, longer commute times, and heightened fuel consumption.

Sunk Costs

A sunk cost is a cost that has been incurred and cannot be recovered. Decisions about project investments should not incorporate sunk costs. For example, when replacing 40-pound airline manuals with iPads, the purchase cost of the paper for the manuals is a sunk cost since it occurred in the past and cannot be changed by any future course of action. Investment decision-makers must only consider relevant costs, and sunk costs are irrelevant.

A sunk cost is a cost that has been incurred and cannot be recovered. Sunk costs are also called "stranded costs". Sunk costs are independent of any event that may occur in the future. While making business decisions, typically a firm considers only future costs because money already spent on the project is now a sunk cost. It is a common business tenet that sunk costs should never be considered in investment decision-making, for instance incorporating already expended research and development millions into future investment decisions. Other sunk costs include the spending on technology once the system is implemented, marketing outlays once the campaign is executed, and training for personnel who leave.

Several years ago, US airlines replaced their heavy paper flight manuals with iPads loaded with special aviation navigation applications. They argue the pilots' use of the 1.5lb iPad, instead of about 38lbs of charts, logbooks and handbooks, will save 16 million sheets of paper and 326,000 gallons of jet fuel annually. Once the decision was made to replace the paper manuals with iPads, the cost of the printed manuals was sunk. The money spent on printing and distributing the manuals is irrecoverable.

In response to economic problems and reduction in traffic, many airlines just park their aircraft. At Mojave Airport, more than 1,000 aircraft ended up in the California desert after their flying days.[6] During a economic boom, airlines may bring them back, but for now, their costs have become sunk.

Assume DirectJet is planning to purchase a $737-400$ at a price of $5 million. The management knows the resale market for this aircraft is not good. If DirectJet is able to resell the aircraft for $2 million, then

$$\textit{Sunk Cost} = \$5,000,000 - \$2,000,000 = \$3,000,000$$

Some but not all fixed costs are sunk. In the DirectJet B737 example, if there were no alternative use or resale opportunity, the cost of the aircraft and related expenses would become sunk and irrelevant to any future decisions.

Believing it is worthwhile to continue with a project even if it is not the best thing to do because one has already invested much money, time, or effort in it is so common it has a name: the sunk cost fallacy or Concorde fallacy.[7] The higher the sunk investment, the more people tend to invest further, even when the return on added investment appears not to be worthwhile. According to researchers Daniel Kahneman and Amos Tversky, a reason people fall prey to the sunk cost fallacy is loss aversion: People tend to have a much stronger preference for avoiding losses than for acquiring gains.[8]

A very apt example of the sunk cost fallacy is the construction of the Concorde supersonic plane. Concorde development began in 1962 based on a treaty between Britain and France and was funded by the UK and French governments. The plane began commercial service in 1976 and flew for 27 years. It cost £1.134 billion to develop the Concorde. Then it cost the company about £654 million (of which only £278 million were recovered through sales) to produce 16

Concorde during 1965–79; this debt was also funded by the two governments.[9] The governments kept "throwing more good money after bad" because they "seemed prepared to pay the prestige premium no matter how high it rose." This was the reason the sunk cost fallacy also came to be known as the Concorde fallacy.

Opportunity Cost

The opportunity cost of an action or a decision is the value of the best alternative foregone, and everything has opportunity costs. One way low-cost airlines keep costs down is by operating young fleets with the most fuel-efficient engines to reduce fuel costs. The tradeoff is that they pay higher monthly aircraft costs for the same reason that a new car is more expensive than a used car.

An airline planning to add a new craft might purchase it or lease it. In this case, the opportunity cost of leasing an aircraft might be the forgone benefits of depreciation tax saving. An opportunity cost for people who delay purchasing airline tickets might be getting nonoptimal seating or inconvenient flight times in exchange for low last-minute fares. For airlines, opportunity costs arise around opportunities that are foregone when they make decisions regarding routes, fleet management, pricing strategies, and other operational aspects. For aircraft manufacturers, opportunity cost arise around making decisions regarding aircraft design, production, and market positioning.

Example 10.7

DirectJet is planning to open a new route from one of two potential markets; the airline has only one aircraft with the needed crew. In trying to decide, DirectJet is basing the decision in part on the accounting costs for one year listed in Table 10.3.

This tells us how much it will cost DirectJet to serve each airport, but to decide which airport to serve, DirectJet should figure out its opportunity cost. The first step is to determine the best alternative for each option. Table 10.4's net gain findings indicate that Airport A's opportunity cost is going to be $59,000 than that for Airport B.

Table 10.3 DirectJet Accounting Costs: Example 10.7

Expenses	*Airport A*	*Airport B*
Landing fees	$648,000	$972,000
Gate fees	219,000	146,000
Airport personnel	150,000	150,000
Miscellaneous	320,000	300,000
Annual Expenses	$1,337,000	$1,568,000

Table 10.4 DirectJet Net Gain: Example 10.7

	Airport A	*Airport B*
Revenue	$1,660,000	$1,950,000
Expenses	$1,337,000	$1,568,000
Net Gain	$323,000	$382,000

Economic versus Accounting Costs

Economists separate the world of cost into explicit costs that vary with the level of output and implicit costs. Explicit costs represent actual out-of-pocket cash outflows that reduce bottom-line profitability. In aviation, these include fuel expenses, gate fees and charges, wages and salaries, and air navigation charges. In economic terms, an implicit cost, also called nonpecuniary cost or implied cost, is the opportunity cost of using your own resources (Chiang, 1984). This is the income the airline loses when it does not fly an aircraft and generate passenger revenue.

For example, Standard & Poor's estimate that the October 2013 federal government shutdown cost the United States $24 billion.[10] And in 2020, millions of US workers were furloughed as COVID-19 brought the economy to a virtual standstill and left nearly 25 million people filing for unemployment benefits.[11]

Example 10.8

After graduation with a master's degree in aerospace engineering, you have been offered a job working for a company that pays you $150,000 annually. In addition, you have the opportunity to start your own business by investing $400,000 that will provide $180,000 year in revenue. You have always wanted to work in your own business. Should you invest in your own business if you can invest your money earning 10% interest? Explain.

Solution:

$$\textit{The opportunity cost of your investment} = 0.10\times(400,000) = \$40,000/\textit{year}$$
$$\textit{The opportunity cost of your time} = \$150,000$$
$$\textit{Total cost including the opportunity cost} = \$190,000\,/\,\textit{year}$$

You should invest in your business if the enjoyment from working for yourself is worth $40,000 a year or more.

Cost of Debt

Business debt is characterized by features such as a commitment to make fixed payments in the future that are tax deductible and the understanding that failure to make the payments can lead to either default or loss of control of the firm to the party the debt is owed to. The cost of debt is generally described as the rate at which the company can borrow long term today, composed of the risk-free rate and a default spread corrected for its tax benefit for the interest payments:

$$k_d = \textit{After}-\textit{tax Cost of Debt}$$
$$k_d = \textit{Long}-\textit{Term Borrowing Rate}\times(1-\textit{Tax Rate})$$

Figure 10.11 Economic cost vs accounting cost.

Cost of Equity

In engineering economics, "equity" often refers to the equity method of project evaluation. The equity of a project represents the investor's asset in the project and is often expressed as a percentage of the total project cost.

Cost of equity is the return a firm theoretically pays to its equity investors, that is, shareholders, to compensate for the risk they undertake by investing their capital. Cost of equity is normally calculated using the capital asset pricing model (CAPM) or the dividend discount model (DDM). It is denoted by the symbol r_e. It is imperative to note that the cost of equity is an estimate and involves some subjectivity in selecting appropriate inputs. Estimating the cost of equity in the air transport industry requires a comprehensive analysis of industry-specific factors, economic conditions, and the financial health of individual companies.

Weighted Average Cost of Capital

The weighted average cost of capital (WACC) is a measure that combines the cost of equity and the after-tax cost of debt based on the existing capital structure in the firm, that is, the ratio of debt to value and equity to value. WACC is an average measure of the payout rate a company expects. A lower WACC indicates cheaper financing and potentially favorable investment opportunities, whereas a higher WACC signals higher risk or inefficiency in capital utilization.

$$WACC = \left(\frac{D}{V}\right) \times k_d + \left(\frac{E}{V}\right) \times r_e$$

where $k_d = After - tax\ cost\ of\ debt$, $r_e = Cost\ of\ equity$, and $V = Total\ value\left(debt + equity\right)$.

SkyFly Airlines is a leading airline operating in a highly competitive market. SkyFly is considering a major expansion project that requires a capital investment of \$3 million. The company's capital structure includes \$2,000,000 in equity and \$1,000,000 in debt, and there are no preferred stocks. The cost of equity is 10%, the cost of debt is 6%, and the tax rate is 30%. The WACC for SkyFly to make this expansion is calculated as follows:

$$k_d = 6\% \times (1 - 0.30) = 4.2\%$$

$$WACC = \left(\frac{\$1,000,000}{\$2,000,000 + \$1,000,000}\right) \times 4.2\% + \left(\frac{\$2,000,000}{\$2,000,000 + \$1,000,000}\right) \times 10\%$$

$$WACC = (0.33) \times 4.2\% + (0.66) \times 10\%$$

$$WACC = 8.09\%$$

The WACC of 8.09% means that SkyFly needs to generate a return of 8.09% on its total capital to cover the costs of both debt and equity financing.

Return on Invested Capital vs WACC

Return on invested capital (ROIC) is a metric that measures the efficiency and profitability of a company in generating returns from its invested capital. ROIC is calculated by dividing the company's net operating profit after taxes (NOPAT) by its average invested capital. It is a key indicator used by investors and analysts to assess a company's ability to utilize its capital effectively to generate profits.

ROIC provides insight into how efficiently an airline utilizes its capital to generate profits. A higher ROIC indicates that the company is generating greater returns than the capital invested, while a lower ROIC suggests inefficiency or underperformance in capital utilization. Here are examples illustrating ROIC:

$$ROIC = \frac{NOPAT}{\text{average invested capital}}$$

If a company has a NOPAT of \$2,250,000 and an average invested capital of \$11,25,000, ROIC is

$$ROIC = \frac{2,250,000}{\$11,250,000}$$
$$ROIC = 0.20 \text{ or } 20\%$$

SkyFly is interested in evaluating its financial performance by calculating ROIC. The relevant financial information for the fiscal year is as follows: debt, \$200 million; equity, \$250 million; non-interest-bearing liabilities, \$100 million; operating income, \$60 million; tax rate, 30%; and total assets, \$500 million.
First, calculate NOPAT:

$$\text{NOPAT} = \$60 \times (1 - 0.30) = \$42$$
$$\text{Invested capital} = \text{total assets} - \text{non-interest-bearing liabilities}$$
$$\text{Invested capital} = \$500 - \$100 = \$400$$
$$ROIC = \frac{\$42}{\$400} = 10.5\%$$

As discussed, WACC is the rate at which a company is expected to pay on average all the security holders in order to finance its assets. As a company continues to increase the invested capital in more projects, it is simultaneously increasing its debt ratio, and an increasing debt ratio increases ROIC but at the same time increases WACC; the optimal debt ratio for any company is ROIC = WACC. This means a company has utilized its profits as much as possible. Any investment beyond this point would result in the WACC being higher than the ROIC, making it a poor investing decision

Example 10.9

Jet Services is an aircraft manufacturing firm headquarter in Brisbane Australia that is trying to decide how much to invest in producing different versions of a certain jet aircraft. Table 10.5 gives the estimated ROIC and WACC for various levels of investment; determine Jet Services' optimal debt ratio. Figure 10.12 shows clearly that ROIC = WACC at a debt ratio of 45% for Jet Services, and any investment beyond this point is a poor decision. Therefore, the company should not invest in any project past the ARJ500.

Cost Categories

The most significant cost for airlines is aircraft operation, which includes fuel expenses, maintenance, crew salaries, and leasing or depreciation costs, with fuel being among the largest operational costs for airlines because as jet fuel prices can fluctuate significantly and have a substantial impact on profitability. Properly categorizing costs allows airline management,

Table 10.5 Jet Services ROIC and WACC Estimates: Example 10.9

Project	*Debt Ratio for WACC*	*WACC*	*Debt Ratio for ROIC*	*ROIC*
ARJ 100	0%	6%	0%	26%
ARJ 200	10%	8%	15%	23%
ARJ300	20%	10%	25%	19%
ARJ 400	30%	12%	32%	16%
ARJ 500	40%	14%	**45%**	**15%**
ARJ 600	50%	16%	57%	12%
ARJ 700	60%	18%	63%	10%
ARJ 800	70%	20%	72%	7%
ARJ 900	80%	22%	81%	5%
ARJ X	90%	24%	90%	3%
ARJ XX	100%	26%	100%	2%

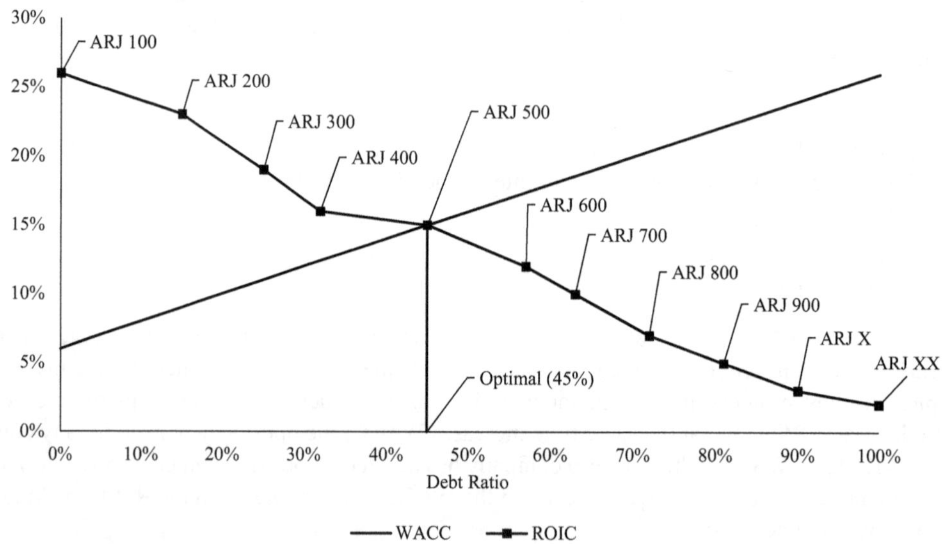

Figure 10.12 ROIC, WACC, and debt ratio: Example 10.9.

investors, and analysts to make informed decisions, optimize resources, and identify areas for improvement. As with other industries, aviation costs can be divided into direct versus indirect.

Direct Costs

All the costs associated with a business can be broadly classified as direct or indirect. The allocation and identification of direct and indirect costs contribute to more accurate profit calculations. An expense that can be traced directly to a specific cost center or activity is called a direct cost. In the airline industry, direct costs include labor, fuel, direct maintenance, and air navigation charges.

Labor and the materials to create specific products constitute the majority of direct costs. While salaries tend to be a fixed cost, direct costs are frequently variable. Determining whether a cost is direct or indirect must be done only by taking into consideration the cost object. A direct cost for one object might be an indirect cost for another. In the airline industry, direct costs include airport landing fees, airframe and power-plant maintenance and repair, commissions, flight and cabin crew expenses, fuel, landing and terminal fees, navigation fees, and station and ground handling service fees.

Direct costs in aircraft manufacturing comprise various expenses that can be explicitly linked to the production of an aircraft: materials, labor, overhead, tooling and equipment, subcontractor costs, quality assurance and testing, and transportation and logistics.

Direct costs in the airline industry encompass a range of expenses directly tied to the operation of flights and the provision of air transportation services. Labor, fuel, navigation and air traffic control charges represent major direct costs in operating an airline.

Indirect Costs

An indirect cost, also known as overhead costs, cannot be directly traced to a specific activity, for example, the wages and fringe benefits of police officers who provide security at the airport or in-flight catering because catering supports the whole system, not just individual flights. Since indirect costs cannot be easily traced to a specific department, project or process, they are usually estimated or allocated using a standard rate for a particular industry.

Also referred to as overhead costs, indirect costs are the ones left over after direct costs have been calculated. They provide an indication of the "real" costs of doing business. The materials and supplies for administrative purposes are examples of indirect costs. Similar to direct costs, indirect costs can be both fixed and variable. Fixed indirect costs include things like rent, and variable indirect costs include the ever-changing costs of electricity and gas. Some examples of indirect costs in the airline industry are salaries; marketing; training and professional development; legal services and compliance with aviation regulations; risk management activities; general and administrative expenses; and parking and passenger services.

Indirect costs are expenses that cannot be directly attributed to a specific project, product, or activity. Instead, these costs support the general operations of an organization and benefit multiple projects or activities. Indirect costs support the overall functioning of the organization rather than a specific task.

Example 10.10

An aircraft manufacturer produces different types of aircraft and incurs different types of costs throughout the year. The following table gives a breakdown about this business's costs break down.

	Direct	Indirect
Variable	• Materials and supplies for a specific aircraft	• Electricity for the corporate office
Fixed	• Rent for a building where only one specific aircraft is manufactured	• Salary of the CEO

Learning Curve Rate

Change occurs rapidly and is in fact inevitable in the dynamic work environments of today, but change induces learning. Improved instructions and repetition allow workers to learn to perform jobs more efficiently and thereby reduce the number of direct labor hours per unit. This process is not true only for the workers but also for the organization as a whole.

The learning curve rate is the percentage reduction in the average cost per unit for each doubling of cumulative production or experience. For example, if the learning curve rate is 80%, for each doubling of cumulative production or experience, the average cost per unit is expected to decrease by 20%. A 90% learning curve denotes a 10% reduction percentage.

The learning effect can be represented by a line called a learning curve, which represents the relationship between the total direct labor per unit and the cumulative quantity of a product or service produced. The learning curve reflects the relationship between experience and productivity: The time required to produce a unit decreases as the operator or firm produces more units.[12]

The idea of learning curves was introduced into economics by Alchian in 1963. Analyzing the data of 22 different US aircraft types produced during World War II, Alchian found that the direct amount of labor required to produce a unit of a special aircraft type regularly declined when the total output of that type increased.[13]

Learning curves were first used by the aircraft industry in the 1930s. The Boeing Co. pioneered the discipline when it discovered that the cost to build new airplanes was highly predictable. The learning curve concept was introduced by T.P. Wright through his groundbreaking empirical study on the productivity of the aircraft industry.

Learning curves enable managers to project the manufacturing cost per unit for any cumulative production quantity. Firms that focus on low prices as a competitive strategy rely on high volumes to maintain profit margins. The target for such firms is to lower labor hours per unit and lower costs per unit by moving down the learning curve as they increase production volume. This tactic makes market entry by competitors difficult because they would incur large losses to lower prices and still face high initial production costs.

The following assumptions typically hold true when observing a learning curve:

- The direct labor required to produce the $(n+1)^{th}$ unit is always less than the direct labor required to produce the nth unit.
- Direct labor requirements will decrease at a declining rate as cumulative production increases.
- The reduction in time will follow an exponential curve.

In other words, the production time per unit is reduced by a fixed percentage each time production is doubled. We can use a logarithmic model to draw a learning curve. The direct labor required for the nth unit is k_n:

$$k_n = k_1 n^b$$

where

- $k_1 = \textit{Direct labor hours required to produce first unit}$
- $k_n = \textit{Direct labor hours required to produce } n^{th} \textit{ unit}$
- $n = \textit{Cumulative number of units produced}$

  $b = \dfrac{\log r}{\log 2}$
- $r = \textit{Learning rate}\left(\textit{as decimal}\right)$

For example, a learning curve with 80% learning rate means that each doubling of cumulative production leads to a 20% reduction in unit cost or time, and a 90% learning curve means that for every time the cumulative quantity is doubled, there is a 10% efficiency gained in the cumulative average production time per unit.

Example 10.11

A component manufacturing company manufactures an electric starter used in jet engines manufactured by GE. The first time the component is produced, it takes 60 labor hours to complete. Based on prior experience, assume the learning rate is 80%. The following equations can be used to calculate the data for the learning curve as follows:

$$\begin{aligned}
k_1 &= 60\ \textit{hours} \\
r &= 80\% = 0.8 \\
b &= \frac{\log r}{\log 2} = \frac{\log 0.8}{\log 2} \\
b &= -0.3219 \\
k_n &= 60 \times n^{-0.3219} \\
k_4 &= 60 \times 4^{-0.3219} = 38.4\ \textit{hours} \\
k_8 &= 60 \times 8^{-0.3219} = 30.72\ \textit{hours}
\end{aligned}$$

Figure 10.13 denotes a typical learning curve and is plotted by calculating the corresponding labor hours for various units based on the formula defined earlier. The lower the learning curve percentage, the steeper the slope of graph, indicating greater improvement in efficiency. In this example, the first 60 hours can be considered the learning period, during which efficiency improved significantly; beyond that, the process becomes standardized.

A learning curve can also reflect factors such as the number of days required for the final assembly for an aircraft in manufacturing, but as the Boeing 787's in Figure 10.14.[14] At the start of production, each aircraft required over 1,000 days in final assembly. Five years of continued production resulted in that time in final assembly for a single aircraft to drop to as low as around 50 days.

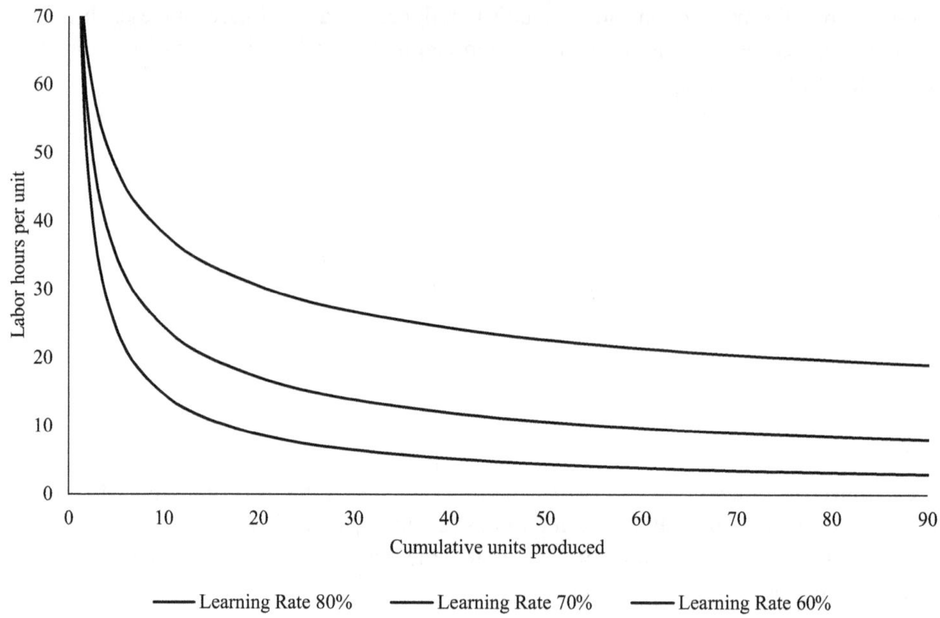

Figure 10.13 Learning curve.

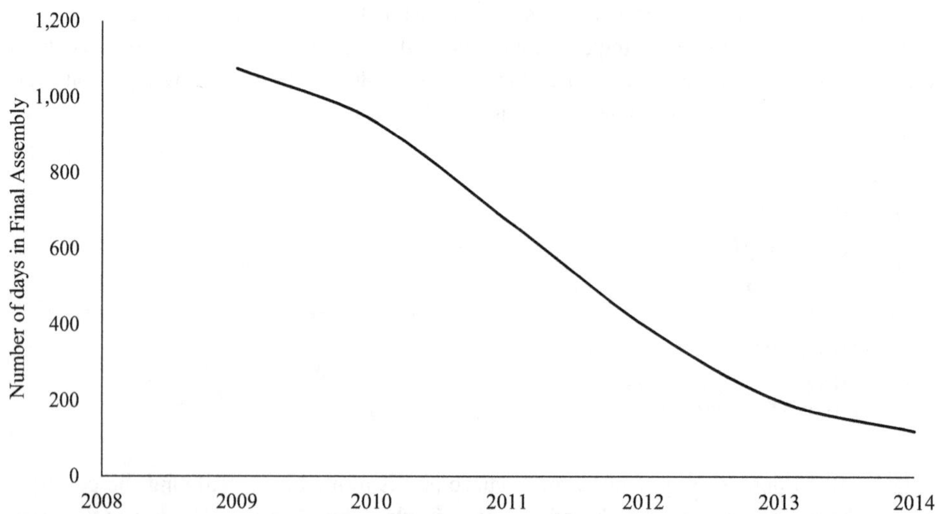

Figure 10.14 Sample learning curve for the Boeing 787.

Source: All Things 787.

Estimating Costs

Engineering economic analysis involves considering present and future economic factors. Hence, it is critical to obtain reliable estimates of future costs, benefits, and other economic parameters. A characteristic of cost estimates is that errors in estimating are typically asymmetric as costs are more likely to be underestimated than overestimated.

Cost estimation involves uncertainties arising from factors such as resource availability and estimator expertise. The quality of a cost estimate increases as the resources allocated to the estimate increase; the benefits expected from improving a cost estimate should in fact outweigh the cost of improving the estimate. A good example of cost estimation is using the Cobb–Douglas production function, which determines total production cost by relating it to labor and capital costs incorporating a productivity factor:

$$TC = AL^{\alpha} K^{\beta}$$

where TC = *Total cost of production*, A = *Productivity factor*, L = *Labor input* (*number of hours*), K = *Capital input*, and α, β = *Output elasticities of labor and capital*. For example, if $\alpha = 0.80$, a 1% increase in labor usage would lead to a 0.80% increase in total cost. The data for the considered example are shown in Table 10.6.

The total cost is found using

$$TC = 100\, L^{0.8}\, K^{0.2}$$

Converting this equation into logarithmic form makes it linear, thereby allowing a regression analysis. The linear equation is as follows, and the results are listed in Table 10.7:

$$Ln(TC) = Ln(100) + 0.8\, Ln(L) + 0.2\, Ln(K)$$

These findings are consistent with the linear equation obtained from the Cobb–Douglas production function. The intercept value (4.6052) obtained in the regression is Ln (100).

Table 10.6 Cobb–Douglas Data Assumptions

L (hours)	*K*	*Total cost*
10	\$100	\$1,585
11	\$200	\$1,965
12	\$300	\$2,284
13	\$400	\$2,580
14	\$500	\$2,862
15	\$600	\$3,137
16	\$700	\$3,407
17	\$800	\$3,673
18	\$900	\$3,936
19	\$1,000	\$4,198

Table 10.7 Regression Analysis Results

	Coefficients	*Standard Error*	*t Stat*	*P*	*Lower 95%*	*Upper 95%*
Intercept	4.6052	2.81E−15	1.60E+15	1.0E−104	4.605	4.605
X Variable 1	0.800	2.90E−15	2.76E+14	2.19E−99	0.800	0.800
X Variable 2	0.200	8.51E−16	2.35E+14	6.65E−99	0.200	0.200

Cost Estimation Methods

In the air transport industry, since operating an aircraft incurs a wide range of costs, cost minimization is essential, but to minimize costs, we have to have a clear understanding of the cost components. The cost components for some projects such as building an aircraft hangar are much simpler and fewer than the components of manufacturing a commercial aircraft. For example, a Boeing 787 Dreamliner has huge cost components. While the aircraft is assembled in the United States, most of the parts come from all over the world.

To reduce its development time and costs, Boeing implemented a worldwide supply chain of approximately 50 strategic partnerships worldwide. These strategic partners are responsible for design, build, and assembly of entire sections of the plane and deliver the complete sections to Boeing's plant in Everett, Washington. This process allows Boeing to assemble these complete sections within three to four days at its plant. While this example is used to magnify the size of the cost components, most manufacturers build components of their products in their factories and need to estimate the component costs as accurately as economically possible. Professional engineers use a number of cost estimation techniques that we discuss in the next sections of the chapter.

Unit Cost

Unit cost is a very preliminary but popular method of estimating the total cost of a project. This method usually provides rough estimates of total costs based on the cost per unit and the total units needed to complete the project. The cost per unit is often available based on similar projects completed in the past, from sources within the company or within the industry. This method is commonly used for preliminary design stage estimates. It is also used by construction companies in building houses, commercial property, factory, parking garage, aircraft hangar, school and university buildings. To get a good estimate of the total cost of any project using unit cost, the cost per unit has to be updated regularly to reflect the current cost. In unit cost method, the total costs is estimated as follows:

$$C_T = C_U \times N$$

where $CT = \textit{Estimated total cost}$, $CU = \textit{Cost per unit}$, and $N = \textit{Number of units needed}$.

There are two approaches used in estimating unit costs: top-down and bottom-up. The top-down approach is based on simply dividing total expenditure (quantum of funding available) for a given project by total units of activity; typically, this approach uses aggregate budgetary data. The main advantages of the top-down approach are the availability of the budgetary data – which means that the cost and time required to estimate unit costs using this approach are minimal – and the simplicity of the calculation.

However, there are also limitations associated with a top-down approach. First, the approach does not identify the main cost drivers and often masks the underlying factors that determine the reason unit costs vary within a single yet heterogeneous group of service users. Second, top-down costing is not a reliable source to forecast changes in costs as a result of changes in user behavior or of possible improvements in outcomes.

The bottom-up approach provides a much more refined outlook than the top-down method. It involves identifying all the resources that are used to provide a service and assigning a value to each of those resources. These values are summed and linked to a unit of activity to derive a total unit cost. This approach gives a basis for determining costs that can be avoided for instance because of reduced demand. Bottom-up cost estimation provides quality assurance because detailed cost data allow for investigating potential errors and testing their impacts. Additionally, the process highlights variations in cost data, enabling practitioners to explore the drivers of variation. Bottom-up estimation is also highly versatile as it enables a practitioner to forecast change in costs as a result of reduced service usage or demand. The main disadvantage associated with the bottom-up approach is that it is labor intensive, and the cost, time, and expertise required to apply it may be prohibitive for providers.

Example 10.12

Sea Breeze Regional Airport (SBR) is a regional airport serving the coastal communities in a 50-mile radius of the City of Sea Breeze, Australia. The airport is extremely convenient to residents of the area and is very quick and efficient. A preliminary estimate for the cost of building an executive hangar space at SBR is \$300 per square foot. Executive hangars are typically about 3,200 square feet. What is the estimated total cost of 20 executive hangars at Sea Breeze Regional?

The estimated total cost per Executive hanger is

$$CT = \$300 \times 3,200 = \$960,000$$

Estimated total cost for 20 executive hangers is

$$\$960,000 \times 20 = \$19,200,000$$

Unit cost can also be used to estimate the total cost of a multicomponent system. To estimate total system cost, first calculate the total cost of each component using component unit cost and the quantity of components needed, then add the total cost of all components.

Example 10.13

A multicomponent system consists of paint materials; sheet metal; and labor for mechanical, electrical, casting, finishing, and painting. The quantity of each component needed and its unit cost are provided in Table 10.8. What is the estimated total cost of the system?

Table 10.9 shows the calculation of the estimated total costs of each component and estimated total cost of the system.

Table 10.8 Components and Unit Costs: Example 10.13

Component	*Quantity Needed*	*Unit Cost*
Paint material	500 gallons	\$95
Sheet metal	2,000 tons	\$62
Labor, mechanical/electrical	1,200 hours	\$85 per hour
Labor, casting	1,500 hours	\$60 per hour
Labor, finishing	1,000 hours	\$50 per hour
Labor, painting	200 hours	\$40 per hour

Table 10.9 Components and Unit Costs: Example 10.13

Component	*Quantity Needed*	*Unit Cost Factor*	$C_T = C_U \times N$
Paint material	500 gallons	\$95	\$47,500
Sheet metal	2,000 tons	\$62	\$124,000
Labor, mechanical/electrical	1,000 hours	\$85 per hour	\$85,000
Labor, casting	1,500 hours	\$60 per hour	\$90,000
Labor, finishing	1,000 hours	\$50 per hour	\$50,000
Labor, painting	500 hours	\$40 per hour	\$20,000
Estimated Total Cost of the System			\$416,500

Cost Index

A cost index is the ratio of the cost of a project today to the cost of a project at a particular time in the past, making the cost index an indicator of the changes in cost over time. Thus, calculating the cost index accounts for inflation to a certain extent. An important quality of a cost index is that it is dimensionless:

$$C_t = C_0\left(\frac{I_t}{I_0}\right)$$

where C_t = *Estimated cost at present time t*, C_0 = *Cost at previous time* t_0, I_t = *Index value at time t*, and I_0 = *Index value at base time* 0.

The widely reported Consumer Price Index (CPI) is an index that denotes changes over time. This index is calculated and published by the US Bureau of Labor Statistics. Table 10.10 presents the CPI for the 21st century to date.

Producer price index (PPI) measures the average change in the selling prices received by domestic producers for their output over time in a particular industry. Tables 10.11–10.13 present PPIs for aircraft engine and engine parts, construction, and wholesale, respectively.

Engineering News-Record generates a construction cost index for building, common labor, skilled labor, and materials. Table 10.14 presents some years' indices with 1930 as a base year.

Example 10.14

EZjET needs to calculate the cost of labor today (in USD) to complete a project compared with the cost of completing the same project in Europe five years ago. The 2010 labor index was 790.60, and today it is 1156.70. The labor cost to complete the project in Europe was €1.5 million. The conversion rate for today is €1 equals \$1.50. The cost index can be used to determine the labor cost of the project today:

$C_t = \textit{The cost that needs to be determined in USD}$
$C_0 = €1{,}500{,}000$
$I_t = 1156.70$
$I_0 = 790.60$

$$C_t = C_0\left(\frac{I_t}{I_0}\right)$$

Table 10.10 CPI for All Urban Consumers: December 2000 to 2023

Year	*CPI*	*Year*	*CPI*
2000*	100.0	2012	156.6
2001	102.8	2013	160.1
2002	107.2	2014	161.7
2003	110.9	2015	163.2
2004	117.1	2016	168.0
2005	123.5	2017	173.2
2006	128.5	2018	178.2
2007	136.8	2019	184.0
2008	136.8	2020	187.4
2009	142.7	2021	206.2
2010	145.9	2022	224.2
2011	152.6	2023	234.1

*2000 is a base year. Indices are unadjusted

Source: Federal Reserve Economic Data and Bureau of Labor Statistics https://fred.stlouisfed.org. Federal Reserve Bank of St. Louis

Table 10.11 PPI for Aircraft Engines and Engine Parts: January 2000–2023

Year	*PPI*	*Year*	*PPI*
2000	100.0	2012	168.1
2001	102.6	2013	174.0
2002	105.3	2014	177.4
2003	110.9	2015	178.2
2004	119.1	2016	183.0
2005	123.8	2017	183.3
2006	128.1	2018	187.3
2007	136.3	2019	190.6
2008	142.4	2020	192.8
2009	152.4	2021	195.9
2010	158.3	2022	202.2
2011	162.7	2023	217.0

*2000 is a base year. Indices are unadjusted.

Source: Federal Reserve Economic Data and Bureau of Labor Statistics https://fred.stlouisfed.org. Federal Reserve Bank of St. Louis

Table 10.12 PPI for Construction: December 2007–2024

Year	*PPI*	*Year*	*PPI*
2007	100.0	2016	117.3
2008	108.0	2017	122.1
2009	102.8	2018	129.4
2010	103.3	2019	135.3
2011	106.6	2020	138.1
2012	108.1	2021	156.9
2013	112.6	2022	189.5
2014	114.7	2023	190.4
2015	117.3	2024	193.4

*2007 is a base year. Indices are unadjusted

Source: Federal Reserve Economic Data and Bureau of Labor Statistics https://fred.stlouisfed.org. Federal Reserve Bank of St. Louis

Table 10.13 PPI for Wholesale Trade: December 2009–2024

Year	*CPI*	*Year*	*CPI*
2009	100.0	2017	120.2
2010	100.8	2018	125.2
2011	104.5	2019	128.3
2012	108.4	2020	132.2
2013	110.2	2021	151.6
2014	112.7	2022	166.7
2015	113.9	2023	164.2
2016	117.9	2024	167.3

*2009 is a base year. Indices are unadjusted

Source: Federal Reserve Economic Data and Bureau of Labor Statistics https://fred.stlouisfed.org. Federal Reserve Bank of St. Louis

Table 10.14 Engineering News-Record Construction Cost Indices for Selected Years

Year	*Index*	*Year*	*Index*
1930	100	1980	3134
1940	139	1990	4629
1950	407	2000	6118
1960	721	2010	8557
1970	1278	2020	11289

Source: https://digital.bnpmedia.com/publication/?i=701229&article_id=3985354&view=articleBrowser

$$C_t = €1{,}500{,}000\left(\frac{1156.70}{790.60}\right)$$
$$C_t = €2{,}194{,}599.04$$
$$C_t = €2{,}194{,}599.04 \times 1.5 = \$3{,}291{,}898.56$$
$$Hence,\ Ct = \$3.29\ million$$

Example 10.15

The average price of an engine in 2009 was about \$11.3 million. The aircraft engine and engine cost indexes were 192.0 and 218.9 for 2009 and 2015, respectively. What is the estimated price of an engine in 2015?

$$C_t = \$11.3\ m\left(\frac{218.9}{192.0}\right)$$
$$Ct = \$12.88\ m$$

Cost Capacity Equation

The cost capacity equation accounts explicitly for economies of scale. This method, which is also called power law or sizing model, estimates the cost of an asset, equipment, or system with different size or capacity than that of a similar one. This model accounts for economies of scale when we are estimating the cost of a larger asset such as a plant, and it accounts for diseconomies of scale when we are scaling down the plant. The cost capacity equation uses a correlating exponent (x) that reflects scale in the capacity or size differences:

$$C_2 = C_1\left(\frac{Q_2}{Q_1}\right)^X$$

where $C_1 = Cost\ at\ capacity\ Q_1$, $C_2 = Cost\ at\ capacity\ Q_2$, and $X = Correlating\ exponent.$

In this model, the correlating exponent can be 1, x > 1, or x < 1. The impacts of the correlating exponent are presented in Table 10.15.

Since economies of scale generally exist when one purchases a larger asset, the correlating exponent should usually be less than 1.

Example 10.16

A turbojet engine with 20,000 pounds of thrust costs $2,000,000. What is the estimated cost of a turbojet engine with 100,000 pounds of thrust if the correlating exponent is 0.60 for the thrust range of 10,000 to 200,000 pounds?

$$C_1 = \$2,000,000\ for\ 20,000\ pounds\ of\ thrust$$
$$C_2 = Estimated\ cost\ for\ 100,000\ pounds\ of\ thrust$$
$$X = 0.6$$
$$C_2 = \$2,000,000 \times \left(\frac{100,000}{20,000}\right)^{0.6}$$
$$C_2 = \$5,253,056$$

The capacity increased by 5 times from 20,000 to 100,000 pounds of thrust, but cost increased only by 2.63 times. This is due to economies of scale with a correlating exponent of 0.60 that is much less than 1.

The cost capacity equation relates the cost of an asset to its size or capacity, but it assumes that the costs of different sizes are current. The correlating exponents usually do not change over time, but the cost of equipment or components change over time. Therefore, one has to combine the cost capacity equation and cost indexing ratio (I_t/I_0) to adjust for time adjustments and obtain the current cost of the equipment. The next equation provides the combined effects of cost capacity equation and cost indexing ratio to estimate the cost at time t for capacity level 2:

$$C_2 = C_1\left(\frac{I_t}{I_0}\right)\left(\frac{Q_2}{Q_1}\right)^X$$

Table 10.15 Possible Values for Correlating Exponent

x = 1	There is a linear relationship among two capacities and there are no economies or diseconomies of scale.
x > 1	Larger capacities will cost more than smaller capacities because of diseconomies of scale.
x < 1	Larger capacities will cost less than smaller capacities because of economies of scale.

Example 10.17

An aerobic digester with a flow rate of 1 million gallons per day (MGD) was installed in 2010 at a cost of $800,000. Estimate the cost of an aerobic digester this year with a flow rate of 5 MGD, assuming that the correlating exponent is 0.20 for range of 0.5 to 20 MGD and the cost index increased from 152 in 2010 to 208 in the current year:

$$C_2 = \$800,000\left(\frac{208}{152}\right)\left(\frac{5}{1}\right)^{0.2}$$
$$C_2 = \$800,000\,(1.3684)(1.3797)$$
$$C_2 = \$800,000\,(1.8880)$$
$$C_2 = \$1,510,385$$

The capacity of the aerobic digester increased by 400%, and the cost index increased by about 37%, but the cost of a new aerobic digester increased by only about 89%. This is because of significant economies of scale or very small correlating exponent.

Cost Factor

The cost factor method is especially useful in estimating total plant cost in processing industries. Both direct and indirect costs can be included. This method is particularly useful when certain factors have a more significant impact on the overall cost, and it helps project managers and estimators allocate resources and budget effectively. The cost factor is commonly the sum of all direct cost components and an indirect cost component:

$$h = 1 + \sum f_i$$

For i = 1, 2, 3 . . . n cost components, including direct and indirect costs.

Total plant cost estimate C_T is equal to overall cost factor (h) × cost of equipment or major component of a plant (C_E):

$$C_T = h \times C_E$$

where

- C_T = *Estimated total cost of a plant*
- C_E = *Cost of equipment or major component of the plant (first cost)*
- h = *Overall cost multiplier*

Example 10.18

A manufacturing company is planning to shift equipment to a new facility. The equipment costs $20 million. A cost factor for all direct costs of 1.74 and an indirect cost factor of 0.35 will make the plant ready to operate. What is the total cost of the plant?

The total plant cost can be estimated as follows:

$$h = 1 + \sum f_i$$
$$h = 1 + 1.74 + 0.35 = 3.09$$

$$C_T = h \times C_E$$
$$C_T = 3.09 \times \$20\ million$$
$$C_T = \$61.8\ million$$

The estimated total cost is \$61.8 million.

In cases when indirect costs are charged separately against direct costs, the cost factor includes only the sum of all direct costs, and the indirect cost are added separately, as follows:

$$h = 1 + \Sigma f_i \quad (only\ direct\ cost\ components)$$
$$C_T = hC_E\left(1 + f_{indirect}\right)$$

Example 10.19

Using relevant information in Example 10.13, consider the delivered equipment cost to be \$20 million. The direct cost factor for installation is 1.20 and for training is 0.54 and an indirect cost factor of 0.3 is applied to all direct costs. In this case, the total cost is estimated as follows:

$$h(direct) = 1 + 1.20 + 0.54 = 2.74$$
$$C_T = hC_E\left(1 + f_{indirect}\right)$$
$$C_T = 2.74 \times \$20\ million(1 + 0.3) = \$71.24\ million$$

Hence the estimated total cost is \$71.24 million.

Indirect Cost Estimation and Allocation

Indirect costs are costs that cannot be directly traced to a production, process, or department. Examples of indirect costs include utilities, administrative costs, IT services, accounting, and marketing functions. Since indirect costs cannot be easily traced, they are usually estimated and allocated using either a standard rate or activity-based method.

Standard rate estimation and allocation can be accomplished using industry-specific rates. For a given industry, the standard rate can be calculated by expressing indirect costs as either a factor of the first cost, the major equipment cost, or the main component cost or as a factor of total direct costs.

$$Standard\ indirect\ cost\ rate = \left(\frac{Total\ expected\ indirect\ costs}{Estimated\ first\ cost}\right)$$

Once the standard rate for indirect cost is calculated, one can use the factor method to estimate the total indirect cost or the total cost of the plant using both direct and indirect costs.

Example 10.20

Martin Aircraft Company (MAC) is planning to manufacture a new aircraft model. The company's total indirect/overhead costs were \$7,639 million, and its total fixed assets were \$14,292 million in 2014. What was the indirect cost rate for MAC based on total fixed assets?

Utilizing the indirect cost estimation equation, calculate the indirect cost rate as follows:

$$DJ\ indirect\ cost\ rate_t = \left(\frac{\$7{,}639\ m}{\$14{,}292\ m}\right)$$

$$DJ\ indirect\ cost\ rate = 0.53$$

Activity-Based Allocation

Activity-based allocation allocates indirect costs to products or services based on the actual activities that drive those costs. Unlike traditional costing methods that use a single, broad allocation base, activity-based allocation considers multiple drivers of indirect costs. In the activity-based method, one would first identify the activities, the cost drivers, and the total volume of those drivers. Then establish the activity-based allocation rate for the cost driver. Finally allocate the total indirect cost by multiplying the volume of each activity by the allocation rate. The activity-based allocation rate can be calculated by dividing total indirect cost of activities by total volume of cost drivers:

$$Activity\text{-}based\ allocation\ rate = \left(\frac{Expected\ total\ indirect\ costs\ of\ activities}{Total\ volume\ of\ cost\ drivers}\right)$$

Example 10.21

A startup airline out of Phoenix, Arizona, established four routes to Los Angeles, Denver, Chicago, and Dallas last year and incurred a total of $2 million in overhead costs. The company wants to use activity-based allocation to allocate the indirect cost among the routes. The cost driver is identified as revenue passenger miles. Table 10.16 presents the available seat miles (ASM) and average load factor for each route. Use the activity-based method to allocate the overhead cost using number of revenue passenger miles.

To calculate the total revenue passenger miles, multiply ASM by the load factor for each route and add them as shown in Table 10.17.

Table 10.16 Available Seat Miles and Load Factor for Each Route: Example 10.21

Route	*Total ASM*	*Average Load Factor*
Chicago	12,000,000	75%
Dallas	15,000,000	78%
Denver	8,000,000	70%
Los Angeles	18,000,000	85%

Table 10.17 Calculating Revenue Passenger Miles: Example 10.21

Route	*Total ASM*	*Average Load Factor*	*Revenue Passenger Miles*
Chicago	12,000,000	75%	9,000,000
Dallas	15,000,000	78%	11,700,000
Denver	8,000,000	70%	5,600,000
Los Angeles	18,000,000	85%	15,300,000
Total revenue passenger miles			41,600,000

The indirect allocation rate per passenger revenue mile is calculated as follows:

$$Allocation\ rate = \left(\frac{\$2,000,000}{41,600,000}\right)$$

$$Allocation\ rate = \$0.048$$

Given the allocation rate of $0.048 per revenue passenger mile, the overhead costs can be allocated to the four routes as shown in Table 10.18.

Airline Cost Structure

The airline industry in the United States is an oligopoly dominated by several major airlines, with industry costs affected by a set of volatile factors. The size and the type of aircraft, fuel efficiency, and distance traveled are some examples of cost factors. The costs of airline resources can be divided into operating and nonoperating, with operating costs being the much larger of the two categories and further divided into direct versus indirect costs. Nonoperating costs are costs not directly linked to the airline's operation but required to conduct business.

Operating Costs

Airline operating costs are the expenses incurred in running an airline, and they are an essential element of overall financial performance. Operating costs can be either fixed or variable, but all relate directly to the core operation of the business. Airline operating costs include aircraft and nonaircraft rental and/or ownership, concessions (food, beverage, etc., fuel, labor, landing fees, maintenance, and transport-related expenses among many others. The air fleets themselves are typically the largest expense, particularly the fuel, followed by labor. Operating costs can be further broken down into direct or indirect costs, with direct expenses such as labor and fuel constituting the greatest portion of operating costs. Airlines for America provides a good overview of airline operating costs (Figure 10.15). In Tables 10.19, we compile operating expenses for Delta gathered from annual company reports.

Direct Operating Costs

Direct operating costs can be directly traced to a specific level of production, which for the airline industry could be a specific airport or specific flight. Table 10.19 shows clearly that labor and fuel are largest direct operating costs for airlines. Some labor costs are fixed (namely wages, salaries, and benefits), while others such as overtime and profit sharing are more likely to be variable. Figures 10.16 and 10.17 present the labor (compiled from annual reports) and fuel costs

Table 10.18 Indirect Cost Allocation across Four Routes: Example 10.21

Route	*Revenue Passenger Miles*	*Allocation Rate*	*Indirect Cost Allocation*
Chicago	9,000,000	$0.04808	$432,720
Dallas	11,700,000	$0.04808	$562,536
Denver	5,600,000	$0.04808	269,248
Los Angeles	15,300,000	$0.04808	735,624

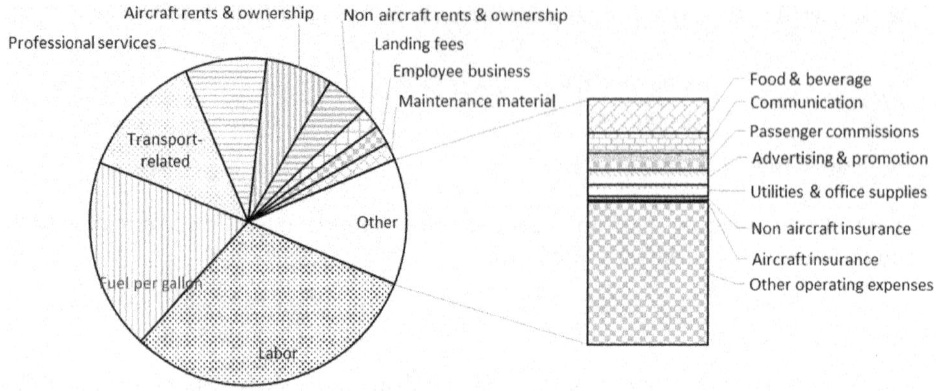

Figure 10.15 Airline operating cost index.

Source: Airlines for America.

Table 10.19 Operating Expenses for Delta Air Lines (in USD millions)

	Year ending Dec. 31	
	2023	*2022*
Aircraft fuel and related taxes	11,069	11,482
Salaries and related costs	14,607	11,902
Ancillary businesses and refinery	4,172	5,756
Aircraft maintenance materials and outside repairs	2,432	1,982
Depreciation and amortization	2,341	2,107
Contracted services	4,041	3,345
Passenger commissions and other selling expenses	2,334	1,891
Landing fees and other rents	2,563	2,181
Profit sharing	1,383	563
Passenger service	1,750	1453
Aircraft rent	532	508
Regional carrier expense	2,200	2051
Other	3,103	1,700
Total operating expense	52,527	46,921

of major US carriers for 2015. The graphs show that each of the two costs form approximately 30% of the total expenses and are the biggest contributors to the overall operating expenses.

Although proper understanding of direct operating costs is important from an external standpoint, internal analysis requires detailed understanding of the basic differences between variable and fixed direct operating costs not only for reducing an airline's cost structure but also for shaping business strategy.

FIXED DIRECT OPERATING COSTS

An airline's fixed direct operating costs are costs of operation that occur whether specific flights are operated. These costs include aircraft leases, terminal leases, and crew salaries. Fixed

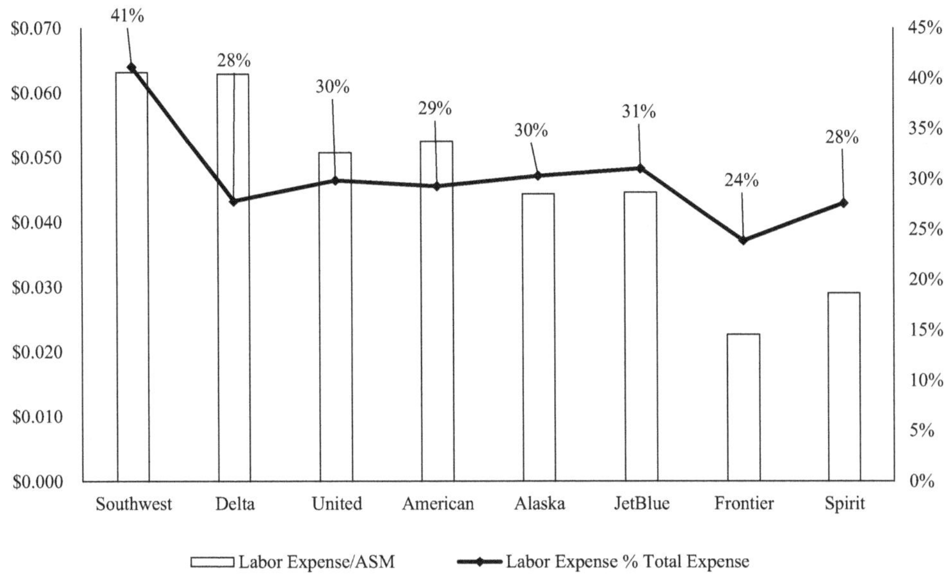

Figure 10.16 Labor costs, 2024.

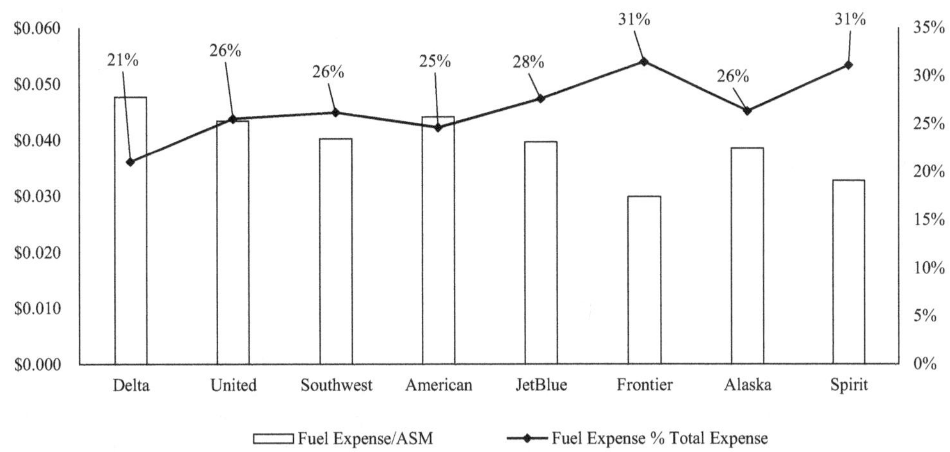

Figure 10.17 Fuel costs, 2023.

operating costs are allocated to flights based on the percentage of operations that the flights make up.

VARIABLE DIRECT OPERATING COSTS

Variable direct operating costs are incurred based on the number of flights an airline operates. Fuel, landing fees, passenger services, and maintenance are all fixed but variable operating costs since they vary depending on the number of flights taken over the course of a year. Some flight crew costs, such as overnight accommodations, could also be deemed variable operating costs.

Airlines should base profitability of flights on variable operating costs because once in operation, the fixed operating costs will be incurred whether or not planes fly. Sometimes a flight is operated even if the direct variable operating costs exceed the revenue, for instance because it feeds passengers feed to a profitable connecting flight, but would be unprofitable without the connecting passengers. Additionally, the direct costs associated with not operating the flight, such as routine maintenance and parking fees, can exceed the financial losses of operating the flight. In such cases, it makes more sense to operate the flight.

Indirect Operating Costs

Indirect operating costs are costs that are not directly related to the core functioning of the airline, such as some administration expenses, personnel training expenses, advertising, and commissions. Indirect costs are necessary for an airline to operate but cannot be directly linked to specific flights because they support all airline operations. The direct impacts of these costs on an airline's operation are negligible, but reducing indirect costs can still significantly lower total operating costs.

Nonoperating Costs

Nonoperating costs are expenses arising from activities not associated with rendering air transport services. Ideally nonoperating costs are related to the financial structuring of the company and are the result of an overarching financial strategy. The most common nonoperating cost in the airline industry is interest, which accounts for airlines' sizeable debt loads. Airline operations are in no way affected by interest expenses incurred even though the debt itself is used to fund the operation of the airline. Other nonoperating costs for an airline include any loss on the sale of aircraft and other assets and foreign currency exchange charges. Another major nonoperating cost is depreciation because asset depreciation has no impact on an airline's operations.

Summary

A thorough understanding of costs in engineering projects is fundamental for effective project management, financial decision-making, risk mitigation, and successful project delivery. This chapter focused on introducing readers to the different types of costs such as fixed and variable; direct and indirect; and total, marginal, and average as well as their varied applications. Engineers must understand costs to negotiate favorable contracts, ensuring that the terms are financially reasonable and align with the project's objectives. A brief discussion about the relationship between economic costs and accounting costs and the possible types of financing options is provided as well, incorporating the cost of capital, the return on investment, and the optimal debt ratio. Understanding the learning curve is a crucial part of cost estimation in any business, and a detailed description regarding the same is provided in the chapter.

Costs tend to decrease as output increases because of the learning effect, which impacts not only the production floor but the whole organization. Different methods of cost estimation are explained to facilitate accurate cost calculation: unit cost, cost index, cost capacity equation, cost factor, and indirect cost estimation and allocation. We introduced the concept of sunk costs in the context of engineering economics, which play a pivotal role in the decision-making process. These are expenditures that have already occurred and cannot be recovered.

The last section of the chapter focuses on the airline cost structure and how it matches up to the previously discussed types of costs. We divided airline costs into operating (costs directly related to the operation of the business such as aircraft rent and ownership costs, catering, fuel expenses, labor costs, landing fees, maintenance costs, nonaircraft rent and ownership, and transport-related expenses), and nonoperating (costs that are not directly associated with the air transport services such as interest, loss on sale of aircraft and other assets, foreign currency exchange charges, and depreciation). Companies that effectively manage cost, emphasize operational efficiency, adjust to market dynamics, and implement strategic cost-cutting measures when necessary are more likely to overcome challenges and ensure their long-term survival in the highly competitive aviation industry.

Discussion Questions and Problems

10.1 Distinguish between economic cost and accounting cost.

10.2 Describe the differences between variable costs and fixed costs.

10.3 Give an example of a fixed cost and a variable cost of an airline.

10.4 Define and give examples of opportunity costs and sunk costs.

10.5 The cost function for a fixed-based operator is given by

$$TC(Q) = 40{,}000 + 30Q^2.$$

Find

- Marginal cost of producing 10 units
- Average cost function
- Average variable cost function
- Average total cost function

10.6 Suppose the cost function is

$$TC(Q) = 50 + Q - 10Q^2 + 2Q$$

- What is the marginal cost of producing a 4th unit?
- What is the marginal cost of producing a 10th unit?

10.7 John is thinking about opening a fixed-based operation (FBO) at a local airport. John estimates that it would cost $8,000,000 per year to rent a hangar and stock it with inventory of parts. In addition, John would have to give up $800,000 per year as a manager for another FBO.

- What are John's explicit costs of running the FBO for a year?
- What are the implicit costs, if any, of running the FBO for a year?
- If John's annual revenue (net other expenses) is $8,450,000, what are his estimated accounting profits? His economic profits?
- Would you advise John to open the FBP? Explain.

10.8 Aviation Supply is a small, North Korean company that provides parts for unmanned aircraft manufacturers. The company's total cost function is given by the following equation:

$$TC = 1{,}500{,}000 + 250 \times Q$$

- Graph the firm's total cost, marginal cost, and average cost.
- Find total fixed cost, total variable cost and average cost for the company's total cost function.

- Break average cost into average fixed cost and average variable cost.
- What happens to average variable cost and average fixed cost as output rises?
- Will average cost ever equal marginal cost?

10.9 Calculate the time required to produce the 10th aircraft if the time to manufacture the first aircraft is three months and the learning rate of production is 0.75.

10.10 A multicomponent system consists of paint materials; sheet metal; and labor for mechanical, electrical, casting, finishing, and painting. The quantity of each component needed and its unit cost are provided in the following table. What is the estimated total cost of the system?

Component	*Quantity Needed*	*Unit Cost Factor*
Paint material	500 gallons	$95
Sheet metal	2,000 tons	$62
Labor, mechanical/electrical	1,000 hours	$85 per hour
Labor, casting	1,500 hours	$60 per hour
Labor, finishing	1,000 hours	$50 per hour
Labor, painting	200 hours	$40 per hour

10.11 The average price of the Rolls-Royce Trent 1000 engine was $16.25 million in 2007. The producer price indices (PPIs) for the engine were 175.9 and 218.9 in 2007 and 2015, respectively. Assuming the price of Rolls-Royce engines increases according to PPI, what was the estimated price of a Rolls-Royce Trent 1000 in 2015?

10.12 The cost of production for 100 electric starter units is $200,000. What is the estimated cost of production of 500 electric starter units if the correlating exponent is 0.7 for a range of production from 100 to 1,000 units?

10.13 A compressor with 2,000 horsepower (hp) was installed at cost of $200,000 in 2010. What is the cost of installing a compressor with 500 hp in this year assuming the correlating exponent is 0.62 for hp range of 200 to 2500 and the cost index has increased from 342 in 2010 to 512?

10.14 A multicomponent system is expected to $400,000 including delivery and installation. The cost factors for the components are provided in the following table. If indirect costs are expressed as a factor of the cost of equipment, what is the estimated total cost of the system?

Components	*Cost Factor*
Concrete	0.85
Sheet Metal	0.46
Construction	1.20
Indirect Labor	0.55
Other Indirect Costs	0.42

10.15 In problem 10.6, recalculate the estimated total cost of the system if indirect costs are expressed as factor of total direct cost.

10.16 A startup airline out of Denver, Colorado, established five routes to Los Angles, Los Vegas, Phoenix, Chicago, and Dallas last year and incurred $4.2 million in overhead costs. The company wants to use activity-based allocation to allocate the indirect cost among the routes. The cost driver is identified as available seat miles (ASM). The following table presents the revenue passenger miles (RPM) and average load factor for each route. Allocate the overhead cost on an activity basis using ASM.

Route	*Total RPM*	*Average Load Factor*
Chicago	450,000	75%
Dallas	574,000	82%
Los Angeles	630,000	70%
Los Vegas	595,000	85%
Phoenix	480,000	80%

10.17 A compressor with 2,000 hp was installed at cost of $200,000. What is the cost of installing a compressor with 500 hp assuming the correlating exponent is 0.32 for hp range of 200 to 2500?

10.18 The price of a B737 MAX engine by CFM, a joint venture between GE and SAFRAN, is about $11 million in 2026. What was the price of the same engine in 2020 if the aircraft engine and engine cost indexes are 197.9 and 217 for 2020 and 2026, respectively?

10.19 An aircraft manufacturing company takes 150 hours to build the first section of a modular wing. The learning curve for constructing additional sections is 75%. How many hours will it take to build the 16th section?

$$k_n = k_1 n^b$$
$$k_{16} = 150 \times 16^{\frac{\log 0.75}{\log^2}}$$
$$k_{16} = 150 \times 16^{-0.4150}$$
$$k_{16} = 47.60\ \textit{hours}$$

10.20 An assembly line requires 200 hours to produce the first unit. The company operates under a 90% learning curve. What is the time required to produce the eighth unit?

$$k_n = k_1 n^b$$
$$k_8 = 200 \times 8^{\frac{\log 0.90}{\log^2}}$$
$$k_{16} = 200 \times 8^{-0.152}$$
$$k_{16} = 145\ \textit{hours}$$

Notes

1 Saddened Lockheed Workers Still View L-1011 with Pride. *Los Angeles Times*, December 8, 1981.
2 Greenwald, J., Hannifin, J. & Kane, J. (1981, December 21). Catch a Falling TriStar. *Time*.
3 The Airbus A350, Up and Away. *The Economist*, June 14, 2013.
4 Aircraft maintenance is typically scheduled to be completed whether the airplane flies or not, as well as scheduled overhauls and avionics updates. Hence, these costs can be considered fixed because they do not necessarily change with aircraft usage.
5 Delta Air Lines is retiring its 747s, older 757s, and domestic 767s to lower its maintenance costs.
6 *BBC*, September 18, 2014.
7 Cambridge Business Dictionary.
8 Tversky, A. & Kahneman, D. (1986). Rational Choice and the Framing of Decisions. *The Journal of Business*, 59(S4).
9 Concorde. F.A.Q.
10 Shutdown Took $24 Billion Bite Out of Economy. *CNN*, October 17, 2013.
11 Furloughed Due to the Coronavirus? *Money Watch*, April 27, 2020.
12 Krajewski, L., Malhotra, M. & Ritzman, P. (2009). *Operations Management, Supplement 1: Learning Curve Analysis* (9th Edition).
13 Hartley, K. (1965). The Learning Curve and Its Application to the Aircraft Industry. *The Journal of Industrial Economics*, 13(2), 122–128.
14 All Things 787.

References

Alchian, A. (1963). Reliability of Progress Curves in Airframe Production. *Econometrica: Journal of the Econometric Society*, 679–693.

Chiang, A. (1984). *Fundamental Methods of Mathematical Economics* (3rd Edition). McGraw-Hill.

Phillip, B. (1998). *Lockheed L-1011 TriStar*. Motorbooks International.

Stratford, A. (1973). *Air Transport Economics in the Supersonic Era* (2nd Edition). London: Macmillan.

Tversky, A. & Kahneman, D. (1974). Judgment Under Uncertainty: Heuristics and Biases. *Science, New Series*, 185(4157).

11 Financial Statements

Financial statements are a collection of reports about a company's operation that provide information on financial activities over the course of a given period. Financial statements are the most important sources of information about companies for a wide variety of stakeholders such as creditors, employees, investors, and tax authorities. Corporations use four types of financial statements to report the financial results of their operations: the balance sheet, the cash flow statement, the income statement. and the statement of retained earnings. The income statement represents a company's revenues and expenses over a given period, whereas the balance sheet is a snapshot of the organization's financial position on a particular day. Another important financial statement is the statement of cash flows, which shows the changes in cash and cash equivalents over the period. In this chapter, we will learn how to read aviation industry financial statements and perform basic financial analysis. We will explore the income statement, the balance sheet, the statement of retained earnings, and the cash flow statement.

The Income Statement: Measuring a Firm's Profits

An income statement, also called an earnings statement, is where you will find a company's profits and losses. It is an accounting statement that matches a company's revenues with its expenses over a period of time, usually a quarter or a year. Income statements begin by listing the company's income from the sale of products or services less total operations costs. The principle of the income statement is a company's clearly stating its earnings and expenses over time including whether activities resulted in profits or losss.

As we described, the income statement is a cumulative account of items through a specific accounting period. Thus, the expenses on a first-quarter income statement equal the cumulative expenses during the first three months of the firm's fiscal year, the expenses on the second-quarter statement equal the cumulative expenses during the second three months of the firm's fiscal year, and so on. We explain the various components of the income statement in the following sections using Boeing's income statement as an example. Table 11.1 presents Boeing's income statement for the year ending December 31, 2023. As shown, Boeing's total revenue was $77,794 million for the year, and the company's cost of goods and services sold

Figure 11.1 Relationship between revenue, expenses, and income.

DOI: 10.4324/9781003469759-11

Table 11.1 The Boeing Company Income Statement – 2023

Consolidated Statements of Operations **The Boeing Company** **For the year ending December 31, 2023** (in millions, except per share data)	
Revenue:	
Sales of products	65,581
Sales of services	12,213
Total revenue	**$77,794**
Expense:	
Cost of products	59,864
Cost of services	10,206
Total costs and expenses	**$70,070**
Other Expense:	
General and administrative expense	5,168
Research and development expense, net	3,377
Loss from operations	**−773**
Interest and debt expense	2,459
Loss before income taxes	**$2,005**
Income tax (expense)/benefit	−237
Net loss	**($2,242)**

was $70,070 million. Subtracting financial cost, interest and debt expenses, and taxes resulted in a net loss for the year of $2,242 million.

Revenue, Sales, or Income

Revenue is the amount of money a company earns over a given period by selling products and services. Airbus's global revenue amounted to €65.4 billion because it delivered a record-setting 735 aircraft to airlines in 2023.[1] Boeing's major sources of income are commercial airplanes; defense, space, and security; and Boeing Capital. Commercial flight is an important revenue source for Boeing; over the next 20 years, Boeing forecasts that long-haul international traffic will grow at about 5% per year.[2] This growth drives the need for about 8,830 new airplanes, valued at approximately $2.7 trillion. This is a major source of revenue for both Boeing and Airbus.

Cost of goods sold (COGS) is the direct costs associated with producing goods and services. COGS includes the cost of materials, labor, and other expenses directly involved in the production process.

Cost of Goods Sold

Whenever a product is manufactured or service is provided, certain direct costs are incurred. These costs are labeled on the income statement as the cost of goods sold (COGS). For the airline industry, COGS includes materials such as fuel, direct labor, and indirect costs. For an aircraft manufacturer, it includes the parts and labor to produce the aircraft. COGS excludes indirect expenses such as distribution and sales force costs.

Table 11.2 gives the cost of goods sold section from Boeing's 2023 income statement.

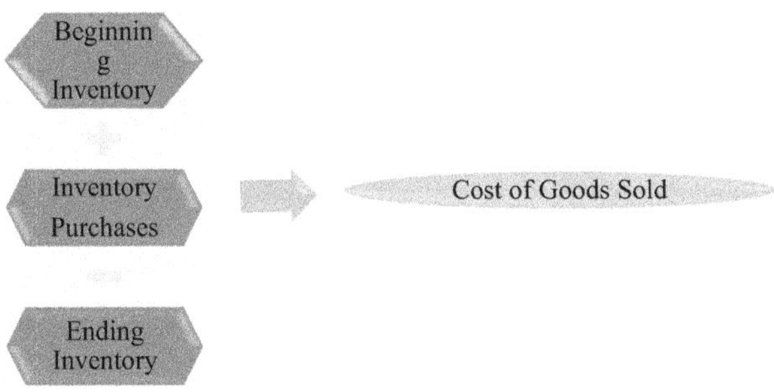

Figure 11.2 Cost of goods sold.

Table 11.2 COGS Section of Boeing's Income Statement, 2023 (in USD)

Cost of products	−59,864
Cost of services	−10,206
Other	0
Total costs and expenses	−70,070

COGS is calculated by starting with the cost of beginning inventory, adding inventory purchased, and then subtracting the cost of ending inventory of finished goods.

Example 11.1

Alpine Aviation sells landing gear for general aviation aircraft at a local airport. A count at the beginning of the year showed that the company held \$800,000 worth of inventory on hand. Over the year, Alpine purchased another \$2,400,000 worth of parts. At the end of year, Alpine had \$600,000 worth of inventory:

$$\text{Cost of Goods Sold} = \$800{,}000 + \$2{,}400{,}000 - \$600{,}000$$
$$\text{Cost of Goods Sold} = \$2{,}600{,}000$$

Example 11.2

Aspen Engineering Company (AEC) manufactures hydraulic parts used primarily in helicopters. AEC has three main products used for light, medium, and heavy lift copters. The company had a beginning inventory of \$700,000 last month and purchased another \$1,500,000 in inventory. Last month was a great month, and Aspen's remaining inventory at the end of the month was \$200,000. We can calculate AEC's COGS as follows:

$$\text{COGS} = \$700{,}000 + 1{,}500{,}000 - 200{,}000$$
$$\text{COGS} = \$2{,}000{,}000$$

Gross Profit (Operating Profit)

Gross profit (Figure 11.3) is the difference between total revenue and cost of goods sold. It represents the company's profit from sales after deducting the costs directly associated with producing the goods.

Figure 11.3 Gross profit.

A firm's gross profit is a measure of its efficiency and lean operation. Creditors, labor groups, investors, and company management tend to pay more attention to the net income because the net income is a good barometer of the company's financial strength and its ability to meet future financial obligations. Table 11.1 shows that Boeing has net sales of $77,794 million and a total COGS of $70,070 million, resulting in a gross profit of $7,724 million for 2023.

Example 11.3

Sanford Regional is a small airport that handles only commuter traffic. During the most recent fiscal year, Sanford generated $40,000,000 in revenue and $10,000,000 in COGS. Sanford's gross profit is

$$\text{Gross profit} = \$40{,}000{,}000 - \$10{,}000{,}000 = \$30{,}000{,}000$$

Operating Expenses

Operating expenses are expenses other than COGS that a company sustains in the normal course of business, for instance in aerospace manufacturing, advertising expenditures, research and development, general and administrative expenses, and depreciation of assets. For airlines, operating expenses include general management, flight personnel, aircraft maintenance, and traffic handling personnel.

Depreciation

Depreciation is part of operating expenses because it is tax deductible. The methods of depreciation are straight-line depreciation (SLD), declining balance, sum-of-years digits, and modified accelerated cost recovery system (MACRS). The US Internal Revenue Service MACRS to calculate depreciation and ensure that tax deduction is uniform for all organizations.

Two of the most basic but important accounting estimates in airline management are aircraft useful life and residual value. These estimates determine effective depreciation rates. Useful lives and residual values of existing aircraft fleets are being increasingly impacted by new-generation aircraft that have lower operating costs and are adversely impacting the value of older aircraft in the secondary market. When deciding to retire aircraft earlier than anticipated, accelerated depreciation may need to be applied prospectively to reduce the carrying value of aircraft.[3]

Different airlines have different depreciation policies based on the type of aircraft and business objectives. Carriers such as Qatar Airways and Emirates Airlines, which are based in the Middle East, are required to depreciate their airplanes using only SLD for a specified duration. This places them at a disadvantage compared with their US counterparts such as United Airlines and American Airlines, since US carriers are allowed to depreciate their assets in an accelerated manner using MACRS. Depreciation is explained in good detail in Chapter 14.

Example 11.4

Jet Propulsion Company purchased several simulators at a total cost of $6,000,000. The installation cost for this equipment was $500,000. The company plans to depreciate the equipment using the MACRS five-year normal recovery period. Prepare a depreciation schedule showing the depreciation expense for each year.

Year	*Depreciation Base*	*Depreciation Rate*	*Depreciation Expense*
0	6,500,000		
1	6,500,000	0.20	$1,300,000
2	6,500,000	0.32	$2,080,000
3	6,500,000	0.19	$1,235,000
4	6,500,000	0.12	$780,000
5	6,500,000	0.12	$780,000
6	6,500,000	0.05	$325,000

Operating Profit

Referring to Boeing's 2023 income statement in Table 11.1, Boeing had a total operating expense of $8,497 million. We subtract the operating expenses from the gross profit of $7,724 million to obtain the operating loss of $773 million. Operating profit presents a more accurate picture of how much money the company made from its operation (Figure 11.4).

Financial Costs

Interest is the cost of borrowing money; it depends on overall firm indebtedness and the interest rate associated with this debt. Companies need capital to maintain business operations and to finance their growth. Start-up airlines borrow money to acquire aircraft, flight equipment, and meet other related expenses. If a debtor is not able to pay the interest but has some assets, creditors might pursue involuntary bankruptcy to get at least some payment. States West Airlines announced that it had a critical shortage of cash and would seek bankruptcy protection if it could not get short-term financing soon.[4] Interest is generally a small fraction of total firm expenses. However, the higher the interest, the higher the risk of financial insolvency.

Income taxes are taxes a government imposes on individuals and businesses carrying out operations in its jurisdiction. Income after deducting the interest can be taxed at the federal, state and/or local levels, and tax rates are available in tax tables published by the respective government agencies (refer to Table 11.9 at the end of this chapter for detailed tax rates). There are strategies for reducing or deferring tax liabilities. For instance, an operating loss can be carried back to the preceding two years and applied against the taxable income in those years and for an immediate tax rebate. IRS stipulates that a loss carryback can be applied only to the two years preceding the loss. For instance, if a company were to record a net operating loss in year seven, the company could apply a loss carryback to years six and five.[5]

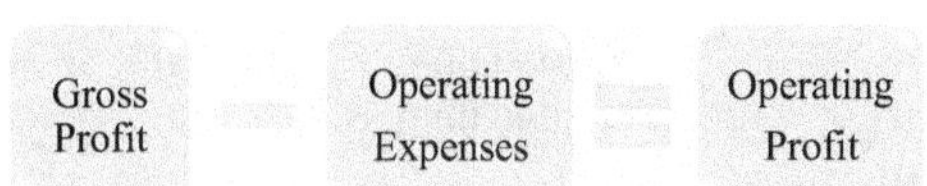

Figure 11.4 Operating profit.

A company may waive to carry loss back and proceeds with loss carryforward up to 20 years. A loss carryforward occurs, when a business carry loss forward to future years and apply it against the net income in those years which reduce the taxable income and consequently pay less taxes in future years.

Example 11.5

DirectJet is a regional carrier with the following pattern of net income/losses over the years 2014 to 2019: They had a large net operating loss in year 2016 and they can offset this loss by means of a loss carryback and a loss carryforward. The schedule of actual earnings for 2020 and 2025 and the expected earnings from 2017 onwards are presented in Table 11.3. Provide a tax carryback and carryforward schedule for DirectJet to help them compensate for the net loss in 2016. Assume they are in the 35% tax bracket. (See Table 11.4 for the answer.)

After loss carryback of $15,000,000 to 2020 and 2021, the rest of the loss is carried forward and applied to net income in 2023 through 2025, which reduced taxable income to 0 in those years. The purposes of carryback and carryforward are to realize the maximum possible tax refunds and to eliminate or reduce future tax liabilities to cover a large loss incurred during a particular year.

Depreciation is another way of reducing effective taxable income. Even though it is not an actual cash expense, Generally Accepted Accounting Principles allow companies to deduct depreciation from revenue. Depreciation refers to accounting for the hypothetical loss in value of an asset upon usage; we discuss it in detail in Chapter 14.

Net Income

Net income/loss (also called net profit or earnings) is the last part of the income statement. It represents the base profit earned by a firm in a given accounting period. Boeing's 2023 operating profit or earnings before interest and taxes (EBIT) was $454 million and loss before taxes was $2,005 million. Boeing paid $237 million in taxes, resulting in a net loss of $2,242 million for the year.

Table 11.3 DirectJet 2023 Income Statement: Example 11.5

Year	*Net Operating Profit/Loss*	*Actual Taxes Paid*
2020	$5,000,000	**($1,750,000)**
2021	$10,000,000	**($3,500,000)**
2022	**($30,000,000)**	
2023	$3,000,000	
2024	$2,000,000	
2025	$10,000,000	**($3,500,000)**

Table 11.4 DirectJet Schedule for Loss Carryforward and Carryback: Example 11.5

Year	*Net Operating Profit/Loss*	*Carryback/ Carryforward*	*Adjusted Taxable Income*	*Tax Refund*
2020	$5,000,000	**($5,000,000)**	$0	$1,750,000
2021	$10,000,000	**($10,000,000)**	$0	$3,500,000
2022	**($30,000,000)**			
2023	$3,000,000	**($3,000,000)**	$0	$0
2024	$2,000,000	**($2,000,000)**	$0	$0
2025	$10,000,000	**($10,000,000)**	$0	$0

Net income divided by the number of outstanding common shares yields the earnings per share, the profit an investor earns for each share of stock owned. Table 11.1 shows that for 2023, Boeing had negative earnings of $2,242 million with basic loss per share of $3.67. This means that if Boeing distributed every dollar of income to its shareholders, each share would lose $3.67.

$$EPS = \frac{Net\ Income}{Number\ of\ Shares\ Outstanding}$$

Corporations may pay part of their earnings as dividends to shareholders as returns on their investment:

$$DPS = \frac{Total\ dividends\ paid}{Number\ of\ Shares\ Outstanding}$$

Boeing did not pay any dividend per share per quarter in 2023.[6] A few airlines such as Southwest and Delta pay dividends regularly,[7] but others such as Boeing pay intermittently.

Delta's 2023 income statement is presented in Table 11.3. For service industries such as airlines, the cost of services sold are included in the total operating expenses.

Table 11.3 Delta Air Lines Income Statement: Year Ending 12/31/2023

Consolidated Statements of Operations Delta Air Lines, Inc. For the year ending December 31, 2023 (in USD millions, except per share data)	
Operating Revenue:	
Passenger	48,909
Cargo	723
Other	8,416
Total operating revenue	**$58,048**
Operating Expense:	
Aircraft fuel and related taxes	11,069
Salaries and related costs	14,607
Ancillary businesses and refinery	4,172
Aircraft maintenance materials and outside repairs	2,432
Depreciation and amortization	2,341
Landing fees and other rents	2,563
Other	15,343
Total operating expense	**$52,527**
Operating Income	**$5,521**
Other Expense:	
Interest expense, net	−834
Gain/(loss) on investments, net	1263
Miscellaneous, net	−342
Total other expense, net	**87**
Income Before Income Taxes	**$5,608**
Income Tax (Provision) Benefit	−999
Net Income	**$4,609**
Earnings Per Share	$7.21
Diluted Earnings Per Share	$7.17
Cash Dividends Declared Per Share	$0.20

In the airline industry, most of the revenue comes from ticket sales but also from cargo and ancillary revenue. Indeed, air cargo is an important revenue source for airlines; over the next 20 years, world air cargo traffic will grow 4.7% per year.[8] Most cargo is carried on large, wide-body aircraft such as the B767, B777, B747, A330, and A380; narrow-body aircraft have significant limitations on the volume and the type of cargo they can carry. Recently, airlines are increasingly depending on revenue from sources other than ticket prices such as ancillary revenue, the revenue from sales of in-flight services. Ancillary revenue is increasingly becoming a major source of income for airlines around the world (Figure 11.5).

This consistent growth in this category indicates that airlines are slowly realizing the potential of this source of revenue and beginning to utilize it. For instance, three and even two decades ago, a ticket price was bundled with services including luggage charges and meals; mor recently, these charges are separate from the ticket and you will pay as you go if you want them. There have also been some innovative methods developed to generate ancillary revenue, such as the "seat-to-seat" service offered by Virgin America Airlines, which enables a passenger to buy a drink for a co-passenger in-flight by looking at a digital seat map. This trend toward increasing revenue from ancillary services is expected to increase in the coming years.

Example 11.6

MyJet Airlines has $5,000,000 of EBIT at year end. Interest for the year was $100,000. The airline expects to distribute $1,000,000 in dividends. Calculate the earnings after taxes for the firm assuming a 30% tax on ordinary income.

Solution:

Earnings before interest and taxes	$1,000,000
Less: Interest	$100,000
Earnings before taxes	$900,000
Less: Taxes (30%)	$270,000
Earnings after taxes	$630,000

Example 11.7

General Engine Manufacturing Company announced $50 million in profit. The company has paid $30 million in operating expenses and $5,000,000 in interest expenses, pays a 30% tax rate, and has declared $5,000,000 in total preferred stock dividends.

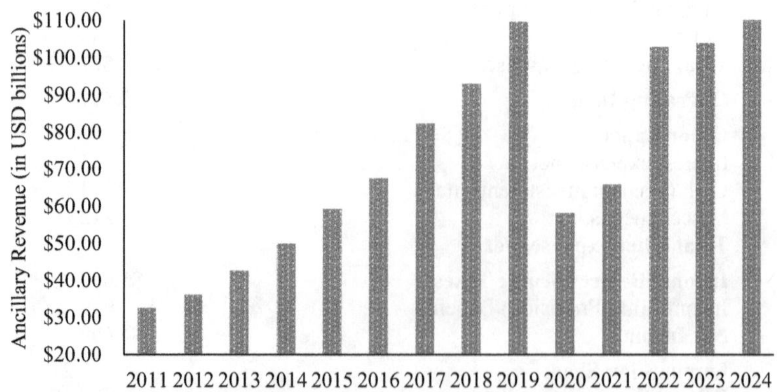

Figure 11.5 Ancillary revenue for global airlines.

a) How much in earnings is available for common stockholders?
b) Calculate the increased retained earnings if the company declared a $5.00 dividend per share of common stock. The company has 1,000,000 shares of common stock outstanding.

a)

Gross profits	$50,000,000
Less: Operating expenses	($30,000,000)
Operating profits	$20,000,000
Less: interest	($5,000,000)
Net profits before taxes	$15,000,000
Less: taxes (30%)	($4,500,000)
Net profits after taxes	$10,500,000
Less: preferred stock dividend	$5,000,000
Earnings available for common stock	$5,500,000

b)

Earnings available for common stock	$5,500,000
Dividend ($5.00), 1,000,000 shares	$5,000,000
Retained earnings	$500,000

The Balance Sheet: Measuring a Firm's Book Value

The balance sheet is a snapshot of a company's finances at a particular point in time; it represents the balance between what the company owns versus what it owes. Balance sheets contain three significant components: total assets, total liability, and stockholder's equity. The left side of the balance sheet lists the total assets, everything the company owns; these include current and noncurrent (fixed) assets. Noncurrent assets are plants and equipment, and nontangible assets are assets that can't be touched but nevertheless exist and have value, such as trademarks and patents.[9] In 1993, Pan Am's name was sold as a nontangible asset for $1.3 million after the airline filed for bankruptcy.[10] The right side of the balance sheet lists the claims against the company, the total liabilities and shareholders' equity. Table 11.4 shows the 2023 balance sheet for a major US airline.

Table 11.4 Delta Air Lines 2023 Balance Sheet

ASSETS	
Current Assets:	
Cash and cash equivalents	$2,741
Short-term investments	1,127
Accounts receivable, net	3,130
Inventory, net	1314
Other current assets	1,957
Total current assets	**$10,269**
Property and Equipment, Net	**$35,486**
Other Assets:	
Operating lease right-of-use assets	7,004
Goodwill	9,753
Identifiable intangibles, net	5,983
Equity investments	3,457
Other noncurrent assets	1,692
Total other assets	**$63,375**
Total assets	**$73,644**

(Continued)

Table 11.4 (Continued)

LIABILITIES AND STOCKHOLDERS' EQUITY	
Current Liabilities:	
Current maturities of long-term debt and capital leases	$2,983
Air traffic liability	$7,044
Accounts payable	4,446
Accrued salaries and related benefits	4,561
Frequent flyer deferred revenue	3,908
Other accrued liabilities	3,476
Total current liabilities	**$26,418**
Noncurrent Liabilities:	
Long-term debt and capital leases	17,071
Pension and post-retirement benefits	3,601
Frequent flyer deferred revenue	4,512
Noncurrent operating leases	6,468
Other noncurrent liabilities	4,469
Total noncurrent liabilities	**$36,121**
Stockholders' Equity:	
Additional paid-in capital	11,641
Retained earnings	5,650
Accumulated other comprehensive loss	-5,845
Treasury stock	-341
Total stockholders' equity	**$11,105**
Total liabilities and stockholders' equity	**$73,644**

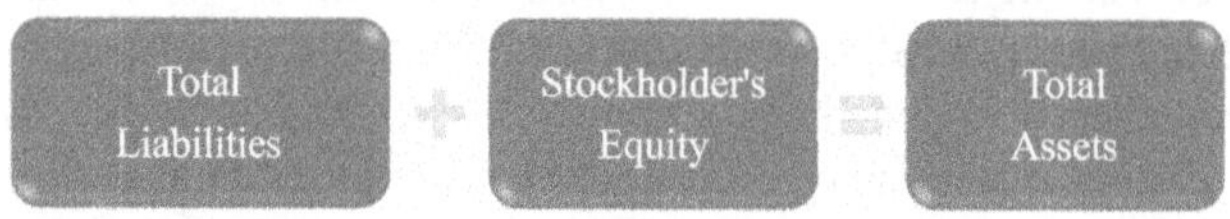

Figure 11.6 Calculating total assets on a balance sheet.

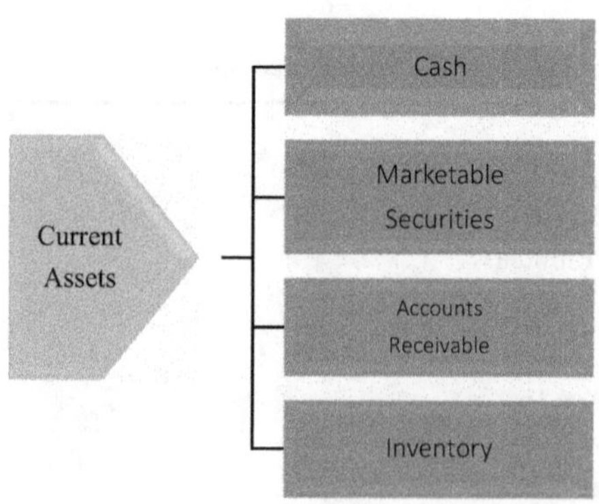

Figure 11.7 Current assets.

A balance sheet is a stock measure statement showing the value of each account on a specific date. These values, particularly liquid assets and liability accounts, may later differ substantially from the balance sheet. Figure 11.6 shows how total assets are calculated on a balance sheet, and Figure 11.7 breaks down current assets.

Current Assets

The first subsection in the balance sheet is the assets, current and noncurrent. Current assets are more liquid and more easily converted into cash, and having sufficient cash and strong current assets is indispensable for the profitability and continuity of an airline. In an industry marked by substantial fixed costs and frequent fluctuations, such financial resources serve as lifelines during challenging times. Cash reserves provide operational resilience, enabling the airline to weather unforeseen shocks like economic downturns or sudden spikes in fuel prices without disrupting services. Moreover, liquidity ensures timely payment of critical expenses, such as fuel procurement, maintenance, and employee salaries, safeguarding the airline's reputation and operational integrity. On a balance sheet, the most liquid assets are listed first and in decreasing order of liquidity such that fixed assets are last. The most liquid asset on the balance sheet is cash and cash equivalents.

Cash and Cash Equivalents

For an industry characterized by razor-thin profit margins and high fixed costs, airlines' having sufficient cash reserves is paramount. It enables them to weather unexpected crises such as spread of communicable disease, economic downturns, or sudden spikes in fuel prices, all of which can profoundly impact cash flows. Companies hold cash for various reasons and in various forms (Figure 11.8), some of which are restricted for special purposes. In the United States, if a company has foreign bank accounts, these accounts must be translated into dollars at the prevailing exchange rate on the balance sheet statement date.

Shortage of available cash and cash equivalents and short-term investments to meet liquidity could force a company into a complex bankruptcy. Wow Air stands out as an example: This low-cost carrier from Iceland abruptly halted flights in March 2019 when it was unable to secure the necessary funds to sustain its operations. Similarly, Thomas Cook Airlines, a prominent British charter and scheduled airline, succumbed to bankruptcy in September 2019, primarily due to cash shortages exacerbated by mounting debt. In India, Jet Airways, once a major player in the aviation industry, grounded its fleet indefinitely in April 2019, citing severe financial distress and a critical lack of cash flow. The demise of Monarch Airlines, a British carrier, in October 2017, and Flybmi in February 2019 further underscored the devastating impact of cash shortages on airline operations.

Marketable Securities (Short-Term Investments)

Some companies temporarily invest excess cash in cash equivalents such as marketable securities (certificates of deposits; T-bills, T-notes, T-bonds, and other US government securities), high-grade corporate commercial paper, and bankers' acceptances (Figure 11.9). These

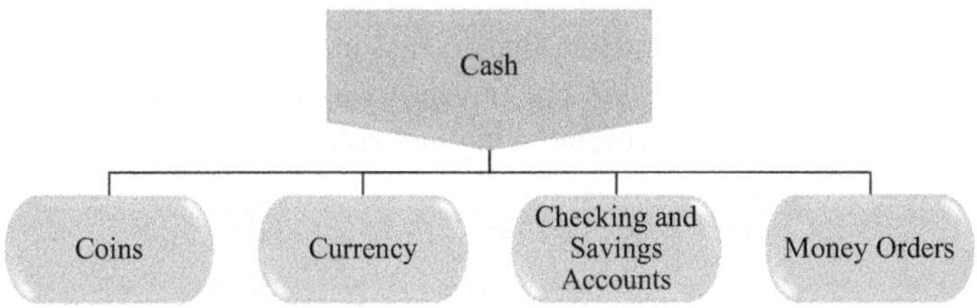

Figure 11.8 Cash: the most liquid asset.

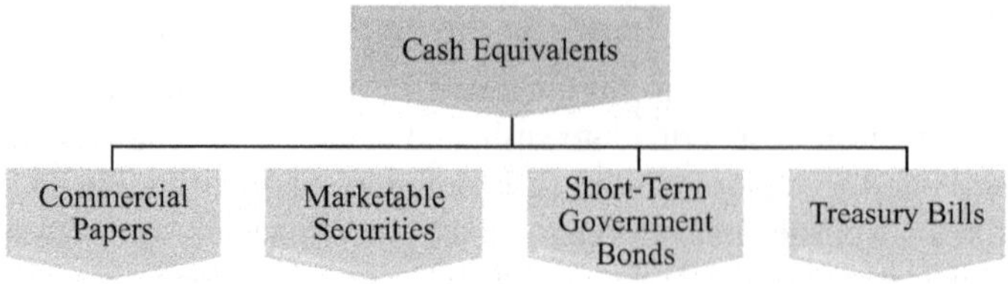

Figure 11.9 Cash equivalents.

short-term investments can earn interest income until the business needs the cash. Appropriate marketable securities are highly liquid and maintain stable market value. It is critical that companies choose the right type of security to make an investment, so that it can ensure a good return. Rather than let the cash remain idle in its bank accounts, Delta Air Lines invests in marketable securities that comprise US government and agency securities, asset- and mortgage-backed securities, corporate obligations, and other fixed-term securities.[11]

Accounts Receivable

The sale of a product or service on credit is shown on the balance sheet as accounts receivable (AR). Credit sales often stipulate payment terms that allow the purchaser to pay within a specified time and may offer a discount as an incentive for early payment. Receivables are the amounts to be collected from any customers, including travel agencies, corporate clients, and government units. AR remains on the balance sheet until it is collected, although notably, some accounts will never be collected and therefore constitute a bad debt, or loss. A company calculates the percentage of possible bad debt (from prior actual experience) and creates a corresponding reserve that is deducted from its gross AR. This reserve is often referred to as an allowance for doubtful accounts:

$$\text{Net Accounts Receivable} = \text{Gross Accounts Receivable} - \text{Allowance for Doubtful Accounts}$$

For an airline, passenger tickets are primarily sold on credit; hence, AR is an important asset, as reflected in Delta's AR of 3,130 million for 2023 (Table 11.5).

Inventories

Inventories are products that need to be stored for future use when needed; for some industries, inventory can be among a company's most expensive assets. For an airline, the main inventories constitute fuel and expendable parts and supplies. For Delta, net inventory amounted to $1,314 million in 2023 (Table 11.5). On the aircraft manufacturing side, inventory comprises the total number of aircraft in production, that is, raw material, parts, works in progress, and finished goods. For example, Boeing had a net inventory of $79,741 million in 2023. This shows the importance of inventory in the manufacturing industry.

Prepaid Expenses

Demand for new aircraft and jet engine orders derives from the perceived future demand for commercial air activities. Generally, airlines are required to make prepayments to sign aircraft

Table 11.5 Delta Air Lines 2023 Cash Flow Statement

Delta Air Lines, Inc. Consolidated Statements of Cash Flows (in millions)	
Cash Flows from Operating Activities:	
Net income	$4,609
Adjustments to reconcile net income to net cash provided by operating activities:	
Depreciation and amortization	2,341
Deferred income taxes	980
Pension, postretirement, and postemployment payments (greater)/less than expense	−121
Changes in certain assets and liabilities:	
Receivables	−7
Fuel inventory	121
Air traffic liability	−1216
Frequent flyer deferred revenue	538
Other, net	($781)
Net cash provided by operating activities	$6,464
Cash Flows From Investing Activities:	
Property and equipment additions:	
Flight equipment, including advance payments	−3,645
Ground property and equipment, including technology	−1678
short-term investments, net	2,235
Other, net	($60)
Net cash used in investing activities	($3,148)
Cash Flows from Financing Activities:	
Payments on long-term debt and capital lease obligations	−4,071
Cash dividends	−128
Proceeds from long-term obligations	878
Other, net	($73)
Net cash used in financing activities	($3,394)
Net (Decrease) Increase in Cash and Cash Equivalents	($78)
Cash and cash equivalents at beginning of period	3,473
Cash and cash equivalents at end of period	$3,395

purchase agreements, then there are structured payments of about 25% of the purchase price, in stages over an 18-month period with the remainder due at delivery. The actual price an airline pays for a given aircraft is not publicly announced, and most payments are proprietary information. Prepaid expenses refer to advance payments made in cash and recorded as assets until they are used or consumed; they expire with time (i.e., rent and insurance) or through use (i.e., supplies). Prepaid expenses increase when the cash paid for expenses exceeds the amount reported on an accrual basis.

Fixed Assets (Noncurrent Assets)

Fixed assets are the second subsection under assets, consisting of equipment, buildings, vehicles, tools, computers, office equipment, leasehold improvements, furniture – in general any items of a fairly permanent nature that are required for the normal operation of a business. A major portion of an airline's fixed assets is aircraft and flight equipment. An airline puts a fixed asset on its balance sheet at historical cost, meaning that its stated value is whatever it cost the company to obtain the asset. The company then depreciates the asset, that is, reduces its reported value over the life of the asset. Accounting standards indicate that balance sheets report the fixed assets at book value, defined as the original historical cost (the purchase price paid by the company) minus allowable depreciation to date. These then appear as net fixed assets on the balance sheet. Boeing's fixed assets include long-term investments, plant and equipment, goodwill and other intangible assets, accumulated amortization, and deferred long-term asset charges. The value of a company's brand name, solid customer base, good customer relations, good employee relations, and any patents or proprietary technology represent goodwill. Goodwill is considered an intangible asset because it is not a physical asset like buildings or equipment. Delta Air Lines recorded $9,753 million in goodwill in 2023 (Table 11.5).

Property, Plant, and Equipment

For an airline, property, plant, and equipment (PP&E) refers to the amount of long-lived noncurrent assets owned by the company and used in principal business operations. Most of the assets of airlines and aircraft and jet engine manufacturers will fall into this category. These companies must continue to buy aircraft to continue their operations, which as mentioned earlier is denoted as net depreciation on the balance sheet. Delta had a net PP&E of $35,486 million in 2023.

Other Long-Term Assets

This mainly refers to investments in other privately or publicly held companies, as these are not easily liquidated and have a life of certainly more than one year. Another long-term asset is deferred taxes, the difference between actual taxes paid and those calculated prior to payment and recorded in the books.

Total Liabilities

Liability represents the amount a company owes to all its creditors, investors, and shareholders. Liabilities are financial obligations of one business entity to others, and there are two main categories: current and long term.

Current Liabilities

Current liabilities denote payments that are due within the next year. Managing current liabilities minimizes risks associated with economic volatility and fuel price fluctuations, bolstering the airline's resilience to unforeseen challenges. Managing current liabilities also enhances creditworthiness, facilitating access to financing for strategic investments and growth initiatives. Delta Air Lines had total current liabilities worth $26,418 million as of December 31, 2023 (Table 11.5). There are three main categories of currents liabilities: accounts payable (AP), accrued expenses, and current portions of long-term debt.

Accounts Payable

AP is one of the most important parts of current liabilities. AP constitutes company purchases made on credit, and it is included under current liabilities because it is expected to be settled by the end of the current year. AP forms the largest portion of current liabilities for an airline, as reflected in Delta's 2023 AP of $4,446 million (Table 11.5).

Accrued Expenses

Accrued expenses are a company's specific direct and operating costs that were not paid at the close of the reporting period. These expenses are usually paid at regular intervals and include such items as utilities, rent, wages and salaries, and taxes. For example, if wages are paid every three weeks and the firm's balance sheet is prepared in the middle of the pay period, wages owed as of that date would be reported as an accrued expense.

Current Portions of Long-Term Debt

At times companies borrow long-term money on installment, making periodic payments over the life of the loan that include principal reduction as well as interest. The current maturities of long-term debt represent the principal portion of these installment payments that is due over the next 12 months. The sum of the current portion of long-term debt and the rest of the long-term debt is the total long-term debt that a company has outstanding at any point in time. Entitling some debt as current is merely a transfer process. Delta had current maturities of long-term debt at the end of 2023 worth $2,983 million (Table 11.5).

Noncurrent Liabilities

Noncurrent liabilities are payments that are not due within the next year or next reporting period. In 2023, the total noncurrent liabilities for Delta Air Lines equaled $36,121 million.

Long-Term Debt

Long-term debt is liabilities with maturities in excess of one year. It is usually used to finance long-term assets such as land, buildings, and equipment. Occasionally, long-term debt is used to finance "permanent" current assets. Long-term debt includes capital lease obligations, corporate bonds, and other long-term leases. Long-term debt is a substantial contributor to noncurrent liabilities; Delta's was $17,071 million in 2023 (Table 11.5). Excessive long-term debt and low liquidity are critical factors leading to an airline's bankruptcy.

Other Long-Term Liabilities

Other liabilities not due over the immediate year include pension and post-retirement benefits for employees and also a separate type of liability specific to airlines called frequent flyer deferred revenue, the mileage credit an airline provides to passengers or sells to credit card companies and other third parties. Pension and post-retirement benefits are the biggest contributors to other long-term liabilities; Delta's for 2023 amounted to $ 3,601 million, nearly 10% of total noncurrent liabilities.

Stockholders' Equity

Stockholders' equity is the third main component of a company's balance sheet. It is the difference between the total assets and the total liabilities and ideally represents what the owners of the company contribute to it (Figure 11.10).

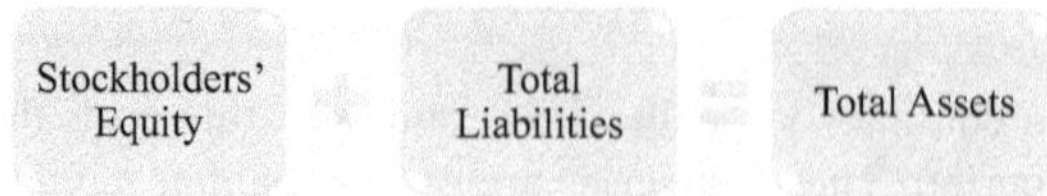

Figure 11.10 Division of assets.

Preferred Stock

Preferred stock or preferred securities share many characteristics of both a stock and a bond. Like bonds, they have a relatively high fixed-rate payment, and like common stock, they are generally listed on a stock exchange. A preferred stock is an equity that may or may not have maturity. Preferred stock can pay either a dividend or interest, usually quarterly or semiannually, and represents nonvoting ownership in a company. These securities are called preferred because preferred shareholders have more rights to a company's assets and cash flows than common shareholders in the event of a bankruptcy or liquidation; however, bondholders' claims are superior to those of preferred shareholders. Preferred stock is usually cumulative, meaning that skipped payments accrue and must be paid when earnings allow.

> *Common stocks and preferred stocks are both types of ownership in a company, but they have distinct characteristics and benefits. Common stock represents ownership in a company and typically comes with voting rights at shareholders' meetings. Shareholders have the right to vote on issues such as the board of directors and major corporate actions. In contrast, preferred stock also represents ownership but usually does not come with voting rights. Instead, preferred shareholders are entitled to fixed dividends, and they have priority over common shareholders when it comes to dividend payments and asset distribution in the event of liquidation.*

Common Stock and Additional Paid-In Capital

Common stock is the shares a company offers in its ownership. It is divided into two components: common stock at par value and additional paid-in capital (or capital surplus). The first component determines the number of shares currently outstanding; the second represents the additional money (above par value) generated when the company actually sold the stock. Delta Air Lines had 1.5 billion shares of common stock authorized on December 31, 2023, at a par value of $0.0001 and paid in additional capital of $11,641 million.

Retained Earnings

Retained earnings are the cumulative total of all net income that has been reinvested into the company. Many companies retain some of their annual profit to fund the expansion (replacement) of assets to reduce their reliance on outside capital markets (Figure 11.11). Delta Air Lines reported 2023 retained earnings of $5,650 million.

Example 11.8

Metro Jet's retained earnings account had a beginning balance of $25,000,000 at the end of 2024. During 2025, Metro Jet earned$75,000,000 of net income and distributed $15,000,000

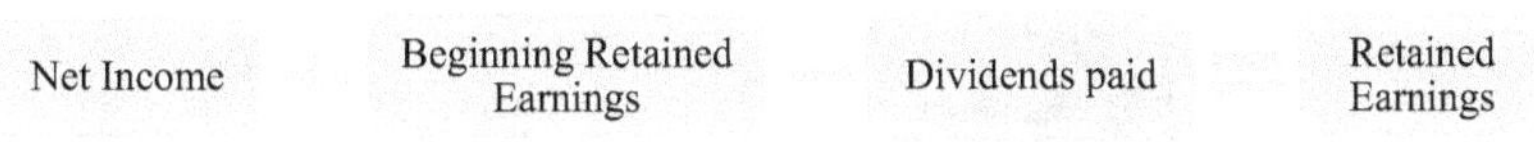

Figure 11.11 Retained earnings.

in dividends among common shareholders. Metro Jet's retained earnings at the end of 2025 are calculated as follows:

Metro Jet Statement of Retained Earnings For the Year Ending December 31, 2025	
Beginning balance	\$25,000,000
+ Net income	\$75,000,000
– Dividends	\$15,000,000
Ending balance	\$85,000,000

Statement of Cash Flows

The statement of cash flows reports the cash generated and used during the time interval specified. A company determines what period its statements will cover. For example, the heading may state "The Fiscal Year Ending December 31, 2025" or "The three months ending September 30, 2025". Because the income statement is prepared under the accrual basis of accounting, the revenues stated may not have been collected; similarly, the expenses reported on the income statement might not have been paid. The cash flow statement primarily integrates all that information to depict the operation of a firm purely based on the inflow and outflow of cash. As a result, investors frequently utilize this important financial statement. It is divided into three sections (Figure 11.12).

Cash Flow from Operating Activities

This section of a cash flow statement consists of a business's revenue-generating activities. Examples of operating activities are cash received and disbursed for product sales, royalties, commissions, fines, lawsuits, supplier and lender invoices, and payroll.

There are two ways to present the cash flow from operating activities, direct and indirect. The direct method requires you to present cash flow information that is directly associated with the items triggering cash flows, but most companies do not maintain records in that format. Hence, they use the indirect method, in which the statement begins with the net income or loss reported on the company's income statement and then make a series of adjustments to this figure to arrive at the amount of net cash provided by operating activities. Some of these adjustments include eliminating noncash expenses such as depreciation and amortization. Making all the necessary changes gives the net cash provided by operating activities. For Delta, the net cash flow from 2023 operating activities was \$6464 million (Table 11.5).

Cash Flow from Investing

Cash flow from investing includes the changes caused in cash flow due to the purchase and sale of long-term assets (fixed assets). It also includes cash inflow from income in investments and

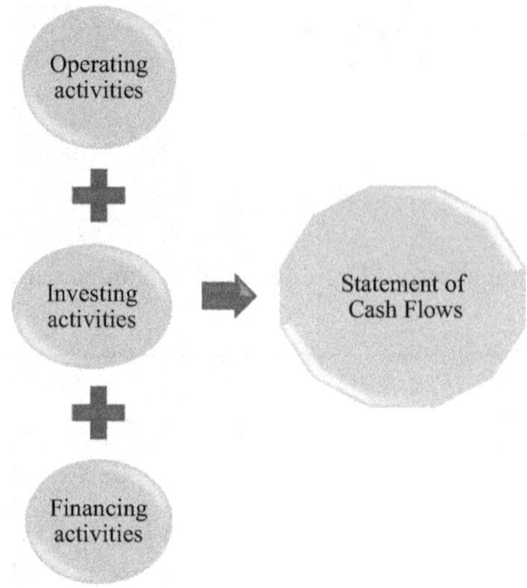

Figure 11.12 The division of cash flow.

cash inflow from disposal of investments. Table 11.5 shows that Delta used $3,148 million in cash flow for investing in 2023. Because it is a cash outflow, it is negative.

Cash Flow from Financing Activities

This section constitutes activities that alter the equity or borrowings of a business. The entries included are the sale of company shares, issuance of debentures and bank loans, the repurchase of shares, and dividend payments. In 2023, Delta Air Lines used $3,394 million in financing activities and, similar to investing, because it is a cash outflow, it is negative.

The sum of the three aforementioned cash flows results in the net increase/decrease in cash and cash equivalents for the corresponding year. For 2023, Delta Air Lines had a net cash decrease of $78 million. This reduced the cash balance to $3,395 million (Table 11.5).

Southwest Airlines was one of the very few airlines in the United States that was able to sustain its profitability during the global economic crisis post-2008. During 2020–23, Southwest took an interesting approach to its statements of cash flows (Table 11.6). The company reported receiving $3,164 million cash from operating activities but spending $2,932 million to purchase in new property and equipment. Southwest supplemented the cash from operating activities by issuing long-term debt and additional shares of common stock (financing activities). It used excess cash to repurchase stock, pay down debt, and pay out dividends. In total, it generated more cash from operating activities than it paid for investing and financing, resulting in a net decrease in cash for 2023. The variations in the net change in cash and cash equivalents over the three years show the progress of Southwest Airlines and the stability they were able to maintain during the period of the global economic crisis. An important part of that stability is attributed to fuel hedging, which Southwest was very active in, enabling them to make considerable profits from their derivatives.

Measuring Free Cash Flow

Free cash flow (FCF) is cash flow available for distribution among all the security holders of an organization and as such is a measuring the ease with which businesses can grow. Investors

Table 11.6 Portion of Southwest Airlines Cash Flow Statement (in USD millions)

Year	*2023*	*2022*	*2021*	*2020*
Cash Flow from Operating activities	\$3,164,000	\$3,790,000	\$2,322,000	\$1,127,000
Cash Flow from Investing Activities	**(\$2,932,000)**	**(\$3,746,000)**	\$(1,264,000	**(\$16,000)**
Cash Flow from Financing Activities	**(\$436,000)**	**(\$3,032,000)**	\$359,000	\$9,658,000
Net Change in Cash and Cash Equivalents	**(\$204,000)**	**(\$29,880,000)**	\$1,417,000	\$8,515,000

and analysts often use FCF analysis to assess a company's ability to sustain dividends, repay debt, and pursue growth opportunities while also evaluating its valuation compared with its FCF generation. There are three different methods for calculating FCF.

- FCF = EBIT × (1 – tax rate) + depreciation & amortization – changes in working capital – capital expenditure
- FCF = net profit + interest expense – net capital expenditure – net change in working capital – tax shield on interest expense
  where net capital expenditure (net CAPEX) = CAPEX – depreciation & amortization and tax shield = net interest expense × effective tax rate
- when profit after tax and debt/equity ratio (d) is available:
  FCF = profit after tax – changes in capital expenditure × (1–d) + depreciation & amortization × (1–d) – changes in working capital × (1–d)

Positive FCF indicates that the company is generating more cash than it is using, which can be a sign of financial strength and flexibility. Conversely, negative FCF may indicate that the company is investing heavily in growth or facing operational challenges.

Example 11.9

DirectJet has an EBIT of \$2,500 million and a depreciation and amortization expense of \$1,600 million for the year ending December 31, 2024. If DirectJet purchased property and equipment worth \$500 million during the same period and it falls under the 35% tax bracket, determine DirectJet's 2024 FCF; assume the net working capital for the considered period to be \$300 million:

FCF = EBIT × (1 – tax rate) + depreciation & amortization – changes in working capital – capital expenditure

$$FCF = \$2{,}500 \times (1 - 0.35) + \$1{,}600 - \$300 - \$500$$

$$FCF = \$2{,}425 \text{ million}$$

DirectJet had a 2024 free cash flow of \$2,425 million.

Common Size Financial Statements

A common size financial statement is one that displays all items on the statement as percentages of a common base figure. This type of statement facilitates easy analysis between companies or between periods of a company. The bias when comparing companies of different sizes for a given period is largely eliminated when they are compared as percentages of a common base figure.

Common Size Income Statement

The base figure utilized for an income statement is the total revenue or total sales. All the items on the income statement are presented as a percentage of total revenue. Table 11.7 shows Delta's 2023 common size income statement. Preparing these statements entails also inadvertently calculating the firm's various margins. For example, the net profit margin is simply the net income divided by sales, for Delta, 7.94% in 2023.

Example 11.10

Phoenix Aviation is a small manufacturer of landing gear for general aviation aircraft. Phoenix believes a market exists for both general aviation and commercial aircraft. The company has hired a consultant to prepare common size income statement. The following table shows the company's income statement.

Phoenix Aviation

	Income Statement		*Common Size Income Statement*	
Total Revenue		$250,000		100%
Cost of Goods Sold		$50,000		
Gross Profit		$200,000		80%
Operating Expenses				
Salaries	$25,000		10%	
Rent	$25,000		10%	
Utilities	$12,500		5%	
Depreciation	*$12,500*		*5%*	
Total Operating Expenses		$75,000		30%
Operating Profit (EBIT)		$125,000		50%
Interest Expense		$25,000		10%
Earnings before tax		$100,000		40%
Taxes		$25,000		10%
Net Income		$75,000		30%

The right side of the income statement, which shows each expense as a percentage of total revenue, is a common size income statement. Phoenix has total revenue of $250,000 and shows operating expenses of $75,000. Therefore, it's operating expenses are $75,000/$250,000 = 30% of total revenue, and the operating profit is 50% of the revenue.

A common size balance sheet expresses each item on the balance sheet as a percentage of total assets. Companies can use these to benchmark their financial structure against industry averages or competitors. This comparison helps in evaluating the company's relative financial health, identifying areas of strength or weakness, and informing strategic decision-making.

Common Size Balance Sheet

The base figure utilized for the balance sheet is the total assets, which will also equal the total liabilities and stockholders' equity. Table 11.8 gives Delta's 2023 common size balance sheet. Common size analysis applied to a balance sheet lends insight into a firm's capital structure and how it compares with rivals. An investor can also identify an optimal capital structure for an industry and compare it

Table 11.7 Delta Air Lines 2023 Income Statement

Consolidated Statements of Operations: Delta Airlines (in millions, except per share data)		
Operating Revenue:		
Passengers	48,909	84.26%
Cargo	723	1.25%
Other	8,416	14.50%
Total operating revenue	$58,048	100.00%
Operating Expense:		
Aircraft fuel and related taxes	11,069	19.07%
Salaries and related costs	14,607	25.16%
Ancillary businesses and refinery	4,172	7.19%
Aircraft maintenance materials and outside repairs	2,432	4.19%
Depreciation and amortization	2,341	4.03%
Landing fees and other rents	2,563	4.42%
Other	15,343	26.43%
Total operating expense	$52,527	90.49%
Operating Income	$5,521	9.51%
Other Expense:		
Interest expense, net	−834	−1.44%
Gain/(loss) on investments, net	1263	2.18%
Miscellaneous, net	−342	−0.59%
Total other expense, net	87	0.15%
Income Before Income Taxes	$5,608	9.66%
Income Tax (Provision) Benefit	−999	−1.72%
Net Income	$4,609	7.94%

Table 11.8 Delta Air Lines 2023 Balance Sheet (in USD millions except share data)

ASSETS		
Current Assets:		
Cash and cash equivalents	$2,741	3.72%
Short-term investments	1,127	1.53%
Accounts receivable, net	3,130	4.25%
Inventory, net	1314	1.78%
Other current assets	1,957	2.66%
Total current assets	**$10,269**	13.94%
Property and Equipment, Net	**$35,486**	48.19%
Other Assets:		
Operating lease right-of-use assets	7,004	9.51%
Goodwill	9,753	13.24%
Identifiable intangibles, net	5,983	8.12%
Equity investments	3,457	4.69%
Other noncurrent assets	1,692	2.30%
Total other assets	**$63,375**	86.06%
Total assets	**$73,644**	100.00%
LIABILITIES AND STOCKHOLDERS* EQITTY		
Current Liabilities:		
Current maturities of long-term debt and capital leases	$2,983	4.05%
Air traffic liability	$7,044	9.56%

(*Continued*)

Table 11.8 (Continued)

Accounts payable	4,446	6.04%
Accrued salaries and related benefits	4,561	6.19%
Frequent flyer deferred revenue	3,908	
Other accrued liabilities	3,476	4.72%
Total current liabilities	**$26,418**	35.87%
Noncurrent Liabilities:		
Long-term debt and capital leases	17,071	23.18%
Pension and post-retirement benefits	3,601	4.89%
Frequent flyer deferred revenue	4,512	
Noncurrent operating leases	6,468	8.78%
Other noncurrent liabilities	4,469	6.07%
Total noncurrent liabilities	**$36,121**	49.05%
Stockholders' Equity[7]:		
Additional paid-in capital	11,641	15.81%
Retained earnings	5,650	7.67%
Accumulated other comprehensive loss	–5,845	–7.94%
Treasury stock	–341	–0.46%
Total stockholders' equity	**$11,105**	15.08%
Total liabilities and stockholder's equity	**$73,644**	100.00%

with that of the firm being analyzed. The common size balance sheet provides a perspective on whether debt is too high, excess cash is being retained, or inventories are growing too high. The goodwill level on a balance sheet also helps indicate the extent to which a company has relied on acquisitions for growth. The current liabilities for Delta Air Lines are 35.97% of the total assets, and goodwill is at 13.24%.

Summary

Financial statements play a pivotal role in the air transport industry, offering a comprehensive view of a company's financial health and performance. Airlines and related businesses rely on financial statements, including income statements, balance sheets, and cash flow statements, to evaluate profitability, liquidity, solvency, and efficiency metrics. These statements serve as critical tools for strategic decision-making, enabling management to assess investment opportunities, allocate resources effectively, and maximize profitability. Moreover, financial statements aid in risk management by identifying and mitigating financial, operational, and market risks. Overall, understanding and applying financial statements enable stakeholders to assess the financial performance, profitability, solvency, and risk of a company, which is essential for making informed decisions, allocating resources efficiently, and maintaining trust and confidence in financial markets.

Discussion Questions and Problems

11.1 Obtain Airbus and Boeing companies' latest financial statements. Whose current assets are likely to be considered the most liquid?

11.2 Analyze Airbus's latest financial statements and decide whether to buy its capital stock or possibly loan money to the company. If you were offered a job at the company, would you accept it or take a job from another organization? Explain your answers.

11.3 What types of financial data will be available on a typical income statement of a business like Pratt & Whitney, Rolls-Royce, or GE Capital?

11.4 DirectJet is a firm with $800 million total revenues, $700 million cost of goods sold, $10,000,000 depreciation expense, and $2,400,000 interest expense. Find the company's operating profit and net income.

11.5 Determine the method or methods of depreciation that Ryanair Airlines uses to depreciate its property, plant, and equipment (PP&E).

11.6 Analyze the information disclosed in the most recent Air France balance sheet on PP&E. Recommend additional data that Air France could include that would be useful to potential investors and creditors.

11.7 Access the most recent financial statements and use the formulas provided in your textbook to calculate the following ratios for Ryanair. (You may have to search around the profit & loss statement and balance sheet to find the appropriate values to enter!)

a) Gross profit margin
b) Operating profit margin
c) Current ratio
d) Debt to assets ratio
e) Total assets turnover
f) Average collection period

11.8 Under MACRS, an aircraft that originally cost $20,000,000, incurred $5,000,000 in repair and overhaul expenses, and has an estimated salvage value of $5,000,000 is being depreciated using a 10-year normal recovery period. What is the annual depreciation amount?

11.9 Fun Air had a cash flow from operating activities of $20,000,000, cash flow from investment activities of −$8,000,000, and cash flow from financing activities of $18,000,000 as of December 31, 2016. What is the impact of these activities on the cash flows?

11.10 Fun Air has just ended the calendar year with total revenue of $30,000,000 and total merchandise purchased of $12,500,000. Although the firm paid in full for the merchandise during the year, it has yet to collect $2,000,000 at year end from the customer. Depreciation and amortization for the year is $3,500,000. What are the net profit and net cash provided by operating activities for the year?

Table 11.9 Tax Rates for 2023

Tax Rate	*Single filers*	*Married filing jointly or qualifying surviving spouse*	*Married filing separately*	*Head of household*
10%	$0 to $11,000	$0 to $22,000	$0 to $11,000	$0 to $15,700
12%	$11,001 to $44,725	$22,001 to $89,450	$11,001 to $44,725	$15,701 to $59,850
22%	$44,726 to $95,375	$89,451 to $190,750	$44,726 to $95,375	$59,851 to $95,350
24%	$95,376 to $182,100	$190,751 to $364,200	$95,376 to $182,100	$95,351 to $182,100
32%	$182,101 to $231,250	$364,201 to $462,500	$182,101 to $231,250	$182,101 to $231,250
35%	$231,251 to $578,125	$462,501 to $693,750	$231,251 to $346,875	$231,251 to $578,100
37%	$578,126 or more	$693,751 or more	$346,876 or more	$578,101 or more

Notes

1 The Airbus Group was known as EADS (European Aeronautic Defense and Space Company) prior to the group's restructuring in January 2014.
2 The Boeing Company (2023). *Long-Term Market. Current Market Outlook.*
3 KPMG (2007). *Components of Aircraft Acquisition Cost, Associated Depreciation and Impairment Testing in the Global Airline Industry* (p. 10).
4 *The New York Times*, December 15, 1992.
5 IRS Publication on Net Operating Loss (NOL). www.irs.gov/publications/p536/ar02.html.
6 The Boeing Company Dividend Date & History.
7 Southwest Airlines and Delta Air Lines annual reports.
8 Boeing World Air Cargo Forecast, 2014–2015.
9 So are investments a company makes.
10 *The New York Times*, December 3, 1993.
11 Delta Air Lines Inc. Form 10-K, SEC Filings.

12 Analyzing Financial Performance

Financial analysis of a company is mainly used to assess to how well it is utilizing its assets and other financial resources to maximize its efficiency and productivity. Financial ratios are useful management tools that help with understanding financial results and trends over time. These ratios are key indicators of organizational performance and allow for comparing performance directly against other businesses regardless of size or market share. Managers also apply financial ratios to determine how efficiently a company's assets are being used. Ratio analysis can be used to pinpoint strengths and weaknesses that form strategies and are also useful in benchmarking performance to industry standards; for instance, one important ratio for airlines is breakeven load factor. In addition to ratios, airlines use income statements to measure how cost of goods sold and operating expenses affect profits. If the costs and expenses of providing a flight were exactly equal to the revenue generated from that flight, there would be neither a profit nor a loss, and net income would be zero.

An important application of financial ratios is in rating credit. Credit ratings are vital in an industry like aviation that is heavily dependent on leasing and external sources of financing. Ratio analysis can be applied to an aircraft, a runway, an employee, a passenger, a market, a company, or even an entire industry. There are a broad range of ratios that we discuss in detail in this chapter.

Liquidity Ratios

If a company consistently maintains a current ratio below 1, it may raise concerns among creditors, investors, and other stakeholders about the company's financial health and ability to meet its short-term obligations. Management must implement strategies to improve liquidity, such as reducing short-term debt, increasing cash reserves, or improving inventory management practices.

Liquidity ratios are used to determine a firm's ability to meet its short-term (usually, within the next reporting period) financial obligations. Investors often consider liquidity ratios when performing a fundamental analysis of a company. Because a company that is consistently facing difficulty in meeting its short-term debt is at a higher risk of bankruptcy, liquidity ratios are a decent measure of whether a company will be able to securely continue as a going concern.

Liquidity is not only a measure of the amount of cash possessed by a company. It is also a measure of how easy it will be for the company to raise enough cash or convert assets classified

DOI: 10.4324/9781003469759-12

as current into cash. Assets like accounts receivable (AR), marketable securities, and inventory are relatively simple for many companies to convert into cash in the short term. Thus, all of these assets go into calculating a firm's liquidity.

Current Ratio

The current ratio (CR) is a financial metric used to assess a company's short-term liquidity and its ability to cover its short-term liabilities with its short-term assets. CR is the most direct liquidity ratio: It measures the ratio of all current assets (CA) to all current liabilities (CL). CR > 1 indicates that a company has more current assets than current liabilities, suggesting it can cover its short-term obligations. However, a very high current ratio may indicate that a company is not efficiently utilizing its assets. When CR < 1, a company will typically have difficulty meeting its short-term obligations with its CA alone.

As of December 31, 2023, Delta Air Lines had CA worth \$10,269 million and CL worth \$26,418 million, for a CR of 0.39.

$$CR = \frac{\$10,269}{\$26,418}$$

$$CR = 0.39$$

Figure 12.2[1] illustrates a comparison of different global airlines' CRs; we gathered the data from the different companies' financial statements. International carriers Ryanair (FR) [1.0] and

Figure 12.1 Current ratio.

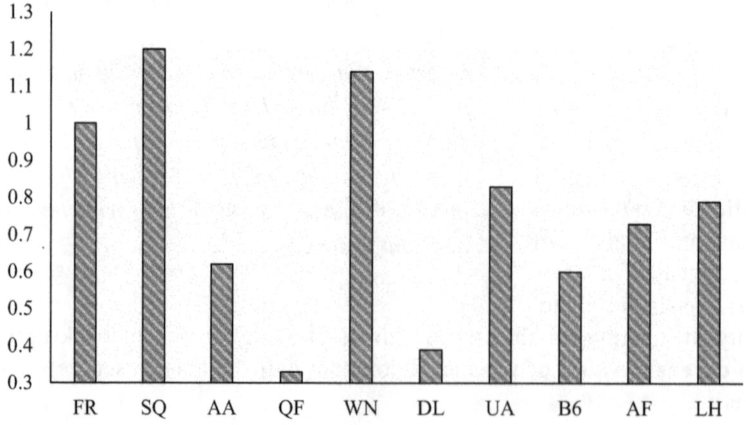

Figure 12.2 Current ratios for global airlines, 2024.

Singapore Airlines (SQ) [1.2] have pretty high CRs. Among the US carriers, American Airlines (AA) [0.62] has a better CR than its peers. The average CR was 0.763.

Example 12.1

DirectJet Airlines has CA worth $13,500 million and L worth $15,000 million; calculate its CR.

$$CR = \frac{\$13{,}500}{\$15{,}000}$$

$$CR = 0.90$$

In this scenario, DirectJet had $0.90 in current assets for every dollar of current liabilities. The company appears to be unable to easily service its short-term debt obligations.

Quick Ratio

Quick ratio (QR; also known as the acid-test ratio) is a measure of a company's ability to meet its short-term obligations using its most liquid assets (near cash or quick assets) that can be quickly converted into cash at close to their book values can be considered quick assets. QR signifies a company's financial strength or weakness; it tells creditors what portion of a company's short-term debt can be settled by the sale of all the company's liquid assets at very short notice.

QR can be given by either of the following two formulas:

$$QR = \frac{Cash + Short - term\ Investment + Accounts\ Receivable}{Current\ Liabilities}$$

$$QR = \frac{Total\ Current\ Assets - Inventory - Prepaid\ Expenses}{Current\ Liabilities}$$

As of December 31, 2023, Delta's quick assets amounted to $6,998 million, while CL amounted to $26,418 million. By dividing, the equation gives us a quick ratio of 0.26.

$$QR = \frac{\$6998}{\$26418}$$

$$QR = 0.26$$

Because we subtracted current inventory, for every dollar of CL, there are only $0.43 dollars of cash, marketable securities, and AR. Both of these ratios indicate that Delta Air Lines has a significant shortage of liquidity.

Figure 12.3 Quick ratio.

Example 12.2

Funjet Airlines has the following assets and liabilities in the year ending December 31, 2024:

Table 12.1 Funjet Airlines Financial Data

Cash	$34,000,000
Marketable securities	$12,000,000
AR	$56,200,000
Prepaid insurance	$9,000,000
Total current assets	$111,590,000
Total current liabilities	$73,780,000

Calculate its QR:

$$QR = \frac{\$34,000,000 + 12,000,000 + 56,200,000}{73,780,000}$$

$$QR = 1.38$$

A quick ratio of 1.38 means that Funjet has $1.38 of liquid assets (cash, marketable securities, and AR) available to cover each $1 of current liabilities.

Asset Management Ratios

Asset management ratios attempt to measure a company's success in managing its assets to generate sales; they are also called efficiency, activity, or turnover ratios. For example, these ratios can help comprehend the success of the firm's credit policy and inventory management.

A company desires high asset turnover ratios because they imply that the assets are being efficiently utilized to produce sales. The higher the asset turnover ratio, the more sales the company is generating from its assets, although this measure is highly industry specific as a low ratio in one industry might be high in another. Hence, it is important to restrict comparisons to within a particular industry.

AR Turnover Ratio

The AR turnover ratio (receivables turnover ratio) indicates the speed with which a company collects its debt, that is, the number of times average receivables are turned over during a year. This ratio determines how fast a company collects outstanding cash balances from its customers during an accounting period. It is an important measure of a company's financial and operational performance and can be used to identify if a company is having difficulties collecting sales made on credit:

$$Accounts\ Receivable\ Turnover\ Ratio = \frac{Annual\ Credit\ Sales}{Accounts\ Receivable}$$

$$ART = \frac{ACS}{AR}$$

DirectJet's net credit sales during 2025 were $58,048 million. Its AR was $3,130 million, and hence the AR turnover ratio becomes 18.55.

$$Accounts\ Receivable\ Turnover\ Ratio = \frac{\$58{,}048}{\$3130}$$

$$Accounts\ Receivable\ Turnover\ Ratio = 18.55$$

Average Collection Period

The receivables turnover ratio is often reported in number of days the credit sales remain in AR before they are collected. This is known as average collection period (ACP). It can be denoted as follows:

$$ACP = \frac{Accounts\ Receivable}{Annual\ Credit\ Sales\ /\ 365}$$

$$ACP = \frac{AR}{ACS\ /\ 365}$$

It is also given by the formula

$$ACP = \frac{365}{ART}$$

DirectJet had an ACP of 19.68 days during 2025:

$$ACP = \frac{365}{18.55}$$

$$ACP = 19.68 \text{ days}$$

On average, DirectJet Airlines has to wait for 19.68 days before its receivables are collected. Whether the AR turnover ratio of 19.68 is good or bad depends on Delta's past ratios, the average for other airlines, and the specific credit terms given to this company's creditors and investors.

Example 12.3

Funjet has an AR turnover ratio of 24.6. Calculate its ACP:

$$ACP = \frac{365}{ART}$$

$$ACP = \frac{365}{24.6}$$

$$ACP = 14.84 \text{ days}$$

The average collection period for Funjet Airlines is 14.84 days.

Inventory Turnover

Inventory turnover is a measure of the number of times inventory is sold or used in a given period such as one year. It is a good indicator of inventory quality (whether the inventory is obsolete or not), efficient buying practices, and inventory management. This ratio is important because gross profit is earned each time inventory is turned over. The inventory turnover ratio is calculated by dividing cost of goods sold by inventory.

The ride-sharing services Uber and Lyft charge higher rates on Saturday nights and at other peak times of demand. Sellers on Amazon.com and other e-commerce sites are increasingly using dynamic pricing to match their inventories with demand. Prices of toll lanes on Southern California freeways move up and down in tandem with traffic.[2] What makes service industries such as airlines so distinct from manufacturing is the high inventory turnover due to the low levels of inventory associated with the service industry.

An airline, as a service-oriented company, does not have costs of goods sold, although some operating expenses such as fuel and administrative expenses can be considered COGS. To illustrate how the ratio is useful, look at Delta's 2023 financial statements. Delta's average inventory was \$1,314 million, and the airline reported COGS of \$47,219 million:

$$ITO = \frac{\$47,219}{\$1,314}$$

$$ITO = 35.94$$

Therefore, the resulting inventory turnover ratio was 35.94.

Example 12.4

AvAir, a general aviation aircraft manufacturing company, has inventory worth \$45 billion during the year 2025, and the cost of revenue for the chosen period is \$76.8 billion. Calculate the inventory turnover ratio:

$$ITO = \frac{\$76.8}{\$45}$$

$$ITO = 1.71$$

AvAir has an inventory turnover ratio of 1.71, which is typical for a manufacturing firm as opposed to the higher values obtained for a service-oriented industry.

Fixed Asset Turnover Ratio

The fixed assets turnover ratio measures how productively a firm manages its fixed assets to generate sales (revenue). If a company has a high fixed asset turnover ratio, it is managing its fixed assets very efficiently. Fixed assets are important because they usually comprise the largest component of total assets. The turnover ratio is calculated by dividing total revenue by net fixed assets:

$$Fixed\ Asset\ Turnover\ Ratio = \frac{Total\ Revenue}{Net\ Fixed\ Assets}$$

$$FAT = \frac{TR}{NFA}$$

Figure 12.4 Inventory turnover.

As of December 31, 2023, with amounts expressed in millions, Delta had net sales, or revenue, of $58,048 million and net fixed assets, or PP&E, of $42,490 million:

$$FAT = \frac{\$58,048}{\$42,490} = 1.366$$

$$FAT = 1.366$$

Delta's fixed asset turnover ratio of 1.366 is high, indicating that the company is quite efficiently managing its fixed assets in order to generate revenue.

Example 12.5

EZjET nurtured revenue of $35,000 million during 2025, and at the end of the year, EZjET owns PP&E worth $24,350 million. Calculate its fixed asset turnover ratio:

$$FAT = \frac{\$35,000}{\$24,350}$$

$$FAT = 1.44$$

EZjET had a reasonable fixed asset turnover ratio of 1.44 for 2025.

Total Asset Turnover Ratio

The total asset turnover ratio measures how effectively the firm manages all its assets to generate revenue. This ratio is calculated by dividing total revenue by total assets.

$$Total\ Asset\ Turnover\ Ratio = \frac{Total\ Revenue}{Average\ Total\ Assets}$$

$$TAT = \frac{TR}{TA}$$

Consider the example of DirectJet for the year ending December 31, 2025. DirectJet had net sales, or revenue, of $58,048 million and average total assets of $81,055 million, giving a total asset turnover of 0.72:

$$TAT = \frac{\$58,048}{\$81,055}$$

$$TAT = 0.72$$

Because airlines have fewer fixed assets, the total asset turnover ratio was lower than the high fixed asset ratio. The higher the total asset turnover ratio, the better and the more efficiently the airline uses the company's asset to generate sales. Table 12.2 shows some total asset turnover ratios for a number of global airlines from 2023. The amounts are shown in the airlines' countries' respective currencies.

Table 12.2 and Figure 12.5 reflect that both Qantas Airways and Delta Air Lines have the highest total asset turnover ratios.

Table 12.2 2023 Total Asset Turnover for Global Airlines

Airline Name	*Airline Code*	*Total Revenue (TR)*	*Total Assets (TA)*	*TAT (TR/TA)*
Deutsche Lufthansa AG	LH	35,442,000	43,335,000	82%
United Airlines	UA	53,717,000	67,358,000	80%
Southwest Airlines	WN	26,091,000	35,369,000	74%
Qantas Airways	QF	19,521,000	19,653,000	99%
British Airways	BA	29,453,000	37,680,000	78%
Emirates Airlines	EK	107,356,000	172,140,000	62%
Delta Air Lines	DL	58,048,000	72,288,000	80%
JetBlue Airways	B6	9,615,000	13,045,000	74%
Air New Zealand	NZ	2,734,000	6,694,000	41%
Ryanair	FR	10,775,200	15,149,800	71%

Source: Compiled from respective annual reports. Reporting periods may slightly vary.

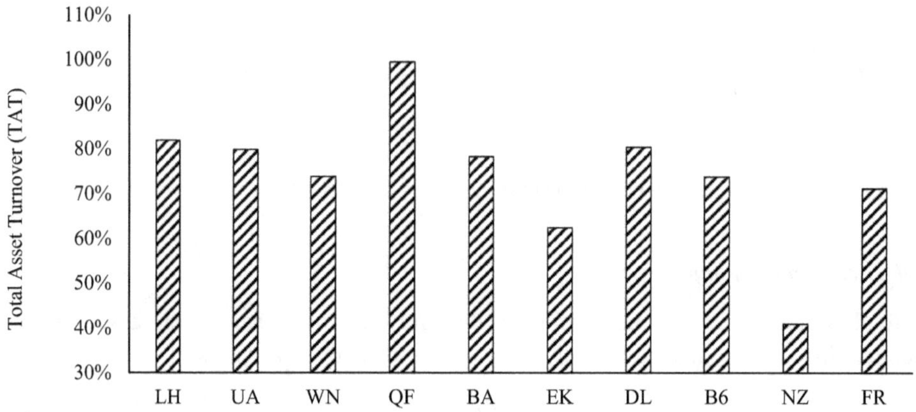

Figure 12.5 Total asset turnover for global airlines, 2023.

Example 12.6

DirectJet has current assets worth \$23 million and noncurrent assets worth \$19 million for 2025 and managed overall sales of \$37 million during the same year. Calculate its total asset turnover ratio:

$$TAT = \frac{\$37,000,000}{\$23,000,000 + \$19,000,000}$$

$$TAT = 0.881$$

DirectJet has a total asset turnover ratio of 0.881.

Financial Management Ratios

Liquidity ratios are concerned only with short-term assets and liabilities, while financial management ratios measure the extent to which firms use long-term debt to finance capital projects. There are many reasons for an airline to file for bankruptcy or go out of business. The high volume of debt makes it more difficult for any company to remain profitable and to pay interest on the debt; for instance, by the end of 1988, Trans World Airlines was facing nearly $4 billion in debt, which forced the airline to file for Chapter 11 bankruptcy in 1992. In 2005, Delta Air Lines was heading into bankruptcy with a remarkably high $28 billion in debt on its balance sheet; since the airline did not have enough cash to meet its financial obligations, it was forced to file for Chapter 11 protection in 2015. Gol Linhas Aéreas, a major Brazilian low-cost carrier, filed for Chapter 11 in the United States on January 25, 2024, although the airline has continued its operations without interruption; This filing was a strategic move to restructure its debts and address financial strains caused by delivery delays of new aircraft and increased costs.

Debt Ratio

A debt ratio is a measure of a firm's total liabilities to its total assets; the ideal is ≥0.5: No more than half of a firm's assets should be financed by debt.

$$D/A = \frac{Total\ Liabilities}{Total\ Assets}$$

Delta had total liabilities worth $69,950 million and total assets worth $81,055 million as of December 31, 2023, for a debt ratio of 0.863:

$$\mathrm{D/A} = \frac{\$69,950}{\$81,055}$$
$$\mathrm{D/A} = 0.863$$

Although this is higher than the ideal, 0.8636 indicates that total assets are greater than total liabilities. For an airline, this is a fair number because most airline operations are financed by debt.

Figure 12.6[3] depicts debt ratios for various global carriers. Singapore Airlines (SQ) is quite close to the ideal debt ratio of less than 0.5. American Airlines (AA) is worse than its US peers. Overall, AA [1.09], Qantas Airways (QF) [1.01], Delta (DL) [0.909] and United Airlines (UA) [0.898] form the higher end of the spectrum.

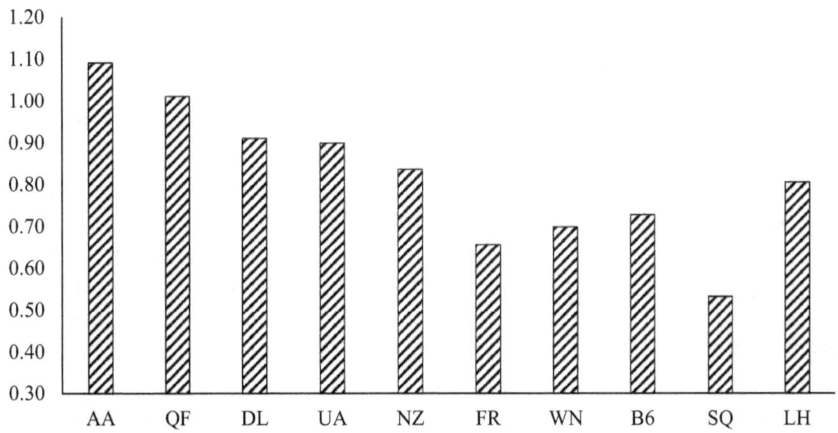

Figure 12.6 Debt ratios for global airlines, 2023.

Source: https://finance.yahoo.com/

Example 12.7

Assume Funjet has the balance sheet shown in Table 12.3 for the year 2025.
Calculate Funjet's debt ratio for 2025:

Table 12.3 Funjet Balance Sheet Data (in USD millions)

Current Assets	$13,500
Current Liabilities	$16,000
Noncurrent Assets	$42,000
Noncurrent Liabilities	$27,500

$$\text{Total Assets} = \$13{,}500 + \$42{,}000 = \$55{,}500 \text{ million}$$

$$\text{Total Liabilities} = \$16{,}000 + \$27{,}500 = \$43{,}500 \text{ million}$$

$$\text{D/A} = \frac{\$43{,}500}{\$55{,}500}$$

$$\text{D/A} = 0.784$$

In this example, 78.40% of Funjet assets have been financed by debt, and therefore only 21.60% was financed by equity capital. A higher percentage indicates greater leverage and risk.

Debt-to-Equity Ratio

The debt-to-equity (D/E) ratio compares a firm's debt with its stockholders' equity. The ideal value for this ratio is 1.0, implying that a company can cover all its debt using its equity.

$$D/E = \frac{\textit{Total Liabilities}}{\textit{Stockholder's Equity}}$$

Consider the example of Delta Air Lines for 2023:

$$D/E = \frac{\$69{,}950}{\$11{,}105} = 6.30$$

This ratio is fairly high: Delta owes $6.30 to creditors for every dollar its shareholders own; in the same period, AA's was $6.33. Historically, airlines have had very high D/E ratios because of the nature of the industry; returns are typically very poor, but the functioning of the industry cannot be avoided. Many airlines have been pushed to bankruptcy because of very high debt and have either ceased operations or reorganized under bankruptcy protection. Airlines such as Braniff,[4] Eastern Airlines, Kiwi International, PanAm, and Southern Air all filed for bankruptcy and ceased operation.

D/E Anomalies in the Airline Industry

D/E Delta Airlines = 6.30
D/E American Airlines = 6.33
Airline industry in general has very high debt due to poor returns

Times Interest Earned Ratio

The times interest earned ratio determines how efficiently a firm can cover the interest payments on its debts. It is the ratio of earnings before interest and tax (EBIT) to interest. Creditors favor companies with much higher ratios because they show that a company can afford to pay its interest payments when they come due. The ratio should ideally be greater than 1.0.

$$TIE = \frac{EBIT}{Interest\ Expense}$$

To illustrate the times interest earned ratio, look at DirectJet's 2025 financial statement and calculate its ratio:

$$TIE = \frac{\$7,638,000}{\$481,000} = 15.88$$

A ratio of 15.88 means that DirectJet Airlines makes enough income to pay for its total interest expense 15.88 times over.

Example 12.8

Assume that a company's net income after tax was \$1,000,000, its interest expense was \$4,000,000, and its income tax was \$6,000,000. Calculate the times interest earned ratio for the company:

$$EBIT = \$1,000,000\,(net\ income) + \$4,000,000\,(interest\ expense) + 6,000,000\,(income\ tax\ expense)$$

$$EBIT = \$11,000,000$$

$$TIE = \frac{\$11,000,000}{\$4,000,000} = 2.75$$

The company had a times interest earned ratio of 2.75.

Profitability Ratios

The airline industry historically has among the average rates of return on capital (ROIC) of any industry and is one of the few that consistently fails to meet its weighted average cost of capital.[5] For the first time, the industry level average ROIC will be in excess of its cost of capital. Profitability ratios link various income statement accounts to show a company's ability to generate profits from its operations and investments in assets. These ratios essentially depict how well companies can achieve profits from their operations.

$$ROIC = \frac{EBIT\,(1 - Tax\ rate)}{Book\ Value\ of\ Equity + Book\ Value\ of\ Debt - Cash}$$

If the airline leases aircraft rather than owning, the formula is

$$Return\ on\ Capital = \frac{(EBIT + operating\ Lease\ Expense - Depreciation\ of\ OL)(1 - Tax\ rate)}{Book\ Value\ of\ Equity + Book\ Value\ of\ Debt - Cash + Present\ Value\ of\ OL}$$

Gross Profit Margin

Gross profit margin (GPM) is the ratio of gross profit (gross sales less cost of sales) to sales revenue. It calculates the percentage by which gross profits exceed production costs, essentially the percentage markup on merchandise from its cost. GPM can vary drastically from one industry to another depending on the type of business:

$$GPM = \frac{Sales - Cost\ of\ Goods\ Sold}{Net\ Sales}$$

For instance, as of December 31, 2023, Delta Air Lines showed a gross profit of $10,829 million, divided by the net sales of $58,048 million, for GPM of 0.1866 or 18.66%:

$$GPM = \frac{\$58,048 - \$47,219}{\$58,048}$$
$$GPM = 0.1866$$
$$GPM = 18.66\%$$

Hence, for every dollar of sales made, a gross profit of $0.1866 is obtained that can be used to cover operating expenses. GPM is a key measure of profitability by which investors and analysts compare similar businesses to the overall industry.

Example 12.9

EZjET has net sales of $160,000,000 and its COGS is $120,000,000. This means its gross profit is $40,000,000, and its GPM is 25%:

$$GPM = \frac{\$160,000,000 - \$120,000,000}{\$160,000,000}$$
$$GPM = 0.25 = 25\%$$

Operating Profit Margin

Operating profit margin (OPM) measures the operating income as a ratio of the net sales. The primary difference is that the operating income considers other expenses as well, not just COGS:

$$OPM = \frac{Operating\ Income}{Net\ Revenue}$$

For 2023, Delta had operating income of $5,277 million and net sales of $58,048 million, for an OPM of 0.0909 or 9.09%.

$$OPM = \frac{\$5,277}{\$58,048}$$
$$OPM = 0.0909$$
$$OPM = 9.09\%$$

Even after all the operating expenses are considered, for every dollar of sales made, an operating profit of 9.09 cents is obtained.

Net Profit Margin

Net profit margin (profit margin or net margin; NPM) is a ratio of profitability calculated as after-tax net income (net profits) divided by sales (revenue). It shows the amount of each sales dollar leftover after all expenses have been paid:

$$NPM = \frac{Net\ Income}{Net\ Revenue}$$

By dividing net profit by total revenue, we can see what percentage of revenue made it all the way to the bottom line, which is good for investors. NPM tells investors which are the most profitable airlines. For instance, Delta in 2023 had net income of \$6,609 million and net sales of \$58,048 million, for NPM of 0.1139 or 11.39%:

$$NPM = \frac{\$6,609}{\$58,048}$$
$$NPM = 0.1139$$
$$NPM = 11.39\%$$

Example 12.10

Using the financial data in Table 12.4, calculate GPM, OPM, and NPM for DirectJet.

GPM:

$$GPM = \frac{Sales - Cost\ of\ Goods\ Sold}{Net\ Sales}$$

$$GPM = \frac{\$50,000,000}{\$52,500,000}$$
$$GPM = 0.9524$$
$$GPM = 95.24\%$$

OPM:

$$OPM = \frac{Operating\ Income}{Net\ Revenue}$$

$$OPM = \frac{\$50,000,000 - 3,750,000 - 3,750,000}{\$52,500,000}$$
$$OPM = 0.8095$$
$$OPM = 80.95\%$$

Table 12.4 DirectJet Financial Data

Sales	52,500,000
Cost of goods sold	2,500,000
Gross profit	50,000,000
Administrative expenses	3,750,000
Selling expenses	3,750,000
Interest on investment	2,500,000
Loss on investment	1,500,000
Income tax	1,250,000

NPM:

$$NPM = \frac{Net\ Income}{Net\ Revenue}$$

$$NPM = \frac{\$50,000,000 - 3,750,000 - 3,750,000 - 2,500,000 - 1,250,000}{\$52,500,000}$$

$$NPM = 0.7381$$
$$NPM = 73.81\%.$$

Return on Total Assets

The return on assets ratio (ROA), often called the return on total assets, is a profitability ratio that measures the net income produced by total assets during a period against the average total assets. This ratio helps both management and investors to see how well the company can convert its investments in assets into profits.

$$ROA = \frac{Net\ Income}{Average\ Total\ Assets}$$

Delta's ROA of 5.69% for 2023 was calculated by dividing the net income of $4,609 million by the average total assets of $81,055 million:

$$ROA = \frac{\$4,609}{\$81,055}$$
$$ROA = 0.0569$$
$$ROA = 5.69\%$$

ROA illustrates how effectively an airline utilizes its assets to generate profits. It shows the return generated by each dollar of asset. Figure 12.7[6] illustrates the return on total assets achieved by various airlines in 2023.

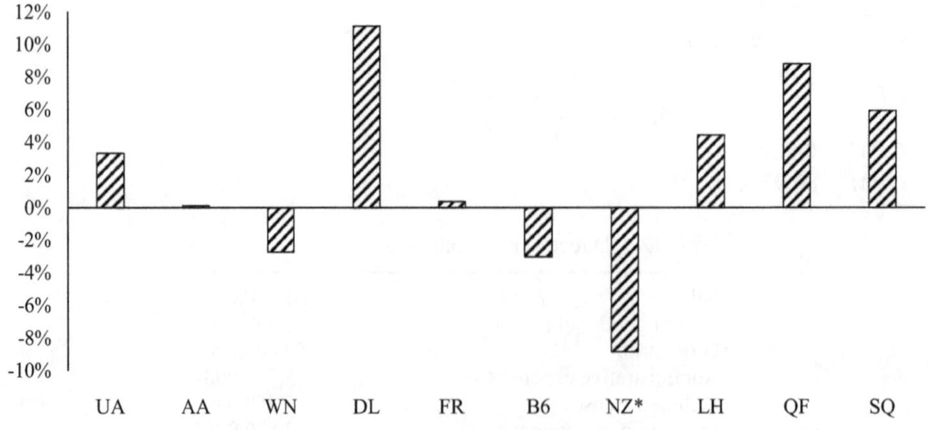

Figure 12.7 Return on total assets for global airlines, 2023. * - 2022

Source: https://finance.yahoo.com/; www.gurufocus.com/

Return on Equity

Return on equity (ROE) is a profitability ratio that denotes the ability of a firm to generate profits from its shareholders' investments in the company. In other words, ROE signifies how much profit each dollar of common stockholders' equity generates. A high ROE suggests that a company is increasing its ability to generate profit without needing as much capital. This is crucial for potential investors because they want to see how efficiently a company will use their money to generate net income:

$$ROE = \frac{Net\ Income}{Average\ Shareholders'Equity}$$

Delta's 2023 ROE of 0.3664 or 36.64% was calculated by dividing the net income of $4,069 million by the average shareholder's equity of $11,105 million:

$$ROE = \frac{\$4,069}{\$11,105}$$
$$ROE = 0.3664$$
$$ROE = 36.64\%$$

In 2023, Delta converted 36.64% of shareholders' equity into net income; for every dollar of shareholder equity, there was a contribution of 36.64 cents into the net income.

Dividend Ratios

Dividend ratios provide insight into the dividend policy of a firm and also possible prospects for future growth. The value of any stock primarily depends on future dividend payments, so it is vital to maintain good dividend ratios to present a profitable picture to potential investors and to existing shareholders. RTX paid its shareholders a dividend of $2.32 per share in 2023. In contrast, American Airlines did not pay its shareholders a dividend, indicating the bleak nature of returns in the airline industry.

Dividend Payout Ratio

The dividend payout ratio (DPR) is the percentage of earnings paid out to shareholders as dividends. Airlines are not generally known for their regular dividend payments, and many airlines do not pay any dividends at all. The ratio also reveals whether a firm can maintain its current level of dividend payouts. If the ratio is greater than 100%, then the company is utilizing its cash reserves to pay dividends. This circumstance may not be sustainable and may result in the eventual termination of all dividends or the financial decline of the company:

$$DPR = \frac{Dividends\ per\ share}{Earnings\ per\ share}$$

Delta's DPR for 2023 was found by dividing the dividends per share, which was $0.2, by earnings per share, which was $6.68:

$$DPR = \frac{\$0.2}{\$6.68}$$
$$DPR = 0.0299$$
$$DPR = 2.99\%$$

A dividend payout ratio of 2.99% is healthy. It indicates that a firm is reinvesting a significant portion of its earnings and only paying out 2.99% as dividends. Delta's dividends per share and earnings per share were provided by NASDAQ.

Dividend Yield

Dividend yield indicates how much a company pays out in dividends each year compared with its share price; it is an important part of the rate of return on an investment. If the price of a stock goes up by 8% in a year while paying a 3% dividend, there is a net 11% earning on the investment:

$$Dividend\ Yield = \frac{Dividends\ per\ share}{Current\ share\ price}$$

Delta's dividend yield for 2023 was calculated as follows:

$$Dividend\ Yield = \frac{\$0.2}{\$40.23}$$

$$Dividend\ Yield = 0.00497 = 0.497\%$$

The yield was just 0.497%; an extremely low dividend yield demonstrate that the airline industry does not possess a high rate of return, in contrast with many other industries.

Example 12.11

FunJet Airlines has a dividend policy of \$0.22 per share and has 790 million shares outstanding. If FunJet earned a net income of \$580 million 2014, calculate the DPR and the dividend yield. Assume the stock price on December 31, 2014, was \$32.71:

$$Earnings\ per\ share(EPS) = \frac{\$580\ million}{790\ million}$$

$$EPS = \$0.73$$

$$DPR = \frac{Dividends\ per\ share}{Earnings\ per\ share}$$

$$DPR = \frac{\$0.22}{\$0.73}$$

$$DPR = 0.3014$$

$$DPR = 30.14\%$$

$$Dividend\ Yield = \frac{Dividends\ per\ share}{Current\ share\ price}$$

$$Dividend\ Yield = \frac{\$0.22}{\$32.71}$$

$$Dividend\ Yield = 0.0067$$

$$Dividend\ Yield = 0.67\%$$

Market Value Ratios

Market value ratios are used to relate an observable market value (i.e., stock price) to values available on a company's financial statements (i.e., book values). Here, we discuss some of these ratios.

Market-to-Book Ratio

Market-to-book ratio relates a company's market value per share to its book value per share. Because the book value reflects historical cost accounting, this ratio signifies management's success in creating value for its shareholders. This ratio is used by "value-based investors" to identify undervalued stocks.

$$\textit{Market-to-book ratio} = \frac{\textit{Price per share}}{\textit{Book value per share}}$$

where

$$\textit{Book value per share} = \frac{\textit{Total Owne's Equity}}{\textit{Number of Shares Outstanding}}$$

Delta's 2023 market-to-book ratio was 2.33, obtained by dividing the market price per share of \$40.23 to the book value per share of \$17.26:

$$\textit{Market-to-book ratio} = \frac{\$40.23}{\$17.26}$$
$$\textit{Market-to-book ratio} = 2.33$$

A ratio of 2.33 indicates that Delta's stock is undervalued and thus is creating a certain value for the shareholders.

Price–Earnings Ratio

The price–earnings (P/E) ratio is calculated by dividing the current market price per share of a stock by earnings per share. The P/E ratio indicates how much investors are willing to pay per dollar of current earnings. Generally, high P/E ratios are associated with stocks with good growth potential.

$$P/E = \frac{\textit{Price per share}}{\textit{Earnings per share}}$$

In 2023, Delta had a market price per share of \$40.23; dividing that by the earnings per share of \$7.17 gives a P/E ratio of 5.61:

$$PE = \frac{\$40.23}{\$7.17}$$
$$PE = 5.61$$

Figure 12.8 is a comparison of the P/E ratios of various global airlines for 2023. Southwest's is by far the highest P/E ratio, indicating maximum growth potential; JetBlue's ratio was the lowest among the US carriers.

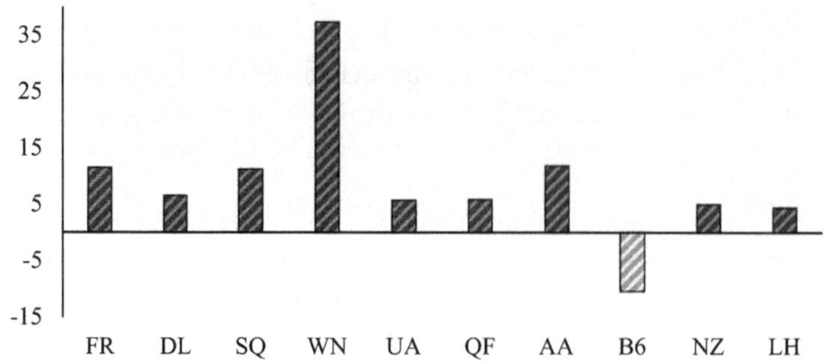

Figure 12.8 Price–earnings ratios for global airlines in USD, 2023.

Dupont System Ratios

The idea of the DuPont system was to combine three critical elements of management, namely, operating management, asset management and the capital structure (financial management), to calculate the two main ratios. The DuPont analysis shows how ROA and ROE can be broken down into subcomponents. Using the DuPont equation, an analyst can easily determine what processes the company does well and what processes can be improved. The equation is called DuPont analysis because DuPont Corporation created it in the 1920s.

Return on Assets

The usual way to calculate ROA, as stated previously, is

$$ROA = \frac{Net\ Income}{Total\ Assets}$$

$$ROA = \frac{NI}{TA}$$

Using the DuPont system, this can be transformed as follows:

$$\text{ROA} = \text{NPM}\left(\frac{\text{NI}}{\text{Sales}}\right) \times \text{TAT}\left(\frac{\text{Sales}}{\text{TA}}\right)$$

The following uses the DuPont system to calculate Delta's 2023 ROA:

$$\text{ROA} = \text{NPM}\left(\frac{\text{NI}}{\text{Sales}}\right) \times \text{TAT}\left(\frac{\text{Sales}}{\text{TA}}\right)$$

$$ROA = 0.0.0794 + 0.803$$

$$ROA = 0.0.0638$$

$$ROA = 6.38\%$$

The product of net profit margin (0.0.0794) and total asset turnover ratio (0.803) results in a ROA of 0.06389 or 6.38%. Table 12.5 and Figure 12.9 show other ROAs calculated with the DuPont system.

Table 12.5 ROAs under the DuPont System for Global Airlines

Airline Name	*Net Income (NI)*	*Total Revenue (TR)*	*Total Assets (TA)*	*NI/TR*	*TR/TA*	*ROA*
UA	2,618,000	53,717,000	67,358,000	5%	80%	3.89%
WN	465,000	26,091,000	35,369,000	2%	74%	1.31%
DL	4,609,000	58,048,000	72,288,000	8%	80%	6.38%
B6	−310,000	9,615,000	13,045,000	−3%	74%	−2.38%
FR	1,313,800	10,775,200	15,149,800	12%	71%	8.67%
NZ	−591,000	2,734,000	6,694,000	−22%	41%	−8.83%
LH	1,921,000	35,442,000	43,335,000	5%	82%	4.43%
EK	10,581,000	107,356,000	172,140,000	10%	62%	6.15%
QF	1,746,000	19,521,000	19,653,000	9%	99%	8.88%

Source: Compiled from respective 10k reports. Reporting periods may slightly vary.

Note: Numbers are in millions of respective local currencies.

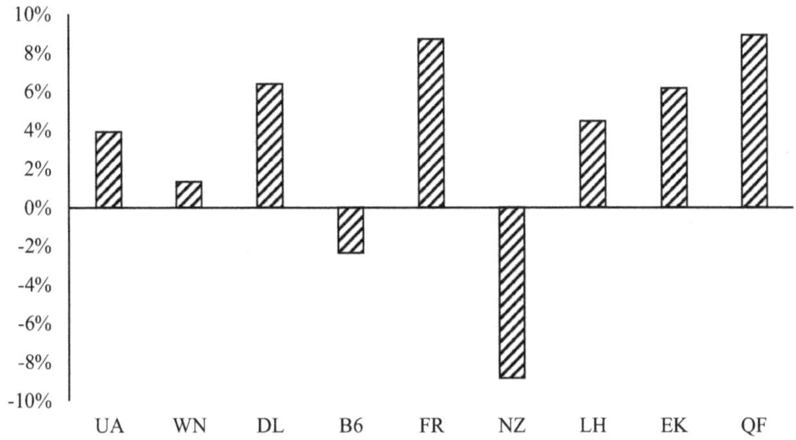

Figure 12.9 ROAs under the DuPont system for global airlines, 2023.

Return on Equity

Consider two companies with the same ROE. The first is well managed (high net-profit margin) and assets are managed efficiently (high asset turnover), but it has a lower equity multiplier than the other company's. An investor is better off investing in the first company because the capital structure can be changed easily but changing management is difficult. The usual way to calculate ROE as stated previously is

$$ROE = \frac{Net\ Income}{Shareholder'\ Equity}$$

$$ROE = \frac{NI}{Shareholder'\ Equity}$$

Using the DuPont system, this can be transformed as follows:

$$ROE = NPM\left(\frac{NI}{Sales}\right) \times TAT\left(\frac{Sales}{TA}\right) \times Equity\ Multiplier\left(\frac{TA}{Shareholders'\ Equity}\right)$$

Consider Delta in 2023. In the DuPont system, ROE is the product between net profit margin (0.0794), total asset turnover ratio (0.803), and equity multiplier (6.51), which is the ratio between total assets ($\$72,288$ million) and shareholders' equity ($\$11,105$ million):

$$ROE = NPM\left(\frac{NI}{Sales}\right) \times TAT\left(\frac{Sales}{TA}\right) \times Equity\ Multiplier\left(\frac{TA}{Shareholders'\ Equity}\right)$$

$$ROE = 0.0794 \times 0.803 \times 6.510$$
$$ROE = 0.41$$
$$ROE = 41\%$$

Delta's 2023 ROE under the DuPont system was 0.41 or 41%.

Example 12.12

The following information is taken from DirectJet's most recent financial statements.

Balance Sheet		*Beginning of Year*	*End of Year*
	Current assets	$21,875,000	$24,500,000
	Total assets	$36,750,000	$42,000,000
	Current liabilities	$9,625,000	$6,125,000
	Total liabilities	$17,500,000	$21,000,000
	Total shareholders' equity	$20,125,000	$25,375,000
Income Statement			
	Net sales		$66,500,000
	Gross profit		$31,500,000
	Operating income		$15,750,000
	Profit		$10,500,000

Calculate the following:

a) Current ratio at year-end
b) Working capital at the beginning of the year
c) Gross profit rate for the year
d) The rate of return on average total assets for the year
e) The rate of return on average total equity for the year

Solutions:

$$a.\ CR = \frac{\$24,500,00}{6,125,000}$$
$$CR = 4$$

$$b.\ Working\ capital = \$21,875,000 - \$9,625,000$$
$$Working\ capital = \$12,250,000$$

$$c.\ Gross\ profit\ margin = \frac{\$31,500,000}{\$66,500,000}$$
$$GPM = 47.4\%$$

$$d.\ ROA = \frac{\$15,750,00}{\$42,000,000}$$

$$ROA = 37.5\%$$

$$ROE = \frac{\$10,500,000}{\frac{\$20,125,000 + \$25,375,000}{2}}$$

$$ROE = 46.20\%$$

A high and stable ROE can signal that the company has a competitive advantage over its competitors. Table 12.6 gives DuPont system ROEs for a number of global airlines.

Figure 12.10 is an illustration of the ROEs for the various airlines. Qantas has a very high return on equity along with Delta Airlines and Emirates. JetBlue and Air New Zealand have the lowest.

Table 12.6 ROEs under the DuPont System for Global Airlines

Airline Name	*Net Income (NI)*	*Total Revenue (TR)*	*Total Assets (TA)*	*Shareholders Equity (SE)*	*NI/TR*	*TR/TA*	*TA/SE*	*ROE*
UA	2,618,000	53,717,000	67,358,000	9,324,000	5%	80%	7.22	28%
DL	4,609,000	58,048,000	72,288,000	11105000	8%	80%	6.51	42%
WN	465,000	26,091,000	35,369,000	10,515,000	2%	74%	3.36	4%
LH	1,921,000	35,442,000	43,335,000	9,709,000	5%	82%	4.46	20%
B6	-310,000	9,615,000	13,045,000	3,337,000	−3%	74%	3.91	-9%
FR	1,313,800	10,775,200	15,149,800	5,642,300	12%	71%	2.69	23%
NZ	-591,000	2,734,000	6,694,000	1,105,000	−22%	41%	6.06	−53%
QF	1,746,000	19,521,000	19,653,000	10,000	9%	99%	1965.30	17460%
EK	10,581,000	107,356,000	172,140,000	27,900,000	10%	62%	6.17	38%

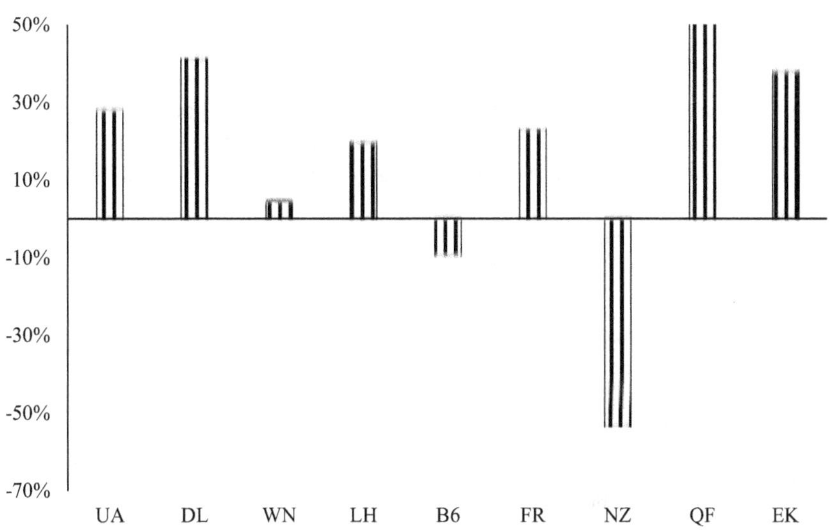

Figure 12.10 ROEs under the DuPont system for global airlines, 2023.

Window dressing refers to the manipulation of financial statements or accounts to present a more favorable picture of a company's financial performance or position than is the case. Off-balance sheet activities refer to the absence of either leased assets or the liabilities under lease contracts on lessees' balance sheets.

Window Dressing

Window dressing refers to actions taken to make financial statements and financial results look better. To improve liquidity ratio, firms often delay payments for equipment, loans, etc. to build up their liquid accounts and thus their liquidity ratios. If possible, it is often more accurate to use other than year-end financial statements to analyze performance. Let us assume that DirectJet wants its balance sheet to look attractive to a potential investor. DirectJet might do some window dressing by disposing of the debt from its balance sheet by leasing aircraft rather than debt financing; because an operating lease is not considered a long-term debt or liability, it does not appear as debt on the financial statement. In some countries, accounting rules encourage airlines to intentionally structure lease obligations as operating leases, thus excluding the obligations from their balance sheets, essentially a form window dressing.

Example 12.13

Table 12.7 presents DirectJet's current balance sheet.

Therefore, the company's debt ratio = $40,000,000/$80,000,000 = 50%. However, DirectJet recently decided to acquire an aircraft for $10,000,000 and capitalized the lease. Table 12.8 presents DirectJet's new balance sheet.

Therefore, the Direct Jet's debt ratio = $50,000,000/$90,000,000 = 55.6%. The airline's financial risk is not different whether the equipment is leased or purchased.

Altman Insolvency Index

Airline industry capital structure and solvency ratio are risky. Both total debt-to-equity and long-term debt-to-equity ratios are very high. The Altman Z score is an analytical representation created by Edward Altman in the 1960s involving a combination of five distinctive financial ratios used for determining the odds of a company's filing for bankruptcy. Altman argued that no single ratio can thoroughly signify the financial status of a firm, and thus, a multivariate approach is needed to ensure that all of the dimensions relevant to insolvency are captured (Gudmundsson, 2002). Most

Table 12.7 DirectJet Current Balance Sheet

Current assets	$30,000,000	Debt	$40,000,000
Fixed assets	50,000,000	Equity	40,000,000
Total assets	$80,000,000	Total claims	$80,000,000

Table 12.8 New DirectJet Balance Sheet

Current assets	$30,000,000	Debt	$50,000,000
Fixed assets	60,000,000	Equity	40,000,000
Total assets	$90,000,000	Total claims	$90,000,000

commonly, a lower score reflects higher odds of bankruptcy. There are several variations of the formulation depending on whether the companies are private or publicly held and also on whether the companies are manufacturers or not.

The Altman Z score, developed by Edward Altman in the late 1960s, is a financial metric used to predict the likelihood of a company facing financial distress or bankruptcy within the next few years. It incorporates several financial ratios to assess a company's financial health and solvency. The Altman Z score is widely used by investors, creditors, analysts, and researchers as a tool for assessing and monitoring financial health and solvency.

Z score for public manufacturing companies is ,calculated as follows:

$$\text{Z-score} = 1.2 \times \text{T1} + 1.4 \times \text{T2} + 3.3 \times \text{T3} + 0.6 \times \text{T4} + 1.0 \times \text{T5}$$

where

$$T1 = \frac{\textit{Working Capital}}{\textit{Total Assets}}$$

$$T2 = \frac{\textit{Retained Earnings}}{\textit{Total Assets}}$$

$$T3 = \frac{\textit{Earnings Before Interest \& Tax}}{\textit{Total Assets}}$$

$$T4 = \frac{\textit{Market Value of Equity}}{\textit{Book Value of Total Liabilities}}$$

$$T5 = \frac{\textit{Sales}}{\textit{Total Assets}}$$

Z scores for public manufacturing companies are divided into zones of discrimination as follows: distress, 1.8 or less; gray, 1.8 to 2.99; and safe, 2.99 or more. Table 12.9 and Figure 12.11 show Altman's Z scores for some of the major aviation manufacturing companies. The aviation industry is not among the most liquid industries, and the table and figure show that the smaller companies such as Lockheed Martin are in a better position with respect to bankruptcy than some of the big companies such as Boeing and Airbus.

Table 12.9 Altman Z Scores for Selected Aviation Manufacturing Companies

Manufacturing Company	*2023*	*2024*
Lockheed Martin	3.97	3.78
General Dynamics	3.43	3.62
Textron Aviation	2.8	2.91
United Technologies	2.11	1.78
Boeing	1.34	1.42
Rolls-Royce	0.08	1.22
Airbus	1.44	1.76
Bombardier	0.32	0.65

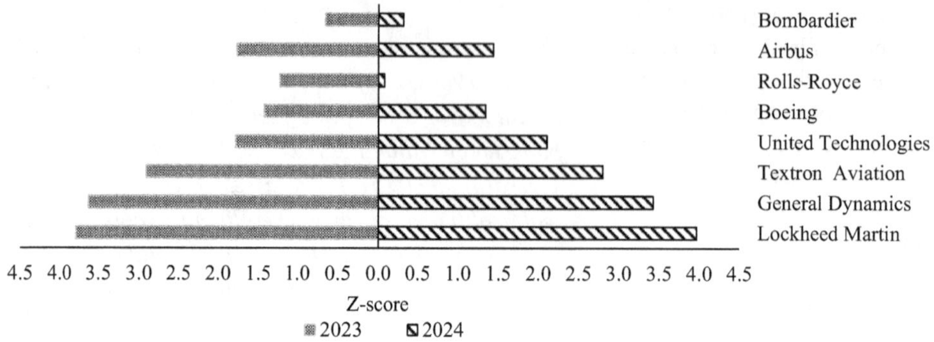

Figure 12.11 Z scores for aviation manufacturing companies.

Source: www.gurufocus.com/

Key Financial Ratios for the Airline Industry

Operational efficiency is another important aspect of any company, particularly an airline. A set of metrics has been devised that can sufficiently provide an insight into the operational efficiency of an airline.

Available Seat Miles[7]

Available seat miles (ASM) is a measure of an airline's passenger carrying capacity. It is calculated as the total number of seats multiplied by the total distance traveled. For instance, a 200-seat aircraft that flies 1,000 miles generates 200,000 ASMs for that particular flight (Figure 12.12).

Revenue Passenger Miles

Revenue passenger miles (RPM) is a measure of production for an airline (Figure 12.13). It is calculated as the number of revenue passengers multiplied by the total distance travelled. For example, 500 passengers flying 8,000 miles generates 4,000,000 RPM. RPM is the basic measure of airline demand. RPM shows how many available seats the airline actually sold compared with its overall capacity. While RPM measures demand, ASM measures supply.

Cost per Available Seat Miles

The primary metric used to measure the cost structure of an airline is cost per available seat mile (CASM or unit cost). CASM is the cost to fly one seat one mile whether it's sold or not, and it is calculated by dividing the total operating cost by the total ASM. The airline industry has successfully reduced its unit costs since 2001. Operating CASM standardizes the direct operational costs incurred on a particular flight. Airlines must reduce CASM to remain competitive and earn profit:

$$CASM = \frac{Total\ Operating\ Cost}{Available\ Seat\ Miles}$$

In 2013, Alaska and Horizon Airlines reduced CASM to remain competitive with lower-cost airlines in the long run. Air Canada is cutting costs by replacing paper manuals with iPads.[8]

Figure 12.12 Available seat miles.

Figure 12.13 Revenue passenger miles.

United completed the installation of a newly designed wingtip curved extension on one of its Boeing 787-800 aircraft. The airline said that it aimed to reduce its fuel costs by $1 billion annually by 2017.[9] American Airlines claims that by switching from paper to iPads, they will save 1.2 million dollars in fuel over the course of a year. Airlines can reduce unit costs in any number of ways. For instance, winglet-equipped aircraft can reduce fuel consumption, and airlines can remove the life rafts on over-land flights. Economy class can be redesigned to accommodate more seating including narrower aisles, and toilets could be smaller. Airlines can reduce the number of flights and fill up aircraft, and pilots can use only one engine to taxi in and one to taxi out.[10] Figure 12.14[11] graphically displays CASM for various global airlines; note that all the CASMs are comparable except for JetBlue and Air New Zealand. A low CASM indicates that costs are minimal.

Revenue per Available Seat Mile

Revenue per available seat mile (RASM) or unit revenue measures the total passenger revenue compared with the overall available seat miles. Figure 12.15[12] is a comparison of RASM for various airlines, and it shows clearly that Delta and United have higher RASMs than the other carriers. The similar RASMs for Southwest, Delta, and United indicate similar choice of routes and hence similar profits.

Revenue per Revenue Passenger Mile or Passenger Yield

Another typical aviation-based ratio is revenue per revenue passenger mile (R/RPM), also referred to as yield; it measures passenger revenue as a ratio of revenue passenger miles, the total miles flown by fare-paying customers not taking into account the empty seats on a particular flight. This is a more accurate measure of airline revenue as it incorporates only those passengers who are contributing to the revenue. Figure 12.16[13] depicts R/RPM for selected global airlines; as with RASM, Delta and United have very similar levels.

Average Stage Length

Average stage length (ASL) refers to the actual length of a particular flight, measured in miles. Higher stage length implies lowers CASM because of fewer takeoffs and landings and therefore fewer costs incurred:

$$ASL = \frac{Total\ Distance\ Flown}{Total\ Number\ of\ Flight\ Segments}$$

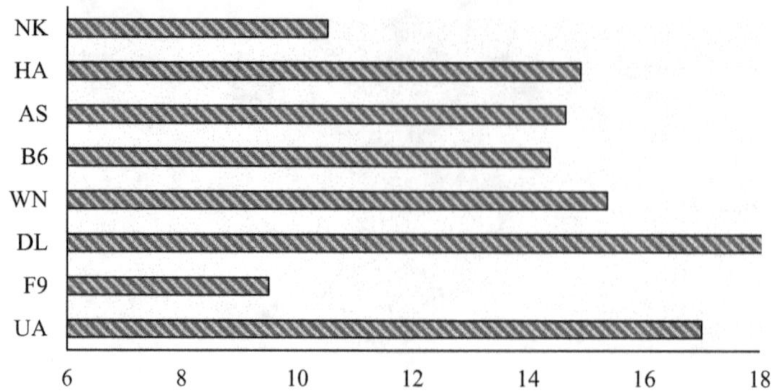

Figure 12.14 CASM (cents) for global airlines, 2024.

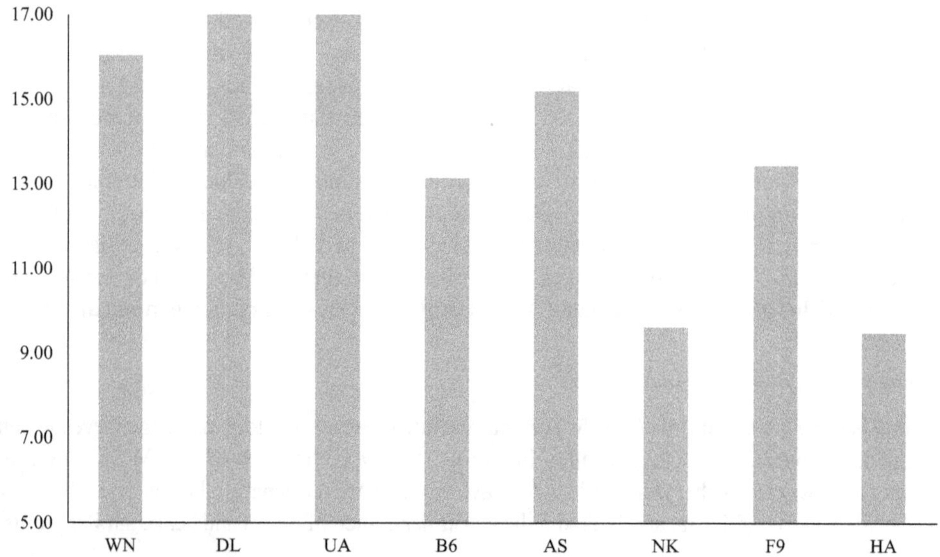

Figure 12.15 RASM (cents) for global airlines, 2023.

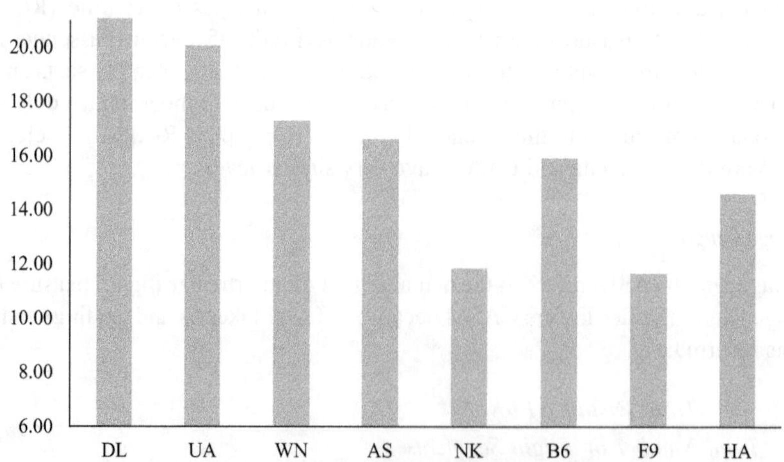

Figure 12.16 R/RPM (cents) for global airlines, 2023.

The ASL for an airline's entire route network is influenced by the mix of short-haul and long-haul flights it operates. Airlines with a focus on short-haul routes have shorter ASL, while airlines specializing in long-haul or international travel have longer ASLs.

For example, DirectJet Airlines operates 500 flight segments in a month, with total distances flown as follows:

250 segments with a stage length of 500 miles each
150 segments with a stage length of 1,000 miles each
100 segments with a stage length of 2,000 miles each

Then

$$ASL = \frac{(250\times 500)+(150\times 1000)+(100\times 2000)}{250+150+100}$$
$$ASL = \frac{475{,}000}{500}$$
$$ASL = 950 \text{ miles}$$

It can be clearly noted from Figure 12.17 that United flies the most international or long-haul flights, while, consistent with its cost structure and planning strategies, Southwest has the lowest ASL.

CASM (Stage Length Adjusted)

Comparing one airline's CASM with that of another offers inaccurate information into which airline is truly more cost efficient. Some serve short-haul distances, and others have vastly different route structures. Operating costs are significantly impacted by the distance flown, and stage-length-adjusted CASM was devised to compare results as if all airlines fly the same distance:

$$CASM_{SLA} = \frac{Length\,of\,haul}{\sqrt{market\ average(stage\ length)}}\times CASM_i$$

where $CASM_i$ = respective carrier unit cost and $CASM_{SLA}$ = stage length adjustment CASM.

Average Daily Block Hour Utilization

Aircraft utilization refers to the average number of block hours that each aircraft flies. Block hours refer to the time between door close (blocks away from the wheels) and door open (blocks

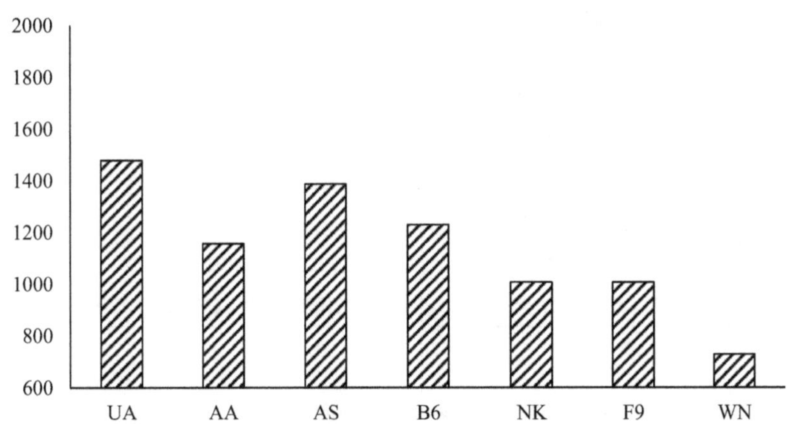

Figure 12.17 Average stage length (miles) for US carriers, 2023.

under wheels). It is measured daily and serves as a measure of the productivity of an airline. Average daily block hours is closely related to ASL. Figure 12.18 shows that Spirit had the maximum average daily block hour utilization of 12.24 hours, while Allegiant Air had the lowest at 7.75 hours. Southwest has a reasonable average block hour per day of 10.51 hours, even though it had the lowest ASL.

Load Factor

Airline load factor is a key performance indicator used in the aviation industry to measure the percentage of total capacity that an airline utilizes. The global airline industry achieved a load factor of 80.3% in 2023[14], while US airlines enjoyed an 82.9% factor on average.[15] Load factor measures and can be calculated using the following formula:

$$LF = \frac{RPM}{ASM}$$

On average, there are 100 passengers on EZjET Airlines flights between New York's JFK airport and Los Angeles' LAX airport. Each leg of the flight covers approximately 2,500 miles, and the airline operates this route with an A-320 NEO aircraft seating 150 passengers.

First, we calculate the ASM for the month. With 30 flights and each flight covering 2,500 miles one way, the round-trip distance amounts to 5,000 miles. Multiplying this by the seating capacity (150 seats) gives the following:

$$\text{ASM} = 30 \times 2{,}500 \times 2 \times 150 = 22{,}500{,}000$$

Next, we calculate RPM:

$$\text{RPM} = 30 \times 2{,}500 \times 2 \times 100 = 15{,}000{,}000$$

Entering these values gives the load factor as follows:

$$LF = \frac{15{,}000{,}000}{22{,}500{,}000} = 66.67\%$$

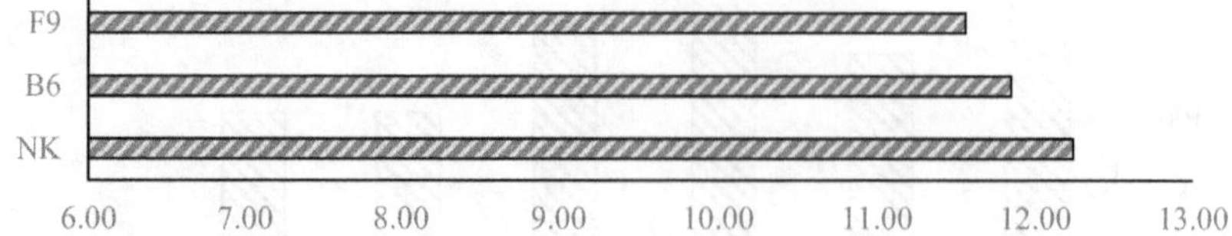

Figure 12.18 Average daily block hour utilization, US carriers, 2024.

Breakeven Load Factor

Breakeven load factor ($LF_{b\text{-}e}$) is the percentage of the seats an airline has in service that it must sell at a given yield, or price level, to cover its costs (Table 12.10). The formula for $LF_{b\text{-}e}$ is

$$LF_{b-e} = \frac{CASM}{R/RPM}$$

Lower breakeven load factors are better for airlines because every seat sold after achieving breakeven is profit generated. Figure 12.19[16] shows that among the US carriers, Frontier had the lowest, and Hawaiian and Delta had considerably high breakeven load factors in 2023.

Summary

Financial analysis plays a crucial role in the air transport industry, providing valuable insights into economic health, operational efficiency, and strategic direction in the industry. This chapter explained in detail all the financial ratios required to assess the current financial standing of any organization. Using financial ratios, stockholders can develop a feel for a company's competitive position, financial strength, and profitability. We described a broad classification of financial

Table 12.10 2023 Breakeven Load Factors for Global Airlines

Carrier Name	*Carrier code*	*CASM*	*Yield (R/RPM)*	*Breakeven Load Factor*
United Air Lines Inc.	UA	16.99	20.07	84.65%
Frontier	F9	9.5	11.65	81.55%
Delta Air Lines Inc.	DL	19.21	21.06	91.22%
Southwest Airlines	WN	15.36	17.29	88.84%
JetBlue Airways	B6	14.37	15.92	90.26%
Alaska Airlines Inc.	AS	14.64	16.61	88.14%
Hawaiian Airlines	HA	14.9	14.59	102.12%
Spirit Air Lines	NK	10.52	11.85	88.78%

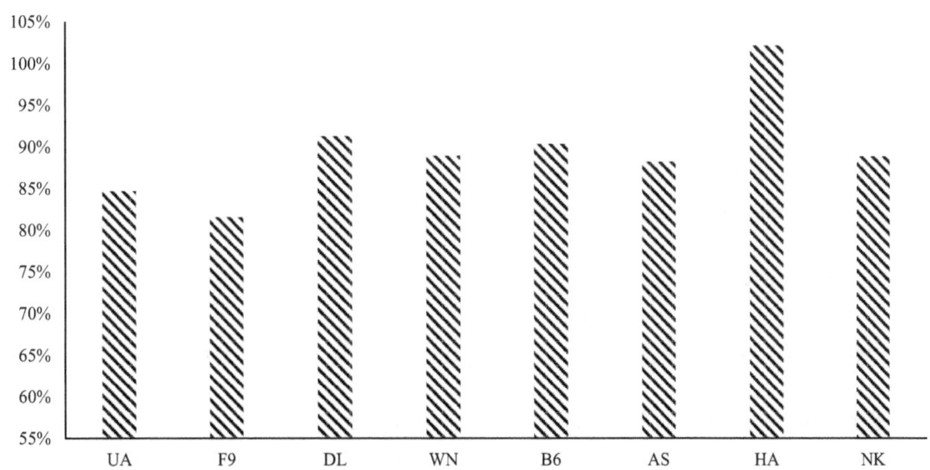

Figure 12.19 Breakeven load factors for various airlines, 2023.

ratios, such as debt management ratios, asset management ratios, profitability ratios, and market value ratios. We also described the Altman Z score, an insolvency index that measures a firm's likelihood of bankruptcy. Finally, we covered aviation-based ratios that convey airlines' financial status.

Discussion Questions and Problems

12.1 Fuel performance for a given flight can be influenced by many factors. Explain some variables that impact airlines' fuel efficiency.

12.2 How do you calculate working capital?

Solution

Working capital = Current assets – Current liabilities

12.3 Your airline has an equity multiplier of 2.50. What is its debt-to-equity ratio?

12.4 An airline has an ROE of 30%. The industry average ROE is 15%. Does this indicate good or poor management of the airline?

12.5 What metrics are most commonly used to evaluate companies in the airline industry?

12.6 Why does an aircraft manufacturer report times interest earned?

12.7 What does it mean when a firm window dresses its financial statements?

12.8 A jet engine manufacturer has $100,000,000 in inventories, a current ratio of 1.2, and a quick ratio of 1.1. What is the firm's net working capital?

12.9 Jet-Tech is a leading commercial aircraft maintenance, repair and overhaul company. Jet-Tech's inventory level of $3,000,000 represents 30 days' sales. What is the annual cost of goods sold? What is the inventory turnover ratio?

12.10 As a credit agency, you are requested to evaluate the balance sheet for PARTS-R-US. From the balance sheet, you acquired the following information:

- Cash and marketable securities = $500,000
- Accounts receivable = $1,000,000
- Inventory = $2,000,000
- Accrued wages and taxes = $400,000
- Accounts payable = $800,000
- Notes payable = $600,000

Calculate PARTS-R-US's current ratio, quick ratio, and cash ratio.

12.11 DirectJet Airlines' financial statements report the following:

- Net sales = $12.0 million
- EBIT = $5.6 million
- Net income available to common stockholders = $3.0 million
- Common stock dividends = $1.0 million
- Total assets = $50 million
- Common stockholders' equity = $20 million with 2 million shares outstanding

Calculate the profit margin, basic earnings power ratio, ROA, ROE, and dividend payout ratio.

12.12 DirectJet reported a D/E ratio of 1.75 times at the end of 2016. If the airline's total debt at year-end was $250 million, how much equity does DirectJet have?

12.13 AVJET provides a full menu of airport services to air carriers at small- to medium-hub airports and general aviation airports. Recent analysis of the company's financial statements revealed that cash makes up 10% of the current assets and accounts receivable makes up another 40%. AVJET's current ratio = 2.0 times and $15 million in current liabilities. Calculate the value of inventory listed on the company's balance sheet.

12.14 Southwest Airlines is a major US airline and the largest low-cost carrier in the world. As of December 2015, Southwest had celebrated 43 consecutive years of profitable operation. Using Southwest's most recent financial statements:

a) Calculate the current ratio
b) Calculate the quick ratio
c) The airline's times interest earned ratio
d) Find the average collection period
e) Calculate the inventory turnover
f) The airline's fixed asset turnover ratio
g) The airline's total asset turnover ratio
h) The airline's return on sales ratio
i) The company's return on equity ratio
j) The company's P/E ratio
k) The company's market to book value
l) Altman Z Score

12.15 Using Southwest's most recent financial statements, calculate the following ratios:

a) Current ratio
b) Quick ratio
c) Inventory turnover
d) Average collection period
e) Fixed asset turnover
f) Return on total asset
g) Return on equity
h) Time interest rate
i) Are the common stockholders receiving a good return on their investment
j) CASM (you need to get ASM data)
k) RPM (you need to find the number of passengers)
l) How is Southwest Airlines financing its assets?

Notes

1 Data is compiled by the authors from respective annual reports. Reporting periods may slightly vary.
2 Why 'Dynamic' Pricing Based on Real-Time Supply and Demand is Rapidly Spreading. *Los Angeles Times*, March 14, 2016.
3 Data is compiled by the authors from respective annual reports. Reporting periods may slightly vary.
4 *The Washington Post*, May 14, 1982.
5 *CAPA*, July 5, 2013.
6 Data is compiled by the authors from respective annual reports. Reporting periods may slightly vary.
7 Sometimes measured as an available seat kilometer.
8 *The Motley Fool*, October 30, 2013.
9 *Forbes*, February 21, 2014.
10 *Daily Mail*, November 5, 2014.
11 Delta Air Lines reported consolidated operations data only as of December 31, 2015.
12 Delta Air Lines reported consolidated operations data only as of December 31, 2015.
13 Delta Air Lines reported consolidated operations data only as of December 31, 2015.
14 IATA, Airlines Continue to Improve Profitability, December 2023.
15 IATA, Air Passenger Market Analysis, 2023.
16 IATA, Air Passenger Market Analysis, 2023.

13 Uncertainty, Risk Analysis, and Simulation

The COVID-19 pandemic brought unprecedented levels of uncertainty to the global community and had a profound impact on the aviation industry, disrupting operations, causing financial losses, and reshaping travel trends. The aviation industry is vastly impacted by external shocks, regulatory reforms, and economic and financial uncertainties. For instance, Russia's invasion of Ukraine had profound impacts on aviation including airspace closures, flight disruptions, safety concerns, and numerous economic consequences.

Risk analysis forms one of the most fundamental aspects of business operation and management. The air transport industry is no exception; companies are exposed to many hazards, such as operational, financial, investment, and political risk. Keeping airline passengers safe while flying efficiently remains paramount, especially in the wake of recent terrorism. The ability to identify and react effectively to potential uncertainty is a major qualification to be a successful business manager. Risk management is an economic issue, as management must balance the costs and benefits associated with risk mitigation. Without proper risk management, an airline would merely rely on fate to avoid financial or operations failures. This chapter focusses on explaining the various methods involved in predicting and analyzing risk.

Decision-making is the process of selecting between different outcomes by setting goals, collecting information, and evaluating alternatives. We all make decisions of varying importance every day; some decisions are simple, and others are more complicated. Jet engine manufacturers face critical decisions when considering propulsion systems such as electronic propulsion, hydrogen fuel cells, or sustainable aviation fuel. To navigate this complex landscape, manufacturers conduct thorough market analyses to gauge demand and regulatory trends, alongside assessing the technological maturity and environmental impact of each option. Performance requirements, including thrust, range, and operational efficiency, are carefully weighed against environmental considerations such as carbon emissions and noise pollution reduction goals. Moreover, regulatory compliance, encompassing safety standards and certification requirements, plays a pivotal role in determining the viability of new propulsion technologies. Risks, including technical challenges, market acceptance, and regulatory uncertainties, must be identified and mitigated through robust risk management strategies to ensure successful implementation. Many managerial decisions are made without knowing in advance what the possible future outcomes will be. For instance, the decision to develop a new aircraft can be made without perfect advance knowledge of whether the manufacturer will reach the breakeven point or whether there will be enough demand to justify a large investment.

When the outcomes are known and the values of the outcomes are certain, the decision-makers know the precise outcome associated with each possible course of action. A decision entails some risk when a single action could result in more than one potential outcome but the probability of each outcome is known; certainty implies that all relevant information is available to

DOI: 10.4324/9781003469759-13

the decision maker. An example of decision-making under certainty includes investment in US government bonds. Every bond is backed by the full faith and credit of the United States government, and the return is known with certainty.[1]

Probability is a foundational concept for making informed decisions, assessing risks, predicting outcomes, and understanding uncertainty in diverse real-world scenarios. The probability of an event is the likelihood or the chance that the event will occur in the future because of an experiment. Probabilities range from 0 to 1, where 0 indicates impossibility and one indicates certainty.

John Maynard Keynes and Frank Knight developed the conceptual distinction between risk and uncertainty; it remains fundamentally correct today (Davidson, 2002). Uncertainty arises when there is more than one feasible possibility, and uncertainty remains as long as the possibilities are not quantified. Once all the options are quantified, uncertainty is modified into risk. Risk can be mathematically measured as the probability of a particular event occurring as opposed to all the possible outcomes. In decision-making under risk, probabilities of events are known precisely by the decision maker. Conversely, in decision-making under uncertainty, the likelihoods of outcomes are not known.

Probability and Business Decisions

Businesses must balance risk and reward when considering any potential project to ensure their viability and success. This balancing act involves assessing the potential benefits or rewards of projects against the associated risks or uncertainties. This tradeoff requires a solid understanding of a project's risk, the organization's strategic objectives, and the prevailing market conditions.

Measuring risk involves assessing the likelihood of adverse events occurring and the potential impacts of those events. Probability concepts are mathematical tools used by decision-makers to identify the degree of risk associated with any project. Probability theory has many practical applications in inventory management, data analysis, revenue management, passenger no-show behavior, and aircraft maintenance and reliability. In finance, probability theory has extensive applications in portfolio management and risk analysis.

Probability is particularly important in quality and biomedical engineering and in estimating the reliability of component and system. Contemporary applications of probability theory run the gamut of business investment including portfolio theory, investment analysis, and capital budgeting. Knowledge of modern probability theory is vital to developing economic modeling and testing the veracity through the analysis of real-world data. Probability and statistics could help to understand the Black–Scholes option pricing model (Black and Scholes, 1973) to develop pricing models for financial assets such as equities, bonds, and the CAPM.

In short, probability is the chance or likelihood that a given event will occur in the future.[2] Events are particular outcomes or series of outcomes. Probability assigns a value to every event, ensuring that the total value of all possible outcomes equals 1. For example, when a single die is thrown, there are six possible outcomes: {1, 2, 3, 4, 5, and 6}, and the probability of any one of them is 1/6. The probability that the experiment results in a successful outcome (A) is

$$P(A) = \frac{\textit{Number of ways event A can occur}}{\textit{Total number of outcomes}}$$

Mathematically, the probability of any event A [denoted as P(A)] is expressed as a number between 0 and 1:

$$0 \leq P(A) \leq 1$$

If P (A) = 0, event A will definitely not occur.
If P (A) = 1, event A will definitely occur.

If the goal for an investment is to produce a minimum 10% return every year on average, and the chances that the goal will not be met are assessed, the event is defined as average annual returns below 10%. Probability concepts are used to assess the chances that an event will take place. If a list of events is mutually exclusive, it means that only one of them can possibly take place. Exhaustive events refer to the need to incorporate all potential outcomes in the defined events.

Example 13.1

Airlines routinely overbook their flights on the expectation that not all ticketed passengers will board, but accurately predicting the number of no-shows has a significant impact on revenue. MyJet tries to combat passenger no-shows by overbooking flights but has noticed that on one day, 121 out of 125 passengers arrived for their flight and the next day, 119 out of 125 passengers made their trip. The two relative frequencies are 121/125 and 119/125, but summing results over many observations, the probability that a MyJet passenger will make their trip is actually 96%.

$$P(\text{Taking the flight}) = \frac{120}{125}$$
$$P(\text{Taking the flight}) = 96\%$$
$$P(No - show) = 100\% - 96\%$$
$$P(No - show) = 4\%$$

Weather conditions, mechanical issues, airspace congestion, crew scheduling, and other issues can cause airlines to experience delays or cancel flights, which also affects the number of no-shows. Knowledge of probability helps revenue managers minimize the cost associated with the possibility that a flight leaves with empty seats. For example, on a flight between Los Angeles and New York, an airline sold 125 tickets; if at the time of departure, only 100 passengers showed up, then

$$P(No - show) = \frac{125 - 100}{125}$$
$$P(No - show) = \frac{25}{125}$$
$$P(No - show) = 20\%$$

Thus, assume you pick a random flight on that route, the probability that a passenger will not show up for this flight is expected to be 20%. To obtain the optimum booking, the airline needs to overbook the flight by 31 seats:

$$125 = Booking \times (1 - no\ show\ rate)$$
$$125 = Booking \times (1 - 0.20)$$

$$Booking = 156$$
$$Overbooking = 156 - 125$$
$$Overbooking = 31$$

Cumulative Probability Distribution

The cumulative distribution function, *x*, is the probability that a real-valued random variable *X* will take a value less than or equal to *x*. Mathematically, the cumulative distribution function f(x) for a random variable X is defined as:

$$f(x) = P(X \leq x)$$

Cumulative probability facilitates decision-making by providing a comprehensive view of the likelihood of different outcomes. For instance, in finance, cumulative probability is used in risk management to assess the probability of portfolio returns falling within a certain range, helping investors make informed decisions about asset allocation and hedging strategies. To better understand cumulative distribution, the probability of filling seats in a particular fare class in a flight can be analyzed.

Example 13.2

Table 13.1 represents the booking pattern for DirectJet Airlines. The revenue manager wishes to determine the cumulative probabilities of filling the allotted number of seats in the $300 fare class (Class Y). Based on historical data, the mean number of bookings was 10 with 3 standard deviations. To determine the probability of filling a seat, the inverse cumulative probability needs to be found because the likelihood of filling more seats is low.

Table 13.1 Cumulative Probability Distribution: Example 13.2

No. of Bookings	*Normal Cumulative Probability*	*Inverse Cumulative Probability*
1	0.0010	0.999
2	0.0040	0.996
3	0.0100	0.990
4	0.0230	0.977
5	0.0480	0.952
6	0.0910	0.909
7	0.1590	0.841
8	0.2520	0.748
9	0.3690	0.631
10	0.5000	0.500
11	0.6310	0.369
12	0.7480	0.252
13	0.8410	0.159
14	0.9090	0.091
15	0.9520	0.048
16	0.9770	0.023
17	0.9900	0.010
18	0.9960	0.004
19	0.9990	0.001
20	1.0000	0.000
Mean	10	
Standard Deviations	3	

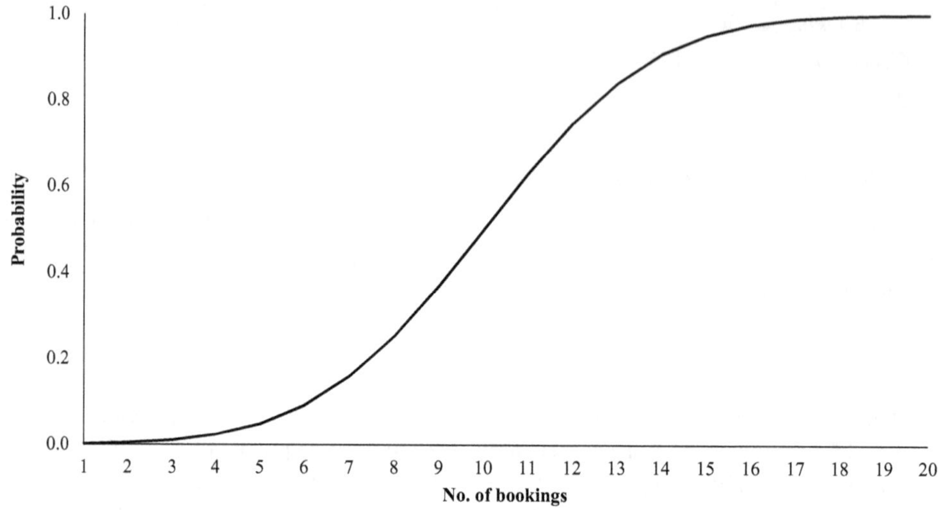

Figure 13.1 Normal cumulative distribution: Example 13.2.

Figure 13.1 is a graphical representation of the cumulative probability distribution of the number of DirectJet bookings presented in the previous table; the table reflects the probability of filling no more than a certain number of seats. For example, the probability of filling seven seats or fewer is 0.159:

$$(X \leq 7) = 0.159$$
$$(X \geq 7) = 0.841$$
$$P(X \leq 7)\ or\ P(X \geq 7) = 100\%$$
$$P(X \leq 7) + P(X \geq 7) = 100\%$$

Figure 13.2 depicts the inverse cumulative probability distribution for the number of bookings from Table 13.1. The inverse cumulative probability denotes the probability of filling at least a certain number of seats. For example, the probability of filling seven seats or more is 0.841.

Joint Probability Distribution

Probability distributions can also be applied to groups of random variables, which gives rise to joint probability distributions. The most common joint probability distribution is a two-dimensional distribution (i.e., only two random variables) but more dimensions (variables) are also possible.

Because all random variables are divided into discrete or continuous, there exist both discrete and continuous joint probability distributions. These distributions are similar to one-variable distributions but have more complex applications. Essentially, joint probability distributions describe situations where both outcomes represented by random variables occur. They are expressed as follows:

$$P(A\,and\,B) = P(A) \times P(B) = P(A \cap B)$$

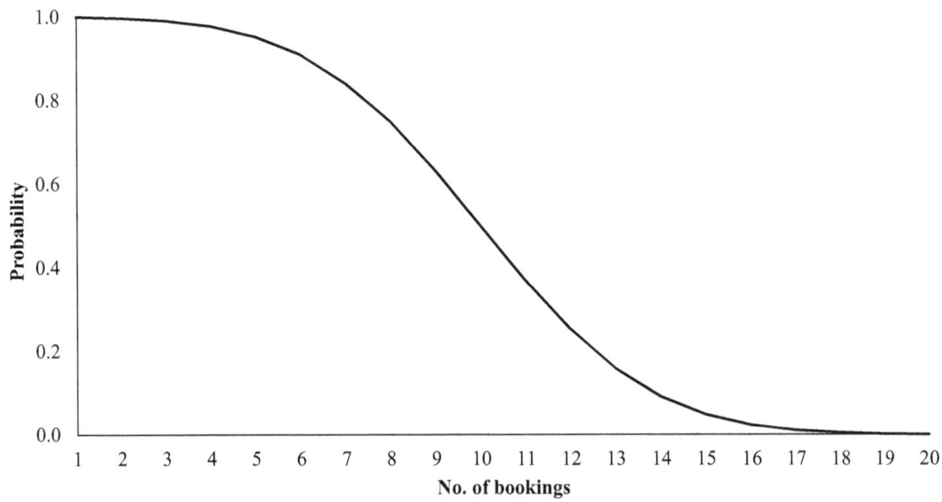

Figure 13.2 Inverse cumulative distribution.

This equation represents the probability that events **A** and **B** occur at the same time. For example, the probability that a playing card will be a black ace:

$$P(Ace\,and\,Black) = P(Ace) \cap P(Black)$$

$$P(A \cap B) = \frac{4}{52} \times \frac{13}{52}$$

$$P(A \cap B) = \frac{1}{52}$$

Example 13.3

Flight delays cost airlines and passengers billions of dollars annually. To identify the major factors that influence flight departure delays, and to develop a strategic departure delay prediction model, a flight dispatcher estimated the probability that two flights will arrive late at the terminal. Assume these two events are independent and give the probability that the two flights will arrive late. The following give the probability of late arrivals:

$$\mathrm{P}\left(\mathrm{FL} - 1_{\mathrm{LAR}}\right) = 0.025$$

$$\mathrm{P}\left(\mathrm{FL} - 2_{\mathrm{LAR}}\right) = 0.035$$

Then the following give the probability that the two flights will arrive late:

$$\mathrm{P}\left(\mathrm{FL} - 1_{\mathrm{LAR}}\right) \cap \mathrm{P}\left(\mathrm{FL} - 2_{\mathrm{LAR}}\right) = \mathrm{P}\left(\mathrm{FL} - 1_{\mathrm{LAR}}\right) \times \mathrm{P}\left(\mathrm{FL} - 2_{\mathrm{LAR}}\right)$$

$$\mathrm{P}\left(\mathrm{FL} - 1_{\mathrm{LAR}}\right) \cap \mathrm{P}\left(\mathrm{FL} - 2_{\mathrm{LAR}}\right) = 875 \times 10^{-6}$$

Measuring Risk and Reward

Risk in traditional terms measures the deviation of the actual outcome from its expected result. Generally, risk has negative connotation, but a risk can also have a positive result. For example, the risk of an investment measures the chance that the investment's actual return will be different from what is expected. An example of risk is drawing an ace from a deck of playing cards. Before we draw, we know in advance what the odds are for each possible outcome, but we do not know what actual card we will draw.

Investors purchase financial assets such as shares of stock primarily to earn a positive rate of return on their investments. Investors like high expected returns but dislike high volatility. Measuring risk and reward, the actual future, however, is uncertain and unpredictable; investors cannot assert with certainty the rate of return their investments will realize.

Risk refers to the dispersion or deviation of returns from the average return of such experiment. Risk also refers to the possibility of loss, harm, or adverse outcomes resulting from uncertain events or conditions. It encompasses both the likelihood and the potential severity of adverse consequences associated with a particular action, decision, or situation.

Managing risk under certainty is not very difficult; you just need to balance your investment to the odds of it paying off. Managing uncertainty is more difficult. The general assumption is that individuals base their decisions on what they expect to happen and their instinct as to what occurs will be close to what they expect to happen. When evaluating potential financial investments, these two dimensions of the decision-making process are called expected return and risk.

Example 13.4

Using simple probability techniques, we can estimate the likelihood of different events occurrence in the future. Assume, two cards are drawn from a deck of ordinary playing 52-card deck without replacement. What is the probability that both cards are a heart?

- There are 13 hearts out of 52 cards total.
  So P (drawing heart on first draw) = 13/52
- After the first draw, there are 12 hearts out of 51 total.
  So, P (drawing heart on second draw) = 12/51

Since the cards are drawn without replacement,
P (both hearts) = P (drawing heart on first draw) × P (drawing heart on second draw)

$$P(H \cap H) = (13/52) \times (12/51)$$

$$P(H \cap H) = \frac{156}{2,652}$$

Hence, the probability of drawing two hearts from a deck of cards, without replacement, is

$$P(H \cap H) = \frac{1}{17}$$

Sample Space

In probability theory, the sample space of an experiment is the set of all possible outcomes for that experiment. Consider the experiment of tossing a die; the typical sample space is {1, 2, 3,

4, 5, 6}. The concept of a sample space is also relevant for experiments where the outcomes are nonnumeric. When determining a sample space, be sure to consider all possibilities. Suppose you reach into your pocket and pull out a coin and you toss the coin three times. In this case, the sample space is

$$\text{SS} = \{\text{HHH, HHT, HTH, HTT, THH, THT, TTH, TTT}\}.$$

$$\text{SS} = \left\{\frac{1}{8}, \frac{1}{8}, \ldots, \frac{1}{8}\right\}$$

The sum of the probabilities of the distinct outcomes within this sample space is

$$Sum = \frac{1}{8} + \frac{1}{8} +, \ldots + \frac{1}{8} = 1$$

Example 13.5

In mathematics, a prime number is a number that can be divided only by 1 or itself. The sample space for choosing a prime number less than 30 at random is given by

$$\text{SS} = \{2, 3, 5, 7, 11, 13, 17, 19, 23, 29\}$$

Example 13.6

A family has four children. Using B to stand for boy and G to stand for girl, provide the sample space for this experiment. What is the probability that all the children are boys?

$$\text{SS} = \{\text{GGGG, GGGB, GGBB, GBBB, BBBB}\}$$

$$P(B \cap B \cap B \cap B) = \frac{1}{2} \times \frac{1}{2} \times \frac{1}{2} \times \frac{1}{2} = 6.25\%$$

Expected Return or Mean

Expected return is the amount of return one would anticipate receiving on an investment that has different potential rates of return.

A return from any investment can be measured by subtracting the amount invested from the final amount realized. For example, if you invested \$100 in the beginning of the year and got a return of \$10 as dividend at the end of the year and finally you sold your investments at the end of the year for \$105, your returns can be presented as follows:

$$\begin{aligned} Return &= \$10(dividend) + (\$105 - \$100) \\ Total\ return &= \$15 \\ Average\ return &= \frac{\$15}{\$100} \\ Average\ return &= 15\% \end{aligned}$$

Expected return is one of the fundamental concepts in engineering economics, in a sense crucial in understanding any investment option. The expected rate of return uses probabilities

Expected return is a fundamental concept in engineering economic and investment decision-making, playing a crucial role in assessing the risk and potential reward of an investment opportunity. Although expected return is an estimate of an investor's expectations of the future, it can be estimated using either ex ante (forward looking) or ex post (historical) data, generally called the average or mean.

$$E(\bar{R}) = \sum_{i=1}^{N} P_i \times R_i$$

to weigh the various return outcomes that an investment may produce. The term mean is used to describe the central tendency of any data set. The mean or the average is calculated by adding up all the numbers and then divide it by the number of observations:

$$\bar{X} = \sum_{n=1}^{n} \frac{X_1 + X_2 + \ldots + X_n}{n}$$

The expected return represents the mean of a possible future return. In simple terms, expected return is the sum of each of the possible outcomes, multiplied by its probability:

$$E(\bar{R}) = \sum_{i=1}^{N} P_i \times R_i$$

where $E(\bar{R})$ = expected return, N = number of possible outcomes, P_i = probability of outcome I, and R_i = return on outcome i.

Example 13.7 Expected Value of Return

When investors who have historical data can examine how the investment has performed in the past and use that as an indication of how it may perform in the future. You intend to invest in three different mutual funds with varying risk. The first mutual fund has 25% probability of providing a 10% rate of return. The second has 50% probability of earning an 8% rate of return, and the last has 25% probability of providing a 12% rate of return. The expected rate of return is

$$E(\bar{R}) = (0.25) \times (10\%) + (0.50) \times (8\%) + (0.25) \times (12\%)$$
$$E(\bar{R}) = 9.5\%$$

Positive return alone does not determine the quality of an investment. The concept that risk and return are positively correlated is one of the most central theories of finance (Danfy, 1975): An investment with a high return most probably entails a high amount of risk as well. Risk factors vary from one type of investment to another. For example, the risk of investing in low-grade securities (junk bonds) can be high, but higher required returns compensate for the higher risk.

Example 13.8

From its hub in Pittsburg, DirectJet serves four different destinations. The airline has noticed that inbound flights are delayed at their origin. Determine the expected number of flights delays if the historical data show the following: 10% of the time, DirectJet has 20 delays; 25% of the time, it has 10 delays; 35% of the time, it has seven delays; and the remaining time, it has three delays:

$$\text{Expected number of delays for January} = (10\% \times 20) + (25\% \times 10) + (35\% \times 7) + (30\% \times 3)$$
$$\text{Expected number of delays} = 2.0 + 2.5 + 2.45 + 0.9$$
$$\text{Expected number of delays} = 7.85 \text{ flights}$$

Example 13.9

Probability is a major part of statistical quality control and statistical process control. A company produces electronic chips by four different processes. Assume that an analyst writes a report on a company and based on the research, he assigns the probabilities in Table 13.2 to the defective items.

The quality controller's expected number of defective items is

$$E(D) = (0.05)\times(10{,}000) + (0.02)\times(25{,}000) + (0.01)\times(15{,}000) + (0.04)\times(20{,}000)$$
$$E(D) = 1{,}950$$

Variance

Variance measures the variation of selected observations from the mean, and it is symbolized by σ^2 (pronounced "sigma squared"). Small variance denotes that numbers in the set are distributed around the mean, and variance of zero indicates that all the values are identical to the mean. When we have historical data, we can study how the observations have varied in the past and use that as to indicate how they may vary in the future. Variation has been studied by scientists, engineers, and statisticians to evaluate performance of projects.

The concept of variance has been also used extensively by engineering economists. Variance of the actual return from the previous calculated expected return denotes the risk involved in that particular decision.[3] The mathematical formula to calculate the variance is

$$\sigma^2 = \frac{\sum_{i=1}^{N} \left[X_i - E(\bar{X})\right]^2}{N}$$

where $E(\bar{X})$ = mean (can also be denoted as μ), N = number of observations, and X_i = value of observation i.

Example 13.10

A random sample of 10 flights reported the number of passenger no-shows shown in Table 13.3. The mean and the variance can be calculated as the table shows.

Table 13.2 Probabilities Assigned to Defective Items: Example 13.9

Process	*Probability of Defective Items*	*Items Produced*
A	0.05	10,000
B	0.02	25,000
C	0.01	15,000
D	0.04	20,000

Table 13.3 Calculating Mean and Variance: Example 13.10

Day	*No shows (X)*	*(X-μ)*	*(X-μ)²*
1	1	−1	1
2	2	0	0
3	6	4	16
4	1	−1	1
5	1	−1	1
6	1	−1	1
7	2	0	0
8	2	0	0
9	1	−1	1
10	3	1	1
Sum	**20**		**22**
Mean (μ)	**2.0**		
Variance (σ²)			**2.2**

Use the "=AVERAGE" function in Excel to find the mean of a set of numbers. Enter the range of numbers (no-shows) in your spreadsheet.

Standard Deviation

In economics and finance, standard deviation (SD) and variance are the terms most used to denote risk associated with a project. SD, denoted by Greek letter "σ" (sigma), measures how spread out the values in a data set are around the mean and is calculated by taking the square root of variance (Bernhard, 1967). The further the data points are, the higher the deviation; closer data points mean a lower deviation. In finance, riskier assets have a higher deviation, while safer bets come with a lower SD.

$$SD(R) = \sigma = \sqrt{\sigma^2}$$

$$SD(R) = \sqrt{Var(R)}$$

Example 13.11

In the past ten days, DirectJet has identified the number of no-show passengers shown in Table 13.4 on one of its domestic flight. First, calculate the mean or expected value. In this case, we are expecting to have four no-shows on average on each flight. Second, subtract the mean from each observation. Third, square each deviation. Finally, the variance is the sum of the last row in this table divided by 10 (i.e., number of observations in days). Once expected return is known, we can calculate variance.

To calculate SD from variance, only take the square root. In our example, the variance was 6.4, and therefore SD is 2.5. SD is expressed in the same units as the mean, whereas variance, in this case the number of no-show passengers, is expressed in squared units. For looking at a distribution, you can use either SD or variance as long as you are clear about what you are intending to achieve.

Variance and SD can also be calculated using Excel functions as illustrated in the following steps.

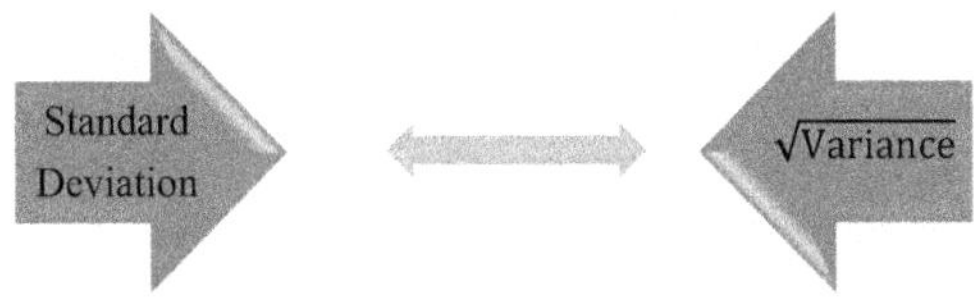

Figure 13.3 The relationship between standard deviation and variance.

Table 13.4 Variance and Standard Deviation: Example 13.11

Day	*No-Shows (X)*	*(X-μ)*	*(X-μ)²*
1	5	1	1
2	2	−2	4
3	7	3	9
4	1	−3	9
5	0	−4	16
6	8	4	16
7	2	−2	4
8	6	2	4
9	5	1	1
10	4	0	0
Sum	**40.0**		**64**
Mean (μ)	**4.0**		
Variance (σ²)			**6.4**
Std. Deviation (σ)			**2.5**

Step 1:

Enter the data from Figure 13.4a into Excel in cells B2 to B11.

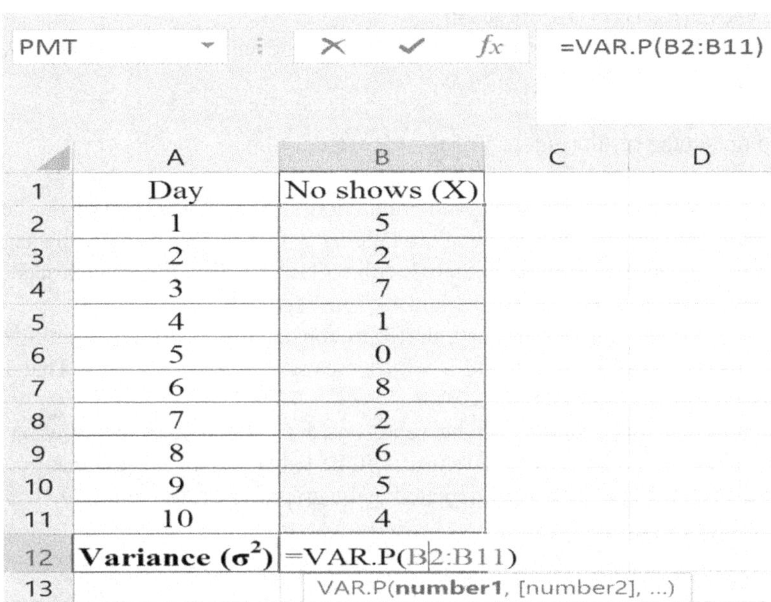

Figure 13.4a Data and formula entry for variance calculation.

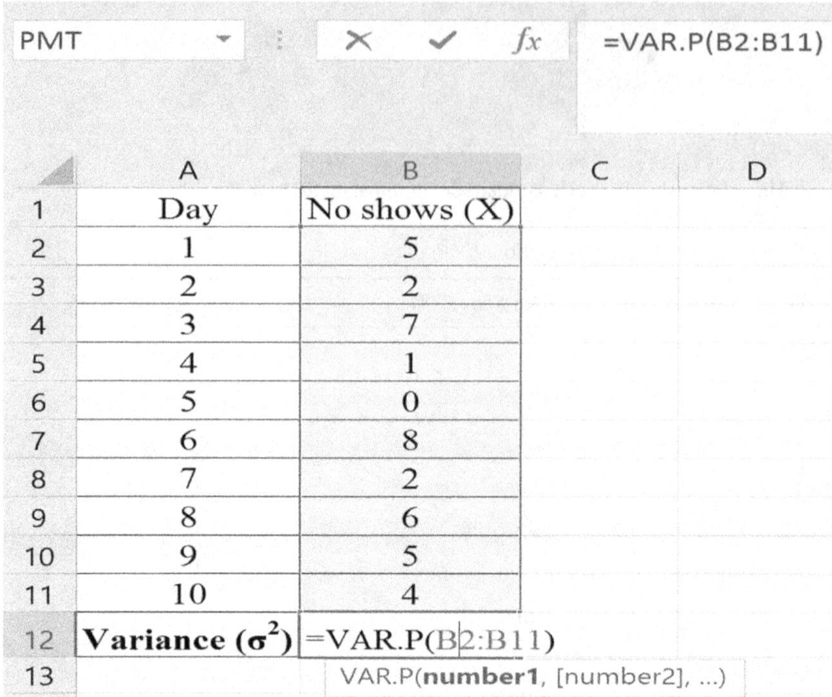

PMT | × ✓ *fx* | =VAR.P(B2:B11)

	A	B	C	D
1	Day	No shows (X)		
2	1	5		
3	2	2		
4	3	7		
5	4	1		
6	5	0		
7	6	8		
8	7	2		
9	8	6		
10	9	5		
11	10	4		
12	**Variance (σ^2)**	=VAR.P(B2:B11)		
13		VAR.P(**number1**, [number2], ...)		

Figure 13.4b Data and formula entry for variance calculation.

Step 2:
Select cell B12 and enter the following formula to calculate statistical variance of a given population: =VAR.P(B2:B11) (Figure 13.4b).
Note: Use the =VAR.P function if you are dealing with the entire population or =VAR.S if you are dealing with the sample.
Step 3:
Hit Enter to obtain the result (Figure 13.5).

Excel =STDEV.P denotes SD of a given population; use =STDEV.P if you are dealing with the entire population or =STDEV.S if you are dealing with a sample. Follow the same steps as for variance but replace the formula in Step 2 with =STDEV.P(B2:B11). The procedure and the result obtained are shown in Figures 13.6 and 13.7 respectively.

Table 13.5 considers the returns for a portfolio consisting of varied probabilities for each return. It shows that variance = 0.0127, which means that SD = 0.1126. That is, the risk involved in investing in this asset is 11.26%.

The probabilities in the table can be represented as the normal distribution shown in Figure 13.8. Sixty-eight percent of the returns will be between one SD less than the mean and one SD more than the mean, as clearly depicted in the graph. The mean return of 10% has a 50% probability of occurring.

Normal Distribution

The normal distribution is the most widely and frequently used in statistics. The shape of the normal distribution resembles that of a bell, which is why it is also referred to as a bell curve

B12 | fx =VAR.P(B2:B11)

	A	B	C	D
1	Day	No shows (X)		
2	1	5		
3	2	2		
4	3	7		
5	4	1		
6	5	0		
7	6	8		
8	7	2		
9	8	6		
10	9	5		
11	10	4		
12	**Variance (σ^2)**	**6.4**		

Figure 13.5 Excel formula results for variance.

PMT | fx =STDEV.P(B2:B11)

	A	B	C	D
1	Day	No shows (X)		
2	1	5		
3	2	2		
4	3	7		
5	4	1		
6	5	0		
7	6	8		
8	7	2		
9	8	6		
10	9	5		
11	10	4		
12	**Std. Deviation (σ^2)**	**=STDEV.P(B2:B11)**		

Figure 13.6 Calculating standard deviation in Excel.

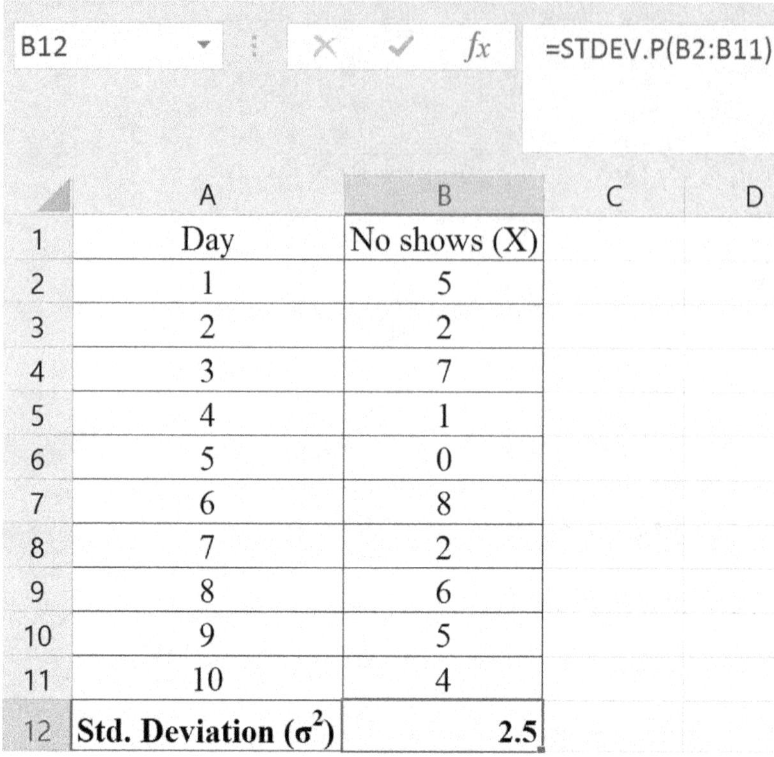

B12 =STDEV.P(B2:B11)

	A	B	C	D
1	Day	No shows (X)		
2	1	5		
3	2	2		
4	3	7		
5	4	1		
6	5	0		
7	6	8		
8	7	2		
9	8	6		
10	9	5		
11	10	4		
12	**Std. Deviation (σ^2)**	**2.5**		

Figure 13.7 Excel standard deviation results.

Table 13.5 Calculating Portfolio Return Variance

$\mathbf{R_i}$	$\mathbf{p_i}$	$\mathbf{E[\bar{R}] = (R_i)(p_i)}$	$\mathbf{(R_i - E[\bar{R}])^2 (p_i)}$
−10%	0.1	−1.00%	0.0040
−5%	0.2	−1.00%	0.0045
18%	0.4	7.20%	0.0026
19%	0.2	3.80%	0.0016
10%	0.1	1.00%	0.0000
Sum	*1*	*10.00%*	0.0127

(Lehmann, 1997). A normal distribution is characterized by two parameters: mean (μ) and SD; the smaller the SD, the more concentrated the data. The normal distribution curve is symmetrical, centered around its mean, and the mean, mode and the median are the same.

$$f(x) = \frac{1}{\sqrt{2\pi\sigma}} e^{\frac{(x-\mu)^2}{2\sigma^2}}$$

The distribution is symmetrical in that it divides data into two equal halves at the mean, so that 50% of the data fall below the mean and 50% above, and the entire area under the normal curve contains 100% of the data (Figure 13.9).

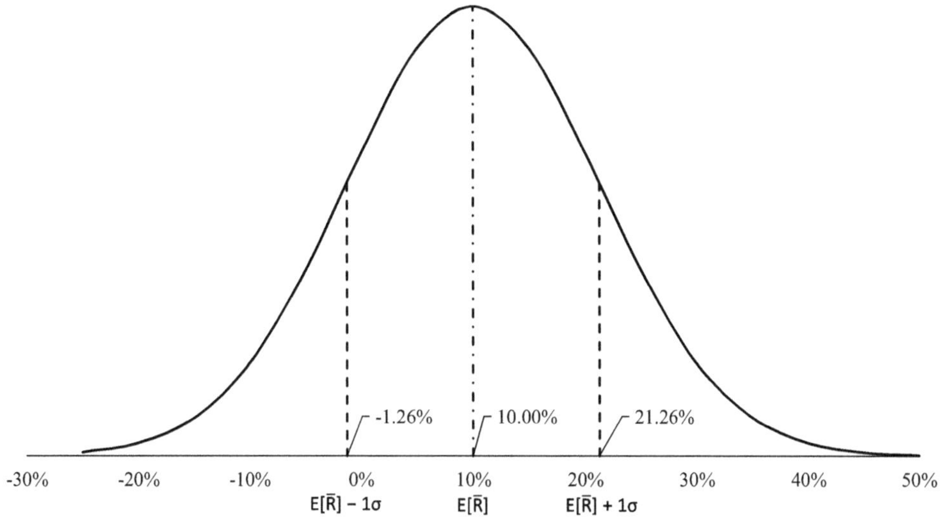

Figure 13.8 Normal distribution for returns.

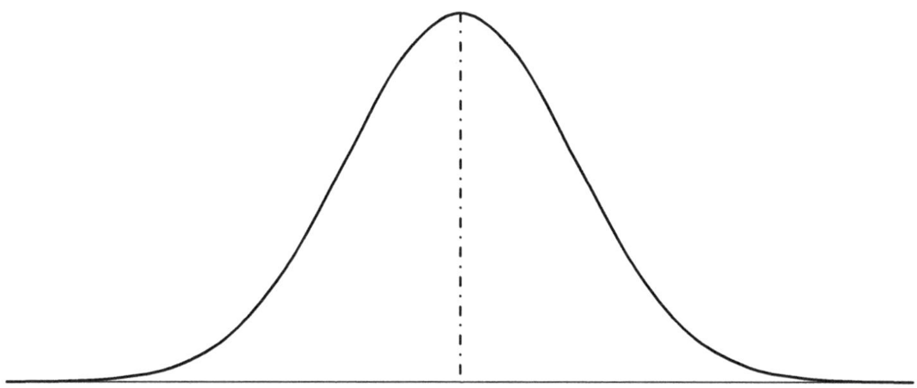

Figure 13.9 Normal distribution.

About 68% of all cases fall within 1 SD of the mean (Figure 13.10):

- $\mu \pm 1\sigma = 68\%$

About 95% of cases lie within 2 SD of the mean (Figure 13.11):

- $\mu \pm 2\sigma = 95\%$

And finally, about 99% of cases lie within 3 SD of the mean (Figure 13.12):

- $\mu \pm 3\sigma = 99\%$

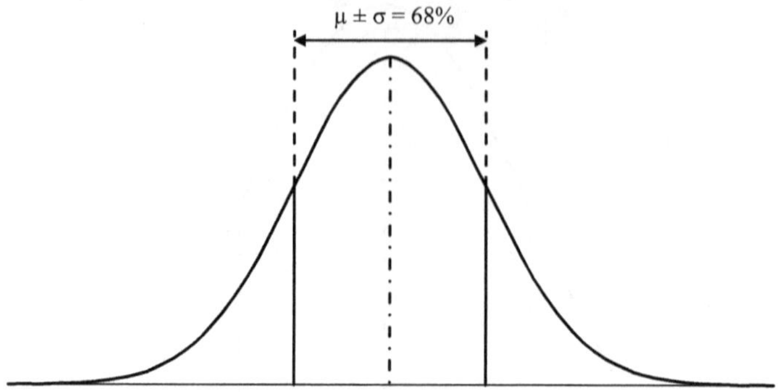

Figure 13.10 Normal distribution (± 1σ).

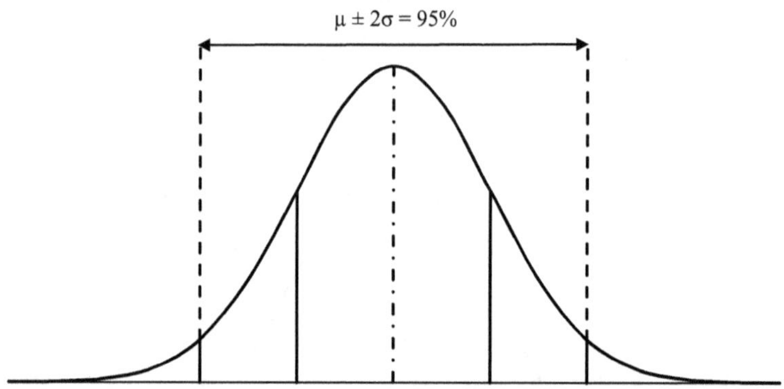

Figure 13.11 Normal distribution (± 2σ).

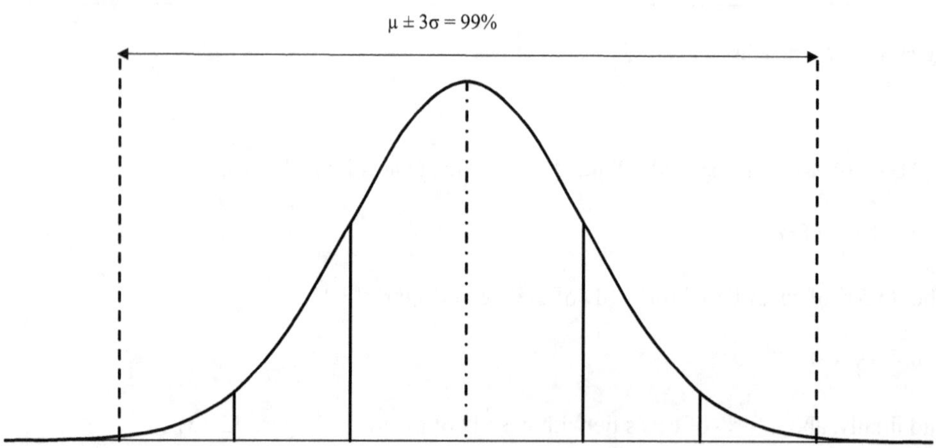

Figure 13.12 Normal distribution (± 3σ).

Example 13.12

Engine life is measured in flight hours and flight cycles.[4] Assume the life of a jet engine is normally distributed with a mean of 30,000 hours and SD of 2,000 hours. Construct a normal distribution interval for this engine:

- 68%: 30,000 ± 2,000 (28,000–32,000)
- 95%: 30,000 ± 2 × 2,000 (26,000–34,000)
- 95%: 30,000 ± 3 × 2,000 (24,000–36,000)

Example 13.13

The total number of passengers for a particular flight at a given time of the day fluctuates day by day; airlines have no way of knowing exactly how many passengers book a given flight. Based on many empirical studies of actual airline passenger records, airlines may choose normal distribution functions to estimate the future number of passengers for a given flight. Airlines regularly estimate the number of no-show passengers to minimize the number of empty seats by overbooking the aircraft. Assume the average number of no-show passengers is distributed normally with a mean of 10 passengers and SD of 6:

- $10 \pm 1 \times 2 = 68\%$
- $10 \pm 2 \times 2 = 95\%$
- $10 \pm 3 \times 2 = 99\%$

In the scenarios in the previous sections, the normal distribution can be calculated in Excel using =NORM.DIST (Figure 13.13). The parameters of the function are the following:

=NORM.DIST (x, Mean, Standard Deviation, "True" for cumulative or "False" for discrete)

Step 1:
Enter mean in cell B1.
Step 2:
Enter standard deviation in cell B2.
Step 3:
In cells A4 to A14, enter 0 to 20 in increments of 2.
Step 4:
In cell B4, enter the formula =NORM.DIST(A4, B1, B2, TRUE).
Note: make sure you "freeze" mean and standard deviation values by typing the dollar sign for both column and row or by simply pressing F4 button.
Step 5:
Drag the formula in Step 4 to cell B14 to obtain results.

The distribution calculated as shown in Figure 13.13 can then be plotted into a graph of a traditional normal distribution.

Standard Normal Distribution

Because μ and σ can have infinitely different values, there are infinite normal distributions. To comparing different distributions possible, normal distributions can be rescaled into a standard

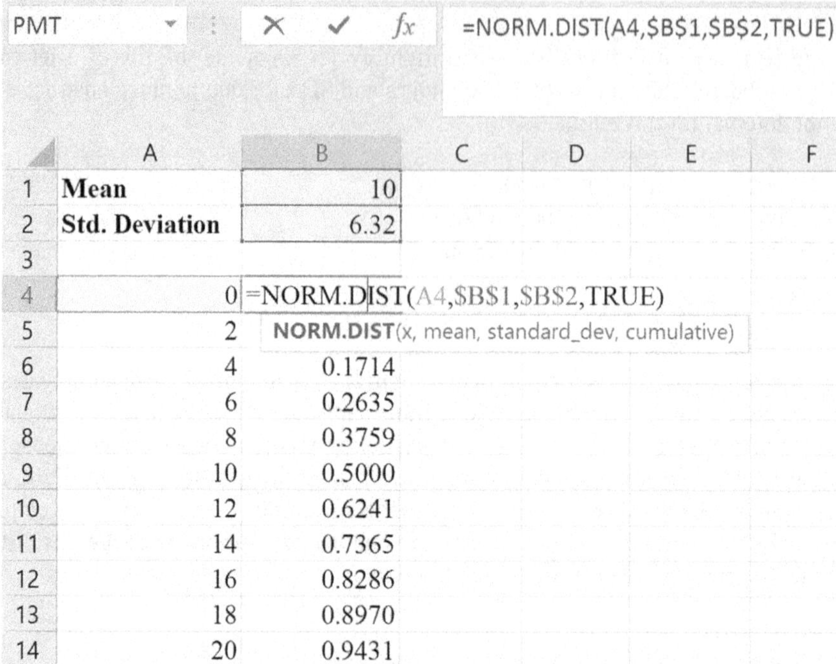

Figure 13.13 Calculating normal distribution in Excel.

form by simple linear transformation. Standardizing a normal distribution facilitates calculating areas under various regions of the curve. If X is a normal random variable with mean μ_x and σ_x, the standard normal variable is calculated as

$$Z = \frac{x - \mu_x}{\sigma_x}$$

If all the values in a distribution are transformed to Z scores, then the distribution will have a mean of 0 and SD of 1. The notation N (μ, σ^2) means normally distributed with mean μ and variance σ^2.

Hence, a normal distribution with ¼= 0, and $\sigma = 1$ is called a standard normal distribution. The main application of a standard normal distribution is that it allows the comparison of two or more normal distributions of different scales. The standard normal distribution ensures that all the normal distributions are converted into normal distributions with a mean of 0 and standard deviation of 1 (Figure 13.14).

A standard normal distribution is a normal distribution with a mean of 0 and a standard deviation of 1. The standard normal distribution is a useful theoretical model in statistics, and it helps us understand probabilities associated with different ranges of values for normally distributed variables.

For example, let's find the probability that X falls between −1 and 1 standard deviation from the mean (i.e., within the interval [−1, 1]). Using the properties of the standard normal distribution, we know that approximately 68% of the data falls within 1 standard deviation from the mean. Therefore, the probability that X falls between −1 and 1 standard deviations is approximately 68%.

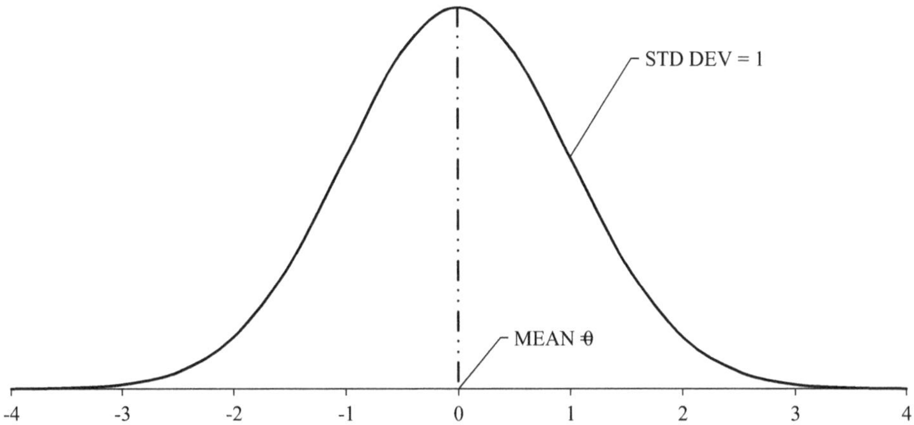

Figure 13.14 Standard normal distribution.

Example 13.14

DirectJet charges five different ticket prices on a given flight on an aircraft with a 100-seat capacity. You believe you will only sell 10% of your seats at \$1,800, 12% at \$1,500, 22% at \$1,200, 24% at \$900, and finally 32% at \$600 (Table 13.6). For this flight, multiply the ticket price number by the probability of selling that seat at the specified price. Make the calculations for each ticket price and add the numbers together to obtain your expected revenue from each seat (Table 13.7), then multiply that number by 100 to get the estimated total revenue from this flight.

Hence the expected per-ticket price for this 100-seat flight is \$1,032. The variance can be calculated by calculating each variance measure and summing them (Table 13.8).

$$\text{Variance} = 155{,}376$$

Hence,

$$\textit{Standard Deviation} = \sqrt{155{,}376}$$
$$\textit{Standard Deviation} = 394.18$$

From the resulting normal distribution, the risk associated with selling the tickets at various prices can be found by converting the normal distribution into a standard normal distribution. For instance, the risk associated with selling the tickets at \$1,400 is

$$Z = \frac{X - \mu}{\sigma}$$
$$Z = \frac{1400 - 1032}{394.18}$$
$$Z = 0.93$$

In the Standard Normal Probabilities Table, Z of 0.93 corresponds to 0.8238 probability. Therefore, the risk associated with selling tickets at \$1,400 is 82.38%. This can be clearly seen in

Table 13.6 Probability Profile for Different Ticket Prices: Example 13.14

Ticket Price	*Probability*
$1,800	0.10
$1,500	0.12
$1,200	0.22
$900	0.24
$600	0.32
Sum	*1.00*

Table 13.7 Calculating the Expected Value of the Ticket

Ticket Price	*Probability*	*Price × Probability*
$1,800	0.10	180.00
$1,500	0.12	180.00
$1,200	0.22	264.00
$900	0.24	216.00
$600	0.32	192.00
Sum	1.00	1,032.00

Table 13.8 Calculating Variance

Ticket Price	*Probability*	*(Value)(Probability)*	*{X-E(X)} ^2*
$1,800	0.10	180	58,982
$1,500	0.12	180	26,283
$1,200	0.22	264	6,209
$900	0.24	216	4,182
$600	0.32	192	59,720
Sum	1.00	1,032	155,376

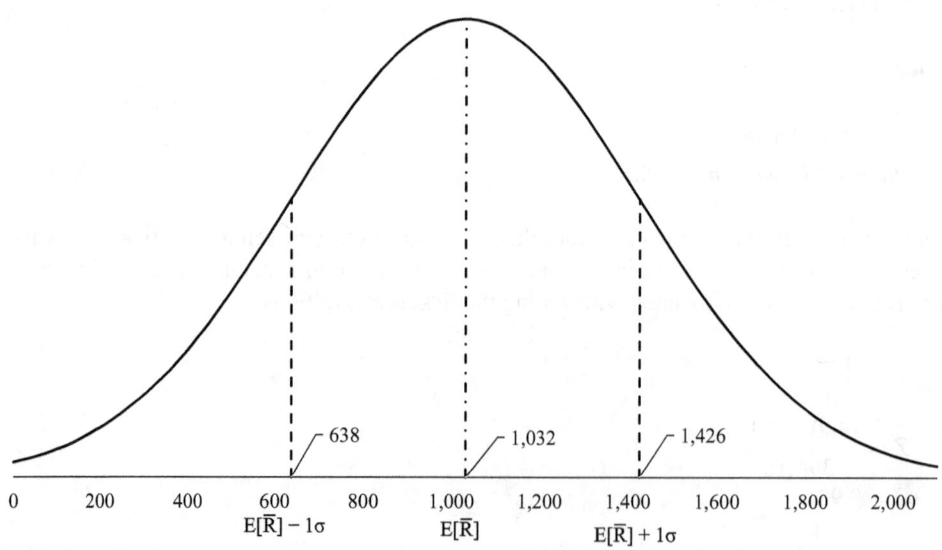

Figure 13.15 Normal distribution of ticket prices.

Figure 13.15, which provides a normal distribution for the ticket prices. Sixty-eight percent of the time, the tickets will be sold at a price that is between one SD above ($1,426.18) and one SD below ($637.82) the mean of $1,032.

A normal distribution can be used as a means of comparison when different sets of data have the same mean but different SDs. In Figure 13.16, the mean of all the three sets of data is 2.0, and the SDs are 1.9, 1.5, and 0.9. The smaller the SD, the narrower the normal distribution curve.

Example 13.15

According to DirectJet's passenger booking report, about 10% of the ticketed passengers do not show up for their flight. Find the probability that 5 or more of the 100 ticketed passengers will not show for their flight. Assume the number of no-show passengers follows a normal distribution.

Solution:

$$\mu = \mathrm{n} \times \mathrm{P}$$
$$\mu = 100 \times 10\% = 10 \text{ passengers}$$
$$\sigma = \sqrt{n \times \mathrm{P} \times \mathrm{q}}$$
$$\sigma = \sqrt{100 \times 0.10 \times 0.90}$$
$$\sigma = \sqrt{9}$$
$$\sigma = 3$$
$$Z = \frac{X - \mu}{\sigma}$$
$$Z = \frac{5 - 10}{3} = -1.67$$
$$P(Z \leq -1.67) = 0.0475$$
$$P(Z \leq -1.67) = 4.75\%$$
$$P(Z \geq -1.67) = 1 - 0.047$$

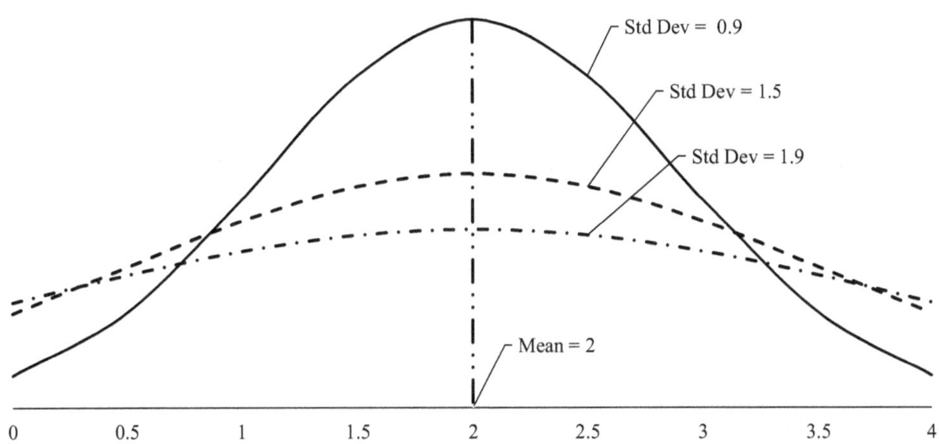

Figure 13.16 Normal distribution with varying standard deviations.

$$P(Z \geq -1.67) = 0.9525$$

$$P(Z \geq -1.67) = 95.25\%$$

The probability that 5 or more of the 100 ticketed passengers will not show up for the flight is 95.25%.

Portfolios

A portfolio is a collection of financial assets (stocks, bonds, bank deposits) or physical assets (aircraft, inventory, equipment, plants). Investors construct portfolios to balance their financial objectives and strategies. Portfolio management aims to maximize returns while minimizing risk. Risk management is a critical aspect of portfolio management that aims to minimize the impact of adverse events on portfolio performance.

> *The fundamental objective of portfolio management is to maximize returns while minimizing associated risks. Diversification, spreading investments across different asset classes and sectors, serves to mitigate risk exposure. For instance, operating a single type of aircraft presents advantages for an airline, but it also comes with inherent risks. If the chosen aircraft type experiences technical issues or maintenance challenges, the airline's entire operation could be affected.*

From an economic point of view, a portfolio is constructed to stabilize the risk of nonperformance of various units of investment. Rational investors select portfolios by evaluating returns as well as risk. Investors may be willing to assume higher risk if they are adequately compensated by a higher expected return. If you own more than one security, undoubtedly, you have an investment portfolio. Aercap's fleet comprises over 1,740 narrow-body and wide-body passenger aircraft, cargo aircraft, and regional and turboprop aircraft from manufacturers such as Boeing, Airbus, and Bombardier. About 300 airline customers finance these aircraft through leases. If Aercap invests in only one type of aircraft, the return will depend solely on that aircraft; if something goes wrong with that aircraft, GE Commercial Aviation Services' entire return will be severely affected. By diversifying the fleet, Aercap can substantially reduce the risk of the single type aircraft (security).

Portfolio Beta

As we described, a portfolio is a specific combination of financial securities, usually defined by portfolio weights that sum up to 1:

$$\mathrm{w} = \{\mathrm{w}_1, \mathrm{w}_2 \ldots \mathrm{w}_\mathrm{n}\}$$

$$\sum_{n=i}^{n} w_i = 1$$

$$w_i = \frac{n_i \times P_i}{n_1 \times P_1 + \cdots + n_m \times P_m}$$

Beta (β) is a measure of the volatility of a security or a portfolio in comparison with the market as a whole; the market's β = 1 because it is being compared with itself. When β is positive, the stock price tends to move in the same direction as the market, and the magnitude of β tells by how much. For instance, β = 2.00 means that if the market's return increases by 10%, the portfolio is expected to increase by 20%. The portfolio beta is a weighted average of the betas of the stocks within the portfolio, and individual stock betas are very important when selecting a portfolio of assets. Generally, a β < 1 indicates that the investment is less volatile than the market.

Calculating the weighted average β of a portfolio allows the investigator to measure the overall risk of the portfolio. The use of a weighted average accounts for the fact that different amounts are invested in each stock, so the betas of the stocks that are owned in larger quantities will have a greater effect on overall portfolio β than those of the stocks owned in fewer quantities:

$$\beta_{Portfolio} = w_1 \times \beta_1 + w_2 \times \beta_2 + \ldots + w_n \times \beta_n$$

Beta measures the responsiveness of a security to movements in the market portfolio. It is calculated using the formula:

$$\beta_i = \frac{Cov(R_i, R_M)}{\sigma^2 (R_M)}$$

where Cov (Ri, RM) = covariance between the return on asset i and the return on market portfolio and $\sigma^2 (R_M)$ = variance of the market.

Thus, β represents the relationship between the expected return on a security and the market return, implying a linear relationship. Most investors use β calculated by a third party, online brokerages give investors extensive data on β, and some free financial news and analysis websites also show current β measurements.

Example 13.16

Your investment account of $500,000 consists of three stocks: 400 shares of stock A, 2,000 shares of stock B, and 1,500 shares of stock C. Your portfolio is weighted as described in Table 13.9; stock A, β = 0.35, stock B, β = 0.5, and stock C, β = 0.76. First, we multiply each individual stock's β by its weight in the portfolio (Table 13.10).

For a real-world example, the betas for selected world airlines are graphed in Figure 13.17.

Table 13.9 Investment Summary: Example 13.16

Asset	*Shares*	*Price per Share*	*Investment*	*Portfolio Weight*
A	400	$500	$200,000	40%
B	2,000	$75	$150,000	30%
C	1,500	$100	$150,000	30%
Total			$500,000	

Table 13.10 Calculating Portfolio Beta: Example 13.16

Projects	*Beta*	*Percentage of Portfolio*	*Beta × % of Portfolio*
A	0.35	40%	0.140
B	0.50	30%	0.150
C	0.76	30%	0.228
		Total portfolio beta	0.518

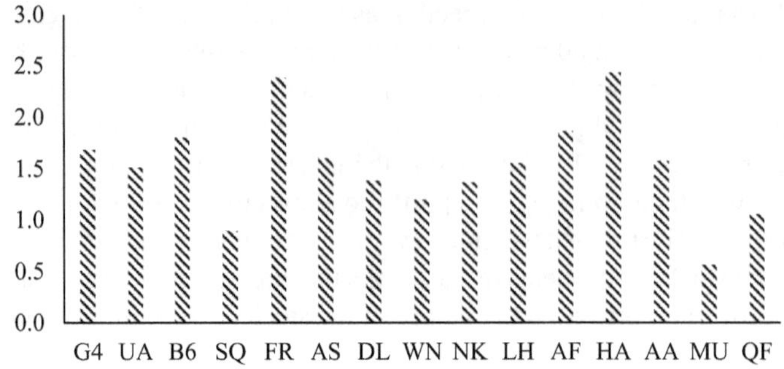

Figure 13.17 Beta for global airlines as of March 2024.

Capital Asset Pricing Model

The capital asset pricing model (CAPM) describes the relationship between risk and expected return and is one of the most significant innovations in portfolio theory; it is based on the relationship between an investment's expected return and the average market return. If this expected return does not satisfy the required return, one should not make the investment. An extension of expected returns is the CAPM, which argues that expected return should be positively related to risk. That is, a risky asset will be purchased only if it promises a high return that compensates for the risk. Building on the earlier work of Harry Markowitz (1952) on modern portfolio theory, William F. Sharpe (1964) and Jan Mossin (1966) independently introduced CAPM, which is represented by the following equation:

$$R_{RE} = R_{RF} + \beta(R_M - R_{RF})$$

where R_{RE} = required rate of return, R_{RF} = risk-free rate of return, R_M = market rate of return, and β = beta. The risk-free rate (R_{RF}) is associated with the returns obtained on government securities such as treasury bills because their returns are the most certain. $R_M - R_{RF}$ is referred to as market premium, which is the difference between the expected return on the market and the risk-free rate.

Example 13.17

CAPM allows for deciding what rate of return you should require for a particular investment. If investment in DirectJet is riskier than the market, naturally you require higher return. Assume your company is planning to invest $100 million in DirectJet equity and assume the following information is provided:

$$R_{RF} = 2\%$$
$$R_M = 10\%$$
$$\beta = 1.5$$

Using CAPM, you should demand the following rate of return to invest in DirectJet:

$$R_{RE} = R_{RF} + \beta(R_M - R_{RF})$$
$$R_{RE} = 2\% + 1.5(10\% - 2\%)$$
$$R_{RE} = 14\%$$

The best way to estimate market risk premium is to use historical data. Once all these parameters are known, the expected return on a security can be estimated using CAPM (Markowitz, 1952). The concept of CAPM can be illustrated better in the following example. If the risk-free rate is 4%, β = 1.5, and the expected market return over the period is 14%, the stock is expected to produce returns as follows:

$$R_{RE} = R_{RF} + \beta \times (R_M - R_{RF})$$
$$R_{RE} = 4\% + 1.5 \times (14\% - 4\%)$$
$$R_{RE} = 19.00\ \%$$

Example 13.18

Assume a risk-free rate of 2.00% and the market required return is 9.00%. DirectJet β = 4, and it offers a return of 17% at the moment. Is DirectJet fairly priced according to the CAPM?

Solution:

$$R_{RE} = 2\% + 4 \times (9\% - 4\%)$$
$$\text{DirectJet's } R_{RE} = 22.00\%$$

This means that the risk-based appropriate return should be 22%. The return of 17% offered by DirectJet is less than the required return. Therefore, DirectJet is not fairly priced according to the CAPM; the current return does not adequately compensate for the risk.

Example 13.19

You own \$200,000 of DirectJet stock that has a beta of 3.0. You also own \$300,000 of EZjET (beta = 1.5) and \$300,000 of FunJet (beta = 0.4). Assume that the market return will be 14% and the risk-free rate is 6%.

a) What is the market risk premium?
b) What is the required rate of return on each stock?
c) What is the required rate of return on the portfolio?

a. Market risk premium = 14% – 6% = 8%

b. $R_{RE(DirectJet)} = 6\% + 3 \times (14\% - 6\%) = 30\%$

$R_{RE(EZjET)} = 6\% + 1.5 \times (14\% - 6\%) = 18\%$

$R_{RE(FunJet)} = 6\% + 0.4 \times (14\% - 6\%) = 9.2\%$

c.
$$\text{Total value} = \$200{,}000 + \$300{,}000 + \$300{,}000 = \$800{,}000$$
$$\text{DirectJet weight} = \$200{,}000 / \$800{,}000 = 25\%$$
$$\text{EZjET weight} = \$300{,}000 / \$800{,}000 = 37.5\%$$
$$\text{FunJet weight} = \$800{,}000 / \$40{,}000 = 37.5\%$$
$$\text{Portfolio beta} = 0.25 \times 3.00 + 0.375 \times 1.5 + 0.375 \times 0.4 = 1.4625$$
$$\text{Required rate of return on the portfolio} = 6\% + 1.4625 \times (14\% - 6\%) = 17.7\%$$

Security Market Line

Capital asset pricing can also be presented graphically. According to CAPM, R_{RE} can be plotted as a function of β. The security market line (SML) plots the expected return of stocks on the

The security market line is a fundamental concept in modern portfolio theory and is used by investors and financial analysts to assess the risk–return characteristics of investment portfolios and make informed asset allocation decisions. The security market line is a graphical representation of the capital asset pricing model with beta on the x-axis and expected return on the y-axis.

y-axis against β on the x-axis. The SML is effective when looking at portfolios composed of different market returns and risk.

In Figure 13.18, expected returns are plotted against the portfolio betas. This SML graph assumes a market return of 14% and a risk-free rate of 4%. The slope of the SML is equal to the market risk premium, and the expected return with $\beta = 0$ is equal to the risk-free rate, while the expected return with $\beta = 1$ has a relative risk equal to the market (14%).

Example 13.20

Use the security market line to determine the required rate of return for Avionics stock. Atlas $\beta = 1.25$, the required return in the market is 12.00%, and the risk-free rate of return is 2.00%.

Solution:

$$R_{RE} = 2\% + 1.25 \times (12\% - 2\%)$$
$$R_{RE} = 14.50\%$$

An investor with a low risk tolerance would choose an investment at the beginning of the SML. An investor with a higher risk tolerance would thus choose an investment higher along the line. If investors' required risk premium changed, the SML slope would change as well.

Example 13.21

Consider three different portfolios of risky assets, airline companies (A), aircraft companies (B), and leasing companies (C), as shown in Table 13.11. These industries were presented to potential

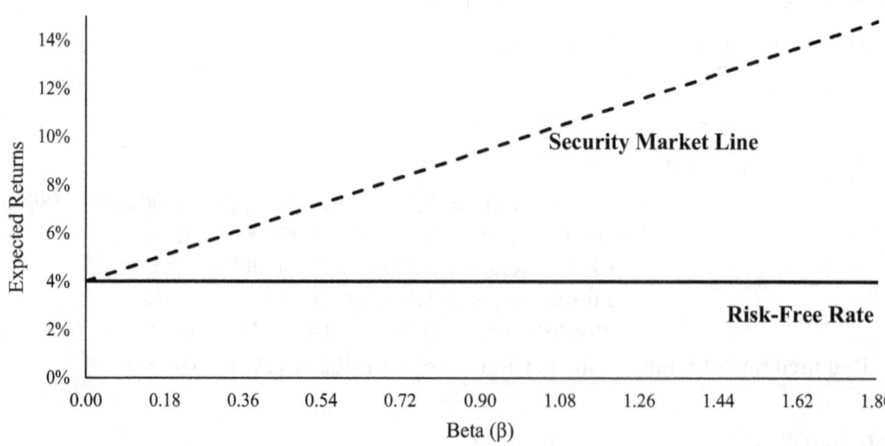

Figure 13.18 Security market line.

Table 13.11 Required Rate of Return under Different Market Premiums: Example 13.21

Required Rates of Return			*Beta*
Portfolio A (12%)	*Portfolio B (6%)*	*Portfolio C (8%)*	
4.00%	4.00%	4.00%	0.0
5.60%	4.40%	4.80%	0.2
7.20%	4.80%	5.60%	0.4
8.80%	5.20%	6.40%	0.6
10.40%	5.60%	7.20%	0.8
12.00%	6.00%	8.00%	1.0
13.60%	6.40%	8.80%	1.2
15.20%	6.80%	9.60%	1.4
16.80%	7.20%	10.40%	1.6
18.40%	7.60%	11.20%	1.8
20.00%	8.00%	12.00%	2.0

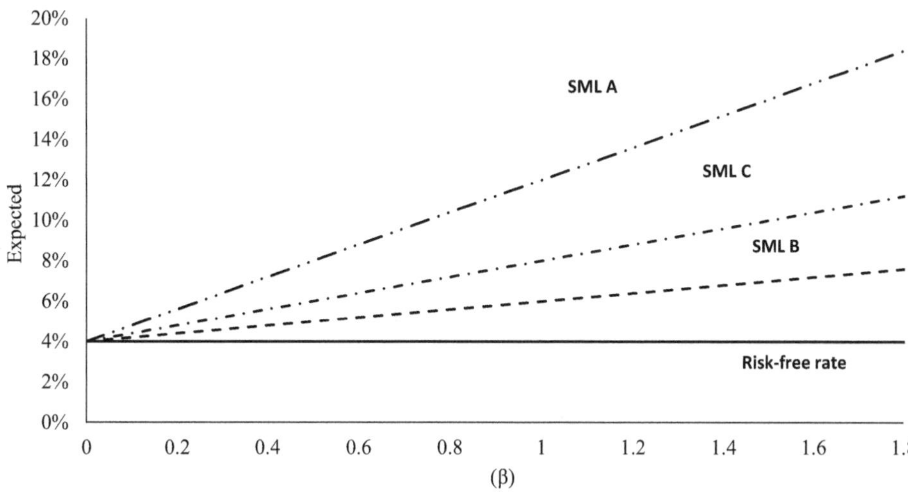

Figure 13.19 Shifts in security market line: Example 13.21.

investors using three different SMLs. Each portfolio is combined with the risk-free asset to create three capital allocation lines: SML (A), SML (B), and SML (C). The risk-free rate is assumed to be 4%, and the market returns are Portfolio A, 12%; Portfolio B, 6%; and Portfolio C, 8%. Figure 13.19 shows clearly that Portfolio A, airline companies, is superior to the other two because it has a greater expected return for any given level of risk. As a result, an investor will choose the portfolio that lies on the security market line for Portfolio A. How the investor combines the risk-free assets and the risky Portfolio A depends on the investor's degree of risk aversion.

Sensitivity Analysis

Sensitivity analysis determines how a variable reacts to changes in other variables. For example, it can assess the uncertainty in a cost–benefit analysis and its impact on study results. Sensitivity analysis shows how project outcomes are affected and how responsive these outcomes are to changes in other factors. Sensitivity analysis here can be broadly classified into breakeven or Monte Carlo analysis.

Breakeven Analysis

The foundation of this type of analysis is to select one variable and change its value while holding the values of other variables constant and observe the amount of change in the results. This is frequently applied to discount rates. Breakeven analysis identifies how great a policy's impact must be for its benefits to equal its costs, that is, to break even. Breaking even results in a net benefit of $0 considering all the existing parameters. Exceeding the breakeven point ensures a profit, whereas failing to reach breakeven ensures a loss.

Breakeven analysis is extensively used in aviation as well; in most cases, an aircraft will not be sustainable unless it breaks even within the first 10 years or so. Indeed, one of the most important parameters in airline operations is the breakeven load factor, the minimum load factor an airline needs to maintain to break even. Anything below this results in a loss for the airline, and market and other changes such as increased fuel or labor prices could raise this breakeven load factor pushing the airline further towards increasing their current load factor. Aircraft manufacturers must also perform breakeven analysis to ensure that their sales meet their costs, as in the next example.

Example 13.22

Air-Ship International, a startup aircraft manufacturer in Latin America, invested close to $20 billion in developing a wide-body aircraft, ASI-333. The aircraft is priced at $350 million. Calculate the breakeven number of aircraft, assuming the variable cost of producing each aircraft is about $250 million:

Profit = total revenue – total cost
Breakeven: total revenue = total cost = $0
Price × quantity = fixed costs + (variable cost × quantity)

$$\mathrm{P} \times \mathrm{Q} = \mathrm{FC} + (\mathrm{VC} \times \mathrm{Q})$$

which implies

$$Q_{BE} = \frac{FC}{P - VC}$$

To calculate the breakeven number of ASI-333, we enter the given information into the previous equation for the following:

$$Q_{BE} = \frac{\$20{,}000 \text{ million}}{(\$350 - \$250) \text{ million}}$$

$$Q_{BE} = 200 \text{ Aircraft}$$

The breakeven number of ASI-333s is 200. Figure 13.20 graphs the breakeven analysis for Example 13.22.

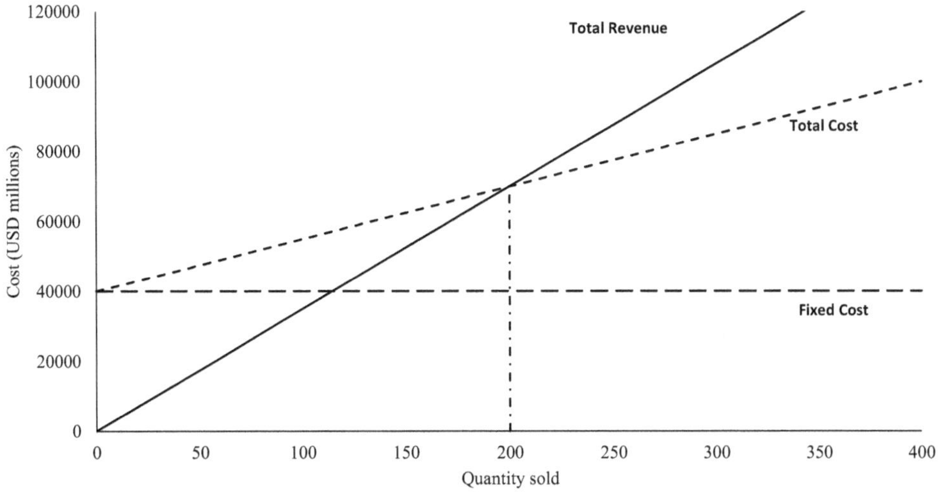

Figure 13.20 Breakeven point from initial assumptions.

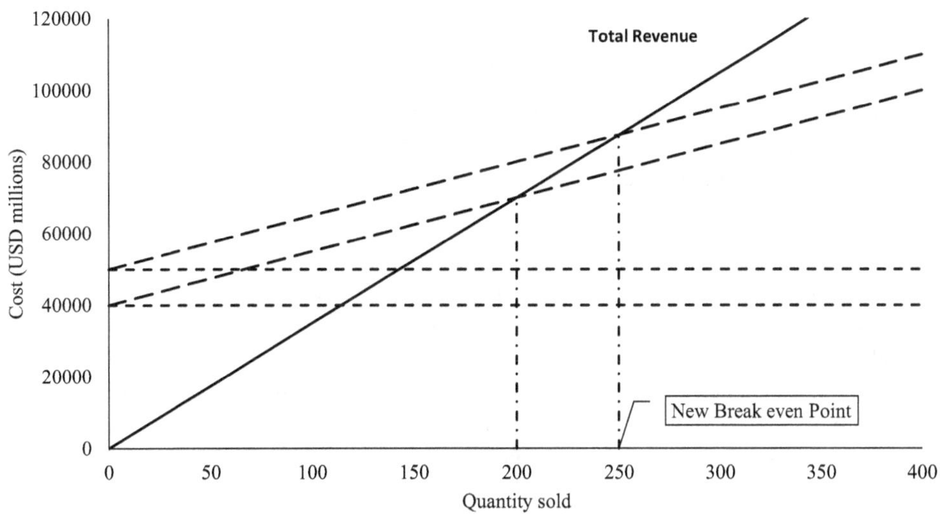

Figure 13.21 Sensitivity analysis scenario 1: Increase in the fixed cost.

Scenario 1:

Now, consider a situation where the fixed cost goes up by $5 billion. Figure 13.21 demonstrates how the breakeven point changes due to this change in the fixed cost. An increase in the fixed cost results in an increase in the quantity required to break even. As seen from the equation derived earlier, fixed cost and quantity are directly related. This increase in the fixed cost by $5 billion increases the breakeven quantity to 250 aircraft.

Scenario 2:

Another possible situation could be an increase in the variable cost of production. The changes in breakeven quantity for various scenarios of variable costs are shown in Figure 13.22.

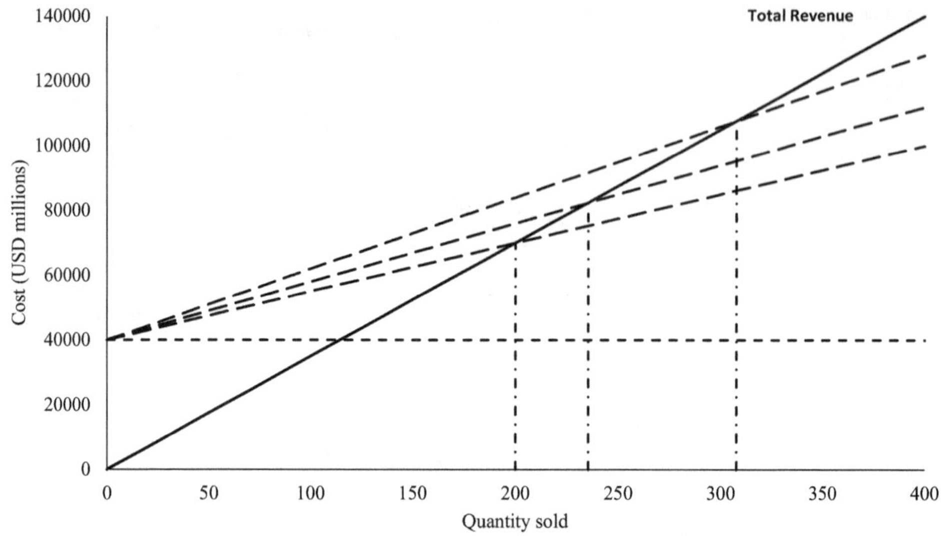

Figure 13.22 Sensitivity analysis scenario 2: Increase in the variable cost.

An increase in variable cost implies that the total cost line becomes increasingly steeper. The equation for quantity shows that increasing variable cost lowers the denominator, which in turn increases the required quantity to break even. Increasing variable cost by $15 million to $265 million makes the required quantity to be 235 aircraft to break even. An increase in variable cost by $35 million, making the variable cost $285 million results in a required quantity of 308 aircraft to break even.

Scenario 3:

The final possible alteration could arise from an increase in the market price of the aircraft. An analysis based on those changes is represented in Figure 13.23. An increase in the market price only alters the total revenue line, keeping everything else the same. As the price increases, the line becomes steeper. The equation for breakeven quantity shows that price and quantity are inversely related: Increasing in price by $25 million lowers breakeven to 160 aircraft, and increasing price by $50 million brings breakeven down to 133 aircraft.

Monte Carlo Analysis

Monte Carlo simulation is a statistical tool employed across diverse fields to quantify uncertainty in outcomes. Simulation can be valuable for better understanding the underlying mechanisms that control a system's behavior. However, using simulation to predict future system behavior can be difficult because for most real-world systems, at least some of the controlling parameters, processes, and events are often stochastic, uncertain, and/or poorly understood. The primary objective of many simulations is to identify and quantify the risks associated with a particular option, plan, or design. Monte Carlo enables decision-makers to make informed choices by considering the inherent uncertainty in their models, thereby enhancing strategic planning, resource allocation, and risk management efforts.

Probabilistic simulation is the process of explicitly representing these uncertainties by specifying inputs as probability distributions. If the inputs describing a system are uncertain, the prediction of future performance is necessarily uncertain. That is, the result of

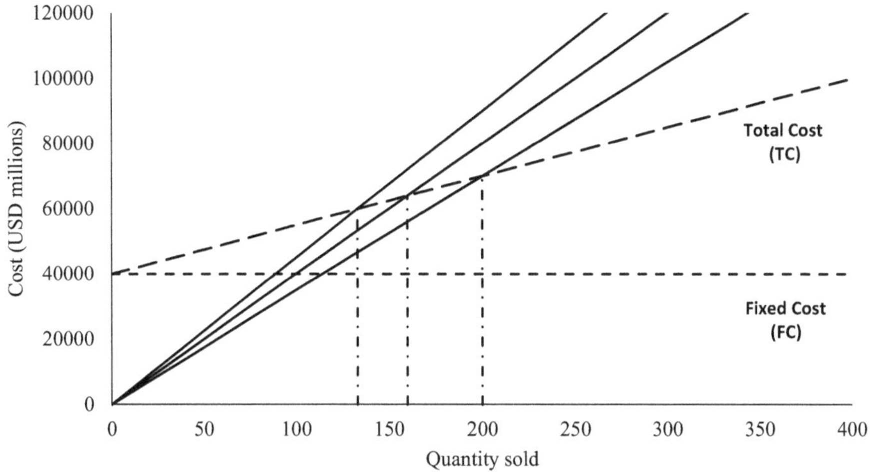

Figure 13.23 Sensitivity analysis scenario 3: Increase in the market price.

any analysis based on inputs represented by probability distributions is itself a probability distribution.[5]

To calculate the probability distribution of predicted performance, it is necessary to translate the input uncertainties into uncertainties in the results. One common technique for translating the uncertainty into various aspects of a system to obtain the predicted performance is Monte Carlo simulation. Monte Carlo simulation furnishes the decision-maker with a range of possible outcomes and the probabilities that they will occur for any choice of action. It shows the extreme possibilities – the outcomes of going for broke and for the most conservative decision – along with all possible consequences for middle-of-the-road decisions.

In Monte Carlo simulation, the entire system is simulated many times. Each simulation is equally likely and is referred to as a realization of the system. For each realization, all of the uncertain parameters are sampled. The system is then simulated through time (given the particular set of input parameters) such that the performance of the system can be calculated. This results in a large number of separate and independent outputs, each representing a possible future for the system (i.e., a possible path the system could follow through time). The results of the independent system realizations are assembled into probability distributions of possible outcomes.

Monte Carlo simulation is based on the fact that each of the inputs that are to be varied in the numerous iterations are randomly assigned a value every time. These inputs are randomized between the specified levels or distributions defined for them. For instance, you can perform this randomization in Excel using "=RANDBETWEEN (bottom, top)". Entering, for instance, =RANDBETWEEN (0,30) in a cell will return a random number between 0 and 30 every time (Figure 13.24).

Every time you execute that function, Excel will give a different number, and if you did so thousands of times, the probability of the occurrence of different numbers can be plotted as a probability distribution, which attempts to quantify the uncertainty.

One good example of the use of simulation is a basic cost estimation for an airplane construction. Consider the project cost data in Table 13.12.

The output obtained for a possible budget from the results of the Monte Carlo simulation is shown in Table 13.13. Figures 13.25–13.27 provide graphical representations of various conclusions about the probability of all possible budget choices.

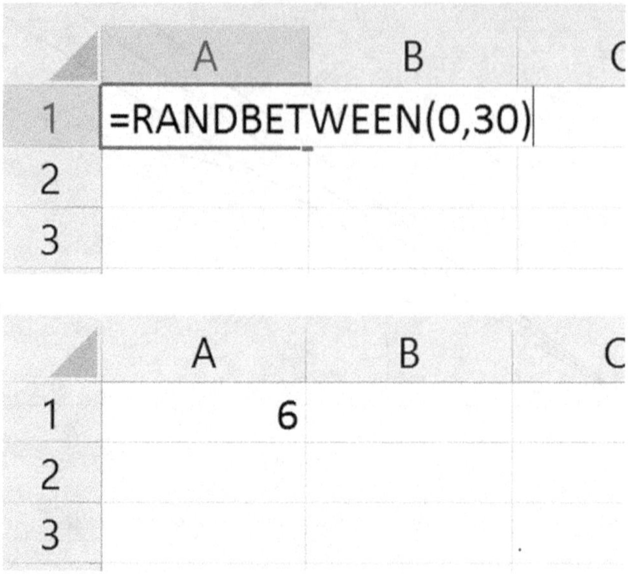

Figure 13.24 Generating a random number in a given range in Excel.

Table 13.12 Project Costs (in USD millions)

Cost Elements	*Base Case*	*Minimum*	*Most Likely*	*Maximum*	*Minimum*	*Most Likely*	*Maximum*
Rent	$2,000	90%	100%	125%	$1,800	$2,000	$2,500
Set-up cost	$5,000	90%	100%	125%	$4,500	$5,000	$6,250
Raw materials	$4,000	90%	100%	125%	$3,600	$4,000	$5,000
Labor cost	$2,000	90%	100%	125%	$1,800	$2,000	$2,500
IT	$1,000	90%	100%	125%	$900	$1,000	$1,250
Vehicles	$500	90%	100%	125%	$450	$500	$625
Marketing	$1,500	90%	100%	125%	$1,350	$1,500	$1,875
Other general overhead	$2,500	90%	100%	125%	$2,250	$2,500	$3,125
Output							
Totals	$18,500						

Table 13.13 Summary of the Analysis

Probability of meeting base case value	4.30%
Total budget required for 95.0% confidence	$20,389
Contingency required for 95.0% confidence	$1,889

Summary

This chapter has covered the essentials of risk and probability. Every business faces risk. Risk management is an economic issue, as the management must balance the cost and the benefits associated with the risk reduction strategy. Businesses experience tremendous challenges throughout the course of their operations. They face the possibility of inadequate profits, change in government regulations and tax policies, restrictions related to international trade, intense competition, market volatility, changes in global economy and many other. To successfully

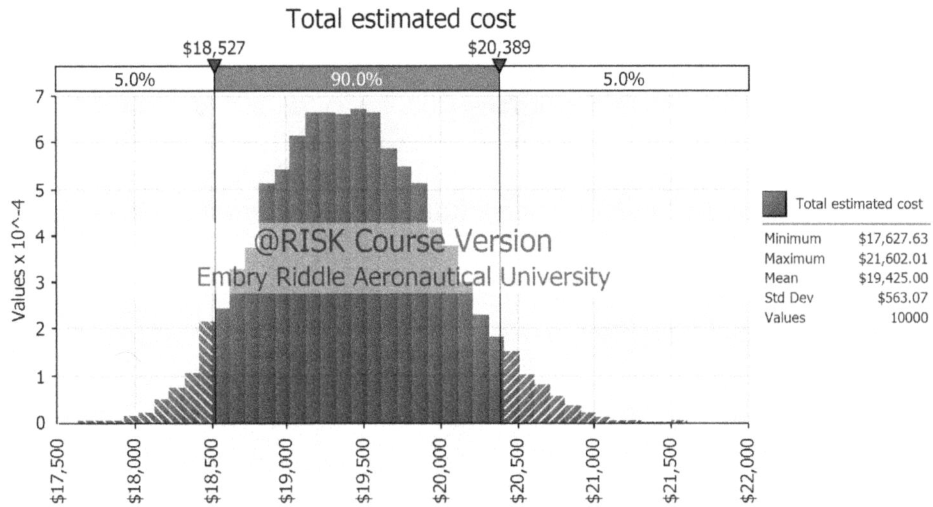

Figure 13.25 Probability density distribution.

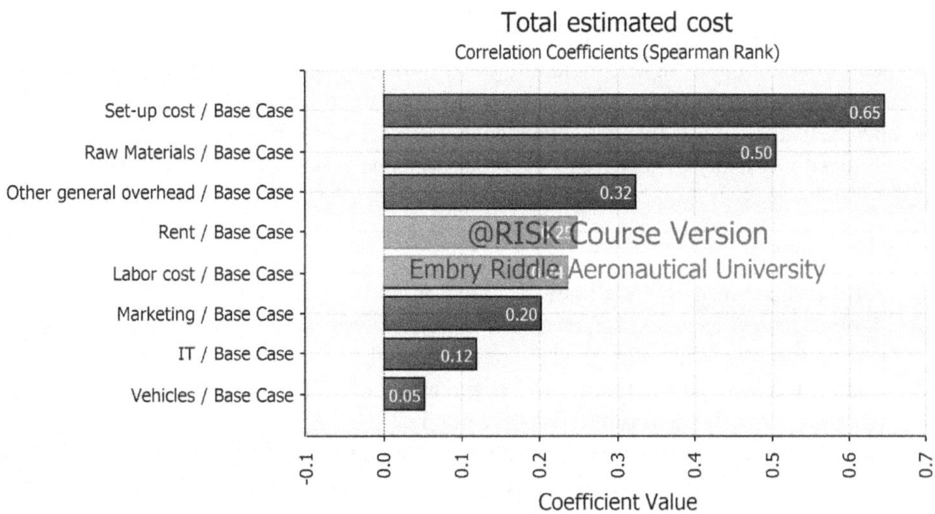

Figure 13.26 Correlation coefficients.

cope with these uncertainties, firms need to know the risk associated with each of the possible outcomes. At this point, an organization or an individual may decide on the return required to adequately compensate for taking the risk. Risk is traditionally associated with probability calculation, and this suggests that an event can be predicted and controlled. A common measure of return volatility is the standard deviation of investment returns. Standard deviation is the square root of the variance of the annual rate of return on investment. Uncertainty, however, is not capable of measurement and deals with possibilities incapable of calculation which are based on guesswork and judgement.[6] An investment portfolio is a collection of securities that together provide an investor with an attractive trade-off between risk and return. In this chapter,

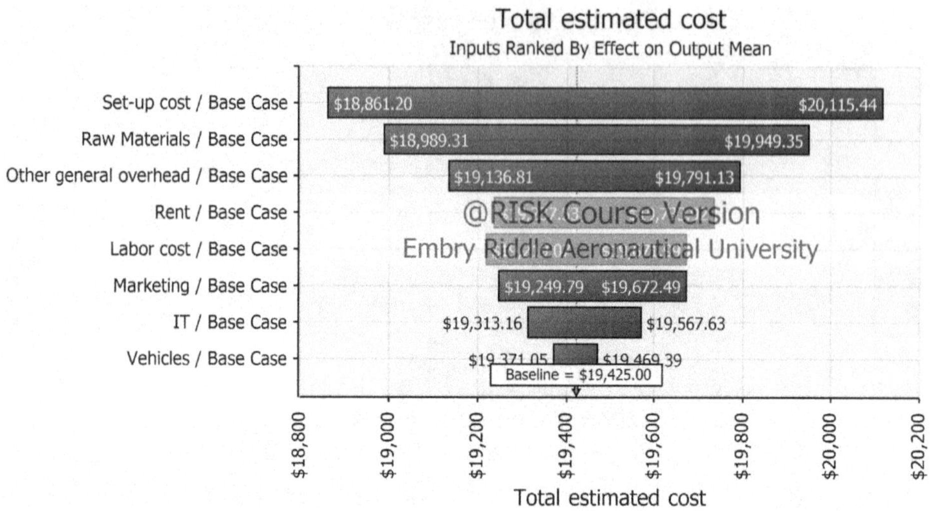

Figure 13.27 Inputs ranked by effect on output mean.

we introduced the students to the CAPM and the security market line (SML) that describe the relation between the risk and the expected return. The concept of the CAPM and the SML is explained throughout the chapter, including the use of expected return, risk-free rate of return, and the risk of investment. This chapter has also discussed the sensitivity analysis, used to determine how "sensitive" a variable is to changes in the other variables, and reflected on two most common sensitivity analysis practices – the breakeven analysis and the Monte Carlo simulation.

Discussion Questions and Problems

13.1 What is the security market line?

13.2 A stock has an expected return of 18%, the risk-free rate is 6.0%, and the market risk premium is 6%. What must the beta of this stock be?

13.3 A stock has an expected return of 12% and a beta of 0.75, and the expected return on the market is 14%. What must the risk-free rate be?

13.4 A die is thrown once. What is the probability of getting a 1?

13.5 The time that it takes to board an aircraft is normally distributed with a mean of 40 minutes and a standard deviation of 15 minutes.

a) What is the probability that a flight can board all of the passengers in less than 20 minutes?
b) Using Excel, draw a normal distribution curve on which this mean and standard deviation are correctly indicated.
c) What is the chance that the flight spends more than an hour at the gate to board all passengers?
d) How often will a flight spend between 30 and 45 minutes at the gate for taking off?

13.6 A stock has a beta of 0.75, the expected return on the market is 12%, and the risk-free rate is 6%. What must the expected return on this stock be?

13.7 Suppose the risk-free rate is 10%. The expected return on the market is 15%. Assume DirectJet equity has a beta of 0.8, what is its expected return based on the CAPM? If another equity has an expected return of 20%, what must its beta be?

13.8 What is the capital asset pricing model?

13.9 Suppose we had the following investments:

Investment	*Amount*	*Expected Return*	*Beta*
Project A	\$20,000.0	8	0.7
Project B	\$25,000.0	12	0.8
Project C	\$40,000.0	15	1.1
Project D	\$30,000.0	18	1.6

a) What is the expected return on this portfolio?
b) What is the beta of this portfolio?

13.10 You own a portfolio that has \$5,800 invested in DirectJet and \$7,800 invested in EZjET equities. If the expected returns on these equities are 6% and 8%, respectively, what is the expected return on the portfolio?

13.11 Go to Yahoo! Finance and download the ending monthly equity prices for The Boeing Company for the last 58 months. Use the adjusted closing price, which adjusts for dividend payments and stock splits. Next, download the ending Dow Jones Transportation Average over the same period. For the historical risk-free rate, download the historical three-month Treasury bill secondary market rate.

a) What are the monthly returns, average monthly returns and standard deviations for Boeing equity, the three-month Treasury bill and the Dow Jones Transportation Average for this period?
b) How do you interpret the weights for the two assets in this case? Explain.

13.12 Your portfolio is comprised of investment in two different jet engine manufacturers. RR Stock has a beta of 1.40 and Stock PW has a beta of 0.9. Suppose $R_{RF} = 2\%$ and $R_M = 12\%$.

a) According to the CAPM, what are the expected returns for each stock?
b) What is the expected return of an equally weighted portfolio of these two stocks?
c) What is the beta of an equally weighted portfolio of these two stocks?
d) How can you use your answer to c) to answer b)?

13.13 EZjET airline estimates that with probability of 0.5 a passenger who purchased a ticket won't take the designated flight. Suppose on their flight from Philadelphia, PA to Phoenix, AZ the airplane can carry 100 passengers and the airline sold 102 tickets.

a) Calculate the probability that exactly 101 passengers will show up to take the flight to four decimal places.
b) Calculate the probability that exactly 102 passengers will show up to take the flight to four decimal places.
c) Calculate to three decimal places the probability that no more than 100 passengers will show up to take the flight and EZjET will not have to ask anyone to give up their seats.

13.14 DirectJet regularly overbooks the flight to balance the cost of empty seats against the cost of overbooking passengers. On the DirectJet flight between Charleroi and Bergamo, the probability of a passenger arriving for a booked flight is 0.8. DirectJet booked 225 passengers and there are 195 seats available on the flight. Assume that data are normally distributed and find the probability that more booked passengers will arrive than there are seats available.

13.15 The TSA rule requires flight schools and flight instructors to provide security awareness training (SAT) to employees and have them take a final exam. The average SAT score was 76 with SD of 5. An A requires a score of 90 or higher; a B is 80–90; a C is 70–80; and a D is 60–70. What is the probability that a randomly selected student scored between a 75 and 99? Assume the variable is normally distributed.

13.16 The variance of Stock A is 0.0016, the variance of the market is 0.0049, and the covariance between the two is 0.0026. What is the correlation coefficient?

13.17 The portfolio's required rate of return is 17%. The R_{RF} = 7 % and R_M = 14%. What is Stock D's estimated beta?

13.18 Given the following data for Jet Leasing Company, calculate the stock variance and standard deviation. The expected return based on the data is 14%.

Aircraft Type	*Probability*	*Return*	*Expected Return (%)*
Regional	10%	0.2	0.02
Narrow-body	40%	0.1	0.04
Wide-body	40%	0.14	0.056
Cargo	10%	0.24	0.024

Notes

1 Decision theory and all related concepts are further discussed in extensive detail in Chapter 15.
2 Olariu, R. F. (2013). Probability. Paper presented at the 8th International Scientific Conference, Defense Resources Management in the 21st Century.
3 Hood, C., Rothstein, H. & Baldwin, R. (2001). *The Government of Risk: Understanding Risk.* Oxford University Press.
4 A flight cycle is a takeoff and landing of a particular aircraft.
5 GoldSim Technology Group (2015). *Probabilistic Simulation.*
6 Gray, J. & Hamilton, J. (2006). *Implementing Financial Regulation: Theory and Practice.*

References

Bernhard, R. (1967). Probability and Rates of Return: Some Critical Comments. *Management Science*, 598–600.

Black, F. & Scholes, M. (1973). The Pricing of Options and Corporate Liabilities. *Journal of Political Economy*, 81(3).

Danfy, J. (1975, September). *Analyzing the Return on Investment.* Management Accounting.

Davidson, P. (2002). *Financial Markets, Money, and the Real World.* Cheltenham, UK: Edward Elgar.

Lehmann, L. (1997). *Testing Statistical Hypotheses* (2nd Edition). Springer.

Markowitz, M. (1952, March). Portfolio Selection. *The Journal of Finance*, 7(1).

Markowitz, M. (1999). The Early History of Portfolio Theory: 1600–1960. *Financial Analysts Journal*, 55(4).

Mossin, J. (1966). Equilibrium in a Capital Asset Market. *Econometrica*, 34(4).

Popescu, A., Keskinocak, P., Johnson, E., LaDue, M. & Kasilingam, R. (2006). Estimating Air-Cargo Overbooking Based on a Discrete Show-Up-Rate Distribution. *Interfaces*, 36(3), 248–258.

Sharpe, F. (1964). Capital Asset Prices: A Theory of Market Equilibrium Under Conditions of Risk. *Journal of Finance*, 19(3), 425–442.

14 Depreciation, Replacement, and Abandonment

Depreciation, abandonment, and impairment are crucial concepts in engineering economics and financial management, particularly for businesses dealing with long-term assets. Abandonment of assets provides financial clarity by removing assets that no longer offer economic benefits, ensuring an accurate representation of the asset base. Impairment accounting ensures that assets are not carried at more than their recoverable amounts, leading to more accurate financial reporting and maintaining stakeholder trust. Regular impairment testing and reporting comply with standards like the International Financial Reporting Standards or Generally Accepted Accounting Principles, ensuring regulatory compliance and financial reporting integrity.

Practically all the assets that a company owns either appreciate or depreciate in value. Depreciation refers to the systematic and rational process of distributing the cost of an asset over the life of the asset. Most types of tangible property such as plants and equipment, buildings, machinery, vehicles, and furniture are depreciable; the value of a physical asset systematically diminishes over time, and predicting the rate of this depreciation is considered critical. Aircraft are high-cost, long-life assets that contain many individual components. Understanding aircraft depreciation is essential for airlines, leasing companies, aircraft manufacturers, and other entities involved in aircraft ownership. The absence of depreciation expense in an income statement would inflate the income of the company.

From the tax point of view and official financial statements, depreciation methods are constrained by legal requirements. For internal purposes, depreciation can even be applied over the economic life of an asset. Economic life of an asset differs from the physical life in the sense that the economic life ends when it costs more to maintain an asset than the asset generates in income. For example, the potential life of an aircraft could be endless, but an airline might replace its old aircraft every six years. Older aircraft are more expensive to operate, but newer aircraft have a higher purchase price and annual depreciation expense. Many airlines such as Flydubai, Emirates and Singapore Airlines do not keep their aircraft more than six or seven years.

Flydubai operates a single-model fleet of 50 Boeing 737-800 Next-Generation aircraft, one of the youngest fleets in the skies with an average age of 3.1 years.[1] Starlux Airlines, a Taiwanese carrier, proudly operates the youngest aircraft fleet in the world as of 2023. With an impressive average aircraft age of just 1.22 years, it has earned the prestigious "ch-aviation World's Youngest Aircraft Fleet Award 2023." Many methods can be used to determine the rate of depreciation, and each produces a different pattern of expenses over time. In this chapter, we focus on some of the major depreciation techniques.

Recognizing the significance of aircraft asset replacement is a critical aspect of sustaining and enhancing the operational efficiency and competitiveness of airlines in the dynamic aviation industry. The continuous evolution of technology, safety standards, and environmental

DOI: 10.4324/9781003469759-14

considerations necessitates a strategic approach to fleet management. Efficient and timely aircraft asset replacement ensures that airlines can stay ahead of regulatory requirements, capitalize on advancements in fuel efficiency and passenger experience, and maintain fleets that align with their long-term business goals. In this context, examining the approaching aircraft replacements of Emirates and SIA Airlines provides uniquely valuable insights into the diverse strategies employed.

Emirates manages a fleet of around 250 aircraft that exclusively comprises A380s and 777s. However, the airline has embarked on an extensive shopping spree, investing significantly in expanding its network and upgrading its aging aircraft fleet. To facilitate this initiative, they have placed orders for approximately 200 new airplanes. This strategic move aims to upgrade and expand their fleet while phasing out their gradually retiring A380s. Notably, the recent acquisitions include 50 A350-900s, 30 787-9s, and 115 777Xs.

SIA Airlines is strategically aiming to retain its aircraft for an estimated 15 years. As part of their expansion plan, the airline is actively growing its fleet of 787-10 aircraft. However, their 777-300ERs are experiencing an extended service period, primarily attributable to delays in the production of the promised 777-9s. In a forward-looking move, SIA Airlines has decided to opt for A350F aircraft to replace their ageing 747-400F. This decision is driven by the substantial reduction in fuel consumption, exceeding 40%, offered by the A350F, aligning with the airline's commitment to modernizing and enhancing efficiency in its fleet.

Depreciation

Depreciation, abandonment, and impairment are important concepts in engineering economics and finance, each serving specific purposes and providing valuable information about the financial health and management of assets within a business. Depreciation can be broadly explained as systematic noncash deductions of allocating the cost of long-lived assets over the useful life of the assets. A long-term asset is an asset with a useful life of more than one year that is acquired for use in the business and is not intended for resale to customers. Each time a company prepares the financial statements for a fiscal year, a depreciation expense is recorded to allocate a portion of the cost of the buildings, machines, or equipment that were purchased in the current year.

Calculating depreciation of an asset involves several key factors, with the book value serving as a central component in the process. The book value is the initial cost of the asset, including any associated expenses to prepare it for use, and serves as the starting point for depreciation calculations. Alongside the book value, other essential elements include the estimated salvage value, which is the anticipated residual value of the asset at the end of its useful life, and the estimated useful life itself, representing the duration over which the asset is expected to be utilized. These factors collectively inform the depreciation expense recognized over each accounting period. By subtracting the estimated salvage value from the book value to determine the depreciable base, and subsequently dividing it by the estimated useful life, businesses can accurately calculate the depreciation expense incurred over time. Thus, while the book value is pivotal in the depreciation calculation, it is integrated with other factors to determine the appropriate depreciation expense for reporting purposes.

The airline industry is characterized by high fixed costs; property, plant, and equipment is one of the largest asset categories for any airline. Depreciation expenses help to reduce the amount of tax that an airline must pay by spreading the initial price of the asset over its useful life. The choice of depreciation method significantly impacts financial outcomes because different methods determine differing amounts for depreciation expense. Although any particular

Depreciation is the loss in the value of property and equipment due to physical deterioration, wear and tear or to obsolescence and lack of adaptability. The airline/aircraft industry has existed long enough for there to be common airplane depreciation life estimates: commercial passenger aircraft: 15–25 years, commercial cargo aircraft: 12–20 years, and private jets: 5–10 years.

method can be used internally, there are specific requirements from government agencies regarding depreciation.

For a taxpayer to be allowed a depreciation deduction for a property, the property must meet all the following requirements.[2] First, the business entity must own the property.[3] However, under a capital lease, the lessee can calculate and record depreciation for the recognized amount of the asset. (A capital lease is a long-term lease agreement with the economic characteristics of asset ownership.) The business entity can also depreciate any capital improvements for property the taxpayer leases. A company must also use the property in business or in an income-producing activity to be allowed a depreciation deduction; if the company uses a property for business and personal purposes, the taxpayer can only deduct depreciation based only on the business use of that property. Finally, the property must have a quantifiable useful life of more than one year.[4]

Depreciation Methodologies

The book value of a physical asset is its original cost minus the related accumulated depreciation. Investors often use book value as one of the metrics to assess whether a stock is undervalued or overvalued. Comparing the book value per share to the market price per share can give an indication of the stock's relative value.

Depreciating assets generate tax deductions and defer tax payments. Let D denote the annual depreciation expense and Tc the company's tax rate. In this case, the company saves (D $\times$ Tc) from the taxes it needs to pay. For a company with the annual depreciation expense of $1 million and a tax rate of 35%, the projected tax shield will be $350,000.

The total depreciation amount charged over an asset's entire useful life (i.e., depreciable amount) is the same irrespective of the depreciation method. However, different depreciation methods do affect the amount of depreciation expense charged in each year of an asset's life. Depreciation benefits business in several different ways. Companies such as airlines and aircraft manufacturers can receive tax benefits for buying plants, equipment, and other physical assets.

To help you understand the concept, let's look at an example of depreciation expense and the impact on after-tax income. In 2024, DirectJet purchased an Airbus A-320NEO for $75,000,000 that it expected to last for 10 years and during the same year was earning $10,000,000 profit a year. Since the aircraft is expected to last 10 years, DirectJet can take the cost of the aircraft and divide it by 10 $\left(\frac{\$75,000,000}{10} = \$7,500,000 \text{ per year}\right)$. Instead of realizing a one-time expense, the airline can subtract $7,500,000 each year for the next 10 years, reporting taxable income of $\$10,000,000 - \$7,500,000 = \$2,500,000$.

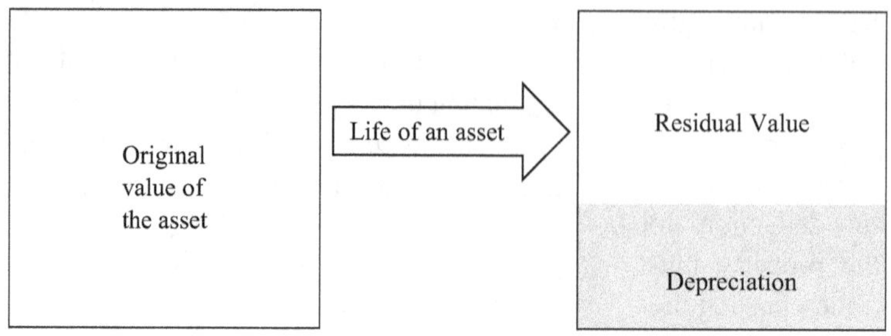

Figure 14.1 Standard deviation vs variance.

Figure 14.2 A company's book value is equal to its total assets less its liabilities.

Depreciation affects a company's profit-and-loss statement as well as the balance sheet. An aircraft's depreciation is derived by estimating both its residual value and its useful life. The residual (or salvage) value is the amount an airline can receive from selling the aircraft at the end of the useful life. Usually, the value of a commercial aircraft depreciates based on an estimated 25-year useful life expectancy, including a capitalized maintenance allowance for wear and tear over the period leading up to the next overhaul. Aircraft components such as engines, spare parts, and undercarriage or landing gear depreciate at different rates. Although a number of different depreciation methods exist, we discuss just a few: straight-line depreciation (SLD), declining balance depreciation (DBD), modified accelerated cost recovery system (MACRS), and sum-of-years digits (SYD)

Straight-Line Depreciation

SLD is likely to be the most common method of matching an asset's cost to the accounting periods in which it is in service. Under the straight-line method of depreciation, each full accounting year is allocated the same amount or percentage of an asset's cost, such that the value either becomes zero at the end of its useful life or reaches a previously set salvage value. SLD is appropriate where economic benefits from an asset are expected to be realized evenly over its useful life. It is also convenient to use where no reliable estimate can be made regarding the pattern of economic benefits expected to be derived over an asset's useful life. SLD assumes that the asset's value decreases by an equal amount each year until it reaches its residual value.

The formula for straight-line depreciation is:

$$Depreciation\ Expense = \frac{Original\ Cost\ of\ Asset - Salavage\ Value}{Useful\ Life}$$

Original cost of an asset includes all costs to bring the project into service: contract fees, cost of permits, engineering expenses, equipment cost, construction insurance, legal charges, supplies and materials, taxes related to the project, etc. Salvage value, also known as residual value or scrap value, is the estimated residual worth of an asset at the end of its useful life. In the context of depreciation, it represents the amount an asset is expected to be worth after it has been fully depreciated. Useful life refers to the estimated duration over which an asset is expected to provide economic benefits and be used by a business, and it is a key factor in determining the annual depreciation expense of an aircraft.

Example 14.1 Depreciation with no salvage value

DirectJet Airlines purchased a Boeing 737 MAX that was valued at $75 million at the time of purchase. Assume that the aircraft has an estimated salvage value of $0.00, and a useful life of 20 years. DirectJet calculates the annual SLD for the aircraft as

$$\textit{Annual depreciation expense} = \frac{\$75,000,000 - \$0.00}{20}$$

$$\textit{Annual depreciation expense} = \$3,750,000$$

Example 14.2 Depreciation with salvage value

In Example 14.1, if the potential salvage value of the aircraft is $10 million, then the depreciation schedule changes as follows:

$$\textit{Annual depreciation expense} = \frac{\$75,000,000 - \$10,000,000}{20}$$

$$\textit{Annual depreciation expense} = \$3,250,000$$

Table 14.1 Straight-Line Depreciation: Example 14.1

Age	*Depreciation Expense*	*Book Value*
0	$0	$75,000,000
1	$3,750,000	$71,250,000
2	$3,750,000	$67,500,000
3	$3,750,000	$63,750,000
4	$3,750,000	$60,000,000
5	$3,750,000	$56,250,000
6	$3,750,000	$52,500,000
7	$3,750,000	$48,750,000
8	$3,750,000	$45,000,000
9	$3,750,000	$41,250,000
10	$3,750,000	$37,500,000
11	$3,750,000	$33,750,000
12	$3,750,000	$30,000,000
13	$3,750,000	$26,250,000
14	$3,750,000	$22,500,000
15	$3,750,000	$18,750,000
16	$3,750,000	$15,000,000
17	$3,750,000	$11,250,000
18	$3,750,000	$7,500,000
19	$3,750,000	$3,750,000
20	$3,750,000	$0

Table 14.2 Straight-Line Depreciation with Salvage Value: Example 14.2

Age	*Depreciation Expense*	*Value*
0	$0	$75,000,000
1	$3,250,000	$71,750,000
2	$3,250,000	$68,500,000
3	$3,250,000	$65,250,000
4	$3,250,000	$62,000,000
5	$3,250,000	$58,750,000
6	$3,250,000	$55,500,000
7	$3,250,000	$52,250,000
8	$3,250,000	$49,000,000
9	$3,250,000	$45,750,000
10	$3,250,000	$42,500,000
11	$3,250,000	$39,250,000
12	$3,250,000	$36,000,000
13	$3,250,000	$32,750,000
14	$3,250,000	$29,500,000
15	$3,250,000	$26,250,000
16	$3,250,000	$23,000,000
17	$3,250,000	$19,750,000
18	$3,250,000	$16,500,000
19	$3,250,000	$13,250,000
20	$3,250,000	$10,000,000

These two examples show that the higher the residual value, the lower the depreciation. Conversely, lower residual value means higher depreciation, and higher depreciation decreases profits or EBIT and thus earnings per share.[5] For example, on January 1, 2024, an airline extended the depreciable lives of its Boeing 737 MAX airplanes from 20 to 23 years. As a result, depreciation expense for the three and nine months ended September 2024 was reduced by $6.4 million and $19.3 million, respectively.[6]

Declining Balance

Declining balance depreciation charges depreciation at a higher rate in the earlier years of an asset, in turn, reducing depreciation as the life of the asset progresses. DBD is an accelerated depreciation method that is particularly applicable for assets that are most useful in their early years of service and that decline in service level over time. This method is particularly useful for assets that lose value quickly after being acquired, such as vehicles and certain types of machinery, and it is calculated as follows:

$$Depreciation\ per\ annum = (Net\ Book\ Value) \times Depreciation\ Rate\ (\%)$$

Net book value is the asset's net value at the start of an accounting period. It is calculated by deducting the accumulated (total) depreciation from the cost of the fixed asset (historical book value). Rate of depreciation is defined according to the estimated pattern of an asset's use over its life term: rate of depreciation = accelerator × straight-line rate. Accelerator can be double, 150% and so on depending on the type of asset and its usability. In that case, for example, for a straight-line depreciation rate of 10%, the double declining balance (DDB) rate will be 2 × 10% = 20%.

Example 14.3

EZjET's fleet manager decided to buy a narrow-body commercial aircraft (A-320 NEO) for $75,000,000 and plans to use the aircraft for 20 years. Because of rapid obsolescence, the airline is planning to depreciate the aircraft under double declining balance. How much depreciation expense should be charged each year?

For the last year, even though the actual depreciation expense should be $1,013,139, we record only an expense of $131,388 to achieve the salvage value of $10 million.

Another DBD method is 150% declining balance. In this technique, the accelerator used is 1.50. However, if 150% DBD were applied, Table 14.4 shows that the value at the end of the 20 years would be $15,772,332 and so a salvage value of $10 million is underpriced. Hence the salvage value should be $16 million.

To achieve the salvage value of $16 million, the actual depreciation expense for year 20 is replaced by $1,051,170.

Modified Accelerated Cost Recovery System

MACRS is the United States tax system's method for recovering the cost of tangible property through annual deductions, and it provides a set of rules specifying the depreciation methods and recovery periods for different types of assets. The IRS provides tables and resources to assist taxpayers in determining the applicable depreciation percentages and recovery periods for different classes of property.

MACRS is the depreciation technique used to calculate taxes in the United States. The Internal Revenue Service Reform Act of 1986 changed the way assets were depreciated, and the Modified Accelerated Cost Recovery System (MACRS)

Table 14.3 DDB Expense Calculation

Age	*Depreciation Expense*	*Book Value*
0	$0	$75,000,000
1	$7,500,000	$67,500,000
2	$6,750,000	$60,750,000
3	$6,075,000	$54,675,000
4	$5,467,500	$49,207,500
5	$4,920,750	$44,286,750
6	$4,428,675	$39,858,075
7	$3,985,808	$35,872,268
8	$3,587,227	$32,285,041
9	$3,228,504	$29,056,537
10	$2,905,654	$26,150,883
11	$2,615,088	$23,535,795
12	$2,353,579	$21,182,215
13	$2,118,222	$19,063,994
14	$1,906,399	$17,157,594
15	$1,715,759	$15,441,835
16	$1,544,183	$13,897,651
17	$1,389,765	$12,507,886
18	$1,250,789	$11,257,098
19	$1,125,710	$10,131,388
20	$131,388	$10,000,000

Table 14.4 150% Declining Balance Calculations

Age	*Depreciation Expense*	*Book Value*
0	$0	$75,000,000
1	$5,625,000	$69,375,000
2	$5,203,125	$64,171,875
3	$4,812,891	$59,358,984
4	$4,451,924	$54,907,061
5	$4,118,030	$50,789,031
6	$3,809,177	$46,979,854
7	$3,523,489	$43,456,365
8	$3,259,227	$40,197,137
9	$3,014,785	$37,182,352
10	$2,788,676	$34,393,676
11	$2,579,526	$31,814,150
12	$2,386,061	$29,428,089
13	$2,207,107	$27,220,982
14	$2,041,574	$25,179,408
15	$1,888,456	$23,290,953
16	$1,746,821	$21,544,131
17	$1,615,810	$19,928,321
18	$1,494,624	$18,433,697
19	$1,382,527	$17,051,170
20	$1,051,170	$16,000,000

has been in use since 1986.[7] Under MACRS, fixed assets are assigned to a specific asset class; the IRS has published a complete set of depreciation tables for each of these classes. Table 14.11 gives a detailed explanation of all the asset classes. A business determines its tax depreciation based on the information in the asset class table. The resulting depreciation is included in the company's income tax return as part of the derivation of taxable income. It is important to note that internally, a company is permitted to use any of the depreciation techniques available, for tax deduction purposes, every company depending on specific asset classes must use MACRS under US law.

Table 14.5 denotes the various rates of depreciation for different useful years or asset classes. Under MACRS, the assets are always completely depreciated, meaning there is no salvage value. Depreciating an asset fully allows for further tax deduction and hence is preferred. MACRS depreciation is calculated using tables that the IRS created for each asset class.[8]

Example 14.4

The example of DirectJet purchasing a Boeing 737 valued at $75 million can be extended to using MACRS. The depreciation schedule assuming a 20-year useful life is given in Table 14.6.

Table 14.5 follows the half-year convention, which denotes that you only get one-half year of depreciation in the first year of ownership regardless of when you purchased the asset during the year. This results in the total depreciation period spanning 21 years because it accounts for a half year of depreciation in both the 1st and 21st years, effectively making the useful life of the asset 20 years. Note also that the aircraft was fully depreciated, giving it zero salvage value at the end of its useful life.

Table 14.5 MACRS Depreciation Rates

Year	*3-Year*	*5-Year*	*7-Year*	*10-Year*	*15-Year*	*20-Year*
1	33.33%	20.00%	14.29%	10.00%	5.00%	3.75%
2	44.45%	32.00%	24.49%	18.00%	9.50%	7.22%
3	14.81%	19.20%	17.49%	14.40%	8.55%	6.68%
4	7.41%	11.52%	12.49%	11.52%	7.70%	6.18%
5		11.52%	8.93%	9.22%	6.93%	5.71%
6		5.76%	8.92%	7.37%	6.23%	5.29%
7			8.93%	6.55%	5.90%	4.89%
8			4.46%	6.55%	5.90%	4.52%
9				6.56%	5.91%	4.46%
10				6.55%	5.90%	4.46%
11				3.28%	5.91%	4.46%
12					5.90%	4.46%
13					5.91%	4.46%
14					5.90%	4.46%
15					5.91%	4.46%
16					2.95%	4.46%
17						4.46%
18						4.46%
19						4.46%
20						4.46%
21						2.23%
Sum	100%	100%	100%	100%	100%	100%

Table 14.6 MACRS Depreciation Expense Calculation

Age	*Depreciation Expense*	*Value*
1	$2,812,500	$72,187,500
2	$5,414,250	$66,773,250
3	$5,007,750	$61,765,500
4	$4,632,750	$57,132,750
5	$4,284,750	$52,848,000
6	$3,963,750	$48,884,250
7	$3,666,000	$45,218,250
8	$3,391,500	$41,826,750
9	$3,346,500	$38,480,250
10	$3,345,750	$35,134,500
11	$3,346,500	$31,788,000
12	$3,345,750	$28,442,250
13	$3,346,500	$25,095,750
14	$3,345,750	$21,750,000
15	$3,346,500	$18,403,500
16	$3,345,750	$15,057,750
17	$3,346,500	$11,711,250
18	$3,345,750	$8,365,500
19	$3,346,500	$5,019,000
20	$3,345,750	$1,673,250
21	$1,673,250	$0

Sum-of-Years Digits

Many assets such as automobiles and computers lose a substantial portion of their value early in their lifetime. SYD is a depreciation technique that allocates a higher depreciation expense in the earlier years of an asset's useful life and gradually reduces it in subsequent years. This method is considered an accelerated depreciation method, like double declining balance.

SYD typically results in higher depreciation expenses in the early years of an asset's life and lower expenses in the later years, reflecting the assumption that assets tend to lose their value more rapidly in their earlier years of use. Assume an asset depreciates from price to salvage value S in N years. Under this method, depreciation is calculated by multiplying book value (V) by the remaining periods of useful life at the start of the period divided by the sum of the digits in the original useful life. For an asset with a five-year useful life, N = 5

- The sum of years is $1+2+3+4+5=15$
- The depreciation in the first year would be
- $\left(\frac{5}{5+4+3+2+1}=\frac{5}{15}\right)=33.33\%$

of depreciable value (V-S). In this methodology, the amount of annual depreciation progressively declines as the asset ages.

$$First-Year=\frac{N}{Sum-of-Years}\times(V-S)$$

$$Second-Year=\frac{N-1}{Sum-of-Years}\times(V-S)$$

$$Final-Year=\frac{1}{Sum-of-Years}\times(V-S)$$

Example 14.5

Using SYD depreciation, find the amount of depreciation to be charged off each year on a flight simulator with a cost of $\$1,000,000$, estimated life of five years, and a trade-in/scrap value of $100,000$. The depreciable base is therefore $\$1,000,000-\$100,000=\$900,00$, and Table 14.7 gives the necessary figures for the calculation. The calculations follow the table.

Table 14.7 Calculating Sum-of-Years Digits Depreciation

Year	*Book Value (V)*	*V-S*	*Depreciation Expense*	*Depreciation Expense*	*Accumulated Depreciation*	*Book Value Year End*
1	$1,000,000	$900,000	0.33	$300,000	$300,000	$700,000
2	$700,000	$900,000	0.27	$240,000	$540,000	$460,000
3	$460,000	$900,000	0.20	$180,000	$720,000	$280,000
4	$280,000	$900,000	0.13	$120,000	$840,000	$160,000
5	$160,000	$900,000	0.07	$60,000	$900,000	$100,000
Sum			100%	$900,000		

Depreciation expense at the end of the

- First year: $\$900,000 \times (5/15) = \$300,000$
  - Book value at the end of the first year: $\$1,000,000 - \$300,000 = \$700,000$.
- Second year: $\$700,000 \times (4/15) = \$240,000$
  - Book value at the end of the second year: $\$700,000 - \$240,000 = \$460,000$.
- Third year: $\$700,000 \times (3/15) = \$180,000$,
  - Book value at the end of the third year: $\$460,000 - \$180,000 = \$280,000$.
- Fourth year: $\$700,000 \times (2/15) = \$120,000$,
  - Book value at the end of the fourth year: $\$280,000 - \$120,000 = \$160,000$.
- Fifth year: $\$700,000 \times (1/15) = \$60,000$,
  - Book value at the end of the fifth year: $\$160,000 - \$60,000 = \$100,000$.

Comparing Depreciation Techniques

In choosing the most suitable depreciation method, businesses should consider factors such as the nature of the asset, its expected usage and obsolescence, financial reporting requirements, tax implications, and the need to accurately match depreciation expenses with revenue recognition. Each method has its advantages and disadvantages, and the decision should be based on the specific circumstances and objectives of the business.

Straight-line depreciation, for instance, is lauded for its simplicity and even for spreading costs across an asset's useful life, making it a popular choice for its straightforwardness. However, its drawback lies in potentially misrepresenting an asset's actual decline in value over time. MACRS depreciation, a method prescribed by tax authorities, can offer tax advantages but may not reflect an asset's true economic depreciation. Consider the example of an asset with an initial cost of \$75,000,000 and a salvage value of \$0, with a useful life of 20 years. All four of the previously discussed depreciation approaches can be applied to the asset and the outcomes in current value can be compared (Table 14.10a,b,c).

The previous tables show clearly that the depreciation recorded every year is different for all four approaches, which changed the current value of the asset over its useful life of 20 years. Notable distinctions include that under MACRS, the total number of years becomes 21 years due to the half year assumptions in year 1 and year 21 and that the salvage value under double declining balance is $\$10,000,000$. Figure 14.3 illustrates the variations in current value.

The figure shows that SYD and double declining balance depreciation correlate closely for the first four years and then begin to diverge. MACRS and SLD are fairly close throughout the life of the asset, as well. This is the reason that sometimes if the straight line offers a higher depreciation, the MACRS rate after that point for certain asset classes is substituted with the straight-line rate.

As a percentage of airline revenue, 6%–8% is typically spent on aircraft depreciation, 3% on leasing, and 2% on interest. In the United States, operators normally use the MACRS deprecitoy in order to depreciate aircraft; this could be different in other parts of the world. Southwest Airlines uses SLD to estimate residual values over periods ranging from 23 to 25 years for flight

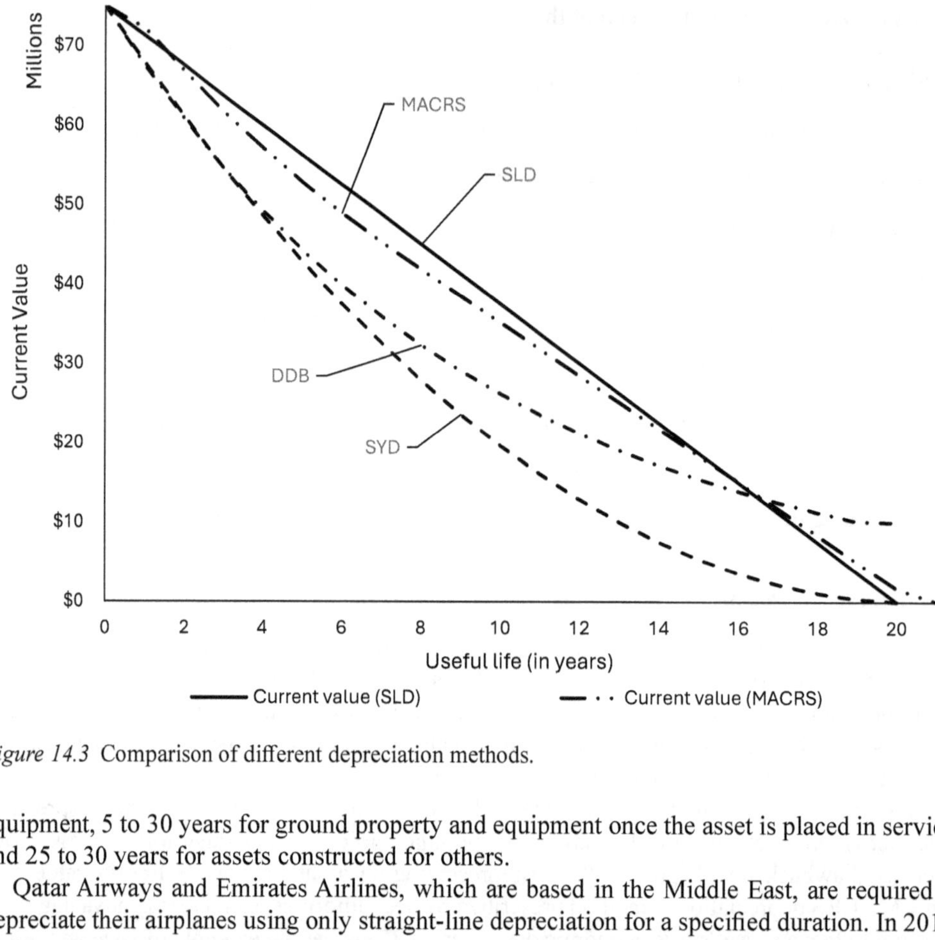

Figure 14.3 Comparison of different depreciation methods.

equipment, 5 to 30 years for ground property and equipment once the asset is placed in service, and 25 to 30 years for assets constructed for others.

Qatar Airways and Emirates Airlines, which are based in the Middle East, are required to depreciate their airplanes using only straight-line depreciation for a specified duration. In 2014, Lufthansa Group extended the depreciation period for its aircraft from 12 to 20 years, reducing their residual book value from 15% to 5% of the purchase price. The changes to its depreciation policy provided a €351 million benefit in 2014. In 2012, the Australian and International Pilots Association called for an acceleration of depreciation rates for aircraft in Australia. It took 10 years for Australian airlines to write off a new aircraft, but although reducing the writeoff period to five years could at least match the rate available to Air New Zealand, it would fall short of matching the investment environment of the major international airlines flooding the Australian market. For example, Singapore Airlines could depreciate its aircraft over three years. In January 2016, Tiger Air reported that changes in accounting estimates for maintenance provisions and aircraft depreciation policy resulted in a Singapore \$3.8 million (US\$2.7 million) increase in aircraft depreciation.

Calculating Depreciation in Excel

Excel and other spreadsheet software are also excellent options for calculating depreciation. Here, we assume the following scenario and calculate the depreciation values according to the various methods explained earlier.

DirectJet has bought a Boeing 777 aircraft for \$7,000,000 and plans to use it for 10 years, following which it plans to sell the aircraft for a salvage value of \$200,000. Calculate straight-line depreciation for each year using Excel's function SLN (). This function requires three parameters: cost, salvage value, and life; cost is the amount paid to buy the asset, salvage value is the value of the asset after depreciation, and life is the useful life of the asset in years. The syntax of the function is =SLN (COST,SALVAGE,LIFE). Figure 14.4a displays how to enter the formula in Excel, and Figure 14.4b shows the result; type the information in Figure 14.4a into your own spreadsheet.

The table in Figure 14.5 can be generated by subtracting the depreciation amount from the current value of each year.

Calculate the depreciation for each year using declining balance and the figures from Figure 14.5 assuming that the aircraft was bought in April. Excel function DB () requires five parameters: cost, salvage value, life, period, and month. We have already explained the first three; period refers to the year of depreciation, and month is the number of months remaining in the year of purchase. The syntax of this function is =DB (COST, SALVAGE, LIFE, PERIOD, MONTH), although month is optional; it is considered 12 if it is left blank. Enter the function in the depreciation amount column (Figure 14.6). The depreciation amount for the last year must be slightly adjusted to account for the salvage value of $200,000 (Figure 14.7).

Double declining balance depreciation can also be calculated in Excel. Instead of the month parameter, there is a parameter FACTOR that is the depreciation rate. Any value can be input for FACTOR, but if it is left blank, a default rate of 200%; to use a 150% depreciation rate, enter 1.5. Using the data from Figure 14.5, calculate double declining balance depreciation using =DBD(COST, SALVAGE, LIFE, PERIOD, FACTOR) (Figure 14.8a). Figure 14.8b gives the results; The salvage value in this case, can be only as low as $751,000 approx. Hence, to obtain a salvage value of $800,000, the depreciation amount for year 10 is adjusted to $139,524.

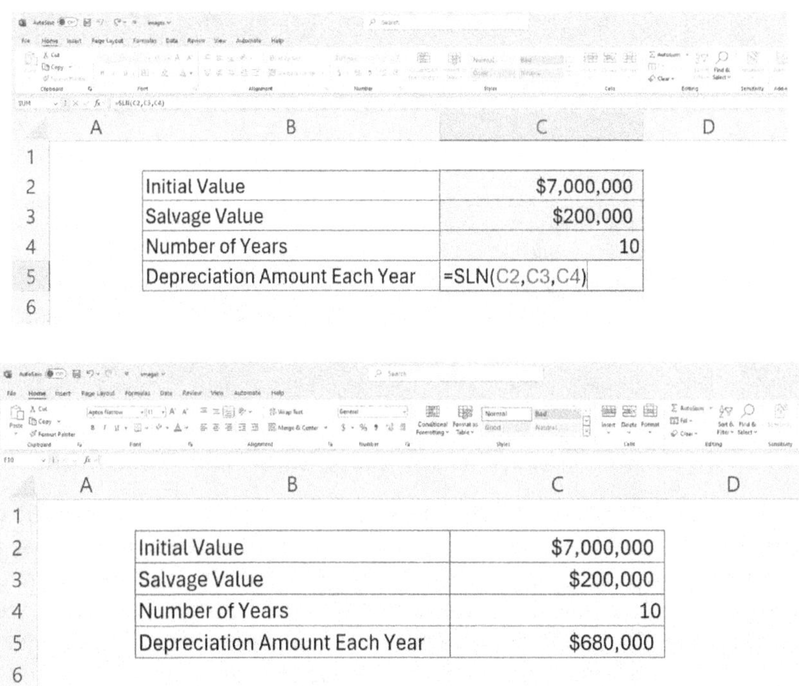

Figure 14.4 Calculating depreciation in Excel.

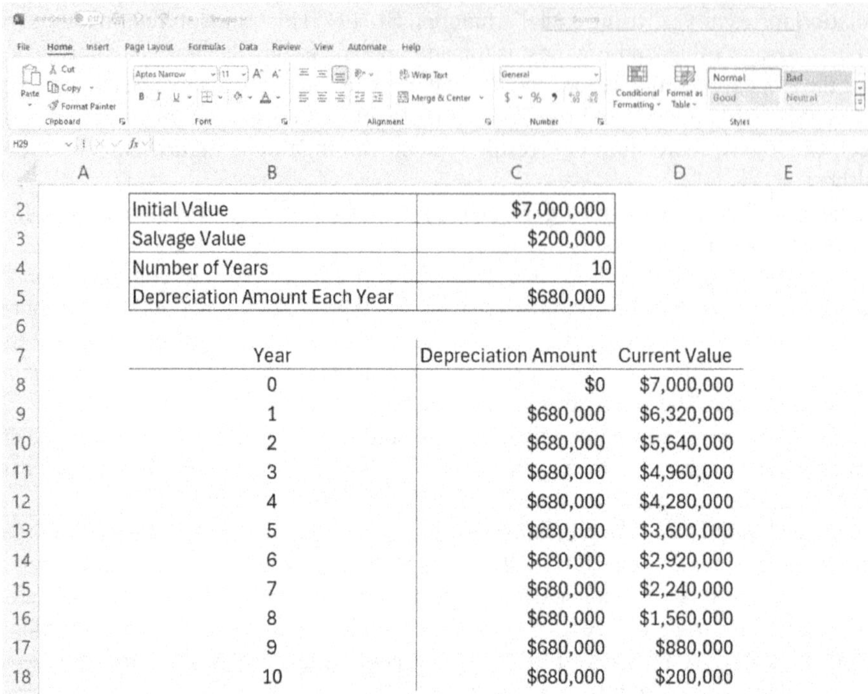

Initial Value	$7,000,000
Salvage Value	$200,000
Number of Years	10
Depreciation Amount Each Year	$680,000

Year	Depreciation Amount	Current Value
0	$0	$7,000,000
1	$680,000	$6,320,000
2	$680,000	$5,640,000
3	$680,000	$4,960,000
4	$680,000	$4,280,000
5	$680,000	$3,600,000
6	$680,000	$2,920,000
7	$680,000	$2,240,000
8	$680,000	$1,560,000
9	$680,000	$880,000
10	$680,000	$200,000

Figure 14.5 Straight-line depreciation.

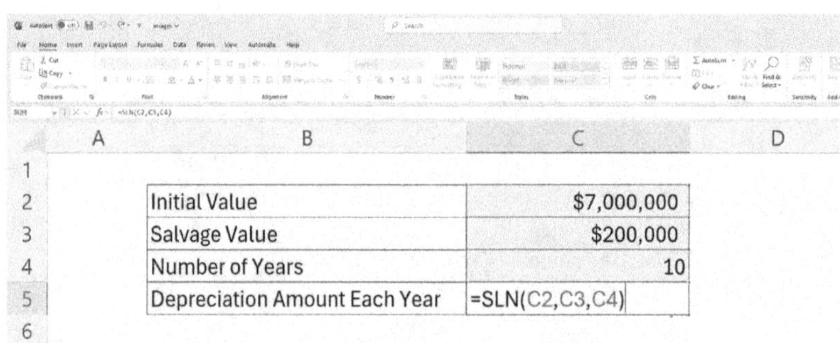

Initial Value	$7,000,000
Salvage Value	$200,000
Number of Years	10
Depreciation Amount Each Year	=SLN(C2,C3,C4)

Figure 14.6 Calculating straight-line depreciation in Excel.

Calculating depreciation using MACRS in Excel is simple and requires no specific functions. The depreciation rates should be taken from the appropriate MACRS table. Here, we are going to use the 10-year rates. Enter the info from Figure 14.9 for Year and MACRS rate on your spreadsheet; for years 7, 8, 9, and 10, note that SLD has to be used as it gives higher values. Enter the formula =B13/4 in cell D13 to obtain the straight-line depreciation value per year for a period of four years without no salvage value, and copy the value in D13 into D14, D15, and D16. This fully depreciates the value of the asset; depreciation for years one to six uses the half-life concept.

In Excel, calculating SYD depreciation is similar to using declining balance except that MONTH is not used: =SYD (COST, SALVAGE, LIFE, PERIOD) (Figure 14.10). This gives the findings in Figure 14.11. The correct salvage value at the end of year 10 is automatically obtained.

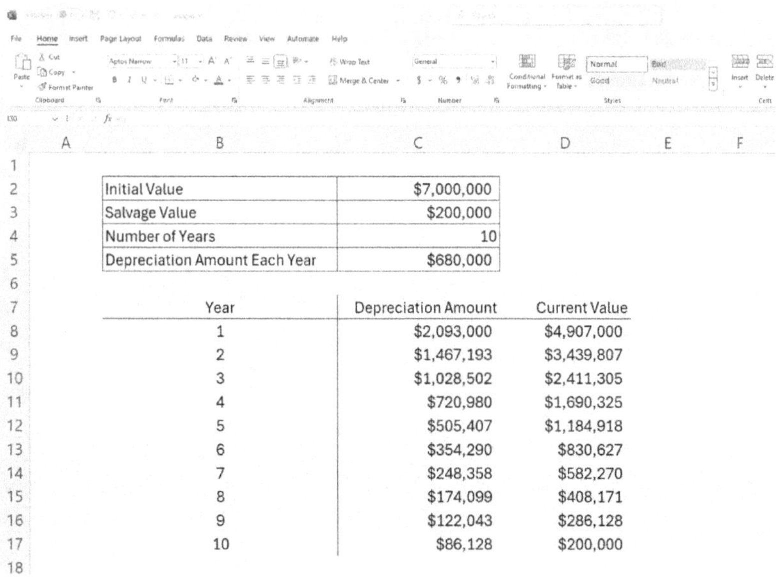

Initial Value	$7,000,000
Salvage Value	$200,000
Number of Years	10
Depreciation Amount Each Year	$680,000

Year	Depreciation Amount	Current Value
1	$2,093,000	$4,907,000
2	$1,467,193	$3,439,807
3	$1,028,502	$2,411,305
4	$720,980	$1,690,325
5	$505,407	$1,184,918
6	$354,290	$830,627
7	$248,358	$582,270
8	$174,099	$408,171
9	$122,043	$286,128
10	$86,128	$200,000

Figure 14.7 Acceleration depreciation.

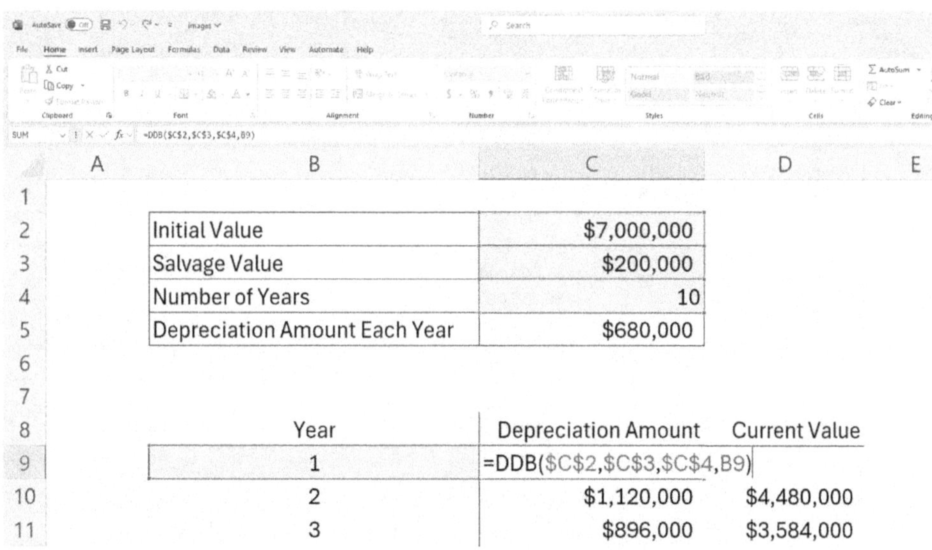

Initial Value	$7,000,000
Salvage Value	$200,000
Number of Years	10
Depreciation Amount Each Year	$680,000

Year	Depreciation Amount	Current Value
1	=DDB(C2,C3,C4,B9)	
2	$1,120,000	$4,480,000
3	$896,000	$3,584,000

Figure 14.8a Calculating double declining balance depreciation in Excel.

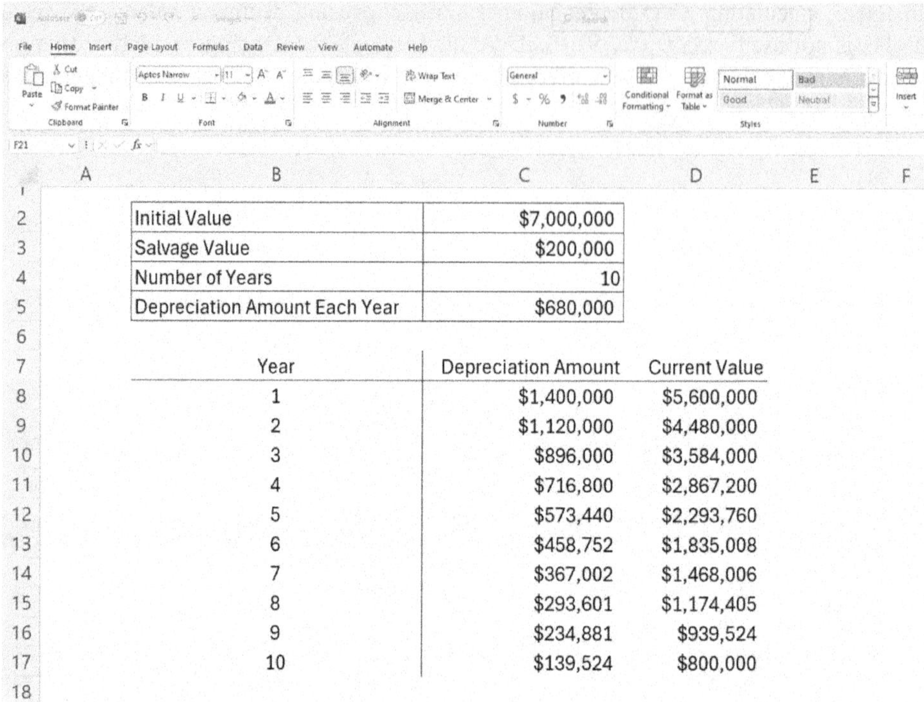

Initial Value	$7,000,000
Salvage Value	$200,000
Number of Years	10
Depreciation Amount Each Year	$680,000

Year	Depreciation Amount	Current Value
1	$1,400,000	$5,600,000
2	$1,120,000	$4,480,000
3	$896,000	$3,584,000
4	$716,800	$2,867,200
5	$573,440	$2,293,760
6	$458,752	$1,835,008
7	$367,002	$1,468,006
8	$293,601	$1,174,405
9	$234,881	$939,524
10	$139,524	$800,000

Figure 14.8b Acceleration depreciation.

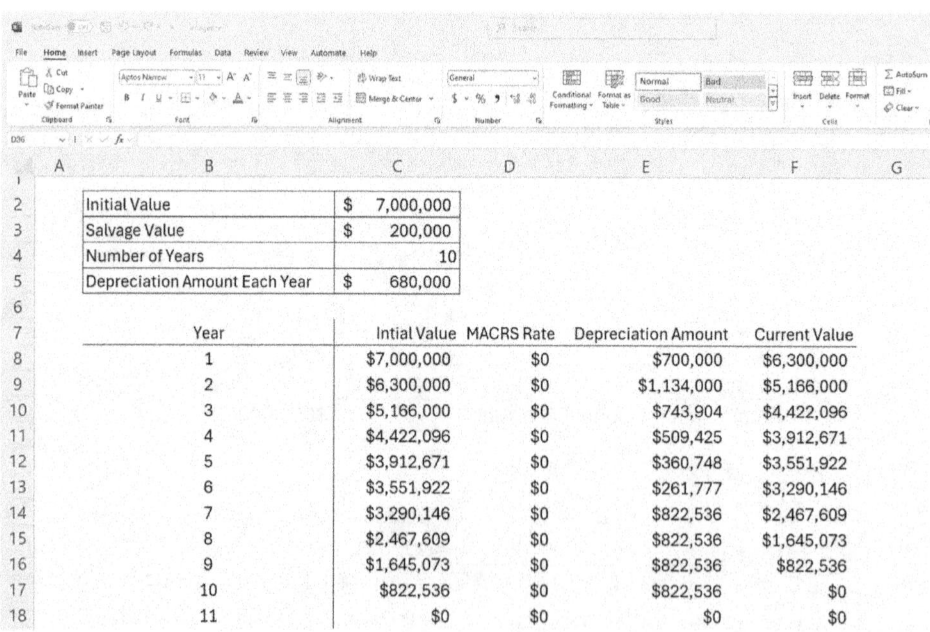

Initial Value	$ 7,000,000
Salvage Value	$ 200,000
Number of Years	10
Depreciation Amount Each Year	$ 680,000

Year	Intial Value	MACRS Rate	Depreciation Amount	Current Value
1	$7,000,000	$0	$700,000	$6,300,000
2	$6,300,000	$0	$1,134,000	$5,166,000
3	$5,166,000	$0	$743,904	$4,422,096
4	$4,422,096	$0	$509,425	$3,912,671
5	$3,912,671	$0	$360,748	$3,551,922
6	$3,551,922	$0	$261,777	$3,290,146
7	$3,290,146	$0	$822,536	$2,467,609
8	$2,467,609	$0	$822,536	$1,645,073
9	$1,645,073	$0	$822,536	$822,536
10	$822,536	$0	$822,536	$0
11	$0	$0	$0	$0

Figure 14.9 Calculating MACRS depreciation in Excel.

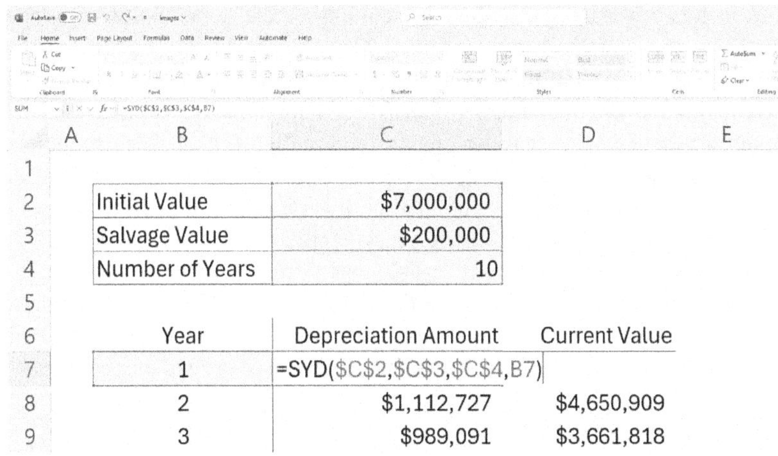

	A	B	C	D
1				
2		Initial Value	$7,000,000	
3		Salvage Value	$200,000	
4		Number of Years	10	
5				
6		Year	Depreciation Amount	Current Value
7		1	=SYD(C2,C3,C4,B7)	
8		2	$1,112,727	$4,650,909
9		3	$989,091	$3,661,818

Figure 14.10 Calculating SYD depreciation in Excel.

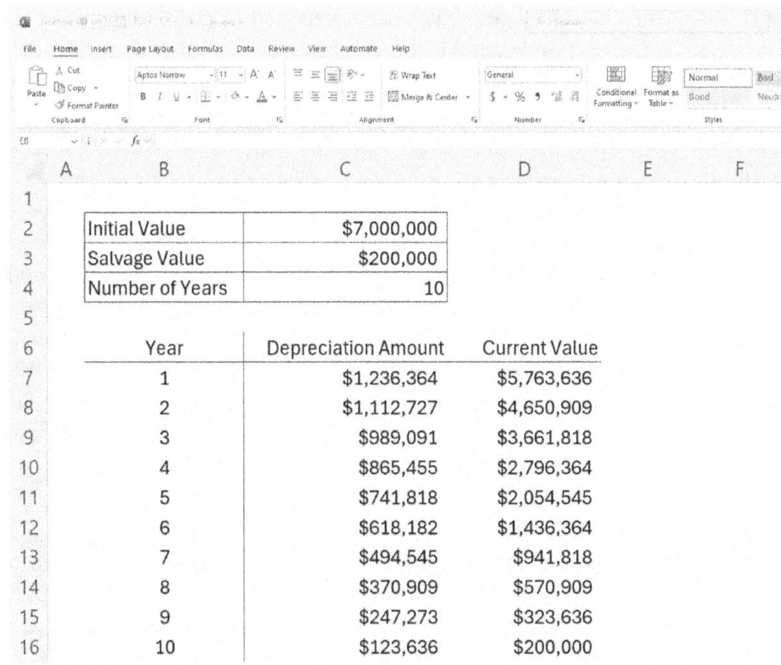

	A	B	C	D
1				
2		Initial Value	$7,000,000	
3		Salvage Value	$200,000	
4		Number of Years	10	
5				
6		Year	Depreciation Amount	Current Value
7		1	$1,236,364	$5,763,636
8		2	$1,112,727	$4,650,909
9		3	$989,091	$3,661,818
10		4	$865,455	$2,796,364
11		5	$741,818	$2,054,545
12		6	$618,182	$1,436,364
13		7	$494,545	$941,818
14		8	$370,909	$570,909
15		9	$247,273	$323,636
16		10	$123,636	$200,000

Figure 14.11 SYD depreciation results in Excel.

Basics of a Replacement Decision

An aircraft replacement decision is always challenging. Fleet reductions are reached by disposing of the surplus aircraft or through aircraft purchase and lease. Scrapping and replacing existing aircraft is generally motivated by the financial and physical deterioration of the aircraft or the availability of newer, more efficient aircraft.

Numerous factors ought to be considered, including purchase price, financing options, ownership costs, operating costs and salvage value. These factors make the replacement decision an economic decision. The cost of maintenance required to keep aircraft airworthy (below the threshold) is a major concern of operators. If an asset is kept too long, its salvage value decreases, and it becomes increasingly expensive to operate. Alternatively, if an asset is replaced too soon, it is too costly from an investment perspective. This is particularly true in case of an asset such as an aircraft because the operating cost of an aircraft is extremely high as the age of the aircraft increases. As the fleet ages, managers often ask when the useful life of an aircraft is over. The typical lifespan of a Boeing 737 is about 25–30 years. Finding the optimum time to replace an aircraft has always been a focus of many studies carried out in the past. According to Boeing's estimate B-737 series aircraft have a lifespan of 90,000 flight cycles or 55,000 flight hours, whichever comes first. The 747 series aircraft had a lifespan of around 35 years or 90,000 flight hours.

Assets may be replaced because of:

- Technological developments

  Technology improvements in aircraft have been the major factor in improving the efficiency of air transport and the growth of the air transport industry. Significant improvements in aircraft design and fuel efficiency have been achieved since the beginning of the commercial aviation industry. For example, the Boeing 787's great fuel efficiency and range flexibility enable airlines to expend the operations and profitably open new routes as well as optimize fleet and network performance.[9] Comparably, the A380's advanced technology resulted in about 20% lower seat-mile costs, while its range is 10% greater than the comparable aircraft.[10]
- An asset at the end of its economic life

  Retirement is part of the aircraft life cycle, and the main reasons behind a decision to retire from an old plane are financial. Older designs are more expensive to maintain and generally less fuel efficient. An increase in fuel prices may have encouraged some airlines to replace the existing fleet with more fuel-efficient ones, aviation consultancy International Bureau of Aviation said. Contrarily, the lower fuel price may very well compensate for the increased maintenance, so management considers using their older fleet.[11] For example, a pair of nearly 50-year-old Vietnam-era OV-10 Bronco turbo-propeller planes were brought out of retirement for service. The estimated cost of flying the more modern jets (like the F-15 or F-35) is $45,000 per hour of flight, while the OV-10 Bronco could cost less than $5,000 per flight.
- Doesn't meet needs, increased demand

  An increase in demand in a certain market could force an airline to switch to a bigger aircraft, and this may normally result in replacement. Also, airlines such as Southwest have been using only one type of aircraft for all their operations; when Southwest acquired AirTran, Southwest was forced to unload the entire fleet of Boeing 717 aircrafts it inherited since it did not match Southwest's policy of only operating the Boeing 737. Flying only Boeing 737s helps Southwest control training, maintenance, and operating expenses, since the smaller Boeing 717 costs more to fly on a per-seat basis.[12]
- Deterioration

  Aircraft are complex machines that comprise many sophisticated parts, components, and systems. As the aircraft age and their use intensifies, they gradually degenerate until they are no longer able to perform. Most aircraft suffer deterioration of their physical condition toward the end of their service life due to high utilization, corrosion, and wear and tear. Drastic deterioration also requires replacement. For example, American Airlines had to replace most of the MD 80s after many years of service, extensive deterioration, and expensive heavy checks. The MD-80 was built by McDonnell Douglas, which was bought by Boeing in 1997.

Figure 14.12 graphically depicts three scenarios: comparing an aircraft's ownership and operating costs (data taken from Table 14.8), when ownership cost drops, and when operating costs might decrease because of lower fuel prices.

In a normal scenario, the life of the aircraft where the ownership cost and the operating cost intersect is 10 years, a reasonable replacement life because beyond this point, the operating cost overshadows the ownership cost. The second scenario involving a drop in ownership cost reduces replacement life to eight years because the operating costs now exceed the ownership cost much sooner than before. In the third possible scenario, the potential decrease in operating cost increases the replacement life to 12 years because it now takes longer for the operating cost to exceed the ownership cost.

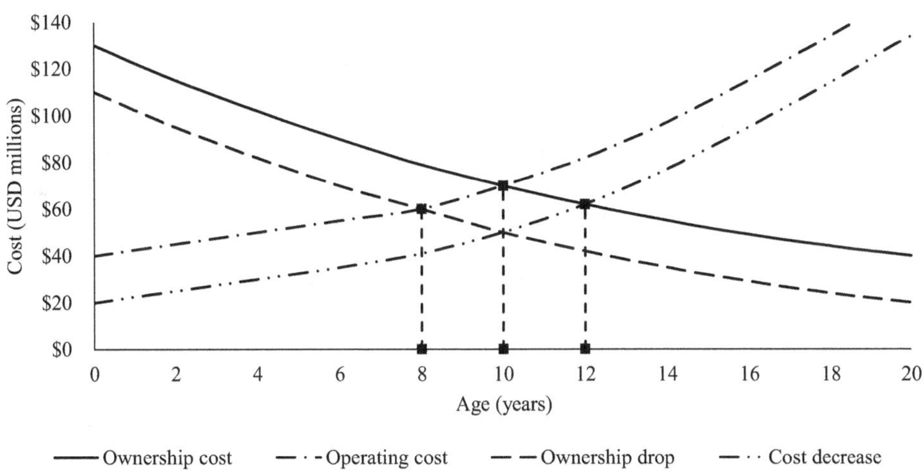

Figure 14.12 Possible changes in economic service life.

Table 14.8 Ownership vs Operating Cost

Age (years)	*Ownership Cost*	*Operating Cost*	*Ownership Drop*	*Cost Decrease*
0	$130	$40	$110	$20
2	$115	$45	$95	$25
4	$102	$50	$82	$30
6	$90	$55	$70	$35
8	$79	$60	$60	$41
10	$70	$70	$50	$50
12	$62	$82	$42	$62
14	$55	$97	$35	$77
16	$49	$115	$29	$95
18	$44	$134	$24	$114
20	$40	$154	$20	$134

Impairment

Impairment refers to a fixed asset that has a market value that has decreased significantly and recognizes a loss in the income statement. The high value of aircraft assets carried on balance sheet coupled with earnings volatility in the industry has historically exposed airlines to potential asset impairments. An aircraft impairment assessment tests the recoverability of the value the aircraft is being carried at in the financial statements. Recoverable amount is the benefits that can be obtained from a fixed asset. Economic benefits are obtained either by selling the asset or using the asset. Recoverable amount equals the higher of the asset's fair value less costs to sell or the value in use (net present value of future cash flows from the asset). Carrying amount refers to the current value of the asset found by subtracting the accumulated value of depreciation from the purchase value of the asset. If the carrying amount exceeds the recoverable amount, an impairment expense amounting to the difference is recognized in the period. If the carrying amount is less than the recoverable amount, no impairment is recognized. The impairment loss is the amount by which the carrying amount of the asset exceeds its recoverable amount (IAS 36.6, IAS 36.8). The process of measuring impairment is illustrated in Figure 14.13.

Assume that in January 2025, DirectJet purchased a Boeing 737-800 MAX for \$75 million. Its estimated useful life at that date was 20 years, and the airline uses straight-line depreciation. In 2025, Boeing embarked on a plan to introduce a more efficient B737, called B-737 TOP. B-737 TOP delivers 8% lower operating costs than its main competitor, and the advanced winglet increases fuel efficiency by 1.8%. DirectJet estimates that it can sell the aircraft for \$70 million, but it must incur costs of \$10,000,000. Alternatively, if DirectJet continues to use it, the present value of the net cash flows the aircraft will generate is \$62 million. The basic rule is to recognize impairment when the carrying amount exceeds the recoverable amount.

First, we need to determine the carrying amount. The aircraft has a cost of \$75 million and useful life of 20 years and has been used for three years so far. This means that accumulated depreciation is \$75/20 × 3 or \$11.25 million. Thus, the carrying amount is \$75 million minus \$11.25 million or \$63.75 million.

Second, we need to determine the recoverable amount. Recoverable amount is the higher of fair value less costs to sell or value in use. Fair value less costs to sell in this scenario is \$70 million minus \$10 million or \$60 million. Value in use is the present value of future cash flows, \$62 million. Recoverable amount is the higher of the two, \$62 million. Carrying

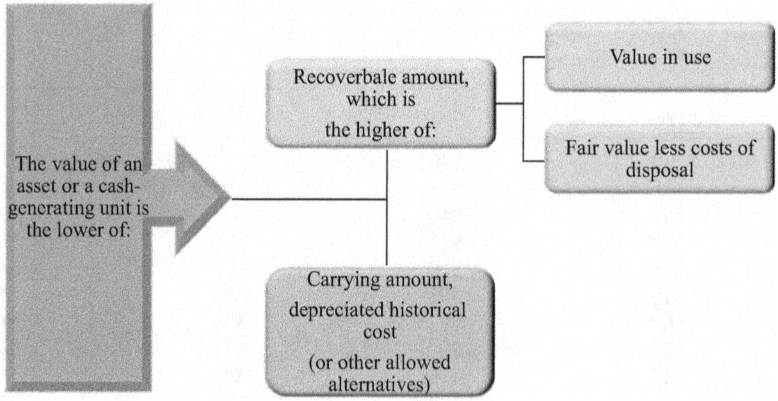

Figure 14.13 Impairment measurement under IAS 36.

amount is $63.75 million, while recoverable amount is $62 million, leaving an impairment loss of $1.75 million.

Example 14.6

A regional airline purchased an aircraft push for $300,000. The truck was depreciated under MACRS as a five-year property (for a five-year property, the MACRS percentages are 20%, 32%, 19.2%, 11.52%, 11.52%, 5.76%). The truck's salvage value is expected to be $50,000 less each year. The O&M costs are expected to be $30,000 per year. Also, the push will generate $135,000 in net present value of future cash flows. The airline decides to sell the truck at the end of two years. Calculate the impairment loss incurred by the airline: Depreciation for year one is calculated as (20% × $300,000) = $60,000. The depreciation schedule for the aircraft push is shown in Table 14.9.

Table 14.9 MACRS Depreciation Schedule: Example 14.6

Year	*Depreciation expense*	*Accumulated Depreciation*	*Value*
1	$60,000	$60,000	$240,000
2	$96,000	$156,000	$144,000
3	$57,600	$213,600	$86,400
4	$34,560	$248,160	$51,840
5	$34,560	$282,720	$17,280
6	$17,280	$300,000	$0

Table 14.10a MACRS Depreciation Schedule: SLD & MACRS

Year	*Straight-Line Depreciation*	*Book Value (SLD)*	*MACRS 20-year rate*	*MACRS Depreciation*	*Book Value (MACRS)*
0	$0	$75,000,000	0%	$0	$75,000,000
1	$3,750,000	$71,250,000	3.75%	$2,812,500	$72,187,500
2	$3,750,000	$67,500,000	7.22%	$5,414,250	$66,773,250
3	$3,750,000	$63,750,000	6.68%	$5,007,750	$61,765,500
4	$3,750,000	$60,000,000	6.18%	$4,632,750	$57,132,750
5	$3,750,000	$56,250,000	5.71%	$4,284,750	$52,848,000
6	$3,750,000	$52,500,000	5.29%	$3,963,750	$48,884,250
7	$3,750,000	$48,750,000	4.89%	$3,666,000	$45,218,250
8	$3,750,000	$45,000,000	4.52%	$3,391,500	$41,826,750
9	$3,750,000	$41,250,000	4.46%	$3,346,500	$38,480,250
10	$3,750,000	$37,500,000	4.46%	$3,345,750	$35,134,500
11	$3,750,000	$33,750,000	4.46%	$3,346,500	$31,788,000
12	$3,750,000	$30,000,000	4.46%	$3,345,750	$28,442,250
13	$3,750,000	$26,250,000	4.46%	$3,346,500	$25,095,750
14	$3,750,000	$22,500,000	4.46%	$3,345,750	$21,750,000
15	$3,750,000	$18,750,000	4.46%	$3,346,500	$18,403,500
16	$3,750,000	$15,000,000	4.46%	$3,345,750	$15,057,750
17	$3,750,000	$11,250,000	4.46%	$3,346,500	$11,711,250
18	$3,750,000	$7,500,000	4.46%	$3,345,750	$8,365,500
19	$3,750,000	$3,750,000	4.46%	$3,346,500	$5,019,000
20	$3,750,000	$0	4.46%	$3,345,750	$1,673,250
21			2.23%	$1,673,250	$0

Table 14.10b MACRS Depreciation Schedule: SYD & DBD

Year	*Sum-of-Years Digits*	*Book Value (SYD)*	*DBD*	*Book Value (DBD)*
0	$0	$75,000,000	$0	$75,000,000
1	$7,142,857	$67,857,143	$7,500,000	$67,500,000
2	$6,785,714	$61,071,429	$6,750,000	$60,750,000
3	$6,428,571	$54,642,857	$6,075,000	$54,675,000
4	$6,071,429	$48,571,429	$5,467,500	$49,207,500
5	$5,714,286	$42,857,143	$4,920,750	$44,286,750
6	$5,357,143	$37,500,000	$4,428,675	$39,858,075
7	$5,000,000	$32,500,000	$3,985,808	$35,872,268
8	$4,642,857	$27,857,143	$3,587,227	$32,285,041
9	$4,285,714	$23,571,429	$3,228,504	$29,056,537
10	$3,928,571	$19,642,857	$2,905,654	$26,150,883
11	$3,571,429	$16,071,429	$2,615,088	$23,535,795
12	$3,214,286	$12,857,143	$2,353,579	$21,182,215
13	$2,857,143	$10,000,000	$2,118,222	$19,063,994
14	$2,500,000	$7,500,000	$1,906,399	$17,157,594
15	$2,142,857	$5,357,143	$1,715,759	$15,441,835
16	$1,785,714	$3,571,429	$1,544,183	$13,897,651
17	$1,428,571	$2,142,857	$1,389,765	$12,507,886
18	$1,071,429	$1,071,429	$1,250,789	$11,257,098
19	$714,286	$357,143	$1,125,710	$10,131,388
20	$357,143	$(0.00)	$131,388	$10,000,000

Table 14.10c MACRS Depreciation Schedule: SLD, MACRS, SYD, DBD

Year	*Book value (SLD)*	*Book value (MACRS)*	*Book value (SYD)*	*Book value (DBD)*
0	$75,000,000	$75,000,000	$75,000,000	$75,000,000
1	$71,250,000	$72,187,500	$67,857,143	$67,500,000
2	$67,500,000	$66,773,250	$61,071,429	$60,750,000
3	$63,750,000	$61,765,500	$54,642,857	$54,675,000
4	$60,000,000	$57,132,750	$48,571,429	$49,207,500
5	$56,250,000	$52,848,000	$42,857,143	$44,286,750
6	$52,500,000	$48,884,250	$37,500,000	$39,858,075
7	$48,750,000	$45,218,250	$32,500,000	$35,872,268
8	$45,000,000	$41,826,750	$27,857,143	$32,285,041
9	$41,250,000	$38,480,250	$23,571,429	$29,056,537
10	$37,500,000	$35,134,500	$19,642,857	$26,150,883
11	$33,750,000	$31,788,000	$16,071,429	$23,535,795
12	$30,000,000	$28,442,250	$12,857,143	$21,182,215
13	$26,250,000	$25,095,750	$10,000,000	$19,063,994
14	$22,500,000	$21,750,000	$7,500,000	$17,157,594
15	$18,750,000	$18,403,500	$5,357,143	$15,441,835
16	$15,000,000	$15,057,750	$3,571,429	$13,897,651
17	$11,250,000	$11,711,250	$2,142,857	$12,507,886
18	$7,500,000	$8,365,500	$1,071,429	$11,257,098
19	$3,750,000	$5,019,000	$357,143	$10,131,388
20	$0	$1,673,250	$0.00	$10,000,000

Table 14.11 MACRS Depreciation Schedule

Asset Class	*Depreciation Period*	*Description*	*Depreciation Method*
3-year property	3 years	Tractor units for over-the-road use, racehorses over 2 years old when placed in service, any other horse over 12 years old when placed in service, qualified rent-to-own property	200% declining balance
5-year property	5 years	Automobiles, taxis, buses, trucks, computers and peripheral equipment, office equipment, any property used in research and experimentation, breeding cattle and dairy cattle, appliances, etc.	200% declining balance
7-year property	7 years	Office furniture and fixtures, agricultural machinery and equipment, any property not designated as being in another class, natural gas gathering lines	200% declining balance
10-year property	10 years	Vessels, barges, tugs, single-purpose agricultural or horticultural structures, trees/vines bearing fruits or nuts, qualified small electric meter and smart electric grid systems	200% declining balance
15-year property	15 years	Certain land improvements (such as shrubbery, fences, roads, sidewalks and bridges), retail motor fuels outlets, municipal wastewater treatment plants, clearing and grading land improvements for gas utility property, electric transmission property, natural gas distribution lines	150% declining balance
20-year property	20 years	Farm buildings (other than those noted under 10-year property), municipal sewers not categorized as 25-year property, the initial clearing and grading of land for electric utility transmission and distribution plants	150% declining balance
Residential rental property	27.5 years	Any building or structure where 80% or more of its gross rental income is from dwelling units	Straight line
Nonresidential real property	39 years	An office building, store, or warehouse that is not residential property or has a class life of less than 27.5 years	Straight line

First, calculate the carrying amount. The aircraft push costs $300,000 and the accumulated depreciation at the end of year two is $156,000. Thus, the carrying amount is $300,000 minus $156,000, $144,000.

Next, calculate the recoverable amount. Fair value less costs to sell in this scenario is $200,000 ($300,000 – $100,000) minus $60,000, which is $140,000. Value in use is the present value of future cash flows, $135,000. The recoverable amount is the higher of the two, $140,000. The carrying amount is $144,000, and the recoverable amount is $140,000, so the impairment loss is $4,000.

Abandonment

The voluntary, intentional, and complete surrender of rights to a certain property/asset without the naming of a recipient as owner is known as abandonment. Acts that imply abandonment include continuous lack of use and/or maintenance and failure to pay property taxes. If there is an entity or individual with a prior interest or claim to that property/asset, it is possible that the property/asset will revert to their ownership. If no owner is apparent, the property/asset will be given to the state. Abandoning a property/asset does not remove the obligations associated with the property unless those are explicitly accepted by the new owner.

Some of the more commonly abandoned properties are mines and oil and natural gas wells. Throughout the world, there are numerous fields of dangerous, exposed holes from mining operations that were abandoned soon after they stopped yielding minerals or coal. For decades, old, abandoned wells have leaked oil, natural gas, and brine into soil and drinking water and also posed explosion risks. The danger of contamination or explosions from abandoned wells has led to aggressive efforts to find and plug old wells. Pennsylvania, the birthplace of the US oil industry, is turning to citizen volunteers, scientists, drillers and archivists to find hundreds of thousands of abandoned wells. It is one of several proving grounds where new technology could lead the way for other states to locate and plug abandoned wells.[13]

Abandonment could also arise from economic losses such that overall expected expenses would exceed the expected long-run revenues, and absorbing the sunk costs would be cheaper than continuing operations. A very appropriate example for this is the impact of the 2008 financial crisis on the construction industry in Spain. Prior to the collapse of the economy, building construction had contributed twice as big a share of gross domestic product in Spain as in other big European countries. The crisis caused this industry to rapidly shrink, and a side effect was the abandonment of thousands of homes, thought to be losing value. The people involved felt that abandonment would incur fewer losses than completing and not selling the houses. Another country that faced similar issues during the financial crisis was Dubai. The striking outcome was the mass abandonment of luxurious cars, which mostly belonged to expatriates who were fleeing the country after being unable to pay their debt or mortgages. Under Sharia law, failure to pay debt is a serious punishable offence.[14]

The abandonment of assets is a prevalent and complex issue in contemporary society. Whether it be the deserted factories standing as silent witnesses to the evolution of industry or the vacant properties scattered across urban landscapes, the act of abandonment is far from unusual. The stories of abandoned assets reflect the dynamic nature of our industry and technological landscapes and rapidly changing global situation to which companies struggle to respond. To illuminate this pervasive trend, we can explore two notable examples that highlight the multifaceted dimensions of asset abandonment.

The Goldin Finance 117 in Tianjin, China, was initially designed to stand as the world's fifth-tallest building, featuring advanced engineering solutions. With an initial estimated cost of around $10 billion, the project faced numerous challenges, including an unstable economic situation in China, stringent regulations, and escalating global tensions. Unfortunately, these factors led to repeated interruptions in construction, ultimately preventing the project's completion. Despite several attempts to sell the unfinished building as a project, none proved successful, leaving the Goldin Finance 117 abandoned.

Second, the H-4 Hercules, known as the Spruce Goose, was a colossal aircraft, the world's largest until 2019; it was requested by the US military during World War II to mitigate naval losses and facilitate the secure transport of personnel and equipment to Europe. Manufacturing initiated during the war; the first aircraft was completed shortly after its conclusion. However, with the war's end rendering the massive aircraft unnecessary, it was retired after its first test flight and left abandoned. The project incurred a cost of $23 million, equivalent to approximately $278 million in current dollars. Despite its ambitious origins and groundbreaking design, the Spruce Goose ultimately became a symbol of a venture abandoned due to shifting geopolitical circumstances.

The aviation industry has had a fair share of abandonment issues as well. Common reasons for aircraft abandonment include aging, damage, lower demand during economic recession, and increasing economical expenses. Abandonment could be short term (where an aircraft will be brought back into operation when it is considered profitable again) or long term (where it is believed that profitability can never be recovered to previous levels). During the financial crisis of 2008, many airlines abandoned aircraft due to financial constraints. Some entire airports have even been abandoned. For example, Don Quixote Airport in the town of Ciudad Real, nearly 150 miles from Madrid, was meant to be a symbol of Spain's economic boom. Instead, the project denounced the country's glaring financial woes when it was ultimately completely shut down in 2012, within three years of its opening.[15]

Aircraft involved in accidents or sustaining significant damage may be deemed uneconomical to repair. In such cases, the aircraft may be abandoned, scrapped, or used for spare parts. As aircraft age, the cost of maintenance and repairs can become economically unsustainable, especially if newer, more fuel-efficient, and technologically advanced aircraft are available. Fuel prices, maintenance expenses, and other operating costs can contribute to the economic decision to retire and abandon an aircraft, particularly if the aircraft is not economically viable to operate. To meet the market conditions in case of a catastrophic drop in demand, airlines abandon aircraft in order to boost their load factor, the percentage of seats with passengers in them. Airlines facing financial difficulties or bankruptcy may be forced to abandon aircraft as part of their restructuring or liquidation efforts. This can happen when the cost of maintaining and operating the aircraft becomes unsustainable for financially troubled carriers. Older aircraft models may become technologically obsolete as newer models with advanced features, improved fuel efficiency, and enhanced safety measures enter the market. According to Boeing, the MAX 8 has a range of 3,550 nautical miles, while the NG's range is 3,060 nautical miles. This increased range is due to a combination of factors, including the increased fuel efficiency and the use of advanced materials in the construction of the aircraft. Airlines may choose to abandon older aircraft in favor of more modern options. On the Airbus aircraft, fuel efficiency improves by some 14–17% on the NEO fleet compared with the CEO fleet.

Abandoned aircraft and plane graveyards exist across the world, from the plane boneyard of Davis-Monthan Air Force Base,[16] Arizona, in the United States to Rinkaby military airfield in Sweden. The largest graveyard for commercial passenger jets in the United States is Mojave Air and Space Port, California. Most of the airplanes that sit in deserted graveyards today date from the Vietnam era or later. They are divided into four categories, depending on their prospects.

Roughly 1,000 planes are preserved for possibly flying again; about 2,000 are maintained for spare parts; about 3,000 are kept in near-ready-to-fly condition; and around 4,000 are destined for future use in museums.

Example 14.7

Jet Aviation Company (JAC) is planning to abandon its only landing gear manufacturing company that is currently in operations. It is June 2024, and JAC plans to continue using the factory until June 30, 2025. The factory, acquired 15 years ago for $100 million, was initially assigned a 20-year estimated useful life, and $5 million in salvage value was estimated. Because of its commitment to a plan to abandon the factory, JAC reduced the factory's estimated remaining useful life from six years to one and will account for the change in estimate in accordance with the policy. Thus, the factory's carrying value of $15.7 million at June 30, 2025, will be depreciated over the next year such that its carrying value will equal $1 million.

Example 14.8

DirectJet purchased an old DC-9 for $36,000,000 and recognizes $3,000,000 of depreciation per year over the following 12 years. After 10 years, the aircraft is not only fully depreciated and because of very high oil prices, it is ready for retirement. DirectJet gives away the aircraft for free and records the following entry:

	Debit	*Credit*
Aircraft		$36,000,000
Accumulated depreciation	$30,000,000	
Loss on aircraft disposal	$6,000,000	

Now assume DirectJet disposes of its $36,000,000 aircraft but does so after six years and sells it for $22,000,000 in cash. In this case, it has already recorded $18,000,000 of depreciation expense. The entry is:

	Debit	*Credit*
Aircraft		$36,000,000
Cash	$22,000,000	$ 4,000,000
Accumulated depreciation	$18,000,000	
Gain on aircraft disposal		

What if DirectJet Airlines had sold the machine for $15,000,000 instead of $22,000,000? Then there would be a loss of $3,000,000 on the sale. The entry would be:

	Debit	*Credit*
Aircraft		$36,000,000
Cash	$15,000,000	
Accumulated depreciation	$18,000,000	
Loss on aircraft disposal	$3,000,000	

The asset write-offs should be recorded as soon after the disposal of an asset as possible because otherwise, the accumulated depreciation and balance sheet will be overstated.

Summary

Depreciation, abandonment, and impairment are important concepts in engineering economics and finance, each serving specific purposes and providing valuable information about the financial health and management of assets within a business. Depreciation is a methodology to allocate the entire cost of depreciable assets to the operating expense for a series of periods. Generally, the depreciation expense is derived by initially estimating both the useful life and the perceived fair market value of the asset at the end of its estimated useful life (residual value). Furthermore, depreciation is the tax deduction given to recover the cost of investments over the tax life of the project. Some international airlines have flexibility in deciding on the effective useful life of their aircraft and their residual value. By decreasing the estimated residual value and reducing the estimated useful life of an asset, companies prospectively record a higher depreciation expense on its income statement. The most common methods of depreciation include straight line, sum-of-years digits, double declining balance, and the Modified Accelerated Cost Recovery System.

Impairment in engineering economics refers to a decrease in the value of an asset on a company's balance sheet. This decrease can occur for reasons such as changes in market conditions, technological obsolescence, regulatory changes, or adverse events affecting the asset's utility or future cash flows. Impairment accounting ensures that assets are not carried at more than their recoverable amount, leading to more accurate financial reporting and maintaining stakeholder trust. Regular impairment testing and reporting comply with standards like International Financial Reporting Standards or Generally Accepted Accounting Principles, ensuring regulatory compliance and financial reporting integrity. Major aircraft lessor Avolon recorded a first-quarter impairment of $304 million to cover the full financial impact of having 10 jets still stuck in Russia following European Union sanctions that forced the termination of all Russian leases.

Proper handling of abandoned assets most of the time is regulated by authorities to ensure compliance with safety, environmental, and industry standards. Failure to comply may result in prosecution and fines. Overall, aircraft abandonment is a complex issue influenced by a combination of economic, regulatory, technological, and environmental factors. In many cases, the decision to abandon an aircraft involves weighing the costs and benefits associated with continued operation, maintenance, or disposal, considering the specific circumstances and objectives of the aircraft owner or operator.

Discussion Questions and Problems

14.1 Explain the concept and the rationale of depreciation.

14.2 Define salvage value or residual cost.

14.3 What is meant by residual value? Could any company suffer from loss of residual value?

14.4 What is the difference between market value and residual value?

14.5 Identify the factors involved in depreciation.

14.6 Flight Services, a provider of maintenance services to commercial airlines, purchased equipment for $1,000,000 with an estimated useful life of three years and a residual value of $5,000. Using straight-line depreciation, complete this table for Flight Services.

Year	*Year-beginning book value*	*Depreciation*	*Accumulated*	*Year-end*
2017	$1,000,000			
2018				
2019				$100,000

14.7 Jet Aviation has purchased a push truck for $1,000,000 a machine that Jet Aviation estimates will have a useful life of five years and a residual value of $46,565. Jet Aviation uses DDB depreciation. Complete this table.

Year	*Year-Beginning Book Value*	*Depreciation Expense*	*Accumulated Depreciation*	*Year-End Book Value*
2022				
2023				
2024				
2025				
2026				
2027				

Next, prepare the adjusting journal entry to record 2022 depreciation expense.

14.8 In January 2024, Jet Aviation purchased a push truck for $1,000,000 that was estimated to have a useful life of five years and a residual value of $100,000. Jet Aviation uses SYD depreciation. Complete the following table.

Year	*Year-beginning book value*	*Depreciation rate*	*Depreciation Expense*	*Accumulated Depreciation*	*Year-end book value*
2024					
2025					
2026					
2027					
2028					

14.9 DirectJet purchased an aircraft simulator to train their new pilots for $800,000, and the simulator is expected to last for seven years; at the end of the seven years, it is expected to have salvage value of $800,000. Use the straight-line method of depreciation to calculate the annual depreciation.

14.10 Air Service Avionic is planning to add a new product to its line. To manufacture this product, the company needs to buy a new machine for $484,000 with an expected five-year life and $15,700 salvage value. All sales are for cash, and all costs are out of pocket except for depreciation on the new machine. Additional information includes the following:

- Expected annual sales of new product $1,870,000,
- Expected annual costs of new product
- Direct materials 455,000
- Direct labor 673,000
- Overhead excluding straight-line depreciation on new machine 337,000
- Selling and administrative expenses 157,000
- Income taxes 34%.

Calculate straight-line depreciation for each year of this new machine's life.

14.11 What is accelerated depreciation using the units of production (units of service) method?

14.12 DirectJet purchased equipment as follows on January 1, 2025:

Cost	$120,000,000
Salvage (residual) value	$ 2,000,000
Estimated life	5 years
Estimated units of production	1,000 units

Complete the following depreciation schedules.

Given the cost information regarding DirectJet's equipment purchase, assume the company uses double declining balance and complete this table:

Year	Calculations	Depreciation Expense	Accumulated Depreciation	End-of-year Book Value
2026	__________	__________	__________	__________
2027	__________	__________	__________	__________

Next, assume DirectJet uses 150% declining balance (1.5 × straight-line rate) and complete this table:

Year	Calculations	Depreciation Expense	Accumulated Depreciation	End-of-year Book Value
2026	__________	__________	__________	__________
2027	__________	__________	__________	__________

Next, assume DirectJet uses sum-of-years digits:

Depreciation		Accumulated	End-of-year	
Year	Calculations	Expense	Depreciation	Book Value
2026	__________	__________	__________	__________
2027	__________	__________	__________	__________

Finally, assume DirectJet uses the straight-line method:

Depreciation		Accumulated	End-of-year	
Year	Calculations	Expense	Depreciation	Book Value
2026	__________	__________	__________	__________
2027	__________	__________	__________	__________

14.13 Assume that an aircraft has a historical cost of \$50,000,000, with an estimated useful life of 25 years, and was 60% depreciated when it was discovered that the haul had structural problem. The estimated cost for maintenance and overhaul is \$10,000,000. The estimated current cost to replace the building is \$75,0000,000. The aircraft is still going to be used. Calculate the impairment value of the aircraft.

14.14 EZjET Airways recently hired a new manager for its struggling finance division. The manager was given responsibility for operating the airline more profitably. A fixed asset with a useful life of three years is purchased on January 1, 2025. Cost of the asset is \$5,000,000, whereas its residual value is expected to be \$1,250,000. Calculate depreciation expense for the years ending December 30, 2025, and December 30, 2026.

Notes

1 *Gulf Digital News*, November 9, 2015.
2 IRS Pub 946.
3 IRS Pub 946.
4 IRS Pub 946.
5 Also known as net income per share.
6 Overview of airline industry depreciation policies. Center for financial research and analysis. December 1999.
7 IRS Pub 946.
8 IRS Pub 946, 2014.
9 Boeing Company Information, September 2015.
10 Eaton's Aerospace Case History Airbus A380 Aircraft, September 2010.
11 How Does an Airline Decide a Plane Is Too Old To Fly? *International Business Times*, March 24, 2015.

12 Southwest to Unload AirTran's Boeing 717s with Delta Leases. *Bloomberg Business*, May 12, 2012.
13 Hoover, S. (2015, July). *Special Report: Uncovering Abandoned Oil and Natural Gas Wells.*
14 Dubai Expats Abandon Cars at Airport Car Park. *The Sunday Times*, February 2009.
15 Rosen, E. (2015, September). *Ghost Airports: Unfinished, Abandoned or Forgotten.*
16 At Davis-Monthan Air Force Base in Arizona, over 4,400 scraped fighter aircraft, bombers, transports, helicopters, and attack jets are kept.

References

Ginnow, A. & Milorad, N. (1985). *Abandonment, Corpus Juris Secundum*. St. Paul, MN, USA: West Publishing.

International Accounting Standards Board (2008). *International Accounting Standard 36 – Impairment of Assets*. London: IASB.

International Accounting Standards Board (2010). *The Conceptual Framework for Financial Reporting*. London: IASB.

Kimmel, D., Weygandt, J. & Kieso, E. (2009). *Accounting Tools for Business Decision Making* (3rd Edition). John Wiley & Sons.

15 Fundamentals of Decision Theory

All business decisions involve some degree of risk, and there is no guarantee of a positive outcome. Decision-making in the air transport industry is a multifaceted process influenced by operational efficiency, financial performance, competitiveness, and the overall experience for both airlines and passengers. Market competition is heavily influenced by decisions on pricing strategies, service quality, and innovative offerings. Fleet management decisions, including the size and composition of aircraft, have implications for operational efficiency, fuel consumption, and maintenance costs. Decisions related to customer experience and innovation, including in-flight services and entertainment, play a vital role in enhancing customer satisfaction and loyalty. Delta Air Lines has undertaken strategic decisions aimed at enhancing customer experience within the air transport industry. Recognizing the importance of customer satisfaction and loyalty, Delta has made pivotal choices across various facets of its operations.

Most business failures, or the lack of corporate success, can be attributed to poorly made decisions without proper evaluation of the future outcomes. The decision by Airbus to produce the A380, while ambitious, has widely been viewed as a strategic blunder for several reasons. The demand for air transportation shifted toward more direct flights, leading to a reduced need for such large-capacity aircraft. In addition, the A380 faced a declining market because of global events such as the economic recession and the COVID-19 pandemic.

Understanding decision theory can help managers make better decisions. The decision to build a new aircraft, develop a new jet engine, or to construct a mega airport begins years before the first phase happens. In 1956, the British government began research into a supersonic aircraft for commercial services (Hooks et al., 2009). The high fuel consumption created a significant price premium for the Concorde's success. The aircraft became very expensive to operate and as a result did not gain interest among airline companies.

The Arab oil embargo of 1973 created a steep rise in fuel prices, and the Concorde looked less attractive: While carrying a full load, Concorde achieved 15.8 passenger miles per gallon (PMPG) of fuel, while the Boeing 747 got 46.4 PMPG; the Boeing 707, 33.3 PMPG; and the McDonnell Douglas DC-10, 53.6 PMPG.[1] The Concorde failed to gain support among the traveling public, and the 2003 decommissioning of the Concorde represented the end of supersonic commercial transport.[2] The 737 MAX, an upgraded version of Boeing's best-selling 737 aircraft, was introduced to compete with Airbus's A320neo, offering improved fuel efficiency and performance. The financial failure of the Boeing 737 MAX represents a significant and complex chapter in aircraft manufacturing, marked by a series of grave technical, managerial, and regulatory missteps. The 737 MAX was grounded worldwide in March 2019, leading to a cascade of financial repercussions for Boeing.[3] This chapter gives a basic idea of how this happended and

DOI: 10.4324/9781003469759-15

provides a critical review of modern decision-making by analyzing selected decision-making environments.

Introduction

As the industry continues to undergo transformative changes, decision-makers in air transport industry play a pivotal role in shaping the future of aviation, balancing innovation, sustainability, and operational effectiveness for the benefit of passengers and stakeholders alike. Even with proven technology, a well-developed capital market, and a highly capable labor force, the air transport industry is continually faced with numerous risks and uncertainty.

Managers often must make decisions when many critical factors are evolving or unknown. For instance, the decision to build a new aircraft must be made in the absence of critical information on demand, air traffic growth, potential mechanical problems, fuel cost, political issues, and the competitive forces of the market. Decision theory is a step toward understanding those conditions.

Decision theory is interpreted in the form of decision analysis, which shows how best to acquire and understand information before planning. For example, in the early 2000s, Boeing faced a strategic decision regarding the design and materials for its new long-range, fuel-efficient aircraft. The company opted for a revolutionary approach by incorporating a significant number of composite materials, such as carbon-fiber-reinforced composites, in the Dreamliner.

The development of the Airbus A380 is another significant example of decision-making in the transport aircraft industry. Airbus faced the challenge of designing an ultra-large, long-range aircraft that could meet the increasing demand for air travel, particularly in the high-capacity, long-haul market. As the aviation industry shifted toward more fuel-efficient twin-engine aircraft, the A380 faced challenges in terms of operating costs and adaptability to changing market preferences. In 2019, Airbus announced the discontinuation of the A380 program, reflecting the evolving landscape of the aviation industry and the company's strategic decision to focus on more fuel-efficient and economically viable aircraft models.

Decisions in the air transport industry are inherently complex, involving a variety of risk and uncertainties. One of the main challenges stems from the long development cycles of aircraft, spanning years from conceptualization to market entry. In total, the development cycle of a commercial aircraft can take approximately 10 to 15 years or even longer, depending on the specific circumstances and challenges encountered during the process. Technological advancements, regulatory changes, and evolving market dynamics introduce uncertainties that can impact the feasibility and success of a particular aircraft program.

Decision-Making

Decision-making is the process of making selections by setting objectives, collecting data, and evaluating potential outcomes. To make a good decision, a manager must evaluate all the potential positives and negatives of each option and consider all conceivable opportunities. Decision-making requires comprehensive knowledge of the subject, transparency of judgement, communication skills, firmness of decision, and successful execution. The practical application of decision-making is aimed at finding tools, methodologies, and software to help business managers make the best decisions. Effective decision-making involves a systematic process that includes several key steps. Initially, it requires the recognition and identification of the problem or challenge at hand. This step involves a thorough understanding of the situation, acknowledging the factors contributing to the issue. Following this, decision-makers must define clear objectives, outlining what they aim to achieve through their choices. This step serves as a guiding framework for evaluating potential alternatives.

- Recognize and identify the problem.

  The first step in decision-making is recognizing that a problem exists. It's crucial to clearly define the problem and understand its nature before moving on to the next steps in the decision-making process.

  For example, an aircraft manufacturer may acknowledge the existing aircraft models faces significant safety issues. This recognition sets the stage for the decision-making process, prompting the manufacturer to explore alternatives and potential solutions to enhance safety.

  The safety concerns related to the Boeing 737 MAX series arose following two tragic accidents: Lion Air Flight 610 in October 2018 and Ethiopian Airlines Flight 302 in March 2019.[4] Both incidents involved the newly introduced Boeing 737 MAX aircraft and led to significant scrutiny and the subsequent grounding of the entire MAX fleet worldwide. Boeing implemented software updates, revised pilot training programs, and enhanced safety features to address the identified issues. The 737 MAX was gradually reintroduced to service after regulatory approvals and comprehensive reviews.
- Define the objectives

  The goal or objective can be an overall purpose of a business initiative or a special project. For example, the primary objective for international strategic alliances in the airline industry is to access the foreign markets, and to benefit from the economies of scale resulting from an increased scope of operations. Airline alliances are marketing, financial, and operational collaborations between two or more airlines. Many airlines have been able to reduce costs by sharing facilities and services, aircraft maintenance, and ground handling in airline alliances.[5]

  Boeing for many years held a monopoly position in very large aircraft with its 747. Airbus didn't have any airplanes to compete with the 747s, and that is why Airbus was motivated to enter this new segment. The primary objective of Airbus in producing large aircraft to compete with the Boeing 747 was to tap into the high-capacity, long-haul market and provide a competitive alternative to Boeing's iconic jumbo jet. Airbus aimed to meet the growing demand for air travel and the increasing need for larger, more efficient aircraft capable of carrying a substantial number of passengers over long distances.[6] While the A380 faced challenges and ultimately did not achieve the anticipated level of success, Airbus's objective in producing large aircraft reflected a strategic response to market demands and competition, with the aim of offering airlines a compelling solution for their long-haul, high-capacity needs.
- Collect the needed data and information

  To make a good decision, we need to collect and gather credible and reliable data. To perform successful decision-making in the aviation industry, various data are required. In the air transport industry, data are sourced from a variety of channels to support strategic decision-making. These sources provide valuable insights into market trends, operational efficiency, safety, customer preferences, and more. The industry employs various methods to collect data that support strategic decision-making. In engineering decision-making, in addition to the following sources, a major source of useful data is in the company's own financial and operational data.

  - Airline for America (A4A)
  - Airline Monitor

- Airports Council International (ACI)
- Air Transport Intelligence
- Bureau of Economic Analysis (BEA)
- Bureau of Transportation Statistics
- Euro-control
- Federal Aviation Administration (FAA)
- International Air Transport Association (IATA)
- International Civil Aviation Organization (ICAO)
- Official Airline Guide
- Organization for Economic Cooperation and Development (OECD)
- Security and Exchange Committee (SEC)
- Transport Canada (TC)
- The Aircraft Owners and Pilots Association
- UK Civil Aviation Authority (CAA)
- US Department of Transportation (DOT)

- Identify and evaluate different alternatives.

  Project managers should regularly evaluate the projects based on their profitability and effectiveness. For example, the airline recognizes the need to update its fleet to meet evolving industry standards, enhance operational efficiency, and address environmental concerns related to fuel consumption. Aircraft manufacturers explore different production strategies before making an investment decision. For example, to develop Airbus A320neo and Boeing 737 MAX series, which are known for their fuel-efficient engines and advanced technologies, manufacturers evaluated many different scenarios. Evaluation criteria included fuel efficiency, range, passenger capacity, maintenance costs, and compatibility with existing infrastructure.
- Implement and follow up on the solution

  After alternatives have been evaluated, the next step is to decide which alternatives are the most acceptable to the company. In response to the need for a streamlined and modernized check-in process, airlines identified a solution: mobile check-in systems. With the objective of improving operational efficiency and enhancing the passenger experience, airlines collected data on passenger preferences and technology adoption trends. The chosen alternative, mobile check-in, was introduced through user-friendly mobile apps and backend system updates. Following implementation, airlines diligently followed up on the solution's effectiveness by monitoring metrics such as user adoption rates, reductions in check-in counter queues, and overall customer satisfaction. This follow-up phase allowed for a thorough evaluation of the impact and facilitated adjustments and improvements based on passenger feedback.

Decision Trees

Decision trees are valuable tools in various domains, including data analysis, machine learning, finance, and business, offering a comprehensive and intuitive approach to understanding and analyzing multifaceted decision-making processes. A decision tree is a graphical tool that uses branching to illustrate a sequential decision process; it describes the decisions to be made, the events that may occur, and the outcomes associated with combinations of decisions and events. A decision tree serves as a powerful visual representation of decision-making processes, organized in a tree-like structure with distinct nodes and branches. These decision nodes branch into chance nodes, representing uncertain events or random outcomes, and outcome nodes, where the results are presented. The branches connecting nodes illustrate the flow of decisions and potential outcomes, providing a clear and systematic depiction of complex decision scenarios. Probabilities are assigned to the events, and respective values are determined for each outcome. The primary objective of a decision tree is to determine the best decisions. Decision trees provide a highly effective structure within which a decision-maker can lay out options and investigate the possible outcomes of choosing those options (Berger, 1985). A balanced picture of the risks and rewards associated with each possible course of action can also be neatly studied.

A decision tree is a graphical representation of a decision-making process, typically used in engineering economics, operations research, and management. It is structured like a tree, with nodes representing decision points, branches representing possible alternatives or outcomes, and leaves representing final decisions or outcomes. Decision trees can be applied in aircraft manufacturing in various ways to optimize processes, improve decision-making, and enhance efficiency.

Example 15.1

Assume that DirectJet has only one seat left in its flight between Philadelphia and Orlando airports. The airline's goal is to make as much as it possibly can from that single seat. DirectJet can either sell the seat now at \$350 or take the chance of selling the seat between now and the date of departure at \$650. DirectJet's dilemma is that if it sets the price at \$650, it has a chance of selling the seat, or the seat may go unsold. On the other hand, if the airline sells the seat at \$350, it loses the opportunity to sell it at \$650, an opportunity cost of \$650 – \$350 = \$300.

The key to determining which situation DirectJet must choose is the actual likelihood of selling the ticket at the higher price. In our scenario, the probability of selling the discounted ticket at \$350 is 100%, and the probability of selling the full price ticket at \$650 is 50%. This of course means that there is also a 50% chance that the ticket will not be sold at the full price. To decide, the expected revenue needs to be calculated. The expected revenue is calculated by simply multiplying the probability of selling the ticket by the ticket price. This process provides expected revenue of \$350 for the discounted ticket and expected revenue of \$325 for the full price ticket; therefore, the discounted ticket should be sold. Figure 15.1 presents DirectJet's decision tree for [].
Decision trees comprise nodes and branches, which we next describe in detail.

Nodes

There are three types of nodes in decision trees: square, round, and terminal. Square nodes are decision nodes, points where choices are to be made. All the possible choices or alternatives

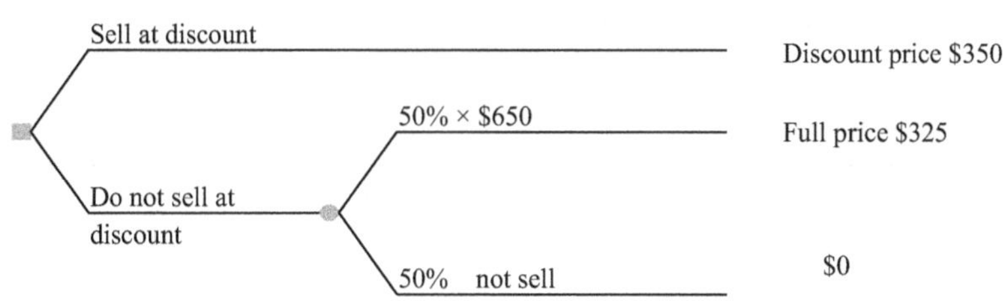

Figure 15.1 Decision tree.

arising from a square node must be mutually exclusive and collectively exhaustive[7]. Round nodes are event nodes, points where an uncertainty is resolved. The round nodes are where the decision-maker learns about the occurrence of an event. Similar to choices arising from a square node, all the possible choices arising from an event node also must be mutually exclusive and collectively exhaustive. An event node is sometimes called a chance node. Each event is assigned a subjective probability, and it is ensured that the sum of all the probabilities is 1. The third node is a terminal node, which represents the result of a combination of decisions and events. Terminal nodes are the endpoints of a decision tree. They are denoted by a triangle or vertical bar on computer-generated diagrams.

Branches

The two types of branches in a decision tree are decision and event branches. Decision branches are the branches extending from the decision nodes, with each branch representing one possible course of action available at that point. Event branches extend from event nodes, and each branch represents one of the possible events that could occur at that point. A major understanding of decision tree components is that the decision nodes and branches represent the controllable factors in a decision problem, while the event nodes and branches represent the uncontrollable factors (see Table 15.1).

Example 15.2

FunJet is a British jet engine manufacturer. The company discovers that a general aviation aircraft manufacturer wants to develop a highly efficient fuel injector for a proposed new jet engine. Because the manufacturers do not have enough research personnel available to develop the new fuel injectors, it will subcontract the development to an independent research firm. The aircraft manufacturers have offered a fixed fee of $250,000 for the best proposal for developing the new fuel injectors. The contract will go to the firm with the best technical plan and the highest reputation for technical competence. FunJet wants to enter the competition.

Management estimates a moderate cost of $50,000 for preparing a proposal, but they are concerned that they may not win the contract. If Funjet decides to prepare a proposal, and if they win the contract, their engineers are not sure about how they will develop the fuel injectors. They are considering three alternative approaches. The first approach is a very expensive mechanical method, and the engineers are certain they can develop a successful model with this approach. The mechanical approach is estimated to cost them $120,000. A second approach involves electronic components. The engineers think that the electronic approach is relatively inexpensive, costing around $50,000 for developing a model of the proposed fuel injectors, but they are not sure that the results will be satisfactory for the contract. A third inexpensive approach uses magnetic components. The magnetic method costs $80,000, which is more than the electronic method, and the engineers think that it has a higher chance of success. Funjet

Table 15.1 Nodes and Branches

Type of Node	*Written Symbol*	*Computer Symbol*	*Node Successor*
Decision	Square	Square	Decision branches
Event	Circle	Circle	Event branches
Terminal	Endpoint	Triangle or vertical bar	Terminal value

Research can work on only one approach at a time and has time to try only two approaches. If it tries either the magnetic or electronic method and the attempt fails, the second choice must be the mechanical method to guarantee a successful model. Create an example decision tree. Figure 15.2 shows the decision tree for this example incorporating all the values associated with each choice or event.

Terminal value (TV) is calculated by determining the sum of all previous choices and events, which led to one terminal node. For example, consider the terminal node that follows electronic failure. The terminal value is obtained by the summing all the previous expenses or rewards, incurred or gained, to reach that result.

$$\text{TV at Electronic Failure} = -\$50{,}000 + \$250{,}000 - \$50{,}000 - \$120{,}000 = \$30{,}000$$

Now consider the various probabilities associated with a certain decision to predict the expected values for the decisions. FunJet management thinks there is a fifty-fifty chance of winning the contract. The engineers think that the inexpensive electronic method has only a 50% chance of satisfactory results; in their opinion, the somewhat more costly magnetic method has a 70% chance of success.

Expected value is the weighted average of the terminal values, which are determined by multiplying the respective probabilities with the terminal values. The expected value for the electronic method is given by:

$$\text{EV}\left(\text{electronic method}\right) = 0.5 \times \$150{,}000 + 0.5 \times \$30{,}000$$
$$\text{EV}\left(\text{electronic method}\right) = \$90{,}000$$

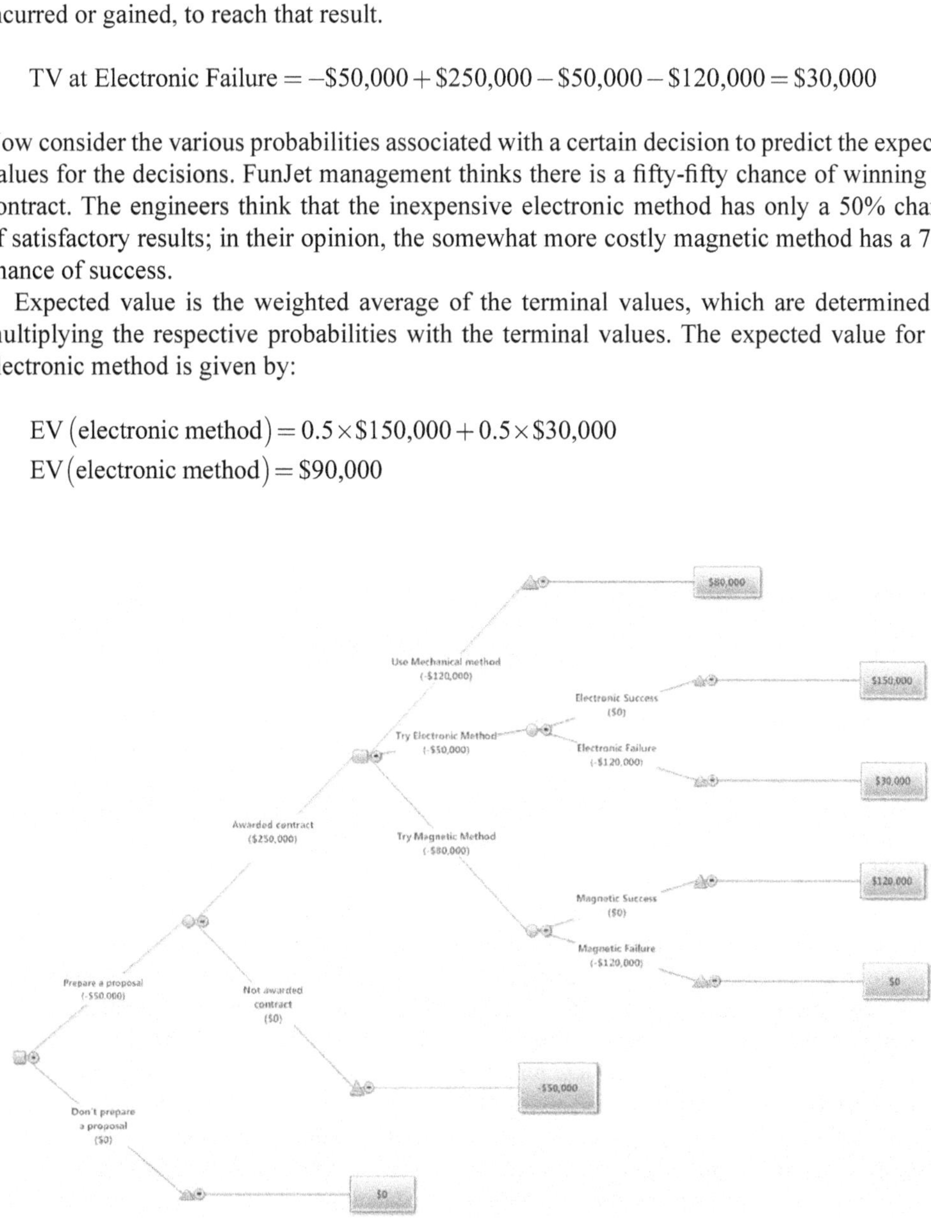

Figure 15.2 Decision tree with terminal values.

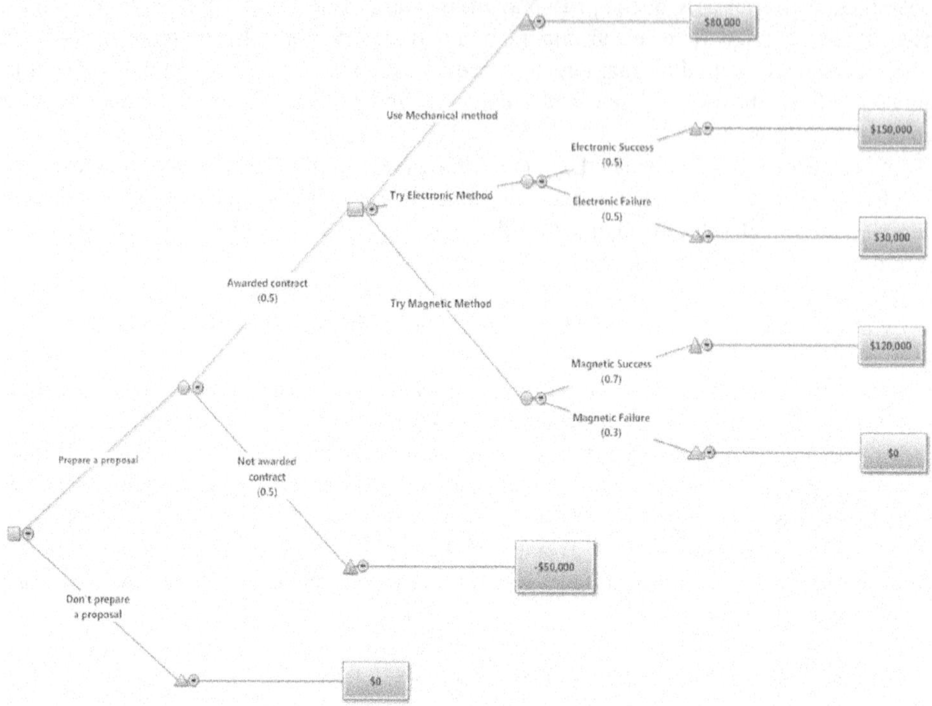

Figure 15.3 Decision tree with probabilities and terminal values (complete tree).

The expected value for the magnetic method is given by:

$$EV(\text{magnetic method}) = 0.7 \times \$120{,}000 + 0.3 \times \$0 = \$84{,}000$$

The expected value for the use of mechanical method is directly the terminal value, $80,000. Because the expected value for the electronic method is highest, the best decision at that node would be to choose the electronic method.

Decision Environment

A decision environment is defined as the collection of information, alternatives, values, and preferences available at the time of the decision. An extensive body of literature has also recognized the importance of decision-making in aviation, with the focus predominantly on airlines and airframe manufacturers. The decisions of aviation management are very much affected by these other players. An ideal decision environment would include all available information, as accurate as possible, at every plausible alternative. Managing uncertainty in decision-making relies on identifying, quantifying, and analyzing the factors that can affect outcomes.

However, there are two major constraints involved in gaining information or identifying alternatives: namely, time constraint and effort constraint. The time constraint implies that a decision must be made by a certain time. The effort constraint reflects the limits of manpower, money, and priorities. Because decisions must be made within this constrained environment, the major challenge of decision-making is uncertainty, and a major goal of decision analysis is

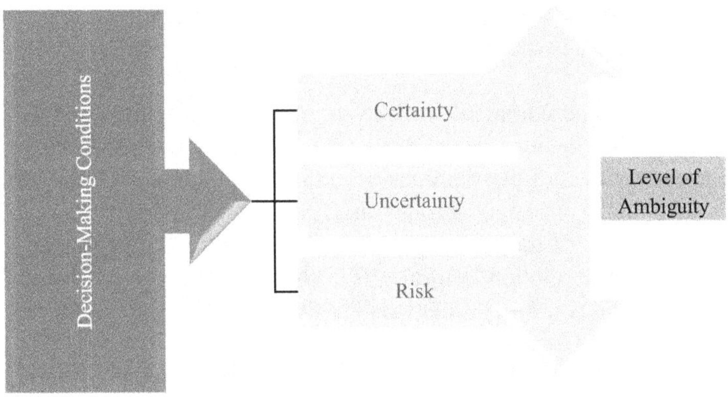

Figure 15.4 The decision-making environment.

to reduce uncertainty. We can almost never have all the information needed to make a decision with certainty, so most decisions involve an undeniable risk and uncertainty. There are three types of environments in which decisions are made: decisions under certainty, decisions under uncertainty, and decisions under risk. We next discuss each in detail.

Decisions under Certainty

> *A decision under certainty is the one in which a decision maker knows with certainty which state of event will occur. In such case, there is no uncertainty or risk involved, and the decision-maker can easily determine which alternative will lead to the desired outcome. Nonetheless, it's important to note that decisions under certainty are relatively rare in real-world situations, and decision-makers often face different degrees of risk and uncertainty.*

Decision-making under certainty refers to a situation where the decision-maker has complete and accurate information about the outcomes of different alternatives. For example, an airline is deciding where to purchase fuel for its fleet of aircraft. The airline may have detailed information on fuel prices, quality, and discounts offered by different suppliers. With certainty about the condition of each aircraft, the fleet manager can plan maintenance schedules to minimize downtime and avoid unexpected breakdowns. The decision is based on accurate knowledge of the maintenance needs of each aircraft. In the above examples, decision-making under certainty enables the decision-maker to analyze and compare alternatives without the need for probabilistic assessments or dealing with unknown variables.

For example, assume a fleet manager deciding when to schedule maintenance for a set of cargo aircraft, where decision-making is under certainty. The manager has precise information on each aircraft's utilization, historical maintenance records, and the expected wear and tear over time. Let's say aircraft A requires maintenance after 10,000 miles with an associated cost of \$50,000, while aircraft B needs maintenance after 8,000 miles with a cost of \$45,000. Under certainty, the decision is straightforward. The fleet manager can compare the exact maintenance requirements and costs for each aircraft and make an informed decision. In this case, aircraft B incurs a lower maintenance cost and requires service at an earlier mileage, making it the optimal choice for scheduling maintenance. The certainty in information enables the fleet manager to efficiently plan maintenance schedules, minimizing downtime and ensuring the fleet's reliable performance.

It is very difficult to find complete certainty in most business decisions. However, almost complete certainty can be noticed in many routine types of decisions. Decisions made under certainty are generally of very little significance to the success of a particular business.

Decision-making under certainty implies that the future state is certain. (This generally means that the probability of the desired future occurrence is 1.0, and all other future events have zero probability). The solution, naturally, is to choose the alternative that gives us the most favorable outcome. Although, many situations are extremely complex, requiring sophisticated mathematical techniques to find the best solution.

One common technique for decision-making under certainty is called linear programming. In this method, a desired outcome (such as profit) can be expressed as a mathematical function (the objective function) of several variables. The solution obtained from the linear programming is in the form of independent variables, also known as decision variables, which serve to maximize the outcome or, in some cases, minimize the cost, subject to certain limits (constraints). There are two major ways to solve a linear programming model, namely, the graphical method and the computer method, which makes use of specific software.

An example for decisions under certainty could be investing in a saving account, buying a certificate of deposit (CD) or the purchase of short-term government bonds, because the payoff for all is insured and guaranteed.

Decisions under Uncertainty

In an environment of uncertainty, multiple events can occur, and the decision-maker has no knowledge or control over which event is likely to take place. Such situations typically arise when the occurrence of the event is determined by external factors. For example, demand for the product, alterations by competitors, etc. are the factors that involve uncertainty. Resource allocation for crew scheduling, aircraft maintenance, and ground operations involves significant uncertainty, requiring effective management to ensure smooth operations. Under uncertainty, the scope to assign probabilities to the events are extremely minimal as well, ensuring that decisions made in this environment are highly volatile. Decision-making under uncertainty is critically important in the aviation industry due to the high stakes involved in safety, financial performance, and operational efficiency. The aviation sector is inherently unpredictable, influenced by a range of factors such as weather conditions, mechanical failures, fluctuating fuel prices, regulatory changes, and geopolitical events. Operational efficiency in aviation is also heavily impacted by uncertainty. Flight planning must account for variables such as weather forecasts, air traffic congestion, and potential delays to optimize routes, reduce fuel consumption, and minimize disruptions.

Under uncertainty, the decision maker has no knowledge of current conditions, or the risks associated with each future outcome. Business decision-making is almost always accompanied by conditions of uncertainty. The air transport industry is constantly evolving with advancements in technology, such as new aircraft models, communication systems, and navigation technologies. Decisions regarding alternative fuel, fleet modernization and technology adoption need to consider uncertainties in technological developments.

In certain situations, a decision maker cannot assess the probability of occurrence for the various future states of nature. Uncertainty occurs when there exists more than one future state of nature but the probabilities of each of the states occurring are not known. The decision maker is forced to choose among several possible approaches for making the decision, because there is no concrete way of arriving at a conclusion. The development of new engine technologies to address climate change introduces several uncertainties in the aviation industry, affecting everything from infrastructure and costs to technological feasibility and regulatory landscapes. Technological feasibility is a primary concern, with many new engine technologies still in experimental or early development stages.

Measuring uncertainty involves assessing the degree of unpredictability or lack of information about a particular situation, event, or outcome.

Example 15.3

To explain the types of decision-making under uncertainty, consider the payoff table for DirectJet Airlines against FunJet Airlines, depicting the payoffs DirectJet is expected to receive based on the pricing behavior of both the airlines. The payoff table is as follows (Table 15.2) and each section describes the various types of decisions which could be made. A payoff matrix is a simplified representation that shows the possible payouts to each airline based on each potential outcome. The two airlines want to decide whether to increase the price, cut the price or keep the same price. The number in each cell is the payoff (profits) to DirectJet Airline when both airlines start a new pricing policy. For example, if both airlines decide to increase the ticket prices, DirectJet makes $12,000,000 profit. If both airlines opt for cutting the price (lower right-hand quadrant) DirectJet loses $5,000,000. Since DirectJet and FunJet are choosing their price levels at the same time, they are unable to detect beforehand the decision of the other.

The types of decisions made under uncertainty are primarily based on attitudes toward risk.

The Optimistic Approach (Maximax)

Maximax principle suggests the player choose the strategy that yields the best of the best possible outcomes. The assumption is that only the best possible scenarios will occur and only the large payoffs are considered, thereby ignoring all the probabilities. The possible outcomes are normally presented in a table format called payoff table. A payoff table consists of columns and rows. Major airlines operate under conditions of oligopoly, where strategy is very important. Because of competition from FunJet Airways, DirectJet has been forced to offer discount flights.

Table 15.2 DirectJet Payoff Table

Funjet	*Pricing Behavior*		
	DirectJet		
	Increase	*Keep it the same*	*Cut*
Increase Price	$12,000,000	$10,000,000	$5,000,000
Keep it the Same	$2,500,000	$6,000,000	$3,000,000
Cut Price	$1,000,000	$4,000,000	−$5,000,000

Note: These values are DirectJet's estimates of profit associated with each alternative.

Under Maximax approach, the best payoff for each alternative should be identified, then the alternative with the maximum payoff is selected. In scenarios marked by uncertainty, decision-makers employing Maximax aim to maximize the potential for the best outcome. This approach aligns with the belief that the most favorable conditions or results will prevail, and decisions are made with the intention of achieving the highest potential payoff.

For example, suppose DirectJet is faced with the following pay-off table (Table 15.3). The manager must choose the pricing strategy: increase the price, keep the same price, or cut the price before he knows the actual demand. So, in this case if the manager employs this rule, he will look at the first row and picks the first course of action, and increase the price since this gives the largest possible return ($12,000,000). To summarize, the airline would optimistically assume that the competitors would raise the prices, resulting in the following maximum payoffs and decisions. For DirectJet, using Maximax criterion would mean increasing average ticket price, because that was the alternative with the highest possible payoff, $12,000,000 per year.

The Conservative Approach (Maximin)

A pessimistic decision maker chooses the conservative approach, which guarantees that the worst outcome would be "least bad". The assumption is that the worst that can happen will, and hence, a decision to choose the best worst-case scenario is made. The maximin criterion results in the maximum of the minimum payoffs. Consider the decision to expand an airline's aircraft fleet, a difficult decision influenced by market dynamics, fuel efficiency, and operational costs. Faced with uncertain economic conditions and potential fuel price fluctuations, the decision-maker adopts a maximin strategy to maximize the minimum potential return on investment. In evaluating options, purchasing smaller, more fuel-efficient aircraft (Option 1) or larger, long-haul aircraft with higher capacity (Option 2), the focus is on minimizing potential losses in adverse conditions. If economic downturns and increased fuel prices materialize, the smaller, fuel-efficient aircraft may incur fewer losses than their larger counterparts. Hence, the maximin decision leads to choosing Option 1, emphasizing flexibility and preparing for the worst-case scenario, ultimately contributing to the airline's long-term sustainability and success in the dynamic air transport industry.

Table 15.3 DirectJet Payoff Table: Maximax Approach

Funjet	*Pricing Behavior*		
	DirectJet		
	Increase	*Keep it the Same*	*Cut*
Increase Price	**$12,000,000**	$10,000,000	$5,000,000
Keep it the Same	$2,500,000	$6,000,000	$3,000,000
Cut Price	$1,000,000	$4,000,000	−$5,000,000

Note: These values are DirectJet's estimates of profit associated with each alternative.

For example, if the DirectJet management is not optimistic, the airline might select the alternative whose worst possible outcome is better than the worst possible outcome from any other alternative. Hence, under maximin criterion, DirectJet should keep the price the same because this worst outcome, $4,000,000, is better than any other alternative's worst outcome.

The Minimax Regret Approach

Another decision-maker may choose the alternative that has the smallest difference between the best and worst outcomes. Regret is considered proportional to the difference between what we get, and the better position that we could have received if a different course of action had been chosen. Regret is also referred to as opportunity cost. The minimax regret rule is derived from the behavior of individuals who spend their post decision time regretting their choices. To solve for the value, Table 15.5, showing the size of the regret, needs to be constructed. This means we need to find the biggest pay-off for each demand row, then subtract all other numbers in this row from the largest number. If the competition increased the ticket price, DirectJet will make a maximum profit of $12,000,000; if DirectJet cuts the price, the opportunity cost would be

$$\$12{,}000{,}000 - \$10{,}000{,}000 = \$2{,}000{,}000$$

Likewise, the regret value for cutting the price is $7,000,000.

If DirectJet used the minimax regret criterion, it would want to minimize that maximum regret and therefore keep the price the same.

Table 15.4 DirectJet Payoff Table: Maximin Approach

Funjet	*Pricing*		
	DirectJet		
	Increase	*Keep it the same*	*Cut*
Increase Price	$12,000,000	$10,000,000	$5,000,000
Keep it the Same	$2,500,000	$6,000,000	$3,000,000
Cut Price	$1,000,000	**$4,000,000**	−$5,000,000

Note: These values are the DirectJet' estimates of profit associated with each alternative.

Table 15.5 DirectJet Payoff Table: Opportunity Cost Table – Minimax Approach

Funjet	*Pricing Behavior*		
	DirectJet		
	Increase	*Keep it the same*	*Cut*
Increase price	$0	$2,000,000	$7,000,000
Keep it the same	$4,500,000	0	$3,000,000
Cut price	$3,000,000	$0	$9,000,000

Note: These values are DirectJet's estimates of opportunity cost associated with each alternative

Equally Likely Approach

A different type of decision maker may assume that all possible states of nature are equally likely and hence set all the probability values to 1/n, where n is the number of possible states of nature, and maximize expected value based on that assumption.

For example, if there are three possible states of nature like in the case of DirectJet and each of the possible outcomes is equally likely, then

$$P_1 = P_2 = P_3 = \frac{1}{3}$$

The equal likelihood criterion multiplies the decision payoff for each pricing behavior by an equal weight, thus assuming that the states of nature are equally likely to occur:

$$\text{Payoff}\left(\text{Increase Price}\right) = \$12,000,000 \times \frac{1}{3} + \$2,500,000 \times \frac{1}{3} + \$1,000,000 \times \frac{1}{3} = \$5,166,666.67$$

$$\text{Payoff}\left(\text{Same Price}\right) = \$10,000,000 \times \frac{1}{3} + \$6,000,000 \times \frac{1}{3} + \$4,000,000 \times \frac{1}{3} = \$6,666,666.67$$

$$\text{Payoff}\left(\text{Cut Price}\right) = \$5,000,000 \times \frac{1}{3} + \$3,000,000 \times \frac{1}{3} - \$5,000,000 \times \frac{1}{3} = \$1,000,000$$

Hence, the option of keeping the price the same is preferred under the equally likely approach because it returns the maximum expected value (Table 15.6).

Example 15.4

Consider an example of an aircraft manufacturing company, FunJet, trying to decide whether they need to research and build a new aircraft to compete in a market which is currently controlled by Airbus. The three possible decisions are don't build, research, and build the FunJet 7E7, or contract out the research and manufacturing to a third party to whom a share of the profit needs to be given. The above decisions along with the three possible market outcomes are illustrated in Table 15.7.

The three possible outcomes could be a result of a reaction from the competitor, in this case Airbus, or could even be an economic crisis or improvement in the market at the time of the launch. For example, if FunJet contracts the research and manufacturing to a third party

Table 15.6 DirectJet Payoff: Equally Likely

FunJet	*Pricing Behavior*			
	DirectJet			
	Increase	*Keep it the same*	*Cut*	*Probability*
Increase price	$12,000,000	$10,000,000	$5,000,000	(1/3)
Keep it the same	$2,500,000	$6,000,000	$3,000,000	(1/3)
Cut price	$1,000,000	$4,000,000	–$5,000,000	(1/3)
Equally likely payoff	$5,166,667	**$6,666,667**	$1,000,000	

Note: These values are DirectJet's estimates of profit associated with each alternative

Table 15.7 FunJet Example: Decision Under Uncertainty

	Small Market Claim	*Moderate Market Claim*	*Large Market Claim*
Don't build	\$0	\$0	\$0
Research and build 7E7	−\$2,000,000	\$26,000,000	\$145,000,000
Contract it to third party	\$20,000	\$12,000,000	\$70,000,000

agreeing to pay them a share of the profits, and this resulted in only a small market claim, the very small profit made would have to be shared with the third party. This implies FunJet only gets a meagre \$20,000 as profit. On the other hand, if FunJet themselves had done the research and built the aircraft, and managed only a small market claim, there would have been an overall loss of about \$2 million because the money spent on research and manufacturing would not be recovered. On the contrary, if FunJet managed a moderate or a large market claim, the profits would be considerably larger because there is no requirement to share the profits with a third party.

The decision an optimistic decision maker would make in such a situation is to use the "Maximax approach," which measures the maximum possible profit in each choice among the possible outcomes and select the maximum among the maximum profits as the best outcome to be chosen. The maximum profits are given in Table 15.8.

Hence under this approach, FunJet would choose to research and build the 7E7 by themselves.

The decision a pessimistic decision maker would make in such a situation is to use the "Maximin approach," which measures the minimum profits made in each choice among the three outcomes and selects the maximum of these minimum profits as the best possible outcome to be chosen. The minimum profits are given in Table 15.9.

Hence under this approach, FunJet would choose to contract the research and manufacturing to a third party.

A more neutral decision maker would choose to use the "equally likely approach," which assigns an equal probability for all the three outcomes in all the cases and chooses the one which gives the maximum expected value in this approach. The values obtained from the approach are illustrated in Table 15.10.

$$E_1 = \frac{-2{,}000{,}000 + 26{,}000{,}000 + 145{,}000{,}000}{3}$$

$$E_1 = \$56{,}333{,}333$$

$$E_2 = \frac{20{,}000 + 12{,}000{,}000 + 70{,}000{,}000}{3}$$

$$E_2 = \$27{,}340{,}000$$

Hence, the option of FunJet doing the research and manufacturing by themselves, gives the highest expected value of \$56,333,333, implying that the best choice in this approach is for FunJet to research and build the 7E7 themselves.

The last course of action a decision maker could take under uncertainty involves the "minimax regret approach." Regret is defined as the difference between the profit from the best alternative and the profit from the chosen alternative, given a particular outcome is fixed. Also, regret can never be negative. The maximum regrets are calculated in a separate matrix and the minimum among the maximums is chosen as the best alternative because it is the option

Table 15.8 FunJet Example: Decision Under Uncertainty – Maximax Approach

	Maximum
Research and build 7E7	**$145,000,000**
Contract it to third party	$70,000,000

Table 15.9 FunJet Example: Decision Under Uncertainty – Maximin Approach

	Minimum
Research and build 7E7	–$2,000,000
Contract it to third party	**$20,000**

Table 15.10 FunJet Example: Decision Under Uncertainty – Equally Likely Approach

	Equally likely (Expected Values)
Research and build 7E7 (E_1)	**$56,333,333**
Contract it to third party (E_2)	$27,340,000

Table 15.11 FunJet Example: Decision Under Uncertainty – Regret Analysis

	Small Market Claim	*Moderate Market Claim*	*Large Market Claim*	*Maximum Regret*
Don't build	$20,000	$26,000,000	$145,000,000	$145,000,000
Research and build 7E7	$2,020,000	$0	$0	**$2,020,000**
Contract it to third party	$0	$14,000,000	$75,000,000	$75,000,000

with the least amount of money lost. The regret analysis for the above example is shown in Table 15.11.

$$Regret = \{Profit\ from\ best\ alternative\} - \{Profit\ from\ chosen\ alternative\}$$

Among the maximum regrets, the minimum is obtained when FunJet chooses to research and build the 7E7 by themselves. Hence, using the minimax regret approach, FunJet must decide to research and build the 7E7 aircraft by itself.

Risk refers to the probability or likelihood of an adverse event or outcome occurring, along with the potential consequences or impact associated with that event. Under risk, the decision maker has some knowledge regarding probability of future outcomes. Effectively managing risk involves identifying potential threats, assessing their likelihood and potential impact, and implementing strategies to mitigate or respond to them.

Decisions under Risk

The main difference between decisions under uncertainty and decisions under risk is that the decision maker under risk has some information about the probability of the possibility of each of the possible outcomes. Under the condition of risk, there is more than one possible event that can take place.

However, the decision maker has adequate information to assign probabilities to the happening or not of each possible event. Such information is generally based on prior experience (French and Insua, 2000). Let us start with an easy question such as: what is the probability of drawing an ace from a shuffled pack of cards? Well, there are 4 aces so the probability of getting an ace would be 4/52, or 1/13. Virtually, every decision in a modern business enterprise is based on interplay of a number of factors and the risks associated with them.

The most common tool used to determine the best decision under risk is calculating the expected value. Let's examine two flight routes, A and B, each with their associated probabilities of on-time arrivals and the likelihood of weather delays. For Route A, there is an 80% chance of on-time arrival and a 20% probability of a weather delay. Conversely, Route B boasts a higher on-time arrival probability of 90% but carries a 10% risk of weather-related disruptions. The decision-maker, aiming to optimize revenue, incorporates not only the probabilities but also the potential revenue loss in case of delays.

If Route A encounters a delay, the revenue loss is $\$20,000$, whereas for Route B, it is $\$10,000$. Through expected value calculations, considering both probabilities and potential losses, Route B emerges as the more favorable choice with an expected revenue of $\$110,000$ compared to Route A's $\$96,000$:

$$EV(A) = (0.8 \times \$100,000) + (0.2 \times (\$100,000 - \$20,000)) = \$96,000$$
$$EV(B) = (0.9 \times \$120,000) + (0.1 \times (\$120,000 - \$10,000)) = \$110,000$$

Therefore, the expected revenue for Route A is $96,000, and for Route B, it is $110,000. Based on these calculations, Route B is the more favorable choice under the risk of weather-related disruptions, as it offers a higher expected revenue compared to Route A. This example underscores how decision-making under risk involves quantifying uncertainties and choosing the option with the higher expected value, navigating the complexities of the airline industry's unpredictable variables.

Example 15.5

In the Funjet example illustrated in the previous section, consider Table 15.7, with the probability of occurrence of the outcomes assigned as follows. The probability of a small market claim is assumed to be 0.6, moderate market claim to be 0.3 and large market claim to be 0.1.

It can be noted that alternative A_3 has a better value than A_1 in all the outcomes and hence A_3 can be considered dominant over A_1, thereby, eliminating A_1. The expected monetary value (EMV) for A_2 and A_3 is calculated as follows:

$$EMV_2 = (0.6 \times -2,000,000) + (0.3 \times 26,000,000) + (0.1 \times 145,000,000)$$
$$EMV_2 = \$21,100,000$$

Table 15.12 Funjet Example: Decision Under Risk

	Small market claim $P_1 = 0.6$	*Moderate market claim* $P_2 = 0.3$	*Large market claim* $P_3 = 0.1$
Don't build (A_1)	$0	$0	$0
Research and build 7E7 (A_2)	−$2,000,000	$26,000,000	$145,000,000
Contract it to third party (A_3)	$20,000	$12,000,000	$70,000,000

$$EMV_3 = (0.6 \times 20,000) + (0.3 \times 12,000,000) + (0.1 \times 70,000,000)$$
$$EMV_3 = \$10,612,000$$

Expected monetary value is the weighted average of a certain outcome based on the probabilities of occurrence of all the events. Purely based on expected monetary value, alternative A_2 is better as it has a higher expected value than A_3. Although a decision maker will choose alternative A_2 only if he/she is ready to accept the risk of losing $2,000,000.

Example 15.6

Another common meaning of risk is variability of outcome, measured by the variance or (more often) its square root, the standard deviation. Consider two investment projects, X and Y, having the discrete probability distribution of expected cash flows in each of the next several years as shown in Table 15.13.

Expected value of cash flows for X and Y are as follows:

$$E_X = (0.1 \times 7,000) + (0.2 \times 7,500) + (0.4 \times 8,000) + (0.2 \times 8,500) + (0.1 \times 9,000)$$
$$E_X = \$8,000$$
$$E_Y = (0.1 \times 6,000) + (0.25 \times 7,000) + (0.3 \times 8,000) + (0.25 \times 9,000) + (0.1 \times 10,000)$$
$$E_Y = \$8,000$$

Although both projects have the same expected cash flows, the expected values of the variances (squares of the deviations from the expected cash flows) differ as follows:

$$V_X = 0.1 \times (7,000 - 8,000)^2 + 0.2 \times (7,500 - 8,000)^2 + 0.4 \times (8,000 - 8,000)^2 + 0.2 \times (8,500 - 8,000)^2 + 0.1 \times (9,000 - 8,000)^2$$
$$V_X = 300,000$$
$$V_Y = 0.1 \times (6,000 - 8,000)^2 + 0.25 \times (7,000 - 8,000)^2 + 0.3 \times (8,000 - 8,000)^2 + 0.25 \times (9,000 - 8,000)^2 + 0.1 \times (10,000 - 8,000)^2$$
$$V_Y = 1,300,000$$

The standard deviations are square roots of the above variance values.

$$\sigma_X = 547.72$$
$$\sigma_Y = 1140.18$$

Table 15.13 Risk as Variance Example

X		*Y*	
Probability	*Cash Flow*	*Probability*	*Cash Flow*
0.10	$7,000	0.10	$6,000
0.20	$7,500	0.25	$7,000
0.40	$8,000	0.30	$8,000
0.20	$8,500	0.25	$9,000
0.10	$9,000	0.10	$10,000

Because project Y has the greater variability (whether measured in variance or in standard deviation), it must be considered to offer greater risk than does project X. Hence, it is a better option to choose project X over project Y.

The Economic Theory of Information

The economics of information is a subdivision of microeconomic theory that analyzes how information and information systems can affect economic decision-making process (Allen, 1990). Information has some special characteristics, such as easy to create but hard to trust and easy to spread but hard to control. These special characteristics (as compared with other types of goods) complicate many standard economic theories. The starting point for economic analysis is the understanding that information has economic value as it enables individuals to make choices that yield higher expected returns compared to a return obtained from a decision or choice made under the absence of information.

Trading of information is not the same as buying and selling most other goods. A number of factors are responsible to make the economics of buying and selling information different from common types of goods. Information is nonrivalrous, implying that consuming information does not exclude another entity from also consuming it. A related characteristic that alters information markets is that information has almost zero marginal cost. This means that duplicating an already existing information costs absolutely nothing or close to nothing. Also, exclusion is not a natural property of information goods. The nature of information is that if it is known, it is difficult to exclude other individuals from its use. Another factor which affects the economics of information is that the degrees of transparency exhibited by the information market are not explicably high, i.e. to evaluate the information, the information must be known, and this forces one to invest in learning it, to evaluate it.

EXPECTED VALUE OF PERFECT INFORMATION

EVPI measures the amount of benefit one can obtain from a decision if the occurrence of each state of nature is always known. The Expected Value of Perfect Information (EVPI) represents the maximum value a decision-maker could achieve if they had access to perfect and complete information before planning. Likewise, EVPI quantifies the potential improvement in decision outcomes through optimal information. EVPI gives a measure of how much an individual is willing to pay for perfect information. Consider a scenario where an aircraft manufacturing company is contemplating the launch of a new aircraft, with potential profits of \$5 billion if successful and a \$1 billion loss if the product fails. With a 50% estimated chance of success and a 50% chance of failure, the initial decision, without perfect information, yields an expected value of \$1 million. However, if the company had access to perfect information, enabling them to know the market conditions with certainty, they could make the optimal decision. In this hypothetical case, discovering favorable market conditions would result in an expected value of \$5 billion. The EVPI is then calculated as the difference between the expected value with perfect information and without perfect information, amounting to \$3 billion. This signifies the potential additional profit the company could secure by possessing perfect information before deciding to launch the new product.

It is mathematically given by the difference between the expected value with perfect information (EV|PI) and the maximum of the expected monetary values among the possible outcomes.

$$EVPI = EV \mid PI - EMV$$

EV WITH PI

EV|PI is the expected value, given the knowledge of perfect information, regarding which outcomes will provide maximum profits based on the choices made. Perfect information is said to be available when a 100% accurate prediction can be made about the future. This concept can be better explained using an example.

Example 15.7

Consider an investment decision that needs to be made between three alternatives, namely, a stock, a mutual fund or a certificate of deposit (CD). Further assume that the market has a 50% chance of increasing, a 30% chance of staying even, and a 20% chance of decreasing. If the market increases, the stock investment will earn \$1,700 and the mutual fund will earn \$1,100. If the market stays even, the stock investment will earn \$500, and the mutual fund will earn \$800. If the market decreases, the stock investment will lose \$1,000 and the mutual fund will lose \$400. The certificate of deposit will earn \$700 independent of the market fluctuation.

The first step is to calculate the expected monetary values for all the three alternatives based on the conditions provided.

$$EMV_{stock} = 0.5\times 1,700 + 0.3\times 500 + 0.2\times(-1,000)$$
$$EMV_{stock} = \$800$$
$$EMV_{MF} = 0.5\times 1,100 + 0.3\times 800 + 0.2\times(-400)$$
$$EMV_{MF} = \$710$$
$$EMV_{CD} = 0.5\times 700 + 0.3\times 700 + 0.2\times 700$$
$$EMV_{CD} = \$$$

The maximum of the calculated expected monetary values is obtained for the stock.

Hence, in this example, $EMV = \$800$

EV|PI can be calculated by assuming the maximum profit in each of the choices given the state of the market is known in advance, i.e. knowledge of perfect information is already given. Hence the maximum profit option under each market state is used to calculate the EV|PI.

$$EV|PI = 0.5\times 1,700 + 0.3\times 800 + 0.2\times 700$$
$$EV|PI = \$1,230$$

From the formula mentioned earlier:

$$EVPI = EV|PI - EMV$$
$$EVPI = 1,230 - 800$$
$$EVPI = \$430$$

The conclusion drawn from this is that if any individual is willing to purchase the perfect information regarding the direction the market will take, the cost of such an information should be less than \$430. If it is priced at anything over the EVPI, it will only result in a loss.

Assume the price for the information was \$410 and the individual purchased it. Then he would expect to make $\$1,230 - \$420 = \$810 > 800$ (EMV). Therefore, by purchasing the information, the individual was able to make \$10 more than if he hadn't purchased the information.

Suppose the price for the information was \$440 and the individual purchased it. Then he would expect to make $\$1{,}230 - \$440 = \$790 < \$800$ (EMV). Therefore, by purchasing the information, he lost \$10 when compared to not having purchased the information.

The third possibility is that the price for the information was \$430, and the individual purchased it. Then he would expect to make $\$1{,}230 - \$430 = \$800 = \$800$ (EMV). Therefore, by purchasing the information, he neither gained nor lost any money when compared to not purchasing the information.

Queueing Theory

Queueing theory is a mathematical discipline that deals with the study of waiting lines, or queues, and the dynamics of entities moving through these queues in a systematic way. Applications of queuing theory helps in planning aircraft maintenance, ground services, and reservation systems, contributing to resource optimization and improved passenger experiences throughout the aviation system.

Queuing theory, a pivotal component of operations research, finds significant applications within the air transport industry, addressing key aspects of operational efficiency and passenger services. The primary objective is to construct a model, so that queue lengths and waiting time can be predicted. Queueing theory is normally considered a branch of operations research, as the results are often used when making business decisions about the resources needed to provide a service. A queueing model has been used to predict how long a plane will wait before takeoff, how long a plane will wait before landing given runway traffic, and weather traffic. The model may help air traffic controller to minimize runway congestion. In airport check-in counters, queuing models optimize the allocation of resources to manage passenger flows during peak and off-peak times, minimizing waiting times. Security checkpoints benefit from queuing theory in designing effective screening processes, considering passenger arrival rates and service times. The boarding and deplaning procedures are enhanced through queuing models, guiding airlines to adopt optimal gate assignments and boarding methods. Baggage claim areas utilize queuing theory to determine the number of carousels and streamline baggage delivery. In flight scheduling and air traffic management, queuing theory contributes to minimizing delays and congestion, ensuring efficient use of airspace and terminals. Additionally, queuing models assist in planning aircraft maintenance, Aircraft deicing, ground services, reservation systems, and ticket counters, collectively improving resource utilization and passenger experience throughout the air transport system.:

- Aircraft deicing
- Aircraft landing queue
- Aircraft waiting for fuel
- Aircraft waiting for parts
- Airport check-in counters
- Airport security checks
- Airport boarder control and immigrations
- Baggage claim
- Passengers waiting for boarding.

The queueing theory was constructed so that the waiting time in the queue can be predicted. Queueing theory was introduced for the first time with the work of Erlang in 1909 (Post et al., 2008). Erlang's work with the Copenhagen Telephone Company is what prompted his initial foray into the field. Erlang studied the problem of determining how many telephone circuits were necessary to provide phone service that would prevent customers from waiting too long for an available circuit. In developing a solution to this problem, he began to realize that the problem of minimizing waiting time was applicable to many fields and began developing the theory further.[8]

Queues are an imminent day-to-day occurrence in a number of different places. The choice to provide too much service involves incurring excessive costs, while not providing enough service capacity causes waiting lines to become excessively long. The ultimate goal or outcome expected from queueing theory, is to achieve an economic balance between the cost of service and the cost associated with the waiting for that service. Queueing theory describes probabilistically and mathematically, the interaction between the arrival process of customers and the service provided to them to manage the system in an efficient manner.

The queueing system consists essentially of three major components:

- The source population and the customer arrival system,
- The servicing system or queue discipline, and
- The condition of the customer's exiting the system.

A detailed discussion on arrival patterns and distribution of arrivals along with some waiting line characteristics and service facility characteristics is carried out in this section.

Customer Arrivals

Customer arrivals at a service system may be drawn from a finite or an infinite population. It is important to distinguish between the two, because the analyses are based on different premises and require different treatments for an optimum solution.

A finite population refers to the limited-size customer pool that utilizes the service and, at times, forms a line. The number of units in a finite population is symbolized by N, and thus N represents the size of the population. The reason this finite classification is important is that when a customer leaves its position as a member for the population, the size of the user group is reduced by one, which reduces the probability of the next requirement of service. An example could be a set of jet engines serviced by a mechanic. The engines form a finite population as customers that require service. If one engine breaks down, the probability of another engine breaking down reduces.

An infinite population is large enough in comparison to the service system, that the population size caused by reductions or additions to the population (a customer requiring service or a serviced customer returning to the population) does not significantly affect the system probabilities. The example for an infinite population, as a modification of the engine example, would be, if there were 100 jet engines serviced by a single mechanic. In this case, the removal of one engine does not largely affect the possible breakdown of another.

Distribution of Arrivals

Waiting line formulas generally require an arrival rate (λ), or the number of units per period, arriving at a service system (such as an average of one every five minutes). A constant arrival distribution is periodic, with the same time between successive arrivals. In reality, only systems subject to machine control have a constant interval period. Variable (random) arrival distributions are more practical and common.

In the context of queueing theory, μ (mu) represents the service rate or the average rate at which entities (such as customers or passengers) are served by the system. It is the reciprocal of the average service time per entity. For example, if the average service time for processing a passenger through a security checkpoint is 30 seconds, then the service rate μ would be $\frac{1}{30\text{ seconds}}$ or approximately 2 passengers per minute.

Hence, ρ (rho) represents the utilization factor of a system. It is the ratio of the arrival rate (λ) to the service rate (μ). Mathematically, ρ is expressed as:

$$\rho = \frac{\lambda}{\mu}$$

Assume an airport security checkpoint processes passengers at an average rate of 100 per hour (¼= 100 passengers/hour). The passengers arrive at the checkpoint with an average rate of 120 per hour (λ = 120 passengers/hour).

The utilization (ρ) is calculated using the formula $\rho = \frac{\lambda}{\mu}$ resulting in ρ =1.2. This implies that the demand for security screening exceeds the checkpoint's capacity, with more passengers arriving than the system can efficiently process. A traffic intensity greater than 1 suggests a potential for congestion and increased waiting times. To optimize the system, airport authorities may need to enhance the service rate (μ) by, for instance, opening additional screening lanes or implementing measures to regulate passenger flow. Managing the traffic intensity is crucial for ensuring the effective operation of the security checkpoint and mitigating congestion challenges in the air transportation environment.

Observation of arrivals at a service facility can be done in two methods.

First, the time between successive arrivals can be calculated and analyzed to see if the times follow any kind of a statistical distribution. Usually, the time between arrivals is assumed to be exponentially distributed.

Second, a certain time length (T) can be set and the number of arrivals entering the system within T is calculated. A typical assumption is that the number of arrivals per time unit is Poisson distributed.

In the first case, when arrivals at a service facility occur in a purely random fashion, a plot of the inter-arrival times yields an **exponential distribution** (Figure 15.4). The probability function for an exponential distribution is as follows:

$$f(t) = \lambda e^{-\lambda t}$$

where λ is the mean number of arrivals per period (t).

Table 15.14 Probabilities for Exponential Distribution

t (minutes)	*Probability that the next arrival will occur in t minutes or more [f(t)]*	*Probability that the next arrival will occur in t minutes or less*
0.0	1.00	0.00
0.5	0.61	0.39
1.0	0.37	0.63
1.5	0.22	0.78
2.0	0.14	0.86

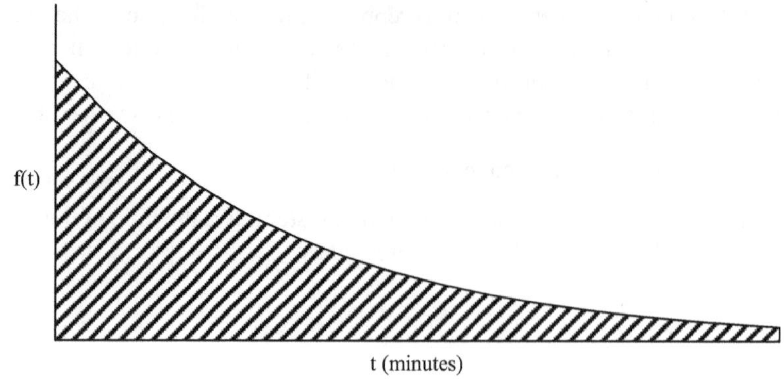

Figure 15.5 Exponential probability distribution.

The summation of the above equation over its positive range is $e^{-\lambda t}$. This integral allows us to calculate the probabilities of arrivals within a specified time. For example, for the case of single arrivals to a waiting line ($\lambda = 1$), the following table can be derived by solving $e^{-\lambda t}$.

In the second case, the number of arrivals (occurrences) during some time T is the primary consideration, and is obtained by determining the probability of exactly n arrivals (occurrences) during T. If the arrival (occurrence) process is random, the distribution is referred to as the Poisson distribution, and the formula is as follows:

$$P_T(n) = \frac{(\lambda T)^n e^{-\lambda T}}{n!}$$

where n is the number of arrivals (occurrences) in a given period T, for which the probability is to be found.

Example 15.8

The annual worldwide average number of airplane crashes of commercial airlines is 3 ($\lambda = 3$). What is the probability that exactly five accidents occur in a given year ($n = 5, T = 1$)?

$$P_1(5) = \frac{(3 \times 1)^5 e^{-3}}{5!}$$

$$P_1(5) = \frac{3^5 \times e^{-3}}{120}$$

$$P_1(5) = 2.025e^{-3}$$

$$P_1(5) = 0.101$$

That is, there is a 10.1% chance that there will be five accidents in any given year.

Hence, it can be noted that the time between arrivals (occurrences) is exponentially distributed and the number of arrivals (occurrences) per unit of time is Poisson distributed.

Another important feature of the waiting structure is the time the customer spends with the server once the service has started. Waiting line formulas generally specify service rate (μ) as the capacity of the server in number of units per period (such as 12 completions per hour).

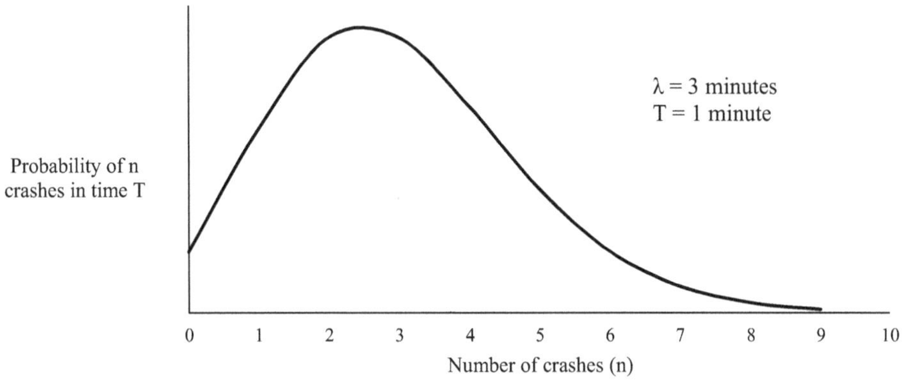

Figure 15.6 Probabilities for Poisson distribution.

A constant service time rule states that each service takes the exact same time. This characteristic is similar to constant arrivals and is generally limited to machine-controlled operations. When service times are random, they can be approximated by the exponential distribution. In this distribution, μ is referred to as the average number of units or customers that can be served per period. Arrival characteristics include arrival patterns, size of arrival units, and degree of patience.

ARRIVAL PATTERNS

The arrival pattern in the context of queuing theory refers to the distribution and timing of entities entering a queue over a period. It plays a crucial role in understanding and managing queues efficiently, particularly in settings such as customer service centers, transportation terminals, or any situation where individuals or entities form lines for service. In various settings such as customer service centers, transportation hubs, or any place where queuing is involved, understanding the arrival pattern is crucial for optimizing resource allocation, managing wait times, and enhancing overall efficiency. For example, in an airport security queue, the arrival pattern may exhibit both random arrivals of passengers entering the queue independently and scheduled arrivals of flights leading to surges in passenger arrivals. Queue management strategies, staffing levels, and operational procedures can be tailored based on a comprehensive understanding of the arrival pattern, contributing to a smoother and more efficient queuing experience.

SIZE OF ARRIVAL UNITS

A single arrival is considered to be one unit. A single arrival scenario in aviation refers to a situation where only one aircraft is arriving at an airport within a specific timeframe. In a typical airport setting, multiple arrivals occur simultaneously, with numerous flights landing and passengers arriving. A single arrival on the floor of the London Stock Exchange (LSE) is 100 shares of stock; a single arrival at an egg-processing plant might be a dozen eggs; a single arrival at a restaurant is a single person.

A batch arrival is some multiple of the unit, such as a block of 1,000 shares on the New York Stock Exchange, a case of eggs at the processing plant, or a party of five at a restaurant.

DEGREE OF PATIENCE

A patient arrival is one who waits as long as necessary until the service facility is ready to serve him or her. There are two types of impatient arrivals. Members of the first type arrive, analyze both the service facility and the length of the line, and then decide to leave. Those under the second type, arrive, view the situation, join the waiting line, and then, after some period, depart. The behavior of the first type is termed **balking**, while the second is termed **reneging**.

Waiting Line Characteristics

Waiting lines hold distinctive characteristics that are integral to the analysis and understanding of queueing systems. The physical configuration of the queue, encompassing the choice between parallel lines, a single or multiple queues, further shapes the waiting line's dynamics. Parameters like queue capacity, or when potential customers opt not to join, and customers leaving the queue prematurely add complexity.

The three important waiting line characteristics are:

- Line Length
- Number of lines
- Queue Discipline

Line Length

A line length is considered infinite if it significantly exceeds the capacity of the service system. Examples of infinite potential length are a line of vehicles stuck in traffic for miles at a certain crossing or lines around the block for theatre tickets. Parking lots, loading docks, and gas stations have limited line capacity caused by legal restrictions or physical space restrictions. These limitations complicate service system utilization, waiting line calculations, and the actual arrival distribution. A particular arrival denied entry into the waiting line because of lack of space may rejoin the population for a later try or may seek service elsewhere. Both actions can significantly affect the queue functions when there is limited capacity.

Number of Lines

The number of lines in a queueing system, as analyzed by queueing theory, is contingent upon several critical factors that collectively shape the system's dynamics. First and foremost, the arrival rate (λ) of customers or entities to the queue plays a pivotal role. Higher arrival rates often result in longer queues, necessitating consideration for the number of lines to accommodate the incoming flow. Equally significant is the service rate (μ), representing the pace at which services are provided to customers. A single line or single file refers to the existence of one line only. The term "multiple lines" refers to the single lines that form in front of two or more servers (counters) or to single lines that converge at some central redistribution point. The disadvantage of multiple lines in a busy facility is that arrivals often shift lines if several previous services have been of short duration or if those customers currently in other lines appear to require a short service time.

Queue Discipline

A queue discipline is a priority rule or set of rules for determining the order of service to customers in a waiting line. The discipline selected can have a vast effect on the system's overall performance. The number of customers in line, the range of variability in waiting time, the average waiting time and the efficiency of the service facility are just a few of the factors affected by the choice of queue discipline.

The major types of queue disciplines are as follows:

- First Come, First Served (FCFS)
- Last Come, First Served (LCFS)

FIRST COME, FIRST SERVED

The FCFS principle is commonly used at various points in the air travel process, including ticket counters, baggage drop-off, and security checkpoints, to manage the flow of passengers efficiently and provide a systematic and equitable service experience. When passengers arrive at the airport and approach the check-in area, they typically form a single queue, and the airline staff assists passengers based on their position in that queue.

The most common queue discipline followed is the first come, first served (FCFS) or first in, first out model. This rule states that customers in line are served purely on the basis of their chronological arrival. This is popularly accepted as the fairest rule, although in practice it discriminates against the arrival requiring a short service time. When checking out at a store that is using first-come, first served as a priority rule, a customer waiting behind another customer with a large number of items waits longer than a customer waiting behind a second customer with only a few items. Although processing is sequential, the wait times vary because of the preceding customer. Check-in process at the airport can be another example of first come, first served model: when no seat reservation option is available, passengers who check-in earlier get into the airplane first. However, there are some situations where the first come, first served rule does not serve as the most effective one. For example, a first come, first-served rule doesn't make sense in a hospital emergency room and in fact, could cause unnecessary deaths.

LAST COME, FIRST SERVED

Last come, first served is a queuing discipline or scheduling policy where the last item or entity to arrive is the first to be served. LCFS contrasts with the more common queuing discipline of FCFS and is not commonly applied in the air transport industry for passenger service processes.

Another major type of queue discipline is the last come, first served (LCFS) or last in, first out (LIFO) model. This rule follows a policy where, the last customer in the queue is served first. A practical example of LIFO is an elevator, where the last person entering the elevator, becomes the first person to leave it, assuming all the members get on and get off the elevator at the same floors. Similarly, at the airport passengers who get on the bus last, will be the first to board the airplane.

Reservations first, emergencies first, highest-profit customer first, largest orders first, best customers first, longest waiting time in line, and soonest promised date are other examples of service disciplines or priority rules. There are two major practical problems in using any rule or discipline: one is ensuring that customers know and follow the rule. Another is ensuring that a system exists to enable employees to manage the line.

Service Facility Characteristics

A queue maybe a single queue or a multiple queue, and the service facility can have one server, or multiple servers. A single service channel may have a single server, or multiple servers. Airport securities may have multiple lines and multiple servers. Aircraft landing at an airport with a single landing strip is an example of a single line and single server.

At busy airports there is usually a long line of aircraft descending towards a runway. If the runway is busy, the air traffic controllers would maintain the aircraft in a holding pattern awaiting their respective landings.

The most important terms associated with determining the different aspects of a single line, single server waiting line, such as, the average number of items in the system, the average time spent by an item at the server, the average number of items in the queue and the average time spent by an item in the queue are illustrated with the help of the following example.

Example 15.9

In Allen Town Regional Airport (ATR), aircraft arrive at an average rate of 20 aircraft per hour and follow a normal distribution. The runway can clear 30 aircraft per hour. Determine the following:

a. The average number of aircraft in the system (the number in the landing area plus the number of aircraft served)

$\lambda = 20$
$\mu = 30$

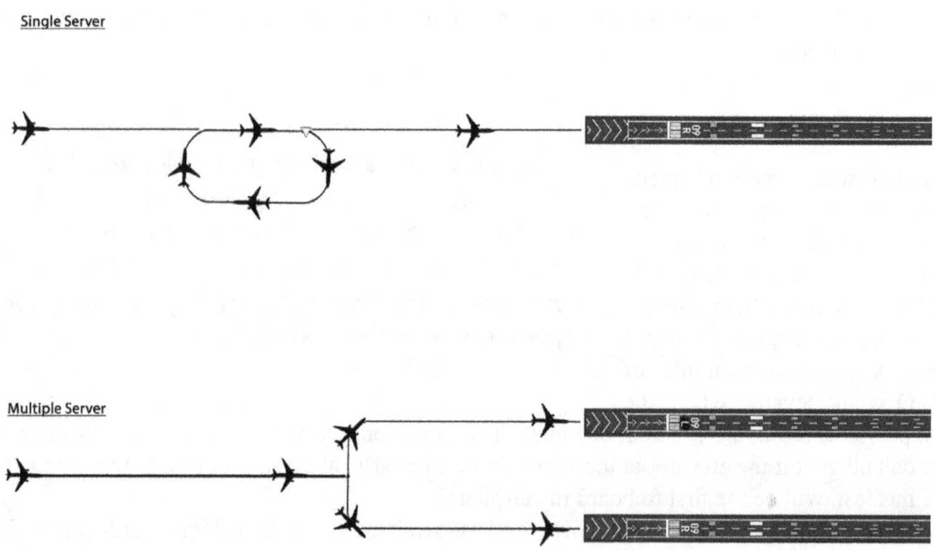

Figure 15.7 Queueing theory.

L is the number of aircraft in the system

$$L = \frac{\lambda}{\mu - \lambda}$$

$$L = \frac{20}{30 - 20}$$

$$L = 2 \text{ aircraft}$$

b. The average time an aircraft spends in the runway (W)

$$W = \frac{1}{\mu - \lambda}$$

$$W = \frac{1}{30 - 20}$$

$$W = 6 \text{ minutes}$$

c. The average number of aircraft in the queue (L_q)

$$L_q = \frac{\lambda^2}{\mu(\mu - \lambda)}$$

$$L_q = \frac{20^2}{30(30 - 20)}$$

$$L_q = 1\frac{1}{3} \text{ aircraft}$$

d. The average time an aircraft spends waiting for clearance

$$W_q = \frac{\lambda}{\mu(\mu - \lambda)}$$

$$W_q = \frac{20}{30(30 - 20)}$$

$$W_q = 4 \text{ minutes}$$

A further extension of waiting line characteristics could be the cost–benefit analysis of adding an additional server to an existing single server system, making it a multiserver system. An illustration of a similar case is presented in example 15.10.

Example 15.10

In the Allen Town Regional Airport (ATR), aircrafts requiring take-off, request for permission to the air traffic control and have to wait for conformation. Aircrafts arrive for take-off in a random (Poisson) fashion at the rate of 40 aircrafts per hour, and a single runway can accommodate take-offs at the rate of 20 per hour (exponential). If the cost to operate a new runway is assumed to be $6,000 per hour and the cost of an aircraft waiting to take-off is $12,000 per hour, determine the optimum number of runways to run the airport efficiently. (Because of the high arrival rate, an infinite source may be assumed.)

- λ = Arrival rate
- μ = Service rate

- L_q = Average number in waiting line

$$\lambda = 40$$
$$\mu = 20$$

In this case we assume the number of servers, i.e. runways to be three because two or less would mean the system is inefficient and would never be satisfied.

Given number of servers (S) equals 3, and λ/μ equals 2, L_q can be found from the table which gives the average number in waiting line for a single-queue, multiserver model.

From that table, L_q was found to be 0.8888 aircrafts waiting all through the day.

Consider a 16-hour day, at \$12,000 per hour, there is a loss of aircraft time worth,

$$0.888 \times 12{,}000 \times 16 = \$170{,}496$$

The next step is to assume the number of servers, i.e. runways to be 4 and recalculate the L_q from the table and compare the cost saved for the aircrafts by adding the runway to the cost of adding the new runway itself.

In this case, with S = 4 and $\lambda/\mu = 2$, L_q was found to be 0.1730.

Consider the same 16-hour day, the loss of aircraft time is now worth:

$$0.1730 \times 12{,}000 \times 16 = \$33{,}216$$

The amount of cost reduced, with respect to the aircraft, by adding a fourth runway would be: \$170,496 – \$33,216, which equals \$137,280.

The cost of adding a fourth runway would be $16 \times 6{,}000$ which equals \$96,000.

Hence by adding the fourth runway, the cost of operation has been saved by:

$$\$137{,}280 - \$96{,}000 = \$41{,}280 \text{ per day.}$$

Therefore, the optimum number of runways required under the given conditions, would be 4 runways.

Cost–Capacity Tradeoff

The cost–capacity tradeoff is a strategic consideration in various industries, encompassing the delicate balance between the cost of providing a service or capacity and the resulting level of capacity. Fixed costs, including infrastructure and facilities, remain constant, while variable costs, such as labor and maintenance, fluctuate with capacity. The decision to increase capacity involves higher fixed costs, requiring substantial investments in facilities and equipment. Conversely, minimizing costs may lead to operating closer to current capacity limits, risking congestion and service quality issues.

Organizations seek the optimal balance where the expense of additional capacity is justified by the benefits of meeting demand efficiently, maintaining service quality, and potentially gaining a competitive advantage. This tradeoff requires continual evaluation and strategic decision-making to align capacity with organizational goals and customer expectations across industries such as transportation, manufacturing, and service provision. It involves making strategic decisions about the optimal balance between costs and the ability to meet demand. A further extension of waiting line and service facility characteristics would be to determine the optimal service capacity that could minimize the aggregate cost (sum of waiting line cost and cost of service capacity). Consider Table 15.15 as an example to demonstrate this cost analysis.

Table 15.15 Cost–Capacity Tradeoff

Service Facility Capacity	*Waiting Line Cost*	*Cost of Service Capacity*	*Aggregate Cost*
0.0	$3,000	$ –	$3,000
0.5	$2,525	$ 60	$2,585
1.0	$2,125	$ 120	$2,245
1.5	$1,788	$ 180	$1,968
2.0	$1,505	$ 240	$1,745
2.5	$1,267	$ 300	$1,567
3.0	$1,066	$ 360	$1,426
3.5	$ 897	$ 420	$1,317
4.0	$ 755	$ 480	$1,235
4.5	$ 636	$ 540	$1,176
4.8	**$ 575**	**$ 575**	**$1,150**
5.0	$ 535	$ 600	$1,135
5.5	$ 450	$ 660	$1,110
6.0	$ 379	$ 720	$1,099
6.2	**$ 354**	**$ 744**	**$1,098**
6.5	$ 319	$ 780	$1,099
7.0	$ 268	$ 840	$1,108
7.5	$ 226	$ 900	$1,126
8.0	$ 190	$ 960	$1,150
8.5	$ 160	$1,020	$1,180
9.0	$ 135	$1,080	$1,215
9.5	$ 113	$1,140	$1,253
10.0	$ 95	$1,200	$1,295

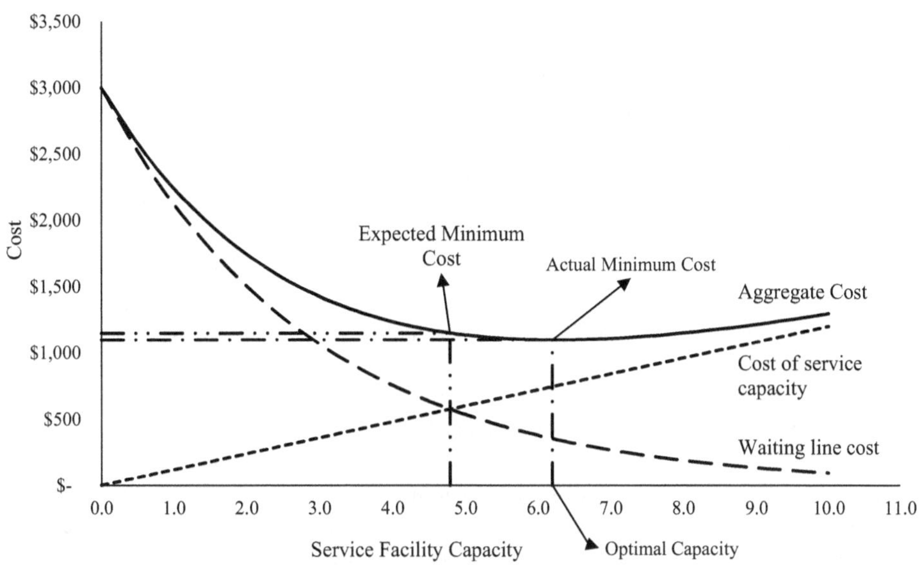

Figure 15.8 Cost vs capacity.

Traditionally, the aggregate cost is assumed to be minimum when the waiting line cost equals the cost of service capacity, although this is true only when the rate of decline in waiting line cost equals the rate of increase in service capacity costs as service capacity increases. Figure 15.8 provides a significant idea of how the trade-off balance needs to be achieved. As the number of servers increases, the cost of service capacity keeps increasing, whereas, the waiting line costs keep decreasing.

In Table 15.14, however, the waiting line cost decreases in an exponential manner while the cost of service capacity is assumed to increase linearly. In such a scenario, as can be seen from both the table and the figure, the optimal capacity is not obtained at the point where the waiting line cost equals the cost of service capacity. It is obtained at a point beyond that due to the fact that, the rate of increase in the cost of service capacity is greater than the rate of decrease in the waiting line cost and so the aggregate cost is lower than the aggregate cost obtained when the two costs are equal. The point where the aggregate cost (sum of the cost of service capacity and the waiting line cost) is found to be minimum is considered the optimal capacity. This is true for any process which utilizes a waiting line or queueing theory model.

Summary

With this chapter, we set out to introduce students and future industry managers to the decision-making environment. Decision-making and risk management are important components of the air transport industry, an industry where the margin for error is very limited. The managerial decision-making models help explain how the decision-making process is used to choose the best alternative.

Most decision-makers rely on emotions in making judgments concerning risky decisions, and the decisions are made based on the decision-maker's intuition. Intuitive decision-making is making decisions based on experience, feelings, and accumulated judgment. In this chapter, we discussed several concepts that prevail in an organization's decision-making. These include decision-making under certainty, decision-making under uncertainty, and decision-making under risk. Consider Airbus's decision to develop Airbus 380. Airbus did not have a product to compete with Boeing's 747 in very large aircraft. In the early 1990s, Airbus developed an aircraft with 500 passenger capacity and a 9,000 -mile range to compete with the Boeing 747. The aircraft cost \$25B to develop, the program has struggled to chalk up the large orders Airbus had envisioned, at \$440 *m* each. The Airbus A380 faced significant economic challenges that ultimately led to its failure to achieve anticipated success. Despite its technological advancements and impressive passenger capacity, the A380 struggled to overcome high development and production costs, making it one of the most expensive commercial aircraft programs in history. Airbus ended manufacture of the A380 in 2021, with just 252 of the 500 passenger double-deckers built. When the pandemic grounded most of the world's passenger planes, some thought it was the end of the massive jet. But post-pandemic, the A380 superjumbo is experiencing a comeback.[9]

In real-life business situations, decisions can often fail because the best alternatives are not clear at the outset, or key factors are not considered as part of the process. Examples may include the Lockheed L-1011 and Concorde. The last part of the chapter provided a brief introduction into queueing theory, a mathematical study of waiting lines or queues, the primary objective of which is to construct a model, so that the queue length and waiting time can be predicted.

Queueing theory is often used when making business decisions about the resources needed to provide a service. Queueing models were used to predict how long a plane will wait before takeoff, how long a plane will wait before landing given runway traffic, and weather traffic. The model can help air traffic controllers minimize runway congestion; aid airlines in estimating queue time and length at the airport check-in counters or at boarding; predict border control and immigration and security queue waiting time and length; and so on. The goal or outcome expected from queueing theory is to achieve an economic balance between the cost of service and the cost associated with waiting for that service. Queueing theory describes probabilistically and mathematically, the interaction between the arrival process of customers and the service provided to them for managing the system in an efficient manner.

Discussion Questions and Problems

15.1 Discuss the differences between decision-making under certainty, risk, and uncertainty and provide examples.

15.2 What is queueing theory?

15.3 Describe the basics of other decision-making techniques.

15.4 SkyJet Services operations manager believes that the probability of a favorable market is exactly the same as that of an unfavorable market: That is, each state of nature has a 0.50 chance of occurring. Can you now determine the EMV for each alternative?

Alternative	*State of Nature*	
	Favorable Market	*Unfavorable Market*
Build a large plant	$200,000	−$180,000
Build a small plant	$100	−$20,000
Do nothing	$0	$0

15.5 What is a decision tree?

15.6 What is the expected value of perfect information?

15.7 What is the expected value under certainty?

15.8 Why are the maximax and maximin strategies considered optimistic and pessimistic, respectively?

15.9 ServiceJet, Inc. is a leading business aviation services company in Hong Kong. ServiceJet offers cost effective maintenance solutions at major airports throughout the Asian Pacific area with the ability to respond quickly to the needs of customers. ServiceJet's demand has increased, aided by the growth of transportation in Asia and the Asia Pacific. To meet the demand, ServiceJet has the alternatives in the next table.

	Demand		
	Increases	*Remain the Same*	*Decreases*
Build New Plant	$122,500,000	$84,000,000	−$105,000,000
Subcontract	$63,000,000	$31,500,000	−$7,000,000
Overtime	$38,500,000	$21,000,000	−$3,500,000
Do nothing	$0	$0	$0

Given the information in the table, determine the appropriate decision under uncertainty using

a) Maximax
b) Maximin
c) Equally likely

15.10 Funjet Airline, a new low-cost airline, started operations in 2015. Funjet has entered several new markets with a new low price. Incumbents may ignore direct price competition and carry on their own strategy as they see fit, or competitors may lower prices and increase services. Funjet created a table of conditional values for the various alternatives (pricing decision) and states of nature (reactions by competitions).

15.11

	Increase the Price	*Competitive Reaction*	
		Keep the Same Price	*Reduce the Price*
Alternatives	$5,500,000	$3,000,000	($500,000)
Increase the Price	$3,500,000	$2,500,000	$1,500,000
Keep the Price Unchanged	$2,250,000	$2,000,000	$1,000,000
Reduce the Price	$0	$0	$0

If the probabilities associated with the states of nature are 0.3 for a big demand, 0.5 for an average demand, and 0.2 for a small demand, determine the alternative that provides FunJet the greatest expected monetary value.

15.12 ServiceJet is considering opening a maintenance base in Inchon International Airport. ServiceJet is faced with significant competition from the regional aircraft maintenance companies. ServiceJet can open a small shop, a large shop, or no shop at all. Because there will be a five-year lease on the building that ServiceJet is thinking about using, he wants to make sure he makes the correct decision. ServiceJet is also thinking about hiring a consulting company to conduct a study on if there is a market for his services. The results of such a study could be either favorable or unfavorable. Develop a decision tree for ServiceJet.

15.13 Geneva Airport Authorities (GAA), a private airport company, is planning on buying a regional airport for $500 million. GAA can finance the investment by borrowing the funds, with an expected annual cost of $50,000,000 to service its debt plus an additional cost of $200,000,000 per year to upgrade the airport facilities. At a contemplated landing fee of $1,000, the probabilities are 0.10, 0.50, and 0.40, respectively, that 600,000 planes, 700,000 planes, or 800,000 planes will land per year. Use a decision tree to determine GAA's optimal action given its desire to maximize expected monetary value and given the option not to make the investment at all.

Notes

1 Is this the End of the Concorde Dream? *The Telegraph*, August 16, 2000.
2 Kumar, S. *Concorde and Supersonic Civil Aviation.* ICFAI Business School Case Development Centre.
3 However, the aircraft was grounded worldwide following two tragic crashes, Lion Air in October 2018 and Ethiopian Airlines in March 2019, which together claimed 346 lives.
4 Doomed Boeing Jets Lacked 2 Safety Features that Company Sold Only as Extras. *The New York Times*, March 21, 2019.
5 Airline alliances tend to lessen competition, increase prices, and naturally helps airlines profits.
6 Norris, G. (2005, June 14). Creating a Titan. *Flight International.*
7 Only one choice can be made at a time, and all the possible choices are included.
8 Queueing Theory, Ryan Berry.
9 The Unlikely Return of the Airbus A380 Superjumbo Jet. *CNBC*, December 19, 2023.

References

Allen, B. (1990). Information as an Economic Commodity. *American Economic Review*, 80(2), 268–273.
Berger, O. (1985). *Statistical Decision Theory and Bayesian Analysis* (2nd Edition). New York: Springer-Verlag.

Chichilnisky, G. *Markets, Information, and Uncertainty*. Cambridge University Press.
French, S. & Insua, D. (2000). *Statistical Decision Theory*. New York: Oxford University Press.
Hooks, M., et al. (2009). *The Concorde Failure to Create a Breakthrough Innovation in the Aircraft Industry, the Tuck School at Dartmouth.*
North, D. W. (1968). A Tutorial Introduction to Decision Theory. *IEEE Transactions on Systems Science and Cybernetics*, 4(3).
Post, J., Gulding, J., Noonan, K., Murphy, D., Bonn, J. & Graham, M. (2008). The Modernized National Airspace System Performance Analysis Capability (NASPAC). In: Proceedings of the 26th Congress of the International Council of the Aeronautical Sciences (ICAS), Anchorage, AK.

Appendices

Appendix A

Tables of Compounding Interest Factors

The tables in Appendix A present compound interest factors at various interest rates for different periods.

Column 1	n	Periods

Columns 2–3 present precalculated values for single payment

Column 2	F/P	Future value of $1 at the end of n periods
Column 3	P/F	Present value of $1 due at the end of n periods

Columns 4–7 present pre calculated values for annuity or uniform series

Column 4	A/F	Annuity of a $1 due at the end of n period (Sinking fund)
Column 5	F/A	Future value of an annuity of $1 at the end of n periods
Column 6	A/P	Annuity of present amount of $1 over n period (Capital Recovery)
Column 7	P/A	Present value of an annuity of $1 over n periods

Columns 8–9 Present pre calculated values for arithmetic gradient series

Column 8	P/G	Present value of an arithmetic gradient series of $1 in the base period increasing by $1 per period for n periods
Column 9	A/G	Annuity or uniform series of an arithmetic gradient series of $1 in the base period increasing by $1 per period for n periods

Table A1 Compound Interest Factors: 0.25%

n	*Single Payment*		*Uniform Payment Series*				*Arithmetic Gradient*	
	F/P	*P/F*	*A/F*	*F/A*	*A/P*	*P/A*	*P/G*	*A/G*
1	1.0025	0.9975	1.00000	1.0000	1.00250	0.9975		
2	1.0050	0.9950	0.49938	2.0025	0.50188	1.9925	0.9950	0.4994
3	1.0075	0.9925	0.33250	3.0075	0.33500	2.9851	2.9801	0.9983
4	1.0100	0.9901	0.24906	4.0150	0.25156	3.9751	5.9503	1.4969
5	1.0126	0.9876	0.19900	5.0251	0.20150	4.9627	9.9007	1.9950
6	1.0151	0.9851	0.16563	6.0376	0.16813	5.9478	14.8263	2.4927
7	1.0176	0.9827	0.14179	7.0527	0.14429	6.9305	20.7223	2.9900
8	1.0202	0.9802	0.12391	8.0704	0.12641	7.9107	27.5839	3.4869
9	1.0227	0.9778	0.11000	9.0905	0.11250	8.8885	35.4061	3.9834
10	1.0253	0.9753	0.09888	10.1133	0.10138	9.8639	44.1842	4.4794

(*Continued*)

Table A.1 (Continued)

n	*Single Payment*		*Uniform Payment Series*				*Arithmetic Gradient*	
	F/P	*P/F*	*A/F*	*F/A*	*A/P*	*P/A*	*P/G*	*A/G*
11	1.0278	0.9729	0.08978	11.1385	0.09228	10.8368	53.9133	4.9750
12	1.0304	0.9705	0.08219	12.1664	0.08469	11.8073	64.5886	5.4702
13	1.0330	0.9681	0.07578	13.1968	0.07828	12.7753	76.2053	5.9650
14	1.0356	0.9656	0.07028	14.2298	0.07278	13.7410	88.7587	6.4594
15	1.0382	0.9632	0.06551	15.2654	0.06801	14.7042	102.2441	6.9534
16	1.0408	0.9608	0.06134	16.3035	0.06384	15.6650	116.6567	7.4469
17	1.0434	0.9584	0.05766	17.3443	0.06016	16.6235	131.9917	7.9401
18	1.0460	0.9561	0.05438	18.3876	0.05688	17.5795	148.2446	8.4328
19	1.0486	0.9537	0.05146	19.4336	0.05396	18.5332	165.4106	8.9251
20	1.0512	0.9513	0.04882	20.4822	0.05132	19.4845	183.4851	9.4170
21	1.0538	0.9489	0.04644	21.5334	0.04894	20.4334	202.4634	9.9085
22	1.0565	0.9466	0.04427	22.5872	0.04677	21.3800	222.3410	10.3995
23	1.0591	0.9442	0.04229	23.6437	0.04479	22.3241	243.1131	10.8901
24	1.0618	0.9418	0.04048	24.7028	0.04298	23.2660	264.7753	11.3804
25	1.0644	0.9395	0.03881	25.7646	0.04131	24.2055	287.3230	11.8702
26	1.0671	0.9371	0.03727	26.8290	0.03977	25.1426	310.7516	12.3596
27	1.0697	0.9348	0.03585	27.8961	0.03835	26.0774	335.0566	12.8485
28	1.0724	0.9325	0.03452	28.9658	0.03702	27.0099	360.2334	13.3371
29	1.0751	0.9301	0.03329	30.0382	0.03579	27.9400	386.2776	13.8252
30	1.0778	0.9278	0.03214	31.1133	0.03464	28.8679	413.1847	14.3130
35	1.0913	0.9163	0.02738	36.5292	0.02988	33.4724	560.5076	16.7454
40	1.1050	0.9050	0.02380	42.0132	0.02630	38.0199	728.7399	19.1673
45	1.1189	0.8937	0.02102	47.5661	0.02352	42.5109	917.3400	21.5789
50	1.1330	0.8826	0.01880	53.1887	0.02130	46.9462	1125.7767	23.9802
60	1.1616	0.8609	0.01547	64.6467	0.01797	55.6524	1600.0845	28.7514
75	1.2059	0.8292	0.01214	82.3792	0.01464	68.3108	2447.6069	35.8305
85	1.2364	0.8088	0.01057	94.5753	0.01307	76.4901	3097.6963	40.4980
100	1.2836	0.7790	0.00881	113.4500	0.01131	88.3825	4191.2417	47.4216
120	1.3494	0.7411	0.00716	139.7414	0.00966	103.5618	5852.1116	56.5084
150	1.4543	0.6876	0.00550	181.7243	0.00800	124.9556	8725.5833	69.8295
200	1.6477	0.6069	0.00386	259.0771	0.00636	157.2363	14341.7851	91.2117
250	1.8668	0.5357	0.00288	346.7158	0.00538	185.7284	20723.4421	111.5793
300	2.1150	0.4728	0.00224	446.0078	0.00474	210.8765	27613.5173	130.9464
350	2.3963	0.4173	0.00179	558.5029	0.00429	233.0730	34804.7642	149.3299
400	2.7149	0.3683	0.00146	685.9567	0.00396	252.6645	42131.5801	166.7491
450	3.0759	0.3251	0.00120	830.3582	0.00370	269.9566	49463.0860	183.2261

Table A2 Compound Interest Factors: 0.50%

n	*Single Payment*		*Uniform Payment Series*				*Arithmetic Gradient*	
	F/P	*P/F*	*A/F*	*F/A*	*A/P*	*P/A*	*P/G*	*A/G*
1	1.0050	0.9950	1.00000	1.0000	1.00500	0.9950		
2	1.0100	0.9901	0.49875	2.0050	0.50375	1.9851	0.9901	0.4988
3	1.0151	0.9851	0.33167	3.0150	0.33667	2.9702	2.9604	0.9967
4	1.0202	0.9802	0.24813	4.0301	0.25313	3.9505	5.9011	1.4938
5	1.0253	0.9754	0.19801	5.0503	0.20301	4.9259	9.8026	1.9900
6	1.0304	0.9705	0.16460	6.0755	0.16960	5.8964	14.6552	2.4855
7	1.0355	0.9657	0.14073	7.1059	0.14573	6.8621	20.4493	2.9801

(*Continued*)

Table A.2 (Continued)

n	Single Payment		Uniform Payment Series				Arithmetic Gradient	
	F/P	P/F	A/F	F/A	A/P	P/A	P/G	A/G
8	1.0407	0.9609	0.12283	8.1414	0.12783	7.8230	27.1755	3.4738
9	1.0459	0.9561	0.10891	9.1821	0.11391	8.7791	34.8244	3.9668
10	1.0511	0.9513	0.09777	10.2280	0.10277	9.7304	43.3865	4.4589
11	1.0564	0.9466	0.08866	11.2792	0.09366	10.6770	52.8526	4.9501
12	1.0617	0.9419	0.08107	12.3356	0.08607	11.6189	63.2136	5.4406
13	1.0670	0.9372	0.07464	13.3972	0.07964	12.5562	74.4602	5.9302
14	1.0723	0.9326	0.06914	14.4642	0.07414	13.4887	86.5835	6.4190
15	1.0777	0.9279	0.06436	15.5365	0.06936	14.4166	99.5743	6.9069
16	1.0831	0.9233	0.06019	16.6142	0.06519	15.3399	113.4238	7.3940
17	1.0885	0.9187	0.05651	17.6973	0.06151	16.2586	128.1231	7.8803
18	1.0939	0.9141	0.05323	18.7858	0.05823	17.1728	143.6634	8.3658
19	1.0994	0.9096	0.05030	19.8797	0.05530	18.0824	160.0360	8.8504
20	1.1049	0.9051	0.04767	20.9791	0.05267	18.9874	177.2322	9.3342
21	1.1104	0.9006	0.04528	22.0840	0.05028	19.8880	195.2434	9.8172
22	1.1160	0.8961	0.04311	23.1944	0.04811	20.7841	214.0611	10.2993
23	1.1216	0.8916	0.04113	24.3104	0.04613	21.6757	233.6768	10.7806
24	1.1272	0.8872	0.03932	25.4320	0.04432	22.5629	254.0820	11.2611
25	1.1328	0.8828	0.03765	26.5591	0.04265	23.4456	275.2686	11.7407
26	1.1385	0.8784	0.03611	27.6919	0.04111	24.3240	297.2281	12.2195
27	1.1442	0.8740	0.03469	28.8304	0.03969	25.1980	319.9523	12.6975
28	1.1499	0.8697	0.03336	29.9745	0.03836	26.0677	343.4332	13.1747
29	1.1556	0.8653	0.03213	31.1244	0.03713	26.9330	367.6625	13.6510
34	1.1848	0.8440	0.02706	36.9606	0.03206	31.1955	499.7583	16.0202
39	1.2147	0.8232	0.02329	42.9441	0.02829	35.3531	649.3883	18.3686
44	1.2454	0.8030	0.02038	49.0788	0.02538	39.4082	815.6087	20.6964
49	1.2768	0.7832	0.01806	55.3683	0.02306	43.3635	997.5116	23.0035
54	1.3091	0.7639	0.01618	61.8167	0.02118	47.2214	1194.2236	25.2899
59	1.3421	0.7451	0.01461	68.4279	0.01961	50.9842	1404.9048	27.5557
74	1.4464	0.6914	0.01120	89.2801	0.01620	61.7257	2112.8455	34.2296
84	1.5204	0.6577	0.00961	104.0739	0.01461	68.4530	2640.6641	38.5763
99	1.6385	0.6103	0.00783	127.6952	0.01283	77.9354	3502.6720	44.9433
119	1.8103	0.5524	0.00617	162.0690	0.01117	89.5238	4758.0988	53.1490
149	2.1025	0.4756	0.00454	220.5070	0.00954	104.8767	6801.9770	64.8569
199	2.6980	0.3706	0.00294	339.6054	0.00794	125.8718	10422.8311	82.8052
249	3.4622	0.2888	0.00203	492.4356	0.00703	142.2329	14062.5690	98.8700
299	4.4428	0.2251	0.00145	688.5512	0.00645	154.9829	17536.4663	113.1510
349	5.7011	0.1754	0.00106	940.2118	0.00606	164.9188	20740.4211	125.7614
399	7.3157	0.1367	0.00079	1263.1493	0.00579	172.6617	23624.3640	136.8246
449	9.3878	0.1065	0.00060	1677.5509	0.00560	178.6957	26173.4775	146.4696

Table A3 Compound Interest Factors: 0.75%

n	Single Payment		Uniform Payment Series				Arithmetic Gradient	
	F/P	P/F	A/F	F/A	A/P	P/A	P/G	A/G
1	1.0075	0.9926	1.00000	1.0000	1.00750	0.9926		
2	1.0151	0.9852	0.49813	2.0075	0.50563	1.9777	0.9852	0.4981
3	1.0227	0.9778	0.33085	3.0226	0.33835	2.9556	2.9408	0.9950

(Continued)

Table A.3 (Continued)

n	Single Payment		Uniform Payment Series				Arithmetic Gradient	
	F/P	P/F	A/F	F/A	A/P	P/A	P/G	A/G
4	1.0303	0.9706	0.24721	4.0452	0.25471	3.9261	5.8525	1.4907
5	1.0381	0.9633	0.19702	5.0756	0.20452	4.8894	9.7058	1.9851
6	1.0459	0.9562	0.16357	6.1136	0.17107	5.8456	14.4866	2.4782
7	1.0537	0.9490	0.13967	7.1595	0.14717	6.7946	20.1808	2.9701
8	1.0616	0.9420	0.12176	8.2132	0.12926	7.7366	26.7747	3.4608
9	1.0696	0.9350	0.10782	9.2748	0.11532	8.6716	34.2544	3.9502
10	1.0776	0.9280	0.09667	10.3443	0.10417	9.5996	42.6064	4.4384
11	1.0857	0.9211	0.08755	11.4219	0.09505	10.5207	51.8174	4.9253
12	1.0938	0.9142	0.07995	12.5076	0.08745	11.4349	61.8740	5.4110
13	1.1020	0.9074	0.07352	13.6014	0.08102	12.3423	72.7632	5.8954
14	1.1103	0.9007	0.06801	14.7034	0.07551	13.2430	84.4720	6.3786
15	1.1186	0.8940	0.06324	15.8137	0.07074	14.1370	96.9876	6.8606
16	1.1270	0.8873	0.05906	16.9323	0.06656	15.0243	110.2973	7.3413
17	1.1354	0.8807	0.05537	18.0593	0.06287	15.9050	124.3887	7.8207
18	1.1440	0.8742	0.05210	19.1947	0.05960	16.7792	139.2494	8.2989
19	1.1525	0.8676	0.04917	20.3387	0.05667	17.6468	154.8671	8.7759
20	1.1612	0.8612	0.04653	21.4912	0.05403	18.5080	171.2297	9.2516
21	1.1699	0.8548	0.04415	22.6524	0.05165	19.3628	188.3253	9.7261
22	1.1787	0.8484	0.04198	23.8223	0.04948	20.2112	206.1420	10.1994
23	1.1875	0.8421	0.04000	25.0010	0.04750	21.0533	224.6682	10.6714
24	1.1964	0.8358	0.03818	26.1885	0.04568	21.8891	243.8923	11.1422
25	1.2054	0.8296	0.03652	27.3849	0.04402	22.7188	263.8029	11.6117
26	1.2144	0.8234	0.03498	28.5903	0.04248	23.5422	284.3888	12.0800
27	1.2235	0.8173	0.03355	29.8047	0.04105	24.3595	305.6387	12.5470
28	1.2327	0.8112	0.03223	31.0282	0.03973	25.1707	327.5416	13.0128
29	1.2420	0.8052	0.03100	32.2609	0.03850	25.9759	350.0867	13.4774
30	1.2513	0.7992	0.02985	33.5029	0.03735	26.7751	373.2631	13.9407
35	1.2989	0.7699	0.02509	39.8538	0.03259	30.6827	498.2471	16.2387
40	1.3483	0.7416	0.02153	46.4465	0.02903	34.4469	637.4693	18.5058
45	1.3997	0.7145	0.01877	53.2901	0.02627	38.0732	789.7173	20.7421
50	1.4530	0.6883	0.01656	60.3943	0.02406	41.5664	953.8486	22.9476
55	1.5083	0.6630	0.01476	67.7688	0.02226	44.9316	1128.7869	25.1223
60	1.5657	0.6387	0.01326	75.4241	0.02076	48.1734	1313.5189	27.2665
75	1.7514	0.5710	0.00998	100.1833	0.01748	57.2027	1917.2225	33.5163
85	1.8873	0.5299	0.00845	118.3001	0.01595	62.6838	2352.6375	37.5318
100	2.1111	0.4737	0.00675	148.1445	0.01425	70.1746	3040.7453	43.3311
120	2.4514	0.4079	0.00517	193.5143	0.01267	78.9417	3998.5621	50.6521
150	3.0673	0.3260	0.00363	275.6419	0.01113	89.8642	5461.5366	60.7754
200	4.4567	0.2244	0.00217	460.8900	0.00967	103.4157	7805.2210	75.4743
250	6.4754	0.1544	0.00137	730.0476	0.00887	112.7424	9884.6048	87.6742
300	9.4084	0.1063	0.00089	1121.1219	0.00839	119.1616	11636.7029	97.6548
350	13.6700	0.0732	0.00059	1689.3361	0.00809	123.5796	13063.4877	105.7091
400	19.8620	0.0503	0.00040	2514.9269	0.00790	126.6203	14197.5098	112.1266

Table A4 Compound Interest Factors: 1%

n	*Single Payment*		*Uniform Payment Series*				*Arithmetic Gradient*	
	F/P	*P/F*	*A/F*	*F/A*	*A/P*	*P/A*	*P/G*	*A/G*
1	1.0100	0.9901	1.00000	1.0000	1.01000	0.9901		
2	1.0201	0.9803	0.49751	2.0100	0.50751	1.9704	0.9803	0.4975
3	1.0303	0.9706	0.33002	3.0301	0.34002	2.9410	2.9215	0.9934
4	1.0406	0.9610	0.24628	4.0604	0.25628	3.9020	5.8044	1.4876
5	1.0510	0.9515	0.19604	5.1010	0.20604	4.8534	9.6103	1.9801
6	1.0615	0.9420	0.16255	6.1520	0.17255	5.7955	14.3205	2.4710
7	1.0721	0.9327	0.13863	7.2135	0.14863	6.7282	19.9168	2.9602
8	1.0829	0.9235	0.12069	8.2857	0.13069	7.6517	26.3812	3.4478
9	1.0937	0.9143	0.10674	9.3685	0.11674	8.5660	33.6959	3.9337
10	1.1046	0.9053	0.09558	10.4622	0.10558	9.4713	41.8435	4.4179
11	1.1157	0.8963	0.08645	11.5668	0.09645	10.3676	50.8067	4.9005
12	1.1268	0.8874	0.07885	12.6825	0.08885	11.2551	60.5687	5.3815
13	1.1381	0.8787	0.07241	13.8093	0.08241	12.1337	71.1126	5.8607
14	1.1495	0.8700	0.06690	14.9474	0.07690	13.0037	82.4221	6.3384
15	1.1610	0.8613	0.06212	16.0969	0.07212	13.8651	94.4810	6.8143
16	1.1726	0.8528	0.05794	17.2579	0.06794	14.7179	107.2734	7.2886
17	1.1843	0.8444	0.05426	18.4304	0.06426	15.5623	120.7834	7.7613
18	1.1961	0.8360	0.05098	19.6147	0.06098	16.3983	134.9957	8.2323
19	1.2081	0.8277	0.04805	20.8109	0.05805	17.2260	149.8950	8.7017
20	1.2202	0.8195	0.04542	22.0190	0.05542	18.0456	165.4664	9.1694
21	1.2324	0.8114	0.04303	23.2392	0.05303	18.8570	181.6950	9.6354
22	1.2447	0.8034	0.04086	24.4716	0.05086	19.6604	198.5663	10.0998
23	1.2572	0.7954	0.03889	25.7163	0.04889	20.4558	216.0660	10.5626
24	1.2697	0.7876	0.03707	26.9735	0.04707	21.2434	234.1800	11.0237
25	1.2824	0.7798	0.03541	28.2432	0.04541	22.0232	252.8945	11.4831
26	1.2953	0.7720	0.03387	29.5256	0.04387	22.7952	272.1957	11.9409
27	1.3082	0.7644	0.03245	30.8209	0.04245	23.5596	292.0702	12.3971
28	1.3213	0.7568	0.03112	32.1291	0.04112	24.3164	312.5047	12.8516
29	1.3345	0.7493	0.02990	33.4504	0.03990	25.0658	333.4863	13.3044
34	1.4026	0.7130	0.02484	40.2577	0.03484	28.7027	446.1572	15.5441
39	1.4741	0.6784	0.02109	47.4123	0.03109	32.1630	570.6616	17.7428
44	1.5493	0.6454	0.01820	54.9318	0.02820	35.4555	705.5853	19.9006
49	1.6283	0.6141	0.01591	62.8348	0.02591	38.5881	849.6237	22.0178
54	1.7114	0.5843	0.01406	71.1410	0.02406	41.5687	1001.5743	24.0945
59	1.7987	0.5560	0.01252	79.8710	0.02252	44.4046	1160.3296	26.1308
74	2.0882	0.4789	0.00919	108.8246	0.01919	52.1129	1667.6484	32.0007
84	2.3067	0.4335	0.00765	130.6723	0.01765	56.6485	2023.3153	35.7170
99	2.6780	0.3734	0.00596	167.8033	0.01596	62.6592	2569.1743	41.0024
119	3.2677	0.3060	0.00441	226.7710	0.01441	69.3975	3298.0585	47.5241
149	4.4044	0.2270	0.00294	340.4379	0.01294	77.2953	4346.5357	56.2328
199	7.2436	0.1381	0.00160	624.3582	0.01160	86.1947	5872.2080	68.1273
249	11.9130	0.0839	0.00092	1091.3026	0.01092	91.6058	7070.4335	77.1832
299	19.5925	0.0510	0.00054	1859.2541	0.01054	94.8960	7963.5107	83.9183
349	32.2225	0.0310	0.00032	3122.2516	0.01032	96.8966	8606.5644	88.8222
399	52.9942	0.0189	0.00019	5199.4175	0.01019	98.1130	9058.3871	92.3261
449	87.1559	0.0115	0.00012	8615.5907	0.01012	98.8526	9370.0943	94.7885

Table A5 Compound Interest Factors: 1.25%

n	*Single Payment*		*Uniform Payment Series*				*Arithmetic Gradient*	
	F/P	*P/F*	*A/F*	*F/A*	*A/P*	*P/A*	*P/G*	*A/G*
1	1.0125	0.9877	1.00000	1.0000	1.01250	0.9877		
2	1.0252	0.9755	0.49689	2.0125	0.50939	1.9631	0.9755	0.4969
3	1.0380	0.9634	0.32920	3.0377	0.34170	2.9265	2.9023	0.9917
4	1.0509	0.9515	0.24536	4.0756	0.25786	3.8781	5.7569	1.4845
5	1.0641	0.9398	0.19506	5.1266	0.20756	4.8178	9.5160	1.9752
6	1.0774	0.9282	0.16153	6.1907	0.17403	5.7460	14.1569	2.4638
7	1.0909	0.9167	0.13759	7.2680	0.15009	6.6627	19.6571	2.9503
8	1.1045	0.9054	0.11963	8.3589	0.13213	7.5681	25.9949	3.4348
9	1.1183	0.8942	0.10567	9.4634	0.11817	8.4623	33.1487	3.9172
10	1.1323	0.8832	0.09450	10.5817	0.10700	9.3455	41.0973	4.3975
11	1.1464	0.8723	0.08537	11.7139	0.09787	10.2178	49.8201	4.8758
12	1.1608	0.8615	0.07776	12.8604	0.09026	11.0793	59.2967	5.3520
13	1.1753	0.8509	0.07132	14.0211	0.08382	11.9302	69.5072	5.8262
14	1.1900	0.8404	0.06581	15.1964	0.07831	12.7706	80.4320	6.2982
15	1.2048	0.8300	0.06103	16.3863	0.07353	13.6005	92.0519	6.7682
16	1.2199	0.8197	0.05685	17.5912	0.06935	14.4203	104.3481	7.2362
17	1.2351	0.8096	0.05316	18.8111	0.06566	15.2299	117.3021	7.7021
18	1.2506	0.7996	0.04988	20.0462	0.06238	16.0295	130.8958	8.1659
19	1.2662	0.7898	0.04696	21.2968	0.05946	16.8193	145.1115	8.6277
20	1.2820	0.7800	0.04432	22.5630	0.05682	17.5993	159.9316	9.0874
21	1.2981	0.7704	0.04194	23.8450	0.05444	18.3697	175.3392	9.5450
22	1.3143	0.7609	0.03977	25.1431	0.05227	19.1306	191.3174	10.0006
23	1.3307	0.7515	0.03780	26.4574	0.05030	19.8820	207.8499	10.4542
24	1.3474	0.7422	0.03599	27.7881	0.04849	20.6242	224.9204	10.9056
25	1.3642	0.7330	0.03432	29.1354	0.04682	21.3573	242.5132	11.3551
26	1.3812	0.7240	0.03279	30.4996	0.04529	22.0813	260.6128	11.8024
27	1.3985	0.7150	0.03137	31.8809	0.04387	22.7963	279.2040	12.2478
28	1.4160	0.7062	0.03005	33.2794	0.04255	23.5025	298.2719	12.6911
29	1.4337	0.6975	0.02882	34.6954	0.04132	24.2000	317.8019	13.1323
34	1.5256	0.6555	0.02378	42.0453	0.03628	27.5605	421.8920	15.3079
39	1.6233	0.6160	0.02005	49.8662	0.03255	30.7185	535.5039	17.4326
44	1.7274	0.5789	0.01719	58.1883	0.02969	33.6864	657.1130	19.5068
49	1.8380	0.5441	0.01492	67.0437	0.02742	36.4755	785.3442	21.5307
54	1.9558	0.5113	0.01308	76.4666	0.02558	39.0967	918.9588	23.5048
59	2.0812	0.4805	0.01156	86.4933	0.02406	41.5600	1056.8434	25.4293
74	2.5075	0.3988	0.00829	120.5960	0.02079	48.0951	1486.6427	30.9105
84	2.8391	0.3522	0.00680	147.1290	0.01930	51.8222	1778.8384	34.3258
99	3.4206	0.2923	0.00516	193.6517	0.01766	56.6126	2213.6565	39.1018
119	4.3854	0.2280	0.00369	270.8317	0.01619	61.7576	2769.7689	44.8490
149	6.3659	0.1571	0.00233	429.2719	0.01483	67.4330	3522.1661	52.2321
199	11.8471	0.0844	0.00115	867.7665	0.01365	73.2473	4515.9916	61.6540
249	22.0477	0.0454	0.00059	1683.8146	0.01309	76.3715	5206.2237	68.1697
299	41.0312	0.0244	0.00031	3202.4984	0.01281	78.0503	5661.0507	72.5308
349	76.3600	0.0131	0.00017	6028.8029	0.01267	78.9523	5950.5502	75.3689
399	142.1077	0.0070	0.00009	11288.6189	0.01259	79.4370	6130.3454	77.1724
449	264.4657	0.0038	0.00005	21077.2542	0.01255	79.6975	6239.9792	78.2958

Table A6 Compound Interest Factors: 1.5%

n	*Single Payment*		*Uniform Payment Series*				*Arithmetic Gradient*	
	F/P	*P/F*	*A/F*	*F/A*	*A/P*	*P/A*	*P/G*	*A/G*
1	1.0150	0.9852	1.00000	1.0000	1.01500	0.9852		
2	1.0302	0.9707	0.49628	2.0150	0.51128	1.9559	0.9707	0.4963
3	1.0457	0.9563	0.32838	3.0452	0.34338	2.9122	2.8833	0.9901
4	1.0614	0.9422	0.24444	4.0909	0.25944	3.8544	5.7098	1.4814
5	1.0773	0.9283	0.19409	5.1523	0.20909	4.7826	9.4229	1.9702
6	1.0934	0.9145	0.16053	6.2296	0.17553	5.6972	13.9956	2.4566
7	1.1098	0.9010	0.13656	7.3230	0.15156	6.5982	19.4018	2.9405
8	1.1265	0.8877	0.11858	8.4328	0.13358	7.4859	25.6157	3.4219
9	1.1434	0.8746	0.10461	9.5593	0.11961	8.3605	32.6125	3.9008
10	1.1605	0.8617	0.09343	10.7027	0.10843	9.2222	40.3675	4.3772
11	1.1779	0.8489	0.08429	11.8633	0.09929	10.0711	48.8568	4.8512
12	1.1956	0.8364	0.07668	13.0412	0.09168	10.9075	58.0571	5.3227
13	1.2136	0.8240	0.07024	14.2368	0.08524	11.7315	67.9454	5.7917
14	1.2318	0.8118	0.06472	15.4504	0.07972	12.5434	78.4994	6.2582
15	1.2502	0.7999	0.05994	16.6821	0.07494	13.3432	89.6974	6.7223
16	1.2690	0.7880	0.05577	17.9324	0.07077	14.1313	101.5178	7.1839
17	1.2880	0.7764	0.05208	19.2014	0.06708	14.9076	113.9400	7.6431
18	1.3073	0.7649	0.04881	20.4894	0.06381	15.6726	126.9435	8.0997
19	1.3270	0.7536	0.04588	21.7967	0.06088	16.4262	140.5084	8.5539
20	1.3469	0.7425	0.04325	23.1237	0.05825	17.1686	154.6154	9.0057
21	1.3671	0.7315	0.04087	24.4705	0.05587	17.9001	169.2453	9.4550
22	1.3876	0.7207	0.03870	25.8376	0.05370	18.6208	184.3798	9.9018
23	1.4084	0.7100	0.03673	27.2251	0.05173	19.3309	200.0006	10.3462
24	1.4295	0.6995	0.03492	28.6335	0.04992	20.0304	216.0901	10.7881
25	1.4509	0.6892	0.03326	30.0630	0.04826	20.7196	232.6310	11.2276
26	1.4727	0.6790	0.03173	31.5140	0.04673	21.3986	249.6065	11.6646
27	1.4948	0.6690	0.03032	32.9867	0.04532	22.0676	267.0002	12.0992
28	1.5172	0.6591	0.02900	34.4815	0.04400	22.7267	284.7958	12.5313
29	1.5400	0.6494	0.02778	35.9987	0.04278	23.3761	302.9779	12.9610
34	1.6590	0.6028	0.02276	43.9331	0.03776	26.4817	399.1607	15.0731
39	1.7872	0.5595	0.01905	52.4807	0.03405	29.3646	502.8576	17.1246
44	1.9253	0.5194	0.01621	61.6889	0.03121	32.0406	612.4955	19.1162
49	2.0741	0.4821	0.01396	71.6087	0.02896	34.5247	726.6884	21.0484
54	2.2344	0.4475	0.01215	82.2952	0.02715	36.8305	844.2184	22.9217
59	2.4071	0.4154	0.01066	93.8075	0.02566	38.9710	964.0189	24.7368
74	3.0094	0.3323	0.00746	133.9633	0.02246	44.5142	1328.3342	29.8407
84	3.4926	0.2863	0.00602	166.1726	0.02102	47.5786	1568.5140	32.9668
99	4.3665	0.2290	0.00446	224.4365	0.01946	51.3991	1915.1133	37.2597
119	5.8811	0.1700	0.00307	325.4071	0.01807	55.3309	2339.7762	42.2869
149	9.1926	0.1088	0.00183	546.1761	0.01683	59.4145	2880.3914	48.4796
199	19.3527	0.0517	0.00082	1223.5158	0.01582	63.2218	3529.2710	55.8236
249	40.7422	0.0245	0.00038	2649.4803	0.01538	65.0304	3927.9175	60.4013
299	85.7722	0.0117	0.00018	5651.4811	0.01518	65.8894	4160.2291	63.1396
349	180.5713	0.0055	0.00008	11971.4206	0.01508	66.2975	4290.9809	64.7231
399	380.1464	0.0026	0.00004	25276.4252	0.01504	66.4913	4362.7800	65.6143
449	800.3003	0.0012	0.00002	53286.6855	0.01502	66.5834	4401.4883	66.1049

Table A7 Compound Interest Factors: 1.75%

n	*Single Payment*		*Uniform Payment Series*				*Arithmetic Gradient*	
	F/P	*P/F*	*A/F*	*F/A*	*A/P*	*P/A*	*P/G*	*A/G*
1	1.0175	0.9828	1.00000	1.0000	1.01750	0.9828		
2	1.0353	0.9659	0.49566	2.0175	0.51316	1.9487	0.9659	0.4957
3	1.0534	0.9493	0.32757	3.0528	0.34507	2.8980	2.8645	0.9884
4	1.0719	0.9330	0.24353	4.1062	0.26103	3.8309	5.6633	1.4783
5	1.0906	0.9169	0.19312	5.1781	0.21062	4.7479	9.3310	1.9653
6	1.1097	0.9011	0.15952	6.2687	0.17702	5.6490	13.8367	2.4494
7	1.1291	0.8856	0.13553	7.3784	0.15303	6.5346	19.1506	2.9306
8	1.1489	0.8704	0.11754	8.5075	0.13504	7.4051	25.2435	3.4089
9	1.1690	0.8554	0.10356	9.6564	0.12106	8.2605	32.0870	3.8844
10	1.1894	0.8407	0.09238	10.8254	0.10988	9.1012	39.6535	4.3569
11	1.2103	0.8263	0.08323	12.0148	0.10073	9.9275	47.9162	4.8266
12	1.2314	0.8121	0.07561	13.2251	0.09311	10.7395	56.8489	5.2934
13	1.2530	0.7981	0.06917	14.4565	0.08667	11.5376	66.4260	5.7573
14	1.2749	0.7844	0.06366	15.7095	0.08116	12.3220	76.6227	6.2184
15	1.2972	0.7709	0.05888	16.9844	0.07638	13.0929	87.4149	6.6765
16	1.3199	0.7576	0.05470	18.2817	0.07220	13.8505	98.7792	7.1318
17	1.3430	0.7446	0.05102	19.6016	0.06852	14.5951	110.6926	7.5842
18	1.3665	0.7318	0.04774	20.9446	0.06524	15.3269	123.1328	8.0338
19	1.3904	0.7192	0.04482	22.3112	0.06232	16.0461	136.0783	8.4805
20	1.4148	0.7068	0.04219	23.7016	0.05969	16.7529	149.5080	8.9243
21	1.4395	0.6947	0.03981	25.1164	0.05731	17.4475	163.4013	9.3653
22	1.4647	0.6827	0.03766	26.5559	0.05516	18.1303	177.7385	9.8034
23	1.4904	0.6710	0.03569	28.0207	0.05319	18.8012	192.5000	10.2387
24	1.5164	0.6594	0.03389	29.5110	0.05139	19.4607	207.6671	10.6711
25	1.5430	0.6481	0.03223	31.0275	0.04973	20.1088	223.2214	11.1007
26	1.5700	0.6369	0.03070	32.5704	0.04820	20.7457	239.1451	11.5274
27	1.5975	0.6260	0.02929	34.1404	0.04679	21.3717	255.4210	11.9513
28	1.6254	0.6152	0.02798	35.7379	0.04548	21.9870	272.0321	12.3724
29	1.6539	0.6046	0.02676	37.3633	0.04426	22.5916	288.9623	12.7907
34	1.8037	0.5544	0.02177	45.9271	0.03927	25.4624	377.8567	14.8398
39	1.9672	0.5083	0.01809	55.2670	0.03559	28.0946	472.5264	16.8191
44	2.1454	0.4661	0.01528	65.4532	0.03278	30.5082	571.3980	18.7293
49	2.3398	0.4274	0.01306	76.5624	0.03056	32.7212	673.1196	20.5714
54	2.5519	0.3919	0.01128	88.6783	0.02878	34.7503	776.5351	22.3461
59	2.7831	0.3593	0.00981	101.8921	0.02731	36.6109	880.6608	24.0546
74	3.6103	0.2770	0.00670	149.1617	0.02420	41.3153	1189.6296	28.7940
84	4.2943	0.2329	0.00531	188.2450	0.02281	43.8361	1387.1584	31.6442
99	5.5707	0.1795	0.00383	261.1811	0.02133	46.8850	1663.6226	35.4830
119	7.8813	0.1269	0.00254	393.2149	0.02004	49.8924	1988.1874	39.8495
149	13.2626	0.0754	0.00143	700.7193	0.01893	52.8343	2377.1241	44.9921
199	31.5754	0.0317	0.00057	1747.1670	0.01807	55.3331	2801.7578	50.6344
249	75.1744	0.0133	0.00024	4238.5380	0.01774	56.3827	3032.5956	53.7859
299	178.9744	0.0056	0.00010	10169.9666	0.01760	56.8236	3151.5970	55.4628
349	426.1003	0.0023	0.00004	24291.4461	0.01754	57.0088	3210.8397	56.3219
399	1014.4549	0.0010	0.00002	57911.7081	0.01752	57.0865	3239.6122	56.7492
449	2415.2030	0.0004	0.00001	137954.456	0.01751	57.1192	3253.3310	56.9569

Table A8 Compound Interest Factors: 2%

n	*Single Payment*		*Uniform Payment Series*				*Arithmetic Gradient*	
	F/P	*P/F*	*A/F*	*F/A*	*A/P*	*P/A*	*P/G*	*A/G*
1	1.0200	0.9804	1.0000	1.0000	1.02000	0.9804		
2	1.0404	0.9612	0.49505	2.0200	0.51505	1.9416	0.9612	0.4950
3	1.0612	0.9423	0.32675	3.0604	0.34675	2.8839	2.8458	0.9868
4	1.0824	0.9238	0.24262	4.1216	0.26262	3.8077	5.6173	1.4752
5	1.1041	0.9057	0.19216	5.2040	0.21216	4.7135	9.2403	1.9604
6	1.1262	0.8880	0.15853	6.3081	0.17853	5.6014	13.6801	2.4423
7	1.1487	0.8706	0.13451	7.4343	0.15451	6.4720	18.9035	2.9208
8	1.1717	0.8535	0.11651	8.5830	0.13651	7.3255	24.8779	3.3961
9	1.1951	0.8368	0.10252	9.7546	0.12252	8.1622	31.5720	3.8681
10	1.2190	0.8203	0.09133	10.9497	0.11133	8.9826	38.9551	4.3367
11	1.2434	0.8043	0.08218	12.1687	0.10218	9.7868	46.9977	4.8021
12	1.2682	0.7885	0.07456	13.4121	0.09456	10.5753	55.6712	5.2642
13	1.2936	0.7730	0.06812	14.6803	0.08812	11.3484	64.9475	5.7231
14	1.3195	0.7579	0.06260	15.9739	0.08260	12.1062	74.7999	6.1786
15	1.3459	0.7430	0.05783	17.2934	0.07783	12.8493	85.2021	6.6309
16	1.3728	0.7284	0.05365	18.6393	0.07365	13.5777	96.1288	7.0799
17	1.4002	0.7142	0.04997	20.0121	0.06997	14.2919	107.5554	7.5256
18	1.4282	0.7002	0.04670	21.4123	0.06670	14.9920	119.4581	7.9681
19	1.4568	0.6864	0.04378	22.8406	0.06378	15.6785	131.8139	8.4073
20	1.4859	0.6730	0.04116	24.2974	0.06116	16.3514	144.6003	8.8433
21	1.5157	0.6598	0.03878	25.7833	0.05878	17.0112	157.7959	9.2760
22	1.5460	0.6468	0.03663	27.2990	0.05663	17.6580	171.3795	9.7055
23	1.5769	0.6342	0.03467	28.8450	0.05467	18.2922	185.3309	10.1317
24	1.6084	0.6217	0.03287	30.4219	0.05287	18.9139	199.6305	10.5547
25	1.6406	0.6095	0.03122	32.0303	0.05122	19.5235	214.2592	10.9745
26	1.6734	0.5976	0.02970	33.6709	0.04970	20.1210	229.1987	11.3910
27	1.7069	0.5859	0.02829	35.3443	0.04829	20.7069	244.4311	11.8043
28	1.7410	0.5744	0.02699	37.0512	0.04699	21.2813	259.9392	12.2145
29	1.7758	0.5631	0.02578	38.7922	0.04578	21.8444	275.7064	12.6214
34	1.9607	0.5100	0.02082	48.0338	0.04082	24.4986	357.8817	14.6083
39	2.1647	0.4619	0.01717	58.2372	0.03717	26.9026	444.3304	16.5163
44	2.3901	0.4184	0.01439	69.5027	0.03439	29.0800	533.5165	18.3465
49	2.6388	0.3790	0.01220	81.9406	0.03220	31.0521	624.1557	20.1003
54	2.9135	0.3432	0.01045	95.6731	0.03045	32.8383	715.1815	21.7789
59	3.2167	0.3109	0.00902	110.8348	0.02902	34.4561	805.7154	23.3838
74	4.3293	0.2310	0.00601	166.4625	0.02601	38.4507	1067.8814	27.7728
84	5.2773	0.1895	0.00468	213.8666	0.02468	40.5255	1230.4191	30.3616
99	7.1026	0.1408	0.00328	305.1297	0.02328	42.9603	1451.0875	33.7774
119	10.5541	0.0948	0.00209	477.7041	0.02209	45.2625	1699.3619	37.5446
149	19.1173	0.0523	0.00110	905.8629	0.02110	47.3846	1979.5279	41.7758
199	51.4558	0.0194	0.00040	2522.7891	0.02040	49.0283	2258.0447	46.0560
249	138.4978	0.0072	0.00015	6874.8883	0.02015	49.6390	2392.0560	48.1891
299	372.7789	0.0027	0.00005	18588.9465	0.02005	49.8659	2453.1894	49.1958
349	1003.3673	0.0010	0.00002	50118.3652	0.02002	49.9502	2480.1170	49.6518
399	2700.6514	0.0004	0.00001	134982.5712	0.02001	49.9815	2491.6872	49.8522
449	7269.0410	0.0001	0.00000	363402.0522	0.02000	49.9931	2496.5676	49.9382

Table A9 Compound Interest Factors: 3%

n	Single Payment		Uniform Payment Series				Arithmetic Gradient	
	F/P	P/F	A/F	F/A	A/P	P/A	P/G	A/G
1	1.0300	0.9709	1.00000	1.0000	1.03000	0.9709		
2	1.0609	0.9426	0.49261	2.0300	0.52261	1.9135	0.9426	0.4926
3	1.0927	0.9151	0.32353	3.0909	0.35353	2.8286	2.7729	0.9803
4	1.1255	0.8885	0.23903	4.1836	0.26903	3.7171	5.4383	1.4631
5	1.1593	0.8626	0.18835	5.3091	0.21835	4.5797	8.8888	1.9409
6	1.1941	0.8375	0.15460	6.4684	0.18460	5.4172	13.0762	2.4138
7	1.2299	0.8131	0.13051	7.6625	0.16051	6.2303	17.9547	2.8819
8	1.2668	0.7894	0.11246	8.8923	0.14246	7.0197	23.4806	3.3450
9	1.3048	0.7664	0.09843	10.1591	0.12843	7.7861	29.6119	3.8032
10	1.3439	0.7441	0.08723	11.4639	0.11723	8.5302	36.3088	4.2565
11	1.3842	0.7224	0.07808	12.8078	0.10808	9.2526	43.5330	4.7049
12	1.4258	0.7014	0.07046	14.1920	0.10046	9.9540	51.2482	5.1485
13	1.4685	0.6810	0.06403	15.6178	0.09403	10.6350	59.4196	5.5872
14	1.5126	0.6611	0.05853	17.0863	0.08853	11.2961	68.0141	6.0210
15	1.5580	0.6419	0.05377	18.5989	0.08377	11.9379	77.0002	6.4500
16	1.6047	0.6232	0.04961	20.1569	0.07961	12.5611	86.3477	6.8742
17	1.6528	0.6050	0.04595	21.7616	0.07595	13.1661	96.0280	7.2936
18	1.7024	0.5874	0.04271	23.4144	0.07271	13.7535	106.0137	7.7081
19	1.7535	0.5703	0.03981	25.1169	0.06981	14.3238	116.2788	8.1179
20	1.8061	0.5537	0.03722	26.8704	0.06722	14.8775	126.7987	8.5229
21	1.8603	0.5375	0.03487	28.6765	0.06487	15.4150	137.5496	8.9231
22	1.9161	0.5219	0.03275	30.5368	0.06275	15.9369	148.5094	9.3186
23	1.9736	0.5067	0.03081	32.4529	0.06081	16.4436	159.6566	9.7093
24	2.0328	0.4919	0.02905	34.4265	0.05905	16.9355	170.9711	10.0954
25	2.0938	0.4776	0.02743	36.4593	0.05743	17.4131	182.4336	10.4768
26	2.1566	0.4637	0.02594	38.5530	0.05594	17.8768	194.0260	10.8535
27	2.2213	0.4502	0.02456	40.7096	0.05456	18.3270	205.7309	11.2255
28	2.2879	0.4371	0.02329	42.9309	0.05329	18.7641	217.5320	11.5930
29	2.3566	0.4243	0.02211	45.2189	0.05211	19.1885	229.4137	11.9558
34	2.7319	0.3660	0.01732	57.7302	0.04732	21.1318	289.5437	13.7018
39	3.1670	0.3158	0.01384	72.2342	0.04384	22.8082	349.7942	15.3363
44	3.6715	0.2724	0.01123	89.0484	0.04123	24.2543	408.9972	16.8629
49	4.2562	0.2350	0.00921	108.5406	0.03921	25.5017	466.3031	18.2852
54	4.9341	0.2027	0.00763	131.1375	0.03763	26.5777	521.1157	19.6073
59	5.7200	0.1748	0.00636	157.3334	0.03636	27.5058	573.0384	20.8333
74	8.9116	0.1122	0.00379	263.7193	0.03379	29.5929	709.6359	23.9800
84	11.9764	0.0835	0.00273	365.8805	0.03273	30.5501	784.5434	25.6806
99	18.6589	0.0536	0.00170	588.6289	0.03170	31.5469	874.7028	27.7271
119	33.7000	0.0297	0.00092	1089.9996	0.03092	32.3442	960.4352	29.6942
149	81.7987	0.0122	0.00037	2693.2905	0.03037	32.9258	1036.8095	31.4892
199	358.5979	0.0028	0.00008	11919.9293	0.03008	33.2404	1089.5147	32.7768
200	369.3558	0.0027	0.00008	12278.5272	0.03008	33.2431	1090.0534	32.7904

Table A10 Compound Interest Factors: 4%

n	*Single Payment*		*Uniform Payment Series*				*Arithmetic Gradient*	
	F/P	*P/F*	*A/F*	*F/A*	*A/P*	*P/A*	*P/G*	*A/G*
1	1.0400	0.9615	1.00000	1.0000	1.04000	0.9615		
2	1.0816	0.9246	0.49020	2.0400	0.53020	1.8861	0.9246	0.4902
3	1.1249	0.8890	0.32035	3.1216	0.36035	2.7751	2.7025	0.9739
4	1.1699	0.8548	0.23549	4.2465	0.27549	3.6299	5.2670	1.4510
5	1.2167	0.8219	0.18463	5.4163	0.22463	4.4518	8.5547	1.9216
6	1.2653	0.7903	0.15076	6.6330	0.19076	5.2421	12.5062	2.3857
7	1.3159	0.7599	0.12661	7.8983	0.16661	6.0021	17.0657	2.8433
8	1.3686	0.7307	0.10853	9.2142	0.14853	6.7327	22.1806	3.2944
9	1.4233	0.7026	0.09449	10.5828	0.13449	7.4353	27.8013	3.7391
10	1.4802	0.6756	0.08329	12.0061	0.12329	8.1109	33.8814	4.1773
11	1.5395	0.6496	0.07415	13.4864	0.11415	8.7605	40.3772	4.6090
12	1.6010	0.6246	0.06655	15.0258	0.10655	9.3851	47.2477	5.0343
13	1.6651	0.6006	0.06014	16.6268	0.10014	9.9856	54.4546	5.4533
14	1.7317	0.5775	0.05467	18.2919	0.09467	10.5631	61.9618	5.8659
15	1.8009	0.5553	0.04994	20.0236	0.08994	11.1184	69.7355	6.2721
16	1.8730	0.5339	0.04582	21.8245	0.08582	11.6523	77.7441	6.6720
17	1.9479	0.5134	0.04220	23.6975	0.08220	12.1657	85.9581	7.0656
18	2.0258	0.4936	0.03899	25.6454	0.07899	12.6593	94.3498	7.4530
19	2.1068	0.4746	0.03614	27.6712	0.07614	13.1339	102.8933	7.8342
20	2.1911	0.4564	0.03358	29.7781	0.07358	13.5903	111.5647	8.2091
21	2.2788	0.4388	0.03128	31.9692	0.07128	14.0292	120.3414	8.5779
22	2.3699	0.4220	0.02920	34.2480	0.06920	14.4511	129.2024	8.9407
23	2.4647	0.4057	0.02731	36.6179	0.06731	14.8568	138.1284	9.2973
24	2.5633	0.3901	0.02559	39.0826	0.06559	15.2470	147.1012	9.6479
25	2.6658	0.3751	0.02401	41.6459	0.06401	15.6221	156.1040	9.9925
26	2.7725	0.3607	0.02257	44.3117	0.06257	15.9828	165.1212	10.3312
27	2.8834	0.3468	0.02124	47.0842	0.06124	16.3296	174.1385	10.6640
28	2.9987	0.3335	0.02001	49.9676	0.06001	16.6631	183.1424	10.9909
29	3.1187	0.3207	0.01888	52.9663	0.05888	16.9837	192.1206	11.3120
34	3.7943	0.2636	0.01431	69.8579	0.05431	18.4112	236.2607	12.8324
39	4.6164	0.2166	0.01106	90.4091	0.05106	19.5845	278.4070	14.2157
44	5.6165	0.1780	0.00866	115.4129	0.04866	20.5488	317.8700	15.4690
49	6.8333	0.1463	0.00686	145.8337	0.04686	21.3415	354.2689	16.6000
54	8.3138	0.1203	0.00547	182.8454	0.04547	21.9930	387.4436	17.6167
59	10.1150	0.0989	0.00439	227.8757	0.04439	22.5284	417.3881	18.5272
74	18.2166	0.0549	0.00232	430.4148	0.04232	23.6276	489.1348	20.7018
84	26.9650	0.0371	0.00154	649.1251	0.04154	24.0729	523.9431	21.7649
99	48.5625	0.0206	0.00084	1189.0613	0.04084	24.4852	561.1647	22.9185
119	106.4063	0.0094	0.00038	2635.1577	0.04038	24.7651	591.1674	23.8710
149	345.1180	0.0029	0.00012	8602.9489	0.04012	24.9276	612.3956	24.5670
150	358.9227	0.0028	0.00011	8948.0669	0.04011	24.9303	612.8107	24.5809

Table A11 Compound Interest Factors: 5%

n	Single Payment		Uniform Payment Series				Arithmetic Gradient	
	F/P	*P/F*	*A/F*	*F/A*	*A/P*	*P/A*	*P/G*	*A/G*
1	1.0500	0.9524	1.00000	1.0000	1.05000	0.9524		
2	1.1025	0.9070	0.48780	2.0500	0.53780	1.8594	0.9070	0.4878
3	1.1576	0.8638	0.31721	3.1525	0.36721	2.7232	2.6347	0.9675
4	1.2155	0.8227	0.23201	4.3101	0.28201	3.5460	5.1028	1.4391
5	1.2763	0.7835	0.18097	5.5256	0.23097	4.3295	8.2369	1.9025
6	1.3401	0.7462	0.14702	6.8019	0.19702	5.0757	11.9680	2.3579
7	1.4071	0.7107	0.12282	8.1420	0.17282	5.7864	16.2321	2.8052
8	1.4775	0.6768	0.10472	9.5491	0.15472	6.4632	20.9700	3.2445
9	1.5513	0.6446	0.09069	11.0266	0.14069	7.1078	26.1268	3.6758
10	1.6289	0.6139	0.07950	12.5779	0.12950	7.7217	31.6520	4.0991
11	1.7103	0.5847	0.07039	14.2068	0.12039	8.3064	37.4988	4.5144
12	1.7959	0.5568	0.06283	15.9171	0.11283	8.8633	43.6241	4.9219
13	1.8856	0.5303	0.05646	17.7130	0.10646	9.3936	49.9879	5.3215
14	1.9799	0.5051	0.05102	19.5986	0.10102	9.8986	56.5538	5.7133
15	2.0789	0.4810	0.04634	21.5786	0.09634	10.3797	63.2880	6.0973
16	2.1829	0.4581	0.04227	23.6575	0.09227	10.8378	70.1597	6.4736
17	2.2920	0.4363	0.03870	25.8404	0.08870	11.2741	77.1405	6.8423
18	2.4066	0.4155	0.03555	28.1324	0.08555	11.6896	84.2043	7.2034
19	2.5270	0.3957	0.03275	30.5390	0.08275	12.0853	91.3275	7.5569
20	2.6533	0.3769	0.03024	33.0660	0.08024	12.4622	98.4884	7.9030
21	2.7860	0.3589	0.02800	35.7193	0.07800	12.8212	105.6673	8.2416
22	2.9253	0.3418	0.02597	38.5052	0.07597	13.1630	112.8461	8.5730
23	3.0715	0.3256	0.02414	41.4305	0.07414	13.4886	120.0087	8.8971
24	3.2251	0.3101	0.02247	44.5020	0.07247	13.7986	127.1402	9.2140
25	3.3864	0.2953	0.02095	47.7271	0.07095	14.0939	134.2275	9.5238
26	3.5557	0.2812	0.01956	51.1135	0.06956	14.3752	141.2585	9.8266
27	3.7335	0.2678	0.01829	54.6691	0.06829	14.6430	148.2226	10.1224
28	3.9201	0.2551	0.01712	58.4026	0.06712	14.8981	155.1101	10.4114
29	4.1161	0.2429	0.01605	62.3227	0.06605	15.1411	161.9126	10.6936
34	5.2533	0.1904	0.01176	85.0670	0.06176	16.1929	194.4168	12.0063
39	6.7048	0.1491	0.00876	114.0950	0.05876	17.0170	224.0054	13.1636
44	8.5572	0.1169	0.00662	151.1430	0.05662	17.6628	250.4175	14.1777
49	10.9213	0.0916	0.00504	198.4267	0.05504	18.1687	273.6418	15.0611
54	13.9387	0.0717	0.00386	258.7739	0.05386	18.5651	293.8208	15.8265
59	17.7897	0.0562	0.00298	335.7940	0.05298	18.8758	311.1846	16.4859
64	22.7047	0.0440	0.00230	434.0933	0.05230	19.1191	326.0064	17.0513
69	28.9775	0.0345	0.00179	559.5510	0.05179	19.3098	338.5731	17.5337
74	36.9835	0.0270	0.00139	719.6702	0.05139	19.4592	349.1665	17.9435
79	47.2014	0.0212	0.00108	924.0274	0.05108	19.5763	358.0521	18.2901
84	60.2422	0.0166	0.00084	1184.8448	0.05084	19.6680	365.4727	18.5821
89	76.8861	0.0130	0.00066	1517.7212	0.05066	19.7399	371.6464	18.8272
94	98.1283	0.0102	0.00051	1942.5653	0.05051	19.7962	376.7651	19.0322
99	125.2393	0.0080	0.00040	2484.7859	0.05040	19.8403	380.9964	19.2032
100	131.5013	0.0076	0.00038	2610.0252	0.05038	19.8479	381.7492	19.2337

Table A12 Compound Interest Factors: 6%

n	*Single Payment*		*Uniform Payment Series*				*Arithmetic Gradient*	
	F/P	*P/F*	*A/F*	*F/A*	*A/P*	*P/A*	*P/G*	*A/G*
1	1.0600	0.9434	1.00000	1.0000	1.06000	0.9434		
2	1.1236	0.8900	0.48544	2.0600	0.54544	1.8334	0.8900	0.4854
3	1.1910	0.8396	0.31411	3.1836	0.37411	2.6730	2.5692	0.9612
4	1.2625	0.7921	0.22859	4.3746	0.28859	3.4651	4.9455	1.4272
5	1.3382	0.7473	0.17740	5.6371	0.23740	4.2124	7.9345	1.8836
6	1.4185	0.7050	0.14336	6.9753	0.20336	4.9173	11.4594	2.3304
7	1.5036	0.6651	0.11914	8.3938	0.17914	5.5824	15.4497	2.7676
8	1.5938	0.6274	0.10104	9.8975	0.16104	6.2098	19.8416	3.1952
9	1.6895	0.5919	0.08702	11.4913	0.14702	6.8017	24.5768	3.6133
10	1.7908	0.5584	0.07587	13.1808	0.13587	7.3601	29.6023	4.0220
11	1.8983	0.5268	0.06679	14.9716	0.12679	7.8869	34.8702	4.4213
12	2.0122	0.4970	0.05928	16.8699	0.11928	8.3838	40.3369	4.8113
13	2.1329	0.4688	0.05296	18.8821	0.11296	8.8527	45.9629	5.1920
14	2.2609	0.4423	0.04758	21.0151	0.10758	9.2950	51.7128	5.5635
15	2.3966	0.4173	0.04296	23.2760	0.10296	9.7122	57.5546	5.9260
16	2.5404	0.3936	0.03895	25.6725	0.09895	10.1059	63.4592	6.2794
17	2.6928	0.3714	0.03544	28.2129	0.09544	10.4773	69.4011	6.6240
18	2.8543	0.3503	0.03236	30.9057	0.09236	10.8276	75.3569	6.9597
19	3.0256	0.3305	0.02962	33.7600	0.08962	11.1581	81.3062	7.2867
20	3.2071	0.3118	0.02718	36.7856	0.08718	11.4699	87.2304	7.6051
21	3.3996	0.2942	0.02500	39.9927	0.08500	11.7641	93.1136	7.9151
22	3.6035	0.2775	0.02305	43.3923	0.08305	12.0416	98.9412	8.2166
23	3.8197	0.2618	0.02128	46.9958	0.08128	12.3034	104.7007	8.5099
24	4.0489	0.2470	0.01968	50.8156	0.07968	12.5504	110.3812	8.7951
25	4.2919	0.2330	0.01823	54.8645	0.07823	12.7834	115.9732	9.0722
26	4.5494	0.2198	0.01690	59.1564	0.07690	13.0032	121.4684	9.3414
27	4.8223	0.2074	0.01570	63.7058	0.07570	13.2105	126.8600	9.6029
28	5.1117	0.1956	0.01459	68.5281	0.07459	13.4062	132.1420	9.8568
29	5.4184	0.1846	0.01358	73.6398	0.07358	13.5907	137.3096	10.1032
34	7.2510	0.1379	0.00960	104.1838	0.06960	14.3681	161.3192	11.2276
39	9.7035	0.1031	0.00689	145.0585	0.06689	14.9491	182.1652	12.1857
44	12.9855	0.0770	0.00501	199.7580	0.06501	15.3832	199.9130	12.9956
49	17.3775	0.0575	0.00366	272.9584	0.06366	15.7076	214.7972	13.6748
54	23.2550	0.0430	0.00270	370.9170	0.06270	15.9500	227.1316	14.2402
59	31.1205	0.0321	0.00199	502.0077	0.06199	16.1311	237.2542	14.7079
64	41.6462	0.0240	0.00148	677.4367	0.06148	16.2665	245.4953	15.0921
69	55.7320	0.0179	0.00110	912.2002	0.06110	16.3676	252.1591	15.4060
74	74.5820	0.0134	0.00082	1226.3667	0.06082	16.4432	257.5167	15.6610
79	99.8075	0.0100	0.00061	1646.7924	0.06061	16.4997	261.8026	15.8671
84	133.5650	0.0075	0.00045	2209.4167	0.06045	16.5419	265.2163	16.0330
89	178.7401	0.0056	0.00034	2962.3351	0.06034	16.5734	267.9249	16.1659
94	239.1946	0.0042	0.00025	3969.9097	0.06025	16.5970	270.0667	16.2720
99	320.0963	0.0031	0.00019	5318.2718	0.06019	16.6146	271.7553	16.3564
100	339.3021	0.0029	0.00018	5638.3681	0.06018	16.6175	272.0471	16.3711

Table A13 Compound Interest Factors: 7%

n	*Single Payment*		*Uniform Payment Series*				*Arithmetic Gradient*	
	F/P	*P/F*	*A/F*	*F/A*	*A/P*	*P/A*	*P/G*	*A/G*
1	1.0700	0.9346	1.00000	1.0000	1.07000	0.9346		
2	1.1449	0.8734	0.48309	2.0700	0.55309	1.8080	0.8734	0.4831
3	1.2250	0.8163	0.31105	3.2149	0.38105	2.6243	2.5060	0.9549
4	1.3108	0.7629	0.22523	4.4399	0.29523	3.3872	4.7947	1.4155
5	1.4026	0.7130	0.17389	5.7507	0.24389	4.1002	7.6467	1.8650
6	1.5007	0.6663	0.13980	7.1533	0.20980	4.7665	10.9784	2.3032
7	1.6058	0.6227	0.11555	8.6540	0.18555	5.3893	14.7149	2.7304
8	1.7182	0.5820	0.09747	10.2598	0.16747	5.9713	18.7889	3.1465
9	1.8385	0.5439	0.08349	11.9780	0.15349	6.5152	23.1404	3.5517
10	1.9672	0.5083	0.07238	13.8164	0.14238	7.0236	27.7156	3.9461
11	2.1049	0.4751	0.06336	15.7836	0.13336	7.4987	32.4665	4.3296
12	2.2522	0.4440	0.05590	17.8885	0.12590	7.9427	37.3506	4.7025
13	2.4098	0.4150	0.04965	20.1406	0.11965	8.3577	42.3302	5.0648
14	2.5785	0.3878	0.04434	22.5505	0.11434	8.7455	47.3718	5.4167
15	2.7590	0.3624	0.03979	25.1290	0.10979	9.1079	52.4461	5.7583
16	2.9522	0.3387	0.03586	27.8881	0.10586	9.4466	57.5271	6.0897
17	3.1588	0.3166	0.03243	30.8402	0.10243	9.7632	62.5923	6.4110
18	3.3799	0.2959	0.02941	33.9990	0.09941	10.0591	67.6219	6.7225
19	3.6165	0.2765	0.02675	37.3790	0.09675	10.3356	72.5991	7.0242
20	3.8697	0.2584	0.02439	40.9955	0.09439	10.5940	77.5091	7.3163
21	4.1406	0.2415	0.02229	44.8652	0.09229	10.8355	82.3393	7.5990
22	4.4304	0.2257	0.02041	49.0057	0.09041	11.0612	87.0793	7.8725
23	4.7405	0.2109	0.01871	53.4361	0.08871	11.2722	91.7201	8.1369
24	5.0724	0.1971	0.01719	58.1767	0.08719	11.4693	96.2545	8.3923
25	5.4274	0.1842	0.01581	63.2490	0.08581	11.6536	100.6765	8.6391
26	5.8074	0.1722	0.01456	68.6765	0.08456	11.8258	104.9814	8.8773
27	6.2139	0.1609	0.01343	74.4838	0.08343	11.9867	109.1656	9.1072
28	6.6488	0.1504	0.01239	80.6977	0.08239	12.1371	113.2264	9.3289
29	7.1143	0.1406	0.01145	87.3465	0.08145	12.2777	117.1622	9.5427
34	9.9781	0.1002	0.00780	128.2588	0.07780	12.8540	134.9507	10.4987
39	13.9948	0.0715	0.00539	185.6403	0.07539	13.2649	149.6883	11.2845
44	19.6285	0.0509	0.00376	266.1209	0.07376	13.5579	161.6609	11.9237
49	27.5299	0.0363	0.00264	378.9990	0.07264	13.7668	171.2417	12.4387
54	38.6122	0.0259	0.00186	537.3164	0.07186	13.9157	178.8173	12.8500
59	54.1555	0.0185	0.00132	759.3648	0.07132	14.0219	184.7496	13.1758
64	75.9559	0.0132	0.00093	1070.7992	0.07093	14.0976	189.3577	13.4319
69	106.5321	0.0094	0.00066	1507.6020	0.07066	14.1516	192.9132	13.6319
74	149.4168	0.0067	0.00047	2120.2406	0.07047	14.1901	195.6407	13.7871
79	209.5648	0.0048	0.00034	2979.4978	0.07034	14.2175	197.7225	13.9069
84	293.9255	0.0034	0.00024	4184.6506	0.07024	14.2371	199.3046	13.9990
89	412.2458	0.0024	0.00017	5874.9397	0.07017	14.2511	200.5024	14.0693
94	578.1960	0.0017	0.00012	8245.6575	0.07012	14.2610	201.4062	14.1229
99	810.9498	0.0012	0.00009	11570.7120	0.07009	14.2681	202.0860	14.1635
100	867.7163	0.0012	0.00008	12381.6618	0.07008	14.2693	202.2001	14.1703

Table A14 Compound Interest Factors: 8%

n	Single Payment		Uniform Payment Series				Arithmetic Gradient	
	F/P	P/F	A/F	F/A	A/P	P/A	P/G	A/G
1	1.0800	0.9259	1.00000	1.0000	1.08000	0.9259		
2	1.1664	0.8573	0.48077	2.0800	0.56077	1.7833	0.8573	0.4808
3	1.2597	0.7938	0.30803	3.2464	0.38803	2.5771	2.4450	0.9487
4	1.3605	0.7350	0.22192	4.5061	0.30192	3.3121	4.6501	1.4040
5	1.4693	0.6806	0.17046	5.8666	0.25046	3.9927	7.3724	1.8465
6	1.5869	0.6302	0.13632	7.3359	0.21632	4.6229	10.5233	2.2763
7	1.7138	0.5835	0.11207	8.9228	0.19207	5.2064	14.0242	2.6937
8	1.8509	0.5403	0.09401	10.6366	0.17401	5.7466	17.8061	3.0985
9	1.9990	0.5002	0.08008	12.4876	0.16008	6.2469	21.8081	3.4910
10	2.1589	0.4632	0.06903	14.4866	0.14903	6.7101	25.9768	3.8713
11	2.3316	0.4289	0.06008	16.6455	0.14008	7.1390	30.2657	4.2395
12	2.5182	0.3971	0.05270	18.9771	0.13270	7.5361	34.6339	4.5957
13	2.7196	0.3677	0.04652	21.4953	0.12652	7.9038	39.0463	4.9402
14	2.9372	0.3405	0.04130	24.2149	0.12130	8.2442	43.4723	5.2731
15	3.1722	0.3152	0.03683	27.1521	0.11683	8.5595	47.8857	5.5945
16	3.4259	0.2919	0.03298	30.3243	0.11298	8.8514	52.2640	5.9046
17	3.7000	0.2703	0.02963	33.7502	0.10963	9.1216	56.5883	6.2037
18	3.9960	0.2502	0.02670	37.4502	0.10670	9.3719	60.8426	6.4920
19	4.3157	0.2317	0.02413	41.4463	0.10413	9.6036	65.0134	6.7697
20	4.6610	0.2145	0.02185	45.7620	0.10185	9.8181	69.0898	7.0369
21	5.0338	0.1987	0.01983	50.4229	0.09983	10.0168	73.0629	7.2940
22	5.4365	0.1839	0.01803	55.4568	0.09803	10.2007	76.9257	7.5412
23	5.8715	0.1703	0.01642	60.8933	0.09642	10.3711	80.6726	7.7786
24	6.3412	0.1577	0.01498	66.7648	0.09498	10.5288	84.2997	8.0066
25	6.8485	0.1460	0.01368	73.1059	0.09368	10.6748	87.8041	8.2254
26	7.3964	0.1352	0.01251	79.9544	0.09251	10.8100	91.1842	8.4352
27	7.9881	0.1252	0.01145	87.3508	0.09145	10.9352	94.4390	8.6363
28	8.6271	0.1159	0.01049	95.3388	0.09049	11.0511	97.5687	8.8289
29	9.3173	0.1073	0.00962	103.9659	0.08962	11.1584	100.5738	9.0133
34	13.6901	0.0730	0.00630	158.6267	0.08630	11.5869	113.7924	9.8208
39	20.1153	0.0497	0.00419	238.9412	0.08419	11.8786	124.2470	10.4597
44	29.5560	0.0338	0.00280	356.9496	0.08280	12.0771	132.3547	10.9592
49	43.4274	0.0230	0.00189	530.3427	0.08189	12.2122	138.5480	11.3451
54	63.8091	0.0157	0.00127	785.1141	0.08127	12.3041	143.2229	11.6403
59	93.7565	0.0107	0.00086	1159.4568	0.08086	12.3667	146.7173	11.8639
64	137.7591	0.0073	0.00058	1709.4890	0.08058	12.4093	149.3085	12.0320
69	202.4133	0.0049	0.00040	2517.6667	0.08040	12.4382	151.2170	12.1574
74	297.4116	0.0034	0.00027	3705.1450	0.08027	12.4580	152.6145	12.2503
79	436.9952	0.0023	0.00018	5449.9402	0.08018	12.4714	153.6327	12.3188
84	642.0893	0.0016	0.00012	8013.6168	0.08012	12.4805	154.3714	12.3690
89	943.4399	0.0011	0.00008	11780.4987	0.08008	12.4868	154.9052	12.4056
94	1386.2227	0.0007	0.00006	17315.2841	0.08006	12.4910	155.2897	12.4321
99	2036.8160	0.0005	0.00004	25447.6997	0.08004	12.4939	155.5657	12.4514
100	2199.7613	0.0005	0.00004	27484.5157	0.08004	12.4943	155.6107	12.4545

Table A15 Compound Interest Factors: 9%

n	*Single Payment*		*Uniform Payment Series*				*Arithmetic Gradient*	
	F/P	*P/F*	*A/F*	*F/A*	*A/P*	*P/A*	*P/G*	*A/G*
1	1.0900	0.9174	1.00000	1.0000	1.09000	0.9174		
2	1.1881	0.8417	0.47847	2.0900	0.56847	1.7591	0.8417	0.4785
3	1.2950	0.7722	0.30505	3.2781	0.39505	2.5313	2.3860	0.9426
4	1.4116	0.7084	0.21867	4.5731	0.30867	3.2397	4.5113	1.3925
5	1.5386	0.6499	0.16709	5.9847	0.25709	3.8897	7.1110	1.8282
6	1.6771	0.5963	0.13292	7.5233	0.22292	4.4859	10.0924	2.2498
7	1.8280	0.5470	0.10869	9.2004	0.19869	5.0330	13.3746	2.6574
8	1.9926	0.5019	0.09067	11.0285	0.18067	5.5348	16.8877	3.0512
9	2.1719	0.4604	0.07680	13.0210	0.16680	5.9952	20.5711	3.4312
10	2.3674	0.4224	0.06582	15.1929	0.15582	6.4177	24.3728	3.7978
11	2.5804	0.3875	0.05695	17.5603	0.14695	6.8052	28.2481	4.1510
12	2.8127	0.3555	0.04965	20.1407	0.13965	7.1607	32.1590	4.4910
13	3.0658	0.3262	0.04357	22.9534	0.13357	7.4869	36.0731	4.8182
14	3.3417	0.2992	0.03843	26.0192	0.12843	7.7862	39.9633	5.1326
15	3.6425	0.2745	0.03406	29.3609	0.12406	8.0607	43.8069	5.4346
16	3.9703	0.2519	0.03030	33.0034	0.12030	8.3126	47.5849	5.7245
17	4.3276	0.2311	0.02705	36.9737	0.11705	8.5436	51.2821	6.0024
18	4.7171	0.2120	0.02421	41.3013	0.11421	8.7556	54.8860	6.2687
19	5.1417	0.1945	0.02173	46.0185	0.11173	8.9501	58.3868	6.5236
20	5.6044	0.1784	0.01955	51.1601	0.10955	9.1285	61.7770	6.7674
21	6.1088	0.1637	0.01762	56.7645	0.10762	9.2922	65.0509	7.0006
22	6.6586	0.1502	0.01590	62.8733	0.10590	9.4424	68.2048	7.2232
23	7.2579	0.1378	0.01438	69.5319	0.10438	9.5802	71.2359	7.4357
24	7.9111	0.1264	0.01302	76.7898	0.10302	9.7066	74.1433	7.6384
25	8.6231	0.1160	0.01181	84.7009	0.10181	9.8226	76.9265	7.8316
26	9.3992	0.1064	0.01072	93.3240	0.10072	9.9290	79.5863	8.0156
27	10.2451	0.0976	0.00973	102.7231	0.09973	10.0266	82.1241	8.1906
28	11.1671	0.0895	0.00885	112.9682	0.09885	10.1161	84.5419	8.3571
29	12.1722	0.0822	0.00806	124.1354	0.09806	10.1983	86.8422	8.5154
34	18.7284	0.0534	0.00508	196.9823	0.09508	10.5178	96.6935	9.1933
39	28.8160	0.0347	0.00324	309.0665	0.09324	10.7255	104.1345	9.7090
44	44.3370	0.0226	0.00208	481.5218	0.09208	10.8605	109.6456	10.0958
49	68.2179	0.0147	0.00134	746.8656	0.09134	10.9482	113.6661	10.3821
54	104.9617	0.0095	0.00087	1155.1301	0.09087	11.0053	116.5642	10.5917
59	161.4966	0.0062	0.00056	1783.2955	0.09056	11.0423	118.6331	10.7435
64	248.4825	0.0040	0.00036	2749.8059	0.09036	11.0664	120.0981	10.8525
69	382.3212	0.0026	0.00024	4236.9020	0.09024	11.0820	121.1286	10.9302
74	588.2485	0.0017	0.00015	6524.9836	0.09015	11.0922	121.8492	10.9851
79	905.0933	0.0011	0.00010	10045.4808	0.09010	11.0988	122.3506	11.0237
84	1392.5982	0.0007	0.00006	15462.2021	0.09006	11.1031	122.6979	11.0507
89	2142.6849	0.0005	0.00004	23796.4993	0.09004	11.1059	122.9377	11.0696
94	3296.7864	0.0003	0.00003	36619.8486	0.09003	11.1077	123.1025	11.0826
99	5072.5145	0.0002	0.00002	56350.1610	0.09002	11.1089	123.2156	11.0916
100	5529.0408	0.0002	0.00002	61422.6755	0.09002	11.1091	123.2335	11.0930

Table A16 Compound Interest Factors: 10%

n	*Single Payment*		*Uniform Payment Series*				*Arithmetic Gradient*	
	F/P	*P/F*	*A/F*	*F/A*	*A/P*	*P/A*	*P/G*	*A/G*
1	1.1000	0.9091	1.00000	1.0000	1.10000	0.9091		
2	1.2100	0.8264	0.47619	2.1000	0.57619	1.7355	0.8264	0.4762
3	1.3310	0.7513	0.30211	3.3100	0.40211	2.4869	2.3291	0.9366
4	1.4641	0.6830	0.21547	4.6410	0.31547	3.1699	4.3781	1.3812
5	1.6105	0.6209	0.16380	6.1051	0.26380	3.7908	6.8618	1.8101
6	1.7716	0.5645	0.12961	7.7156	0.22961	4.3553	9.6842	2.2236
7	1.9487	0.5132	0.10541	9.4872	0.20541	4.8684	12.7631	2.6216
8	2.1436	0.4665	0.08744	11.4359	0.18744	5.3349	16.0287	3.0045
9	2.3579	0.4241	0.07364	13.5795	0.17364	5.7590	19.4215	3.3724
10	2.5937	0.3855	0.06275	15.9374	0.16275	6.1446	22.8913	3.7255
11	2.8531	0.3505	0.05396	18.5312	0.15396	6.4951	26.3963	4.0641
12	3.1384	0.3186	0.04676	21.3843	0.14676	6.8137	29.9012	4.3884
13	3.4523	0.2897	0.04078	24.5227	0.14078	7.1034	33.3772	4.6988
14	3.7975	0.2633	0.03575	27.9750	0.13575	7.3667	36.8005	4.9955
15	4.1772	0.2394	0.03147	31.7725	0.13147	7.6061	40.1520	5.2789
16	4.5950	0.2176	0.02782	35.9497	0.12782	7.8237	43.4164	5.5493
17	5.0545	0.1978	0.02466	40.5447	0.12466	8.0216	46.5819	5.8071
18	5.5599	0.1799	0.02193	45.5992	0.12193	8.2014	49.6395	6.0526
19	6.1159	0.1635	0.01955	51.1591	0.11955	8.3649	52.5827	6.2861
20	6.7275	0.1486	0.01746	57.2750	0.11746	8.5136	55.4069	6.5081
21	7.4002	0.1351	0.01562	64.0025	0.11562	8.6487	58.1095	6.7189
22	8.1403	0.1228	0.01401	71.4027	0.11401	8.7715	60.6893	6.9189
23	8.9543	0.1117	0.01257	79.5430	0.11257	8.8832	63.1462	7.1085
24	9.8497	0.1015	0.01130	88.4973	0.11130	8.9847	65.4813	7.2881
25	10.8347	0.0923	0.01017	98.3471	0.11017	9.0770	67.6964	7.4580
26	11.9182	0.0839	0.00916	109.1818	0.10916	9.1609	69.7940	7.6186
27	13.1100	0.0763	0.00826	121.0999	0.10826	9.2372	71.7773	7.7704
28	14.4210	0.0693	0.00745	134.2099	0.10745	9.3066	73.6495	7.9137
29	15.8631	0.0630	0.00673	148.6309	0.10673	9.3696	75.4146	8.0489
34	25.5477	0.0391	0.00407	245.4767	0.10407	9.6086	82.7773	8.6149
39	41.1448	0.0243	0.00249	401.4478	0.10249	9.7570	88.0908	9.0285
44	66.2641	0.0151	0.00153	652.6408	0.10153	9.8491	91.8508	9.3258
49	106.7190	0.0094	0.00095	1057.1896	0.10095	9.9063	94.4715	9.5365
54	171.8719	0.0058	0.00059	1708.7195	0.10059	9.9418	96.2763	9.6840
59	276.8015	0.0036	0.00036	2758.0149	0.10036	9.9639	97.5072	9.7861
64	445.7916	0.0022	0.00022	4447.9157	0.10022	9.9776	98.3400	9.8561
69	717.9518	0.0014	0.00014	7169.5178	0.10014	9.9861	98.8996	9.9038
74	1156.2685	0.0009	0.00009	11552.6852	0.10009	9.9914	99.2735	9.9359
79	1862.1820	0.0005	0.00005	18611.8201	0.10005	9.9946	99.5221	9.9576
84	2999.0628	0.0003	0.00003	29980.6275	0.10003	9.9967	99.6866	9.9720
89	4830.0206	0.0002	0.00002	48290.2056	0.10002	9.9979	99.7950	9.9816
99	12527.8294	0.0001	0.00001	125268.2940	0.10001	9.9992	99.9130	9.9921
100	13780.6123	0.0001	0.00001	137796.1234	0.10001	9.9993	99.9202	9.9927

Table A17 Compound Interest Factors: 11%

n	*Single Payment*		*Uniform Payment Series*				*Arithmetic Gradient*	
	F/P	*P/F*	*A/F*	*F/A*	*A/P*	*P/A*	*P/G*	*A/G*
1	1.1100	0.9009	1.00000	1.0000	1.11000	0.9009		
2	1.2321	0.8116	0.47393	2.1100	0.58393	1.7125	0.8116	0.4739
3	1.3676	0.7312	0.29921	3.3421	0.40921	2.4437	2.2740	0.9306
4	1.5181	0.6587	0.21233	4.7097	0.32233	3.1024	4.2502	1.3700
5	1.6851	0.5935	0.16057	6.2278	0.27057	3.6959	6.6240	1.7923
6	1.8704	0.5346	0.12638	7.9129	0.23638	4.2305	9.2972	2.1976
7	2.0762	0.4817	0.10222	9.7833	0.21222	4.7122	12.1872	2.5863
8	2.3045	0.4339	0.08432	11.8594	0.19432	5.1461	15.2246	2.9585
9	2.5580	0.3909	0.07060	14.1640	0.18060	5.5370	18.3520	3.3144
10	2.8394	0.3522	0.05980	16.7220	0.16980	5.8892	21.5217	3.6544
11	3.1518	0.3173	0.05112	19.5614	0.16112	6.2065	24.6945	3.9788
12	3.4985	0.2858	0.04403	22.7132	0.15403	6.4924	27.8388	4.2879
13	3.8833	0.2575	0.03815	26.2116	0.14815	6.7499	30.9290	4.5822
14	4.3104	0.2320	0.03323	30.0949	0.14323	6.9819	33.9449	4.8619
15	4.7846	0.2090	0.02907	34.4054	0.13907	7.1909	36.8709	5.1275
16	5.3109	0.1883	0.02552	39.1899	0.13552	7.3792	39.6953	5.3794
17	5.8951	0.1696	0.02247	44.5008	0.13247	7.5488	42.4095	5.6180
18	6.5436	0.1528	0.01984	50.3959	0.12984	7.7016	45.0074	5.8439
19	7.2633	0.1377	0.01756	56.9395	0.12756	7.8393	47.4856	6.0574
20	8.0623	0.1240	0.01558	64.2028	0.12558	7.9633	49.8423	6.2590
21	8.9492	0.1117	0.01384	72.2651	0.12384	8.0751	52.0771	6.4491
22	9.9336	0.1007	0.01231	81.2143	0.12231	8.1757	54.1912	6.6283
23	11.0263	0.0907	0.01097	91.1479	0.12097	8.2664	56.1864	6.7969
24	12.2392	0.0817	0.00979	102.1742	0.11979	8.3481	58.0656	6.9555
25	13.5855	0.0736	0.00874	114.4133	0.11874	8.4217	59.8322	7.1045
26	15.0799	0.0663	0.00781	127.9988	0.11781	8.4881	61.4900	7.2443
27	16.7386	0.0597	0.00699	143.0786	0.11699	8.5478	63.0433	7.3754
28	18.5799	0.0538	0.00626	159.8173	0.11626	8.6016	64.4965	7.4982
29	20.6237	0.0485	0.00561	178.3972	0.11561	8.6501	65.8542	7.6131
34	34.7521	0.0288	0.00326	306.8374	0.11326	8.8293	71.3724	8.0836
39	58.5593	0.0171	0.00191	523.2667	0.11191	8.9357	75.1789	8.4133
44	98.6759	0.0101	0.00113	887.9627	0.11113	8.9988	77.7534	8.6404
49	166.2746	0.0060	0.00067	1502.4965	0.11067	9.0362	79.4686	8.7944
54	280.1824	0.0036	0.00039	2538.0218	0.11039	9.0585	80.5976	8.8975
59	472.1236	0.0021	0.00023	4282.9422	0.11023	9.0717	81.3335	8.9657
64	795.5558	0.0013	0.00014	7223.2345	0.11014	9.0795	81.8094	9.0104
69	1340.5578	0.0007	0.00008	12177.7980	0.11008	9.0841	82.1151	9.0394
74	2258.9178	0.0004	0.00005	20526.5256	0.11005	9.0869	82.3102	9.0581
79	3806.4079	0.0003	0.00003	34594.6171	0.11003	9.0885	82.4342	9.0701
84	6414.0186	0.0002	0.00002	58300.1695	0.11002	9.0895	82.5127	9.0778
85	7119.5607	0.0001	0.00002	64714.1881	0.11002	9.0896	82.5245	9.0790

Table A18 Compound Interest Factors: 12%

n	*Single Payment*		*Uniform Payment Series*				*Arithmetic Gradient*	
	F/P	*P/F*	*A/F*	*F/A*	*A/P*	*P/A*	*P/G*	*A/G*
1	1.1200	0.8929	1.00000	1.0000	1.12000	0.8929		
2	1.2544	0.7972	0.47170	2.1200	0.59170	1.6901	0.7972	0.4717
3	1.4049	0.7118	0.29635	3.3744	0.41635	2.4018	2.2208	0.9246
4	1.5735	0.6355	0.20923	4.7793	0.32923	3.0373	4.1273	1.3589
5	1.7623	0.5674	0.15741	6.3528	0.27741	3.6048	6.3970	1.7746
6	1.9738	0.5066	0.12323	8.1152	0.24323	4.1114	8.9302	2.1720
7	2.2107	0.4523	0.09912	10.0890	0.21912	4.5638	11.6443	2.5515
8	2.4760	0.4039	0.08130	12.2997	0.20130	4.9676	14.4714	2.9131
9	2.7731	0.3606	0.06768	14.7757	0.18768	5.3282	17.3563	3.2574
10	3.1058	0.3220	0.05698	17.5487	0.17698	5.6502	20.2541	3.5847
11	3.4785	0.2875	0.04842	20.6546	0.16842	5.9377	23.1288	3.8953
12	3.8960	0.2567	0.04144	24.1331	0.16144	6.1944	25.9523	4.1897
13	4.3635	0.2292	0.03568	28.0291	0.15568	6.4235	28.7024	4.4683
14	4.8871	0.2046	0.03087	32.3926	0.15087	6.6282	31.3624	4.7317
15	5.4736	0.1827	0.02682	37.2797	0.14682	6.8109	33.9202	4.9803
16	6.1304	0.1631	0.02339	42.7533	0.14339	6.9740	36.3670	5.2147
17	6.8660	0.1456	0.02046	48.8837	0.14046	7.1196	38.6973	5.4353
18	7.6900	0.1300	0.01794	55.7497	0.13794	7.2497	40.9080	5.6427
19	8.6128	0.1161	0.01576	63.4397	0.13576	7.3658	42.9979	5.8375
20	9.6463	0.1037	0.01388	72.0524	0.13388	7.4694	44.9676	6.0202
21	10.8038	0.0926	0.01224	81.6987	0.13224	7.5620	46.8188	6.1913
22	12.1003	0.0826	0.01081	92.5026	0.13081	7.6446	48.5543	6.3514
23	13.5523	0.0738	0.00956	104.6029	0.12956	7.7184	50.1776	6.5010
24	15.1786	0.0659	0.00846	118.1552	0.12846	7.7843	51.6929	6.6406
25	17.0001	0.0588	0.00750	133.3339	0.12750	7.8431	53.1046	6.7708
26	19.0401	0.0525	0.00665	150.3339	0.12665	7.8957	54.4177	6.8921
27	21.3249	0.0469	0.00590	169.3740	0.12590	7.9426	55.6369	7.0049
28	23.8839	0.0419	0.00524	190.6989	0.12524	7.9844	56.7674	7.1098
29	26.7499	0.0374	0.00466	214.5828	0.12466	8.0218	57.8141	7.2071
34	47.1425	0.0212	0.00260	384.5210	0.12260	8.1566	61.9612	7.5965
39	83.0812	0.0120	0.00146	684.0102	0.12146	8.2330	64.6967	7.8582
44	146.4175	0.0068	0.00083	1211.8125	0.12083	8.2764	66.4659	8.0308
49	258.0377	0.0039	0.00047	2141.9806	0.12047	8.3010	67.5929	8.1427
54	454.7505	0.0022	0.00026	3781.2545	0.12026	8.3150	68.3022	8.2143
59	801.4258	0.0012	0.00015	6670.2153	0.12015	8.3229	68.7443	8.2596
64	1412.3862	0.0007	0.00009	11761.5513	0.12009	8.3274	69.0177	8.2880
69	2489.1070	0.0004	0.00005	20734.2249	0.12005	8.3300	69.1855	8.3056
74	4386.6570	0.0002	0.00003	36547.1417	0.12003	8.3314	69.2880	8.3165
79	7730.7885	0.0001	0.00002	64414.9040	0.12002	8.3323	69.3503	8.3231
84	13624.2908	0.0001	0.00001	113527.4232	0.12001	8.3327	69.3880	8.3272
85	15259.2057	0.0001	0.00001	127151.7140	0.12001	8.3328	69.3935	8.3278

Table A19 Compound Interest Factors: 13%

n	*Single Payment*		*Uniform Payment Series*				*Arithmetic Gradient*	
	F/P	*P/F*	*A/F*	*F/A*	*A/P*	*P/A*	*P/G*	*A/G*
1	1.1300	0.8850	1.00000	1.0000	1.13000	0.8850		
2	1.2769	0.7831	0.46948	2.1300	0.59948	1.6681	0.7831	0.4695
3	1.4429	0.6931	0.29352	3.4069	0.42352	2.3612	2.1692	0.9187
4	1.6305	0.6133	0.20619	4.8498	0.33619	2.9745	4.0092	1.3479
5	1.8424	0.5428	0.15431	6.4803	0.28431	3.5172	6.1802	1.7571
6	2.0820	0.4803	0.12015	8.3227	0.25015	3.9975	8.5818	2.1468
7	2.3526	0.4251	0.09611	10.4047	0.22611	4.4226	11.1322	2.5171
8	2.6584	0.3762	0.07839	12.7573	0.20839	4.7988	13.7653	2.8685
9	3.0040	0.3329	0.06487	15.4157	0.19487	5.1317	16.4284	3.2014
10	3.3946	0.2946	0.05429	18.4197	0.18429	5.4262	19.0797	3.5162
11	3.8359	0.2607	0.04584	21.8143	0.17584	5.6869	21.6867	3.8134
12	4.3345	0.2307	0.03899	25.6502	0.16899	5.9176	24.2244	4.0936
13	4.8980	0.2042	0.03335	29.9847	0.16335	6.1218	26.6744	4.3573
14	5.5348	0.1807	0.02867	34.8827	0.15867	6.3025	29.0232	4.6050
15	6.2543	0.1599	0.02474	40.4175	0.15474	6.4624	31.2617	4.8375
16	7.0673	0.1415	0.02143	46.6717	0.15143	6.6039	33.3841	5.0552
17	7.9861	0.1252	0.01861	53.7391	0.14861	6.7291	35.3876	5.2589
18	9.0243	0.1108	0.01620	61.7251	0.14620	6.8399	37.2714	5.4491
19	10.1974	0.0981	0.01413	70.7494	0.14413	6.9380	39.0366	5.6265
20	11.5231	0.0868	0.01235	80.9468	0.14235	7.0248	40.6854	5.7917
21	13.0211	0.0768	0.01081	92.4699	0.14081	7.1016	42.2214	5.9454
22	14.7138	0.0680	0.00948	105.4910	0.13948	7.1695	43.6486	6.0881
23	16.6266	0.0601	0.00832	120.2048	0.13832	7.2297	44.9718	6.2205
24	18.7881	0.0532	0.00731	136.8315	0.13731	7.2829	46.1960	6.3431
25	21.2305	0.0471	0.00643	155.6196	0.13643	7.3300	47.3264	6.4566
26	23.9905	0.0417	0.00565	176.8501	0.13565	7.3717	48.3685	6.5614
27	27.1093	0.0369	0.00498	200.8406	0.13498	7.4086	49.3276	6.6582
28	30.6335	0.0326	0.00439	227.9499	0.13439	7.4412	50.2090	6.7474
29	34.6158	0.0289	0.00387	258.5834	0.13387	7.4701	51.0179	6.8296
34	63.7774	0.0157	0.00207	482.9034	0.13207	7.5717	54.1430	7.1507
39	117.5058	0.0085	0.00112	896.1984	0.13112	7.6268	56.1150	7.3576
44	216.4968	0.0046	0.00060	1657.6678	0.13060	7.6568	57.3349	7.4881
49	398.8813	0.0025	0.00033	3060.6258	0.13033	7.6730	58.0783	7.5692
54	734.9130	0.0014	0.00018	5645.4849	0.13018	7.6818	58.5259	7.6187
59	1354.0296	0.0007	0.00010	10407.9202	0.13010	7.6866	58.7927	7.6487
64	2494.7118	0.0004	0.00005	19182.3985	0.13005	7.6892	58.9505	7.6666
69	4596.3448	0.0002	0.00003	35348.8062	0.13003	7.6906	59.0432	7.6773
74	8468.4674	0.0001	0.00002	65134.3643	0.13002	7.6914	59.0974	7.6836
84	28746.7831	0.0000	0.00000	221121.4087	0.13000	7.6920	59.1471	7.6894
85	32483.8649	0.0000	0.00000	249868.1918	0.13000	7.6921	59.1496	7.6897

Table A20 Compound Interest Factors: 14%

n	*Single Payment*		*Uniform Payment Series*				*Arithmetic Gradient*	
	F/P	*P/F*	*A/F*	*F/A*	*A/P*	*P/A*	*P/G*	*A/G*
1	1.1400	0.8772	1.00000	1.0000	1.14000	0.8772		
2	1.2996	0.7695	0.46729	2.1400	0.60729	1.6467	0.7695	0.4673
3	1.4815	0.6750	0.29073	3.4396	0.43073	2.3216	2.1194	0.9129
4	1.6890	0.5921	0.20320	4.9211	0.34320	2.9137	3.8957	1.3370
5	1.9254	0.5194	0.15128	6.6101	0.29128	3.4331	5.9731	1.7399
6	2.1950	0.4556	0.11716	8.5355	0.25716	3.8887	8.2511	2.1218
7	2.5023	0.3996	0.09319	10.7305	0.23319	4.2883	10.6489	2.4832
8	2.8526	0.3506	0.07557	13.2328	0.21557	4.6389	13.1028	2.8246
9	3.2519	0.3075	0.06217	16.0853	0.20217	4.9464	15.5629	3.1463
10	3.7072	0.2697	0.05171	19.3373	0.19171	5.2161	17.9906	3.4490
11	4.2262	0.2366	0.04339	23.0445	0.18339	5.4527	20.3567	3.7333
12	4.8179	0.2076	0.03667	27.2707	0.17667	5.6603	22.6399	3.9998
13	5.4924	0.1821	0.03116	32.0887	0.17116	5.8424	24.8247	4.2491
14	6.2613	0.1597	0.02661	37.5811	0.16661	6.0021	26.9009	4.4819
15	7.1379	0.1401	0.02281	43.8424	0.16281	6.1422	28.8623	4.6990
16	8.1372	0.1229	0.01962	50.9804	0.15962	6.2651	30.7057	4.9011
17	9.2765	0.1078	0.01692	59.1176	0.15692	6.3729	32.4305	5.0888
18	10.5752	0.0946	0.01462	68.3941	0.15462	6.4674	34.0380	5.2630
19	12.0557	0.0829	0.01266	78.9692	0.15266	6.5504	35.5311	5.4243
20	13.7435	0.0728	0.01099	91.0249	0.15099	6.6231	36.9135	5.5734
21	15.6676	0.0638	0.00954	104.7684	0.14954	6.6870	38.1901	5.7111
22	17.8610	0.0560	0.00830	120.4360	0.14830	6.7429	39.3658	5.8381
23	20.3616	0.0491	0.00723	138.2970	0.14723	6.7921	40.4463	5.9549
24	23.2122	0.0431	0.00630	158.6586	0.14630	6.8351	41.4371	6.0624
25	26.4619	0.0378	0.00550	181.8708	0.14550	6.8729	42.3441	6.1610
26	30.1666	0.0331	0.00480	208.3327	0.14480	6.9061	43.1728	6.2514
27	34.3899	0.0291	0.00419	238.4993	0.14419	6.9352	43.9289	6.3342
28	39.2045	0.0255	0.00366	272.8892	0.14366	6.9607	44.6176	6.4100
29	44.6931	0.0224	0.00320	312.0937	0.14320	6.9830	45.2441	6.4791
34	86.0528	0.0116	0.00165	607.5199	0.14165	7.0599	47.6053	6.7431
39	165.6873	0.0060	0.00085	1176.3378	0.14085	7.0997	49.0312	6.9060
44	319.0167	0.0031	0.00044	2271.5481	0.14044	7.1205	49.8753	7.0045
49	614.2395	0.0016	0.00023	4380.2819	0.14023	7.1312	50.3675	7.0630
54	1182.6656	0.0008	0.00012	8440.4687	0.14012	7.1368	50.6511	7.0972
59	2277.1216	0.0004	0.00006	16258.0117	0.14006	7.1397	50.8129	7.1169
64	4384.4032	0.0002	0.00003	31310.0228	0.14003	7.1412	50.9045	7.1283
69	8441.7938	0.0001	0.00002	60291.3846	0.14002	7.1420	50.9560	7.1347
74	16253.9530	0.0001	0.00001	116092.5212	0.14001	7.1424	50.9847	7.1383
84	60257.0009	0.0000	0.00000	430400.0064	0.14000	7.1427	51.0096	7.1415
85	68692.9810	0.0000	0.00000	490657.0073	0.14000	7.1428	51.0108	7.1416

Table A21 Compound Interest Factors: 15%

n	*Single Payment*		*Uniform Payment Series*				*Arithmetic Gradient*	
	F/P	*P/F*	*A/F*	*F/A*	*A/P*	*P/A*	*P/G*	*A/G*
1	1.1500	0.8696	1.00000	1.0000	1.15000	0.8696		
2	1.3225	0.7561	0.46512	2.1500	0.61512	1.6257	0.7561	0.4651
3	1.5209	0.6575	0.28798	3.4725	0.43798	2.2832	2.0712	0.9071
4	1.7490	0.5718	0.20027	4.9934	0.35027	2.8550	3.7864	1.3263
5	2.0114	0.4972	0.14832	6.7424	0.29832	3.3522	5.7751	1.7228
6	2.3131	0.4323	0.11424	8.7537	0.26424	3.7845	7.9368	2.0972
7	2.6600	0.3759	0.09036	11.0668	0.24036	4.1604	10.1924	2.4498
8	3.0590	0.3269	0.07285	13.7268	0.22285	4.4873	12.4807	2.7813
9	3.5179	0.2843	0.05957	16.7858	0.20957	4.7716	14.7548	3.0922
10	4.0456	0.2472	0.04925	20.3037	0.19925	5.0188	16.9795	3.3832
11	4.6524	0.2149	0.04107	24.3493	0.19107	5.2337	19.1289	3.6549
12	5.3503	0.1869	0.03448	29.0017	0.18448	5.4206	21.1849	3.9082
13	6.1528	0.1625	0.02911	34.3519	0.17911	5.5831	23.1352	4.1438
14	7.0757	0.1413	0.02469	40.5047	0.17469	5.7245	24.9725	4.3624
15	8.1371	0.1229	0.02102	47.5804	0.17102	5.8474	26.6930	4.5650
16	9.3576	0.1069	0.01795	55.7175	0.16795	5.9542	28.2960	4.7522
17	10.7613	0.0929	0.01537	65.0751	0.16537	6.0472	29.7828	4.9251
18	12.3755	0.0808	0.01319	75.8364	0.16319	6.1280	31.1565	5.0843
19	14.2318	0.0703	0.01134	88.2118	0.16134	6.1982	32.4213	5.2307
20	16.3665	0.0611	0.00976	102.4436	0.15976	6.2593	33.5822	5.3651
21	18.8215	0.0531	0.00842	118.8101	0.15842	6.3125	34.6448	5.4883
22	21.6447	0.0462	0.00727	137.6316	0.15727	6.3587	35.6150	5.6010
23	24.8915	0.0402	0.00628	159.2764	0.15628	6.3988	36.4988	5.7040
24	28.6252	0.0349	0.00543	184.1678	0.15543	6.4338	37.3023	5.7979
25	32.9190	0.0304	0.00470	212.7930	0.15470	6.4641	38.0314	5.8834
26	37.8568	0.0264	0.00407	245.7120	0.15407	6.4906	38.6918	5.9612
27	43.5353	0.0230	0.00353	283.5688	0.15353	6.5135	39.2890	6.0319
28	50.0656	0.0200	0.00306	327.1041	0.15306	6.5335	39.8283	6.0960
29	57.5755	0.0174	0.00265	377.1697	0.15265	6.5509	40.3146	6.1541
34	115.8048	0.0086	0.00131	765.3654	0.15131	6.6091	42.1033	6.3705
39	232.9248	0.0043	0.00065	1546.1655	0.15065	6.6380	43.1374	6.4985
44	468.4950	0.0021	0.00032	3116.6334	0.15032	6.6524	43.7235	6.5725
49	942.3108	0.0011	0.00016	6275.4055	0.15016	6.6596	44.0506	6.6146
54	1895.3236	0.0005	0.00008	12628.8243	0.15008	6.6631	44.2311	6.6382
59	3812.1728	0.0003	0.00004	25407.8188	0.15004	6.6649	44.3296	6.6512
64	7667.6412	0.0001	0.00002	51110.9414	0.15002	6.6658	44.3830	6.6583
69	15422.3653	0.0001	0.00001	102809.1017	0.15001	6.6662	44.4117	6.6622
74	31019.8852	0.0000	0.00000	206792.5680	0.15000	6.6665	44.4271	6.6643
85	144316.6470	0.0000	0.00000	962104.3133	0.15000	6.6666	44.4402	6.6661

Table A22 Compound Interest Factors: 16%

n	Single Payment		Uniform Payment Series				Arithmetic Gradient	
	F/P	P/F	A/F	F/A	A/P	P/A	P/G	A/G
1	1.1600	0.8621	1.00000	1.0000	1.16000	0.8621		
2	1.3456	0.7432	0.46296	2.1600	0.62296	1.6052	0.7432	0.4630
3	1.5609	0.6407	0.28526	3.5056	0.44526	2.2459	2.0245	0.9014
4	1.8106	0.5523	0.19738	5.0665	0.35738	2.7982	3.6814	1.3156
5	2.1003	0.4761	0.14541	6.8771	0.30541	3.2743	5.5858	1.7060
6	2.4364	0.4104	0.11139	8.9775	0.27139	3.6847	7.6380	2.0729
7	2.8262	0.3538	0.08761	11.4139	0.24761	4.0386	9.7610	2.4169
8	3.2784	0.3050	0.07022	14.2401	0.23022	4.3436	11.8962	2.7388
9	3.8030	0.2630	0.05708	17.5185	0.21708	4.6065	13.9998	3.0391
10	4.4114	0.2267	0.04690	21.3215	0.20690	4.8332	16.0399	3.3187
11	5.1173	0.1954	0.03886	25.7329	0.19886	5.0286	17.9941	3.5783
12	5.9360	0.1685	0.03241	30.8502	0.19241	5.1971	19.8472	3.8189
13	6.8858	0.1452	0.02718	36.7862	0.18718	5.3423	21.5899	4.0413
14	7.9875	0.1252	0.02290	43.6720	0.18290	5.4675	23.2175	4.2464
15	9.2655	0.1079	0.01936	51.6595	0.17936	5.5755	24.7284	4.4352
16	10.7480	0.0930	0.01641	60.9250	0.17641	5.6685	26.1241	4.6086
17	12.4677	0.0802	0.01395	71.6730	0.17395	5.7487	27.4074	4.7676
18	14.4625	0.0691	0.01188	84.1407	0.17188	5.8178	28.5828	4.9130
19	16.7765	0.0596	0.01014	98.6032	0.17014	5.8775	29.6557	5.0457
20	19.4608	0.0514	0.00867	115.3797	0.16867	5.9288	30.6321	5.1666
21	22.5745	0.0443	0.00742	134.8405	0.16742	5.9731	31.5180	5.2766
22	26.1864	0.0382	0.00635	157.4150	0.16635	6.0113	32.3200	5.3765
23	30.3762	0.0329	0.00545	183.6014	0.16545	6.0442	33.0442	5.4671
24	35.2364	0.0284	0.00467	213.9776	0.16467	6.0726	33.6970	5.5490
25	40.8742	0.0245	0.00401	249.2140	0.16401	6.0971	34.2841	5.6230
26	47.4141	0.0211	0.00345	290.0883	0.16345	6.1182	34.8114	5.6898
27	55.0004	0.0182	0.00296	337.5024	0.16296	6.1364	35.2841	5.7500
28	63.8004	0.0157	0.00255	392.5028	0.16255	6.1520	35.7073	5.8041
29	74.0085	0.0135	0.00219	456.3032	0.16219	6.1656	36.0856	5.8528
34	155.4432	0.0064	0.00104	965.2698	0.16104	6.2098	37.4441	6.0299
39	326.4838	0.0031	0.00049	2034.2735	0.16049	6.2309	38.1963	6.1302
44	685.7274	0.0015	0.00023	4279.5465	0.16023	6.2409	38.6045	6.1857
49	1440.2619	0.0007	0.00011	8995.3869	0.16011	6.2457	38.8227	6.2160
54	3025.0421	0.0003	0.00005	18900.2629	0.16005	6.2479	38.9380	6.2321
59	6353.6219	0.0002	0.00003	39703.8867	0.16003	6.2490	38.9983	6.2407
60	7370.2014	0.0001	0.00002	46057.5085	0.16002	6.2492	39.0063	6.2419

Table A23 Compound Interest Factors: 17%

n	Single Payment		Uniform Payment Series				Arithmetic Gradient	
	F/P	P/F	A/F	F/A	A/P	P/A	P/G	A/G
1	1.1700	0.8547	1.00000	1.0000	1.17000	0.8547		
2	1.3689	0.7305	0.46083	2.1700	0.63083	1.5852	0.7305	0.4608
3	1.6016	0.6244	0.28257	3.5389	0.45257	2.2096	1.9793	0.8958
4	1.8739	0.5337	0.19453	5.1405	0.36453	2.7432	3.5802	1.3051

(Continued)

Table A.23 (Continued)

n	*Single Payment*		*Uniform Payment Series*				*Arithmetic Gradient*	
	F/P	*P/F*	*A/F*	*F/A*	*A/P*	*P/A*	*P/G*	*A/G*
5	2.1924	0.4561	0.14256	7.0144	0.31256	3.1993	5.4046	1.6893
6	2.5652	0.3898	0.10861	9.2068	0.27861	3.5892	7.3538	2.0489
7	3.0012	0.3332	0.08495	11.7720	0.25495	3.9224	9.3530	2.3845
8	3.5115	0.2848	0.06769	14.7733	0.23769	4.2072	11.3465	2.6969
9	4.1084	0.2434	0.05469	18.2847	0.22469	4.4506	13.2937	2.9870
10	4.8068	0.2080	0.04466	22.3931	0.21466	4.6586	15.1661	3.2555
11	5.6240	0.1778	0.03676	27.1999	0.20676	4.8364	16.9442	3.5035
12	6.5801	0.1520	0.03047	32.8239	0.20047	4.9884	18.6159	3.7318
13	7.6987	0.1299	0.02538	39.4040	0.19538	5.1183	20.1746	3.9417
14	9.0075	0.1110	0.02123	47.1027	0.19123	5.2293	21.6178	4.1340
15	10.5387	0.0949	0.01782	56.1101	0.18782	5.3242	22.9463	4.3098
16	12.3303	0.0811	0.01500	66.6488	0.18500	5.4053	24.1628	4.4702
17	14.4265	0.0693	0.01266	78.9792	0.18266	5.4746	25.2719	4.6162
18	16.8790	0.0592	0.01071	93.4056	0.18071	5.5339	26.2790	4.7488
19	19.7484	0.0506	0.00907	110.2846	0.17907	5.5845	27.1905	4.8689
20	23.1056	0.0433	0.00769	130.0329	0.17769	5.6278	28.0128	4.9776
21	27.0336	0.0370	0.00653	153.1385	0.17653	5.6648	28.7526	5.0757
22	31.6293	0.0316	0.00555	180.1721	0.17555	5.6964	29.4166	5.1641
23	37.0062	0.0270	0.00472	211.8013	0.17472	5.7234	30.0111	5.2436
24	43.2973	0.0231	0.00402	248.8076	0.17402	5.7465	30.5423	5.3149
25	50.6578	0.0197	0.00342	292.1049	0.17342	5.7662	31.0160	5.3789
26	59.2697	0.0169	0.00292	342.7627	0.17292	5.7831	31.4378	5.4362
27	69.3455	0.0144	0.00249	402.0323	0.17249	5.7975	31.8128	5.4873
28	81.1342	0.0123	0.00212	471.3778	0.17212	5.8099	32.1456	5.5329
29	94.9271	0.0105	0.00181	552.5121	0.17181	5.8204	32.4405	5.5736
34	208.1226	0.0048	0.00082	1218.3684	0.17082	5.8541	33.4748	5.7182
39	456.2980	0.0022	0.00037	2678.2238	0.17037	5.8695	34.0235	5.7967
44	1000.4098	0.0010	0.00017	5878.8809	0.17017	5.8765	34.3088	5.8383
49	2193.3464	0.0005	0.00008	12896.1553	0.17008	5.8797	34.4549	5.8600
54	4808.7980	0.0002	0.00004	28281.1647	0.17004	5.8811	34.5288	5.8711
59	10543.0397	0.0001	0.00002	62011.9984	0.17002	5.8818	34.5659	5.8768
60	12335.3565	0.0001	0.00001	72555.0381	0.17001	5.8819	34.5707	5.8775

Table A24 Compound Interest Factors: 18%

n	*Single Payment*		*Uniform Payment Series*				*Arithmetic Gradient*	
	F/P	*P/F*	*A/F*	*F/A*	*A/P*	*P/A*	*P/G*	*A/G*
1	1.1800	0.8475	1.00000	1.0000	1.18000	0.8475		
2	1.3924	0.7182	0.45872	2.1800	0.63872	1.5656	0.7182	0.4587
3	1.6430	0.6086	0.27992	3.5724	0.45992	2.1743	1.9354	0.8902
4	1.9388	0.5158	0.19174	5.2154	0.37174	2.6901	3.4828	1.2947
5	2.2878	0.4371	0.13978	7.1542	0.31978	3.1272	5.2312	1.6728
6	2.6996	0.3704	0.10591	9.4420	0.28591	3.4976	7.0834	2.0252
7	3.1855	0.3139	0.08236	12.1415	0.26236	3.8115	8.9670	2.3526

(*Continued*)

Table A.24 (Continued)

n	Single Payment		Uniform Payment Series				Arithmetic Gradient	
	F/P	P/F	A/F	F/A	A/P	P/A	P/G	A/G
8	3.7589	0.2660	0.06524	15.3270	0.24524	4.0776	10.8292	2.6558
9	4.4355	0.2255	0.05239	19.0859	0.23239	4.3030	12.6329	2.9358
10	5.2338	0.1911	0.04251	23.5213	0.22251	4.4941	14.3525	3.1936
11	6.1759	0.1619	0.03478	28.7551	0.21478	4.6560	15.9716	3.4303
12	7.2876	0.1372	0.02863	34.9311	0.20863	4.7932	17.4811	3.6470
13	8.5994	0.1163	0.02369	42.2187	0.20369	4.9095	18.8765	3.8449
14	10.1472	0.0985	0.01968	50.8180	0.19968	5.0081	20.1576	4.0250
15	11.9737	0.0835	0.01640	60.9653	0.19640	5.0916	21.3269	4.1887
16	14.1290	0.0708	0.01371	72.9390	0.19371	5.1624	22.3885	4.3369
17	16.6722	0.0600	0.01149	87.0680	0.19149	5.2223	23.3482	4.4708
18	19.6733	0.0508	0.00964	103.7403	0.18964	5.2732	24.2123	4.5916
19	23.2144	0.0431	0.00810	123.4135	0.18810	5.3162	24.9877	4.7003
20	27.3930	0.0365	0.00682	146.6280	0.18682	5.3527	25.6813	4.7978
21	32.3238	0.0309	0.00575	174.0210	0.18575	5.3837	26.3000	4.8851
22	38.1421	0.0262	0.00485	206.3448	0.18485	5.4099	26.8506	4.9632
23	45.0076	0.0222	0.00409	244.4868	0.18409	5.4321	27.3394	5.0329
24	53.1090	0.0188	0.00345	289.4945	0.18345	5.4509	27.7725	5.0950
25	62.6686	0.0160	0.00292	342.6035	0.18292	5.4669	28.1555	5.1502
26	73.9490	0.0135	0.00247	405.2721	0.18247	5.4804	28.4935	5.1991
27	87.2598	0.0115	0.00209	479.2211	0.18209	5.4919	28.7915	5.2425
28	102.9666	0.0097	0.00177	566.4809	0.18177	5.5016	29.0537	5.2810
29	121.5005	0.0082	0.00149	669.4475	0.18149	5.5098	29.2842	5.3149
34	277.9638	0.0036	0.00065	1538.6878	0.18065	5.5356	30.0736	5.4328
39	635.9139	0.0016	0.00028	3527.2992	0.18028	5.5468	30.4749	5.4941
44	1454.8168	0.0007	0.00012	8076.7603	0.18012	5.5517	30.6750	5.5253
49	3328.2685	0.0003	0.00005	18484.8251	0.18005	5.5539	30.7731	5.5408
54	7614.2721	0.0001	0.00002	42295.9563	0.18002	5.5548	30.8207	5.5485
59	17419.6101	0.0001	0.00001	96770.0563	0.18001	5.5552	30.8436	5.5522
60	20555.1400	0.0000	0.00001	114189.6665	0.18001	5.5553	30.8465	5.5526

Table A25 Compound Interest Factors: 19%

n	Single Payment		Uniform Payment Series				Arithmetic Gradient	
	F/P	P/F	A/F	F/A	A/P	P/A	P/G	A/G
1	1.1900	0.8403	1.00000	1.0000	1.19000	0.8403		
2	1.4161	0.7062	0.45662	2.1900	0.64662	1.5465	0.7062	0.4566
3	1.6852	0.5934	0.27731	3.6061	0.46731	2.1399	1.8930	0.8846
4	2.0053	0.4987	0.18899	5.2913	0.37899	2.6386	3.3890	1.2844
5	2.3864	0.4190	0.13705	7.2966	0.32705	3.0576	5.0652	1.6566
6	2.8398	0.3521	0.10327	9.6830	0.29327	3.4098	6.8259	2.0019
7	3.3793	0.2959	0.07985	12.5227	0.26985	3.7057	8.6014	2.3211
8	4.0214	0.2487	0.06289	15.9020	0.25289	3.9544	10.3421	2.6154
9	4.7854	0.2090	0.05019	19.9234	0.24019	4.1633	12.0138	2.8856
10	5.6947	0.1756	0.04047	24.7089	0.23047	4.3389	13.5943	3.1331

(*Continued*)

Table A.25 (Continued)

n	Single Payment		Uniform Payment Series				Arithmetic Gradient	
	F/P	P/F	A/F	F/A	A/P	P/A	P/G	A/G
11	6.7767	0.1476	0.03289	30.4035	0.22289	4.4865	15.0699	3.3589
12	8.0642	0.1240	0.02690	37.1802	0.21690	4.6105	16.4340	3.5645
13	9.5964	0.1042	0.02210	45.2445	0.21210	4.7147	17.6844	3.7509
14	11.4198	0.0876	0.01823	54.8409	0.20823	4.8023	18.8228	3.9196
15	13.5895	0.0736	0.01509	66.2607	0.20509	4.8759	19.8530	4.0717
16	16.1715	0.0618	0.01252	79.8502	0.20252	4.9377	20.7806	4.2086
17	19.2441	0.0520	0.01041	96.0218	0.20041	4.9897	21.6120	4.3314
18	22.9005	0.0437	0.00868	115.2659	0.19868	5.0333	22.3543	4.4413
19	27.2516	0.0367	0.00724	138.1664	0.19724	5.0700	23.0148	4.5394
20	32.4294	0.0308	0.00605	165.4180	0.19605	5.1009	23.6007	4.6268
21	38.5910	0.0259	0.00505	197.8474	0.19505	5.1268	24.1190	4.7045
22	45.9233	0.0218	0.00423	236.4385	0.19423	5.1486	24.5763	4.7734
23	54.6487	0.0183	0.00354	282.3618	0.19354	5.1668	24.9788	4.8344
24	65.0320	0.0154	0.00297	337.0105	0.19297	5.1822	25.3325	4.8883
25	77.3881	0.0129	0.00249	402.0425	0.19249	5.1951	25.6426	4.9359
26	92.0918	0.0109	0.00209	479.4306	0.19209	5.2060	25.9141	4.9777
27	109.5893	0.0091	0.00175	571.5224	0.19175	5.2151	26.1514	5.0145
28	130.4112	0.0077	0.00147	681.1116	0.19147	5.2228	26.3584	5.0468
29	155.1893	0.0064	0.00123	811.5228	0.19123	5.2292	26.5388	5.0751
34	370.3366	0.0027	0.00051	1943.8771	0.19051	5.2489	27.1428	5.1711
39	883.7542	0.0011	0.00022	4646.0748	0.19022	5.2572	27.4372	5.2190
44	2108.9501	0.0005	0.00009	11094.4741	0.19009	5.2607	27.5779	5.2423
49	5032.7008	0.0002	0.00004	26482.6356	0.19004	5.2621	27.6441	5.2534
54	12009.8039	0.0001	0.00002	63204.2309	0.19002	5.2627	27.6749	5.2587
55	14291.6666	0.0001	0.00001	75214.0348	0.19001	5.2628	27.6786	5.2593

Table A26 Compound Interest Factors: 20%

n	Single Payment		Uniform Payment Series				Arithmetic Gradient	
	F/P	P/F	A/F	F/A	A/P	P/A	P/G	A/G
1	1.2000	0.8333	1.00000	1.0000	1.20000	0.8333		
2	1.4400	0.6944	0.45455	2.2000	0.65455	1.5278	0.6944	0.4545
3	1.7280	0.5787	0.27473	3.6400	0.47473	2.1065	1.8519	0.8791
4	2.0736	0.4823	0.18629	5.3680	0.38629	2.5887	3.2986	1.2742
5	2.4883	0.4019	0.13438	7.4416	0.33438	2.9906	4.9061	1.6405
6	2.9860	0.3349	0.10071	9.9299	0.30071	3.3255	6.5806	1.9788
7	3.5832	0.2791	0.07742	12.9159	0.27742	3.6046	8.2551	2.2902
8	4.2998	0.2326	0.06061	16.4991	0.26061	3.8372	9.8831	2.5756
9	5.1598	0.1938	0.04808	20.7989	0.24808	4.0310	11.4335	2.8364
10	6.1917	0.1615	0.03852	25.9587	0.23852	4.1925	12.8871	3.0739
11	7.4301	0.1346	0.03110	32.1504	0.23110	4.3271	14.2330	3.2893
12	8.9161	0.1122	0.02526	39.5805	0.22526	4.4392	15.4667	3.4841
13	10.6993	0.0935	0.02062	48.4966	0.22062	4.5327	16.5883	3.6597
14	12.8392	0.0779	0.01689	59.1959	0.21689	4.6106	17.6008	3.8175

(*Continued*)

Table A.26 (Continued)

n	Single Payment		Uniform Payment Series				Arithmetic Gradient	
	F/P	P/F	A/F	F/A	A/P	P/A	P/G	A/G
15	15.4070	0.0649	0.01388	72.0351	0.21388	4.6755	18.5095	3.9588
16	18.4884	0.0541	0.01144	87.4421	0.21144	4.7296	19.3208	4.0851
17	22.1861	0.0451	0.00944	105.9306	0.20944	4.7746	20.0419	4.1976
18	26.6233	0.0376	0.00781	128.1167	0.20781	4.8122	20.6805	4.2975
19	31.9480	0.0313	0.00646	154.7400	0.20646	4.8435	21.2439	4.3861
20	38.3376	0.0261	0.00536	186.6880	0.20536	4.8696	21.7395	4.4643
21	46.0051	0.0217	0.00444	225.0256	0.20444	4.8913	22.1742	4.5334
22	55.2061	0.0181	0.00369	271.0307	0.20369	4.9094	22.5546	4.5941
23	66.2474	0.0151	0.00307	326.2369	0.20307	4.9245	22.8867	4.6475
24	79.4968	0.0126	0.00255	392.4842	0.20255	4.9371	23.1760	4.6943
25	95.3962	0.0105	0.00212	471.9811	0.20212	4.9476	23.4276	4.7352
26	114.4755	0.0087	0.00176	567.3773	0.20176	4.9563	23.6460	4.7709
27	137.3706	0.0073	0.00147	681.8528	0.20147	4.9636	23.8353	4.8020
28	164.8447	0.0061	0.00122	819.2233	0.20122	4.9697	23.9991	4.8291
29	197.8136	0.0051	0.00102	984.0680	0.20102	4.9747	24.1406	4.8527
34	492.2235	0.0020	0.00041	2456.1176	0.20041	4.9898	24.6038	4.9308
39	1224.8096	0.0008	0.00016	6119.0482	0.20016	4.9959	24.8204	4.9681
44	3047.7183	0.0003	0.00007	15233.5916	0.20007	4.9984	24.9196	4.9856
49	7583.6985	0.0001	0.00003	37913.4923	0.20003	4.9993	24.9644	4.9935
54	18870.6685	0.0001	0.00001	94348.3427	0.20001	4.9997	24.9844	4.9971
55	22644.8023	0.0000	0.00001	113219.0113	0.20001	4.9998	24.9868	4.9976

Table A27 Compound Interest Factors: 21%

n	Single Payment		Uniform Payment Series				Arithmetic Gradient	
	F/P	P/F	A/F	F/A	A/P	P/A	P/G	A/G
1	1.2100	0.8264	1.00000	1.0000	1.21000	0.8264		
2	1.4641	0.6830	0.45249	2.2100	0.66249	1.5095	0.6830	0.4525
3	1.7716	0.5645	0.27218	3.6741	0.48218	2.0739	1.8120	0.8737
4	2.1436	0.4665	0.18363	5.4457	0.39363	2.5404	3.2115	1.2641
5	2.5937	0.3855	0.13177	7.5892	0.34177	2.9260	4.7537	1.6246
6	3.1384	0.3186	0.09820	10.1830	0.30820	3.2446	6.3468	1.9561
7	3.7975	0.2633	0.07507	13.3214	0.28507	3.5079	7.9268	2.2597
8	4.5950	0.2176	0.05841	17.1189	0.26841	3.7256	9.4502	2.5366
9	5.5599	0.1799	0.04605	21.7139	0.25605	3.9054	10.8891	2.7882
10	6.7275	0.1486	0.03667	27.2738	0.24667	4.0541	12.2269	3.0159
11	8.1403	0.1228	0.02941	34.0013	0.23941	4.1769	13.4553	3.2213
12	9.8497	0.1015	0.02373	42.1416	0.23373	4.2784	14.5721	3.4059
13	11.9182	0.0839	0.01923	51.9913	0.22923	4.3624	15.5790	3.5712
14	14.4210	0.0693	0.01565	63.9095	0.22565	4.4317	16.4804	3.7188
15	17.4494	0.0573	0.01277	78.3305	0.22277	4.4890	17.2828	3.8500
16	21.1138	0.0474	0.01044	95.7799	0.22044	4.5364	17.9932	3.9664
17	25.5477	0.0391	0.00855	116.8937	0.21855	4.5755	18.6195	4.0694
18	30.9127	0.0323	0.00702	142.4413	0.21702	4.6079	19.1694	4.1602
19	37.4043	0.0267	0.00577	173.3540	0.21577	4.6346	19.6506	4.2400

(*Continued*)

Table A.27 (Continued)

n	Single Payment		Uniform Payment Series				Arithmetic Gradient	
	F/P	P/F	A/F	F/A	A/P	P/A	P/G	A/G
20	45.2593	0.0221	0.00474	210.7584	0.21474	4.6567	20.0704	4.3100
21	54.7637	0.0183	0.00391	256.0176	0.21391	4.6750	20.4356	4.3713
22	66.2641	0.0151	0.00322	310.7813	0.21322	4.6900	20.7526	4.4248
23	80.1795	0.0125	0.00265	377.0454	0.21265	4.7025	21.0269	4.4714
24	97.0172	0.0103	0.00219	457.2249	0.21219	4.7128	21.2640	4.5119
25	117.3909	0.0085	0.00180	554.2422	0.21180	4.7213	21.4685	4.5471
26	142.0429	0.0070	0.00149	671.6330	0.21149	4.7284	21.6445	4.5776
27	171.8719	0.0058	0.00123	813.6759	0.21123	4.7342	21.7957	4.6039
28	207.9651	0.0048	0.00101	985.5479	0.21101	4.7390	21.9256	4.6266
29	251.6377	0.0040	0.00084	1193.5129	0.21084	4.7430	22.0368	4.6462
34	652.6834	0.0015	0.00032	3103.2545	0.21032	4.7546	22.3929	4.7097
39	1692.8927	0.0006	0.00012	8056.6321	0.21012	4.7591	22.5526	4.7389
44	4390.9278	0.0002	0.00005	20904.4180	0.21005	4.7608	22.6229	4.7519
49	11388.9358	0.0001	0.00002	54228.2658	0.21002	4.7615	22.6533	4.7576
54	29539.9664	0.0000	0.00001	140661.7448	0.21001	4.7617	22.6663	4.7601
55	35743.3594	0.0000	0.00001	170201.7112	0.21001	4.7618	22.6678	4.7604

Table A28 Compound Interest Factors: 22%

n	Single Payment		Uniform Payment Series				Arithmetic Gradient	
	F/P	P/F	A/F	F/A	A/P	P/A	P/G	A/G
1	1.2200	0.8197	1.00000	1.0000	1.22000	0.8197		
2	1.4884	0.6719	0.45045	2.2200	0.67045	1.4915	0.6719	0.4505
3	1.8158	0.5507	0.26966	3.7084	0.48966	2.0422	1.7733	0.8683
4	2.2153	0.4514	0.18102	5.5242	0.40102	2.4936	3.1275	1.2542
5	2.7027	0.3700	0.12921	7.7396	0.34921	2.8636	4.6075	1.6090
6	3.2973	0.3033	0.09576	10.4423	0.31576	3.1669	6.1239	1.9337
7	4.0227	0.2486	0.07278	13.7396	0.29278	3.4155	7.6154	2.2297
8	4.9077	0.2038	0.05630	17.7623	0.27630	3.6193	9.0417	2.4982
9	5.9874	0.1670	0.04411	22.6700	0.26411	3.7863	10.3779	2.7409
10	7.3046	0.1369	0.03489	28.6574	0.25489	3.9232	11.6100	2.9593
11	8.9117	0.1122	0.02781	35.9620	0.24781	4.0354	12.7321	3.1551
12	10.8722	0.0920	0.02228	44.8737	0.24228	4.1274	13.7438	3.3299
13	13.2641	0.0754	0.01794	55.7459	0.23794	4.2028	14.6485	3.4855
14	16.1822	0.0618	0.01449	69.0100	0.23449	4.2646	15.4519	3.6233
15	19.7423	0.0507	0.01174	85.1922	0.23174	4.3152	16.1610	3.7451
16	24.0856	0.0415	0.00953	104.9345	0.22953	4.3567	16.7838	3.8524
17	29.3844	0.0340	0.00775	129.0201	0.22775	4.3908	17.3283	3.9465
18	35.8490	0.0279	0.00631	158.4045	0.22631	4.4187	17.8025	4.0289
19	43.7358	0.0229	0.00515	194.2535	0.22515	4.4415	18.2141	4.1009
20	53.3576	0.0187	0.00420	237.9893	0.22420	4.4603	18.5702	4.1635
21	65.0963	0.0154	0.00343	291.3469	0.22343	4.4756	18.8774	4.2178
22	79.4175	0.0126	0.00281	356.4432	0.22281	4.4882	19.1418	4.2649
23	96.8894	0.0103	0.00229	435.8607	0.22229	4.4985	19.3689	4.3056

(*Continued*)

Table A.28 (Continued)

n	*Single Payment*		*Uniform Payment Series*				*Arithmetic Gradient*	
	F/P	*P/F*	*A/F*	*F/A*	*A/P*	*P/A*	*P/G*	*A/G*
24	118.2050	0.0085	0.00188	532.7501	0.22188	4.5070	19.5635	4.3407
25	144.2101	0.0069	0.00154	650.9551	0.22154	4.5139	19.7299	4.3709
26	175.9364	0.0057	0.00126	795.1653	0.22126	4.5196	19.8720	4.3968
27	214.6424	0.0047	0.00103	971.1016	0.22103	4.5243	19.9931	4.4191
28	261.8637	0.0038	0.00084	1185.7440	0.22084	4.5281	20.0962	4.4381
29	319.4737	0.0031	0.00069	1447.6077	0.22069	4.5312	20.1839	4.4544
34	863.4441	0.0012	0.00026	3920.2006	0.22026	4.5402	20.4582	4.5060
39	2333.6375	0.0004	0.00009	10602.8978	0.22009	4.5435	20.5763	4.5287
44	6307.1411	0.0002	0.00003	28664.2779	0.22003	4.5447	20.6262	4.5385
49	17046.3618	0.0001	0.00001	77478.9175	0.22001	4.5452	20.6469	4.5426
54	46071.3413	0.0000	0.00000	209410.6423	0.22000	4.5454	20.6554	4.5443
55	56207.0364	0.0000	0.00000	255481.9837	0.22000	4.5454	20.6563	4.5445

Table A29 Compound Interest Factors: 23%

n	*Single Payment*		*Uniform Payment Series*				*Arithmetic Gradient*	
	F/P	*P/F*	*A/F*	*F/A*	*A/P*	*P/A*	*P/G*	*A/G*
1	1.2300	0.8130	1.00000	1.0000	1.23000	0.8130		
2	1.5129	0.6610	0.44843	2.2300	0.67843	1.4740	0.6610	0.4484
3	1.8609	0.5374	0.26717	3.7429	0.49717	2.0114	1.7358	0.8630
4	2.2889	0.4369	0.17845	5.6038	0.40845	2.4483	3.0464	1.2443
5	2.8153	0.3552	0.12670	7.8926	0.35670	2.8035	4.4672	1.5935
6	3.4628	0.2888	0.09339	10.7079	0.32339	3.0923	5.9112	1.9116
7	4.2593	0.2348	0.07057	14.1708	0.30057	3.3270	7.3198	2.2001
8	5.2389	0.1909	0.05426	18.4300	0.28426	3.5179	8.6560	2.4605
9	6.4439	0.1552	0.04225	23.6690	0.27225	3.6731	9.8975	2.6946
10	7.9259	0.1262	0.03321	30.1128	0.26321	3.7993	11.0330	2.9040
11	9.7489	0.1026	0.02629	38.0388	0.25629	3.9018	12.0588	3.0905
12	11.9912	0.0834	0.02093	47.7877	0.25093	3.9852	12.9761	3.2560
13	14.7491	0.0678	0.01673	59.7788	0.24673	4.0530	13.7897	3.4023
14	18.1414	0.0551	0.01342	74.5280	0.24342	4.1082	14.5063	3.5311
15	22.3140	0.0448	0.01079	92.6694	0.24079	4.1530	15.1337	3.6441
16	27.4462	0.0364	0.00870	114.9834	0.23870	4.1894	15.6802	3.7428
17	33.7588	0.0296	0.00702	142.4295	0.23702	4.2190	16.1542	3.8289
18	41.5233	0.0241	0.00568	176.1883	0.23568	4.2431	16.5636	3.9036
19	51.0737	0.0196	0.00459	217.7116	0.23459	4.2627	16.9160	3.9684
20	62.8206	0.0159	0.00372	268.7853	0.23372	4.2786	17.2185	4.0243
21	77.2694	0.0129	0.00302	331.6059	0.23302	4.2916	17.4773	4.0725
22	95.0413	0.0105	0.00245	408.8753	0.23245	4.3021	17.6983	4.1139
23	116.9008	0.0086	0.00198	503.9166	0.23198	4.3106	17.8865	4.1494
24	143.7880	0.0070	0.00161	620.8174	0.23161	4.3176	18.0464	4.1797
25	176.8593	0.0057	0.00131	764.6054	0.23131	4.3232	18.1821	4.2057
26	217.5369	0.0046	0.00106	941.4647	0.23106	4.3278	18.2970	4.2278
27	267.5704	0.0037	0.00086	1159.0016	0.23086	4.3316	18.3942	4.2465

(*Continued*)

Table A.29 (Continued)

n	Single Payment		Uniform Payment Series				Arithmetic Gradient	
	F/P	P/F	A/F	F/A	A/P	P/A	P/G	A/G
28	329.1115	0.0030	0.00070	1426.5719	0.23070	4.3346	18.4763	4.2625
29	404.8072	0.0025	0.00057	1755.6835	0.23057	4.3371	18.5454	4.2760
34	1139.6560	0.0009	0.00020	4950.6783	0.23020	4.3440	18.7573	4.3180
39	3208.4801	0.0003	0.00007	13945.5655	0.23007	4.3465	18.8449	4.3357
44	9032.8522	0.0001	0.00003	39268.9225	0.23003	4.3473	18.8803	4.3430
49	25430.2401	0.0000	0.00001	110561.9135	0.23001	4.3477	18.8945	4.3459
50	31279.1953	0.0000	0.00001	135992.1536	0.23001	4.3477	18.8960	4.3462

Table A30 Compound Interest Factors: 24%

n	Single Payment		Uniform Payment Series				Arithmetic Gradient	
	F/P	P/F	A/F	F/A	A/P	P/A	P/G	A/G
1	1.2400	0.8065	1.00000	1.0000	1.24000	0.8065		
2	1.5376	0.6504	0.44643	2.2400	0.68643	1.4568	0.6504	0.4464
3	1.9066	0.5245	0.26472	3.7776	0.50472	1.9813	1.6993	0.8577
4	2.3642	0.4230	0.17593	5.6842	0.41593	2.4043	2.9683	1.2346
5	2.9316	0.3411	0.12425	8.0484	0.36425	2.7454	4.3327	1.5782
6	3.6352	0.2751	0.09107	10.9801	0.33107	3.0205	5.7081	1.8898
7	4.5077	0.2218	0.06842	14.6153	0.30842	3.2423	7.0392	2.1710
8	5.5895	0.1789	0.05229	19.1229	0.29229	3.4212	8.2915	2.4236
9	6.9310	0.1443	0.04047	24.7125	0.28047	3.5655	9.4458	2.6492
10	8.5944	0.1164	0.03160	31.6434	0.27160	3.6819	10.4930	2.8499
11	10.6571	0.0938	0.02485	40.2379	0.26485	3.7757	11.4313	3.0276
12	13.2148	0.0757	0.01965	50.8950	0.25965	3.8514	12.2637	3.1843
13	16.3863	0.0610	0.01560	64.1097	0.25560	3.9124	12.9960	3.3218
14	20.3191	0.0492	0.01242	80.4961	0.25242	3.9616	13.6358	3.4420
15	25.1956	0.0397	0.00992	100.8151	0.24992	4.0013	14.1915	3.5467
16	31.2426	0.0320	0.00794	126.0108	0.24794	4.0333	14.6716	3.6376
17	38.7408	0.0258	0.00636	157.2534	0.24636	4.0591	15.0846	3.7162
18	48.0386	0.0208	0.00510	195.9942	0.24510	4.0799	15.4385	3.7840
19	59.5679	0.0168	0.00410	244.0328	0.24410	4.0967	15.7406	3.8423
20	73.8641	0.0135	0.00329	303.6006	0.24329	4.1103	15.9979	3.8922
21	91.5915	0.0109	0.00265	377.4648	0.24265	4.1212	16.2162	3.9349
22	113.5735	0.0088	0.00213	469.0563	0.24213	4.1300	16.4011	3.9712
23	140.8312	0.0071	0.00172	582.6298	0.24172	4.1371	16.5574	4.0022
24	174.6306	0.0057	0.00138	723.4610	0.24138	4.1428	16.6891	4.0284
25	216.5420	0.0046	0.00111	898.0916	0.24111	4.1474	16.7999	4.0507
26	268.5121	0.0037	0.00090	1114.6336	0.24090	4.1511	16.8930	4.0695
27	332.9550	0.0030	0.00072	1383.1457	0.24072	4.1542	16.9711	4.0853
28	412.8642	0.0024	0.00058	1716.1007	0.24058	4.1566	17.0365	4.0987
29	511.9516	0.0020	0.00047	2128.9648	0.24047	4.1585	17.0912	4.1099
34	1500.8500	0.0007	0.00016	6249.3751	0.24016	4.1639	17.2552	4.1440
39	4399.9295	0.0002	0.00005	18328.8731	0.24005	4.1657	17.3202	4.1578
44	12898.9437	0.0001	0.00002	53741.4321	0.24002	4.1663	17.3456	4.1633
49	37814.8666	0.0000	0.00001	157557.7776	0.24001	4.1666	17.3553	4.1654
50	46890.4346	0.0000	0.00001	195372.6442	0.24001	4.1666	17.3563	4.1656

Table A31 Compound Interest Factors: 25%

n	*Single Payment*		*Uniform Payment Series*				*Arithmetic Gradient*	
	F/P	*P/F*	*A/F*	*F/A*	*A/P*	*P/A*	*P/G*	*A/G*
1	1.2500	0.8000	1.00000	1.0000	1.25000	0.8000		
2	1.5625	0.6400	0.44444	2.2500	0.69444	1.4400	0.6400	0.4444
3	1.9531	0.5120	0.26230	3.8125	0.51230	1.9520	1.6640	0.8525
4	2.4414	0.4096	0.17344	5.7656	0.42344	2.3616	2.8928	1.2249
5	3.0518	0.3277	0.12185	8.2070	0.37185	2.6893	4.2035	1.5631
6	3.8147	0.2621	0.08882	11.2588	0.33882	2.9514	5.5142	1.8683
7	4.7684	0.2097	0.06634	15.0735	0.31634	3.1611	6.7725	2.1424
8	5.9605	0.1678	0.05040	19.8419	0.30040	3.3289	7.9469	2.3872
9	7.4506	0.1342	0.03876	25.8023	0.28876	3.4631	9.0207	2.6048
10	9.3132	0.1074	0.03007	33.2529	0.28007	3.5705	9.9870	2.7971
11	11.6415	0.0859	0.02349	42.5661	0.27349	3.6564	10.8460	2.9663
12	14.5519	0.0687	0.01845	54.2077	0.26845	3.7251	11.6020	3.1145
13	18.1899	0.0550	0.01454	68.7596	0.26454	3.7801	12.2617	3.2437
14	22.7374	0.0440	0.01150	86.9495	0.26150	3.8241	12.8334	3.3559
15	28.4217	0.0352	0.00912	109.6868	0.25912	3.8593	13.3260	3.4530
16	35.5271	0.0281	0.00724	138.1085	0.25724	3.8874	13.7482	3.5366
17	44.4089	0.0225	0.00576	173.6357	0.25576	3.9099	14.1085	3.6084
18	55.5112	0.0180	0.00459	218.0446	0.25459	3.9279	14.4147	3.6698
19	69.3889	0.0144	0.00366	273.5558	0.25366	3.9424	14.6741	3.7222
20	86.7362	0.0115	0.00292	342.9447	0.25292	3.9539	14.8932	3.7667
21	108.4202	0.0092	0.00233	429.6809	0.25233	3.9631	15.0777	3.8045
22	135.5253	0.0074	0.00186	538.1011	0.25186	3.9705	15.2326	3.8365
23	169.4066	0.0059	0.00148	673.6264	0.25148	3.9764	15.3625	3.8634
24	211.7582	0.0047	0.00119	843.0329	0.25119	3.9811	15.4711	3.8861
25	264.6978	0.0038	0.00095	1054.7912	0.25095	3.9849	15.5618	3.9052
26	330.8722	0.0030	0.00076	1319.4890	0.25076	3.9879	15.6373	3.9212
27	413.5903	0.0024	0.00061	1650.3612	0.25061	3.9903	15.7002	3.9346
28	516.9879	0.0019	0.00048	2063.9515	0.25048	3.9923	15.7524	3.9457
29	646.2349	0.0015	0.00039	2580.9394	0.25039	3.9938	15.7957	3.9551
34	1972.1523	0.0005	0.00013	7884.6091	0.25013	3.9980	15.9229	3.9828
39	6018.5311	0.0002	0.00004	24070.1243	0.25004	3.9993	15.9714	3.9935
44	18367.0992	0.0001	0.00001	73464.3969	0.25001	3.9998	15.9895	3.9976
49	56051.9386	0.0000	0.00000	224203.7543	0.25000	3.9999	15.9962	3.9991
50	70064.9232	0.0000	0.00000	280255.6929	0.25000	3.9999	15.9969	3.9993

Table A32 Compound Interest Factors: 30%

n	*Single Payment*		*Uniform Payment Series*				*Arithmetic Gradient*	
	F/P	*P/F*	*A/F*	*F/A*	*A/P*	*P/A*	*P/G*	*A/G*
1	1.3000	0.7692	1.00000	1.0000	1.30000	0.7692		
2	1.6900	0.5917	0.43478	2.3000	0.73478	1.3609	0.5917	0.4348
3	2.1970	0.4552	0.25063	3.9900	0.55063	1.8161	1.5020	0.8271
4	2.8561	0.3501	0.16163	6.1870	0.46163	2.1662	2.5524	1.1783
5	3.7129	0.2693	0.11058	9.0431	0.41058	2.4356	3.6297	1.4903
6	4.8268	0.2072	0.07839	12.7560	0.37839	2.6427	4.6656	1.7654

(*Continued*)

Table A.32 (Continued)

n	Single Payment		Uniform Payment Series				Arithmetic Gradient	
	F/P	P/F	A/F	F/A	A/P	P/A	P/G	A/G
7	6.2749	0.1594	0.05687	17.5828	0.35687	2.8021	5.6218	2.0063
8	8.1573	0.1226	0.04192	23.8577	0.34192	2.9247	6.4800	2.2156
9	10.6045	0.0943	0.03124	32.0150	0.33124	3.0190	7.2343	2.3963
10	13.7858	0.0725	0.02346	42.6195	0.32346	3.0915	7.8872	2.5512
11	17.9216	0.0558	0.01773	56.4053	0.31773	3.1473	8.4452	2.6833
12	23.2981	0.0429	0.01345	74.3270	0.31345	3.1903	8.9173	2.7952
13	30.2875	0.0330	0.01024	97.6250	0.31024	3.2233	9.3135	2.8895
14	39.3738	0.0254	0.00782	127.9125	0.30782	3.2487	9.6437	2.9685
15	51.1859	0.0195	0.00598	167.2863	0.30598	3.2682	9.9172	3.0344
16	66.5417	0.0150	0.00458	218.4722	0.30458	3.2832	10.1426	3.0892
17	86.5042	0.0116	0.00351	285.0139	0.30351	3.2948	10.3276	3.1345
18	112.4554	0.0089	0.00269	371.5180	0.30269	3.3037	10.4788	3.1718
19	146.1920	0.0068	0.00207	483.9734	0.30207	3.3105	10.6019	3.2025
20	190.0496	0.0053	0.00159	630.1655	0.30159	3.3158	10.7019	3.2275
21	247.0645	0.0040	0.00122	820.2151	0.30122	3.3198	10.7828	3.2480
22	321.1839	0.0031	0.00094	1067.2796	0.30094	3.3230	10.8482	3.2646
23	417.5391	0.0024	0.00072	1388.4635	0.30072	3.3254	10.9009	3.2781
24	542.8008	0.0018	0.00055	1806.0026	0.30055	3.3272	10.9433	3.2890
25	705.6410	0.0014	0.00043	2348.8033	0.30043	3.3286	10.9773	3.2979
26	917.3333	0.0011	0.00033	3054.4443	0.30033	3.3297	11.0045	3.3050
27	1192.5333	0.0008	0.00025	3971.7776	0.30025	3.3305	11.0263	3.3107
28	1550.2933	0.0006	0.00019	5164.3109	0.30019	3.3312	11.0437	3.3153
29	2015.3813	0.0005	0.00015	6714.6042	0.30015	3.3317	11.0576	3.3189
30	2619.9956	0.0004	0.00011	8729.9855	0.30011	3.3321	11.0687	3.3219
31	3405.9943	0.0003	0.00009	11349.9811	0.30009	3.3324	11.0775	3.3242
32	4427.7926	0.0002	0.00007	14755.9755	0.30007	3.3326	11.0845	3.3261
33	5756.1304	0.0002	0.00005	19183.7681	0.30005	3.3328	11.0901	3.3276
34	7482.9696	0.0001	0.00004	24939.8985	0.30004	3.3329	11.0945	3.3288
35	9727.8604	0.0001	0.00003	32422.8681	0.30003	3.3330	11.0980	3.3297

Table A33 Compound Interest Factors: 35%

n	Single Payment		Uniform Payment Series				Arithmetic Gradient	
	F/P	P/F	A/F	F/A	A/P	P/A	P/G	A/G
1	1.3500	0.7407	1.00000	1.0000	1.35000	0.7407		
2	1.8225	0.5487	0.42553	2.3500	0.77553	1.2894	0.5487	0.4255
3	2.4604	0.4064	0.23966	4.1725	0.58966	1.6959	1.3616	0.8029
4	3.3215	0.3011	0.15076	6.6329	0.50076	1.9969	2.2648	1.1341
5	4.4840	0.2230	0.10046	9.9544	0.45046	2.2200	3.1568	1.4220
6	6.0534	0.1652	0.06926	14.4384	0.41926	2.3852	3.9828	1.6698
7	8.1722	0.1224	0.04880	20.4919	0.39880	2.5075	4.7170	1.8811
8	11.0324	0.0906	0.03489	28.6640	0.38489	2.5982	5.3515	2.0597
9	14.8937	0.0671	0.02519	39.6964	0.37519	2.6653	5.8886	2.2094
10	20.1066	0.0497	0.01832	54.5902	0.36832	2.7150	6.3363	2.3338

(*Continued*)

Table A.33 (Continued)

n	Single Payment		Uniform Payment Series				Arithmetic Gradient	
	F/P	P/F	A/F	F/A	A/P	P/A	P/G	A/G
11	27.1439	0.0368	0.01339	74.6967	0.36339	2.7519	6.7047	2.4364
12	36.6442	0.0273	0.00982	101.8406	0.35982	2.7792	7.0049	2.5205
13	49.4697	0.0202	0.00722	138.4848	0.35722	2.7994	7.2474	2.5889
14	66.7841	0.0150	0.00532	187.9544	0.35532	2.8144	7.4421	2.6443
15	90.1585	0.0111	0.00393	254.7385	0.35393	2.8255	7.5974	2.6889
16	121.7139	0.0082	0.00290	344.8970	0.35290	2.8337	7.7206	2.7246
17	164.3138	0.0061	0.00214	466.6109	0.35214	2.8398	7.8180	2.7530
18	221.8236	0.0045	0.00158	630.9247	0.35158	2.8443	7.8946	2.7756
19	299.4619	0.0033	0.00117	852.7483	0.35117	2.8476	7.9547	2.7935
20	404.2736	0.0025	0.00087	1152.2103	0.35087	2.8501	8.0017	2.8075
21	545.7693	0.0018	0.00064	1556.4838	0.35064	2.8519	8.0384	2.8186
22	736.7886	0.0014	0.00048	2102.2532	0.35048	2.8533	8.0669	2.8272
23	994.6646	0.0010	0.00035	2839.0418	0.35035	2.8543	8.0890	2.8340
24	1342.7973	0.0007	0.00026	3833.7064	0.35026	2.8550	8.1061	2.8393
25	1812.7763	0.0006	0.00019	5176.5037	0.35019	2.8556	8.1194	2.8433
26	2447.2480	0.0004	0.00014	6989.2800	0.35014	2.8560	8.1296	2.8465
27	3303.7848	0.0003	0.00011	9436.5280	0.35011	2.8563	8.1374	2.8490
28	4460.1095	0.0002	0.00008	12740.3128	0.35008	2.8565	8.1435	2.8509
29	6021.1478	0.0002	0.00006	17200.4222	0.35006	2.8567	8.1481	2.8523
35	36448.6878	0.0000	0.00001	104136.2508	0.35001	2.8571	8.1603	2.8562

Table A34 Compound Interest Factors: 40%

n	Single Payment		Uniform Payment Series				Arithmetic Gradient	
	F/P	P/F	A/F	F/A	A/P	P/A	P/G	A/G
1	1.4000	0.7143	1.00000	1.0000	1.40000	0.7143		
2	1.9600	0.5102	0.41667	2.4000	0.81667	1.2245	0.5102	0.4167
3	2.7440	0.3644	0.22936	4.3600	0.62936	1.5889	1.2391	0.7798
4	3.8416	0.2603	0.14077	7.1040	0.54077	1.8492	2.0200	1.0923
5	5.3782	0.1859	0.09136	10.9456	0.49136	2.0352	2.7637	1.3580
6	7.5295	0.1328	0.06126	16.3238	0.46126	2.1680	3.4278	1.5811
7	10.5414	0.0949	0.04192	23.8534	0.44192	2.2628	3.9970	1.7664
8	14.7579	0.0678	0.02907	34.3947	0.42907	2.3306	4.4713	1.9185
9	20.6610	0.0484	0.02034	49.1526	0.42034	2.3790	4.8585	2.0422
10	28.9255	0.0346	0.01432	69.8137	0.41432	2.4136	5.1696	2.1419
11	40.4957	0.0247	0.01013	98.7391	0.41013	2.4383	5.4166	2.2215
12	56.6939	0.0176	0.00718	139.2348	0.40718	2.4559	5.6106	2.2845
13	79.3715	0.0126	0.00510	195.9287	0.40510	2.4685	5.7618	2.3341
14	111.1201	0.0090	0.00363	275.3002	0.40363	2.4775	5.8788	2.3729
15	155.5681	0.0064	0.00259	386.4202	0.40259	2.4839	5.9688	2.4030
16	217.7953	0.0046	0.00185	541.9883	0.40185	2.4885	6.0376	2.4262
17	304.9135	0.0033	0.00132	759.7837	0.40132	2.4918	6.0901	2.4441
18	426.8789	0.0023	0.00094	1064.6971	0.40094	2.4941	6.1299	2.4577
19	597.6304	0.0017	0.00067	1491.5760	0.40067	2.4958	6.1601	2.4682

(*Continued*)

Table A.34 (Continued)

n	*Single Payment*		*Uniform Payment Series*				*Arithmetic Gradient*	
	F/P	*P/F*	*A/F*	*F/A*	*A/P*	*P/A*	*P/G*	*A/G*
20	836.6826	0.0012	0.00048	2089.2064	0.40048	2.4970	6.1828	2.4761
21	1171.3556	0.0009	0.00034	2925.8889	0.40034	2.4979	6.1998	2.4821
22	1639.8978	0.0006	0.00024	4097.2445	0.40024	2.4985	6.2127	2.4866
23	2295.8569	0.0004	0.00017	5737.1423	0.40017	2.4989	6.2222	2.4900
24	3214.1997	0.0003	0.00012	8032.9993	0.40012	2.4992	6.2294	2.4925
25	4499.8796	0.0002	0.00009	11247.1990	0.40009	2.4994	6.2347	2.4944
26	6299.8314	0.0002	0.00006	15747.0785	0.40006	2.4996	6.2387	2.4959
27	8819.7640	0.0001	0.00005	22046.9099	0.40005	2.4997	6.2416	2.4969
28	12347.6696	0.0001	0.00003	30866.6739	0.40003	2.4998	6.2438	2.4977
29	17286.7374	0.0001	0.00002	43214.3435	0.40002	2.4999	6.2454	2.4983
30	24201.4324	0.0000	0.00002	60501.0809	0.40002	2.4999	6.2466	2.4988

Appendix B

Solutions to Selected Problems

Chapter 2

2.2

$$\begin{aligned} I &= (\$10{,}000)\times(0.05)\times(4) \\ I &= \$2{,}000 \end{aligned}$$

2.4

$$\begin{aligned} F_n &= P + P\times(i)\times(n) \\ \$14{,}000{,}000 &= P + P\times(0.05)\times(8) \\ \$14{,}000{,}000 &= 1.4\times P \\ P &= \$10{,}000{,}000 \end{aligned}$$

2.6

$$\begin{aligned} F_n &= P\times(1+i)^n \\ F_6 &= \$100\times(1+0.08)^6 \\ F_6 &= \$100\times(1.5869) \\ F_6 &= \$158.69 \text{ million} \end{aligned}$$

2.10

$$P = F\times\frac{1}{(1+i)^n}$$

$$P = \$2{,}000{,}00\times\frac{1}{(1+0.08)^5}$$

$$P = \$2{,}000{,}000\times[0.6806]$$

$$P = \$1{,}361{,}166$$

Alternatively,

$$\begin{aligned} P &= F\ (P/F,\ i,\ n) \\ P &= \$2{,}000{,}000\ (P/F, 8\%, 5) \end{aligned}$$

From Table A14 for 8%, enter interest factor (P/F, 8%, 5) 0.6806 in the alternative equation and calculate

$$P = \$2,000,000 \times (0.6806)$$
$$P = \$1,361,166$$

2.12

Since payments are not uniform, first calculate the future value of each payment at the end of year four; then simply add them:

$$F_n = P \times (1+i)^n$$

Future value of the first payment at the end of year $4 = \$50,000 \times (1+0.10)^3$

$$= \$50,000 \times (1.331)$$
$$= \$66,550$$

Future value of the second payment at end of year $4 = \$65,000 \times (1+0.10)^2$:

$$4 = \$65,000 \times (1+0.10)^2$$

Future value of the third payment at end of year $4 = \$80,000 \times (1+0.10)^1$

$$= \$80,000 \times (1.10)$$
$$= \$88,000$$

Future value of the fourth payment at end of year $4 = \$100,000$:

$$\text{Total future value} = \$66,550 + \$78,650 + \$88,000 + \$100,000$$
$$\text{Total future value} = \$333,200$$

2.14

Using rule 72 for compound interest,

$$n = \frac{72}{12} = 6 \text{ years}$$

Chapter 3

3.2

$$A = F \times \left[\frac{i}{(1+i)^n - 1} \right]$$

$$A = \$400,000 \times \left[\frac{0.08}{(1+0.08)^{18} - 1} \right]$$

$$A = \$400{,}000 \times \left[\frac{0.08}{3.9960 - 1}\right]$$

$$A = \$32{,}000$$

$$2.9960$$

$$A = \$10{,}681$$

Alternatively,

$$A = F(A/F, i, n)$$

$$A = \$400{,}000 \times (A/F, 8\%, 18)$$

From Table A14 for 8%, interest factor $(A/F, 8\%, 18)$is 0.0267.

$$A = \$400{,}000 \times (0.0267)$$

$$A = \$10{,}680$$

3.5

We compare the two alternatives on a present value basis.
First, we calculate the present leasing cost (P_L) for 10 years:

$$P_L = \$100{,}000(P/A, 6\%, 10)$$

$$P_L = \$100{,}000 \times (7.3601)$$

$$P_L = \$736{,}010$$

Second, we calculate the present cost of building the hangar and the maintenance cost (P_B):

$$P_P = \$960{,}000 + \$5{,}000(P/A, 6\%, 10) - \$500{,}000(P/F, 6\%, 10)$$

$$P_P = \$960{,}000 + \$5{,}000 \times (7.3601) - \$500{,}000 \times (0.5584)$$

$$P_P = \$960{,}000 + \$36{,}801 - \$279{,}200$$

$$P_P = \$717{,}601$$

Building is cost efficient.

3.8

$$P_G = \$100{,}000(P/A, 8\%, 5) + \$20{,}000(P/G, 8\%, 5)$$

$$P_G = \$100{,}000 \times (3.9927) + \$20{,}000 \times (7.3724)$$

$$P_G = \$399{,}270 + \$147{,}448$$

$$P_G = \$546{,}718$$

3.11

$$F_G = A(F/A, i, n) + G/i\,[F/A, i, n) - n]$$

$$F_G = \$12{,}000(F/A, 10\%, 25) + \$1{,}200/0.10[F/A, 10\%, 25) - 25]$$

$$F_G = \$12,000 \times (98.3471) + \frac{\$1,200}{0.10} \times [98.3471 - 25]$$
$$F_G = \$1,180,165 + \$880,165$$
$$F_G = \$2,060,330$$

Alternatively, one may calculate the present value of investments and then calculate that future amount at the end of 20 years.

$$P_G = \$12,000(P/A, 10\%, 25) + \$1,200(P/G, 10\%, 25)$$
$$P_G = \$12,000 \times (9.0770) + \$1,200 \times (67.6964)$$
$$P_G = \$108,924 + \$81,236$$
$$P_G = \$190,160$$
$$F_{20} = 190,160 \times (1 + .10)^{25}$$
$$F_{20} = 190,160 \times (10.8347)$$
$$F_{20} = \$2,060,327$$

3.14

Total contributions to retirement account in the first year $= \$120,000 \times (0.04 + 0.04) = \$9,600$.

$$P_g = \$15,000 \times \left[\frac{1 - \left\{ \frac{1 + 0.04}{(1 + 0.10)} \right\} \wedge 30}{0.10 - 0.04} \right]$$

$$P_g = \$15,000 \times \left[\frac{1 - 0.1859}{0.06} \right]$$
$$P_g = \$15,000 \times (13.5683)$$
$$P_g = \$203,524.50$$

The accumulation at the end of 30 years is

$$F_{30} = \$203,524.50 \times (1 + 0.10)^{30}$$
$$F_{30} = \$203,524.50 \times (17.4494)$$
$$F_{30} = \$3,551,380$$

3.17

The payments for the first five years are the same amounts, an annuity of \$40,000 per year for five years. The payments for the next five years are on an arithmetic gradient with the base amount of \$60,000 in year six increasing by \$20,000 per year through year 10:

$$P_T = P_A + P_G$$
$$P_T = \$40,000(P/A, 8\%, 5) + \{[\$60,000(P/A, 8\%, 5) + \$20,000(P/G, 8\%, 5)] \times (P/F, 8\%, 5)\}$$

$$P_T = \$40,000(3.9927) + \{[(\$60,000 \times 3.9927) + (\$20,000 \times 7.3724)] \times 0.6806\}$$
$$P_T = \$159,708 + [(\$239,562 + \$147,448) \times 0.6806]$$
$$P_T = \$159,708 + (\$387,010 \times 0.6806)$$
$$P_T = \$159,708 + \$263,399$$
$$P_T = \$423,107$$

Chapter 4

4.2

a. Nominal rate per month $= 18\% / 12 = 1.5\%$

$$i_{effective} = \left(1 + \frac{0.015}{30}\right)^{30} - 1$$
$$i_{effective} = 1.0151 - 1$$
$$i_{effective} = 0.0151$$
$$i_{effective} = 1.51\%$$

b. Nominal rate per quarter $= 4.5\%$

$$i_{effective} = \left(1 + \frac{0.045}{90}\right)^{90} - 1$$
$$i_{effective} = 1.0460 - 1$$
$$i_{effective} = 0.0460$$
$$i_{effective} = 4.60\%$$

c. $i_{effective} = \left(1 + \frac{0.18}{360}\right)^{360} - 1$

$$i_{effective} = 1.1972 - 1$$
$$i_{effective} = 0.1972$$

4.5

$$0.1956 = (1 +)^{12} - 1$$
$$1.1956 = (1 +)^{12}$$
$$(1.1956)^{1/12} = \left(1 + \frac{\text{r}}{12}\right)$$
$$1.015 = 1 + \frac{\text{r}}{12}$$
$$0.015 = \frac{\text{r}}{12}$$
$$r = 0.17998$$
$$r = 18\%$$

4.8

$$\text{Effective rate} = \left(1 + \frac{0.08}{4}\right)^4$$

Effective rate = 8.2432%

$$P = \frac{\$5,000,000}{(1+0.082432)^6}$$
$$P = \frac{\$5,000,000}{1.60844}$$
$$P = \$3,108,610$$

4.11

In this example, PP < CP, and we need to calculate quarterly payments to match the compounding period:

$$\text{quarterly payment} = \$200,000 \times 3 = \$600,000$$

Now we can rewrite the problem as Kazak Airline is depositing $600,000 per quarter for four years. Now PP = CP, and we can calculate the future value of all payments at the end of four years at 8% per year compounded quarterly:

$$F = A\left(F/A\,\frac{i\%}{4}, n\times 4\right)$$
$$F = \$600,000\left(F/A, \frac{8\%}{4}\, 4\times 4\right)$$
$$F = \$600,000(F/A, 2\%, 16)$$
$$F = \$600,000 \times (18.6393)$$
$$F = \$11,183,580$$

4.14

a. Nominal rate per month $= \frac{18\%}{12} = 1.5\%$

b. Effective rate per month $= e^{0.015} - 1 = 1.151\%$

c. Nominal rate per quarter $= \frac{18\%}{4} = 4.5\%$

d. Effective rate per quarter $= e^{0.045} - 1 = 4.603\%$

e. Semiannual nominal rate $= \frac{18\%}{2} = 9\%$

f. Semiannual effective rate $= e^{0.09} - 1 = 9.417\%$

g. Effective rate per year $= e^{0.18} - 1 = 19.722\%$

Chapter 5

5.3

$$\text{Bond price} = \$50 \times \frac{1}{0.04}\left[1 - \left[\frac{1}{(1+0.04)^4}\right]\right] + \frac{\$1,000}{(1+0.04)^4}$$

$$\text{Bond Price} = \$1,036.20$$

5.12

$$\text{P} = \$100(P/A,14\%,5) + \$1,000(P/F,14\%,5)$$
$$\text{P} = \$862.71$$

5.17

$$\text{P} = 300,000(P/A,12\%,6) - 50,000(P/G,12\%,6) = \$786,800$$

5.18

$$\text{A} = 100,000 \text{ and i} = 0.05.$$
$$\text{CC} = 100,000/0.05 = \$2,000,000$$

Chapter 6

6.2

$$\text{AW} = -\$5,000,000(,10\%,10) - \$400,000 + \$1,500,000$$
$$\text{AW} = -\$5,000,000(0.16275) - \$400,000 + \$1,500,000$$
$$\text{AW} = -\$813,750 - \$400,000 + \$1,500,000$$
$$\text{AW} = \$286,250$$

Since $\text{AW} > 0$, this project is economically justified.

6.4
Since revenues are constant per year, calculate the AW of all costs and add it to the annual revenue:

$$\text{AW}_{\text{System}} = -\ \text{AW}_{\text{Cost}} + \text{AW}_{\text{Revenue}}$$
$$\text{AW}_{\text{Cost}} = -\$4,000,000(\text{A/P}, 8\%, 10) - [\$500,000(\text{P/F}, 10\%, 4) + \$600,000(\text{P/F}, 10\%, 8)] \times [(\text{A/P}, 8\%, 10)] + \$200,000(\text{A/F}, 8\%, 10)$$
$$\text{AW}_{\text{Cost}} = -\$4,000,000\,(0.14903) - [\$500,000\,(0.7350) + \$600,000\,(0.5403)] \times [(0.14903)] + \$200,000(0.06903)$$
$$\text{AW}_{\text{Cost}} = -\$596,120 - [\$367,500 + \$324,180] \times [0.14903] + \$13,806$$
$$\text{AW}_{\text{Cost}} = -\$596,120 - \$103,081 + \$13,806$$
$$\text{AW}_{\text{Cost}} = -\$685,395$$

To calculate the annual worth of the project, simply add AW of costs to AW of revenue:

$$AW_{System} = -\$685,395 + \$1,200,000$$
$$AW_{System} = +\$514,605$$

Since project AW is greater than zero, this project is economically justified.

6.6

$$CR = [-\$4,000,000 - \$500,000\ (P/F\ 12\%, 5)][(A/P\ 12\%, 10)] + \$200,000\ (A/F\ 12\%, 10)$$
$$CR = [-\$4,000,000 - \$500,000\ (0.5674)][(0.17698)] + \$200,000\ (0.05698)$$
$$CR = [-\$4,000,000 - \$283,700][(0.17698)] + 11,396$$
$$CR = -\$758,129.23 + 11,396$$
$$CR = -\$\ 746,733.23$$

6.8

$$CR = -\$2,000,000\ (0.17401) + \$2,000,000(0.10)\ (0.09401)$$
$$CR = -\$348,020 + \$18,802$$
$$CR = -\$329,218$$

Since this is a cost-based project and there is no annual revenue, we use annual operating cost (AOC) instead of NACF:

$$A\ of\ AOC = -\$100,000 - \$50,000\ (A/G\ 9\%,\ 8)$$
$$A\ of\ AOC = -\$100,000 - \$50,000\ (3.0985)$$
$$A\ of\ AOC = -\$100,000 - \$154,925$$
$$A\ of\ AOC = -\$254,925$$
$$AW = -\$329,218 - \$254,925$$
$$AW = -\$584,143$$

6.10

$$AW = CR + A\ of\ NACF$$
$$CR = -\$1,100,000\ (A/P,\ 10\%, 10) + \$80,000\ (A/F, 10\%, 10)$$
$$CR = -\$1,100,000\ (0.16275) + \$80,000\ (0.06275)$$
$$CR = -\$179,025 + \$5,020$$
$$CR = -\$174,005$$

$$A\ of\ NACF = (\$300,000 - \$100,000) + (\$75,000 - \$50,000)\ (A/G, 10\%, 10$$
$$A\ of\ NACF = (\$200,000) + (\$25,000)\ (3.7255)$$
$$A\ of\ NACF = \$200,000 + \$93,137.50$$
$$A\ of\ NACF = \$293,137.50$$

$$AW = -\$174,005 + 293,137.50$$
$$AW = \$119,132.50$$

Since AW is greater than 0, the project is economically justified.

Chapter 7

7.7

$$PW = -\$10{,}000{,}000 - \$400{,}000\ (P/A,\ i^*, 10) - \$50{,}000\ (P/G,\ i^*, 10) + \$2{,}500{,}000\ (P/A,\ i^*, 10) = 0$$
$$PW = -\$10{,}000{,}000 + (\$2{,}500{,}000 - \$400{,}000)\ (P/A,\ i^*, 10) - \$50{,}000\ (P/G,\ i^*, 10) = 0$$
$$PW = -\$10{,}000{,}000 + \$2{,}100{,}000\ (P/A,\ i^*, 10) - \$50{,}000\ (P/G,\ i^*, 10) = 0$$

Try $i^* = 10\%$

$$PW = -\$10,000,000 + \$2,100,000\,(6.1446) - \$50,000\,(22.8913)$$
$$PW = -\$10,000,000 + \$12,903,660 - \$1,144,565$$
$$PW = \$1,759,095 > 0$$

Try $i^* = 12\%$

$$PW = -\$10,000,000 + \$2,100,000 \times (5.6502) - \$50,000 \times (20.2541)$$
$$PW = -\$10,000,000 + \$11,865,420 - \$1,012,705$$
$$PW = \$852,715 > 0$$

Try $i^* = 14\%$

$$PW = -\$10,000,000 + \$2,100,000 \times (5.2161) - \$50,000 \times (17.9906)$$
$$PW = -\$10,000,000 + \$10,953,810 - \$899,530$$
$$PW = \$54,280 > 0$$

Try $i^* = 15\%$

$$PW = -\$10,000,000 + \$2,100,000 \times (5.0188) - \$50,000 \times (16.9795)$$
$$PW = -\$10,000,000 + \$10,539,480 - \$848,975$$
$$PW = -\$309,495 > 0$$

i*	PW
14%	$54,280
14% + X%	0
15%	−$309,495

$$\frac{X}{1} = \frac{\$54,280}{\$363,775}$$

$$X\% = \frac{\$54,280}{\$363,775} = 0.15\%$$

Therefore, ROR (i*) = 14.15%. Since ROR > MARR, this project is economically justified.

7.11

	Hangar A	*Hangar B*	*Δ B-A*
First cost	−\$2,000,000	−\$3,000,000	−\$1,000,000
Annual operating cost	−\$500,000	−\$200,000	\$300,000
Deposit return	\$400,000	\$800,000	\$400,000
Life, years	10	10	10

$$PW\Delta = -\$1,000,000 + \$300,000\ (P/A, \Delta i^*, 10) + \$400,000\ (P/F, \Delta i^*, 10) = 0$$
$$\text{Try}\Delta i^* = \text{MARR} = 12\%$$
$$PW\Delta = -\$1,000,000 + \$300,000\ (P/A, 12\%, 10) + \$400,000\ (P/F, 12\%, 10)$$
$$PW\Delta = -\$1,000,000 + \$300,000 \times (5.6502) + \$400,000 \times (0.3220)$$
$$PW\Delta = -\$1,000,000 + \$1,695,060 + \$128,800$$
$$PW\Delta = \$823,860 > 0$$

Since at Δi^* equal to MARR, the PW of Δ project is positive; $\Delta i^* >$ MARR, Δproject is economically justified, and therefore, the hangar with the higher first cost, hangar B, should be selected.

7.17

We calculate the ROR for each project by setting the PW of all cash flows to 0 and solve for i*:
New Parking Garage

$$PW = -\$120 - 5\ (P/A, \Delta i^*, 20) + \$25\ (P/A, i^*, 20) = 0$$
$$\$120 = (\$25 - \$5)\ (P/A, i^*, 20)$$
$$\$120 = \$20\ (P/A, i^*, 20)$$
$$(P/A, i^*, 10) = 6$$

i*	*(P/A i*, 20)*
15%	6.2593
15% + X%	6.0000
16%	5.9288

$$\frac{X\%}{1\%} = \frac{0.2593}{0.3305}$$

$$X\% = \frac{0.2593}{0.3305} = 0.78\%$$

Therefore, ROR = i* = 15.78% > MARR, and New Parking Garage is economically justified.
Expanding Existing Terminal

$$PW = -\$540 - 25\ (P/A, i^*, 25) + \$85\ (P/A, i^*, 25) = 0$$
$$\$540 = (\$85 - \$25) \times (P/A, i^*, 25)$$
$$\$540 = \$60\ (P/A, i^*, 25)$$
$$(P/A, i^*, 25) = 9$$

i*	(P/A, i*, 25)
10%	9.0770
10% + X%	9.0000
11%	8.4217

$$\frac{X\%}{1\%} = \frac{0.0770}{0.6553}$$

$$X\% = \frac{0.0770}{0.6553} = 0.12\%$$

$$\text{ROR} = i^* = 10.12\% < \text{MARR}$$

Expanding Existing Terminal is not economically justified.
Building New Terminal

$$\text{PW} = -\$780 - \$30\,(P/A, i^*, 25) + \$150\,(P/A, i^*, 25) = 0$$

$$\$780 = (\$150 - \$30)\,(P/A, i^*, 25)$$

$$\$780 = \$120\,(P/A, i^*, 25)$$

$$(P/A, i^*, 25) = 6.5$$

i*	(P/A, i*, 25)
14%	6.8729
14% + X%	6.5000
15%	6.4641

$$X = \frac{0.3729}{0.4088}$$

$$X = 0.91\%$$

Therefore, ROR = i* = 14.91% > MARR, and Building New Terminal is economically justified. Of the three projects, building the new parking garage and the new terminal are economically justified, and Legacy Regional Airport should only undertake those two projects.

Chapter 8

8.8

$$\text{AW of Benefits} = \$150\,\text{m}$$

$$\text{AW of Disbenefits} = \$10\,\text{m}$$

$$\text{AW of AOC} = \$25\,\text{m}$$

$$\text{AW of P} = \$800\,\text{m}\,(0.10) + \$100\,\text{m}\,(A/F, 10\%, 10) = \$80\,\text{m} + \$100\,\text{m}\,(0.06275)$$

$$\text{AW of P} = \$80\,\text{m} + 6.275\,\text{m} = 86.275\,\text{m}$$

$$B/C = \frac{\$150\,\text{m} - \$10\,\text{m}}{\$86.275\,\text{m} + \$25\,\text{m}} = \frac{\$140\,\text{m}}{\$111.275\,\text{m}}$$

$$B/C = 1.26 > 1$$

Because the B/C ratio of the new terminal is greater than 1, it is economically justified.

8.13

$$\Delta \text{ Project} = \text{Bridge B} - \text{Bridge A}$$

Note in Table C1 that the implied benefit is the different public user travel costs.

Table C1 The Cash Flows for Δ Project

	Bridge A	*Bridge B*	*Δ Project B-A*
First cost	\$50m	\$80m	\$30M
Annual operating cost (AOC)	\$4m	\$5m	1\$
Repair cost every 10 years	\$2m	\$2.5	\$.5m
Users travel costs per year	\$20m	\$10m	\$10m (benefits)
Estimated life, years	∞	∞	∞

$$\begin{aligned}
AW_{\Delta P} &= \$30\,(0.08) = \$2.4 \\
AW_{\Delta AOC} &= \$1 \\
AW_{\Delta RC} &= \$10\,M\,(A/F, 8\%, 10) = \$10\,(0.06903) = \$0.6903 \\
AW_{\Delta B} &= \$10\,m \\
\Delta B/C &= \frac{\Delta B - \Delta D}{\Delta TC - \Delta S} \\
\Delta B/C &= \frac{\$10\,m - \$0\,m}{\$2.4\,m + 1 + \$0.6903} = \frac{\$10\,m}{\$4.0903\,m} = 2.44 > 1
\end{aligned}$$

Because the ΔB/C ratio is greater than 1, the Δ project is economically justified, and bridge B should be selected.

8.15

For simplicity, all values are converted to AW:

$$\begin{aligned}
\text{AW of P for CAE} &= \$300\text{m}\,(0.08) = \$24\,\text{m} \\
\text{AW of P for CBE} &= \$400\text{m}\,(0.08) = \$32\,\text{m} \\
\text{AW of P for NRW} &= \$500\text{m}\,(0.08) = \$40\,\text{m}
\end{aligned}$$

$$\begin{aligned}
\text{AW of D for CAE} &= \$15\,\text{m}\,(0.08) = \$1.2\,\text{m} \\
\text{AW of D for CBE} &= \$20\,\text{m}\,(0.08) = \$1.6\,\text{m} \\
\text{AW of D for NRW} &= \$18\,\text{m}\,(0.08) = \$1.44\,\text{m}
\end{aligned}$$

Table C2 presents the cash flows for the two different options.

Table C2 The Cash Flows for Concourse Expansion vs New Runway

	Concourse A Expansion	*Concourse B Expansion*	*New Runway*
AW of First cost, P	\$24m	\$32m	\$40m
AW of AOC	\$15m	\$20m	\$25m
AW of Benefits, B	\$85m	\$100m	\$120m
AW of Disbenefits, D	\$1.2m	\$1.6m	\$1.44m
Life, Years	∞	∞	∞

Because these projects are benefit-based alternatives, Do-nothing becomes an option. Table C3 shows the different cash flows.

$$\Delta\text{Project} = \text{CAE} - \text{Do} - \text{nothing}\Delta$$

Table C3 The Cash Flows for Do-Nothing, New Economy Parking Garage, and Δ Project

	Do-Nothing (DN)	*Concourse A Expansion (CAE)*	*Δ Project CAE – DN*
AW of P	\$0	\$24m	\$24m
AW of AOC	\$0	\$15m	\$15m
AW of Benefits	\$0	\$85m	\$85m
AW of Disbenefits	\$0	\$1.2m	\$1.2m
Life, Years	∞	∞	∞

$$\Delta\text{B/C} = \frac{\$85\,\text{m} - \$1.2\,\text{m}}{\$24\,\text{m} + \$15\,\text{m}} = \frac{\$83.8\,\text{m}}{\$39\,\text{m}}$$

$$\Delta\text{B/C} = 2.14 > 1$$

Because ΔB/C > 1, the Δ project is economically justified. DN is eliminated, and CAE survives. Now, we compare CAE with CBE.

$$\Delta\text{Project} = \text{CAE} - \text{CBE}$$

Table C4 presents the relevant cash flows.

Table C4 The Cash Flows for CAE, CBE, and Δ Project

	CAE	*CBE*	*Δ Project CBE – CAE*
AW of P	\$24m	\$32m	\$8m
AW of AOC	\$15m	\$20m	\$5m
AW of benefits	\$85m	\$100m	\$15m
AW of disbenefits	\$1.2m	\$1.6m	\$0.4
Life, Years	∞	∞	∞

$$\Delta\text{B/C} = \frac{\$15\,\text{m} - \$0.4\,\text{m}}{\$8\,\text{m} + 5\,\text{m}} = \frac{\$14.6\,\text{m}}{\$13\,\text{m}}$$

$$\Delta\text{B/C} = 1.12 > 1$$

Because ΔB/C > 1, the Δ project is economically justified. The CAE is eliminated, and the CBE survives. Now, we compare the CBE with the NRW.

$$\Delta\text{Project} = \text{CAE} - \text{CBE}$$

Table C5 presents the relevant cash flows.

Table C5 The Cash Flows for Concourse A Expansion, Concourse B Expansion, and Δ Project

	Concourse B Expansion (CBE)	*New Runway (NRW)*	*Δ Project NRW – CBE*
AW of P	\$32m	\$40m	\$8m
AW of AOC	\$20m	\$25m	\$5m
AW of benefits	\$100m	\$120m	\$20m
AW of disbenefits	\$1.6m	\$1.44m	–\$0.16m
Life, Years	∞	∞	∞

$$\Delta B/C = \frac{\$20\,m - (-\$0.16\,m)}{\$8\,m + \$5\,m} = \frac{\$20.16\,m}{\$13\,m}$$

$$\Delta B/C = 1.55 > 1$$

Because ΔB/C > 1, the Δ project is not economically justified. Therefore, the CBE is eliminated, and the New Runway survives. Guangzhou International Airport should select the New Runway.

Chapter 9

9.1

a.

$$Q_{BE} = \frac{\$1,500}{\$0.9 - \$0.5}$$

$$Q_{BE} = 3{,}750 \text{ units}$$

b.

$$\text{Profit} = 4{,}000 \times (\$900{,}000 - \$500{,}000) - \$1{,}500{,}000$$

$$\text{Profit} = \$1{,}000{,}000$$

9.3

$$\text{Load Factor (LF)} = \frac{1{,}957 \text{ million}}{2{,}284 \text{ million}}$$

$$\text{LF} = 0.85 \text{ or } 85\%$$

$$\text{CASM} = \frac{\text{Total Costs (TC)}}{\text{Available Seat Miles (ASM)}}$$

$$\text{CASM} = \frac{\$365 \text{ million}}{2{,}284 \text{ million}}$$

$$\text{CASM} = \$0.1598$$

$$\text{RRPM} = \frac{\text{Total Revenue (TR)}}{\text{Revenue per Passenger Mile (RPM)}}$$

$$\text{RRPM} = \frac{\$388 \text{ million}}{1{,}957 \text{ million}} = \$0.1983$$

$$\text{Breakeven Load Factor } (LF_{B\text{-}E}) = \frac{\$0.1598}{\$0.1983}$$
$$LF_{B\text{-}E} = 0.81 \text{ or } 81\%$$

Since LF > $LF_{B\text{-}E}$, the route is economically justified.

9.7

$$\text{Variable cost per unit } (V) = \frac{6 \times 8 \times \$50}{8} = \$300$$

$$AW = 0$$
$$[-\$12{,}000{,}000 - \$1{,}000{,}000\ (P/F, 8\%, 4)] \times [A/P, 8\%, 10] + \$2{,}000{,}000\ (A/F, 8\%, 10)$$
$$-\$500{,}000 - \$300\ Q + \$15{,}000\ Q = 0$$

$$[-\$12{,}000{,}000 - \$1{,}000{,}000\ (0.7350)] \times [0.14903] + \$2{,}000{,}000\ (0.06903)$$
$$-\$500{,}000 + (\$15{,}000 - \$300)\ Q = 0$$

$$-1{,}897{,}897 + 138{,}060 - 500{,}000 + \$14{,}700\ Q = 0$$
$$\$2{,}259{,}837 = \$14{,}700\ Q$$
$$Q_{BE} = 153.73$$

9.9

$$-\$24{,}000Q = -\$12{,}000{,}000\ (A/P, 10\%, 10) + \$12{,}000{,}000 \times (0.08) \times (A/F, 10\%, 10)$$
$$\$300{,}000 - \$12{,}000\ Q$$
$$-\$12{,}000Q = -\$12{,}000{,}000\ (0.16275) + \$12{,}000{,}000 \times (0.08) \times (0.06275) - \$300{,}000$$
$$-\$12{,}000Q = -\$1{,}953{,}000 + \$60{,}240 - \$300{,}000$$
$$-\$12{,}000Q = -\$2{,}192{,}760$$
$$Q = \frac{-\$2{,}192{,}760}{-\$12{,}000}$$
$$Q_{BE} = 182.73$$

9.11

We first calculate the cumulative NACFs (Table C6).

Table C6 Cumulative NACFs

Year	*NACF*	*Cumulative NACF*
0	–\$8,100,000	–\$8,100,000
1	\$2,000,000	\$6,100,000
2	\$1,750,000	\$4,350,000
3	\$1,500,000	\$2,850,000
4	\$1,250,000	\$1,600,000
5	\$1,000,000	\$600,000
6	\$750,000	–\$150,000
7	\$500,000	
8	\$500,000	
9	\$500,000	
10	\$500,000	

$$N_P = 6 - \left(\frac{\$150,000}{\$750,000}\right)$$
$$N_P = (6) - 0.2$$
$$N_P = 5.8 \text{ years}$$

9.14

$$Q_{BE} = \frac{FC}{P-V} = \frac{16,000 \text{ million}}{P-170 \text{ million}}$$
$$Q_{BE} = 200 \text{ units}$$
$$200\,(P-170) = 16,000$$
$$200\text{ P} - 34,000 = 16,000$$
$$200\text{ P} = 16,000 + 34,000 = 50,000$$
$$P = \frac{50,000}{200}$$
$$P = \$250 \text{ million}$$

9.15

$$\text{Load Factor (LF)} = \frac{RPM}{ASM}$$
$$\frac{RPM}{56,000 \text{ million}} = 80\%$$
$$RPM = 56,000 \times 80\%$$
$$RPM = 44,800 \text{ million}$$

$$R/RPM = \frac{\text{Total Revenue}}{RPM} = \frac{5,376 \text{ million}}{44,800 \text{ million}} = 0.12$$
$$LF_{B\text{-}E} = \frac{CASM}{RRPM} = 70\%$$
$$CASM = LF_{B-E} \times R/RPM$$
$$CASM = 70\% \times 0.12$$
$$CASM = 0.084$$

10.6

Marginal cost is the first derivative of the total cost function:

$$MC = 1 - 20Q + 6Q^2$$
$$MC\,(Q{=}4) = 1 - 2(4) + 6\,(4)^2$$
$$MC\,(Q{=}4) = 89$$
$$MC\,(Q{=}10) = 1 - 2(10) + 6\,(10)^2$$
$$MC\,(Q{=}10) = 581$$

10.10

Component	*Quantity Needed*	*Unit Cost Factor*	$C_T = C_U \times N$
Paint material	500 gallons	\$95	\$47,500
Sheet metal	2,000 tons	\$62	\$124,000
Labor, mechanical/electrical	1,000 hours	\$85 per hour	\$85,000
Labor, casting	1,500 hours	\$60 per hour	\$90,000
Labor, finishing	1,000 hours	\$50 per hour	\$50,000
Labor painting	500 hours	\$40 per hour	\$20,000
Estimated total cost of the system			\$416,500

10.13

$$C_2 = \$200,000\left(\frac{512}{342}\right)\left(\frac{500}{2000}\right)^{0.62}$$
$$C_2 = \$200,000\,(1.4971)(0.4234)$$
$$C_2 = \$200,000\,(0.6339)$$
$$C_2 = \$126,780$$

10.14

$$h = 1 + 0.85 + 0.46 + 1.20 + 0.55 + 0.42 = 4.48$$
$$C_T = h \times C_E$$
$$C_T = 4.48 \times \$400,000$$
$$C_T = \$1,792,000$$

10.16

Route	*Total RPM*	*Average Load Factor*	*Total ASM*
Chicago	450,000	75%	600,000
Dallas	574,000	82%	700,000
Los Angeles	630,000	70%	900,000
Los Vegas	595,000	85%	700,000
Phoenix	480,000	80	600,000
Total ASM			3,500,000

$$\text{Allocation rate per ASM} = \left(\frac{\$4,200,000}{3,500,000}\right) = \$1.20$$

Route	*Total ASM*	*Allocation Rate*	*Indirect Cost Allocation per Route*
Chicago	600,000	\$1.20	\$720,000
Dallas	700,000	\$1.20	\$840,000
Los Angeles	900,000	\$1.20	\$1,080,000
Los Vegas	700,000	\$1.20	\$840,000
Phoenix	600,000	\$1.20	\$720,000
Total indirect cost			\$4,200,000

Chapter 11

11.4

$$\text{Operating Income} = \$800 - \$700 - \$10 = \$90\,\text{m}$$
$$\text{Net Income} = (\$90 - \$2.4)(1 - .21) = \$69.20\,\text{m}$$

11.9

$$\text{Free Cash Flow} = \$20 - \$8 + \$18 = \$30\text{m}$$

Chapter 12

12.8

$$\begin{aligned} CR &= \frac{CA}{CL} = 1.2 \\ CR &= 1.2 \times CL \\ QR &= \frac{CA - Inventory}{CL} \\ \frac{1.2 \times CL - 100,000,000}{CL} &= 1.1 \\ 1.2 \times CL - 1.1 \times CL &= 100,000,000 \\ CL &= \$1,000,000,000 \\ CA &= \$1,200,000,000 \\ NWC &= \$200,000,000 \end{aligned}$$

12.9

$$\text{Annual cost of goods sold} = \$3{,}000{,}000 \times \frac{365}{30}$$
$$\text{Annual cost of goods sold} = \$36{,}500{,}000$$
$$\text{Inventory turnover} = \frac{\$36{,}500{,}000}{\$3{,}000{,}000} = 12 \text{ times per year}$$

12.10

$$\begin{aligned} Current\ Ratio &= \frac{\$500,000 + \$1,000,000 + \$2,000,000}{\$400,000 + \$800,000 + \$600,000} = 1.94 \\ Quick\ Ratio &= \frac{\$500,000 + \$1,000,000 + \$2,000,000 - \$2,000,000}{\$400,000 + \$800,000 + \$600,000} = 0.83 \\ Cash\ Ratio &= \frac{\$500,000}{\$400,000 + \$800,000 + \$600,000} = 0.28 \end{aligned}$$

12.11

$$Profit\ Margin = \frac{\$3\,\text{m} - \$1\,\text{m}}{\$12\,\text{m}} = 16.67\%$$
$$ROA = \frac{\$3.0}{\$50\,\text{m}} = 6.00\%$$
$$ROE = \frac{\$3.0}{\$20\,\text{m}} = 15.00\%$$
$$Dividend - Payout = \frac{Dividends\ Paid}{Net\ Income} = \frac{\$1.0\,\text{m}}{\$3.0\,\text{m}} = 33\%$$

12.12

$$\frac{\$250\,\text{m}}{Equity} = 1.75$$
$$\text{Equity} = \$142.90\ \text{m}$$

12.13

$$Current\ Ratio = \frac{Current\ Assets}{Current\ Liabilities}$$
$$2.0 = \frac{Current\ Asset}{\$15}$$
$$\text{Current Assets} = \$30\ \text{million}$$
$$\text{Cash} = 10\% \times 30 = \ \$3\ \text{million}$$
$$\text{Accounts Receivable} = 40\% \times 30 = \$12\ \text{million}$$
$$\text{Inventory} = \$30 - (\$3 + \$12) = \$15\ \text{million}$$

Chapter 13

13.13

a. $P(x = 101) = 0.95^{101} = 0.0056$

b. $\text{P}(\text{x} = 102) = 0.95^{102} = 0.0053$

c. $\text{P}\ (0\text{£x £}100) = \text{binomcdf}\ (102{,}0.95{,}100) = 0.9660$

13.14

$$\mu = n \times q$$
$$\mu = 225 \times 0.80 = 180$$
$$\sigma = \sqrt{n \times p \times q}$$
$$\sigma = \sqrt{225 \times 0.8 \times 0.2}$$
$$\sigma = 6$$

13.16

$$\text{Correlation coefficient} = 0.0026 / (0.04 \times 0.07) = 0.9286$$

13.18

$$\sigma^2 = (0.10) \times (0.2 - 0.14)^2 + (0.40) \times (0.1 - 0.14)^2 + (0.40) \times (0.14 - 0.14)^2 + (0.10) \times (0.24 - 0.14)^2$$

$$\sigma^2 = 0.002$$

Given that variance, the standard deviation of JLCs stock is simply the square root of the variance:

$$\sigma^2 = 0.045$$

Chapter 14

14.2

The salvage value is an estimate of the amount that is potentially achievable when the asset is retired from service.

14.5

The initial cost, estimated salvage value, estimated useful life, and depreciation method.

14.6

Annual depreciation expense:

$$Annual\ Depreciation = \frac{\$1,000,000 - \$100,000}{3} = \$300,000$$

Year	*Year-Beginning Book Value*	*Depreciation*	*Accumulated*	*Year-End*
2017	$1,000,000	$300,000	$300,000	$700,000
2018	$700,000	$300,000	$600,000	$400,000
2019	$400,000	$300,000	$900,000	$100,000

14.7

a.

$$1/5 \text{ years} = 20\% \text{ straight-line rate} \times 2 = 40\% \text{ DDB rate}$$

Year	*Year-Beginning Book Value*	*Depreciation Expense*	*Accumulated Depreciation*
2022	*$1,000,000*	*$400,000*	*$400,000*
2023	600,000	$240,000	640,000
2024	360,000	$144,000	784,000
2025	216,000	$86,400	870,400
2026	129,600	$51,840	922,240
2027	77,760	$31,104	953,344

2022: \$1,000,000 beginning book value $\times$ 40% DDB rate = \$400,000
2023: \$600,000 beginning book value $\times$ 40% DDB rate = \$1240,000
2024: \$360,000 beginning book value $\times$ 40% DDB rate = \$144,000
2025: \$216,000 beginning book value $\times$ 40% DDB rate = \$86,400
2026: \$129,600 beginning book value $\times$ 40% DDB rate = \$51,840
2027: \$77,760 beginning book value $\times$ \$15,000 residual value = \$31,104

b.

Depreciation Expense	\$400,000
Accumulated Depreciation	\$400,000

14.8

Year	*Year-Beginning Book Value*	*Depreciation Expense*		*Accumulated Depreciation*
2024	\$900,000	1/3	\$300,000.00	\$300,000
2025	\$900,000	4/15	\$240,000.00	\$540,000
2026	\$900,000	1/5	\$180,000.00	\$720,000
2027	\$900,000	2/15	\$120,000.00	\$840,000
2028	\$900,000	1/15	\$60,000.00	\$900,000

Sum-of-the-years's denominator $\left[\left(n\left(n+1\right)\right)/2\right]=\left(5\times 6\right)/2=15$

\$900,000 $\times$ 5/15 = \$300,000 first 12 months' depreciation
\$900,000 $\times$ 4/15 = \$240,000 second 12 months' depreciation
\$900,000 $\times$ 3/15 = \$180,000 third 12 months' depreciation
\$900,000 $\times$ 2/15 = \$120,000 fourth 12 months' depreciation
\$900,000 $\times$ 1/15 = \$60,000 last 12 months' depreciation

Depreciation expense:

$2017:(\$900,000\times 5/15)=\$300,000$
$2018:(\$900,000\times 4/15)=\$240,000$
$2019:(\$900,000\times 3/15)=\$180,000$
$2020:(\$900,000\times 2/15)=\$120,000$
$2021:(\$900,000\times 1/15)=\$60,000$

14.13

Component Cost of Repair and Overhaul	*Amount*
Aircraft historical cost	\$50,000,000
Accumulated depreciation	–\$30,000,000
Carrying value of impaired asset	\$20,000,000
Restoration cost (\$10,000,000)/replacement cost (\$75,000,000)	13.33%
Impairment loss = carrying value (\$20,000,000) multiplied by restoration cost ratio (13.33%)	\$2,666,000

Chapter 15

15.1

Suggested answer
Certainty:

- The decision maker has complete knowledge about the problem and knows about the results.
- Investing in government bonds, insured savings account.

Uncertainty

- The decision maker must decide when the outcome and the probabilities of the possible outcomes are not known.

Risk

- The decision maker must decide when the outcome is not known with certainty but probabilities can be assigned to the various outcomes.
- Aircraft accidents, number of passenger no-shows on a given flight.

15.6

EVPI quantities how much better decisions a decision maker could make with the ability to always know when each state of nature would occur.

Appendix C

Major Excel Project for Airport

COMPUTER PROJECT
MICROSOFT EXCEL ASSIGNMENT

Greenville Airport Construction
Redford Airport Authority

Greenville Airport Construction: Microsoft Excel Project

Redford Airport Authority is considering constructing a reliever airport in Greenville County, about 40 miles away from Redford International Airport (RIA) to reduce current congestion at RIA. This facility will accommodate up to an additional 30 million enplanements (# of passengers boarding the planes) at ultimate buildout in five years. The following are costs associated with construct the Greenville Airport; all costs and revenues occur at the end of the year unless the beginning of the year is specifically stated:

- Purchase of 15,000 acres of land at \$100 million in Greenville County to be paid today (time 0).
- Environmental assessment for \$30 million due in year one.
- Airfield improvements including taxiway, ramps, access roads, airfield storm drainage, and fencing at \$150 million due in year two.
- Construct two terminals with 25 gates each as well as supporting spaces at \$400 million in year three, \$500 million in year four, and \$600 million in year five.
- Construct parking garage and rental car facilities for \$80 million in year four.
- Construct concession areas in both terminals for \$100 million in year four and \$125 million in year five.
- Construct two parallel runways at the following costs:

  Runway A $(150\text{ ft} \times 15{,}000\text{ ft})$ \$400 million in year 4

  Runway B $(150\text{ ft} \times 12{,}000\text{ ft})$ \$300 million in year 5

- \$50 million in other capital equipment at the end of each of the five years of construction.
- Maintenance and recurring expenses are \$100 million in the first year of airport operation (year 6) and increase 5% per year thereafter.

Enplanement revenue is expected to be $15 million in the first year of operation (year 6) with 5% increase per year, and the following are expected airport revenues and fees:

- Passenger facility charges of $4.50 per enplaned passenger.
- Estimated landing fees of $50 million in year 6 with 15% increase per year.
- Estimated net revenue from parking structure of $50 million in year 6 with 10% increase per year up to maximum of $100 million.
- Estimated annual advertising revenue of $400 million for years six to eight, $450 million for years 9–12, and $500 million for years 13–15, with the airport receiving 85%.
- Estimated annual food revenue of $200 million for years six to eight, $250 million for years 9–12, and $300 million for years 13–15; the airport's concession is 15%.
- Estimated gate use revenue of $40 million in year six to increase by 10% per year through year 15.
- Estimated annual alcohol revenue of $180 million for years six to eight, $280 million for years 9–12, and $380 million for years 13–15 with airport concession of 18%.
- Estimated annual gift and general merchandise revenue of $300 million for years six to eight, $400 million for years 9–12, and $500 million for years 13–15 with airport concession of 12%.
- Annual airport revenue from car rental concession is $6 per rental day. The annual car rental days are estimated to be 10 million for years six to eight, 20 million for years 9–12, and 30 million for years 13–15.
- Redford Authority also agreed to sell the Greenville Airport to Greenville County at the end of 10 years of airport operation at an expected price of $1500 million.

Assuming that Redford's MARR is 8% and using Excel functions, complete the following:

- Calculate the total annual investment (cost) per year through year five.
- Calculate the PW of annual investments (costs) occurring in the first five years. This is considered the first cost.
- Calculate the net annual cash flow per year for the first 10 years of operations.

(Years 6–15).
Use the information you just calculated and the following techniques to evaluate the project:

- Calculate the PW (NPV) of all cash flows.
- Calculate the ROR (IRR) of all cash flows.
- Calculate the modified B/C ratio.
- Calculate the no-return payback period.

Add a brief statement at the bottom of the page indicating whether you recommend that Redford construct the Greenville Airport.

Glossary of Terms

A

Accounts Payable Money the company owes to another party.

Accounts Receivable Monies due from customers because of credit sales. On a balance sheet, AR is often recorded as an asset because it represents a legal obligation for the customer to pay cash for its short-term debts.

Aircraft Utilization Aircraft block hours divided by the number of aircraft days assigned to service on air carrier routes and presented in block hours per day.

Air Carrier Any airline that undertakes directly, by lease or by other arrangement, to engage in air transportation.

Airport Improvement Program Provides grants for public-use airports that are included in the National Plan of Integrated Airport Systems. These grants are given to public and private owners and entities for planning and development.

Air Traffic Control A service operated by appropriate authority to promote the safe, orderly, and expeditious flow of air traffic.

Amortization Repayment of loan principal and interest.

Ancillary Revenue Revenue from nonticket sources such as commissions from hotel bookings, baggage fees, onboard food, premium seat assignments, and early boarding fees.

Annuity A series of consecutive payments of equal amounts.

Asset An item of economic benefit to an institution.

Available Seat Miles A passenger airline's carrying capacity, calculated as

$$ASK = number\ of\ seats \times number\ of\ kilometers\ flown$$

Average Stage Length The average distance flown per aircraft departure, calculated as

$$\text{ASL} = \frac{Plane\ Miles}{Departures}$$

Average Collection Period The average time receivable accounts have been on the books, calculated as

$$ACP = \frac{ACR \times 365\ \text{days}}{Credit\ Sales}$$

B

Balance Sheet A financial summary of a company's assets, liabilities, and shareholder equity at a specific point in time.

Bankruptcy A legal status of being unable to pay creditors. There are two basic bankruptcy proceedings. Chapter 7 bankruptcy is called liquidation. Chapter 11 bankruptcy allows an airline to reorganize and refinance to be able to prevent final insolvency.

Block Hour The airline industry's basic measure of aircraft utilization, it is the time from the minute the aircraft door closes at departure of a revenue flight until it opens at the arrival gate.

Book Value An asset's original cost minus accumulated depreciation.
Breakeven The point where total costs and total revenue are equal:

$$Q_{B-E} = \frac{FC}{Price - VC}$$

Breakeven Load Factor The load factor that covers the necessary operating costs for scheduled traffic revenue:

$$\text{Break-Even}_{\text{LF}} = \frac{CASM}{R / RPM} = \frac{CASM}{Yield}$$

C

Capital Any financial or income property or physical goods used to generate income by investing in a business.
Capital Lease A financial lease that typically lasts for the life of the asset, with the lease payments covering the price of the asset and the lease generally being noncancellable.
Carrying Costs The costs associated with carrying inventories. For most inventories, these include warehouse, damage, obsolescence, shrinkage, and relocation costs.
Commuter Air Carrier A passenger air carrier operating aircraft with 30 seats or fewer and performing at least five scheduled roundtrips per week. It operates for hire or compensation under FAR Part 135.
Computer Reservation System A system that provides travel agencies with airline schedules, fares, and seat availability and enable travel agents to book seats and issue tickets.
Cost per Available Seat Mile A measure of airline efficiency represented in cents and calculated as follows:

$$\text{CASM} = \frac{Operating\ Costs}{ASM}$$

Cost of Capital The overall financial cost to an airline, expressed as a percentage and considering its capital structure, the interest rate it pays on debt, and the cost of its equity.
Current Assets Assets that can be converted into cash without significant loss of value in a very short period.

D

D-Check A process of more or less taking apart an entire airplane for inspection and overhaul; also known as a heavy maintenance visit.
Degree of Financial Leverage Financial leverage involves using debt to finance the project, and will include higher expenses before interest and taxes, and DFL is the percentage change in earnings per share for a given percentage change in EBIT:

$$DFL = \frac{Q(P-V)}{Q(P-V) - FC - I}$$

Degree of Operating Leverage Operating leverage involves using a large proportion of fixed costs in the firm's operations, and DOL measures the degree to which a project incurs a combination of fixed and variable costs:

$$DOL = \frac{Q(P-V)}{Q(P-V) - FC}$$

Depreciation The reduction in the price of an asset during its estimated useful life due to wear and tear, age, deterioration, and obsolescence.
Deregulation The lifting of U.S. government regulation of airline routes and charges under the Airline Deregulation Act of 1978.

Discount For a debt security, the difference between the promised future payment and the present value.

Dry Lease A leasing arrangement between two airlines where the first airline (lessee) leases an aircraft from the second (lessor). Under dry lease, the lessee pays for the crew, fuel, and maintenance.

E

Economy of Scale The increasing efficiency of production as the number of goods being produced increases.

Enplanement The boarding of scheduled and nonscheduled service aircraft by domestic, territorial, and international revenue passengers for intrastate, interstate, and foreign commerce including in-transit passengers.

Essential Air Service The program intended to guarantee small communities a minimal level of scheduled air service. EAS subsidizes commuter airlines to serve the rural communities across the country that otherwise would not receive any scheduled air service.

Equipment Trust Certificate A financial security under which a trust of investors purchases the aircraft and then "leases" it to the operator on condition that the airline will receive title upon full performance of the lease.

F

Federal Aviation Administration The U.S. government agency responsible for air safety and operation of the air traffic control system.

Federal Air Regulation Title 14 of the U.S. government's Code of Federal Regulations governing all the rules regarding aviation in the U.S.

Financial Lease See **Capital Lease**.

Financial Leverage The amount of debt a business uses in its capital structure. In aviation, an airline with high leverage is more vulnerable to downturns in the business cycle because it must continue to service its debt regardless of how bad business is.

Financial Risk The risk that an airline may not have sufficient cash to meet current financial obligations.

Fixed-Base Operator A commercial business granted the right by an airport to operate on the airport and provide aeronautical services such as fueling, hangaring, parking, aircraft rental and maintenance, and flight instruction.

Fixed Cost Costs that do not change as volume changes. Fixed costs cannot be eliminated in the short run.

Freight Any commodity other than mail and passenger baggage transported by air.

Future Value The value that a current investment grows to at a given interest rate over a specified period.

Future Value of an Annuity The future value of a series of consecutive equal payments.

Goodwill Customer loyalty and patronage developed with continuous business under the same name over a period of time; goodwill serves as a business advantage.

Gross Domestic Product The total output of goods and services produced by all the different productive resources within a given country, valued at market prices.

H

Half-Life The point in the life of a component like a jet engine that when it is exactly midway between scheduled overhaul and replacement.

Hedging A financial strategy used to minimize and transfer risk, similar buying insurance.

Hub and Spoke A system under which many airlines designate an airport as a hub through which they transit passengers from spoke (origin) to spoke (destination).

I

Internal Rate of Return The discount rate that makes the net present value of all cash flows from a project 0.

Income Statement A financial statement that summarizes a business's various transactions during a specified period, showing the net profit or loss based on the fundamental accounting equation

Income = Revenue – Expenses

In-Transit Passengers Revenue passengers on board international flights who pass through an airport for nontraffic purposes domestically.

L

Lease A contract granting use or occupation of property during a specified period in exchange for specified lease payments.

Lessee A person who leases a property from its owner (lessor).

Lessor The owner of an asset who grants another party lease rights to the asset.

Leverage The use of debt to supplement investment.

Liquidity The ability of an asset to be converted into cash quickly and without any loss of value.

Load Factor The ratio of revenue passenger miles over available seat-miles, representing the proportion of aircraft seating capacity that is actually sold and utilized.

M

Major Airlines Airlines earning revenues of $1 billion or more annually in scheduled service.

Modified Accelerated Cost Recovery System The U.S. tax depreciation system, which allows for more depreciation toward the beginning of the life of the capital asset and allows the tax-deductible depreciation expense to be taken sooner.

N

National Plan of Integrated Airport Systems A program that identifies more than 3,300 airports that are eligible to receive federal grants under the Airport Improvement Program based on their significance to national air transportation.

Net Present Value The total present value of all cash inflows and outflows.

Net Profit Margin Net profit (or loss) after interest and taxes as a percentage of operating revenues.

Nonscheduled Service Revenue flights not operated as regular scheduled service, such as charter flights, and all nonrevenue flights incident to such flights.

O

Operating Expenses Expenses incurred in performing air transportation based on overall operating revenues and expenses.

Operating Lease A short-term lease, for example, an aircraft which has an economic life of 30 years may be leased to an airline for four years on an operating lease.

Operating Leverage The extent to which a firm utilizes its fixed assets.

Operating Profit Margin Operating profit (i.e., operating revenues minus operating expenses) as a percentage of operating revenues.

Operating Revenues Revenues from business operations and related incidental services.

Options A contract that gives the holder the right but not the obligation to buy or sell a security at a predestined price for a given period.

Overbooking When more seats have been booked on a flight than seats allowable for sale.

P

Payback Period The time required to recover an initial investment.

Par Value The amount of money the investor will receive once the bond matures, same as the face value, principal value, or maturity value of the bond.

Passenger Load Factor The ratio of revenue passenger miles over available seat-miles, representing the proportion of aircraft seating capacity that is actually sold and utilized:

$$LF = \frac{RPM}{ASM} \times 100$$

Passenger Name Record A record of each passenger's travel requirements containing all information necessary for processing reservations.
Passenger Revenue per Available Seat Mile The average revenue received by the airline per unit of capacity available for sale.
Preferred Stocks A hybrid security combing some of the characteristics of bonds and common stocks but that usually carries no voting rights.
Prime Rate The rate that a commercial bank charges its most creditworthy customers.
Profitability Ratios A group of ratios used to assess the returns on assets, sales, and invested capital.

R

Return on Investment The percentage earned on a company's total capital, calculated by dividing the total capital by the earnings before interest, taxes, or dividends.
Revenue Management A management approach to optimizing revenue that is based on managing revenues for different market segments or from different sources of funding around capacity and timing (yield management).
Revenue Passenger Enplanement The total number of revenue passengers boarding aircraft including origination, stopover, or connecting passengers.
Revenue Passenger Load Factor The ratio of revenue passenger miles over available seat miles, representing the proportion of aircraft seating capacity that is actually sold and utilized.
Revenue Passenger Miles A principal measure of an airline's turnover, calculated by summing the products of the revenue aircraft miles flown and the number of revenue passengers carried on that route.
Revenue per Available Seat Mile The revenue in cents received for each seat mile offered, calculated by dividing operating income by available seat miles and not limited to ticket sales revenue.
Revenue Ton Mile One nonmetric ton of revenue traffic transported one mile.
Risk Aversion The propensity of investors or individuals to avoid risk unless it is properly compensated.
Risk-Free Assets Assets free of risk of default.
Risk Premium The minimum difference an investor requires before investing in a risky investment.

S

Safety Stocks The inventory that is held in addition to what is regularly needed to protect against being out of stock.
Secondary Market The markets for securities that have already been issued and traded among investors with no proceeds going to the company.
Straight-Line Depreciation Depreciation calculated by taking the purchase price of an asset less the salvage value and dividing it by the total productive years the asset can be reasonably expected to benefit the company.
Sunk Costs A cost that has already been incurred and consequently cannot be recuperated.

T

Treasury Bills Short-term obligations of the federal government. They mature in one year or less, and like zero-coupon bonds, they do not pay interest prior to the maturity.
Treasury Notes Short-term obligations of the federal government that mature in two to ten years.

V

Variable Costs A cost that changes in proportion to a change in a company's activity or business.

W

Walk-Away Lease A lease that allows the airline to return the aircraft at specified times without penalty.
Warrant A security issued by a company along with a bond or preferred stock that gives the holder the right to buy a specific amount of securities at a specific price.

Weighted Average Cost of Capital The average rate of return a company is expected to pay its shareholders for using their capital, calculated by simply multiplying the cost of each item of capital by its weighted representation in the overall capital structure:

$$WACC = \frac{D}{A} \times k_d \times (1 - T) + \frac{E}{A} \times k_e$$

where A= company's market value and E= market value of the firm's equity.

Wet Lease A leasing arrangement between a lessor and a lessee to lease an aircraft and crew from the second party that operates services on behalf of the first party.

Wide-Body Aircraft A commercial aircraft with two aisles.

Working Capital The amount of liquidity assets an airline has on hand to meet its short-term financial obligations.

Y

Yield A unit of airplane prices, defined as average revenue per revenue passenger mile or revenue ton mile.

Index

Note: page references to non-textual content such as Figures will be in *italics*, followed by the letter '*f*', whereas those for Tables will be in *italics* followed by the letter '*t*'.

For Product Safety Concerns and Information please contact our EU
representative GPSR@taylorandfrancis.com
Taylor & Francis Verlag GmbH, Kaufingerstraße 24, 80331 München, Germany

www.ingramcontent.com/pod-product-compliance
Lightning Source LLC
LaVergne TN
LVHW080802011026
849160LV00015B/1511
* 9 7 8 1 0 3 2 7 4 5 4 0 4 *